The FOUNTAIN *of* AGE

Betty Friedan

SIMON & SCHUSTER
New York   London   Toronto   Sydney   Tokyo   Singapore

SIMON & SCHUSTER
SIMON & SCHUSTER BUILDING
ROCKEFELLER CENTER
1230 AVENUE OF THE AMERICAS
NEW YORK, NEW YORK 10020

DESIGNED BY EVE METZ
MANUFACTURED IN THE UNITED STATES OF AMERICA

1   3   5   7   9   10   8   6   4   2

LIBRARY OF CONGRESS CATALOGING-IN-PUBLICATION DATA
FRIEDAN, BETTY.
THE FOUNTAIN OF AGE / BETTY FRIEDAN.
P.   CM.
INCLUDES BIBLIOGRAPHICAL REFERENCES AND INDEX.
1. OLD AGE—UNITED STATES.   2. AGED—UNITED STATES.
3. AGED WOMEN—UNITED STATES.   4. AGING—SOCIAL ASPECTS—
UNITED STATES.   5. AGEISM—UNITED STATES.   I. TITLE.
HQ1064.U5F753   1993
305.26′0973—DC20   93-4090
CIP
ISBN: 0-671-88098-5

A version of Chapter 9 was previously published in
Ladies Home Journal, September 1984.

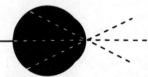

**This Large Print Book carries the
Seal of Approval of N.A.V.H.**

Also by BETTY FRIEDAN

The Second Stage
It Changed My Life
The Feminine Mystique

On my kitchen wall in Sag Harbor,
where we all get together,
are Hebrew letters from a song celebrating
"from generation to generation."

This book is dedicated
to the memory of my mother, Miriam,
and my father, Harry,
who made a larger life possible for me.

And for Daniel, Jonathan, Emily
and Rafael, Caleb, Nataya, David, Isabel, Lára,
Birgitta, and Benjamín,
whose mother and grandmother I am.

Contents

Author's Note

I started this search in what I thought was merely theoretical excitement when I saw that first clue that didn't fit the accepted truth about women on the brink of age—those women who "didn't have menopause." I pursued that clue in growing personal dread, because in my fifties I didn't even want to think about age. I was locked in my own denial. I had to break out of my personal denial before I could truly take in and exult over the stories of the surprisingly many women, and also men, whom I found in their sixties, seventies, eighties, and even nineties continuing to grow, and living with vitality a different kind of age.

I am first of all indebted to those strangers and friends who shared their personal truth with me. From Helen and Dick Dudman, Kathleen MacPherson and the Mitchells in Maine to Sam Jaffe, Rita Lowenthal, Madeleine Stoner, and Cecelia Hurwich in California, Edward Bernays in Boston, Ida Davidoff in Connecticut, Earl Arthurs in North Carolina, and all the others—some of whose names have been changed to protect their identities—who surprised me so. As with *The Feminine Mystique,* I made this search into the strange discrepancy between the dread image of age and the vital reality of these women and men simply as a writer on the track of a story, using my own combination of personal truth and hunch (my historical Geiger counter, I sometimes call it), of journalistic observation and investigative research, drawing on my training as a psychologist and a social scientist to follow clues where they led me in the massive controlled research of gerontology.

I am not myself a gerontologist, of course, but I had powerful guidance from others in this field. First of all, from Robert Butler, my now beloved friend and mentor who was then head of the National Institute on Aging, who wanted to "get me interested in age because," he said, "all the policy and research has been done in terms of men when most of those in age are women." Of course, he can't be held responsible for the way I ran with that.

I could not have spent the years it took me to wade through the data and interview the researchers and over one hundred women and men living their personal age in so many states without the support of the National Endowment for the Humanities, whose then chief, Joe Duffey, said it didn't matter that I wasn't a Ph.D. gerontologist. I am deeply grateful for the even more generous support I got from the Ford Foundation, and most especially my officer there, Terry Saario, and from Jonathan Cole, then head of the Center for Social Science at Columbia University, who gave me an academic home.

I am also grateful to James Birren, then head of the Ethel Percy Andrus Gerontology Center at the University of Southern California, its current chief, Ed Schneider, and to William Alonso of the Center for Population and Development Studies at Harvard, who welcomed me as a senior fellow.

My dear friend Mogey Lazarus aided my search enormously when he and Bob Butler made me part of the team for the Salzburg Seminar on Health, Productivity and Aging and then named me to the LORAN Commission of the Harvard Community Health Plan.

My own dread of age and personal denial became more acute at first as I plunged into the gerontological research. But this dread gave way to growing excitement as I found in many studies implications for a new truth about age that belied its definition only as decline and deterioration from youth—even though the authors of the research themselves may not have spelled out these implications or the dry facts may not have pierced through because they simply did not fit that dread mystique that is responsible for our own and society's fear of age.

The eminent gerontologists who gave me pieces of this different view of age—David Gutmann of Northwestern; Gisela Labouvie-Vief of Michigan; Robert Kastenbaum of Arizona; Myrna Lewis of New York; Marjorie Kantor of Fordham; Bernice Neugarten and Helena Lopata of Chicago; Marian Diamond of Berkeley; Robert Binstock of Case Western Reserve; Ellen Langer and John Rowe of Harvard; Dr. David Lehr of Miami; Marian Diamond and Margaret Clark of Berkeley; Vern Bengtson, Margaret Gatz, Ruth Weg, Tuck Finch and Leah Buturain of Andrus; Paul Costa of Baltimore; George Maddox and E. Palmore at Duke; Lissy Jarvik of UCLA; Dr. Harold Dupuy; and so many others—may be surprised to be described as an underground. Many of them are card-carrying members of the gerontological establishment. They cannot be blamed for my revolutionary interpretation of their work, though I hope one day they will be celebrated for it.

I hope my personal guides, who shared with me the good and different age they were living at the moment in time when I found them, were able to continue living that good age and to die, as many have since I met them, in the midst of life, though the way things are now in this society I'm afraid they may not have.

I had throughout these ten years the invaluable manuscript birthing help of my beloved assistant, Margaret Peet. I am grateful for the steadfast support of Jim Silberman during the long years when I couldn't finish this book, and I am indebted indeed to my agents, Emilie Jacobson and Peter Ginsberg, of Curtis Brown, and to Alice Mayhew, Eric Steel, and my friend and invaluable manuscript editor, Burton Beals, of Simon & Schuster, for seeing me through to the end.

I must say that as I worked on this book I experienced a delicious sea change, which I hope you will also experience as you read it.

Sag Harbor, New York
June 1993

Preface

When my friends threw a surprise party on my sixtieth birthday, I could have killed them all. Their toasts seemed hostile, insisting as they did that I publicly acknowledge reaching sixty, pushing me out of life, as it seemed, out of the race. Professionally, politically, personally, sexually. Distancing me from their fifty-, forty-, thirty-year-old selves. Even my own kids, though they loved me, seemed determined to be part of the torture. I was almost taunting in my response, assuring my friends that they, too, would soon be sixty if they lived that long. But I was depressed for weeks after that birthday party, felt removed from them all. I could not face being sixty.

I thought back to the years that followed the publication of *The Feminine Mystique*, when I went through my forties and into my fifties with all the zest and exhilaration of reborn women for whom the movement opened up a whole new future. I forgot about growing older. Age didn't concern me, personally, at all. But, even in those heady years, I did notice something out of the corner of my mind's eye that got me thinking about some change in the aging process that might take place as a result of what was happening to women.

After the book was published, I began looking for new patterns in women who had moved beyond what I had called the feminine mystique— that definition of women solely in terms of their sexual relation to men and their biological role as mothers. When I lectured in Oklahoma, or Texas, or Illinois, I would ask my university hosts to gather those women in town who were combining marriage and motherhood with some profession or serious pursuit beyond the home. The few women they were able to find, back then, with serious jobs involving long-term commitment, were usually older than I. My generation had given up its own ambitions for three or four babies when the men came home from World War II to take our jobs. The younger women, who never had the ambitions which that mystique denied, had abandoned their own educations to put their husbands through engineering or law school, and had acquired even earlier those babies, that suburban house with its appliances, that then defined women's fulfillment. The few "career women" to be found in America thirty years ago—when that feminine mystique had made "career" and "women's rights" dirty words—were likely to be "freaks" who had not married or had children. Women who combined professions with motherhood were not numerous enough in any city to constitute a pattern. They certainly had no sense of pioneering. They had been invisible women in their offices back then, juggling home and children and job so unobtrusively that the boss wouldn't notice.

They were older, in their fifties most of them, but I had noticed something about the way they looked. The tone of their skin, their eyes, and their voices seemed somehow more vibrant, more alive than those of the frustrated younger suburban housewives I had been interviewing for *The Feminine Mystique.* When I asked them, in passing, about their menopause, one after another said, "I didn't have menopause." I got this response from woman after woman in such groups—sure, she was in her fifties, she didn't deny it, but she "never had menopause." I began to wonder if I was dealing with some biological freaks. And then, of course, closer questioning revealed that they had, in fact, stopped menstruating, though they weren't sure exactly when, because they had been so busy with their jobs and their teenage kids. But they simply hadn't suffered any of the dreaded debilitating symptoms that were then expected to accompany that supposed "end of life as a woman."

At that time, if menopause was talked about at all—and like other aspects of female biology, this shameful sexual sickness was better not discussed—the end of a woman's childbearing function was seen as ultimate trauma, the end of her sexual function, her life as woman. She was told to expect painful, even agonizing, physiological symptoms and depressions that might send her to bed for weeks, even years, sometimes requiring hospitalization. A high proportion of the beds in mental hospitals were in fact filled by women suffering "involutional melancholia," as it was then called. Mournful books were written about "leftover years to live." A male gynecologist made millions selling women hormone extracts to keep them "forever female," artificially inducing that cycle of bleeding each month, though reproduction itself was no longer possible. Only later would it emerge that the hormones which prolonged that bloody illusion of sexual nubility might also hasten death from cancer.

The women I met had taken no such hormones. Their failure to experience traumatic menopause simply didn't fit the conventional or clinical image of the "climacteric" of a woman's life. My inner Geiger counter clicked at that, and I went to see some of the leading gynecologists, as well as psychoanalysts who were considered experts on menopause. In Chicago, the psychoanalyst Theresa Benedek said that while there were great individual differences in the intensity of the symptoms, the depression, and the duration of the mourning, the irreversible loss of the sexual function that defined woman's psyche was for every woman a drastic ending. The death, indeed, of her life as a woman. Her biological "sex role," which defined her, was finished. Some adjusted to the loss, sublimated in gardening, good works, their grandchildren; others did not.

But in the 1960s, women, myself included, were moving beyond that definition of ourselves solely in terms of our biological sexual role. In the great wave of consciousness-raising that was now taking place from suburban dining tables to church basements, women were taking steps to change their lives—going back to school, getting up the courage to look for jobs, asserting their own personhood. Then the pattern I had seen in those few exceptional women in Oklahoma, Texas, and Illinois in 1964 became a great wave, cresting across the nation, as women in their thirties, forties, fifties—with young children, or teenagers, or kids already grown—went back to school, became visible in offices, started law school, theological school, businesses of their own, ran for political office, and embarked on serious new directions in church or volunteer work. And I began to wonder: When women grow beyond the limits of their biological role and find new purposes for their lives, could that larger human dimension change the very biology of the aging process?

About that same time, I got a call from Dr. Robert Butler, then head of the National Institute on Aging. Would I come to see him in Washington? He wanted to get me interested, politically, in the problems of age. Because women are, in fact, the great majority of the old, the problems of age are really women's problems, he said. Yet most of the policies and programs and research on age had been designed by and about and for men.

Well, the problems of age didn't interest me, personally *or* politically. Reading the paper, I skipped stories about nursing home scandals. In the women's movement, age didn't seem to count; we all felt young. But, as Butler spoke, I remembered those changes I had begun to notice in the way women were aging—that vanishing menopause—during the early years of the women's movement. I asked him if that change was being studied, and what it meant. Could women's aging process actually be affected by that change in their definition of themselves? And why were women now living so much longer than men? They hadn't at the turn of the century. But long after women stopped dying in childbirth, even in the last twenty years in America, the gap between men's life expectancy and women's had continued to widen. If the change in women's role could have had a dramatic effect on the aging process, I asked, could some comparable change in the masculine role help men to live longer? Butler said most of the research on aging didn't deal with questions like that.

My Geiger counter was clicking again. I needed some new question to work on myself. Not that I was particularly interested in age. Not that the problems of women which had absorbed my energy and passions for twenty years had all been solved. Not that the women's movement was over. But I now saw it as only the first stage of a revolution—not a war of women against men but an evolutionary breakthrough freeing us from those polarized masculine and feminine sex roles that once might have been important for human survival, specializing women for nurture and men for fighting off marauders and dominating prey, but that were now getting in everyone's way.

Come to think of it, what had really caused the women's movement was the *additional years of human life.* At the turn of the century, women's life expectancy was forty-six; now it was nearly eighty. Our groping sense that we couldn't live all those years in terms of motherhood alone was "the problem that had no name." Realizing that it was not some freakish personal guilt but our common problem as women had enabled us to take the first steps to change our lives. We had to move into the world of men because all the world outside the home was man's world then. But I sensed a dead end. I saw younger women, dressed for success in those dark gray suits, trying to be superwomen, to "have it all" in professions based on the lives of men who had wives to take care of the details of life. Women were smoking more now, and getting lung cancer more often. Did women really want to live, and die, like men? Among my own friends, some of the men were having heart attacks, triple bypasses, high blood pressure, strokes, Parkinson's disease. Others were facing crises of forced retirement from their professions. Would men live longer, like women, if they broke out of their traditional sex role as we have ours? It was as if these new years of life were forcing us to transcend polarized masculine and feminine sex roles geared to reproduction. Career vs. childrearing wasn't the question any more. But there was no model for living those new years of life in either the man's or the woman's sex role. Was the very transcending of those sex roles an evolutionary breakthrough?

Robert Butler gave me a list of the few places in this country where research on human aging was going on that might shed light on my questions. I began using my lecture trips to seek out experts—the gerontologists and geriatricians, the gerobiologists and geropsychiatrists. There were conferences, for the aging field was beginning to take off. There was research money. Young men and women were beginning to make careers of age. But the questions most of them were dealing with—incontinence in nursing homes, senile dementia of the Alzheimer's syndrome, the effect of age on insulin dosage for diabetics, precise quantitative measurements of memory loss—were not the questions that interested me. I sought out the psychologists who had done the major longitudinal studies at the University of California, Harvard, and Duke, following people from childhood or adolescence who were now in their seventies and eighties. Some of those studies had been done only on men. The questions I asked the researchers about sex roles were not questions they had asked in their studies.

So, I began my own search for answers, seeking out women and men who were breaking through conventional expectations of decline and deterioration in age—vital people over sixty-five. I followed men through and past the supposed trauma of retirement, and women after widowhood, in New York, Boston, Los Angeles, Seattle, Long Island. I interviewed couples in a retirement hotel and a trailer community in Sarasota, Florida, and at Leisure World in Laguna Hills, California, and went back to see my own high school classmates in Peoria, Illinois. I began to recognize some new dimension of personhood, some strength or quality of being in people who had crossed the chasm of age—and kept on going and growing. It surprised me.

To be honest, I dreaded doing those interviews at first. I had no wish to wallow personally in the dreariness of age. I didn't really want to look at or listen to those finished old people. Even "vital" ones. I didn't want to be contaminated by them. I was interested in theoretical questions. I surely didn't want the physical aura of age to rub off on me. During those first months of interviewing "them," I felt alternating currents of dread, fascination, and a strange pleasureful ease—and then an increased franticness, as if I had to keep rushing away from something I was getting nearer and nearer to myself. I couldn't bear to listen to much of what went on at the conferences on aging. It was so grim: the bed-wetting of old people in nursing homes; the depressing effect on "family caretakers" of Alzheimer's victims who finally lose the memory of their own names; the crisis looming in Social Security when the younger generation refuses to shoulder an increasing burden as more and more people live into their eighties and longer.

I began finding excuses not to pursue the answers to my questions. Yet I kept being drawn back, feeling I was on the track of something important. I kept stumbling on more surprises— like studies of the trauma of retirement in men or widowhood or the "empty nest" in women where, in fact, the expected symptoms never materialized in many of those studied.

Why not?

Another fact I stumbled on in those first months of my new search: when a man's wife dies, he is more likely to die within the next two years than are other men his age—unless he remarries, at which point his life expectancy goes back to normal. But if her husband dies, a woman, whatever her grief, is not as likely to die within the next two years. I suppose I was surprised, after all the years I had spent fighting for women's access to opportunity and power only open to men before, to find some strength in women, as we face age, that men seem to lack.

About this time, two massive sets of data were released that confirmed my own initial hunches about a vital change in women's aging. Twenty years earlier, the Midtown Manhattan Longitudinal Study had shown that women's mental health sharply deteriorated with age: there was progressive impairment in every decade after the age of twenty, and drastic impairment after forty, compared to men. A similar finding was reported by the National Center for Health Statistics. But when these studies were repeated, a few years ago, the results were so remarkably different that, at first glance, the epidemiologists and psychologists wondered whether mental health might not necessarily deteriorate with age at all. But then they looked closer and saw that the improvement had taken place only among women. Women in their forties and fifties, even in their sixties, were now enjoying mental health as good as or better than that of women in their twenties and thirties. In fact, the younger women today were showing more signs of stress. That decline in every decade after twenty, and that drastic deterioration after forty, no longer seemed to be taking place among American women. Men showed no such improvement.

More surprises. Studies were showing men now suffering greater "empty nest" crises than their wives, who were going on to other pursuits, without depression, when the kids left home. Men—even very successful men who had been concentrating on the career rat race, with little time for family—were now clutching at the kids as they took off. All around me, men my age and older were leaving their wives of thirty and forty years to start new families with young wives. They were sharing the care of their babies, these new fathers of fifty and sixty and seventy, as they never had in that first nest. Some of the discarded, older wives were desperately dyeing their hair, having their faces lifted, and looking for younger men to compete with those "re-born" husbands. But others were suddenly let-ting that brassy red or jet black hair grow out white, and moving on to projects of their own that they hadn't dared to try before.

The split was fascinating. Why were many women and men frantically denying, avoiding, refusing to admit their age, enduring deep de-pression at its prospect, while others crossed the age divide and found beyond it previously denied aspects of themselves? Could a woman, released from her previous feminine role, find strengths in herself she had sought before from men; could a man discover and/or develop sen-sitivities in himself that he had once sought only in women? Is integration of our masculine and feminine qualities a possible stage of develop-ment in age? And finally, might a new dimension of our humanity emerge with age? None of the measures then used in studies of aging showed any positive change. Still, those measures of human development, psychological growth, and mental capacity had been defined and standard-ized (mostly in male terms) on characteristics that could be studied in children with numerical precision. Muscular strength, numerical skills, abstract thought, and rote memory were at their peak in youth. If something new did emerge with age, or became integrated in a new way, it wasn't showing up on those scales, which only measured qualities that peaked in youth.

I knew I couldn't continue asking questions about age in abstract intellectual terms. The dread and denial they aroused in me were getting too intense to allow me to hone in on them. The fact was, I was getting too close to my own sixtieth birthday. I knew my writing about women had come from my own life. But I certainly wasn't prepared to identify with "them," the "aging" men and women I had started interviewing the previous winter in Florida, for instance. After all, I was only . . . fifty-eight? . . . fifty-nine?

In the months that followed my sixtieth birthday, I grimly forced myself to study age, head on. I took a fellowship at Harvard, where I would teach a seminar but otherwise be free to use the resources of that great university. I would immerse myself in state-of-the-aging-art: medical, clinical, physiological, psychological, social policy. I would pursue systematically my interviews of men and women who had apparently transcended age to achieve the strengths that interested me. But in this greatest of all American universities, the only official studies of age had to do with Alzheimer's disease, "health policy" governing nursing homes, and "ethical issues"—such as whose consent is needed to turn off those machines and pronounce the body-without-human-consciousness dead.

Looking around the paneled room at my first

Harvard meeting on "Ethical Issues in the Care of the Aged," I realized that, aside from my own, there was only one white head of hair. It belonged to a man who was a pioneer in the study of age and was about to retire (it seemed gerontologists must also retire at sixty-five). These bright young turks of the new aging field were mostly men who maybe started out in psychiatry, doing post-docs in "geropsychiatry" (there was a lot of research money available for Alzheimer's syndrome studies), and a few women staking out new turf as legal-medical "ethicists." Listening to these experts on aging talk about "them"—the problems of those sick, helpless, senile, incontinent, childlike, dependent old people, all alone, or draining the finances of their families, a burden on the Social Security system and the hospitals—I thought how different their concerns were from those of the women and men who had been telling me about surprising changes in their own lives since they turned sixty, seventy, eighty.

And then I was struck by *déjà vu*. I remembered those early conferences twenty-five years ago or more on the "woman problem." Male "experts" on women had talked about "them," those frustrated housewives who couldn't seem to adjust to their role as women. How could they be gotten off their husbands' and children's backs? Now, at the aging conference, I heard myself asking how people in their thirties and forties could identify the crucial questions and ethical issues for people over sixty-five. "Them." Wasn't it like having a bunch of men define the problems of women? Why weren't older people here identifying the questions? I stopped short of identifying myself as one of "them," but for a minute I felt the passion of true engagement, true excitement, and adventure stirring in me.

The room grew quiet. People looked uneasy. Behind their polite smiles and startled stares was the unspoken question, *Why does she have to intrude her feminist bias?* But I wasn't talking about women just then. For a moment there I had started talking about age the way feminists talk about women, from the gut! *Why, of course, she's getting old herself,* I could almost hear them thinking. Gray hair or no, some of the men directing this project were in their fifties, heading into their sixties like me. Why did none of them ever say "us" about age?

Suddenly self-conscious, I felt that maybe I shouldn't cross that line either. There was a divide here that clearly none of us intended to cross. Listening to the jargon, I sensed some necessary wall, some imperative that even those who make a career of studying age had to put between themselves and its reality. What was everybody so afraid of? What were we all denying? I realized that my own peers in that paneled room sounded even more distant and abstract about these dreary problems of aging than the medical young turks and post-docs who were enthusiastically categorizing them under new labels on large charts. At least the young gerontologists sounded smugly compassionate talking about "them," the objects of their new expertise. But why did we all seem to feel the need to distance ourselves from age, the closer we got to it? And yet there was this secret fascination.

At another conference on age, devoted exclusively to Alzheimer's, a statistic pierced through the drone: only 5 percent of people over sixty-five in America today suffer from this disease. And it *is* a disease, the experts now know, not the normal aging we must all anticipate. And suddenly I had another question to add to my growing list: Why was such a preponderance of the research money and gerontologists' attention being devoted to a disease afflicting a relatively small percentage of the population over sixty-five? Was it because such a mammoth publicity campaign for that terrible loss of human memory and personhood kept "us" from having to identify with age ourselves? It surely reinforced our terror and denial of age.

Considering the preponderance of papers and sessions on nursing homes at gerontological conferences, I was also amazed to learn at Harvard that only 5 percent of Americans over sixty-five are, in fact, in nursing homes, and less than 10 percent will ever be. Could such concentration on the victims of the most extreme ravages of senility, the sick, helpless old who can no longer function as persons in society, build up into an anathema of age that blinded those who made its policies and treated its problems, and even older people themselves, to the new possibilities of personhood in the years of life beyond sixty, seventy, eighty?

That year at Harvard, I wanted to learn what the behavioral sciences and the humanities had to say about the potentials of those added years of human life. There was a seminar on "Loneliness" that might be pertinent, I thought, and one on "Stages of Adult Life"—though that seemed to end at fifty. At the divinity school, a lively bunch of feminist theologians invited me to a seminar on female spirituality and God-experience. But when I asked if there was a seminar on spiritual development in the late stages of life, they studied the catalogue and found "Funeral Services" and "Concepts of the Afterlife."

A number of older graduate school mothers were taking the "Life Stages" course with the young Harvard undergraduates, but when they plotted the trajectories of their lives so far, the lines didn't fit into the life-course theories of Daniel Levinson, Erik Erikson, and others. Their plot of life's stages had charted a straight line of development from youthful preparation, to identity and intimacy and adult potency, to midlife peak and crisis, with age only as descent to death. That seemed to describe men's lives. The women's trajectory seemed to show a different kind of curve, with interruptions, changes, a less orderly, more complex development. It started earlier, later, stopped, shifted, went along a plateau, and then might leap ahead. It was continually interrupted, but continued longer. Was that sense of age as decline—an abrupt descent from human potency to helpless, passive, solitary senility—a man's trajectory, based on male sexual strength that declines with age? I now know that the study of age had begun with those dread declining curves of intelligence and strength as measured on male patients isolated in "old people's homes." But taking clues from women and men whose lives have not followed this pattern, why not now look at these new years of life in terms of continued or new roles in society, another stage in personal or even spiritual growth and development?

The next fall, I went back to Harvard. At the invitation of the Center for Population Studies, I organized a seminar on "Growth in Aging," inviting psychologists and other social scientists whose work had implications for continued evolution of the self. I also invited a few of those gerontology turks officially working on "aging and health policy" at the medical school. They weren't interested. In fact, the very term "growth in aging" outraged some of the senior behavioral scientists, especially those advanced in age themselves. B. F. Skinner got especially cross with me. There could be some behavioral conditioning to offset the effects of the decline. You could hang your umbrella on the doorknob to remind you to take it along in case of rain, and make lists, and so on. But age and growth were a contradiction in terms, he insisted.

Searching now for clues beyond the limits of gerontology, the academic study of aging, I started auditing the basic Harvard courses on evolution. Since human beings are the only species with such a long span of life after reproduction, is age simply an accidental byproduct, or an evolutionary breakthrough? I spent some delightful hours with E. O. Wilson and Stephen Jay Gould, over sandwiches amid their skeletons and fossils, speculating about all this. I also noticed a few other white-haired oddities in the rows of blue-jeaned young at those evolution lectures. And I found a little-publicized enclave of retired citizens, a de facto Harvard experiment in "growth in aging." The group was permitted to use the basement of one of the Harvard buildings. Members led each other in study groups of whatever interested them and could audit undergraduate courses. Later I would find, in Los Angeles and other cities, a veritable fountainhead of retired men and women participating in such experiments.

In the next three years, as I began to speak up at conferences, I continued to encounter this strange predilection of gerontological experts for dealing with age only in terms of pathology, and what appeared to be a serious discomfort with any view of positive aspects of aging. Asked to give the banquet speech at the (primarily male) Western Gerontological Association Convention in Albuquerque, New Mexico, in 1983, I queried mildly, "Why can't men age more like women?" A few of the women took me aside afterward to tell me, with great amusement, how I had threatened the men. They themselves had loved it.

"But why were the men uncomfortable?" I asked. "I didn't attack them. I deliberately stayed away from feminist issues."

"It wasn't your feminism," one of the women said. "You were so *personal.* You talked about their *own* aging. That's not the way it's done in gerontology."

At some conferences, sessions on "The Problems of Older Women" were initiated. For the first time, the National Institute on Aging convened experts to deal with the "problem" of women living so much longer than men; the "problem" of menopause and other female "diseases" of age, such as osteoporosis; the burden long-living women place on the Social Security system; and finally, what was to be done with all those women with no one to take care of them, now that their husbands were dead and their daughters and daughters-in-law were working?

Those sessions wallowed in the miseries of women in age: women as victims and as burdens. Nobody ever talked about the strengths that allowed women to live so much longer than men and how they might be used, and even emulated by men to live longer themselves. Nor was there discussion of circumstances or policies that might nourish such strengths, or make use of them for the benefit of the women themselves or of society.

Sessions on "the sexual problems" of age were also initiated. Research now indicated that people might have an active sex life into their seventies and eighties, even into their nineties. Maggie Kuhn, feisty founder of the Gray Panthers, interrupted the polite jargon about women's problems at a Washington conference to ask with whom women were going to have sex until eighty or ninety, with so many men their age dead: ten widows for every widower, and that widower marrying a younger woman. Everyone laughed uneasily when Kuhn said that we shouldn't kid ourselves, that if we were going to have sex, it would have to be with younger men, someone else's husband, other women, masturbation. No kidding, she said, and went on to describe how she had organized a commune and worked out a non-exclusive, part-time arrangement with a younger, married lover, rather than give up sex.

"What a character!" people said. Still, it was

easier to talk about "sex in aging" than to break through the resistance to consideration of "productive" use of those new years.

Just about this time, it was discovered that the old were not as poor as they had once been—what with Social Security, pensions, and countless new retirement villages that enabled them to live comfortably in California, Arizona, Florida, and on the outskirts of cities. But not even the women's movement raised an outcry when, in the last years of the losing battle for ERA, "minimal" Social Security was eliminated for those who had no earnings record, which meant no security in age for divorced women who had spent many years as housewives. The "bag lady" was replacing the "dirty old man" as the obscene joke of age. But with more and more muttering about the unfairness of burdening the younger generation with the escalating Social Security claims of those growing millions of people living into their eighties and nineties—the fastest-growing group in the population—even a feminist might think twice about calling attention to the fact that most of those living longer happened to be women, many barely covered by Social Security. The economic problems were real enough, for all too many women at least. But was the "problem" of age really getting more tax money to pay the doctors and the hospitals and the nursing homes and the bills for those machines? Not to speak of the lawyers to wrangle over when the machines get turned off? Or was the problem finding ways to utilize our added years of life in new and productive ways?

In the summer of 1983, Robert Butler asked me to join a group of scholars conducting a seminar on "Health, Productivity, and Aging" in Salzburg, Austria. The "fellows" attending were young doctors and officials heading or developing government programs in a number of European and Latin American countries as well as Egypt, Jordan, Israel, and the United States. Again I found that despite the announced focus of the seminar, there was a stubborn resistance to the very notion of "productive aging." Day after day, when the participants broke into discussion groups after each lecture, they only wanted to talk about Alzheimer's, senility, and nursing homes. They vehemently objected to discussing age in terms of any kind of "productivity." And they became very hostile indeed, almost hysterical, when I suggested an exercise in thinking of themselves at sixty-five or seventy, imagining the flesh of their underarms slightly more flabby, their eyesight or hearing a little dimmer, visualizing themselves carrying on in their present or new work, at play, in sex, in politics, whatever. In other words, they refused to contemplate any possibility of productive aging with which they could identify themselves. "Old people have earned the right to rest and be taken care of at that age," they said piously. Clearly they did not want to think about people over sixty-five except as helpless patients, clients of their compassionate care.

Deliver me from such compassion, I thought. It reminded me of pre-feminist "protection" of women, the old "protective" laws sheltering women from the burdens of earning, voting, participating in society in equality with men. Even so, I began to find a few people who were thinking about new possibilities for the added years of life and arguing about them. At the gerontological conventions in San Francisco in 1984 and New Orleans in 1985, I attended sessions in which researchers reported the development of new kinds of "cognitive capacity" in age—kinds of intelligence that developed and grew in ways that more than compensated for rote memory losses. These reports elicited active hostility from many of the participants. Citing years of research, they insisted that there was not and could not be any real change in personality, capacity, or mental functioning after forty. Not much after twenty, actually, except gradual decline.

Was I kidding myself about the possibilities? Maybe not. I began to find an underground of respectable biologists and psychologists, in Berkeley, Los Angeles, Chicago, Boston, whose data showed the development and emergence of various strengths in age. Some seemed to have a hard time getting their findings published in the gerontological journals. Some who were still bucking for tenure published only work that did not challenge the conventional wisdom about age—and were *waiting* to publish their more controversial studies. But even when such studies were published, they didn't seem to carry much weight against the dominant view of age as decline.

What were the motives that made all these "experts" want to keep the aging out of the places where the productive activities of society go on? Out of the activities that earn money and status? Well, if you were intent on making a successful professional career or building a lucrative business out of nursing homes, geriatric care, or other "help" for the aging, the more helpless the better. Far less trouble to keep them sedated, in beds and wheelchairs in expensive nursing homes, than to deal with their diverse reality and figure out ways to keep them productive in the community. Better to keep the elderly playing golf in retirement villages. Who really wants old people around, reminding you that you won't always be thirty-five, or forty-five years old? Who wants old people talking back to you about what kind of care they would prefer—as women, the handicapped, and other previously passive groups had begun to do?

I myself shrank from the polite or almost

sneering tone of voice, the glazed eyes that avoided mine, the mixture of condescension, pity, revulsion, when people heard I was doing research on age. "I'm not really interested in age," I insisted. "Just what keeps some women and men growing and developing past sixty while others deteriorate."

"You mean the fountain of youth," a woman said, turning away, avoiding my eyes, lighting her cigarette. "I hope it's in time for me."

"It's not the fountain of youth," I said one night, talking to Mike, who looked older than his seventy-odd years, a red-faced, overweight, wheezing, retired Chicago builder who refused to quit smoking and drinking when his doctor said he should. He kept writing into the night the poems he'd dreamed of when he was young, even in the hospital, after his heart attack. Funny, punny aphorisms to celebrate approaching death.

And it's not living forever, either, I realized, laughing at Mike's latest graveyard ditty, which he could barely wheeze out. "It's something else that can happen in age—if you let it," I said, "but it's not holding on to youth."

And Mike smiled. "The fountain of age?"

One September I signed up for a new program called "Going Beyond," sponsored by Outward Bound. The group proposed to put people "55-plus" through the same kind of wilderness-survival ordeal with which it had toughened generations of young people for the Peace Corps. I told myself I would find there older people from various backgrounds seeking new adventures, not clients for nursing homes and geriatric care. I went to buy a spare pair of glasses and to have my prescription checked. Lately, I had been seeing four moons when I looked up at the sky. The optometrist said, "Your eyesight has changed drastically. You'd better see a surgeon. I think you've got a cataract."

I took the Outward Bound wilderness survival trip anyhow. I survived the white-water rafting, and mountain cliff rappelling, and twenty-four hours alone in the wilderness in a crashing thunderstorm. I learned to use a compass to find my way in the forest without a trail, a feat dreamed of in childhood but never tried before. And knew I had dipped indeed into what I had begun to call the fountain of age. But on the top of that Tennessee mountain, I saw those four moons. So again I discontinued my search. How in all honesty could I go on speculating about the fountain of age when I was losing my own eyesight? Cataract means old. Cataract means deterioration. And I wasn't even sixty-five! Who was I kidding about growth in age?

For weeks I refused even to think about cataract surgery. But when I had to stop driving my car because I couldn't see the white line, finally I scheduled the operation for later that fall, but didn't mention it to anyone. When I confessed to my children and friends that I was scared about the operation, they all came around. And when the doctor took the bandage off, the day after the lens implant, I saw more clearly than I had in years. Medical advances like that lens implant were surely part of the fountain of age, I thought. They truly prolonged and enhanced our human functioning.

So I resumed interviewing vital older people and attending conferences and seminars on aging where the image of "them" was always strangely discrepant from the reality I was observing. One day during a discussion of "those poor old senile people" in nursing homes, I suddenly heard myself saying, "Let's not talk about 'them,' let's talk about 'us.'" I had come to understand, through my own experience, the panic that trapped those of us who are growing older into clutching at the illusion of physical youth. We cannot play the old games, or at least we cannot play them in the old way. We've lost the stomach for some, though we can't always bear to admit it. But was there any other way to work, to love, to continue finding the respect, the intimacy, and the sense of purpose we still needed? Now that I could honestly think about "them" as "us," I came to realize that the fountain of age didn't mean, *can't* mean, the absence of physiological, emotional, or situational change. But it takes so much effort to hold on to the illusion of youth, to keep the fear of age at bay, that in doing so we could fail to recognize the new qualities and strengths that might emerge.

I got a glimpse of the possibilities when I interviewed an eighty-five-year-old woman in a Florida retirement hotel. A former college teacher recovering from a stroke, she was teaching French to neighbors in their eighties who planned to visit France for the first time. I got a glimpse of it in a man in his early seventies, a cynical, pugnacious, go-getting Hollywood agent who had no use for love after his wife died and refused to have the operation he needed on a deteriorated disk until it was almost too late. The first operation didn't work. After the second one, walking again, driving, swimming half a mile every day, he shook his fist and had an angry dialogue with God every morning when the pain was really bad. Then he discovered how to live with that pain. To his surprise, he even felt sexy again, and reached out for love.

I talked to women surviving cancer of the breast, or a heart attack, or widowhood or divorce from men who had been their whole lives. Some had been obsessed with the rage at dependence that feminism unleashed. I saw one of them, discarded by the husband whose success she had never forgiven, forgo a fourth face-lift and start a business of her own when she was sixty. Another, after a heart attack, admitted her dissatisfaction with her career and her grief over the husband she had lost, and went on a pilgrimage to Jerusalem. She said she wanted to study Hebrew, but what she was looking for was some new way to be comfortable in herself, beyond husband or career.

Sometimes my search would slip out of focus or become obscured by doubts and complexities. Who were we kidding, these men who had lived only for success, we women whose lives had been dominated by the pursuit of love even as we accomplished new things in the world outside of the home? Did I really believe that there might be life beyond retirement from the power-sex race? *How? Where?* And if I was honest about "us," how could there be a fountain of age without men as objects of our dreams of love? How to face the reality that there might never again be a man to fill that longing for romance, sexual passion, transcendent bliss, not to speak of something so mundane as marriage? Was feminine solidarity an adequate answer to the rage we felt about men our age to whom we had become sexually invisible? If we didn't want to be defined solely as sex objects, that didn't mean we wanted permanently to eliminate the pleasures of being one.

I was, in any event, feeling better about myself as a woman, more at ease about growing older. In fact, I was taking new delight and comfort in my new and old men friends, without wanting or expecting the friendship to end in bed, much less marriage. This comfort made me feel closer to them and perhaps freer to be myself than I had ever been—before or after feminism. In sex, too, was it necessary to free ourselves from old expectations, the fantasies of youth? Was it possible to stop playing sexual games at some point and risk new honesty about our feelings? Knowing that we can survive alone but have the power of honest friendship, can we let go of the old fantasies and the desperate denial they breed, allowing something new to emerge?

More questions; still no answers. But at least I could now see that as long as we strained to hold on to the illusions and expectations of youth—thinking only in youth's terms of what we wanted and expected of ourselves—we were trapped in an increasingly desperate game we could only lose. Even if society allowed both men and women to keep playing for power, sex, and career, was that what we still really wanted and needed? The pursuit of youth was blinding us to the possibilities of age. Could denial of our own aging block further growth, foreclose the emergence of a new life otherwise open to us?

I had a hunch that there was a chain of denial that had to be broken to release us from that dread of dreary, helpless, sick, lonely age, which was both cause and effect of our entrapment within the values and perceptions of youth. As long as we flailed fruitlessly within the binds of that youth trap, the potential of those uncharted years couldn't emerge. We would not use the freedom of age to make our own choices about spending that bounty of time. But who set that trap, and how could we break free, separating out the complex actualities of biological aging from the pathologies, confronting the losses we dreaded, distinguishing what is biologically programmed and irreversible from what is open, up to us? I suspected that we might be able to face the realities of age if we had the courage to take the responsibility for making choices that we never before had to make about our own lives.

By denying the real infirmities of age, we become its passive victims, forfeiting choice. And that realization also opened up a host of new questions. Could we conceive of a kind of health care in age that aims beyond diagnosis and "cure" of terminal disease, with concomitant machine-sustained life or nursing home confinement, to a goal of continued human functioning with whatever infirmities exist? Could we use new technology not simply to prolong life but to promote its human ends? Is it simply death that inspires the denial of age, or is the obsessive dread of age itself much of what we fear about death?

Finally, what do we actually experience as we go through the process of growing old? How much of what we see is imposed by our society's views, how much is self-imposed? What do we see when we look at age in its own terms? What do we see when we look at vital women and men who neither deny age nor wallow in its victim state but continue to develop and grow? If, in fact, new visions, new values, new states of personal realization emerge in this stage of life, what are the implications for our own and society's approach to the "problem" of age? What further reaches of human growth can we envision? And what public policies in health care, housing, education, in labor, industry, church and synagogue and government, might nourish the emergence and societal use of these new dimensions in human vitality? What paths can we all take to defy the self-fulfilling prophecy of decline?

I have discovered that there is a crucial difference between society's image of old people and "us" as we know and feel ourselves to be. There are truly fearful realities reflected—and imposed —by that image. To break through that image, we must first understand why, how, and by whom it is perpetuated. We must also glimpse some new possibilities and new directions, both as individuals and as a society, that belie that image. I have found the answers to many of the questions that motivated my quest to distinguish the truth from the lies, the realities from the myths, about age. I have also found that there are choices we can make along the journey we all, sooner or later, must take that truly open surprising new possibilities.

Part I

The Age Mystique

Denial
and the
"Problem"
of Age

At the start of my quest, I sat at my desk trying to make sense of some strange discrepancies between image and reality in the pile of clippings and studies I had been accumulating about age. On the one hand, despite continued reports of advances in our life expectancy, there was a curious *absence*—in effect, a blackout—*of images of people over sixty-five,* especially older women, doing, or even selling, anything at all in the mass media. On the other hand, there was an *increasing obsession with the problem of age* and how to avoid it personally, through diet, exercise, chemical formulas, plastic surgery, moisturizing creams, psychological defenses, and outright denial—as early and as long as possible. And there seemed to be a *growing impatience for some final solution* to that problem—before the multiplying numbers of invisible, unproductive, dependent older people, unfortunately living beyond sixty-five, placed an "intolerable burden" on their families and society with their senility, chronic illnesses, Medicare, Meals on Wheels, and nursing homes.

Consider the following, a random selection from my pile:

ITEM: In a recent study of characters appearing in prime-time network television drama monitored for one week in a major city, of 464 role portrayals, only seven (or 1.5 percent) appeared to be over sixty-four years of age. Another study found that only two out of one hundred television commercials contained older characters.[1]

ITEM: In an analysis of 265 articles on aging in a large midwestern newspaper, none depicted older people still active in their communities. All dealt with the "problem" of age: nursing homes, or retirees reminiscing about the "good old days."[2]

ITEM: In a nationwide survey of American adults conducted for the National Council on Aging to determine popular images of aging, Louis Harris found the great majority of Americans agreed that "most people over 65" were *not* very "physically active," *not* very "sexually active," *not* very "open-minded and adaptable," *not* very "useful members of their communities."[3]

ITEM: Only 8 percent of people over sixty-five in the Harris Poll found the term "old" acceptable to describe themselves. A majority of those over sixty-five also objected to "older American," "golden-ager," "old-timer," "aged person," even "middle-aged person." Barely half of the people over sixty-five accepted the terms "senior citizen," "mature American," or "retired person" for themselves.[4]

ITEM: In some senior citizen clubs, the members are fined if they use the word "old." "Before new business, the president calls for leftover business. It's as if being old is a disgrace."[5]

ITEM: "Forever Young," a cover story in *New York* magazine subtitled "Plastic Surgery on the Fast Track" (June 9, 1986), revealed that in 1984, 2,700 certified plastic surgeons operated on 477,000 people to make them look younger. Between 1981 and 1984, according to the American Society of Plastic and Reconstructive Surgeons, the number of cosmetic operations increased by 61 percent. Most of these patients were over fifty, and most were women, but "both sexes are seeing cosmetic surgeons at an earlier age."

The uneasiness I had earlier felt when I admitted to people that I was working on a book about age came back to me as I started a systematic

53

search through magazines I occasionally read, even wrote for, looking for images of people who might be sixty-five or more. I went through the major mass-market magazines for August 1986—fashion, general, women's, men's, news —studying every ad or illustration showing identifiable faces. The *non-existence* of images that were not "young" was dismaying: the seeming disappearance of people who could be over sixty-five, except for those extremely rich or famous—and they were shown "young." I started to cheat, shifting my count to "over sixty" where the age was known. I even considered stretching my "older" category to include people who might be fiftyish, if there was gray in their hair, or lines on their faces, or any visible sign of "maturity"—as, for instance, Jackie Kennedy, Jack Nicholson, Michael Caine, the Marlboro Cowboy.

Here was what I found:

• In *Vogue,* of 290 identifiable faces in ads, there was only *one* of a woman who might have been over sixty—in a tiny snapshot of "me and granny" among the 38 snapshots in the double-page Albert Nipon ad of a young woman growing up: "Show me the child and I'll give you the woman." There were four older men—Ronald Reagan, Gene Autry, a white-haired boss buying drinks for a young woman and man, and another white-haired man getting on a plane after three younger men.

• Out of 200 faces in the illustrations in *Vogue,* less than ten might have been over sixty: one white-haired hairdresser (the "Busy Women's Power Styler"); one "oil empress of Texas"; "one of the richest men in the country," Paul Mellon, and his wife; the author J. D. Salinger in a picture of himself as a young man; a grizzled Texan "contemporary cowboy"; and a balding British male author. All of these were miniatures in the front or back-of-the-book columns—none of the full-page fashion ads showed a woman even conceivably fifty.

• Of the 116 identifiable faces in the *Vanity Fair* illustrations, there were two women clearly over sixty—the Queen Mother and Imelda Marcos—and ten older men, all powerful or famous.

• In the *Ladies Home Journal,* of 72 faces in ads, two might have been in their sixties—old-style grandparents in a candy ad. Of 74 faces in illustrations, six were over sixty—Ronald and Nancy Reagan, several of Queen Elizabeth, and the late Rock Hudson.

• The men's magazines practiced almost the same denial of age. In *Esquire,* of 201 images in ads, three, or 1 percent, were conceivably over sixty. The Marlboro cowboys were more vague of feature and seemed more "young" than heretofore. The Hathaway Shirt man with the eyepatch, whom I recalled as a handsome mature man—fiftyish—was now a baby-faced yuppie!

• In *Fortune,* out of 49 images in ads, three were conceivably over sixty—Walter Cronkite (though not a recent, white-haired photo), a baseball coach, and a vague drawing of a symphony conductor with a "young" face and a misty halo of white hair. Of the article illustrations, 11 out of 129 were mature men (including the head of General Motors, four Justices of the Supreme Court, and two "quality gurus" brought back in their eighties to advise companies in crisis).

• In *Psychology Today,* whose market was well-educated adults, out of 21 identifiable faces in ads, the only one not "young" was the Marlboro Cowboy. Of 66 figures in illustrations, only two had white hair—a historic photograph from November 6, 1946, showing an admiral in uniform and his wife cutting a cake in the shape of an atom bomb.

• In *Time,* there were *no* faces over sixty in the ads. Of 125 people in the news photographs, 12 men might have been over sixty, and another five—at least mature—were world leaders. There were no faces at all of older women.

The magazines I had picked were not those specifically geared to "young" men or women, but it was quite clear that editors, art directors, ad agency executives, and advertisers shared a belief that the face of anyone "older" (than sixty, fifty, forty?) was an object of revulsion to Americans, which had to be hidden from view in order to sell the product—even when the prospective buyers were in or approaching that age range themselves. Even in the ads in *Ms.* magazine, I was amazed to discover that there was not one image of an older woman. I asked Gloria Steinem, *Ms.*'s editor (who had openly admitted to being over fifty herself), about this. She said it bothered her, too, but the advertisers simply refused to use older women as models. "We do try to run articles about the plight of older women," she said.

An ad in *Vogue* and *Vanity Fair* for a facial mask "that virtually reverses the effects of age on surface skin" showed clay smeared over a young face that was, in fact, taut and unlined beneath. An ad in *Ladies Home Journal,* "Don't just cover your gray—mousse it," showed the faces of two women who could have been in their twenties; another, "How to relieve arthritis pain," showed a young, unlined woman's face under streaked platinum hair, despite grotesquely twisted muscles X-rayed under the skin of her arms and legs.

Even articles that dealt with people known to be in their sixties were, for the most part, illustrated with pictures of those same people in their youth. The main illustration in a *Vanity Fair* article on Imelda Marcos showed her at forty-five. A *Vogue* article on Jean Harris, in August 1986, did not show her white-haired present self in prison, or in the dramatic years of her midlife murder trial, but a brown-haired, younger picture "taken six years before Hy's death." Four out of six illustrations for the article on Rock Hudson's death from AIDS were of the "young" Rock Hudson.

The exceptions that prove the rule were, of course, Ronald and Nancy Reagan. But there was no gray in Nancy's hair, no lines crinkling the tight skin of her face when she smiled. The ages of the Reagans were known—she then in her sixties, he in his seventies—but daily denied by their air-brushed "photo opportunities." In his old movies, or as he was shown challenging Walter Mondale to arm-wrestle, or chopping wood at Camp David, Ronald Reagan was forever young, while Nancy, like the models and actresses in those ads, was giving us daily proof that the lines and experience of sixty years of living can indeed be erased from a woman's face.

The reality of our own government headed by a man in his seventies was not surprising in a decade when the life expectancy of Americans had been breaking through to a new high every year, with people living into their eighties and nineties the fastest-growing group in the population. The reality of "the graying of America" rendered doubly strange this insidious, pervasive media blackout of images of older people active in the work, play, love, and sports of everyday American life, even in consuming the products our society sells.

Coincidentally in this same decade, there was increasing media attention to the "plight" of the elderly, to age as a "problem." The biggest folder in my research file of news clips and magazine articles on "the graying of America" was, in fact, about nursing homes: exposés of the plight of helpless, senile, dependent, solitary, sick, poor old people. There were many reports about that terrible senility of Alzheimer's disease and the grisly details of its progressive destruction of memory, intelligence, personal identity. There were also more and more reports of the increasing cost to society of Social Security and Medicare, and the burden on families of taking care of those vastly increasing numbers of "unproductive" older people.

The perennial newsmagazine stories ominously proclaiming "the graying of America" managed somehow to twist even positive news about aging into a "plight" or "problem." For news stories dealing with the work of the Senate Committee on Aging, which, under the leadership of Senator Claude Pepper, was proposing positive measures to keep older people actively engaged in their communities, the most frequent headline was in fact "Plight of the Elderly." A *Newsweek* cover story (January 24, 1983) was headlined: "The Social Security Crisis: Who Will Pay?", with subheads, "The Growing Burden on the Young" and "The Mounting Worries of the Old." An inverted triangle showed a single twenty-year-old on the bottom, then a man and woman in their thirties, groaning under the weight of four gloomy "golden-agers" on their backs. An article entitled "The Old Folks" in *Forbes* that winter, purporting to dispel the "myth that they're sunk in poverty," ended: "The trouble is there are too many of them . . . God bless them."

The "problem of age" or "the plight of the elderly" was often presented in praiseworthy, compassionate terms, as, for instance, in the Emmy Award–winning documentary "What Shall We Do About Mother?" (August 2, 1980), Marlene Sanders's examination of America's aging population on "CBS Reports":

No longer able to care for themselves, yet too poor for private nursing homes and too wealthy for government assistance, millions of America's elderly face bleak futures, and the responsibility of care often falls on their children. . . . Claire Brown's mother has already exhausted her savings in a private nursing home. At eighty-five, she is a victim of advanced senility. "You can't communicate with her," says Claire Brown. "It's a big decision when you have to put somebody in any kind of facility, you know. You're acting like a person's keeper." . . . Today we ask the question on behalf of our parents; tomorrow, it will be our children asking it about us.

An ad for a new volume in the Institute of Medicine series on America's aging read: "The percentage of Americans age 65 and older will likely double within the next 50 years. Many people in this age group will continue to lead healthy active lives. *But how will our society cope with the many others for whom old age will spell chronic illness, disability and dependence?*"

The italics, the emphasis, is the ad's, not mine.

Putting together all these stories about the "plight" of the elderly and their increasing numbers beside their strange disappearance from images of active American life, I began to sense something sinister about the impatience of Americans for some "final solution" to the "problem of age," and the frantic obsession of Americans generally with denying their own aging. The blackout of images of women or men visibly over sixty-five, engaged in any vital or productive adult activity, and their replacement by the "problem" of age, is our society's very definition of age. Age is perceived only as decline or deterioration from youth. An observer from another planet might deduce from these images that Americans who can no longer "pass" as young have been removed from places of work, study, entertainment, sports— segregated in senior citizens' "retirement villages" or nursing homes from which, like concentration camps, they will never return. Is that the reality, or is the "plight" of the elderly a way

61

to displace or deny our own aging? Older people rendered helpless, childlike, and deprived of human identity or activities don't remind us of ourselves. The "problem" of age can be shifted onto "them" and kept away from us. Clearly, the image of age has become so terrifying to Americans that they do not want to see any reminder of their own aging. What *is* the final solution to such a problem?

Staring at these images—and thinking about what they leave out—I realized that I had been on this road before. I remembered when some thirty years ago I had suddenly sensed there was something missing in the image of woman in the women's magazines I was then reading and writing for. That image defined a woman only in sexual relation to a man—as wife, mother, sex object, server of physical needs of husband, children, home. But I had heard women groping to articulate a "problem that had no name," because it didn't have to do with husband, children, home, or even sex. And I realized that the image of women we all accepted left out woman *as a person,* defining herself by her own actions in society. I asked myself what it meant, this discrepancy between the reality of our being as women and the image by which we were trying to live our lives. I began to call that image the "feminine mystique," and to figure out how it had come about and what it was doing to us. I began to see the "woman problem," as it was called then, in new terms. And to see how that feminine mystique masked, even created, the real problems.

So now I asked why there was no image of age with which I could identify the *person* I am today. What did the image of the "plight" or "problem" of age leave out? What explained the absence of any image of older people leading active and productive lives? The image of age as inevitable decline and deterioration, I realized, was also a mystique of sorts, but one emanating not an aura of desirability, but a miasma of dread. I asked myself how this dread of age fitted or distorted reality, making age so terrifying that we have to deny its very existence. And I wondered if that dread, and the denial it breeds, was actually helping to *create* the "problem" of age.

I could already see, from the panic that kept dogging my own search, that the mystique of age was much more deadly than the feminine mystique, more terrifying to confront, harder to break through. Even as age came closer and closer to me personally, I kept asking myself if denial isn't better, healthier. Did I really want to open this sinister Pandora's box? For there was truly nothing to look forward to—nothing to identify with, nothing I wanted to claim as "us" —in the image of age as decay and deterioration. Perhaps, I thought, age becomes more terrifying the more it is denied? Still, wasn't it better, wiser, healthier to try to think and act "young" as long as we can? Or was the terrifying mystique of age—and the real "plight" of the elderly—somehow created by our obsession with and idealization of youth, and the refusal even to look at the reality of age on its own terms?

We who are now approaching age can hardly remember a time when older people were respected, looked up to, venerated for their wisdom. We can't see ourselves in biblical images of prophets with white beards, or in the anthropological lore of times before literacy, before printing press, radio, television, computer, when the elders were the repositories of the accumulated knowledge, wisdom, history, and traditions of the tribe. Or even in the earlier history of our own society, when the elders owned and controlled the land. It was the young, after all, who left Europe and Africa for America, who went west on the wagon trains.

If we were the children or grandchildren of immigrants—if we went from small town to big city to seek a job or profession our parents never even dreamed of—if we were the first in our family to go to college, medical school, law school, or get a job in an industry like television that didn't even exist before—youth, young adulthood, meant for us the open world, the road to kinds of freedom, power, wealth, knowledge, status unimaginable to them. Upward mobility, the sociologists called it, the American dream.

And our parents wanted it for us—expected us to move beyond them. They worshipped our youth, and this shift from veneration and respect for age to the obsession with and emulation of youth escalated during our lifetimes with the babies we produced in such numbers in the 1940s and 1950s—that enormous demographic bulge that skewed the American population curve and became the unprecedented youth market of the 1960s and 1970s. The media fed that shift. An analysis of American magazine fiction between 1890 and 1955 found an increasing tendency to characterize young adulthood as the best years of life. In the sixties and seventies, when the postwar baby boomers ignited the "generation gap," the shift was vastly accelerated. The "youth market" now set the styles—music, haircuts, jeans—the eighteen-to-forty-nine market that every movie, magazine, television program, and ad campaign targeted.[6]

One does not need to be a marketing expert to know that marketers are enchanted . . . obsessed with young consumers. . . . Most major marketers limit their efforts to only three out of five of their potential customers by directing their marketing activities to consumers under the age of 49. They cross that age barrier only on such items as denture cleansers, laxatives, tonics, arthritis remedies, and other products that are clearly designed to relieve the aches and pains of old age. In effect, two out of every five American adults are invisible consumers. . . . Perhaps one reason over-49s are invisible is that very often only their hairdressers know for sure. . . .[7]

Those of us then in our forties and fifties became invisible in other ways. Between 1969 and 1971, CBS cleared the decks of such prime-time series as "Green Acres," "Beverly Hillbillies," "Red Skelton," and "Gomer Pyle" because their audiences "skewed" over the forty-nine level. By the mid-1970s television networks had canceled the few programs with older men or women in them like "The Waltons." And a movie, *Logan's Run*, in which Michael York played a thirty-year-old man of the future whose age marks him for execution by the state, was piloted for a continuing television series. The blackout of images of people over forty-nine—much less sixty-five—in and as targets of print advertising, TV commercials, television programs, and movies was in place by the beginning of the 1980s.

Thus in strange reverse correlation with the actual demographic shift, as increasing millions now lived well beyond their sixties the proliferation of programs that dealt with the "problem" of age and the stepped-up sales pitch for products that promised to stop aging all underlined the message that age was acceptable *only if it passed for or emulated youth.* In the fifteen years prior to 1985, the over-sixty-five segment of the population increased by more than 35 percent, to over 30 million persons, with over $200 billion to spend.[8] But even the advertising and media campaigns that began to be specifically directed at those multiplying older consumers were permeated by, and perpetrated, the denial of age. The Clairol slogan, "You're not getting older, you're getting better," said, in effect, that *we dare not age—nothing about "old" can be better.* It promoted denial of the very fact of aging.

Consider, also, the "special issues" that were put out once or twice a year by the fashion magazines geared to "over 40 and sensational!" I leafed through one of them (*Harper's Bazaar,* September 1982) with the cover banner: "How to Look Younger Every Day." The issue included:

• Stop-the-clock beauty book: great over-40 beauties tell you how to take off inches, wrinkles, years.
  • Your first face-lift: what can go wrong.
  • Could you be an alcoholic?
  • Can sex cure arthritis?

The articles on menopause, "Having My First Baby at 40," and an article on going back to college were fine. But the *images*—the 200-odd pictures of women wearing the clothes in the fashion pages and ads, which are what the magazine is all about—were models in their twenties and thirties.

The beauty section, "Over 40 and Fabulous," showed some women who really were over forty and did look fabulous: Princess Grace, Julie Andrews, Barbara Walters, Dina Merrill. "Being over 40 can mean looking and feeling healthier, happier and more beautiful than ever before," the writer proclaimed. But what was being sold by these superwomen was the fountain of youth: a career of looking forever young.

The caption "Keeping skin moist and supple can become a problem as you get older" was placed opposite a picture of one woman, whose face, over sixty, in fact, showed no wrinkles at all (the caption did not mention her plastic surgery).

"With the passing years, skin's soluble collagen breaks down, causing it to sag and wrinkle. . . . One of the first areas to show signs of age is the neck" (picture of Capucine's neck with no sags or wrinkles).

"Tiny expression lines around the eyes are a common problem as the years go by" (picture showing no expression lines around Joanna Carson's eyes).

Toward the back of the magazine were pictures of "five beauties who still have the enviable faces and figures that made them top models" in their twenties. Then why weren't these women, now in their forties and fifties, used to model the "over-40 and fabulous" fashions the magazine was selling, instead of twenty-year-olds? Because, in fact, those "forever young" models didn't look that good—they didn't look *alive,* like the natural young ones. And without those "expression lines," they didn't look vitally aging either. After a while, the absence of any marks of human experience and personality on the tautly stretched skin of such multiple-face-lifted models truly evoked, in me at least, that dread of age. It was a breakthrough, of course, for an American fashion magazine to go on for so many pages about being over forty as "fabulous," as opposed to the blackout. But the overwhelming effect of such images is to create, especially in women, a devastating terror of not being young—and thereby to sell billions of dollars of skin and beauty cosmetics and surgical procedures, building whole industries on that fear, that desperate illusion of stopping age.

By the mid-1980s, estimates of how many cosmetic surgeries were done each year in the United States swung from 60,000 to 2 million face-lifts, rhytidectomies, literally, "wrinkle re-movers," which, at an average cost of $5,000, totaled $300 million to $10 billion. In her book *Mirror, Mirror: The Terror of Not Being Young* (1983), the California psychologist Elissa Mel-amed claimed that the fear of aging was striking women at an ever earlier time of life.

The physical trauma of plastic surgery was not minimized by the women described in "Forever Young," the *New York* magazine cover story of June 9, 1986. The woman is "tied to a table, her arms bound," as "the man jabs [a needle] into [her] right breast . . . about a dozen times, and then makes an incision . . . a deep pocket inside her breast." There is ". . . a terrible hissing sound, like that of a hot poker being held to the flesh. . . . [He] stuffs something that looks like a flattened jelly doughnut . . . into the woman's right breast, then another into the left." The woman then thanks the man "for making her 36B breasts a fuller 36C." This woman, who "has paid $4,700 and gone through 90 minutes of surgery" in order to make her breasts "more like they were when I was a teenager," was twenty-nine at the time!

Doctors also recommended getting an early start, and then frequent "renewals" of the face-lift. One surgeon told Melamed:

It seems that the longer a patient waits to have the primary rhytidectomy, the more likely he or she is to develop early recurrence of the deformity [i.e., the wrinkles, the expression lines?]. I believe it is advantageous to do the initial procedure at a relatively early age, such as the fourth or even the third decade [the twenties!].

. . . The patient who wants to look as good two years later . . . should be told that an early secondary operation will be needed. . . . People who want to "fix" their ages might benefit from a second renewal operation three to four years later and perhaps even a third renewal operation five to seven years after the second one.[9]

"Even the best face-lifts don't last more than eight to ten years," the article continued, "but doctors say getting three face-lifts in a lifetime is no big deal." An older woman visited the same surgeon once a month for "a nip, a tuck . . . an injection of collagen . . . into the lines between her eyebrows. . . . Cosmetic surgery has been a success for this woman. Though she's probably in her seventies, she doesn't look old. The problem is, she doesn't look real either. But she's got high cheekbones, a clean neckline and no wrinkles. As she is injected with Valium to dull the pain of the collagen injection, she talks about a friend of hers who is dating a 28-year-old man. 'And she's my age,' she says."[10]

Though doctors are supposed to inform women of the possible risks of such surgery—facial paralysis, infection, bleeding, skin perforation, hair loss, blindness, and even death from a blood clot migrating to the lungs—studies have shown that women prefer to gloss over or deny the danger. Only three out of twenty women in one study remembered even three of the risks they had been warned about.

Another woman admitted to this terror of age

—at thirty-six. In the "Hers" column of *The New York Times* (January 16, 1986), Katha Pollitt, whose work was printed that year in an anthology of "younger poets," wrote:

As a poet, I may be younger, but as I am a woman I am definitely older. As a sex object, to put it bluntly, I am depreciating by the day.

Today I am urged on every side to fight the encroaching decay of my person with large investments of energy, time and money. I should slather my face with makeup by day and collagen cream by night. I should take up running or aerobic dancing and resign myself to 1,200 calories a day for life. I should dye my hair. Advertising, which features no female who looks one minute over 25, tells me this, and so do women's magazines which treat beauty care and dieting as a female moral duty. . . . I did dye my hair. . . . But basically, I don't want to do many of these things. . . .

Does this mean I accept my age gracefully? No, actually I'm furious . . . and frightened— when I think of the time down the road when I'll be elderly in more than the obstetrical sense. Will I end up tied to a bed in some horrible nursing home?

Pollitt discounted the recent false "vogue" for older women as sex symbols. ("What does that vogue really mean? Joan Collins and Linda Evans may be goddesses after 40, but what makes them 'beautiful' is primarily that they don't look middle-aged, they look embalmed. These actresses' popularity is no tribute to mature femininity, but to the dubious arts of the makeup man and, I suppose, the plastic surgeon.") She was especially furious when she thought of how different aging is for women as opposed to men, who can "acquire progressively younger wives with each marriage."

In that futile search for images of women over sixty, fifty, forty in major mass-market magazines, I also got furious at ads showing a handsome white-haired man, clearly over fifty, even over sixty, putting a luxurious mink coat over the bare shoulders of a blonde in her twenties. Or the personal ads: "Divorced male, 65, seeks slim, beautiful, warm, intelligent, charming female 35–45." But I was not at all sure that the older man, denying his age, was much better off than the woman denying hers—except, of course, economically. And in fact, by the end of the 1980s, the men's magazines were pushing plastic surgery, hair transplants, and tasteful ways to hide the gray. An *Esquire* cover story, "How a Man Ages" (May 1982), pictured a man in bathing trunks, pensively twentysomething, getting paunchier, flabbier, and dimmer as he progressed in a series of pictures, to age thirty, forty, fifty, sixty, seventy: "the catalog of decay."

30. In most ways he is at his peak . . . and yet he can see the first lines on his forehead, he can't hear quite as well as he could . . . and his degeneration has just begun. . . . 40. He's an eighth of an inch shorter than he was ten years ago, and each hair follicle has thinned two microns. . . . All over he's begun to feel the weight of time's passage; his stamina is greatly diminished. . . . 50. His eyes have begun to fail him . . . his erections have dipped below the horizontal mark. . . . 60. By now he has shrunk a full three-quarters of an inch, he has trouble telling certain colors apart . . . trouble making distinctions among the different foods he tastes. . . . 70. His heart is pumping less blood, his hearing is worse, vision weakening still, yet if he's made it thus far, say the statistics, he'll live another 11 years.[11]

Does the ability of men to keep on replaying the youthful child-rearing role, with younger wives, really keep them from aging? As Pollitt said, "We can't do anything about the fact that a man can father a whole second family while collecting Social Security. . . . At least, we can stop glorifying female youth to ourselves. We can stop thinking that wrinkles make men more interesting, but make women look ugly." We might also spare ourselves any feelings of spite or envy of that man, who, notwithstanding his greater economic power, may get pretty tired and scared, obsess about impotence, and die before his time, even if he succeeds in denying his own age. He can still expect to die eight years sooner than the woman his age.

Even so, the denial of age seems more desperate in women's magazines. An article (*McCall's,* January 1987) on *"Dallas'* sexy superstar" began:

"Twenty-seven . . . again!" Linda Gray said joyfully (yes, joyfully) when photographer Greg Gorman surprised her on her 46th birthday with a lavish cake.

The determination not to take age too seriously, but instead to play lightheartedly with the idea of time passing, might well be what keeps women like Linda . . . indefinitely young. No doubt it has helped Linda Gray redefine for all of us what it means to be 46 in 1987. Why, it just means being 27 nineteen times in a row! "In my mind, *I am* 27," she admits, laughing some more.

Even feminists have not often challenged the dread of age among women. Gloria Steinem, celebrating her fiftieth birthday at a big gala in the ballroom of the Waldorf-Astoria, remarked that she had been worried that fifty was "serious, grown-up, and finally old." But not to worry: "Fifty is what 40 used to be. Romance is still possible since women of 50 are now able to 'choose younger men.' "

One feminist, Jane O'Reilly, took issue with Steinem:

But is that all there is to say? . . . It seems to me that "grown-up" is a word that should be coherent at the age of 50, and not accompanied by a girlish giggle.

I think it is important to say that 50 is not a delayed 40. . . . Let there be less marveling at our wonderful preservation and more respect for the maturity of our mind and spirit. . . . Fifty is 50, and to deny that is to deny wisdom, experience and life itself.[12]

The fact is, however, the dread of age has become so ingrained in our consciousness that even those who study or report on age seem to seek only the fountain of youth. I got a call from a *Time* researcher who was gathering material for a cover story on "changing attitudes about age." She was told to call me because she had heard that I'm "very active and energetic" and "look very good for my age." She said, compassionately, that she knew I was over sixty but had heard that I "still do a lot of things, like jogging." I groaned. I had just sprained my ankle, jogging. "Isn't it nice for you," she asked, "that attitudes are changing and older people are now being allowed to do young people's things?"

• • •

If there are few, if any, positive images of age in the mass media, there is no lack of negative ones. Summing up the results of their Media Watch in the late 1970s, the Gray Panthers' nationwide volunteer force monitoring television found older people depicted as "ugly, toothless, sexless, incontinent, senile, confused and helpless. . . . Old age has been so negatively stereotyped that it has become something to dread and feel threatened by." In a survey conducted by *Retirement Living* (April 1976) on a cross section of people under and over sixty-five, the most common adjectives used to describe the way people over sixty were depicted on television were "ridiculous," "decrepit," and "childish." At least most of the younger people in the survey, 70 percent, considered such an image "unfair"—but nearly half of the people over sixty-five accepted it! Even graduate students in psychology, enrolled in a course on the aging process, agreed by as high as 90 percent that older people "have lost most of their teeth," are "forgetful," "like to doze in a rocking chair," are "lonely," "repeat themselves," "walk slowly," "have poor coordination," "dislike any changes," are "set in their ways," and "like to think about the good old days."[13]

In studies over the past twenty years, young people, middle-aged people, doctors, occupational therapists, nurses, institutionalized older persons, and even *gerontologists* saw older people as childlike, mentally incompetent, unattractive, lonely, dependent, and powerless. A survey by the Andrus Gerontology Center of the University of Southern California in 1977 of public and private sector decision makers who made policy for the elderly in Los Angeles County found that they vastly overestimated the dependency of people over sixty-five: they thought five times as many were in institutions compared to the actual statistic of 4.9 percent. Only one out of ten decision makers was aware of this reality. Some thought 50 percent or more of people over sixty-five were in nursing homes.

If age itself is defined as "problem," then those over sixty-five who can no longer "pass" as young are its carriers and must be quarantined lest they contaminate, in mind or body, the rest of society. The increasing attention paid to nursing homes by media and politicians— including compassionate or sensational exposés—assumes increasing *acceptance* of the nursing home as an appropriate answer to "What shall we do about Mother?" And such an assumption spreads the "final solution" mentality. For though only 1 million, or less than 5 percent, of those over sixty-five are in nursing homes, 60 percent of those now in nursing homes are supposedly suffering from irreversible senile dementia, Alzheimer's disease. Little attention is paid to the fact that the very incarceration of older people in those nursing homes often causes depression or other mental or physical deterioration that can be mistaken for senility. Thus to base our main image of age on nursing homes is to reify—and even make a self-fulfilling prophecy of—that terrifying image of incontinent, senile age.

The very creation of gerontology and geriatrics as fields of medical specialization, and the multiplicity of "experts" and programs they have spawned for the care of the infirm elderly, has also fostered the aged-as-sick-dependent approach: compassionate ageism. And here again image converges into terrible reality. For the basic thrust of the nursing home and most programs which institutionalize and "treat" the "problem" of age, is to reduce women and men alike to that helpless, passive, dehumanized state which the age mystique defines—a depersonalized, sick, untouchable image from which we understandably avert our eyes.

There has been a recent upsurge of interest in the "right to die" for elderly people who are terminally ill. But is this philosophy a new, sophisticated confrontation of our mortality and control of our own death? Or are the older persons in our society who kill themselves—or voluntarily become nursing home statistics to avoid being a burden to their children—merely conforming to our society's implied "final solution" to the "problem" of age? Some non-conforming gerontologists have suggested that "the quiet death, the suicide to avoid burdening, the failure to have adequate health care and the abdication to nursing home admission all represent . . . forms of altruistic suicide." [14]

There was a national outcry when Governor Richard D. Lamm of Colorado remarked that the elderly have a responsibility to "bow out" of life and not continue using national resources needed by the young—that is, a "duty to die" and allow the next generation to build their lives. The shock at a politician expressing out loud a sentiment that had previously merely been implied or hinted at by the media caused Lamm to insist later that he had merely meant that the elderly have a "right to die" and not be kept alive artificially on machines. [15]

"It is inconceivable that older people would be rounded up, carted off and killed," the sociologists Jack Levin and Arnold Arluke wrote in an op-ed piece in The New York Times during one of those periodic flare-ups of "age problem" consciousness that occurs when Social Security comes up for congressional renewal:

It is hard to imagine that our retirement communities and nursing homes could become the concentration camps of the future. Indeed, it may never happen—at least, not deliberately. Yet there is strong evidence that increasing numbers of frail, disabled and financially dependent elders, most of whom are over 75, are even now, as a result of our social policies, being isolated from society and dying prematurely. . . .

A *de facto* mass extermination may already be taking place. . . . Some researchers suggest that transplanting elders to nursing homes or retirement communities shortens their lives. Indeed, it is hard to imagine the systematic extermination of elders without their first being segregated from society. . . .

The intellectual justification for a final solution can already be observed in our changing attitude toward aging. . . . Hitler's scientists justified his "final solution" on the basis of physical anthropology. Our sciences of biology, psychology, sociology and even gerontology describe old age as a period of deterioration and decline. Could today's scientific thought be used to justify *de jure* extermination of the elderly in the future? [16]

The horror among young people and old—and especially among gerontologists and other professionals trained to treat the "problem" of age —when such implications are spelled out points to the ambivalence in our very denial. Consider, for instance, the uneasiness among gerontologists at the Cumming and Henry "disengagement" theory—one of the very few comprehensive theories of aging advanced in this century. They hypothesized that it is "functional" for both society and the individual for older people to voluntarily retire, retreat, "disengage" from active involvement in society, awaiting death (in their sixties—with a quarter of their possible life span still to live?). Was that too clear a rationalization for the total exclusion of the visibly old: a "final solution" of the age problem? Given that prospect, the only alternative to "disengagement" is, indeed, stepped-up, youth-aping activity.

As I continued this search, I expected the exploding reality of millions of healthy, active Americans living to an ever-advancing age to break through the youth-obsessed grayout of the media. Instead, even news reports of developments opening up new vistas for age got the "problem" treatment, and as the bulging baby-boom population approached fifty, fantasies of a literal return to youth became a movie and television formula.

Thus, in the fall of 1992, major newspapers and newsmagazines reported new scientific developments implying that "humans could live to be 200, 300 or more." But even if "we could not merely live much longer, but do so in good health," one reporter brooded, "What would marriage be like, for instance, if 'until death do us part' meant 100 years together? Could the workplace employ people for 80 to 100 years? How would a planet groaning with people absorb masses of elders who did not . . . feel a duty to die?"[17]

"CAN WE STOP AGING? There are scientists who believe we can and will—but would we really want to?" a *Life* cover questioned (October 1992), quoting scientists' predictions that

> possibly in 30 years we . . . will be in a position to double, triple, even quadruple our maximum life span of 120 years. It's possible that some people alive now may still be alive 400 years from now. . . . They [scientists] foresee a Malthusian nightmare, an appalling population explosion that could break the world's economy and ravage its environment. . . . The brave new world that emerged, they say, would be a dreary, overcrowded zoo of ancient mutants, a monotonous community of smooth-faced Dorian Grays enduring eternal youth on a planet where time no longer ticked and death alone offered relief from boredom.

A *Newsweek* cover (December 7, 1992) showed a sweating young man with some gray hairs clapping one hand to his aching head and groaning, *"Oh, God . . . I'm really turning 50!"* Noting that on or about their birthdays, the 2.7 million Americans who turned fifty that year received an offer to join the American Association of Retired Persons (AARP), *Newsweek* reported:

Not since the Selective Service Board sent "greetings" to 18-year-old men during the Vietnam War has a birthday salutation been dreaded by so many. . . . They are responding with ever more exaggerated forms of foreboding. . . . Dr. Mel Bircoll, 52, considered the father of the cosmetic pectoral implant, the calf implant and the fat implant (which he layers into facelifts to avoid the "overstretched look"), says his clients used to start at 55. Now they come to him at about 45.

Hollywood has been playing to this intensifying dread of age with fantasies of a literal return to youth in such films as *Peggy Sue Got Married*, *Back to the Future*, *Forever Young*, and Stephen King's *Golden Years*, in which a "lively and crusty old codger, pondering retirement in his own good time" from the government laboratory where he's still working at seventy, finds after a lab explosion his failing eyesight restored and his white hair returning to its original brown. Under the headline "He's Not Getting Better, He's Only Getting Younger," a critic noted, "Mr. King, it seems, has decided to have a go at the old fountain-of-youth routine that seems to be curiously obsessive these days, permeating everything from the 'Back to the Future' movies to television series like the short-lived 'My Life and Times.' Perhaps it has something to do with the boom in cosmetic surgery and its promise to make all of us look like escapees from a wax museum."[18]

Nostalgia movies like *Tough Guys* made aging Burt Lancaster and Kirk Douglas objects of sentimental ridicule. Paul Newman, over sixty-five now, still plays attractive, distinguished older men, or older men losing their power. But a recent study found older women in movies today shown as "hags, nags, witches or worse." Men who earned the Academy Award for best actor averaged forty-five; best actress winners were closer to thirty-five. There are "old bag" roles aplenty, the "less attractive, less desirable, opinionated and eccentric" older women—as played by Jessica Tandy in *Driving Miss Daisy*, who "proves her incompetence in the very first scene when she backs the car off the road."[19]

The unexpected success of even that movie about age did not seem to affect the movie and television industry's obsession with youth. Angela Lansbury, whose "Murder, She Wrote" has for the last ten years been one of the top ten programs on television, complained publicly about her "invisibility" to the network brass because of their blind spot about age. She felt that network executives never even watched her show because it was about a woman over sixty, and that in their obsession with youth they were "cut off from their audience." It seemed that "Murder, She Wrote" ranked in the top five shows among viewers fifty-five and older, while it ranked 108th among adults eighteen to thirty-four. But the average household income was an unusually high $60,000 for the older audience. Although "this represents a very attractive audience for products," a network executive insisted, "For now and for the foreseeable future, the younger audience will still be the most desirable audience for advertisers." As Lansbury tartly commented: "The networks seem to be chasing people 20 and under. Why? They don't buy anything. They eat cereal. They drink Coke."[20]

CBS belatedly wooed back Lansbury, deciding to make a more conscious play for the older market. "Golden Girls," which metamorphosed into "Golden Palace," was the only other exception to the universal grayout of older women on network TV. Strong women generally have also begun to disappear, displaced by super-macho young males and high school studs. But by the end of 1992, critics reported: "Both ABC and NBC, which started the season sworn to a youth-oriented programming strategy, have begun to bring in reinforcements [male] that are decidedly gray around the temples: Ben Matlock, Lieutenant Columbo and Perry Mason." "The Roundtable," a show about twentysomething police detectives, lasted only five weeks. The ratings nearly doubled when NBC brought in old Perry Mason to plug the hole.[21]

As the market potential of that exploding older audience becomes clearer, the schizophrenic split seems to intensify. When Grace Mirabella was abruptly dismissed at fifty-nine as editor of *Vogue* after seventeen brilliant years on the job, she started *Mirabella* in 1989, aiming at those "over 40 and fabulous" women the other fashion magazines have stopped wooing in their "effort to court younger readers."[22] Meanwhile, *Modern Maturity*, owned by AARP, recently became the nation's largest-circulation periodical.[23] It refuses to carry ads which show older people in negative, stereotyped, frail images. But *Longevity*, another magazine playing to the age market, defines itself as a "practical guide to the art and science of staying younger." A recent cover (October 1992) showed a bra slipping off the luscious breasts of thirty-something Cindy Crawford ("Cindy Crawford's Thigh Anxiety") with the lines: "10 Years Younger in 10 Minutes, Amazing Makeup Makeovers" and "Youth Serum, Hot on the Trail of the De-Aging Hormone."

In fact, the advertisers, who control the media image, seem to be gearing up to appeal to that burgeoning older market by pandering to their disdain for oldness. As Ken Dychtwald put it in *Age Wave*: "Who says you ever have to stop being a cover girl?"[24] Instead of celebrating new realities of age, the sell is eternal, attractive youth. In a more recent advertising campaign for Quaker Oats, Wilford Brimley, the veteran character actor who was rejuvenated in *Cocoon*, was transformed from a low-key old guy sitting at a kitchen table or walking his dog on a city street to a reborn cowboy, "aggressively active in Western settings—riding horses, digging postholes to build a corral—accompanied by a soundtrack of pounding hoofbeats." One media critic opined: "Among those marketing to the mature, it's fairly common knowledge that those over 45 want to identify with those who are 10 years younger." Advertising aimed at older Americans must now depict them as "take-charge doers, almost as frantically busy as their young professional children." [25] Explaining why "one minute the guy's in a rocking chair and the next minute he's riding the range," Leda Sanford, advertising director of *Modern Maturity*, said: "It's because people realize the boomers are on the horizon and they're not going to accept a negative image of aging."

An exception that proves the rule is a new British magazine called *The Oldie*, which "promises to 'out' people who lie about their age. . . . It wants to be a sort of *Rolling Stone* for the graying set. Mixing humor and rant with serious reportage, it wants to do battle with the cult of youth. 'I call it hip replacement—putting hip into old,' said Emma Soames, formerly the editor of *Tatler*." Actually, *The Oldie* started out as a joke, but surprisingly, people took it seriously—and put up the money to publish it.[26]

The denial of age carried to its extreme is, finally, the unadulterated horror of second childhood, a vision of ourselves regressing to a childlike state. If we are banished from previous adult roles after sixty-five, and denied the very possibility of future growth or the use of mature abilities in society, when we can no longer ape youth, we can only regress to second childhood. Gerontologists have pointed out that the television image of people over sixty-five is distinctly reminiscent of the "terrible two" toddler. That "second childhood" note is explicit, or barely disguised, in movies, commercials, and ads, and even in professional medical journals dealing with people over sixty-five; it can be heard in the tone of voice that doctors, social workers, and other geriatric practitioners often use when talking to "senior citizens" themselves.[27] Consider:

• The movie *Harold and Maude*, in which Ruth Gordon plays a fey, childlike, white-haired old woman egging on a teenage dropout in his adolescent rebellion.
• The scene in *On Golden Pond* where Henry Fonda and his new step-grandson sneak off to go fishing, like two naughty little boys when Mother is not looking.
• Ads for the movie *Just You and Me, Kid* that show teenager Brooke Shields and octogenarian actor George Burns playing stickup: "the story of two juvenile delinquents."

• A feature entitled "The Fun Life for Young and Old" in the *Boston Globe*, offering "a guide to August activities for senior citizens and children"—a puppet show, a magic act, etc.

• The "Kiddies Menu" of a Massachusetts ice-cream parlor chain, showing a white-haired old man hand in hand with a little boy, offers as bill of fare "for all kids under 10 and over 65": a "hot doggie," "kiddieburger," or "peanut butter and jelly samwitch."

• A poster, "*Have a Senior Birthday Party at McDonald's*," offers to provide cake, party favors, and paper hats for the "birthday kid" who is "young at heart."

• In a professional journal, a Melloril ad "for the agitated geriatric" shows an old man angrily waving his fist. "TANTRUMS," the ad admonishes.

• A pharmaceutical ad for the stool softener Doxidon shows a smiling bifocaled older woman: "Minnie moved her bowels today. The day started right for Minnie. That young doctor fella gave her Doxidon to take last night, and it worked! . . . Minnie figures she's got the smartest doctor in town."

• A suburban newspaper reports that the patients at a local nursing home "held their *very own* Christmas party," exclaiming, incredulously, that the patients "planned the party, made the invitations, decorated the cookies made by the chef, and took part in the entertainment which included group singing of Christmas carols."[28]

I felt uncomfortable at the movie *Cocoon* watching Don Ameche and all those silly old people trying to become twenty-five again, watching them dive into the swimming pool where cocoons preserve beings in space in perpetual embryonic youth against age and death. Was it merely a lighthearted scene, a futurist fantasy, a caricature of the way many old people behave, or the ultimate denial of age? Diving into that literal fountain of youth, *denying age*, those silly old people making love and dancing again as if they were twenty-five repelled me. Since we cannot ever be twenty-five again in real life, when we pursue the fountain of youth do we think we can somehow escape our human condition, denying the reality of death?

It now horrifies me that, in the spring of 1986, *You're Only Old Once!* by Dr. Seuss, "a book for obsolete children," was number one on bestseller lists for some weeks. I bought it, thinking it might be a satire or a humorous attack on the denial of age, or a celebration of the joys and values of maturity. But it was, indeed, what it said it was, "a book for obsolete children"—the kind of versifying my four-year-old grandson had already outgrown. Following the "obsolete child," perky in his wheelchair, through his checkup by the experts at the Golden Years Clinic, "through all the stops along Stethoscope Row to finally being 'properly pilled' and 'properly billed,' Dr. Seuss lightens the aches and pains of growing old," as the blurb proclaimed.

Why is this "second childhood" image of age so repulsive? A gerontologist has said that it suggests that older people "are losing, or have lost, the very things a growing child gains. It implies a backward movement to earlier developmental stages." [29] And, of course, the pervasive attempt of older people to emulate or pass for young logically culminates in "second childhood": mockery and denial of our adult personhood and the years of risk, pain, joy, and learning that got us there, a denigration of our grown-up selves. Some gerontological services almost seem to encourage us to go to bed meekly, like good children.

In this light, the recent proliferation of programs that provide compassionate services and patronizing diversions for older people, once they accept passive senior citizen status and segregation, became suspect in my eye. A nurse/social worker who had grown uneasy about those programs, which she herself had been trained to administer, Connie Eaton Cheren of Champaign, Illinois, wrote me:

So many of these programs are really ageist and work toward increased dependence of the elderly and increased segregation as opposed to working toward integration and independence. I worry sometimes about the giant network that has been established to help with "problems" of the aged, i.e., senior centers, nutrition meal sites, etc. It seems to me they have added to the problem and now work toward securing enough resources to keep themselves and their programs funded.

Immersing myself in the state of the art of gerontology, I was surprised to find, in so much of its literature, the same "compassionate," patronizing, contemptuous image of the poor childlike senior citizen as in that menu offering "samwitches" to senior "kiddies." For instance, a book by Martha T. John entitled *Teaching and Loving the Elderly* proposed, as tools for teaching the elderly, a spelldown, "including the following words: sparrow, hyacinth, dandelion . . . a diagram of the parts of a bird; a crossword puzzle including such answers as gizzard, ostrich. . . . 'Place a mark by each colony that was one of the original thirteen,' 'sing the first verse of the national anthem.' " The very discussion of age as a false barrier was entitled "Can They Learn?" The author's answer: "Some elderly can and do welcome the challenge of learning and acquiring an education." With a third-grade lesson plan? She simply did not see them as persons like herself.[30]

Reviewing this book in the *International Journal of Aging and Human Development,* the gerontologist Nancy Datan put her finger on her colleague's blind spot: "Her earnest, undoubtedly well-intentioned book is permeated by the very ageism she explicitly rejects. Yet . . . this book is firmly anchored in contemporary gerontology. . . . We have let loose upon the world the disquieting conviction that the old are people other than ourselves—we, the experts, will do well by them, but we certainly will never be them."

I began to wonder why people would voluntarily put themselves into an age ghetto, paying hundreds of thousands of dollars to wall themselves off from the rest of society. Is it because they *accept* that senior citizen stigma and voluntarily retreat from its pain? They also help the rest of the community to deny its own aging even further. Some gerontologists suggest that an important appeal of a retirement community like Leisure World in California or Sun City in Arizona is its promise to separate old people from the prejudice and discrimination of young people. Jack and William C. Levin maintain that "the everyday indignation experienced by the elderly in their dealings with the young can be minimized where almost everyone shares the stigma of aging and seeks to avoid its most painful consequences. But, of course, isolation also contributes to the belief that the aged are a separate or different kind of people from the rest of society and reduces the visibility of people who are exceptions to the stereotypes of old age."[31]

The process encouraged by acceptance of the mystique of age is not static. It seems, finally, to make a self-fulfilling prophecy of isolation, passivity. To "play the role of age" as it is defined today can mean literally to give up life. Thus Jerry Jacobs's study of the relatively well-to-do retirement community he called Fun City found that half of its 5,600 residents accepted the fact that they had come there "to retire" (i.e., "to withdraw from society"). Only a small minority of them became active participants in Fun City's "fun" (the club activities in the promotion brochure). According to one estimate, some 25 percent of Fun City's aged never even left their homes.[32]

Ironically, the refusal to accept the stereotype also has its consequences. The secret problems of excessive drug and alcohol use in age that I was told about, in confidence, by a distinguished mental health pioneer, himself retired to Sun City in Arizona, have long been recognized by gerontologists—but they are carefully kept out of the "retirement village" image. Certain symptoms of senility—such as chronic forgetfulness, incompetence at performing simple tasks, infantile behavior, even incontinence— "may actually represent a form of refusal to accept the aged status," gerontologists have suggested.[33] Less severe forms of illness may also represent an escape hatch for older people who have been isolated from society—it keeps them involved with the doctor, at least. "No one knows how many of the illnesses associated with old age have been caused or exaggerated by a desire to escape from the role requirements of the aged status."[34]

When the gerontologist Robert Kastenbaum surveyed a large cross section of people on the age they "expect to live to" and the age they "want to live to," one out of four wanted to die before their time.[35] In fact, the suicide rate for people over sixty-five has been increasing steadily in America—only 11 percent of the population, they account for roughly 25 percent of reported suicides. The suicide rate is highest among older white men—45.9 per 100,000 aged seventy-five to seventy-nine. Despite the "compassionate" moaning over the "problems" of older women, the suicide rate for women actually decreases with age—from 9 per 100,000 at sixty-five to 4.2 at eighty-five.[36] But that dread mystique of age so skews our thinking that what's questioned is not why men kill themselves to avoid the "problem" of age but why, in effect, women don't.

The dynamics by which the age mystique distorts our view of aging and is reinforced by our dread were illuminated in a series of experiments by the Harvard psychologist Ellen Langer, the Yale psychologist Judith Rodin, and their associates. They tested the image of age among three groups of people: those from 25 to 40; 40 to 60; and over 70. People over sixty-five were perceived by the two younger groups as passive, alone, sick, miserable, unpleasant, incompetent, and so on. People who themselves were over seventy were much more likely to visualize older people engaged positively and actively with other people—doing, working, playing—and not as isolated or sick. But when scenes were presented to all three groups depicting people variously described as "age 35" or "age 75"— for example, a man goes to the store with a list of groceries and he comes back without coffee and peanut butter—all three groups were more likely to say the seventy-five-year-old was "senile," the thirty-five-year-old simply "forgot." And the middle-aged and older groups were much more likely than the younger group to see those behaviors in the seventy-five-year-old as signs of "senility."

"The older one gets, the more frightened one is of being or becoming senile or showing other presumably age-related negative traits," Langer and Rodin concluded. "This fear is likely to motivate older people to distance themselves, psychologically, from older people with difficulties such as forgetfulness, by evaluating them as negatively as possible and thereby making them very different from themselves." They found that older people overestimated even very slight changes in their own capacities, and the "effects of this awareness may be more debilitating than the change itself." It caused confused, fearful behavior that "actually confirmed prevalent stereotypes of old age and led to lowered self-esteem and diminished feelings of control."[37]

They added: "Any such fears the elderly have about themselves are exacerbated by the dearth of appropriate role models who could serve as counter examples of what life after seventy might be like." The slowing down of *normal* aging, which usually does not occur before the eighties, can be compensated for by people who actively identify with their own aging. It is cause for panic only among those who deny age. Then, signs of normal aging are misinterpreted as signs of senility, and old people are "helped" to become progressively more dependent. As people expect less of them, they expect less of themselves—and get out of the habit of thinking. They allow themselves to be cared for, and are finally unable to care for themselves. Gerontologists agree that institutionalization, even in the best nursing homes, is the surest way to speed the decline of memory and to hasten confusion and disorientation. "Senility is a garbage-can diagnosis for people . . . after 65," said the gerontologist Muriel Oberleder. "The classic problems—disorientation, incontinence, depression—are symptoms of anxiety at any age. . . . Sometimes senile behavior allows someone to hide their terror of being old and dying helplessly by just avoiding reality. Most senile people are terrified people."[38]

Depression—which is anger turned against the self—is, in fact, a response to this powerlessness. Isn't it the denial of the personhood of age—not seeing those over sixty-five as people, in their own concrete particularity—that causes that misdiagnosis of depression, so much more prevalent in older people than in the population at large, as senility? Depression should not be surprising in any *person* suddenly stripped of power, of job or earnings, of a sense of productivity and purpose; in any person who suffers the increasing isolation and "sense of no-goodness" that results from others' avoidance of the old. But it is those who so fear their own aging that they must repress and deny all thought of it —those who are *alienated from their own experience* as they continue to try to pass as young —who may be at highest risk of depression.

All forms of denial of age, it seems to me, ultimately spring that dread trap we try to avoid. How long, and how well, can we really live by trying to pass as young, as all those articles and books like Muriel Oberleder's *Avoid the Aging Trap* seem to advise?[39] By the fourth face-lift (or third?) we begin to look grotesque, no longer human. Obsessed with stopping age, passing as young, we do not seek new functions in the years of life now open to us beyond the sexual, childrearing, power-seeking female and male roles of our youth. Seeing age only as decline from youth, we make age itself the problem—

and never face the real problems that keep us from evolving and leading continually useful, vital, and productive lives. Accepting that dire mystique of age for others, even as we deny it for ourselves, we ultimately create or reinforce the conditions of our own dependence, powerlessness, isolation, even senility. We can then feel "compassionate" about those "problems" of aging which are too expensive ever to solve once we cast people over sixty-five out of productive roles in society. And we can continue denying our own age a little longer by walling off the "senior citizens" in retirement villages and nursing homes from which they never return. But if we alienate ourselves from the actuality of our own experience, in those years of denial, passing for young, and never let ourselves see new possibilities, new qualities emerging and evolving in ourselves that might be different from "young"; if we avoid thinking about age except in terms of its most pathological problems, from which we can usually distance ourselves, ultimately we may become what we most fear.

Until we break through that dread age mystique, we can't even see the problems straight. In a Louis Harris Poll for the National Council on Aging, done in 1975 and repeated in 1981, the majority of young and middle-aged people (eighteen to sixty-four) were convinced that people over sixty-five had "very serious problems" of loneliness, poor health, not enough money to live on, and fear of crime. Most people over sixty-five also thought at least half of their own age peers had "very serious problems" in these areas—but none of these items were reported by the majority as a "very serious problem" personally. A significant number of those over sixty-five did have some problems, but they were not the same ones both the young and older people thought "most older people" suffered. "The message that emerges here is that the older public, like the young, has bought the negative image of old age," the gerontologist Vern Bengston concluded. "They apparently assume that most old people are miserable and that they are merely exceptions to the rule. Myth has replaced reality."[40]

Thus, despite their own acceptance of the "problem" myth for older people generally, the majority of people over sixty-five in that Harris Poll described *themselves* as "very open-minded and adaptable" (63 percent), and "very good at getting things done" (55 percent), but only one out of three of the young and middle-aged could see people over sixty-five in such effective terms. Bengtson, a social psychologist at the Andrus Gerontology Center, warned that when society sees older people "as merely a problem, and not as part of the solution to any of society's problems," this generates "a sense of guilt and pity among the young, and not a

sense of appreciation for the talents and energies that older people can still contribute to society." The consequences of such an attitude
are real, indeed. In effect, young and middle-
aged people begin to "discourage, even punish,
any behavior on the part of the aged that is active, effective or competent. In turn, the aged
come to accept the negative stereotype and to
act in accordance with the role of senior citizens." [41]

A feminist theologian described her own shriveling experience with the "compassionate"
(contemptuous) age-pedestal in the women's
movement itself. "I celebrated my seventieth
birthday during a large conference of women
ministers where I had been invited to speak.
Suddenly I realized that I was segregated at the
beginning of the conference with two other
older women and labeled 'Our Foremothers.' As
the conference proceeded, it was obvious that a
great cleavage appeared because of this label-
ing. 'We' were not considered to be in the mainstream of the conference thought—though later
many women said I was far more radical than
any other person on the program. I never felt
the real pinch of ageism until, in the feminist
movement (which is now my life), my own sisters
began to call me mother." [42]

It is subtle, the shriveling effect of this kind of
honorable dismissal. People never understood
why I would involuntarily glower when being in-

troduced as "the mother of the women's movement" (occasionally, lately, the "grandmother"). Technically, maybe I was the mother—and proud of it—but it put a damper on my fire to be so introduced before, for instance, a speech in which I was trying to challenge my middle-aged sisters to get out of their single-issue rut and into a second stage of feminism, dealing with the new problems of home and work facing our daughters. Does denial of our own approaching age foster an inability to evolve in larger thought?

Or take dancing. I was nearly fifty before I was liberated enough to discover that I could dance. Now I love to dance! I was too self-conscious when I was young, too stiff. But in recent years, on a dance floor where most of the people were young, when, whirling around, I saw them smiling—suddenly, I felt funny dancing. I liked it when my friend Bel Kaufman, who wrote *Up the Down Staircase* in her sixties, began to throw private dances for her friends to dance until 2:00 A.M.—with no young people sneering at us.

As a matter of fact, the more we deny our own age in order to pass as young, the more we give credence to that dread aura of age. And the more we exaggerate that poor, fearful, passive, sick, lonely, helpless, senile image—in order to distance ourselves from it—the more we justify the actual exclusion of people over sixty-five from the work and play and other activities of society. The reason younger people buy this stereotype, gerontologists say, is that older people are no longer seen as part of the action; the media image simply omits the "over-49 demographic." And, in fact, older people usually do not seem to be present in most of the places where younger people work, eat, dance, play tennis, or otherwise compete.

Well, of course they are not present if they have been forced to retire from jobs at sixty-five or pushed out of community leadership. So, those of us who want to stay in the mainstream of society have to "pass" as young. We make ourselves less conspicuous with our white hair dyed black or red, our faces lifted, having gotten rid of those "expression lines." But as long as we do "pass" for young, the increasing millions of us who are, in fact, moving vitally through our later years will not alter people's negative image of age. And therefore there *still* will be no image or role model of older people behind the television mike, or on the dance floor, or scuba diving, or doing other useful or enjoyable things.

So, again, only the "problems"—the *truly* helpless, dependent, sick, isolated, senile ones —are actually seen as "old." And the more guilty and "compassionate" people are made to feel about the "problem" and "plight" of the elderly, the more they want to avoid them and actively resist personal identification with them. The more people over sixty-five become unfamiliar "others," like any segregated minority group, the more they make the rest of us uncomfortable. And the older we get ourselves, the more we exaggerate *their* "problems," and deepen that aura of guilt and pity, to keep ourselves as distant as possible from the contamination of age.

The tendency of people in middle age (forty to sixty) to exaggerate the expectation of dread decline after sixty-five that Langer and Rodin found is a basic part of the age mystique. For the professionals who deal with the "problems" of the aging—the experts and researchers who study and label them, the doctors, nurses, and social workers who treat them, the employers and supervisors who hire and fire them—tend themselves to be in, or on the verge of, middle age. In one study, ostensibly of interviewing methods, half of a group of middle-aged professionals were told they were going to interview a person forty-two years old; the other half were told the person was seventy-one. The questions they chose to give the older person were easier, even when she was described as "above average for her age." Thus, the kind (or lack) of treatment older persons might get from doctors or social workers and the kind (or lack) of demands that society at large might make on them, as a result of this age mystique, further lowers self-esteem and could actually bring about a decline in competence, Langer and her colleagues concluded.[43]

In another study, groups of psychiatrists, psychologists, and physicians were given seven case histories describing "pathological" behavior—the patient variously described as "in his sixties or seventies" or "young." When the individual was described as in his sixties or seventies, the same behavior was much more likely to be diagnosed as "organically based" impairment requiring heavy drug treatment or institutionalization than when the patient was described as "young." The "young," but not those over sixty, were more likely to be diagnosed as suffering from depression that could be treated, in the community, by long- or short-term therapy. (In real situations, when depressed older people are diagnosed—or, too often, misdiagnosed—as senile, individual or group therapy is rarely prescribed.)

Recent research indicates that even among the 5 percent of the population diagnosed as "senile," for every four correctly diagnosed as suffering from irreversible senile dementia, Alzheimer's disease—which, as the National Institute on Aging keeps saying, "is an abnormal condition of the aging brain . . . not a natural consequence of aging"—there is at least one older woman or man misdiagnosed because of a "confusional state" that could be caused by overmedication, wrong drug combinations, or depression. Dr. Richard Besdine of Harvard Medical School estimated that misdiagnoses of "irreversible dementia" may account for 300,000 wasted lives and 100,000 needless institutional-izations each year. One quarter of all drug pre-scriptions are written for persons over sixty-five. Although it is now known that a normal dose for a forty-year-old could be an overdose for a seventy-five-year-old, older people may take five or six different medications every day. In nursing homes, geriatric professionals are likely to see almost any condition as caused simply by aging itself—and so they treat it with drugs to keep the patient quiet. Thus, physical health problems that could be treated, and the depression or loss of competence caused by a hostile environment, are accepted as inevitable results of aging.

If we could, in fact, pass for "young" into our eighties, could succeed in denying age until we die, and never become "old," if we could find that fountain of youth, to be honest, wouldn't we want to? Staring at all these images of deteriora-tion and decline, sensing the power they have over us in the need to deny age, I again felt un-certainty about going on with this quest. Should we, must we confront age, even our own aging, as it really is?

As long as the dread mystique of age remains in place, it seemed to me, at first glance, that people heading into or beyond their sixties *should* avoid accepting their own age as long as they can, and however they can, as a matter of personal survival. In fact, gerontologists have found some evidence that people who don't think of themselves as "old"—and, certainly now most people don't at sixty-five, and many don't at eighty—do better in age. In one study in which large numbers of people over sixty-five, asked to identify themselves in terms of age, checked off "middle-aged," the people willing to label themselves "old" or "elderly" actually had a higher mortality rate. Many did not live until the restudy, which took place ten years later.[44]

The denial of age, after all, is a defense mechanism to avoid the negative role of senior citizens. As the gerontologist Jack Levin put it, "Given the severe stigma of aging and the negative connotations associated with it, a middle-aged self-concept may actually sustain morale."[45] Studies of nursing home residents have shown that "socially uninvolved or disengaged individuals tend to classify themselves as old, whereas individuals who remain socially active avoid the self-designation of old age." Yet such denial accepts, and in the end reinforces, that dread mystique of age as isolated, helpless, an inevitable decline into senility. It justifies the desperation to pass as young, to ward off the terror of aging. But as long as we acquiesce in that dread, as long as age itself is defined as sickness, doctors may not diagnose or even treat ailments in people over sixty-five that can be cured. And social workers, psychotherapists, employers, policymakers will not deal with our real needs and our real abilities for intimacy, work, involvement, respect and self-respect, which may or may not be the same as the needs and abilities of the young, but nevertheless are vital to our lives.

It becomes harder and harder to "pass" as young, denying so much of one's self, living in fear of the day when our defenses falter and we fall or slip into a necessary admission that we are, in fact, over sixty-five. We have reason to feel terror at the prospect of slipping into that abyss of age which we have helped create. "I feel sad about losing my youthful looks," a fifty-two-year-old woman wrote of her "Experience with Ageism." "I never learned to appreciate my body and my looks until I was in my mid-thirties and there was such a short time to rejoice. I have not let myself go. . . . But when people's eyes slide over me and look away because they see an aging woman with whom they think they can't relate, then I want to yell at them, 'Hey! I'm an interesting person and we could share real things. . . .' For myself, I fear sick old age more than I fear death!" [46]

The equation of age with deterioration has become so pervasive that gerontologists are surprised to find "capacity for growth and new activities" even in some who accept that senior citizen status after they have entered the ghettos of retirement communities. "Re-engagement may be found where it is least expected to occur," the Levins noted,[47] implicitly recognizing that the "retirement village" is not supposed to offer real social involvement. They found "surprising" numbers of Fun City residents employed in part- or full-time jobs, despite the absence of civil service, industry, or major retail stores. Retired admirals paint houses, retired colonels pump gas or transcribe math problems into Braille for the blind, while housewives act as realtors. Other well-to-do residents work as handymen or gardeners.[48]

It is our drive for continued involvement in life that is denied by the compassionate "problem of age" mystique. Our own refusal to renounce that involvement in life is what makes us deny age; that core of ongoing life is hard to kill. Gerontologists were, again, *surprised* to report the experience of seventy-eight older people who got themselves reemployed or remarried after the loss of job or wife, "average" men and women from all walks of life, "who exhibited the kind of capacity for growth and new activities in later life that we believe to be much more widespread than has been recognized."[49]

Why have gerontologists not looked seriously at abilities and qualities that may develop or emerge in women or men in the later years of life, and contemplated new possibilities for their use? Why is the political programming for age confined to those proliferating care services that work toward increased dependence and segregation of the elderly, as opposed to the continued integration of people over sixty-five into roles in society, in which they can continue to function as independent persons and make their own choices?

Why the increasing emphasis by professional age experts and the media—and public acceptance—on the nursing home as the locus of age when, in fact, more than 90 percent of those over sixty-five continue to live in the community? Why the preoccupation, professional and political, with senility, Alzheimer's disease, when less than 5 percent of people over sixty-five will suffer it? Why the persistent image of age as "sick" and "helpless," as a burden on our hospitals and health care system, when, in fact, people over sixty-five are less likely than those who are younger to suffer from the acute illnesses that require hospitalization? Why the persistent image of those over sixty-five as sexless when research shows people capable of sex until ninety, if healthy and not shamed out of seeking or otherwise deprived of sex partners? Why the persistent fear of mental incompetence, loss of memory and intelligence in age when research shows, for healthy people into their eighties, no deterioration in either basic mental competence or intelligence if they continue to be challenged? Why don't most people know that current research shows some *positive* changes in certain mental abilities, as well as muscular, sexual, and immune processes, that can compensate for age-related declines?

What are we doing to ourselves—and to our society—by denying age? (Peter Pan and Dorian Gray found it hell staying "forever young.") Is there some serious foreclosure of human fulfillment, forfeiture of values, in that definition of age as "problem"? For society, for ourselves? In fact, the more we seek the fountain of perpetual youth and go on denying age, defining age itself as "problem," that "problem" will only get worse. For we will never know what we could be, and we will not organize in our maturity to break through the barriers that keep us from using our evolving gifts in society, or demand the structures we need to nourish them.

I think it is time we start searching for the fountain of age, time that we stop denying our growing older and look at the actuality of our own experience, and that of other women and men who have gone beyond denial to a new place in their sixties, seventies, eighties. It is time to look at age on its own terms, and put names on its values and strengths as they are actually experienced, breaking through the definition of age solely as deterioration or decline from youth. Only then will we see that the problem is not age itself, to be denied or warded off as long as possible, that the problem is not those increasing numbers of people living beyond sixty-five, to be segregated from the useful, valuable, pleasurable activities of society so that the rest of us can keep our illusion of staying forever young. Nor is the basic political problem the burden on society of those forced into deterioration, second childhood, even senility. The problem is not how we can stay young forever, personally—or avoid facing society's problems politically by shifting them onto age. The problem is, first of all, how to break through the cocoon of our illusory youth and risk a new stage in life, where there are no prescribed role models to follow, no guideposts, no rigid rules or visible rewards, to step out into the true existential unknown of these new years of life now open to us, and to find our own terms for living it.

This is not to deny genuine problems of people over sixty-five—problems of food, housing, economic support, intimacy, medical care, purpose, and respect—but we can only deal with those once we have stopped defining age itself, the aged themselves, as the problem. Only then can we stop that desperate pursuit of "fountain of youth" fantasies and gain some control over the realities of our own aging.

It was not easy to break through my own denial of age. Pangs of doubt, pain, and fear kept erupting, clouding a vision of new freedom that I glimpsed, making me lose hold of that grounding in new reality. But I began to sense, more and more surely from the experience of those who had already accepted that reality, that it is *the affirmation of age on its own terms,* the embrace of our own aging in its new reality, that enables us to face and deal with the genuine problems of forced retirement, divorce or renewal of forty- or fifty-year marriages, widowhood, social denigration and dismissal, compassionate contempt in services and housing, and health.

I started my quest for the fountain of age by simply looking for people who seemed to be "vitally aging" as compared to the image of deterioration and decline that seemed to be the norm. Not geniuses like Picasso or Casals or Einstein, but my own friends and neighbors, and women and men in other cities, who were facing the realities of aging with new and different patterns of purpose and intimacy. I had myself so accepted the image of deterioration and decline that I expected such vitally aging people to be *exceptional.* Even though our society's dread of age, its dreary or blanked-out image of the aging, seemed to deny their very existence, even with so many elements of society seeming to conspire to prevent them from continuing to use their human abilities after sixty-five, I found that *they were everywhere.*

Could I, or any of us, look forward to an age that we can be comfortable with, surprise ourselves with, not have to deny? I realized that the people from whom I got hints of possible new patterns in age were hardly scientific proof of the existence of a fountain of age. I broadened my search for biological, psychological, and sociological evidence of emergent modalities in the later years of life other than simulation of or decline from youth. And I found, even in the research that posed questions about "them" instead of "us," that such evidence did exist.

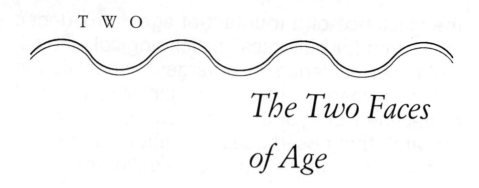

The Two Faces of Age

"We study what we are afraid of, and gerontologists are no exception," said my friend David Gutmann, geropsychologist at Northwestern Medical School, admitting that the science of gerontology has shared, worked within, and perpetuated the conventional American view of "aging as catastrophe, aging as wasteland."

Geropsychologists . . . enact their special version of gerophobia by elaborating the doctrine of catastrophic aging, by portraying the aged as needy of services, and by playing down the developmental possibilities of late life. . . .

The conventional psychology of aging is almost completely devoted to a study of its discontents: aging as depletion, aging as catastrophe, aging as mortality. At best the aged are deemed barely capable of staving off disaster, but they are certainly not deemed capable of developing new capacities or of seeking out new challenges by their own choice (and even for the sheer hell of it).[1]

Was that what I was doing, I wondered—studying what I was afraid of? If so, what better way to exorcise my own demons? Gutmann's words were hardly reassuring, for they confirmed my suspicion that the science of gerontology itself was perpetuating the fear and dread of age. And in speaking to many gerontologists personally, attending their lectures and seminars, immersing myself in that medical specialty, I found ample additional evidence of the view of age as pure pathology. Yet I also found glimmers of another approach: the study of age as a state of becoming and being, not merely as ending. Among gerontologists I found too an am bivalence, an uncertainty, as if the mirror of age reflected two images. At the opening session of the Salzburg Seminar on Health, Productivity, and Aging in 1983, Robert Butler stated:

From the biological perspective, aging is a predictable, progressive, universal deterioration of various physiological systems, mental and physical, behavioral and biomedical. . . .

. . . At the same time there is clear evidence, though more elusive and more difficult to measure, of concurrent psychosocial growth in capacities for strategy, sagacity, prudence, wisdom [in age].[2]

Those two seemingly contradictory statements, made by Dr. Butler, Brookdale Professor of Geriatrics and Adult Development at Mount Sinai School of Medicine in New York and former director of the National Institute on Aging, sum up the dichotomy in scientific thinking about age. For lately gerontologists have begun to puzzle over the fact that some people don't show "universal deterioration." While research on aging has "emphasized losses," John Rowe, an eminent gerontologist who left Harvard to be head of Mount Sinai Hospital, said flatly, "in many data sets that show substantial average decline with age, one can find older persons with minimal physiologic loss, or none at all, when compared to the average of their younger counterparts."[3]

Only within the past few years have gerontologists admitted that previous assumptions about age as genetically programmed catastrophic decline were based on pathological aging. "Many prevailing ideas and facts about aging and the aged come from studies of the sick and institutionalized," the National Institute of Mental Health pointed out in its revised *Introduction to the Study of Human Aging.* "Because of the nature of the studies and of the populations studied, the dominant theme has been one of *decline.* Thus cerebral metabolism and circulation have generally been regarded as declining with advancing age; senility, regression, and rigidity are often regarded as unavoidable concomitants of growing older."[4]

Those first studies were done, for the most part, on men—men without families or resources for living in their own communities who, earlier in the century, filled the old people's homes. The assumption, for instance, that the cessation of testosterone function and ending of sexual capacity is an inevitable accompaniment of age in men was based on studies of institutionalized men who were cut off from sexual activity. Even in the last twenty years, when studies of "normal human aging" have brought healthy older people living in their own communities into the laboratory for regular testing, there has been an assumption of systematic, genetically programmed decline with age, reversing, in effect, the process of growth and development in infant and child. The first studies of "normal human aging," both at the National Institute on Aging and the National Institute of Mental Health, were also done only on men, so that the findings could be compared with those earlier studies of institutionalized men, in order to separate out effects of pathology.

It was assumed that the increases in blood pressure, weight, and cholesterol levels found in such studies were the irreversible programmed changes of "normal aging," as was progressive impairment in the capacity to metabolize glucose or carbohydrates, with increased risk of stroke; progressive decline in bone density, with increased risk of fractures; and decline in cognitive capacities, as measured in tests of intelligence. The "substantial variability" found on all such tests—*much more variability than was found in studies of younger age groups*—was ignored or dismissed as an accident of heredity.

But men aging in the community did not show the same loss of testosterone or sexual capacity as the institutionalized men. They continued to be sexually active in varying degrees into their eighties. Nor did older men in good physical shape show the carbohydrate intolerance supposedly caused by biological aging. Their performance on glucose tolerance tests was identical to that of young athletes.[5] A progressive decline in bone density (osteoporosis) so severe as to result in fractures at a slight fall had been considered a factor of "normal aging" ("by age 81 one-third of women and one-sixth of men will have suffered a hip fracture"). More recent studies showed a "remarkable variance" in the emergence of osteoporosis, "a common, crippling and expensive disorder previously considered to represent the normal aging process. The marked reductions in bone density associated with 'usual' aging may be in large part preventable or modifiable."[6] Other recent research suggested that even those declines attributed to "normal" aging may also have been exaggerated, since *in some environments such declines do not occur.* And in the last decade what had seemed normal and irreversible aging decline has, in fact, been reversed with changes in diet, exercise, lifestyle, or environment.

Lately, Rowe and some of his colleagues at Harvard and elsewhere have begun to go beyond the distinction between "pathological" and "normal" aging: what has been considered "normal" is merely "usual" aging, which includes *elements not previously considered pathological in age that can, in fact, be prevented, modified, or reversed.* They would further distinguish between "usual aging" and "successful aging." Certain impairments considered "normal" in our society (those increases in blood pressure, body weight, and cholesterol, for instance), which "had been interpreted as age-intrinsic, are turning out to be usual in prosperous industrial countries but not in pastoral and traditional agricultural societies." Further, "normal" aging implies something that is biologically programmed, an inevitable and irreversible component of aging. There is also an "implication of harmlessness, of lack of risk . . . and the related implication that, risky or not, what is normal is somehow natural and therefore is or should be beyond purposeful modification." But if cutting out smoking and red meat, or exercising or taking calcium, does, in fact, prevent or reverse that kind of decline—making heart attack or osteoporosis less "usual"—it is clearly not a necessary part of aging.[7]

These revised perceptions about aging were surely a dramatic shift, I thought; but even Rowe's concept of "successful aging" was limited to "people who show little or no loss in various functions compared to youth." Then I stumbled on a small but growing underground in gerontology that was questioning whether measuring age—"normal" or "pathological," "usual" or "successful"—only in terms of decline from youth was blinding us to the full human potential of the new years of life beyond our youth: the third age, as the French call it.

It is necessary to keep reminding ourselves that of all the millennia of life on earth, only the women and men now alive can expect a vital third to half of life *after* they have reproduced. It is only in this century that our life expectancy has moved from forty-six to nearly eighty years, and the fastest-growing part of the population is now people over eighty, most of whom are women. Why are we not looking at age as a new, evolving stage of human life—not merely as a decline from youth, but as an open-ended development in its own terms, which, in fact, may be *uniquely ours to define?*

Past theories of aging do not help us much in answering that question, for it was deemed functional for society and for the aging individual to "disengage" voluntarily from his or her various roles in society to prepare for death— or alternatively, to simulate or keep up youthful activity, or develop mechanisms to compensate for loss of youthful powers as long as possible. Only recently have maverick gerontologists begun to ask if the long period of age after reproduction might not be as important as that long period of childhood *in making us human.* Other species do not have such a long period of youth—or of age.

The public policies of compassionate ageism and the scientific parameters of gerontology, no less than outright age discrimination in industry and profession and the social exclusion of older people from the mainstream of the community, have reinforced the terror of age: the weak, catastrophic, victim face of age. But there *is* evidence, even from the accumulated research originally intended to measure the rate and extent of that supposedly programmed decline from youth, for another, strong and vital, face of age. In my search through the literature of gerontology, I discovered some paradoxes and unexpected findings that cannot be explained by that view of age as programmed decline. They were my first clues to the possibility of new and different kinds of growth after our reproductive prime.

1. *The decline in various capacities with age, which had been studied by comparing average tendencies within different age groups, has turned out not to be universal and predictable—as it would be if it were biologically programmed.*
The biological programming of growth seems to end with reproduction. But in our other physical functions and physiological processes—hearing or sight, muscular strength or coordination, digestion, heart or lung capacity—studies reveal that deterioration is not necessarily uniform or progressive. In men or women aging in their own communities, in recent decades, decline seems to take place much more variously and later and later in life, and much of it can be reversed.

After sixty, people's capacities, and their impairment, seem to depend on their particular environments, changes in society, and their own individual choices and patterns even more than does earlier development. The differences between individuals (that is, the variability within an age group in both mental and physical capabilities) seem to *increase* with age. Does our biological programming end with reproduction? Perhaps because we are released from those reproductive sex roles in work and parenting, which dictate common behavior, and have no further role defined for us by society, individual choices (and serendipity) count more in age. The difference between those who do decline with age and those who persist in vital activity or even show further development is greater than earlier differences.

2. *The progressive deterioration in both mental and physical capacities that appeared in earlier studies of cross sections of Americans at different ages disappeared when healthy people aging in their own communities, and not institutions, began to be studied longitudinally—at fifty, sixty, sixty-five, seventy, eighty, etc.*

The earlier decline in intelligence tests, for instance, was a factor of the different educational level of the older immigrant generations compared to the sons and daughters they sent to college. When education was held constant, the decline in cognitive capacity was insignificant well into the eighties.

The major longitudinal studies—at Duke, the National Institute on Aging study in Baltimore, the National Institute of Mental Health study in Philadelphia—done in the last twenty-five years did not show evidence of the declines in intelligence-test functioning, cognitive skills, and even memory that had appeared in all previous cross-sectional studies of aging. In these studies, groups of people of different ages—forty, fifty, sixty, seventy, eighty—were tested simultaneously and compared in their performances, which were progressively poorer for each older age group. Now, the men who were studied at eighty-one in the National Institute of Mental Health study were compared with their own performances at seventy-five and seventy, five and ten years earlier. The "pattern of decline of cognitive . . . capabilities generally associated with advanced aging" was "neither extensive nor consistent," the researchers reported. "Most of the decreases in level of functioning were small and not statistically significant. There were a number of tests in which no decline in performance was evident. On a few others there was a noticeable improvement in functioning."[8]

Further, this National Institute of Mental Health study of men in whom "age was relatively uncontaminated by the diseases and infirmities so common in the elderly" led to the "unexpected" finding that aging need not result in decline in cerebral blood flow and metabolic rate. In healthy men of seventy or eighty, these functions were not different from the level observed in men fifty years younger.[9]

Finally, of the forty-seven men originally tested in the 1956 National Institute of Mental Health study, twenty-three were still living at the time of the follow-up in 1967—nearly twice as many as the number of survivors predicted by the life expectancy tables based on previous averages.[10] In almost every major study of aging in recent years, there has been the puzzling disappearance or even reversal of that decline in intellectual functioning, or cerebral blood flow, or life satisfaction found in previous sixty- or seventy- or eighty-year-olds compared to younger groups. And this improvement emerged not only between different cohorts—those seventy in 1987 compared to those seventy in 1967 or 1977 —but among those who survived, compared to their own performance on the tests five and ten years earlier. In fact, such *mental functioning,* which does not decline and even improves with age, would seem to be an essential clue to vital aging.

The survivors in the National Institute of Mental Health's Eleven-Year Follow-up Study had in the original tests "demonstrated higher intellectual capacities than the non-survivors, particularly with respect to the effective use of stored information," "flexibility of mind set and actions," and "greater ideational freedom, imaginativeness and organization of ideas." The investigators, intent merely on charting the rate of normal aging decline in the absence of disease, were struck in that follow-up study not only by the high number who did survive to an average age of eighty-one—twice the statistical expectation—but by the remarkably high quality of mental functioning . . . despite their fairly advanced age. Their performances remain, to a considerable extent, close to what they were more than a decade earlier. Declines, of course, are evident but what stands out are [their] residual capabilities. This is a matter which has received relatively limited attention in gerontological research. . . . The aged may be getting less credit than they deserve for the extent of their intellectual, perceptual, and personality strengths and capabilities [including] the acquisition by the elderly of new knowledge, concepts and skills.[11]

K. Werner Schaie and Gisela Labouvie-Vief did a longitudinal series of cross-sectional studies on successive cohorts of individuals across the adult age range. Cross-sectional comparisons between age groups in 1963 showed significantly lower scores in many cognitive capacities for the older groups (sixty, seventy, eighty, etc.), the kind of finding commonly interpreted as reflecting declines with advancing age. But when the same subjects were retested seven years later, the now sixty-seven- and seventy-seven-year-olds did not show the decline from *their own earlier scores* that would have been predicted from the earlier cross-sectional comparisons.[12]

The longitudinal data showed that declines in

both "crystallized intelligence" (verbal) and "fluid intelligence" (reasoning and spatial tests) occurred at *substantially later ages* than had been predicted from the cross-sectional comparisons of age groups where the older groups had less education. Time and again, other researchers have also reported the puzzling finding that tests repeated seven and ten years later on successive new cohorts reaching sixty, seventy, or eighty do not show the predicted decline, and some even show an improvement. It has thus become clear that much of the cognitive loss after sixty that had been considered intrinsic to aging is caused by other factors, such as educational differences, and *may therefore be preventable.* In fact, when Schaie and his colleagues pinpointed the people in their longitudinal study with a clear pattern of age decline in fluid intelligence and gave them five training sessions, even those who were previously declining in cognitive function showed substantial improvement—and retained that improvement.

The most comprehensive large-scale study of aging to date was done over a fifteen-year period, beginning in 1970, by Alvar Svanborg and his colleagues on the population of the city of Gothenburg in Sweden, where three successive cohorts were studied at ages seventy, seventy-five, and eighty-one. Swedes are among the longest-lived people in the world; the large, systematically sampled groups of seventy-year-olds were representative of the total population of that industrial city of approximately one million.

This famous Swedish study found no measurable decline in many biological functions (e.g., immune response) until after age seventy, and very little decline by eighty-one. Cognitive abilities were intact to at least age seventy-five (and still intact in almost all those who had reached eighty-one), though speed at rote tests declined. And, again, those who reached seventy in 1977 did better in intelligence and memory tests (verbal meaning, reasoning, spatial ability) than those who became seventy in 1971. The previously assumed declines in intelligence and memory after sixty failed to show up. Svanborg and his colleagues concluded that changes in society in these years were actually changing the aging process:

It is a paradox in our societies that the intellectual function of the elderly improves. We seem just now to live in a period of human history when both the rate and/or manifestations of aging . . . are undergoing marked and rapid changes. The vitality of old people in Sweden today seems to be greater than what it was only five to ten years ago. In other words, we are experiencing rapidly occurring age cohort differences [which] are obvious effects of a changing environment.[13]

The combined thrust of the Swedish, Duke, National Institute on Aging, and National Institute of Mental Health studies of "normal aging" and other recent research is inescapable: *physical and mental decline with aging is not inevitable.* The current research summarized by Rowe shows that the majority of elderly are capable of engaging in all types of normal physical activity up until the age of eighty-five. The research of James Birren, a pioneer gerontologist and the founding head of Andrus, counters the belief that age involves a gradual mental decline: between twenty-two and sixty-five, the vocabulary of an average college graduate doubles from approximately 22,000 to 45,000 words, and for cohorts at that educational level, "neither memory loss nor a decline in mental activity is inevitable after 65."

And as more and more people live beyond eighty—the fastest-growing group in the population—recent investigations have begun to include larger numbers of very old individuals. This research shows that "individuals at the age of 100 can be highly competent and effective in their performance of intellectual tasks," Birren reported.[14]

3. *The gradual disengagement from society and decline in social activities that had been considered a "functional" and "normal" adjustment to age by gerontologists was not the pattern found among the healthy survivors in these major longitudinal studies of "normal human aging."*

"Disengagement" theory, as propounded by Cumming and Henry in 1961[15]—the most famous theory in American gerontology—claimed that social activity tends to decline among elders, as they "disengage" from previous roles in society and social ties and prepare for death. Further, such disengagement was considered a normal, healthy adjustment to age, "functional" for both the individual and society. In the early 1960s, in their cross-sectional study of two hundred healthy middle-class residents of Kansas City over age fifty, Cumming and Henry found few of those over age seventy-five reported high social activity (between 8 and 27 percent, depending on the measure) compared to those aged fifty to fifty-four (between 61 and 86 percent).

Cross-sectional studies, comparing patterns of activity among different age groups at that time, seemed to show participation rising to a peak around age forty and then declining after forty-five. But more recent longitudinal studies of people at the same socioeconomic levels actually reveal "stable or increasing levels of membership and participation after age 45 through at least ages 75–80. Only after age 80 does infirmity and limitations in mobility begin to lower participation appreciably."[16] When socioeconomic status is controlled, those over sixty-five have the highest voting rate of any age group.

The Duke Longitudinal Studies showed slow average declines in total social activities (mean sum of intimate contacts, number of leisure social activities, number of organizations belonged to, and number of meetings attended) from age fifty to seventy-five. The decrease was greater for men than for women, and was greatest during the period of retirement, in the men's sixties. But many of the participants reported no declines and some reported increases in social activity. Only half reported declines of one or more hours per week. In their seventies, two thirds of the men but only two fifths of the women said they were attending clubs less now than at age fifty-five. And almost two fifths of the women said they were attending more than at age fifty-five.

Greater social activity tends to "maintain health by stimulating more physical and mental activity, by providing a social network . . . and by maintaining a sense of self-esteem and social worth," the researchers concluded. Those who did *not* survive their seventies, in the National Institute of Mental Health study, were the ones who earlier "tended toward withdrawal from social contacts." [17]

Contrary to disengagement theory, a number of studies done by Chicago gerontologists found that activity in society became *more important* with increasing age. There was a strong positive correlation between total activity in social roles and life satisfaction among Chicago teachers and steelworkers, a finding confirmed by an international study of six nations. [18] The

Duke Longitudinal Studies provided evidence that more social activity also tends to predict better physical function and health, higher happiness ratings, and greater longevity. These studies showed that "some types of social activity appear not to decline with age. Contacts with friends and relatives appear not to decline until the eighties. Participation in voluntary organizations tends to be stable or increase until the eighties, when socioeconomic status is controlled. This is true of religious and political activity as well." Even in types of social activity that showed "gradual decreases," the researchers found "substantial minorities who maintain or increase their social activity as they age." [19]

In the Duke studies, another surprise was a *negative* correlation between employment and longevity among the men. Those who retired did not die sooner. The crucial factor was "work satisfaction" and "choice" or "control of retirement." The researchers concluded that "unless one derives some satisfaction from work, employment . . . may reduce longevity. Apparently persons who have to work out of necessity and derive no satisfaction from it tend to die earlier than expected. In other words, satisfying work tends to increase longevity, but unsatisfying work tends to reduce longevity." [20]

4. *Activity in society of some complexity, using cognitive ability and involving choice, is*

evidently a crucial clue to longevity and vital aging.

The strongest predictor for survival in the twenty-five-year National Institute of Mental Health Longitudinal Study—better than any other factor, except smoking, to indicate who would survive until eighty-one—was "highly organized behavior." [21] Of all fifteen variables studied, two were found to be as good as all the variables taken together: *the degree of organization and complexity of a person's daily behavior,* and cigarette smoking. These two variables correctly predicted about 80 percent of both survivors and non-survivors.

When first studied at ages sixty-five to seventy-five in 1956, half of the group were genuinely involved in social contacts beyond the immediate family circle, and were rated satisfied and interested in life. Only 11 percent of the group carried on at the level of chores and routines, while nearly half (42 percent) had new, complex, absorbing activities to report. The *survivor* group in the next decade "did not move toward less complexity in daily behavior . . . or toward passivity or toward narrowed social contacts." [22] The critical distinction between the men who survived the next decade and those who did not was the degree of "behavioral organization: the survivors were carrying on more organized and complex living than the men in the non-survivor group. . . . Survivors showed more social interaction, were more active and more satisfied in outlook when they were studied in 1956 than were the men who did not survive to 1967." [23]

But deaths and departures of wives and close friends had a deteriorative effect, "which seemed to be more devastating as the men grew older. Also, different aspects of the individual's behavior and attitude tended to become more closely interrelated . . . increasing the men's vulnerability to critical events as aging advanced. [Those] who continued to maintain their involvement in living did so with greater expenditures of effort. An intact and supportive intimate social environment was [an] important factor in resisting assaults in old age and thus a significant factor in survival." (It should be noted that women—who were not a part of this study— show a much greater ability to re-create such an intimate social environment after the death of a spouse, even though they have less probability of remarriage; this may be a factor in their greater ability to survive. In other studies, women also showed a higher level of social activities and organized behavior.)

The link between greater organization of behavior and survival makes biological sense. "The central nervous system influences other organs through neuronal and hormonal controls that affect development of fatal conditions," the study explained. Evidently the more complex the organization of behavior and mental status, the less likely a pathological or fatal hormonal response to stress among these aged men.[24]

5. *An accurate, realistic, active identification with one's own aging—as opposed both to resignation to the stereotype of being "old" and denial of age changes—seems an important key to vital aging, and even longevity.*

To what degree did the significantly greater-than-expected survival rate and high level of emotional health and cognitive status of those men who were followed from an average age of seventy to eighty-one years in the National Institute of Mental Health study derive from the very fact of their participation in this study? It gave them a conscious identification with, interest in, awareness of, and pride in their own aging. The researchers noticed the men's pride in being part of the study but did not relate it to the surprising vitality of their continued life involvement and their unpredicted lack of decline. Even men who showed signs of organic impairment were able to maintain their level of activity and to compensate for or overcome decline because *they realistically monitored their own aging.* They became aware of other complex changes in themselves that could override decline. They changed the focus of their activities, shifting purposes and grounds for their own self-esteem.

"The stereotype which visualizes old age as inevitably a period of depressing decline was refuted by these men's reported experiences of the aging process. The analysis showed that the men frequently reported favorable changes as they aged, especially in the social and emotional sphere of their lives." For some of these men, there was "an exhilarating new sense of success starting in old age," according to the NIMH study. "A continued interest in using the mind as a satisfying instrument in an environment where there was some sense of purpose appeared to substantially influence the men's level of mental performance," superimposing on the physiological state of the brain.[25] All six of the men whose mental-status test performance improved between seventy and eighty-one had "lively interests in maintaining their mental abilities and lived in environments where keeping their minds active was meaningful."

Denying the stereotype of "the old person who has deteriorated mentally but refuses to give up responsibilities which he or she can no longer handle," the men in this study "generally succeeded in maintaining or withdrawing from activities as their mental capacities dictated. They accomplished this through insightful self-monitoring of their mental capacities which they used to guide their behavior." Without exception, these men "easily acknowledged objective evidence of physical decline." Even at eighty-one, none had any incapacitating chronic medical disease, though reduced hearing or vision, dizzy spells, impotence, and tremors were each mentioned by a few. "They had come to terms with the expectation of physical problems . . . with a matter-of-factness suggestive of a description of a machine that was showing signs of wearing out. There was no sense of hopelessness in their acceptance and no instances of panic about physical deterioration." They did not deny their changes from youth, nor equate or confuse them with sickness.[26]

On the other hand, men who had not fully come to terms with their age were depressed, "experiencing what they saw as discouraging diseases or physical difficulties." *An active, realistic acceptance of age-related changes*—as opposed to denial or passive resignation—was thus the key to a continued vital involvement in life, a very different face of age than disengagement and decline. "Life for a majority of the men," the researchers reported, "was characterized by vitality, interest and enjoyment during most of old age." The crucial key to these men's successful "personal adaptability" to age was "having goals until the end of life." And this involved "modifying goals to fit the needs of age or finding new ones."[27]

There were some men in this study who did not succeed in maintaining goals. Of these men, the researchers noted:

We suspect that perhaps half of the men could have had even more successful lives in their later years had they been prepared upon retirement to take up a substantial part of their new free time with some special interest. . . . Subjects voluntarily offered the thought that their reduction of responsibilities had not been well matched to the high level of mental capacity they maintained. They said that in retrospect they might have been wise to plan more demanding activities for their later years.[28]

Realistic monitoring of their own aging would have ruled out "getting senile" as a valid reason for retirement. But even if they had not been forced to retire, for how many would simply continuing on the same job have been a sufficient goal for the years after sixty-five? "New socially and personally useful roles need to be developed for the growing numbers of men and women who have many years to live in retirement," Butler and his colleagues concluded.[29]

For my own search, the trouble with all these studies of "normal aging" was that they necessarily could only describe "adaptations" to forced retirement from jobs, to the lack of roles in our society for people over sixty-five, to the resultant depression often misdiagnosed as organic brain syndrome, and to illnesses equated

140

with age and therefore untreated—or to changes overtreated as illness when age is denied. The very concept of "normal aging" denied the *developmental possibilities* of age as a unique period of human life.

The qualities that may emerge in people who continue to develop after sixty-five are the uncharted terrain in studies of human aging. Until now, theorists of aging have at the most envisioned an elimination of pathology—a squaring of the curve, as it were, so that more people could live to the limits of "normal aging," presumably set by the genes. It was clear even in these studies—as evidenced by the surprising improvements with age measured in the successive cohorts and in some individuals in every cohort—that some of what had been considered "normal" decline was not, in fact, set by the genes. Are there capacities that actually improve or emerge with age? If there is new or continued growth or development in small but significant numbers of people after sixty-five, after seventy, up into the eighties, why has it not been apparent before? What would cause or prevent its emergence?

Putting all this together, I began to wonder if age, in fact, may offer the opportunity to develop values and abilities, for each of us and for society, that are not visible or fully realized in youth. The reason these developments do not show up on the usual scales of measurement is that all such scales have been based on qualities that are characteristic of youth or young adulthood —and simple, easily measured, grossly visible separate qualities, at that. I was struck, looking into the Baltimore Longitudinal Study of the National Institute on Aging, by the multiplicity of single measurements of blood pressure, muscle tone, function of this organ or that, various easily measured and graphed kinds of physical strength or cognitive abilities on the tests each man was subjected to when he came back to Baltimore every five years, then every two, then each year. And, by contrast, how little the researchers knew about these aging individuals' more complex qualities, and how they functioned as men (and later the women also) in their daily lives, their intimacies, their goals and purposes.

Research cited here has shown that individuals over sixty-five who do not decline seem to become more *integrated* in their various characteristics as they get older. They also become *increasingly individual* and different from others who decline; they continue to develop on the basis of their own accumulated and increasingly divergent experience. In this increasing integration, traumas, declines, or deficiencies in one sphere are compensated for by another. Further, as more than one of these researchers has groped to articulate, something emerges that is more than or different from these separate measurable traits. The "integration" of age seems to transcend the youthful qualities; the transformation is real.

In infancy and childhood, growth takes place in all dimensions, physical, mental, and emotional; development is quick, vivid, clearly measurable in gross changes in the body and in specific basic skills. The "quiet ripening of . . . mental and spiritual capacities" or "gradual shift in appetites and interests" that psychologists like Erik Erikson, Birren, and Gutmann sense as subtle signs of late-life development are not only less vivid but "easily obscured by visible, tangible changes in the aging body, which seems to register decay rather than growth." It occurs to me, further, that the very precise, quantitative scales medical researchers and psychologists use to measure discrete functions or skills might miss the integrative emergence of new qualities in age. From my own interviews, which their data confirm, it is clear that *integration*—making it possible for people to transcend some physical impairments, to become more themselves, more "of one piece" in later life—may not only be less observable in gross physical measurements, but may not register at all on scales standardized for youth or young adults. The very traits that emerge may not have been that visible or seemed that important before, or may even have been deliberately omitted from the focus of the measuring instrument.

The age "crossover" that Gutmann found in

certain societies he categorized in terms of "reclaimed powers" from the early parental role of the other sex.[30] In age, the man can reclaim his "feminine" side, which had to be repressed to allow him to protect his young as warrior; the woman can reclaim her assertive, aggressive, masculine side, which had to be repressed for her to stay close to the young she must nurture. Now, in reclaiming and integrating their suppressed masculine and feminine sides, these elders play a larger parental role that helps to keep the whole tribe human, and the species to survive.[31] Even Erik Erikson's postulation of "generativity" versus "stagnation" imparts to age merely sublimation of the parental role, and his *Vital Involvement in Old Age* argues a recapitulation of youthful stages.

But I submit that scales of "growth" based on childhood or youth—and even capacities defined by the parental roles that peak in midlife—may not give us the lenses we need to discern or comprehend the capacities that mark growth in the third of life after parenting is complete. Since our kind of post-parental age is uniquely human, we might expect it to bring to full realization our unique humanness. We might even expect it to have a unique function in our survival and evolution as a species. I would speculate quite simply that to fulfill our human life span, to realize our full human potential in age, we might have to use in new ways—or integrate, to new simplicity—the complex functioning of our unique human capacities, male and female.

This would require not a denial of age but an active affirmation of its unique human dimensions. We have barely even considered the possibilities in age for new kinds of loving intimacy, purposeful work and activity, learning and knowing, community and care. We have hardly explored the transcendental reaches of ultimate self-realization in age that go beyond "normal" aging. For to see age as continued human development involves a revolutionary paradigm shift.

We can begin that exploration by considering one inescapable conclusion that has, in fact, been borne out by the scientific studies: *The exercise of our unique human capacity for mindful control is key to vital age versus decline.* Consider that in the longitudinal studies, it was organized human behavior—complex, purposeful activity, the web of intimate social ties, connectedness beyond family—that distinguished between those who survived beyond seventy-one and those who did not. The biology of this distinction manifested itself in complex ways, with different diseases. But it comes down to this: the brain and the immune system, which are powerfully affected by emotions, control and affect all our organs, and thus our susceptibility to disease. Legally and medically in this era when machines can keep us breathing when we can no longer function as human beings, "brain death" now defines the end of our personal human existence. *In a very real sense, the life of our brain —which powers that organized, complex, purposeful behavior and the ties it sustains (and that sustain it)—is the key to vital aging.*

Much research done in the last ten years, in nursing homes, retirement communities, and among individuals suffering various traumatic events in age, has revealed that autonomy or control—that is, the extent to which we are able to make our own decisions and choices about our activities and when and how we engage in them—affects not only our performance and well-being in age, but the basic physiology of our aging.

Ellen Langer of Harvard, Judith Rodin of Yale, and their colleagues did an experiment on control at one of the best nursing homes in Connecticut, where the patients, aged sixty-five to ninety, were randomly assigned to two different floors. The patients on one floor were told by the administrator: "You should be deciding how you want your rooms to be arranged . . . whether you want to rearrange the furniture. You should be deciding how you want to spend your time . . . whether you want to visit your friends . . . in your room or . . . theirs. . . . We're showing a movie two nights next week, Thursday and Friday . . . decide which night you'd like to go, if you choose to see it at all."

Each resident on that floor was shown some small green plants and told to choose which one they wanted. "The plants are yours to keep and take care of as you'd like." But the residents on the other floor were told: "We've tried to make your rooms as nice as they can be. . . . We want to do all we can to help you. . . . We're showing some movies next week. We'll let you know which night you're scheduled to go." And each resident was handed a plant "to keep. The nurses will water and take care of them for you."

Three weeks later, the first group showed a significant improvement in alertness, activity, and general well-being, as rated by nurses and themselves, while the comparison group showed a negative change. All but one of the first group, who had arranged their own rooms, chose their own movies, and watered their own plants, showed improvement in physical and mental well-being, whereas only 21 percent of the comparison group showed any improvement. This study and other research suggested to Langer and Rodin that "senility and diminished alertness are not an almost inevitable result of aging. In fact, it suggests that some of the negative consequences of aging may be retarded, reversed or possibly prevented by returning to the aged the right to make decisions and a feeling of competence." [32]

A year and a half later, when the investigators returned to the nursing home, only seven of the forty-seven residents (15 percent) who had watered their own plants and chosen their own movies had died. Twice that number (30 percent —thirteen out of forty-four) had died in the group where the nurses did these things for them. There had been no other difference between the two groups, who originally had roughly the same overall health status and had been institutionalized the same amount of time. The survivors who exercised their own choices were now significantly superior to the others on measures of physical and psychological health.[33]

Another group of experiments conducted by Ellen Langer showed that environments which induce "mindlessness"—a reduced level of mental activity after many repetitions of a particular experience so that behavior becomes automatic—reduce self-confidence, make people less willing to risk doing anything for themselves, and finally create the mental deterioration implied by the false connotation of the old as "senile." She cited clinical cases indicating that, in the extreme, mindlessness may lead to death.

Since "mindfulness" can only take place in situations which are new or require effort to master, older people who accept their "deteriorated" status may indeed be reduced to mindlessness; given no opportunities for new and challenging experience, they sink into brain-numbing passivity. The nursing home residents who did not have to take care of their own plants or decide which movie to go to simply did not have to think as much as the others. Environments like nursing homes which "do not necessitate or allow for conscious, active, cognitive work" may pathologically prevent some minimum amount of mental activity essential for human survival, Langer and her colleagues suggested.

A number of other experiments by the same team showed that young and middle-aged people are, in fact, likely to assume that older people are "senile," "childlike," "helpless," and otherwise "incompetent" because of the pervasive image of age as decline. In turn, feeling avoided leads to older people's withdrawal from involvement in activities, reduced feelings of control, and self-induced helplessness; hence to mindlessness and actual incompetence. When older people attribute these problems to "aging" rather than to the concrete circumstances, they do not take steps to change the circumstances that may be causing the "inevitable" decline.

Langer and her colleagues took people the week after entering a nursing home, who accepted the fact of aging itself as the cause of all their problems, and gave one group some information about slippery floors in the nursing home causing falls, and being awakened at 5:30 A.M. causing weariness. This realization alone resulted in an increase in active participation and sociability, and improvement in health and stress indices, for this group compared to others. Understanding how circumstances in the nursing home could be causing some of their problems gave those resigned nursing home patients new feelings of control, which changed their behavior, and reversed some of the deterioration.[34] In another study involving two nursing homes, the patients in one were invited to join a council of residents to have a voice in larger matters of scheduling, meal planning, rules, and so on. Again, the group with some control over the circumstances of their lives showed increased activity, healthier patterns of eating and sleeping, and decreases in helplessness and despair.

The effect of losing control over their own lives was infantilizing: "learned helplessness." In Langer's experiments, even the usual deterioration in health brought about by admission to a nursing home was moderated when individuals were given some control over the move—choice about the timing, which of several institutions, a say in their own living arrangements, and so forth. Langer warned: "In situations in which people over time gradually and insidiously lose control, they don't take risks and they retreat into an all too familiar world. When people feel they can exercise some control over their environment, they seek out new information, plan, strategize—they behave mindfully." It was this mindful enactment of control that yielded the psychological and physical consequences experienced by the nursing home patients who arranged their own rooms, chose their own movies, and took care of their plants.

If such seemingly minor changes could reverse deterioration in nursing home patients, Langer speculated, then much of the accepted experience of "old age" may be an artifact. She advertised in the paper for healthy men over sixty-five to take part in an experiment in a different kind of aging. She took the group for a week to the New Hampshire woods, where they were given complete control over organizing their meals and activities, where they would sleep, and so on. By the end of the week, they were playing football, and had so dramatically reversed their own "normal" aging that she feared loss of credibility if she published the results. Her experiment did not, however, *deny* age. "I wouldn't suggest that they could live forever that way," she told me. "Their hair stayed white, after all."

In "usual" or "normal" aging, economic stringencies, forced retirement, deaths of people with whom one is connected, fear of mugging, loss of access to driving or public transportation, all deprive people of control over their lives and environment. The extreme, of course, is placement in an institution. But if small changes in the practices of nursing homes that gave the patients more control over their lives were enough to reverse some of the deterioration, public policies that give older people more control over their lives in their own communities might prevent much of the deterioration that leads to nursing home admissions. In Sweden, such a simple intervention as lowering the height of steps on buses and publicizing their easy use gave older people more confidence and mobility to leave their homes and travel about the city—to museums, movies, parks. Perhaps this contributed to the amazing lack of deterioration Svanborg found among the eighty-year-old Swedes aging in their own communities.

I had another hunch in studying paradoxes related to the presence or absence of intimate bonds in age. *Since the continued exercise of our unique human capacity for caring, intimacy, love is key to vital aging versus decline, we must be able to evolve beyond the sexual and family ties of youth.* A number of epidemiological studies have shown that *connectedness* (social support and caring ties or networks) has a direct effect on mortality. Studies in Alameda County, California, over a nine-year period showed men and women at the bottom of a social network index (including spouse, extended family, close friends, church and other group membership) were more than twice as likely to die as those with the strongest social ties (a ratio of 2.3 for men, 2.8 for women). A similar significant link between social connectedness and mortality was found in studies carried out in Michigan and North Carolina.[35] The ability to sustain or create bonds beyond the family was an even more important factor than family bonds in successful aging in some of those studies. Patients' rate and degree of recovery from heart attacks, injuries, and various physical illnesses, including cancer remission, have been found to be improved by informal "supportive behavior" from friends, relatives, or members of their social groups.

The life-and-death importance of connectedness was also revealed in studies over many years showing that widowers are 40 percent more likely to die in the first six months after their spouse's death than other men their age. The widower's mortality returns to that of other men his age if he remarries—or after he survives five years alone. A great many widowers die from heart disease, but higher death rates and higher rates of symptoms for any disease were also found after the death of their wives.[36]

The critical importance of autonomy and connectedness in vital aging, as shown by the statistics of excess mortality and morbidity in their absence, must have a physiological basis. Medical researchers have found that ulcerative colitis, leukemia, cervical cancer, and heart disease are all linked to a feeling of helplessness and loss of hope experienced by the patient before the onset of the disease. A number of studies have linked such factors to immunological processes and susceptibility to infectious diseases, as well as to heart disease, diabetes, arthritis, and cancer. Other studies have found specific reductions in lymphocyte response after the death of a spouse. From these studies, John Rowe, then head of Harvard Medical School's Division on Aging, concluded: "To the extent that older people are placed in situations where they lack control over their lives, and to the extent that the forms of support available to them are not control-enhancing, we would predict [such] physiologic changes ... with consequent increases in morbidity and passivity." He also believed that such research helped explain the great variability on physiological measures of older people, which "appears to increase with increasing age."[37] Without social roles to support them, older people are on their own in finding ways to keep control over their lives and the connectedness that sustains them.

Perhaps the most frightening aspect of aging is the physical deterioration of the brain—again inevitable, according to some experts. But in my search, I discovered evidence from other experts that seemed to prove the opposite. *The presumed loss of brain cells with age does not take place in normal aging. Vital new brain connections can continue to develop until the end of life and even reverse deterioration. The plasticity of the brain makes either decline or further growth possible but not programmed in age.*

Was it possible, I wondered, that we could control mental development in age as much as or more than we have already begun to control physical decline? During the last several years, as people have changed their diets to include more vegetables, fish, and chicken instead of red meat, and jogging and exercise classes have become a way of life, there has been a dramatic decline in heart attack rates. Experimental results on the effects of exercise in increasing bone density have shown it is also possible to reverse osteoporosis.

But even if we exercise and diet, and stop smoking and drinking, and our arteries remain unclogged and our muscles firm, how can we deny the inevitable mental deterioration as our brains begin to shrink and we lose all those brain cells with every year of advancing age? For we learned early in science that the nerve cells in the outer layers of the brain, the cerebral cortex, cannot divide after birth, and do not replace themselves, and that we lose 100,000 nerve cells a day after age thirty. In fact, recent experiments have shown that normal healthy brains do not necessarily lose nerve cells with age. The brain and its neurons may shrink in dimension from loss of the dendrites connecting brain cells with each other; but even in late age, the brain can develop new dendrites (connections) under conditions that stimulate growth.

Since the 1960s, Marian Diamond and her colleagues in the Department of Physiology and Anatomy at Berkeley have been studying rats under conditions of varying stimulation. At first they were simply interested in the effects of the environment on the brains of very young rats. Instead of the standard laboratory condition of three rats to a small cage, they put some rats in isolation in bare small cages, and others in larger cages holding twelve rats, with many objects and mazes to explore, climb in and out of, and manipulate. All the rats were fed the same diet, but the "enriched" rats were petted and otherwise treated with tender loving care when they were fed. And the objects in their cages were changed every week. Those first experiments showed a significant increase in the size of the brain in every dimension of the neurons, and above all, in the number of dendrites between cells in the occipital region of the cerebral cortex, and in the glial cells supporting them, among the rats in the enriched conditions from 25 to 105 days. In rats, the brain starts to shrivel after 26 to 41 days, when they become sexually mature.

Diamond's group repeated the experiment

with rats from 112 to 142 days. Given the maximum life span of rats of approximately 1,000 days, compared to 100 years in humans, these rats were the equivalent of eleven to fourteen years old. At 142 days, the "enriched" rats' brains were not only larger than those of the rats in the bare cages, but also larger than those of the control group of "enriched" rats that were autopsied at 112 days. It was clear that not only was the shriveling halted under the stimulating conditions, but actual growth took place in the brains of these rats long after they reached sexual maturity. Then the same experiment was done with rats at 600 days, the equivalent of 60 human years. After 30 days under stimulating conditions with other rats, every one of the "enriched" rats, upon autopsy, had a thicker cortex than the standard rats.

It is hard to find rats over 700 days old. But in another experiment, geriatric rats were taken out of the bare wire cages a foot square in which they had spent their entire lives and put, at 766 days (equivalent of seventy-five human years), into the larger, yard-square cage with stimulating mazes, wheels, blocks and ladders, and other rats. They lived in these cages until 900 days, when a few began to die. All the rats were then autopsied, and those "ninety-year-old" rats who had been thus stimulated showed, again, increased thickening of the cortex compared to the isolated rats in the bare cages. From the equivalent of seventy-five to ninety human years —far beyond the normal rat life span—their brain cells had increased in both size and activity, and the glial cells that support brain activity had multiplied accordingly. The brain cells of the "ninety-year-old" rats also showed a lengthening of the tips of the dendrites, allowing more communication with other brain cells, which induces further growth. And, in fact, those geriatric rats, despite the deterioration that had already taken place, became significantly smarter in learning how to make their way through a maze.[38]

I have seen Marian Diamond several times in California over the last few years. Like any scientist, she is cautious in the interpretation of her findings. She does not claim that her rats' brains became "young" again—but they did start growing and developing new dendrites and glial cells, long after the rat brain was supposed to reach its maturity, and even after deterioration had begun. "We learned that the outer layers of the brain could retain their plasticity even in very old age," she said. "By having lived in conditions which offered an opportunity for constant exploration and novelty in the objects of various shapes and sizes, these animals could then utilize the changes that had occurred in their brains to solve new problems which they encountered in the mazes."[39]

Further upsetting conventional wisdom about

the brain's deterioration, Diamond and her colleagues actually counted the nerve cells in the rats' brains: even in the non-enriched standard conditions, the number of cells in the brains of rats that were the equivalent of ninety human years was virtually the same as in the "sixty-year-old" brain and the "ten-year-old" brain.

Diamond said:

It is essential to challenge many of the myths about the aging human brain. For example, where did the statistics come from that we are losing 100,000 nerve cells a day after age 30? In 1955, one investigator estimated the loss of nerve cells in the human cortex between 20 and 80-years-of-age was about 3 percent. Then, another scientist found a 10 percent decrease on the surface area of the brain between 20 and 76 years of age. Finally, a third individual, by using these data, calculated that the daily cell loss is 100,000. One of these scientists, however, has recently acknowledged that these data are inaccurate, because no account was taken of the many variables involved in altering brain structures, such as nutrition, illness, physical and mental activity.[40]

Those claims had been made on the basis of autopsy of fewer than ten human brains, and the brains then available for autopsy tended to be those of unclaimed corpses, mostly the bodies of institutionalized men from the VA and other hospitals. The few brains in that study were undeniably "shrunken" at seventy-six and eighty years. In the midst of our discussion, Dr. Arnold Scheibel, Marian Diamond's husband, who is himself a distinguished brain researcher at UCLA, proudly showed me a recent picture of the "luscious, rounded, rich, heavy brain of an active sixty-five-year-old man."

Marian Diamond explained that scientists now know that most of the loss in brain cells takes place in the embryo before birth:

It is essential to understand that since most nerve cells do not divide after they are formed, an excessive number of cells is produced in the embryo to allow for a greater selection during functional organization. The greatest loss of nerve cells is actually as the embryo is developing, and the nervous system is reorganizing to meet its changing needs. You lose 50 percent of your nerve cells before you are born.

In our own studies with controlled laboratory conditions, we have learned from counting cells in the rat cortex, the number of nerve cells does not significantly decrease after early adulthood. We counted brain cortical cells in the healthy 904-day-old rat, equivalent to a 90-year-old human being, and found no significant loss compared with the 600-day-old animal (60 years) which was not significantly different from the 100-day-old animal (equivalent to a 10-year-old child). Other investigators have also reported similar findings that contradict earlier nerve cell loss data. In the more recent medical texts, one now reads that the healthy elderly person's brain is very similar to a healthy younger person's.[41]

And yet, when Diamond began presenting her data from these experiments in which brains long past maturity began developing new dendrites in response to the "enriched" environment, and those "75- to 90-year-old" nerve cells began increasing in size instead of shriveling, her colleagues expressed disbelief, even outrage. "Young lady, that brain cannot change," a leading scientist said, pounding the table, when she first presented her findings in 1963. "There still are non-believers, even though by now a number of experiments have shown the lifelong plasticity of the brain, and these experiments have been repeated and verified," Diamond told me. "The brain is so plastic, it's unbelievable. It seems that we can change the brain at any age, depending on how we use it." Even if some brain cells are lost in age, in conditions of less perfect health, the brain's plasticity can compensate, she stressed. Other researchers have shown that brain cells, within limits, can re-arrange themselves to compensate for a brain injury.

Early brain development is more dependent on experience than had previously been thought; it is not just programmed in the genes. At UCLA, Arnold Scheibel has found that the cells in the speech centers of infants' brains undergo a growth burst in which they form many new con-nections to other cells, just at the time the infant is beginning to respond to voices, between six and twelve months. This growth accelerates be-tween twelve and eighteen months, when the infant begins to grasp that words have mean-ings. Part of the explosion of growth is stimu-lated by the adults' talking to the infants, Scheibel said. "The dendrites' projections are like muscle tissues. They grow the more they're used. Even in old age," he added, "if you learn a new language, it's dendritic fireworks."

Why, then, the persistence of the belief not only in the inevitable physical deterioration of the brain in age, but also in its functions? My search led me to a mountain of experiments and tests that seemed to prove that deterioration beyond question—until I came to an interesting realiza-tion: *The age-programmed declines in memory and cognitive function may be artifacts of tests geared to youth.* For I found that in other labora-tories, students of the psychology of aging have begun to have second thoughts about the research that over the years has established a pattern of age-programmed universal and irreversible decline in cognitive function and memory.

Early studies of adult cognition were launched during the heyday of logical empiricism, in a simplistic and mechanical attempt to make psychology "scientific." Intelligence tests were devised to measure the development of logical, objective, rational thought, free from the influence of background, values, religion, environment, specifically divorced from any context of personal experience or meaning. Proficiency on such tests was quickly established to peak in adolescence, and to decline progressively and severely in age.

New research has led to new questions. If biological growth continues into adulthood and beyond, given proper conditions of stimulation—as in the studies of the "75- to 90-year-old" rat brains—why shouldn't psychological growth also continue into late life? Was it adequate to define "maturity" by a twenty-year-old's performance on those abstract tests measuring abilities that peak at youth—or did that prematurely foreclose the model of human development? Should adulthood be seen as the *cessation of growth and development* (and therefore the beginning of decline), or as a life stage programmed only for plasticity (and therefore open to further growth or decline)?

While unitary measures of intelligence such as

those used on IQ tests continued to show a steady decrement from the twenties onward, during the 1970s a number of psychologists began to discover that what was being measured was not unitary "intelligence" at all.[42] It seemed that "fluid" and "crystallized" intelligence show different aging patterns. "Crystallized" intelligence, which involves experience, meaning, knowledge, professional expertise, wisdom, increases throughout adulthood. "Fluid" intelligence, which involves tests of memory and abstract problem solving divorced from meaningful or cultural context, seems to show profound age differences between younger and older adults. Older people do not do as well as younger ones on tests of immediate recall of lists of random numbers or words, spatial relations, and abstract reasoning, while they "typically perform well in tests of stored information." It was assumed that the "abstract" tests measured the "aging of those brain centers responsible for either the most complex or the most hierarchically superior mental operations." Intellectual aging was thus seen as regression from "higher" to "lower" levels of functioning. The aging individual "functions at a more concrete, lower level of organization."[43]

But in 1974, Werner Schaie and his colleagues began systematically to investigate a phenomenon evident ever since the first life-span studies of aging: the striking discrepancies between cross-sectional and longitudinal studies of intellectual development and aging. The cross-sectional studies invariably reported earlier and more dramatic declines than the longitudinal ones. Schaie and Labouvie-Vief performed fourteen-year follow-up studies on different age cohorts, ranging from twenty-five to eighty-one, and found that each respective cohort did not decline, but stayed relatively stable in its actual performance on tests of verbal meaning, word fluency, reasoning, and so on, until well into the seventies. In a cross section of any single year— for instance, 1963—sixty-year-olds scored significantly lower than fifty-year-olds, who appeared to score lower than forty-year-olds, etc. But people who hit fifty, sixty, and seventy in 1970 scored significantly higher than people who hit fifty, sixty, and seventy in 1963. Each later cohort or generation tended from the start to test at systematically higher levels than earlier ones.

They concluded that "most of the adult life span is characterized by an absence of decisive intellectual decrements. In times of rapid cultural and technological change, it is primarily in relation to younger populations that the aged can be described as deficient." But it is "erroneous," Schaie and Labouvie-Vief insisted, to interpret such cross-sectional age differences as indicating *changes or declines* in intelligence caused by age itself.[44] Further, the higher educational level of the later cohorts seemed to affect not only the "crystallized" intelligence on the verbal tests but "fluid" reasoning, which had been considered the purest indicator of the aging brain's decline. (Computer-educated and computer-user generations will undoubtedly score even higher on such tests when they hit sixty and seventy.) While these tests made clear that "significant decrements are considerably delayed" into the far end of the seventies, such differences did not account for all of the supposed decline with age, especially after seventy.

Then, Paul Baltes and Gisela Labouvie-Vief began to question the very conceptualization of "intelligence" and "cognitive competence" that had been the focus of those tests and, above all, their standardization on the performance of youth. And the eminent biologist J. F. Fries, with other researchers, took another look at the biological data that had seemed to show that aging was simply a gradual unraveling or reversal of the processes of gradual maturation that peak in youth. For the problems on which the older people showed deficiencies were, quite simply, the *problems of youth*. They dealt with the matter of childhood and school, not with problems and material from the adult world; for example, "two excellent reports indicating clear cut significant decreases in problem solving in older years, as shown by an alphabet maze and a puzzle board." [45]

But intelligence, though it has come to mean "that which intelligence tests measure," is supposedly a vital aspect of biological adaptation. If, in fact, the *very nature of biological aging* has changed as a result of historical changes in society and environment, specifically, the lengthening of the life span—and if intelligence is "the ability to negotiate environmental demands successfully"—that curve of mental development which peaks in youth would seem to be prematurely foreclosed. If growth can continue beyond youth, in adults who face problems more complex than puzzle boards, ought it not to be investigated on its own terms?

Further, the very basis of the biological model of reversal—gradual, genetically programmed growth and development from birth to the early twenties mirrored in gradual programmed deterioration ending in terminal decay—has changed dramatically in recent decades. The "squaring" of the mortality curve as interpreted by J. F. Fries [46] means that, while the maximum life span has remained fixed at 100 years, the *accelerated decline* which used to mark aging *sets in at a later age.* Thus, the view of *gradual aging* must be displaced by the concept of "a vigorous adult life span followed by a brief and *precipitous senescence.*" [47]

In actuality, the changes in mortality rates reflect profound changes in the very causes of aging as well. As Fries has pointed out, acute disease has been virtually eliminated, replaced by chronic disease and accident as the major causes of death. Since chronic disease is strongly affected by lifestyle, diet, exercise, smoking, as well as "psychological coping mechanisms," Fries and his colleagues maintain that aging must now be viewed as a highly variable and idiosyncratic process, whose rate and specific course are under the control of non-biological factors, including "choice" and "assumption of personal responsibility." Labouvie-Vief summed it up: "The very concept of biological causation thus shifts. . . . The individual not only passively submits to a predetermined aging program, but also—within limits—actively participates in its course, affecting it through his or her own behavior and decision making." [48]

Yet I found that the "decline" model persists despite the evidence that refutes it. With surprisingly little impact, Birren, Baltes, Schaie, Labouvie-Vief, and others have questioned the whole body of research that had established the view of a biologically programmed, steadily deteriorating decline in intellectual adaptability with advancing age. They reexamined the evidence of atrophy of brain weight from young adulthood to the mid-eighties, loss of neuron cells, and other changes in the brain that had seemed essentially irreversible, restricting intellectual adaptability in age. Birren drew attention to the fact that neither the decline in intelligence nor the biological changes on which it was supposed to be based were normally distributed through the aging years, but were found in groups suffering pathology *in the months or years just before death.*[49] While earlier research had indicated diminished cerebral blood flow as key to intellectual decline, more recent data revealed that this relation did not hold for older people in reasonably good health.

Even more significantly, declines were revealed to be a function of *distance from death,* not chronological age, the dramatic changes occurring primarily in the years immediately preceding death. As for the supposed atrophy of the brain in age, that data came from people suffering dementia. Only a slight reduction in brain weight was found in a normal sample of adults over sixty-two compared to those under fifty—and even this was found only in males.[50]

It seems that as we ascended the evolutionary scale, the significant factor was the relative amount of cerebral cortex, which is the structural basis for brain plasticity. It is highest in humans because the specific interconnections between neurons are virtually unlimited and highly influenced by experience. One would predict that the plasticity of those "ninety-year-old" rat brains that Marian Diamond found when her rats were placed in stimulating environments would be even greater for human brains. In fact, recent research on a sample of normal adults at 79.6 years revealed dendritic branching more extensive than in middle-aged subjects (51.2 years). On the other hand, a group of seventy-six-year-olds with senile dementia displayed markedly less dendritic branching.[51]

Yet despite all such recent evidence which shows that presumed decline of intelligence with age to be an artifact of specific pathology, or of the different educational experiences of different generations, the decline model remains. When psychologists did a careful study of intellectual aging, adjusting for educational level across age groups, and discovered that the seemingly age-related declines previously shown on the intelligence test used were essentially eliminated, they found it "surprising" that such evidence "has not eroded belief in the decline hypothesis."[52]

I, too, found it surprising. For decades, cross-sectional results had confirmed the expected pattern of loss of intellectual performance with age, beginning in early adulthood around age thirty. Why didn't the expectation change when the longitudinal follow-up data did not show the same decline patterns? Schaie and his colleagues, as of 1984, had followed for twenty-eight years more than two thousand subjects, measured repeatedly on a large battery of intelligence tests. New cohorts were added at seven-year intervals, from 1956 on, and the results should have revolutionized our conception of the decline of intelligence in age. Schaie found that the average decline in his subjects was relatively small from age sixty to eighty; in fact, about one third of seventy-year-olds performed above the mean of young adults in intelligence tests.

The most notable finding was the *substantial variability* in the overall course of intellectual aging, between individuals—and between generations. "Depending upon conditions of health, work context and similar factors, aging decline can begin for different persons during the fourth, fifth, sixth, seventh or even eighth decade of life," Baltes summed up the results.[53]

More recent research has revealed a dynamic whereby "normal" aging can indeed induce decline. Vern Bengtson has posited the relationship between aging and intellectual functioning as a feedback loop, which actively induces vulnerable older people into a role of social and intellectual incompetence. "Once begun, this loop initiates a cycle of self-fulfilling prophecies that is buttressed by mythologies and stereotypes surrounding socially held views of 'normal aging.'"

Not only do institutions such as nursing homes "actively discourage competent behavior," but the individual patients themselves "internalize negative expectations," surrendering to negative stereotypes of aging and thereby contributing to their own decline. Labouvie-Vief and Baltes have stated that similar effects might well explain part of the apparently "normal" decline in cognitive functioning in the late sixties to early seventies in those studies done mainly on men who were then undergoing forced retirement. So they and their colleagues began to do a different kind of research into changes in intelligence in late life. They reasoned that "if deficits are indeed induced by . . . a general restriction of environmental complexity, they are not necessarily irreversible and can possibly be reversed." [54]

Baltes and his colleagues at the Max Planck Institute for Neurological Research in Berlin and at Pennsylvania State University undertook some ten "cognitive training" studies involving a total of about one thousand people between sixty and eighty years of age with above-average health and education. These older people were given five to ten training sessions over several months on reasoning problems similar to those in tests of "fluid" intelligence, which, according to previous theory, irreversibly and sharply declines with age. When they were then tested for "fluid" intelligence, they showed a significant improvement. The gain was approximately as great as the *loss* reported in previous research on aging. [55] Further, the gain was maintained in follow-up studies six months later. The people in this study represented 50 to 75 percent of all the sixty- to eighty-year-olds living in Berlin and rural Pennsylvania. Regardless of their age, educational level, health, or initial level of performance, "fluid" intelligence increased with training, even in their eighties.

The Baltes group then extended their research on intellectual plasticity and reserve capacity to memory. They gave healthy people sixty-seven to seventy-eight years old training on the sorts of tests used to assess memory loss with age: repetition of strings of digits or random words. After thirty sessions of memory training, every one of those sixty-seven- to seventy-eight-year-olds was able to repeat at least thirty words and strings of digits as long as forty in the correct order, though they were presented only once. These were healthy older people living in the community, not residents of nursing homes or Alzheimer victims. Their performance after the training sessions was so strikingly different from the memory loss usually shown at that age that the researchers speculated whether "the everyday world of many older persons is indeed one that generates intellectual atrophy, due to lack of experiences and demands conducive to high intellectual performances."[56]

Corroborating studies by the Max Planck Institute indicated that the intellectual plasticity observed in older people thus challenged had a measurable counterpart in physiological brain functioning. Evidently the brain is not fixed in structure by early adulthood, as had previously been assumed. Other research suggests that growth *and* deterioration of brain structures occur throughout the life span, depending on environmental stimulation. The kind of recovery and compensatory response often found in older patients after sudden brain damage indicates further reserves of plasticity that are not drawn upon in the "normal" roles of even healthy people over sixty-five.

On the basis of such testing of people aged sixty-eight to eighty living the "normal" life of the aging in our society, Baltes concluded:

> Certainly there is decline in old age, especially at maximum limits of functioning in the basic mechanics of intelligence. However, for most normal elderly people there is also great reserve capacity and potential for new learning and growth. . . . If provided with cognitive enrichment and practice, most elderly people up to age 75 or so are capable of remarkable gains and peaks of intellectual performance, including in those areas of functioning such as memory where the typical expectation is one of early and regular decline.[57]

But the "aging of intelligence" as shown by these word and digit tests, Baltes suggested, "is but a sample of what is possible in principle.

Existing limits in a given society or in given science are not absolute or necessary ones. In this sense, the search for the range and limits of intellectual plasticity . . . has also opened up new social vistas on what the aging of intelligence could be like if conditions were different." [58]

The resistance even to talking about further growth in age must be confronted before we are able to envision new possibilities—for ourselves or for society. As it is now, the weak face of age embodied in the mystique inspires such visceral dread that the strong face can only be seen in terms of youth.

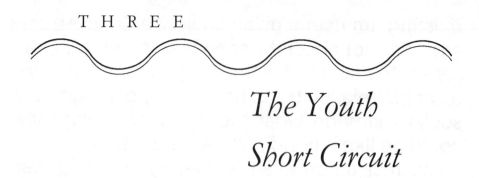

The Youth
Short Circuit

As I continued my search for scientific proof that further development is, in fact, possible in age, I became aware of a glitch so obvious we don't see it, a short circuit closing off both the way many gerontologists view age and the way our society as a whole perceives it. Just as darkness is sometimes defined as the absence of light, so age is defined as the absence of youth. Age is assessed not by what it is, but by what it is not. To conceive of development beyond youth seemed to involve a paradigm shift that was strangely difficult. For instance, the "testing the limits" of intelligence and memory in age had been done on digit and random word tests, deliberately stripped of meaning, emotional content, memory associations, and historical context—the kind of "problems" used to test intelligence in youth. Older people, in fact, do progressively worse on such tests as they age; since most never come into contact with such tests after they leave school, the older they get, the more remote and rusty they become in whatever skills these tests test. But as Paul Baltes showed, specific training sessions on such rote and memory problems could make any reasonably healthy older person perform as well as or better than young people on those tests; that remarkable improvement with practice held up to age eighty.

But Baltes, along with Schaie, Labouvie-Vief, and others, I also found, had become increasingly restive about what was being measured with these tests. Baltes warned:

> . . . what we know about psychometric intelligence in the older adult is based on instruments and models developed for the young. In other words, we know how to compare the older person with the young in youth-oriented tasks and settings. But we have relatively few instruments that would tell us much about the unique nature of intellectual behavior . . . in the older adult.

This critical view has been expressed by a number of researchers over the past twenty-five years, with no effect. The tests are still in use.

Moreover, as Baltes pointed out, some of the most aggressive proponents of the concept of intellectual aging as a programmed decline continue to base their own research and interpretation "almost exclusively on the use of the test instruments developed in the context of young adults, where academic performance served as the major validation criterion."[1]

None of these tests measured intelligence as it is actively used *after* youth. They were not based on asking: What are the unique settings and tasks related to the intellectual behavior of the older person? What are the intellectual tasks of advancing adulthood and how are those tasks related to the systems of earlier life? To what degree is it perhaps necessary for the older adult to unlearn (rather than passively forget) knowledge and skills acquired in the first part of the life course? Could some of these differences be not primarily a matter of decline but of further development? Is it possible, as Baltes suggested, that aging brings qualitative changes in thinking that "may mimic decrements but in fact signal adaptive reorganization to meet the demands of later life?"

Researchers have known for years that if tests are constructed to tap knowledge relevant to adult life—the use of the Yellow Pages of a telephone directory, for instance—the usual decline found with increasing age seems to be reversed. The young always excelled in tests dealing with the usual school-based forms of information. But older adults excelled on information about modes of transportation, finance management, health and disease, and so on.

Jean Piaget and others who studied the development of thought in children and adolescents postulated a movement from the concrete to the hypothetical, abstracted from the context. Proficiency in the tests they developed involved the ability to deliberately strip the material of meaning, feeling, considerations of context and consequence. Such tests did indeed predict effective adaptations of young people to college and professional school. And when they were used on older adults, age seemed to bring about a "regression" from that purely abstract problem solving to more concrete, practical, contextual thinking. Was this actually a regression to a kind of second childhood, as it was at first interpreted, or was something else happening?

It seems to be a fact that older adults do not do so well on tests that are stripped of meaning, although, as we have seen, with sufficient training sessions on this kind of material, their supposed "cognitive deficits" disappear. When older adults insisted on giving meaning to these tests, they were seen as suffering from an "erosion of higher abstract levels . . . a 'return' to the concrete." But Labouvie-Vief and others now suggest that declines on such tests of cognitive abilities useful in the school years may sometimes indicate that an individual "is evolving a different and *higher* level of structural organization. As such new forms of organization are negotiated, initial skills may be reshaped and transformed, some being affirmed and enhanced, others denied and delegated to atrophy. . . . Indeed, under certain circumstances the insistence that abstractions must be related back to specific social contexts can be argued to constitute a higher level of psychological maturity than the pure exercise of logic so often found in youth."[2]

Instead of looking for "the one correct solution," older people, given problems that are inherently open-ended and ambiguous, seemed to seek dimensions from their actual experience of life that might remove the ambiguity. They seemed to have discarded the "pure" logic of adolescent youth that had served as the measurement standard for intelligence. Labouvie-Vief and others now saw that pure logic as "a merely budding, but not yet mature, mode of thinking." But it is still the standard against which older adults' thinking is judged as regressive, deteriorating, in decline. For instance, in a study in which young and older adults were presented with logically inconsistent statements, the younger ones took the information presented as given, and proceeded from there to reach conclusions. The older adults questioned the premises, went beyond the information given, and expanded upon it on the basis of their own personal experience and knowledge that might resolve the inconsistencies. The researcher, however, concluded that this approach demonstrated a failure to comprehend the material logically, as well as a regressive tendency to allow "interference" from one's real-world knowledge.[3] One elderly subject complained: "I know what you want me to do, but it just isn't true."

In one such experiment, older adults were presented with a green surface (a "meadow") on which miniature houses could be arranged in different ways. They were then asked whether the spatial arrangement of houses would affect the amount of grass left to mow. The older subjects did not give the "correct" mathematical solution—that the spatial arrangement does not affect the total surface left. Instead, they noted that mowing many small spaces between the individual houses rather than one large open space would, of course, be harder and take more time!

In another experiment, Labouvie-Vief and her colleagues had forty-five young men (mean age 22.3 years) and forty-five elderly men (mean age 74.2 years) listen to a taped fable, "The Wolf and the Crane," and then recall it. The story tells of a wolf who gets a bone stuck in his throat. Offering a reward, the wolf convinces a crane to stick its neck down his throat and dislodge the bone.

The crane succeeds and asks for the reward. Its reward, the wolf replies, is to survive sticking its neck down a wolf's throat.

When asked for a summary of the story, it appeared that the elderly subjects' attention to detail was qualitatively different from that of the younger. Their summaries emphasized the metaphorical or moral meaning of the story. For instance, one said: "The moral of the story as I understood it was that people should not seek a reward for their well doing, but to be content with having done a good deed."

These spontaneous reflections on the moral of the fable for life did not reflect a deficit in recall. For when the instructions were changed to "recall as much as you can," the performance of the older people was as high as that of the younger ones on the details previously omitted from the metaphorical focus. Labouvie-Vief pointed out that "the older adults are not, therefore, suffering from a lack of flexibility. It might be suggested that flexibility is lacking on the part of the younger ones as they do not show any sensitivity to changes in the recall instructions. Instead, they may reflect rote or surface-bound memory not present in the old."

In fact the elderly, but not the young, went *beyond* the text. They related the information as a whole to dimensions of real-world knowledge, stressing its moral and metaphorical values. In contrast to this quite active interpretive process,

Labouvie-Vief said that the young men could be characterized as passively taking in new information "as is" and compartmentalizing it, rather than integrating it fully with previous knowledge and experience.[4]

Is cognitive "maturity" what is really being measured by the ability to "abstract" facts from values, to brush aside one's real-world knowledge, one's emotions, intentions, and actions? "By that criterion," as Labouvie-Vief remarked, "many mature and aging adults fail miserably. They insist on meaning. They are unwilling to sever form from context, to dissociate structure from function, to isolate thinking from its application. As a result, they have been said to return to the concrete."[5]

In a more complex view of development, such so-called declines may, in fact, indicate that the individual is evolving a different and higher level of structural organization. Certain losses may be essential to continued growth. Young children, for instance, do better than older children and adults on tests involving memory of incidental details—of shape or color of blocks or toys, etc. This ability declines when the older child discovers that he or she should pay less attention to details irrelevant to the task at hand.

The "concreteness" of age, in Labouvie-Vief's view, is not at all the same as the child's, nor is it a regression from the abstract thought of youth. It is a developmental advance on the youth's acceptance of problems at face value, on youthful performance motivated out of compliance with authority and youth's search for the one "correct" solution. When older people insist on evaluating these same tasks within larger social contexts, aware of their uncertainties, ambiguities, and contradictions, participating rather than submissively complying in the task, should such a complex interfacing be considered "regression," or a higher mode of human knowing, unique to age?

Labouvie-Vief said of these older subjects that "their sometimes passionate concerns with morals and ethics, it could be maintained, are no more indices of deterioration than the moral concerns of an aging Albert Einstein or Bertrand Russell are fully captured by being called the ranting of senility. Indeed, a widening of the concept of truth to encompass morals and ethics appears to be the very hallmark of the generative concerns of the autonomous self in age."[6]

During the year I spent at Harvard immersing myself in the state-of-the-art study of age, I became increasingly restive with the medical school's gerontological focus on Alzheimer's and nursing home policy, and I decided to audit a psychology course on "Adult Development" and everything I could find on evolution. Those human years after sixty that interested me are, after all, a relatively new phenomenon in the evolution of life. At the turn of the century, remember, life expectancy was only forty-six years.

In the "Adult Development" class at the school of education, where Harvard undergraduates were joined by a number of older women returning to school for degrees after their kids were grown, our young instructor, Henry Lasker, told us: "Until seven or eight years ago, there wasn't supposed to be such a thing as adult development." When he asked the class to list adjectives describing adults and we replied with "mature," "grown-up," "independent," "stable," "secure," "responsible," "no longer a child," he pointed out that most of these adjectives were heavy and static, implying full growth and maturity at the end of childhood, not showing at all that adulthood is *a period of continued change.*

Of course, until recently, psychologists thought that full personal, social, emotional, and intellectual as well as physical development was reached by the early twenties. Freud believed that the lines of development were set before the age of six, and even the most rigorous psychoanalysis could not change them much after thirty. To apply the word "development" to adults is still considered questionable by some psychologists. Adult development, to those psychologists who now study it, constitutes relatively stable *shifts* beyond that childhood model of biologically programmed, straight-line, cumulative development.

Our class studied the work of those psychologists who have begun to postulate life stages and phases of development, tracing the life course beyond childhood in longitudinal studies of Harvard men followed from college, Californians followed from childhood, and Kansas City residents followed from midlife through their adult years. It quickly emerged that the main developmental studies of "life stages" and "phases" so far had been based chiefly on white, middle-class men, and such studies usually seemed to end before age. They assumed that adult "development" terminated with the midlife crisis at forty to forty-five. And although these studies explicitly dealt with *adult* development, the measures were still taken from *youth.*

Carl Jung is probably the father of the modern study of adult development. During his thirties, Jung was a disciple of Freud's. Approaching forty, he split from Freud, believing that Freud was too narrowly focused on childhood development and its influence on adult problems. Jung thought attention should be paid to development in "the second half of life," after the emotional involvements and parental conflicts of childhood are resolved and the demands of family and work met. Only after forty, Jung believed, could the developmental process of "individuation" begin, extending over the second half of the life cycle.

I went to see the three men who did the main contemporary studies of life stages: George Vaillant at Harvard; Roger Gould in Los Angeles; and Daniel Levinson at Yale. It seemed significant to me that all three were in their early forties when they laid down their rubrics, as was Erik Erikson. I was a graduate student in psychology at Berkeley in 1943 with Daniel Levinson and his brilliant wife Maria, who collaborated in his research during the forty-odd years of their marriage. We studied together with Erikson at Berkeley. We were/are the same age. Rereading Danny's preface to *The Seasons of a Man's Life* as I was undertaking my own search for the meaning of our new third age, I was taken aback by his gloomy, desperate clinging to youth. He was nearing sixty when I saw him again at Yale. Some months later I learned that he had left Maria for a much younger woman to whom he is now married. He wrote in that preface:

Adults hope that life begins at 40—but the great anxiety is that it ends there. . . . The most distressing fear in early adulthood is that there is no life after youth. Young adults often feel that to pass 30 is to be "over the hill." . . . The middle years, they imagine, will bring triviality and meaningless comfort at best, stagnation and hopelessness at worst. . . . At 46, I wanted to study the transition to middle age in order to understand what I had been going through myself.[7]

When Levinson got the message that people in their twenties no longer considered him of their generation, he responded at first with puzzlement, irritation, or depression. He wanted to say: "This is ridiculous! I haven't really changed —I am still with you, not with them. The 'you' . . . is the youthful generation in society and the youthful parts of the self. The 'them' . . . refers to the 'old,' the generation that has lost its place in society and its capacity for youthful pursuits."[8]

Levinson came to see the crucial generation as middle adulthood—the generation of "dominance" in career and family—and he embraced Erikson's concept of "generativity versus stagnation" as its main task ("to become generative a man must know how it feels to stagnate—to have the sense of not growing, of being static, stuck, drying up, bogged down in a life full of obligations and devoid of self-fulfillment"). He placed Jung's "individuation" (the developmental process through which a person becomes more uniquely individual) at around forty. And while he said that "individuation" holds the possibility of "continuing self-renewal" and "may continue through the afternoon and evening of life,"[9] in effect, he ended it in the fifties.

At around 60, there is . . . the reality and the experience of bodily decline. . . . Even if he is in good health and physically active, he has many reminders of his decreasing vigor and capacity. . . . He is also likely to have at least one major illness or impairment—heart disease, cancer, endocrine dysfuntion, defective vision or hearing, depression. . . . To approach 60 [is] to feel that all forms of youth —even those seemingly last vestiges remaining in middle age—are about to disappear, so that only "old age" remains.

In late adulthood a man can no longer occupy the center stage of his world. . . . Moving out of center stage can be traumatic. A man receives less recognition and has less authority and power. His generation is no longer the dominant one. As part of the "grandparent" generation, he can at best be moderately helpful to his grown offspring and a source of indulgence and moral support to his grandchildren. . . . In his work life, too, there will be serious difficulties if a man holds a position of moral authority beyond age 65 or 70. . . . Even when a man has a high level of energy and skill, he is ill-advised to retain power well into late adulthood.

What does development mean at the very end of the life cycle? It means that a man is coming to terms with the process of dying and preparing for his own death. . . . He must come finally to terms with the self—knowing it and loving it reasonably well, and being ready to give it up.[10]

For Levinson, the measure of development, even in age, was in some basic way managing to hold on to youth:

The internal Young has great energy and capacity for further development in many directions. The internal Old has attained a high degree of structure, has gone as far as he can in realizing his potential, and can now develop no further . . . peak levels of functioning. . . . The decline is normally quite moderate . . . but it is often experienced as catastrophe. A man fears that he will soon lose all the youthful qualities that make life worthwhile. When youth is totally lost, all that is left is to be totally old.[11]

Similarly, Roger Gould in his *Transformation: Growth and Change in Adult Life* could not see beyond the giving up of the "false assumptions" of childhood, which occupy us from sixteen to forty-five: "I'll always belong to my parents and believe in their world" . . . "Doing things my parents' way, with willpower and perseverence, will bring results" . . . "My loved ones can do for me what I haven't been able to do for myself" . . . "Life is simple and controllable." He wrote:

By about 50 we complete the work of dismantling the last false assumption. . . . Events are forcing us to accept that there never will be any magical powers with which we can bend the world to our will. With that, we make the final passage from "I am theirs" to "I own myself." ... We step from the intense heat of the mid-life period to a cooled-down, post-mid-life attitude. We live with a sense of having completed something, a sense that we are whoever we are going to be.[12]

Gould was forty-three when he finished that study. The end of adult development could not be delayed much further, he felt. "For some men the disillusionment with the 'magical' payoff of work is delayed to the late forties or early fifties. ... For some women the excitement of a new career ... can lend a temporary new sense of power just as the old power of youthful attractiveness fades."[13]

George Vaillant took charge of the Grant Study of 268 Harvard men, who had been followed from their college years, 1939–42, at their twenty-fifth reunion when they were forty-six. He, himself then thirty-three, was so "alarmed" by his first interviews of these men that he told his department chief:

I don't want to grow up; these men are all so ... so depressed. ... As I was to learn, the men were by no means despairing; but like any child first discerning the facts of life, I had subtly distorted what I had seen. . . . The Grant Study men had grown up enough to acknowledge real pain that the caterpillar in me still denied.[14]

But to Vaillant, too, "adult development" climaxed in the mid-forties. "How can I marshal evidence that adults continue to grow at the same time that their bodies seem to shrivel?" It surprised him to find "a progressive maturation of adaptive modes" in these men.

As adolescents, the Grant Study men were twice as likely to use immature defenses as mature ones; in middle life they were four times as likely to use mature defenses. . . . The facts that dissociation, repression, sublimation and altruism appeared to increase in middle life and that projection, hypochondriasis and masochism were most common among adolescents, are at variance with many popular conceptions. . . . We sometimes think of the young as dreamy artists and the middle-aged as hypochondriacal martyrs.[15]

Although he also found a deepening appreciation of human relationships and an increasing sense of comfort with other people, comparing fifty to twenty-five, he reported incredulously a female colleague's suggestion that "this trend toward greater interpersonal comfort may increase until age 70."

Other recent studies, concerned less with age than with the "evolution of the self," "adaptive strategies," and "moral growth," provide a more open-ended view of maturity, especially studies now involving women. In adolescence, when our public and private selves divide, these studies see authority rather than self regulating our behavior, and life is lived out automatically and compulsively rather than freely and consciously. Jane Loevinger's work on ego development, and Bernice Neugarten's on transcending polarized sex and age roles, have shown that midlife rather than childhood or adolescence represents the pivotal time of individuation, autonomous self-definition, and conscious choice.[16] From the childish morality of avoiding guilt and conforming to the majority, to the adult's response to the needs of the community and the demands of her own conscience, they suggest that moral or ego development follows a fixed sequence, although the age at which any given shift occurs varies widely among individuals. Aspects important in one stage may decline or be discarded in another; turmoil may signal the transition to a more advanced stage; regression may occur; the evolution may be reversible.

But implicit in all these studies is the sense that *maturity*—whether it begins or ends at forty-five—brings somehow a resolution or integration of the childish split between instinctual conflicts (Freud's shameful id), the private and public selves (ego), and morality (superego). Beyond the acquisition of skills, knowledge, and money, transcending the previous masculine/feminine polarization, one finally moves in a more autonomous, integrated, conscious, and flexible way as a generative and responsible member of the human community. Yet even if these psychological models, so far, have seemed to end by fifty —mainly because of the blind spot of their creators—they hint at a new basis for looking at age, other than that of linear decline. Development had previously been seen as a kind of linear accumulation, in which lower-level responses are retained as higher stages are added, from infancy to that youthful peak, now extended to midlife. The only patterns possible in that model are either continued additions onto the top of the pyramid or deletions of stages from the top down. Aging is simply considered development-in-reverse, in a first-in/last-out sequence, a return to the childlike state.

But what if those years after fifty are, rather, an additional stage of development? Regression is possible, but so is further growth, along the lines of that individuation and generativity which all of these studies have discerned at the midlife "transition" from youthful polarizations and rigid conformity. If one applies to age the new knowledge of the non-linear, dynamic nature of development—of the brain, the biological organism, and of the self—it becomes clear that development can continue, with losses, gains, reorganization, depending on what one's environment permits and what one chooses to do. (Indeed, it now appears that the traditional linear model is no longer valid even for studying childhood development. Recent research shows that development in childhood is characterized not just by gain, and does not consist of a mere cumulative layering of stages, but at each stage brings a dynamic reorganization.) [17]

To make a leap here, I would suggest that the extreme variability found in age—people from sixty until just before death are more different from each other than at any other time in life—shows that the process of *individuation,* becoming more oneself, which those studies of male development discerned at forty-five, and which I found so striking in my own interviews of women and men at sixty-five, seventy, and eighty, shapes our third age uniquely, *unless we succumb in stagnation or denial to the self-fulfilling prophecy of age as decline and despair.*

All of the more recent evidence that I had so far collected suggested that it is evidently the nature of our human biology—and above all, our human brain—that development can indeed continue beyond childhood and youth, *beyond midlife,* up to and beyond the seventies. It can continue until the very end of life, given purposes that challenge and use our human abilities; given the exercise of that individuation, that autonomy, that can be ours at childhood's end.

But that is merely the jumping-off point. Our biology evidently makes it possible but does not determine it. Mindless conformity to the standards of youth can prohibit further development, and that denial can become mindless conformity to the victim-decline model of age. It takes a conscious breaking out of youthful definitions—for man or woman—to free oneself for continued development in age. It was not an accident, it seemed to me, that the people who participated year after year in the longitudinal studies of aging survived significantly longer than they were expected to. They surprised the researchers with a minimum of decline, no matter what tests were used, and with those unpredicted signs of further hard-to-define development. They were so removed from the usual pattern that the researchers in each study kept thinking they must be making errors of selection. But since this phenomenon was found again and again in such studies, it seemed more likely that it was caused by these individuals' participation in the study of aging itself. Those who consciously affirmed and studied their own aging in an open-ended way, as a new period of development, simply continued to find ways to keep on developing.

It was also a noteworthy aspect of these studies that mental decline, when it did take place, was a predictor of approaching death, even if no disease had yet been diagnosed. In sum, our development does not necessarily end at any age, according to these studies. We can continue to develop in our eighties, even into our nineties. We can use our own unique mix of human energies and abilities for purposes we now have to find for ourselves, as long as our environment permits it, until a short period just before death.

But that is not the way we look at age in America today. As things are now, we have good reason to fear age. We have seen and are shown only the losses and declines it can impose. We have therefore averted our eyes from the face of age. How can we honestly affirm our own age? It takes a most heroic act for an individual in America today to break through the dread mystique of age. In fact, it still takes a heroic scholar to break through the model of decline and study age professionally as another period of human development, to see its unique emergent aspects.

When Lissy Jarvik, now professor of neurophysiology at the University of California at Los Angeles Medical School, began her trail-blazing study of aging twins twenty-five years ago, the so-called last age of man, "sans teeth, sans everything," was genuinely accepted, even by scientists. The old woman in her dotage, the old man in his second childhood, were seen as the norm. Senility was considered inevitable: its dictionary definition was "infirmity due to old age." Studying 268 twins living in communities around New York over a twenty-year period, Jarvik and her colleagues attempted to separate biologically determined aging of the brain and its consequences from environmental influences. They found that intellectual decline after the age of sixty was neither inevitable nor necessary. When it happened, it seemed to predict mortality, or dementia, and to be accompanied by chromosome reduction. But it did not happen in "normal aging," as had always been assumed. In fact, on the average, there was no significant intellectual decline in the twins from age sixty-four to seventy-three, and on some tests they showed improvement. Entering their seventies, they performed like other normal adults in their fifties on the Wechsler intelligence scale. From seventy-three to eighty-four years, they showed a slight but significant average decline. But in their seventies, the *standard deviation* from the average, or the differences between the twins, was the highest ever shown on that test.

Still, Lissy Jarvik warned me, "It was the author of that test who defined senescence as the normal cognitive deterioration of aging." At first, as those twins moved through their seventies, they seemed to show an annual decline of 2 percent on digital tests, 10 percent on verbal syllogisms. Then the researchers began to notice that the twins in whom these declines appeared were the ones who were no longer alive five years later. They checked back and found that eleven of the fifteen twins who had died within five years showed a critical deterioration in intellectual capacity, compared to only four out of forty-six who were still alive. In other words, even among identical twins, critical loss in mental ability was a function not of age but of approaching death.[18]

In the Duke studies also, deterioration in indices of mental ability, life satisfaction, and participation correlated not with chronological age but with nearness to death. "Disengagement" and "decline," therefore, can be seen not as normal aging, but as cause-and-effect indices of approaching death. It is only in the period just before death that the pattern of people aging in the community resembles the decline of the men originally studied in institutions, whose pathological deterioration was taught for so many years as the norm.

George Maddox, who pioneered those studies, told me how that happened:

Twenty-five years ago, when you wanted to study aging, you took the convenient sample, going to those institutions where the elderly were already assembled. One aspect of aging, impairment, was indeed assembled there. Whatever normal aging meant, how could you find out from concentration on pathology?

That simple-minded equation of aging with disease and pathology will lead to conclusions that are badly distorted. You will get what you are looking for. In concentrating on the stereotype, by looking at aging in institutions, you take the eye away from reality.

In the Duke studies, we saw—and didn't take seriously enough, at first—the incredible variability of older people in the community. When you've seen one older person, you haven't seen them all. Older people do not become more alike by becoming old. In many areas, they become more varied. The more you study the actual behavior and health of older people, the more you see that aging is a social and not just a biological phenomenon. These terrible things you see happening to some people in age are not the inevitable ticking of the biological clock. Age is not a time bomb. Even the new emphasis on age as a crisis, the midlife crisis, etc., is misleading. When you come to one of these life crises or transitions that are supposed to be so traumatic, the people who cope, grow.

On my visit to Duke, the eminent Erdman Pallmore recalled the surprise they all experienced when they began to study the people aging in their own communities, as opposed to institutions:

We could have found that the community was merely one giant institution, but we did not. That image of the aged as sick, lonely, helpless was so far off reality that it's a wonder we all kept on teaching it so long. The same forces, of course, are at work with age as in the stereotyping of race and sex. One has to *retain attentiveness,* be constantly on guard, to avoid slipping into stereotypes. But you don't undo stereotypes just by giving people information. What social scientists call the "unambiguous" stereotype is so powerful that it drives out evidence that doesn't fit it. Scientific research no longer supports that blacks or women or older people are the way we've always thought of them *by nature.*

If you look at what's happening to older people themselves, it becomes harder and harder not to see that large numbers of chronologically old people are not, in fact, impaired. In our own studies, we just didn't find those problems other gerontologists found when they studied the institutionalized elderly. But by then a whole profession had built up around gerontology, an establishment of supposed advocacy for the aged which exaggerates the problems to gain support for the victims, and this just strengthens the stereotype. The false idea of older people as sick, senile, miserable, and alone leads to real discrimination in employment, and compulsory retirement. The idea that illness and decline is just part of growing old means that older people don't seek, or get, as good health care, or continued education.

And finally, you make people so ashamed of being old that they disassociate themselves from the different *reality of their own aging* in false self-hatred. That conspiracy to pretend we are not old, so that when you see a vigorous, vital seventy-year-old going down the street, you "don't think of her as old." Only when you see her in a wheelchair! It's so easy not to *see* old people except as stereotypes.

Thus, I began to understand the denial, the avoidance, the positive revulsion toward age manifest in our society even among social scientists, psychologists, and gerontologists who make their living studying age. Commenting on the dearth of cross-cultural anthropological studies of aging that would enable Americans to test their own stereotypes, Margaret Clark, the eminent Berkeley anthropologist, said: "My own experience with American subjects, including some anthropologists . . . is a common view that not only old age, but even late maturity, is a horrible state; one shouldn't really think about it or look at it too closely—as though it were the head of Medusa. To contemplate later life is often seen as a morbid preoccupation—an unhealthy concern, somewhat akin to necro-philia."

Further, anthropologists and psychologists have long tended to accept the Freudian view of personality as a system which is open during infancy and childhood, but closed and fixed fairly early in life, with any personal change in adulthood seen as essentially superficial. Even the more recent students of "adult develop-ment" have considered it as ending with the "midlife crisis" at forty-five. The ideal still seems to be "staying young" as long as possible.

But evidence is beginning to appear that those who stop there—at the insistent holding on to youth, whether personally or professionally—never do break through to the *strong face of age.* As part of the recent studies in aging at the Langley Porter Neuropsychiatric Institute in San Francisco, Margaret Clark conducted intensive interviews with eighty people over sixty, half of whom had been free of any treatment for mental or emotional problems in their later lives; the other half had been institutionalized for psychi-atric disorders for the first time after the age of sixty. She found that those who held most tenaciously to certain values of their youth were the most likely candidates for psychiatric break-down in age. "The mentally healthy aged seem able to meet unpleasant but alterable circum-stances with action, and unalterable ones with flexibility and forbearance. The mentally ill, by contrast, value aggressiveness as such. . . . They must *do* something, and they are less likely to admit that there are circumstances beyond their control." [19]

The self-esteem of the healthy older group seemed linked to "the fruitfulness of a search for meaning in one's life in the later years," as compared to the mentally ill, who were still pursuing the values of their youth. The healthy group had "a broader perspective, which they call by different names: wisdom, maturity, peacefulness, or mellowing. They feel released and freed in some basic sense from earlier social imperatives. The mentally ill group are still driven to compete; ambition is a central value, and failure to achieve leads to self-recrimination." [20]

The group that had not broken down in age seemed to focus on aspects of themselves that were "continuous or evolving" rather than on those they had lost. More important, according to Clark, "they were able to substitute a new set of achievable gratifications and sources of pride to replace old ones which were no longer available to them." The mentally ill sample, on the other hand, failed to perceive alternatives, which left them with merely a "retrospective or deteriorative view of the self." For those who rigidly clung to the values of youth, denying age, "time was the enemy." For those who identified with their evolving selves in later life, the time left was "cherished and enjoyed." The person who rigidly clings in age to the competitive, aggressive, future-oriented, and acquisitive values of his or her youth is "today's best prospect for geriatric psychiatry," Clark concluded. But since these values of youth are the dominant values of American society, she conceded that where the aging individual was released from those earlier adult roles without a new basis for self-esteem, he or she often suffered "a serious, stress-ridden discontinuity."[21]

That singularly astute gerontologist Bernice Neugarten remarked on her own and her colleagues' amazement, some twenty years ago, when studies of expected traumatic crises of middle and old age—menopause, retirement, widowhood—were not, in fact, experienced as crises, or traumatic, if they were anticipated and, in effect, "rehearsed" as part of the life cycle.[22] Another astute gerontologist, Robert Kastenbaum, suggested that aging as decline, as opposed to development, "begins when novel events and situations are treated as though repetitions of the familiar." Through the process of "habituation," those who cling to the responses of youth may forfeit the flexibility to change that is essential for vital age:

At any given adult year some people are older than others. Their balance has shifted more drastically toward habituation. . . . It is easier ... to treat new stimuli, situations, people, and events as though they were essentially repetitions of those already experienced. ... Life and one's own self are made to seem more stable by reducing acknowledgement of change through hyperhabituation ... "nothing new here!" ... perhaps missing a critical threat or a golden opportunity.

Hyperhabituation becomes an increasing liability as we move from early to late adulthood. Development is sacrificed for the illusion of stability. ... What we need is the ability to observe change quickly and accurately, the better to adapt and develop. What we practice, however, is ... a disposition toward clinging to the past. ... Opinions, belief systems, and routines of daily life as well as the roles one insists on playing all may be put in the service of protecting against the experience of loss—and, in a literal sense, limit also the "experience of experience."

A hyperhabituated person has a markedly reduced exchange with the external world and also seems unable to call on neglected inner resources that might renew personal development.

In this way, holding on to youth and denial of age leads to mental and emotional "stagnation," Kastenbaum maintained. "Failure to adapt to

changing conditions in turn leads to many negative outcomes, such as institutional placements
that could have been avoided, chronic disabilities that could have been prevented or treated,
and the proverbial lives of quiet desperation that
might instead have flourished into advanced
age."[23]

James Birren in his emphasis on wisdom, and
Erik Erikson in the late-life expansion of the psychological model of the life cycle that he originally put forward in his early forties, have both
suggested that the developmental *tasks* of late
life involve a clear shift from the values of youth.
But Birren warned that "mere stretching of our
definitions and criteria of mental health," which
were derived from study and treatment of the
young, will not "provide an orientation for late
life."

Despite the emphasis on environmental mastery . . . "good mental health" in the older
person might require . . . a shift in the focus
of activity over which the individual aims to
attain mastery. . . . Autonomy and self-actualization may take different directions upon
retirement than they do for the late adolescent. Retirement or loss of physical capacities may require an individual to give up roles
and activities in which there have been a
great amount of investment. He must then
satisfy his competence and environmental

mastery needs . . . with alternative activities. . . . The mental health movement has never paid sufficient attention to the fact that the goals of life shift with age.[24]

Only a few very wise psychological theorists, in their own old age, have said flatly, like Jung, that problems are likely if we try to live the "afternoon of life" by the "chart of the morning." While it is necessary for the young and the early middle-aged to turn themselves outward and strive for achievement, Jung felt that the older person must devote serious attention to the inner life. Jung insisted that aging individuals run into difficulties when they refuse to see that the second half of life is not governed by the same principles as the first.

For Erikson, each stage has its own task: for infancy, trust; for school age, competence; for adolescence, identity; for early adulthood, intimacy versus isolation; for middle age, generativity versus stagnation; and for old age, wisdom—integrity versus despair. When Erikson first developed his theory with his wife Joan, in their forties, they saw the final stage of wisdom as simply an objective reconciliation of life in the face of death. Now in their eighties themselves —the only life-span theorists so far to look back from that peak personally—they have tried to spell out the ways in which each earlier stage of life is recapitulated in the wisdom of old age.

During this stage, they say, the aging individual should gain an understanding and acceptance of his (or her) life as a product of his own choices and work, the dignity of which he is willing to defend. Failure to achieve this "integrity" leads to despair, vindictiveness, depression, suicide, or a deep fear of old age and death. They propose an elegant transformation of each previous stage in age: the infant's sense of trust becomes age's appreciation of human interdependence; childhood's increasing control over bodily functions versus shame is mirrored in age's acceptance of bodily deterioration; childhood's playfulness becomes age's resilience, empathy, and humor; youth's competence becomes age's humility, comparing one's early hopes and dreams with the life one actually lived, with, finally, a realistic appreciation of one's true abilities and limitations. In age, identity is defined by other ways than mastery and abstract knowledge—by feelings, intuitions, intimacy, by tenderness, "coming to terms with love expressed and unexpressed during one's entire life"; and midlife "stagnation" is resolved by generativity as opposed to greed and self-absorption.

The final phase of life, in which integrity battles despair, culminates in wisdom. The Eriksons believe that the integrity that results in a sense of completeness—of personal wholeness—is strong enough to offset the psychological pull of inevitable physical disintegration.[25] And for the Eriksons also, while the thrust is personal *reconciliation* to the integrity of one's life as it has been lived and the reality of one's own disintegrating body, the task of generativity and wisdom somehow involves transcending the greedy, shallow values of one's own society in larger responsibility to the human race.

Studying all this, although I felt, increasingly, that it is a desecration of age, a rigid truncation, to restrict or test it by the tasks of youth, I still could not see what age might be if it could indeed live out and fully use its own unique wisdom. What might age mean for men or women no longer driven by parental caveats and the guilts and conflicts and competitive tests of youth, freed from the compulsions of conformity to career and family roles, if beyond that midlife crisis, they were challenged by roles that used the wisdom of their unique lifetime's experience in, and for, society?

At gerontological conferences, I often sought out the unpublicized sessions on "Late-Life Art." They were held in small, dark rooms, down obscure back hotel corridors, not very well attended, considering the standing-room-only ballroom sessions on new developments in Alzheimer's disease or nursing home management. I usually ran into the by now familiar faces of my gerontological underground—James Birren,

Rick Moody of Brookdale, Robert Kastenbaum, Nancy Datan, David Gutmann. The gerontological establishment had refused to let them set up a division of humanistic studies of aging; it was dismissed as "not scientific." But the questions they dealt with seemed pertinent to my own search for the fountain of age.

In artists who went on working throughout a long life—Michelangelo, Rembrandt, Beethoven, Yeats, Picasso—was there a continued or new development in their art that hinted at possible further stages of human growth in age? From these sessions I learned that late-life creativity is considered strongly suspect among gerontologists, controversial and certainly not biologically programmed or universal. But I also learned that artistic or scientific creativity does not uniformly peak in youth. As Elliot Jacques pointed out, a number of scientists and artists have flowered and done their best work by their late thirties. Of these an unusually large number die in their forties; of those who survive and transcend the midlife crisis, some develop profound new directions.

At one such session, someone said of Yeats: "In youth, his metaphor of self was escape, in age it was encounter. His mind worked harder and harder as his body declined. By his seventies, his language revealed the height of its powers. He now stood for something beyond himself: the Irish people." Rick Moody traced the late-life development of Beethoven, from the virtuoso technical brilliance of the sonata *Appassionata* at thirty-four to the contemplative Quintet in A Minor, No. 2, of his age, and the loosening of form to celebrate the human voice in his great Ninth Symphony, long after he was completely deaf. Someone else contrasted the youthful idealism of Michelangelo's *Pietà* sculpted at twenty-five with the groping toward new form of his *Pietà* at eighty-nine, as if his earlier style had become meaningless to him.

Grappling with such comparisons, I began to make my own—in museums and galleries in New York, Los Angeles, Madrid, where I could find retrospectives of late-life art. Was this an explosion beyond previous limits in age—or a condensation into something simple, intimate, vulnerable, something intensely emotional, and personal, not hiding anything and yet reaching finally beyond the self? A lengthening or loosening of structure, an enmeshing of figures into one another, losing their separateness and glowing from within? A getting beneath or beyond surface appearance—decorative detail, idealization, heavy heroics—to deep, somber, undecorated inner reality, as in Rembrandt's last self-portraits or T. S. Eliot's poems: "At last, the true distinguished thing?"

Not all artists or scientists continue to develop in creativity as they age, we are often reminded. Wordsworth grew stale. But I found that the people who do keep on developing—sometimes after a hiatus, a period of stagnation—celebrate the distinctive voice of age. They also seem ready to risk the large questions, putting it all together, that they would have been afraid to ask in youth—questions they often do not finish answering. And this, of course, was deemed a decline from their surer, earlier peaks. Einstein, for instance, after his monumental contribution of relativity, spent the end of his life in what seemed a futile attempt at a unified field theory, uniting the principles of gravity, electromagnetism, and the interactions of strong and weak particles into a single, comprehensive explanation of the universe. That work, considered a "failure" unfinished at his death, is now being carried forward by my son's generation of theoretical physicists, on the cutting edge of superstring theory. And those who decried Einstein's final attempt at a unified field theory as a decline from his youthful peak are having second thoughts.

And yet many an outraged gerontologist insists: "There's no such thing as late-life art. There are just artists who get old and refuse to stop working in age, when they should." Why do some artists and scientists struggle to keep on, often after deafness, strokes, severe physical impairment? Perhaps because for them the mind *(the self)* is not impaired in age but continues to grow and develop. For those who don't stop, may not something new emerge? Why does that prospect seem to threaten us so? Why do we feel such a need to diminish or disparage the very possibility of continued or new creativity in age?

And how, finally, do we put together all of the research on age until now—the well-documented curves of deterioration and decline of older people in institutions removed from society; the increasing mental and physical vitality of each generation to reach ever-lengthening age in the community over this century; the enormous variability of people over sixty in our society today; the evidence of untapped limits of plasticity and potential for change after childhood, even after midlife, depending on what one's environment permits or demands; the clear hints of an emergent wisdom in maturity that differs from youth as against the strange resistance in ourselves and those who study age to *conceive* of a life beyond youth in truly different terms? How do we get beyond our strange reluctance to really look at that strong face of age, our inability to see age on its own terms of trust, competence, identity, intimacy, generativity, and integrity; our failure to imagine new powers of creativity; our holding on to that dread view of age as solely a decline from youth, no matter what the evidence of another possibility?

Even the most prescient of those who have studied aging until now can only view it as it is actually experienced in our society today. They can only surmise the damage imposed by the lack of purposeful roles for older people in our society, the restricted, isolating environment even for those still living in the communities of the young, the forces that *impose* a victim state upon us. But if caged old rats and nursing home patients could reverse supposedly irreversible geriatric deterioration with simple tasks, giving them new control and challenge in their very late days; if eighty-year-olds, given new training, could recover the total amount of supposed decline even on those abstract tests geared to youth; if some different wisdom or integrity does emerge in age that is not measured in such tests of youth—what could age be if we were able to identify those unique capacities as they emerged in ourselves, and could obtain the conditions necessary for them to flourish? As it is now, we can only get hints by testing the waters of that rich variability, and giving *names* to what we see in those who continue to grow and develop, even in environments that expect or prescribe nothing but decline.

This *is* the condition now under which all of us still approach age, not just in the extremes of nursing homes, but in our own towns and offices, and at gerontological conferences. The victim face, the problem face, the expectation of that dread decline prevails, drowning, distorting the very evidence that denies it. What "surprised" the researchers on age—the crises that turned out not to be so traumatic after all, the stubborn exceptions and deviations from the general decline that were dismissed before as probable errors of design or sample, even the work of those "exceptional" geniuses that broke new ground in age—all these are merely hints that something else is possible.

We have to take these hints more seriously, in ourselves and in the research, to break through the dread mystique of age. For that mystique which locks us in, clinging desperately to the limits of youth, is so strong now that it is barely affected by this new knowledge, even in the science of gerontology. Still thinking of ourselves as young, we are surprised at first and then learn gradually to expect and fear the pain of being treated as "old." Well, we must still expect that. But the real surprise is that "something else" which emerges. Do others feel it, too? Why does no one talk about it publicly? If staying "young" as long as possible is the only way to stave off that dread, who will dare to name the strengths of age?

At a gerontological conference in Washington, D.C., in 1988, I ran into my friend David Gutmann, doing his annual count of papers dealing with irreversible disorders of age, such as Alzheimer's dementia, compared to "functional" problems that could be treated or solved. The ratio was two to one. "For every paper on life span development, there are now seven on incontinence," he said. "Death is big this year." He is full of black humor. "Elder abuse is coming on strong." Of course, as he pointed out, incontinence and elder abuse are easier for graduate students to measure than, for instance, wisdom.

I dropped in on a session where T. Kahana of Case Western Reserve was discussing "Late Life Coping and Adaptation to Extreme Stress." "Often the research doesn't look for positive characteristics that may come from the struggle," she said. "We get the impression of something else, some strength that isn't completely clear on the stress test scores but we shouldn't perhaps talk about this. We don't want to make people feel guilty if they don't have enough strength."

I wandered through a poster session, where the papers were pinned on walls in rows: "Under-Treatment and Over-Treatment of the Acutely Ill Elderly" . . . "Regressive Intervention and the Dying Role" . . . "Empowerment of the Elderly in the Health Care System: Potential and Pitfalls" . . . "Empowerment of the Elderly: A Right or a Duty?" They seemed, not so subtly, to want to limit the empowerment of the elderly. The authors stood by to explain their papers, and one said: "Some older people don't want to make their own choices. It's not sensible to assume everybody wants to make their own choices about the end of life. Some people are not capable of being empowered. Should we force them to be autonomous, whether they want to be or not? Let's talk about the right of the elderly to give up empowerment and autonomy, and the responsibility of professionals and institutions to make the decisions for them. Why should we force decisions on older people?" Why indeed.

I went into an unusual session on the implications for society of increasing the life span. Here another friend, Roy Walford, an eccentric, brilliant pathologist at UCLA who was accepted, in his sixties, as an "astronaut" for the biosphere experiment, explained that his experiments extending the life span of rats through "undernutrition" (an enriched diet of restricted calories) imply that people could live to 150 years, a century and a half, without aging at current rates. (After his scientific work, *Maximum Life Span,* based on that research, was published, Walford wrote a simple diet book telling people how they could extend their own life span. He arbitrarily called it *The 120 Year Diet,* thinking people wouldn't believe the real implications of his research for extending our maximum life span to 140, possibly 180 years. In fact, *The 120 Year Diet* was not the best seller he expected it to be. He would stand around in bookstores and hear people say, "I wouldn't *want* to live to 120 years, would you?")

At the gerontological session, Walford predicted that extending the life span would lead to greater diversity within society, with multiple careers, intergenerational marriages, extended social networks, and more creativity and innovation. ("Very old people get quite radical in their ideas," he pointed out, "freed as they are of societal constraints.") He also made the point that such caloric restriction would delay the onset of the degenerative diseases of aging, which now occurs between sixty and eighty. Thus, extending the life span in this way would create not a tribe of helpless, decrepit centenarians but of very, very old people who remain productive, functional, creative, and wise for 120 years and more.

But the very idea of extending the life span seemed strangely threatening to the other distinguished gerontologists and young turks of that burgeoning profession in the hall. Dr. Leonard Hayflick of the Center for Gerontological Studies at Gainesville, Florida, warned that such research was heading humanity toward a "gerontological winter," conjuring up the specter of "miserable" people like his own patients, losing their vision, hearing, and reflexes, their heart and lung capacity, and mental powers—"people who never died, just got older and older and more disabled." Dr. Nancy Dubler, gerontological ethicist at Montefiore Hospital in New York, said disapprovingly: "I'm not sure the banishment of death to its furthest point is ever a good goal. Perhaps there is an obligation on the part of the old to step aside and die in their time, and turn over their assets to the younger generation." Others expostulated, with visible agitation, that it wasn't fair to put that kind of burden on insurance companies, the Social Security system, the federal budget. Some suggested that such research on extending the life span should not be encouraged, funded—even permitted.

How, then, do we move beyond the youth model of decline that blinds so many gerontologists and society itself? Our species is unique, we must keep reminding ourselves, not only for a prolonged infancy which requires parental nurture, but for an increasingly prolonged period of human maturity and age after the reproductive years and parental roles are over. And those years, too, must be seen as an essential stage of human evolution. For me, evolution is not just an abstract concept: it is what I have experienced and observed in women over the past twenty-five years, since I myself, at forty, broke through the feminine mystique (which was, of course, a youth model, defined by men). Thinking of how I and other women moved through our forties, fifties, sixties in this time of evolutionary breakthrough—redefining ourselves as women, re-creating ourselves as people, accepting challenges we never even dreamed of in our youth—I sense the sheer absurdity of women thinking of those years after the reproductive "end" in terms of an irreversible deterioration into passive helplessness, according to that young man's model of age.

Under the rubric of "age," it seemed necessary to cite the enormous variability of people's performance from existing gerontological research, the number of cases where such decline does *not* take place, to show that deterioration is not necessarily "normal" or even usual, and thus surely not biologically programmed. Switching to my personal knowledge of women in the years of the movement, I know that in my gut. Women have *evolved* in these years—at thirty and forty, and at fifty, sixty, seventy, and beyond —in thought and behavior; in the homes and offices of every community; in politics and in society itself. Aging is just "something else" now for many women. Our thinking about evolution has thus far been in terms of reproduction and survival of the species. Is it merely an accidental byproduct of advanced male technology that our species, and especially women, have all those new years beyond their reproductive possibility? Evolution happens that way.

One way to open our minds, at least, to what may lie ahead in age for both men and women is to ask in all seriousness why women now live so much longer than men. And why do women now do so much better in their later years than men, in terms of vital age, despite economic problems? They didn't twenty-five years ago. Looking at women's different, changing experience of age, can we find a hint of the new paradigm beyond youth? Can we find clues to longer life and new roles for men? And if the breakthrough that women have succeeded in making from their previous reproductive role—which has dramatically changed our own aging—were emulated by men, what significance would it have for their own survival, and for the evolution of our species?

Part II

Strengths That Have No Name

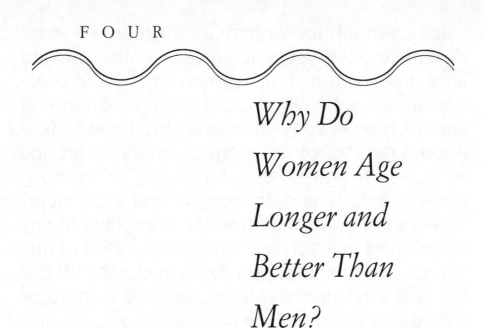

FOUR

*Why Do
Women Age
Longer and
Better Than
Men?*

There is an increasing divergence in the life expectancy of women and men in America today. At the turn of the century, life expectancy for both men and women was roughly the same —forty-five years for men, one year more for women. By 1930, deaths of women in childbearing had been basically eliminated, but the age gap between women and men at death continued to increase—by 1950 it was five years; now it is eight. If this trend continues, it is estimated that by 2020 there will be a twelve-year difference in the life expectancy of women and men.

Since World War II, according to Svanborg's studies in Sweden, longevity has increased twice as much for women as for men—7 years in females, 3.5 years in males. At the present time, three out of four women who die in Sweden are seventy-two or more; the corresponding age for men is sixty-six years. "We need to find out the reason for the increasing sex difference in rate of aging and longevity," Svanborg pointed out. "The data indicate that a considerable part of this sex difference is explainable by differences in lifestyles."[1] In the first third of this century, women stopped dying in childbirth. *But the sex difference in life expectancy is increasing now mainly after the childbearing years, and most dramatically after sixty-five.* A seventy-five-year-old woman alive today can expect to live two years more than a seventy-five-year-old woman three decades ago. For men, on the other hand, hope of further life expectancy at ages above sixty-five "has been counterbalanced by an increased death rate in the 45-to-65 age interval."[2]

This difference in life expectancy between male and female is present in all species from birth, but it becomes most striking in human beings *after* the reproductive years. It is vastly higher in industrialized countries, and seems highest in countries where there has been a breakthrough in women's sex role and some movement toward equality. In Jordan, life expectancy at birth is 52 years for women and 56 years for men; in Egypt, the life expectancy at birth is

53.8 for women and 51.6 for men; in Italy, it is 74.9 for women and 69 for men; in France, 77.2 for women, 69.2 for men; in Israel, 75 for women, 71.5 for men; and in Finland, 77.1 for women, 68 for men.

In the United States, the average life expectancy for a white baby girl born in 1981 was 78.3 years, nearly eight years longer than the boy (average male life expectancy was 70.7 years). According to most recent figures from the U. S. Bureau of the Census and the National Center for Health Statistics, a woman who was 65 at the beginning of this decade could expect to live an average of 18.6 more years (a man 14.2 years). The fastest-growing age group in the United States and in the world are women over 85.

These differences are so striking that one wonders why there hasn't been a major public outcry as to why men are dying younger than women in this country. In fact, the first scientific conference on "Gender and Longevity: Why Do Women Live Longer Than Men?" was sponsored by the National Institute on Aging and the National Institute of Child Health and Human Development in Washington, D.C., in September 1987. As the gerontologist Lois Verbrugge pointed out there, sex differences were until recently "expected and unquestioned in all aspects of life, including mortality." Statistics revealed such differences, increasing over the century, but they were taken for granted "and not given further scrutiny in science or public policy. . . . Sex differences are now considered open for policy intervention, to reduce disadvantages in risks or outcomes for one group or the other, and thereby make health and length of life not only better but more similar."[3]

At first there seemed to be a contradiction in these statistics—men die younger, but women report more illnesses. Thus, women appear sicker in the short run, but are less likely to die when ill. Further, women are "much more active in personal health care." The fact that women seemed to get sick more often than men, spend more days in bed, and visit doctors more often actually hid a basic and increasing male disadvantage. Examining mortality data from the National Center for Health Statistics (1958–72), covering 99 percent of the non-institutionalized civilian population of the United States, Verbrugge found that for all causes of death combined, female rates were only 56–64 percent of male rates. Per 100,000 population, 343 to 402 more males than females died each year. Males showed *increasingly* higher death rates than females for most leading causes of death in the period 1958–72—heart disease, cancer, cardiovascular problems, accidents, pneumonia, arteriosclerosis, emphysema. Only in suicide, peptic ulcer, and diabetes were women "catching up" with men. Further, male mortality rates rose sharply for heart and other important diseases in that period, beginning in the late 1950s, after what had seemed a stationary level.[4]

Chronic conditions, which women once seemed to suffer more frequently, now render a far higher (and increasing) number of men unable to carry on major activities. The difference widens for every successive age group—some 28 percent of all men sixty-five and over were so disabled that they could not do strenuous work of any kind, compared to only 8 percent of women that age. In this period, women were diagnosed more often for cancer—but more men were dying from cancer. Evidently women are more likely to report symptoms of cancer and hypertension in time for them to be treated; for most leading causes of deaths, men now show excess rates of morbidity (sickness) as well as mortality (death). And the sicker sex (now men) has higher death rates in the more recent studies.

Lately, psychologists have been investigating why women seem to report more illnesses, go to doctors, and take to their beds more often, obscuring the actual and increasing male disadvantage in mortality. They speculate that women are more sensitive to changes in their own health and body signals, that women may be more willing than men to report illness, that girls are more socialized than boys to take caring measures when ill, and that women have more flexible roles and fewer time constraints than men. Even in conditions where women seem to report more sickness, their strikingly lower mortality rates highlight a worsening situation for men.

However, until 1970, women certainly seemed sicker than men. They were also diagnosed as having more neurotic symptoms and nervous disorders than men. And the predominance of women's doctor visits, psychological and physical symptoms, and complaints somehow obscured the significance of their living so much longer. Feminism, in its newly awakened and articulated anger at women's oppression and inequality in society, gave credence to this view of woman-as-victim. At least, it was no longer taken for granted, by feminists or social scientists, that women should be sicker than men. And, in fact, some of the evident sickness was surely caused by the narrow sex role and the inequality we were rebelling against.

The eminent anthropologist Ruth Benedict blamed women's greater psychological impairment on the *discontinuities* of women's lives. A girl grows up going to school, playing games with boys, competing for good grades. Then, at thirteen, she has to start playing dumb, to attract boys. She goes to college, starts a job, and abruptly, in her twenties, has to put ambition aside and leave the world she had been working in, all its busyness and conviviality, for the isolation of her own home, and her role as wife and mother. And then, suddenly, at forty-five or fifty, all that is over: menopause, the "empty nest," her role is finished.[5] It was not really questioned, during those years, why a great preponderance of beds in mental hospitals were filled with women suffering "involutional melancholia." If woman's role in life is limited solely to housewife/mother, it clearly ends when she can no longer bear more children and the children she has borne leave home.

But the studies done since the 1960s on women aging in America are full of new contradictions, paradoxes—*surprises.* In the years that women have been breaking through the feminine mystique, they have apparently stopped suffering a lot of those symptoms of impaired mental health and even physical distress that obscured their survivor's strengths. In fact, the actual experience of women in the last twenty-five years who *continued developing* after their childbearing years has defied the expected trauma of empty nest, menopause, even widowhood. If the study of age had begun with women —my generation of women, moving and growing through changes we ourselves were continually creating—that dread mystique of age as drastic decline from the peak of youth might never have embedded itself in our national psyche.

During these years, as a matter of fact, psychologists, gerontologists, and social scientists were puzzled by the absence of trauma, pathology, and impairment when they started seriously studying the aging of women. For example, when the researchers went back twenty years later to follow up the groundbreaking Midtown Manhattan Longitudinal Study, originally done in 1954, they were surprised to discover that mental health no longer seemed to deteriorate with age. But when they looked closer, the surprising change had taken place only for women. Twenty years earlier, the mental health of women had shown increasing impairment each decade after twenty, and drastic decline after forty, compared to men. In those twenty years, the percentage of women suffering impaired mental health after forty had been cut more than half—from 21 to 8 percent—whereas men's impairment remained at 9 percent. This remarkable improvement was sustained into the women's sixties.

While there was some question as to the validity of the Midtown Manhattan follow-up sample, the same striking differences between women and men and evidence of new patterns of aging among women in this twenty-year period were also revealed in studies at the National Center for Health Statistics, challenging the previous assumptions of declining mental health and increased impairment and depression with age.[6]

During this same period, the American Psychiatric Association discontinued use of the diagnostic term "involutional melancholia." This supposedly menopause-connected illness was no longer filling the mental hospitals. Women in the United States no longer seemed to suffer involutional melancholia after their childbearing years were over, or if they did, it was clearly pathological, not a natural product of menopause. When I first caught a glimpse of that phenomenon twenty-five years ago, interviewing "exceptional" older women (ones combining motherhood with career) who claimed they "did not have menopause," life for most American women did supposedly peak in their twenties. According to the gynecological texts, women so free of the usual symptoms that they claimed not to have gone through menopause though they had ceased menstrual bleeding had to be "freaks."

Looking for scientific explanation of this phenomenon, I stumbled across a reference to some research done originally in Germany by a psychologist, now dead, Charlotte Buhler. She was perhaps the first to chart the total life course of different types of people. Buhler found that certain groups of people—athletes, housewives —whose lives were lived according to physiological functions that crest in youth, showed a pattern of development that rose quickly to a peak in their twenties and then declined rapidly. Others—businessmen, for instance—displayed what was then considered the normal aging pattern: a relatively quick rise to a developmental peak in the thirties, gradually declining in the forties, and then an increasingly rapid decline to senility and death. But there were some whose life course moved much more slowly to a peak in middle or late years that hardly declined at all, until just before death. In Buhler's study, these were artists, philosophers, or political leaders, men who kept growing in their creative work or in response to historical challenges, building on and moving beyond their past body of work.

I tracked down Charlotte Buhler in Los Angeles, where she spent the last years of her life teaching at the University of Southern California Medical School and practicing psychotherapy. When her secretary phoned my hotel to tell me Dr. Buhler was driving over to pick me up, I was rather alarmed. According to the dates of her original research, she must have been in her late eighties. I went down to the lobby to wait, apprehensively. Suddenly, there was a flurry at the entrance and a red-headed woman, with that wonderful creamy Viennese skin, sprang across the hotel lobby, kissed me effusively on each cheek, and led me quickly out to her sporty new American car.

Telling me of the new work she was doing with groups of midlife women, Buhler had clearly not yet peaked in her own life course. In her original research, done in the 1920s and 1930s in Germany and Austria, no women had shown that non-deteriorative pattern of aging. She herself had been trained as a psychoanalyst in the Freudian tradition, which assumed that woman's personality is "fixed" and not really susceptible to change after thirty. Neither the ego psychologists nor Erik Erikson or Abraham Maslow were at that time applying concepts of self-realization to women. The studies of "adult development" were just starting, and only on men. But without fanfare or foundation grants, Buhler herself, in her eighties, was using my book *The Feminine Mystique* to help women in their forties conceive of further directions of growth beyond that early housewife peak. She was sending women out in middle age to start directing movies and new mental health clinics, while she herself, in widowhood, had just moved with great gusto into an airy high rise off Sunset Boulevard, getting rid of the heavy dark furniture of her European past after her husband's death. "But, of course," she said, "when women no longer define themselves as housewives and mothers, and find new purposes, their life course is very different. It no longer peaks at twenty. After that it depends on what they do with themselves."

Some years later when I asked Dr. Harold Dupuy, who had done the follow-up Midtown Manhattan Study, why American women were no longer suffering that mental health impairment every decade after twenty, and that drastic decline after forty—why in fact, women in their forties, fifties, and sixties today were in as good or better mental health as young women in their twenties and thirties—he said, "It is surely related to the great change in women's life that you know about, which has not happened to men. Beginning with the vote, the movement for equality was good for women's mental health. It is better for women to have control over their lives."

In the 1980s, Rosalind Barnett and Grace Baruch of the Wellesley Center for Research on Women compared women aged thirty-five to fifty-five in all sorts of combinations of roles and found, instead of the expected decline of mental health with age, that most women experienced a sense of resurgence, of revitalization, a new sense of self and self-worth in midlife that gave them great confidence.[7] By the 1980s, what characterized American women facing age was an *openness to change,* a flexibility, an eagerness for challenge. When asked about age, these women, at fifty-five, said, "Well, I've lived through all this change and my life is so much better now, so the next change is not a great fear for me. Why should I be afraid of it?"

The entrance of increasing millions—by now a majority—of women into jobs and professions and decision-making roles in society was, of course, the most striking change of those years. But in the national longitudinal studies, housewives as well as working women experienced the same dramatic improvement in mental health after midlife. In the Baruch and Barnett study, I was struck by the fact that the sense of self-worth and openness to change was found most strongly not among lifelong professional women with the highest status, but among women who had lived some years as housewives and then moved into jobs. Women who had been in careers all along had a strong sense of self-worth and control over their lives, but they didn't have the same sort of zest for change, the confidence in their ability to master challenges and move on to new things in age, that was evident among women who had come from a more traditional housewife role to new growth in midlife.

The Baruch and Barnett study showed that those women who *combined* marriage, motherhood, and work were in the greatest state of psychological well-being. Of the factors necessary for psychological well-being, the most important, in this study, was a sense of control over one's life. The woman who was just a housewife did not have as much sense of control over her life as the woman who combined marriage or motherhood with profession. The second most important factor was intimacy. Women who were neither married nor mothers suffered for lack of intimacy. Combining marriage and/or motherhood with job or profession seemed to give women greater control over and more pleasure in their lives, buffering the more burdensome part of either role. Despite the media moaning over "superwoman" stress, and the impossibility of "having it all," that juggling evidently offered more than a face-lift to women moving into age.

These surprising changes in women's aging bear further study. For they suggest that certain strengths of women that have not been conceptualized before—or have been viewed only as unfortunate deficiencies and discontinuities, stemming from women's biological reproductive role—may contribute to superior vitality and longevity in age. And if the movement of women to equality and full participation in society enhances these strengths, as it seems to, how do we account for this?

Some twenty-odd years ago, when Bernice Neugarten began investigating the actual experience of women at menopause, that "change of life" was so feared and dreaded, so shrouded in revulsion and shame, that most women didn't talk about it. Dr. Robert Wilson, in his book *Feminine Forever,* was urging that menopause be regarded as a hormone-deficiency disease, to be treated or cured by giving estrogen to every woman over forty, so that she would continue her menstrual bleeding even if she could no longer conceive.

There was a great deal of medical literature on the symptoms of menopause and their treatment. It was not noticed or considered significant that most of these symptoms came from women hospitalized for hysterectomies or involutional melancholia (at that time, 25 to 30 percent of American women aged fifty to sixty-four suffered a surgical rather than a natural menopause). The eminent psychoanalyst Helene Deutsch described the mastering of psychological reactions to menopause as one of the most difficult tasks of any woman's life—"because it signifies that reproductive life has come to an end, it is a potential threat to a woman's feminine identity." The few large-scale studies of the 1950s and 1960s indicated that 85 percent of women had some symptoms at menopause, though, significantly, only 10 percent were incapacitated. Neugarten reported:

More recent estimates are that perhaps 75% of all women experience some disturbance or discomfort during the climacterium, even though, in the absence of disease, relatively few seem to bring these troubles to the doctor. Some psychologists have written that, because it is a visible sign that the reproductive life has come to an end, the menopause is a critical event in the life of the middle-aged woman and a major threat to her adjustment. Some psychotherapists have observed that the menopause presents a particular threat to a woman's self-concept if reproduction and motherhood have been her primary symbols of worth . . . or if the menopause signifies a loss of sexual attractiveness or sexual interest.[8]

But when she herself began interviewing women before, during, and after menopause, *women who were not hospitalized* (in two Chicago neighborhoods, one working-class, one upper-middle-class, two-thirds housewives, one-third working women, all living at home with husbands and children), Neugarten found virtually no psychological problems or crisis caused by menopause itself. When asked what changes in middle age worried them most, only four women out of the one hundred even mentioned menopause.

A few confessed to considerable fear before they actually experienced the "change" themselves: "I would think of my mother and the trouble she went through, and I wondered if I would come through it whole or in pieces" . . . "I knew two women who had nervous breakdowns, and I worried about losing my mind" . . . "I thought menopause would be the beginning of the end . . . a gradual senility, closing over, like the darkness."

Two out of three of the women interviewed about their own menopause felt it had no effect on or even caused a positive improvement in their physical and emotional health, and that it either had no effect or gave greater importance to their sexual relations. Three out of four agreed that "women are generally calmer and happier after the change of life than before," and "a woman feels freer to do things for herself." Even after considerable time, in two different interviews, only one third could think of any way that a woman's physical or emotional health was adversely affected by the "change of life." About three fourths felt that women have a relative degree of control over their "symptoms" at menopause and need not even expect them. And they did not experience menopause as "a major loss of feminine identity, irrespective of the severity of their symptoms."

"Our initial hypothesis was wrong," Neugarten concluded in 1970. "Now that the study is completed, we wonder that we should ever have formulated such naive hypotheses . . . [we found] no evidence to support a crisis view of the climacterium."[9]

Why was menopause supposed to be such a crisis? It is not so surprising, when you think of how and why women were valued in the past—and how that has changed. In a study of nearly 1,200 middle-aged women of five Israeli subcultures, women in every cultural group from the most traditional (with eight children) to the most modern (with two), emphatically welcomed the cessation of their fertility. But women of the two most traditional groups—Muslim Arabs and Near Eastern Jewish immigrants from settings where the role of women had altered little since biblical times—did suffer some of those negative expectations.[10] In another study comparing Japanese and Canadian women in the 1980s, 78 percent of the Canadian women but only 55.8 percent of the Japanese women felt that menopause did not change a woman in any important way. Nearly a quarter of the Japanese women interviewed by Margaret Lock gave unsolicited comments like "One becomes a man," or "One loses one's sacred function as a woman," or one's "value as a woman decreases" at menopause.[11]

After four articles in the *New England Journal of Medicine* in the mid-seventies postulated a link between estrogen replacement therapy and uterine cancer, menopause became a feminist issue. It was then discovered that the high incidence of menopausal problems came mainly from studies of women who had had hysterectomies. In feminist consciousness-raising groups, women began comparing notes on their own fears about menopause and their actual experience, beginning to help each other break though the dread of "end of life as a woman" which menopause represents only if one is still locked within the feminine mystique.

"Love My Menopause? You Must Be Crazy!"

Rosetta Reitz wrote in the feminist journal *Prime Time* (April 1976).

By loving your menopause, your hot flashes and yourself entirely, you will be doing the exact opposite of what the culture teaches —which is to hate your menopause, fear your hot flashes, because you are in your middle years and aging. You are not only invisible but valueless because you are not wanted as a sex object nor can you any longer be "a servant of the species." . . .

As much as I am against estrogen replacement therapy, I can understand how and why five million women are currently sucked into taking it. The fear of aging in some of us is almost as powerful as the fear of cancer and death. . . . To be taking estrogen makes a woman feel she is doing something for herself. . . . If there were an initiation rite connected with menopause—say, becoming a wise-older-woman—the whole business would be easier.

A woman wrote me from Virginia Polytechnic Institute in Blacksburg, Virginia, where, at fifty-four, after thirty years of raising children, she was working on a Ph.D.: "I've been remembering how we are all so forgiving of pregnancy (little foot kicking my liver) because of the anticipated birth of a child. . . . Can we be as forgiving of menopause, giving birth to ourselves?"

The second presumed "crisis" for aging women —the "empty nest"—also turned out to be a "surprise" when Neugarten and others investigated the actual experience of women in this period before and after their youngest child left home. In the first studies, women who had continued to concentrate on home and children during the 1960s and 1970s when other women were moving into careers were, indeed, often fearful or depressed in anticipation of the "empty nest." But five and ten years later, even these women seemed stronger than men of their age. Could the continual need to change, the continual beginnings and ends confronting women in their reproductive role, have strengthened them for age? [12] In fact, I found many studies indicating that women experiencing the most change and discontinuity were the most vital in later life. It was the ones who held on most tenaciously to the early roles—or had been forced to stay in or repeat the "cluttered nest" past its time, and thereby kept from moving on —who seemed the most frustrated, angry, and depressed.

In Neugarten's "empty nest" study, she separated the women into those who were primarily home-oriented, community-oriented, work-oriented, or mixed home–community-oriented,

and asked whether they had expanded, constricted, or shifted their roles and activities (as
wife, mother, homemaker, grandmother, daughter, worker, church or club member, citizen,
friend) over the past five to ten years as children
left home. Some women were "statics" or "con-
strictors," others "expanders" or "shifters." As
it turned out, the actual measures of psychological well-being among these women whose roles
were changing "showed again that our initial
hypothesis was wrong." Rather than being a
stressful period for women, the empty nest or
post-parental stage in the life cycle was associated with a somewhat *higher* level of satisfaction. When people whose youngest child was
about to leave home showed serious problems,
those problems were not related to the departure of their children.

During the 1970s, as the redefinition of ourselves as women spread through the generations, a very interesting longitudinal study was
done by Marjorie Fiske and her colleagues at the
University of California Medical School in San
Francisco. It examined men and women in four
supposedly critical periods, before and after the
"empty nest" and "retirement." The samples
were drawn from the middle and lower middle
class in a big city—not the groups leading
movements of social change or with the education to get the most benefit from them. The men
were for the most part in civil service and other

white- and blue-collar jobs; the women defined themselves primarily as housewives even when they held jobs. At first glance, the middle-aged women whose last child was about to leave home seemed to be in the deep trouble that had been predicted for the "empty nest." These middle-aged women (average age forty-eight) had far more psychiatric symptoms than anyone else across the four life stages, were most preoccupied with fears, stress, and problems, and were most likely to be ranked "low" in adaptive measures by the psychologists. The middle-aged men, while suffering from "job boredom," were still mainly focused on work and "providing sufficient income to maintain a comfortable lifestyle." They appeared "well adapted." Even men already suffering from rather severe physical ailments seemed to be "denying to themselves and others that they have any problems at all."

The middle-aged women confronting the empty nest appeared to be in a more critical period, with diffuse stresses and "malaise" alternating with anxiety. They were much more "apprehensive about their pending transitions" than their male counterparts. But ten years later, these older women were *less likely* to be suffering from a wide array of symptoms. A significant proportion of these older women (average age fifty-eight) had now become more assertive, more likely to rate themselves fairly high on traits that had been considered masculine, "to call themselves boss in the family, and to be strongly motivated to do something on their own, outside of the family sphere." Their "marital problems" and "psychiatric symptoms," which had seemed so much greater than the men's, had diminished or disappeared. They had a stronger self-concept, but had "role conflicts" about what they could actually do— which were caused as much by their husbands' needs and demands as by social strictures.[13] Only about half as many of the older men remained at all concerned with social and political issues; the others were "resigned," whereas nearly half of the older women had become *more* concerned with sociopolitical matters.

Nearly twice as many of the women whose youngest child had left home, in comparison with men at the same stage, reported themselves as happier five years later. All but one of these happier women had made expansive changes in their lives, which they themselves had initiated: new training, new jobs, new houses, new husbands or boyfriends, or lengthy trips abroad. In contrast, older men for whom the stage of active parenting was about to cease seemed to be mustering their strength to get through another ten or fifteen years on the job, so that their lifestyle would not have to be too drastically altered at retirement.[14]

Thus the women who, approaching the empty nest, showed those "signs of being in a painful if not critical stage"—who "expressed a desire for growth and self-assertion, a wish to break out of the family confines but could envisage few realistic possibilities for doing so"—were better off than the unchallenged men. "The mixture of strain and boredom in the middle-aged men struck us as a threat to their mental and possibly their physical health in succeeding years," Fiske reported.[15]

In another Bay Area study, women were invited to join a group to explore their "empty nest" problems with other middle-aged women. The researchers noted:

All the women had heard or read that . . . the empty nest . . . was a "crisis" period during which they were supposed to experience depression or anxiety. The majority expressed puzzlement and confusion and even guilt because they were "feeling better than ever," "taking care of myself for once," "much freer and in charge of my own time." Some worried that there was something abnormal about them . . . they shouldn't be feeling as good as they did. But most exulted in the fact that they had some free time in which to explore themselves, take classes and workshops, and—often for the first time—enter the job market. One woman described herself as a yucca plant "finally blooming after 50 years."

One woman asked where the "brainwashing" about midlife crisis was coming from. Only two women reported an increase in depression (which one attributed to a recent divorce, another to a radical mastectomy operation).[16]

But the emptying of the nest did appear to create *conditions of change,* which showed increasing impact as these women moved through it. What the women experienced, finally, was increased activity, increased excitement, increased overall happiness, a decrease in depression, and an increase in pride. No such change was found for men. Other, more recent studies have shown men reacting more acutely than women to the empty nest as they focused less on job success and sought belatedly the intimacy with their children which men of those generations had left to their wives.

One group in Los Angeles did an ingenious investigation, comparing white women with Mexican-American women, who presumably avoid the empty nest altogether, since they continue raising children and then their daughters' children through the middle years and beyond. With 65 percent of the Mexican-American women aged forty-five to seventy-four but only 25 percent of the white women reporting someone eighteen or younger living at home, the Mexican-American woman seemed assured of "a mother role over a large part of her life-time." Nearly half of the Mexican-American women were raising grandchildren (44 percent) compared to just 3 percent of the white women.[17]

The researchers had predicted lower morale for the "empty nest" women, especially for the Mexican-Americans, for whom the loss of value when they had to give up the maternal role was expected to be drastic. Their hypothesis turned out to be curiously wrong. Among the Mexican-American women aged forty-five to fifty-four, almost one fourth of those still caring for children or grandchildren reported "sadness"—twice as many as the "empty nest" women. The researchers speculated that the sadness might be due to "feelings that one is living out of one's time and one's place." Margaret Clark, who found a similar phenomenon among Mexican-American women in San Francisco, told me that with all the value supposedly placed on the maternal role, it seemed to go against some deep human grain for women to keep repeating it—as if some larger, more mysterious force was urging them on to different growth.

In another study of black grandmothers, Vern Bengtson found a positive anger among women who were expected by their daughters to resume or continue the role they thought they had finished. Said a fifty-six-year-old great-grand-mother, "My daughter and granddaughter keep making these babies and expect me to take care of them. I ain't no nursemaid; I ain't old; and I ain't dead yet."[18] A similar surprise was recently reported over today's Soviet grandmothers' new lack of enthusiasm for the babushka role.[19]

Widowhood, which in many studies women feared even more than an illness that might cause their own deaths, was also "surprising" in its actual effects on women compared to men, and compared to its traumatic specter. When Helena Lopata started her groundbreaking study of Chicago widows in the 1960s, she expected to find a drastic identity crisis. Since the roles of wife and mother were considered "the basic and only really important ones for adult women," and "becoming Mrs. Harry Jones wipes out the whole past of Mary Smith, her family, her ethnic and personal achievement identities," she predicted that "the abrupt ending of marriage through the death of the husband would result in a dramatic identity reformulation."[20]

Coming out of the feminine mystique era, the educated woman was expected to be even more traumatized by her loss of identity as widow because she had given up previous career interests to define herself totally as wife: "She assigns the role of wife first place in a rank order of importance. . . . The more educated woman feels that she influences her husband's performance at work . . . through entertainment . . . by understanding his problems and being able to discuss them. She shares with him a definition of the world . . . and builds a set of social relations which involve him, including couple friendships, neighboring, membership in voluntary associations, etc." Reporting on such a woman becoming widowed in the 1960s, Lopata enumerated the expected "losses":

Living alone, as most older widows do, she gradually loses the memory of her husband's definitions. She will often report that, as new situations arise, she tries to imagine what her husband would have said were he alive, but the dialogue becomes difficult over time. . . . She has no object for her work. . . . Many widows report strong feelings of inadequacy and frustration because of their inability to handle money transactions or maintain an automobile. . . . Widows feel very unfeminine doing things previously undertaken by the husband. . . . Without her husband, people do not treat her the same way. . . . Some report being literally shunned, because the late husband's friends are made so uncomfortable by her presence. . . . To the extent to which their world was built around him and his outside identities, [they] report a decrease in social life . . . are afraid to go out at night alone, hesitant about entering public places without a male escort . . . and in general helpless in many social situations.[21]

And indeed, right after the death of their husbands, the Chicago widows of that previous generation had many such "complaints" about the problems of widowhood: "a feeling of incompetence and incompleteness as persons, being shunned by others and experiences of strain in social interaction [with] strong stigmatic aspects." But, again, the changes in these women, after the "initial grief work is completed," came as a revelation to the widows, their friends, and to the researchers themselves. The overwhelming majority became "more independent and competent now than while their husbands were living" (63 percent); in addition, many became "freer and more active" (47 percent) and "more socially engaged" (31 percent). Only 18 percent viewed the major change in negative terms. Lopata concluded:

The overwhelming proportion of widows who recognize or admit change in their personalities or identities consider themselves fuller and freer people than before the death of their husbands. They have rounded out their personalities, previously restricted or limited as a result of marriage. This does not mean necessarily that they had bad marriages, as these are the very same individuals who list loneliness, rather than money or other troubles as the worst problem of widowhood, and miss their husbands most as a person or a partner, rather than as a breadwinner.[22]

Until recently, the fact of widowhood only interested researchers in terms of women's adjustment to the overwhelming "loss" of the husband who defined them. The "strengths" that were revealed or elicited by this loss were another surprise. (It still surprises *me* that researchers never questioned the astounding frequency of widowhood—41 percent of women aged sixty-five to seventy-four were widowed at the last census—in terms of men's deficiencies in the survivor strengths.)[23] New research has revealed that older women "adjust" to the death of a spouse and, with whatever grief or pain, move on to new strengths afterward, with less apparent difficulty than younger women—*and than men at any age.*[24] It is striking, as we have already seen, that if a man's wife dies, he is much more likely to become sick and die himself within the next two years, from any number of diseases, than other men his age. This vulnerability disappears only if he remarries—or after he survives five years alone. No such drastic toll on women's lives takes place with widowhood, whether or not they remarry (and they are much less likely to remarry, given the declining numbers of men still alive after sixty).

• • •

The one "loss" expected to be traumatic for men—and until recently only studied in men—was retirement. And here again there were surprises and paradoxes, especially when one compares the experience of women and men. Early studies of retirement included women only in their reaction as wives toward the retirement of their husbands. It was assumed that working was not very important for a woman, and retirement not a significant stage for her, but that for men retirement from work would be as traumatic a loss of identity as the empty nest and widowhood for women. In much of the research literature, retirement was conceptualized as a "crisis," with the result that the findings seemed to contradict each other. Neugarten reported that some investigators were unprepared for their discovery of no significant losses in life satisfaction or no increased rates of depression following retirement.

"A surprisingly large proportion of workers in all industries are choosing to retire earlier and earlier, with the determining factor being level of income," she stated, finding even more surprising the fact that nearly 70 percent of persons who retired as planned were content in their retirement, compared with less than 20 percent of those who retired unexpectedly because of poor health or loss of job.[25] But, again, men compared to women seemed deficient in some basic strength to survive retirement. It is a fact that a woman who reaches sixty-five can expect to live an average of nineteen more years, but a man only fourteen more. Could the very discontinuity and change that has taken place in women's roles over a lifetime—*their continual practice in retirement and disengagement, shift and reengagement*—account for their greater flexibility and resilience in age?

A young graduate student, Chrysee Kline, found that women between the ages of fifty and sixty who had returned to or started careers after their children entered school, or who combined homemaking and work, had higher life satisfaction in age; the lowest satisfaction was evident among women in a single continuous role—either homemaker or worker—throughout their adult life.

> While some wives may retire as many as three different times during a lifetime, these retirements obviously differ from the retirement of a man who at a relatively advanced age and with declining physical health is facing a single, final separation from his central life role as a wage-earner and principal provider for his family.
>
> The striving of women for permanence is dead-ended numerous times during the life cycle, resulting in role discontinuity or change in life situation. . . . From education to marriage, there is a strong role discontinu-

ity; for the woman who disbands her work role to give priority to roles of mother and housewife, there is discontinuity when the children leave home. . . . The discontinuity of widowhood is 70% more likely to be suffered by women.

Women have therefore become accustomed to change and impermanence. Thus, women are not as devastated as men are likely to be when old age, another impermanence, separates them from the productive, involved, financially independent world of middle age; and the adoption of new roles . . . should be relatively more facile for women than for men.[26]

Another study showed that both women and men who had experienced a considerable amount of change (in residence, marital status, work involvement) showed "high morale" in age, compared to those experiencing only a small degree of change in life. But almost twice as many women as men experienced such changes. Instead of bemoaning the "discontinuities" of women's life, this researcher raised the question whether women or men "actually benefit from working in one occupation for more than perhaps 10 years." Do women really want straight-line careers like men? "Perhaps the seeming goal to attain the same rigid, life-long role to which most males in our society are now subjected should be reconsidered by women's activist groups," she warned. If change and discontinuity strengthens women for age, "then a new system of career flexibility should be adopted as the new battle cry by men and women alike." [27]

Another loss for aging women that research has found to be "less problematical than expected" was that of youthful beauty. The traditional definition of femininity did indeed doom women to premature aging compared to men, for women as sex objects had to be "young." ("In short, men mature while women get old.") The fear of this loss has been an obsession for middle-aged women; but older women, surprisingly, transcend it. In one study, where young, middle-aged, and older men and women were asked to rate pictures of women for attractiveness and for youthfulness, middle-aged women were most likely to perceive "attractive" faces as younger than their actual age, but older women did not.[28] More recently, Susan Jacoby wrote in a "Hers" column in *The New York Times* (August 28, 1988):

I look in the mirror. There they are, those cruelly and accurately named crows-feet at the corners of the eyes. They were scarcely visible ten years ago. . . . There are deep horizontal lines crossing my forehead and creases at the corners of my mouth. All caused not by the villainous sun but by immoderate laughing, frowning and reading.

The wrinkles aren't exactly pretty but they are—well, *dear* is as good a word as any to describe them. If I managed to eradicate them with this ever-so-scientific improvement on old-fashioned vanishing cream, would my face be as unmistakably mine?

I have noticed this serene, strong awareness of their own appearance in its unique reality among all the women I have interviewed who have grown beyond the obsession with youth. They seem comfortably, vitally who they are— "I've stopped worrying about how I look. I like the way I look now." Some suddenly stopped dyeing their hair, or refused another face-lift. Other researchers have noted this increased self-awareness, this freeing ease and comfort with one's self, which leads to new, sometimes startling frankness, and lessened conformity to the expectations and sanctions of others: the older woman becomes a "truthteller."

But despite all the evidence of the evolving self of women, aging is still perceived as an aberration, defined by loss. Lillian Rubin, in her book *Women of a Certain Age* (1979), claimed that the new psychological and post-feminist bemoaning of women's conflicting roles and midlife crises rested on the same unspoken assumptions as the old ones:

> Think about the language we unquestioningly use. . . . Not *the awakening,* not *the emergence,* not words that might suggest that inside that house all those years there lived someone besides a mother; no, we say *the empty nest.* . . . Indeed, the very words *empty nest* conjure up a vision of a lonely, repressed woman clinging pathetically and inappropriately to a lost past—a woman who has lived for and through her children, a woman incapable of either conceiving or deserving a "room of her own." [29]

Even for the women Rubin studied who had defined themselves only as wives, mothers, housewives, "there are possibilities that, until now, existed only in fantasy . . . the possibility for adventure, for freedom . . . for the development of a self only hinted at in earlier life stages. . . . The ending, then [of active mothering], is difficult, not because the children are gone, but because it brings with it a beginning. The beginning has the potential for adventure and excitement, but . . . also the possibility of failure." As one woman put it:

> The children's leaving hasn't been traumatic at all. What has been and still is traumatic is

trying to find the thing I want to do, and being able to pursue it to a successful conclusion. I'm an artist—a good one, I think. But it's hard to make the kind of commitment that real success requires. I'm afraid of what it'll do to my marriage, and also to the rest of my life. And I suppose I'm afraid to really try and fail. What's painful right now is not knowing what I'll be doing, or even what I can do. And from 45 to 75 is a lot of years if I don't have something useful to do.[30]

The few recent studies that exist of women's reaction to retirement from their jobs suggest that women who do not want to retire suffer more distress and depression than men. These were often women who had put all their energies into job or career, foregoing marriage and/or children, or women who came late into careers only after their children were grown. This may be the converse of evidence that the "empty nest" could, in fact, be more painful for men than women. The surprise here may simply come from the fact that, until recently, women haven't been expected to be that involved in their work, or men in their children, and both sexes must face, late, unrealized feelings or parts of themselves they will no longer have the chance to express and satisfy—in that job, with these children, at least.

On the other hand, the "losses" involving

physical disabilities and incapacities that may come with age, again, do not have the same profound and disastrous effect on women's adjustment and sense of satisfaction as ill health seems to have on many men. In fact, women who either continue working into old age despite physical disabilities or choose to retire for this reason maintain a sense of purpose, connectedness, and control more easily than men. As one researcher put it, for men, "ill health is one condition that precludes adjustment. . . . For many of the women one wouldn't have even guessed which were the seriously disabled from listening to them." The researcher concluded the women seem to have some capacity not shared by males to transcend their biology and adjust to life's changing demands despite ill health.[31] But these researchers also warn against the countermyth that age is "not a crisis; it's a growth opportunity." Real losses *are* incurred; each transition may involve a genuine struggle to create life anew. And the distress and depression reported in previous studies of menopause, widowhood, and "involutional melancholia" really happened—not as a consequence of the "change of life" but, we can see in retrospect, of the lack of alternative roles.[32]

And yet for women who kept facing and surviving these struggles—with each "change of life" continually having to reinvent themselves and find new purposes for their lives instead of that single, career-dominated pattern expected of men—age itself seems to have become simply another transition. I have noticed among my own friends how delighted women are at becoming grandmothers, at fifty-five (or more likely sixty-five, when our kids finally get around to it), compared to some husbands, who still deny their aging, or start babies over again with younger wives. I have also watched my men friends, in their sixties, facing business takeovers, loss of power, and retirement with surprising serenity, discovering a serious new interest in their own children and grandchildren.

The brilliant gerontologist Nancy Datan commented before her own premature death that the only gerontologist she knew who was actually planning rather than denying her retirement happened to be a woman (it was Bernice Neugarten).

> At sixty, she has begun to jog; she looks foward to an opportunity to open doors into academic fields she has not been able to explore; and she plans to return to a novel she had begun some fifteen years ago, and had not had time to finish. . . . She returned to school at forty (after her children were in school), completed her graduate training, is currently a department chairman. . . . Her professional success [is considered] all the more remarkable because she began her ca-

reer relatively late. . . . Perhaps the very opposite is true: that precisely because she had reared a family, she brought to her graduate studies a sensitivity to intergenerational relations which could not be found in a younger person.

Nancy Datan was one of the first people I met in that gerontological underground who saw through the male blinders and the youth blinders. She proposed that a woman's life cycle can be "a continuous series of careers which come to an end followed by new careers; that childbearing and childrearing, rather than locking women into traditional roles, force them to consider and reconsider new beginnings." And she stressed that "continuous involvement with a constantly changing family is a constant stimulus to enlarged horizons." [33]

Now I want to speculate further on some traits women may bring with them from their traditional female role into their lives today that could be conducive to their greater vitality, their longer life expectancy, and better health in age. I also want to speculate as to what aspects of the traditional male role, however conducive to survival in an earlier period of human history, might explain men's greater vulnerability at this same moment in our society. And then I want to speculate on how transcending their traditional role and integrating opportunities previously open only to men has been conducive to health and vital aging in women, and how this transcendence and integration might happen in men.

Consider studies of coronary heart disease, which is now the leading killer in America and some of the other highly industrialized nations. Coronary heart disease has been striking men in a ratio of about eight to one, compared to women. It was commonly predicted that as women moved into traditionally male jobs and professions, they would start suffering the so-called Type A, hard-driven, competitive personality syndrome that seems to be found among men more subject to heart disease. The cardiologists I interviewed had expected women to suffer more heart attacks and were, again, "surprised" when they didn't.

It turned out that the only women who suffered more heart attacks were those in low-paying, dead-end, stressful clerical or service jobs, with bosses who elicited an enormous amount of anxiety and hostility. The Framingham and other studies indicated that such women with no control over their work life and a lot of suppressed hostility, as well as overwhelming family responsibilities at home, had almost twice the incidence of heart disease of other women. In the eight-year Framingham Study, other working women did not show a significantly high incidence; in fact, single women who had been longest in the work place had the lowest incidence of coronary disease. Svanborg's data from the study of the entire population of Sweden, where the proportion of women in the work force has risen from 30 to over 60 percent of all adult women, showed no increase in coronary heart disease or related stress diseases.

So the mystery deepens: for whatever reason, women are living longer than men, and the lead is increasing with each census. And as women's experience begins finally to be taken seriously —by ourselves and by society—we must claim and explore our new strengths in age. Instead of deploring the great "problem" of so many women living so much longer than men (such a burden on our resources!), gerontologist Myrna Lewis noted that such women are "the first great group of human beings in history to live such long lives in such large numbers. These are biological pioneers." [34]

Are women's bodies, no longer under threat from repeated risks in giving birth, showing an evolutionary strength at the end of the life cycle? Are women by their nurturing of children better trained than men in building life—sustaining ties with others? Since women appear to have both more chronic and more acute temporary diseases and symptoms, and yet live so much longer, are they simply more sensitive to what is really going on—in their bodies and in their selves? In any event, whatever these strengths, they increase or become more visible as women age, and they have somehow been enhanced by the changes over the last decades of our movement to equality.

Depression is defined as anger turned against the self. Women under the confines of the feminine mystique took out their anger, even their blocked healthy aggression, on their own bodies —in self-denigration, headaches, depression. And not just anger, but any aggressive, assertive need to write their own story in life. Behind the image of the tranquil white-haired old woman, serenely crocheting in her rocking chair while waiting to hand out cookies to the neighbor's children, lurked the witch—the old woman as an aggressive, dominating, irascible fury. Research has shown an actual strong relationship between "irascibility" and longevity.[35] Could that very rage, long buried in women, which we have now managed to express, breaking down the barriers and the false images that once made us turn it against ourselves, be part of the fountain of age?

In this light, let us reconsider the evident change in women's aging process over these last twenty years or so; the appearance of new zest and sense of self in women in midlife, and the disappearance of impairment and depression supposedly ushered in by menopause and the end of childbearing.[36] In these years, women felt as if we became more "whole." We became more fully, freely *ourselves,* by daring to become more assertive in the world, by turning outward that energy we once took out in rage on our own bodies, or covertly on men and children. In that period of "consciousness-raising," we claimed our own real feelings, our problems, and our total state—the rages and angers and humiliations, the passivities and dependencies, that had been encouraged in us so long and still held us back. And then we began to reclaim and redefine our denigrated strengths as women. (Some, in the beginning at least, just *reacted,* exchanging the mask of passive, helpless pseudo-femininity for defensive, machismo fake-masculinity.)

In the more recent period, as women have engaged in such large numbers on new paths of self-realization, new conflicts between the sexes have appeared in late life—some of them merely transitional phenomena caused by that excessive reaction; others perhaps because women have made this evolutionary leap in advance of men. Some women appeared to be moving into a brand new zest in living their own lives, while their husbands succumbed to heart attacks or strokes, or seemed to retreat into retirement, or depart on a futile search for the fountain of youth. Some men in their fifties and sixties seemed to be going through the male equivalent of what I called "the problem that has no name" that women were going through twenty-five years ago. Perhaps the male "midlife crisis"—which emerged about the time we were starting the women's movement—is a signal of the urgency of the sex role revolution, for men as well as women.

Do men now have to break consciously out of the previous confines of their masculine definition—as women had to break through the feminine mystique—even to live the new years of life *which should be men's as well as women's,* much less live and use them fully? Is the bridging of the polarization between men and women, and between the "masculine" and "feminine" sides of our personhood, a key to the fountain of age?

It has been noted by various investigators that a sex role crossover seems to take place in the years after parenthood. David Gutmann found evidence across many cultures that later in life men develop passive, nurturing, or contemplative "feminine" qualities and women develop bold, assertive, commanding, or adventurous "masculine" qualities. His hypothesis was that the qualities that men and women needed to suppress in themselves in order to play the polarized, separate roles of passive nurturer and aggressive, dominant hunter-fighter (required for survival of the species in primitive societies) had to be lived vicariously through the "other" in the parenting years; but could be claimed and developed for the self, after parenting was over. He cited much evidence that primitive societies expected and accommodated this development, using older men's new contemplative, nurturing, and spiritual mode to deal with their gods, and letting women take over active tribal responsibilities previously sacred to men.[37] Women's recent urgent and zestful move into "masculine" activity and competition in the modern world could thus be seen as an evolutionary response to the increasingly long span of life after parenting. Whether or not the survival of the species in our technological society still requires men to suppress their "feminine" and women to suppress their "masculine" potential during the parenting years, the liberation and integration of formerly suppressed sides of the self do seem to be keys to vital age.

If there is, as there seems to be, a *further stage of growth,* beyond what had previously been considered the masculine and feminine peaks, men and women appear to have reached it by different paths that ultimately involve a "crossover." I think that much of the paradoxical, superficially conflicting data in the recent studies I have cited where expected pathologies failed to appear may be explained by the fact that some women and men are moving beyond these polarized masculine and feminine sex roles, while others, holding on to them, are thrown into crises by the "change of life." There is much confusing evidence of stresses and symptoms that may signal the transition from a mode that is appropriate for an earlier stage of life but that does not enhance growth or survival if prolonged. In some of these studies, the "problems" or "stresses" which women were expected to suffer, facing menopause or the "empty nest," or men, facing retirement, did not appear at all. In others, the "stresses" were not harbingers of the pathologies expected but instead turned out, in follow-up studies five or ten years later, to have been harbingers of new growth or adjustment.

It is clear from these studies that women and men have suffered unnecessary pain and self-doubt when stages of their own development were misunderstood as *absolutes* of their masculinity or femininity, and the impulses to further growth were stifled or doubted as "sick" deviations. From the research on the "empty nest," menopause, and widowhood to the studies of men in retirement, again and again the finding emerges that the difference between knowing and planning, and not knowing what to expect (or denial of change because of false expectations) can be the crucial factor between moving on to new growth in the last third of life, or succumbing to stagnation, pathology, and despair.

If there is, indeed, this need in the last third of life for people to live out their unexpressed side, it is clearly easier now, in our society, for a woman simply to move over into the man's world and express her previously underdeveloped "masculine" qualities—even if the jobs she can get are not high in pay and status—than it is for an older man to find any role in society in which he can express his more "feminine" side. Reading the crossover studies, I began to sense the appeal to some men of a nurturing role, with the babies of those new young wives, that they were too consumed with career to play in the families of their younger fatherhood. "I've done with that," says the older ex-wife, who is on to some new quest and as incredulous at her ex-husband's delight in diapering again as he was about her gusto at the office meeting. "I've had all that."

When Cecelia Hurwich went back to graduate school, nearing sixty, she had been rather frantically denying "qualms" of anxiety, even terror, about her own aging. She had been preoccupied with preserving her beautiful figure and complexion, and very proud of her sexual involvement with men much younger than herself. "But I worried about how I would feel when I could no longer be so physically active. I was keenly aware that now, when I walk into a room, I am usually one of the oldest persons present; no longer do eyes look up when I enter."

She decided to do her master's thesis on "Vital Women in Their Seventies and Eighties," hoping to counter the negative image that she shared about the dreariness of aging women. She was expecting to find a simple physical answer, in terms of diet and exercise, as to why some older women were vitally living their age and others were not. But when she finished intensive oral histories of ten extremely vital women in the Bay Area of California, she found to her surprise that neither diet nor exercise, nor their bodies altogether, were a major concern to any of them.

Five of the women had, in fact, what others would consider "health problems," yet they were "in no way disengaged from life." Sex and children, again to her surprise, were not a major concern. Childrearing had been a part of life for these women, but for six of the seven mothers, though glad they had children, it was not "the most fulfilling thing" in their lives. There was no common pattern to their sexual stories, which ranged from brief early marriages ending in divorce or wartime death of spouse to "marriages without desire because it was expected of their generation" to "lifelong growth-enhancing unions." Some had divorced to "pursue their own interests, growth and development." For half the women, sex remained a part of life at seventy or older; for the other half, it did not. But the essence of their vital aging was something beyond that.

One of Hurwich's biggest surprises was that almost all of these women repeatedly stated that "old age is the best time in life." She reported, with disbelief, that as far as she could ascertain, in these women the expected deterioration of memory, intelligence, productivity, and the ability to learn "has not been evidenced":

> They do not expect their mental energies to diminish and it has not happened. They continue to take risks and resist norms which they find limiting. . . . Now in their seventies and eighties, none of the women look forward to dying but neither do they fear it. . . . They feel they have living yet to do. These women have adapted to the physical, mental and psychological changes they experienced throughout their lives. They have retained their zest regardless of their chronological age or the state of their health. They demonstrate that with the later years come increasing wisdom, integrity and creativity.[38]

In contrast to the "disengaged older women" of the gerontological literature Hurwich had studied, these women all had *active purposes* in their age—seven still continuing their careers "through choice," the others "active in their communities." All refused to conform to "traditional sex-role stereotypes for the seventy- and eighty-year-old woman" in their choice of lifestyles and range of many friends "across a wide variety of ages." Four women counted their grandchildren as "particularly close friends." Why did these women experience "growth, change and aliveness" in age instead of boredom, retreat, and stagnation? They did not seem to share any patterns of diet, exercise, health, childhood, or other such factors—except that none of them had passively accepted "traditional female role prescriptions." And all of them seemed to share, in age, the traits of "trust, risk-taking, adaptability, non-conformity and the ability to live in the present." [39]

In the midst of her still unfinished attempt to figure out the source of the mysterious strength such women experienced in age, Hurwich became aware that she herself was in "a different place."

Halfway through these interviews something happened to me. A door opened and life suddenly took on new meaning. I discovered that I was like the women I was studying! The kind of vital later years they are enjoying I too can look forward to.

Facing seventy now herself, Cecelia sat in my apartment in New York, on her way back to California from a hiking trip in Switzerland. She told me how her own life has changed enormously since she started studying age in women (and stopped denying her own). She looked back now on herself at fifty:

I didn't know what was wrong with me. I had a powerful, successful husband, a lovely home, great kids. I didn't know why I was so depressed. I never told how old I was anymore, and yet I was so obsessed with my own aging. But I had no identity of my own.

At fifty, she started on her hiking expeditions. Her daughter had just dropped out of high school, so she took her backpacking through India—and when her daughter chose to go home to finish school (she became an environmental lawyer), Cecelia went further into India alone, teamed up with some artists, and set up an export handcraft business. And then she went back home and had a face-lift without telling anyone.

I felt so funny about it. It made me look younger, but I wouldn't do it again. I hadn't quite come out of the closet yet about my age. Maybe I didn't want anyone to know I was fifty because by now I was divorced and maybe thinking about myself looking for a man.

She didn't think she would be accepted for the master's program at Antioch West when she gave her age—and she didn't know why she had decided to do her thesis on aging in women.

I was so unhappy about how old I was, but people at the school knew my age, and they wanted me! When I got my degree, I remember saying, "I'm sixty-one, I've got a new career and the rest of my life ahead of me," and feeling so *excited!*

But it was her study of those vital older women that made her affirm her own aging, as growth:

I am less concerned with decoration, the outside, and more concerned with the inside now, myself and others. I'm in some kind of a quest for more meaning in whatever I do. I'm less and less interested in small talk. I didn't expect that this time in life could be so good, so rewarding. The connection with nature and going back to school opened a whole new side of life for me. I have such a different mix of friends now, not all of them liberal, they don't all see things the same way; the richness of the mix delights me. And this comfort now with being my age, growing older.

When I finish my dissertation I'm going to study Russian, and start painting again, and take piano lessons so I can play jazz. The man I live with now is such a good companion. He's a retired educator, he remodels and builds things, takes pleasure now in working with his hands, and growing things in my garden. My house has never been in such good repair. He's a lot more relaxed and laid back than I am. I used to feel I had to go to everything, and now I don't unless I really want to.

For so long, I was driven by wanting everyone to love me. That's no longer an issue somehow. By choice, I decided I wanted to be a single woman the rest of my life. From there, I'll make my friendships, choose the persons I want to be close to. The three men I was close to wanted to get married, I didn't. Within a year, they all got married. Men need to be married more than women, maybe. But it's nice, living with Don. I love the morning, taking a walk with him in the morning. Maybe I'll change my mind, who knows? Men worry about getting old, not having someone there to take care of them. But we all have to face death alone. The biggest challenge is these next years, the seventies and eighties, now that I am who I am.

I met Kathleen MacPherson in the fall of 1988 at a conference of nurse practitioners and midwives on "Women Growing Older: Breaking the Rules." Dean of a school of nursing in Maine, she spoke on the "Politics of Hormone Replacement Therapy," warning the nurse practitioners about the drug companies' new hype to get them to prescribe heavy doses of estrogen-progesterone to all older women, ostensibly to prevent osteoporosis. Approaching her sixties, MacPherson wanted to get out of administration now and spend more time on her own, writing and teaching. "After raising two kids, being dean is like housekeeping all over again, attention to detail, a lot of things to do with no relation to each other, monitoring other people's work, no time to think about anything beyond the day's chores. It's like going back to the days with little kids when you had no time for yourself."

A nurse since eighteen, married to a dominating, controlling man, MacPherson gave up a bitter divorce battle for custody of her children because it was "destroying" them, and lived by herself during the fifteen years of her own midlife, getting her doctorate in urban sociology, teaching in France, becoming a feminist, and writing a dissertation on the myths and realities of menopause and hormone replacement therapy.

Those fifteen years alone gave me strength. I had had a childlike dependence on my husband. I finished my Ph.D. when I was fifty-four. Then I used men as "rest for the warrior," but I never took them seriously. And then I watched my parents fall apart. They had been so independent, so integrated, so sure of themselves—watching them disintegrate was the most painful experience of my life. My father, to the end, denied age, denied death. He tried to keep his lifestyle the way it had always been, until it all collapsed. He died of a heart attack.

My mother, on the other hand, has been making concessions all along. When she developed a chronic disease in her late forties, rheumatoid arthritis, she gave up driving a car, going to all the meetings she used to go to, by increments. She could accept the constraints of the condition, whereas he denied until the day he died that he'd even had a heart attack, that he had a terminal cardiac disease. My mother was willing to do some bargaining. At eighty-eight now and in a nursing home, she is more resilient, she rolls with the punches— boy, does she want to live, even on lesser terms. When she kept falling and they strapped her in her bed or a chair, she consciously taught herself how not to fall to get her freedom back.

MacPherson was, in fact, using her own resilience to negotiate an age on very different terms from her father's rigid, doomed, and desperate denial or her mother's passive "concessions":

Heading for sixty now myself, I have very consciously designed my own age. After living alone so long, I wanted more in my life, someone to settle down with. I knew what kind of a man I wanted, and I found him, and as soon as I heard he was divorced, I found a pretext to drop him a note. Of course, he's not security, he warned me he'll probably die before I do, but after all these years of being alone, I don't have that fear. I'm having a surprising, wonderful time with him, and I'm willing to take the gamble. I'm not afraid of being alone. I'm not rich but I feel secure.

It wasn't all easy when I was alone, between relationships, years without sex—you can live through it. He has his own research, of long duration, on agricultural economy, and he's not a bit threatened by my career. He always comes down to support me when I give a paper like this. He's the first man I haven't gotten into a competitive thing with. He'd like me to spend more time with him, and that's the next step of my development. I'm going to give up the administration and restructure space between me and all these organizations overcommitting my time. I don't brood about age myself. I just keep on changing.

• • •

In age, what seemed most important to the many vital women I have interviewed, and others have studied, was not marriage and children or questions of body and beauty—the traditional female concerns—but "quests" that sometimes intersected with "male" careers but had developed more deviously, randomly, serendipitously, into self-chosen purpose and structure. What also seemed important were new forms of intimacy—with men, even their own husbands; with other women; with their own grandchildren—across traditional lines of sex and age. Most of them, after they had married and had children, had moved unevenly, and late, into their careers. And they had continued to develop new purposes and projects long past the conventional retirement age for men.

But what had once seemed exceptional, in these women, has now become a massive pattern as women move into jobs and professions, early or late, juggling their careers with childbearing and childrearing, marriage and motherhood, not "just like men" but in ways that demand, and perhaps enhance, some new integration of male and female skills and strengths. At this point in history, enormous numbers of women, liberated early or late from the rigidities of the old, passive, female sex role, seem to be making the "crossover" that may be a key to vital age more easily than men.

But where are the new roles for men? Does there merely *seem* to be a crossover because, with age, men simply lose their power, control, and "dominance," and are forced into the kind of submissive passivity that women have had a lifetime to adjust to? Or is there more to it than that?

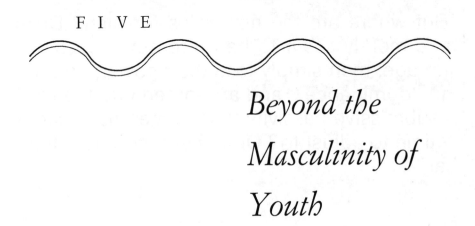

Beyond the Masculinity of Youth

In all the debate about women and men, sex roles and sex, over the last thirty years, it is never pointed out that all our assumptions and definitions of masculinity are based on *young men*— just as what I called the feminine mystique, which defined women only in sexual relation to men, was based on young women in their childbearing years. The crisis in identity for women, trying to live within that role, as their life span increased to nearly eighty years, was caused, in effect, by those new decades of life beyond the biological possibility of childbearing. Further, the Industrial Revolution actually intensified the polarization of sex roles, removing the important work, which women and men used to share, away from the home altogether, leaving women only their sexual and child-nurturing function, and defining men solely in terms of their wage-earning role. The dominance that defined masculine superiority when the work of the society required physical mastery of earth and elements, animals and enemies, was, in fact, a young man's strength, as nubility was a young woman's. With the Industrial Revolution, maleness came to be identified with *success,* dominance in the job role. Its end with the onset of age was arbitrary but as brutally abrupt a termination of men's identity thus defined as menopause used to be for women.

The women's movement focused on the damage done to women, deprived of opportunities to develop skills, strengths, and confidence to move in the complex mainstream of modern society, encouraged to suppress their own ambition and project power and competence onto men, relying on husbands and children to define their sense of self and worth. But what of boys forced to put aside their dependence on the mother earlier and more fully than little girls, denying childish vulnerability and longing in order to establish that tough, independent masculine identity? As psychologists are beginning to realize, that early independence demanded of boys often interfered with men's capacity for affection or intimacy later in life.[1] Men's subjection to success also removed them from continual experiences of intimacy with their own children. And competition defined their relationships with other men.

But the domination that men were brought up to exert is not as functional today as it was in the cave-man era and the early Industrial Revolution. Men's dominance over things—which led to the great technological advances of industrial society—also put them into routinized, computerized corporate offices, factories, and professions that increasingly abstracted them from dealing with life itself. Men in the factory or corporate office undergoing post-industrial technological change were already in trouble with a masculinity based on dominance, even before the male "midlife crisis" exploded into national consciousness. (It is a paradox that this crisis occurred among men at about the same time women began marching for equality in society.) And what of men at retirement age and beyond? How functional is that "masculine mystique"?

Over the years, psychologists have believed, on the basis of studies of childhood development and adolescence, that clear and appropriate sex role typing is crucial to personal adjustment and mental health in both men and women. Since men in our society, by and large, "are expected to take the more ascendant-dominant sexual role, and vice versa for the female," those who departed from these expectancies would be more prone to "personal maladjustments" than those who fulfilled them, so the argument went, and it was held especially true for boys—boys tested in kindergarten, in grades four to six, in junior high school, and in later adolescence—in a number of studies begun more than half a century ago. Thus, it was a revelation when Jeanne Block reported in a lecture at the University of California, Berkeley, in 1972, on studies following up these boys and girls into their fifties and sixties, that the hyper-masculine boys and hyper-feminine girls who had seemed the best adjusted in junior high scored significantly lower in psychological functioning later on, in adulthood. It seemed that "unmitigated masculinity" for boys and "unqualified femininity" for girls was a relatively youthful stage of development. Those who did not go on to make that shift or "crossover" accepting both masculine and feminine impulses were, in effect, stunted or handicapped in their later development.

"For men whose self and sex role definitions have changed little since adolescence, the first signs of age in our youth—emphasizing culture may be particularly threatening," Block said. "Because their sense of personal adequacy has depended upon their physical prowess, dominance, appearance, and sexual exploits, age may be regarded as the enemy robbing them of the foundations of their masculine sex role definition, and their selfhood." [2]

Two modalities essential to all living organisms—"agency" and "communion"—were polarized in that youthful definition of "masculinity" and "femininity," Block speculated, attempting to explain why "the present American cultural emphasis on masculine machismo and feminine docility appears to impede the development of mature ego functioning."[3] Psychologists such as Jane Loevinger, concerned with the larger dimensions of ego development, have been saying for some time that the highest stages of maturity involve transcending the conformity to rigid sex roles, in order to achieve an autonomous, self-directed integration of values of "agency" and "communion."[4] But "ego strength" itself has been masculine in its definition, as David Gutmann and others have observed. It has not included the "flexibility and resiliency" that is the hallmark of the masculine-feminine crossover.

In early studies of sex roles and the aging process, it seemed that women were much more handicapped by their femininity from achieving the ego strength essential to the integration of "agency" and "communion." But in the years since the women's movement, younger women have broken through the feminine mystique to a larger definition of self, and the midlife crossover has been made with great zest by increasing numbers of women in my generation and those that followed it. For the first generation of women dressing for success, "communion" was perhaps suppressed and "agency" exaggerated. But it is clearly easier for women now to integrate masculine values of "agency" than for men to move beyond them. Recent researchers have found evidence of the crossover so much more visible in women than men that Nancy Datan before her death in 1986 suggested that midlife androgyny might be "for women only." [5]

The liberation of men from the mandate to masculine dominance was supposed to be the other side of women's liberation. Many young men in the 1960s forswore the machismo whose exaggeration masks the excess vulnerability that such a definition of masculinity both causes and suppresses. But in the eighties, this development among men was blurred by the new surge of competitiveness of the Reagan-Bush era, which also spurred women's crossover into careers. However, most women never expected their career roles to define them fully, nor could they easily sustain any illusion of dominance. Most women, after all, still had to "juggle" with the changing demands of husband, children, teenagers, home, and washing the pantyhose. Domestic life sustains its demands on women, in or out of career, marriage, divorce, widowhood.

In the massive longitudinal studies at the Institute of Human Development, the University of California, Berkeley, where men and women were studied periodically from seventh grade into age, those who were psychologically healthier at fifty revealed increasingly similar characteristics, no longer polarized by sex. But the two sexes did not reverse roles. From adolescence through their forties, women became increasingly feminine and men increasingly masculine; but by fifty, each was allowing qualities conventionally assigned to the opposite sex to emerge: "Women who were psychologically healthier became more assertive with age while remaining nurturant and open to their feelings. Men became more giving and expressive while they continued to be ambitious and assertive."[6]

Only the psychologically less healthy women remained as dependent and passive at fifty as they had been in adolescence. And they were the most "anxious" about facing age. Those women who held on to dependent aspects of the female role were inhibited from later life development. But the less healthy men were beginning to die. Could the new permission for men to soften their macho image and open themselves up to emotionality, tenderness, and intimacy give them those new years of age that women, but not men, enjoy today? Given the overwhelming dominance of masculine values in our society, female flexibility has surely made it much easier for women to move into men's active mastery in late life, or earlier, than for men to make a comparable crossover. Yet, for women to *define themselves* now in terms of those polarized career roles would be to give up what seems at the moment to be their evolutionary advantage.

The competitive orientation toward achievement and dominance may seem stronger than ever among the young today, but it is increasingly maladaptive, incongruous, even dangerous in terms of the changing social realities, especially for older men. As demands for labor shift in our increasingly technological world, and as the jobs now open to either men or women no longer define identity in terms of dominance or even lifelong professional or corporate career, career shifts or "retirement" may be expected to come earlier in life. Thus the flexibility in response to the discontinuities, uncontrollable changes, and exigencies of life so long experienced by women now emerges as an essential strength in age, for men as well as women.

The integration of masculine and feminine strengths is where all the psychologists striving to conceptualize highest levels of self-actualization and human development end up—from Jung to Erikson, Maslow, Loevinger, Gutmann, Birren, and Block. I don't like the word "androgyny." But the women and men I have interviewed all seem to experience this sure, uncramped, new sense of self as the "surprise" of their own age. It is not the way they felt before. Even if they have been moving toward it all along, backward and forward, they realize that they are "in a new place." And that place involves flexibility, being able to deal with complexity and change, to have some control over one's environment, and yet not to have one's well-being depend on absolute control. It also involves a new ease in risk taking.

There seems to be a release from the old imperatives of dominance and power, of competitive appearance and performance, of self-abnegation and manipulation, of conformity and mask, of illusion and self-deceit. There is a new ease of responsiveness and an unarmored vulnerability that relaxes old, no longer necessary defenses. Such ease appears to come at least in part from no longer being bound by the old restrictions of masculine and feminine competition. Evidently, this requires an ability to risk changes in life and then to have the sense, from having risked *and mastered* changes, that one can move easily, again, to new challenges and new changes.

Women who lived through the identity crisis of the women's movement and managed to define themselves anew face the unknown of a further transformation in age with a by now familiar mix of fear and fascination. The changes women have made all through their lives, the risks they have taken, demanding and learning to juggle new roles in society beyond their biological one, have put them today in a place where age may hold much less fear than it does for men.

I had been invited as a guest speaker to a dinner meeting of the Senior Executive program. I was spending my year at Harvard as a fellow at the Institute of Politics of the Kennedy School of Government, and I supposed the invitation was a concession to the fact that a few women were now present in this previously all-male senior executive group. I agreed to talk to them about the changing roles of women and men if they would talk to me about the personal changes in the second half of life I assumed they had come to this retreat to plan. But, in fact, their program seemed to be geared merely as an antidote against burnout, to help them renew flagging energy for their business careers. When I asked them around the table to tell me what each of them was planning to do, after or beside their present jobs, most of them—then in their late forties, fifties, or sixties—had no such plans. "Retirement is for the birds," said one in disgust. "I intend to die making a deal." When I asked how many honestly felt that way, about half the group raised their hands. But there were others who seemed to be probing for something different. A distinguished-looking Air Force officer, out of uniform in this educational retreat, said:

I want to have new goals for myself. Guys that try to hold on to the power I've had die. I don't necessarily want a new career, though. I'm tired of routines that I don't control myself.

A government administrator said:

I went through a hell of an identity crisis when I was sixty. Four years ago I still felt a tremendous burning ambition. Now I feel that my career has peaked out. I've reconciled myself to that now. I can be reasonably content with the kind of work I'm doing to bring younger people along, without feeling I'm competitive with them.

A senior trade commissioner said:

In the last six months I've been asking myself, is this all there is to it? In the beginning, when I was doing my own work, I felt more in control than after I got promoted. What happens if I do this the rest of my life?

It is not easy for men to shift from the power race. Yet some men do. Dr. A. Baird Hastings,

eighty-six when I talked to him several years before his death, moved out to La Jolla, California,
at sixty-five, retiring after twenty-three years as
head of the biochemistry department at Harvard.
He started over again, as it were, doing basic
laboratory research full time at the Scripps
Clinic. When he had to retire there at seventy, he
became Research Associate in Neuroscience,
appointed annually without reimbursement. His
life has been full of shifts, he told me, beginning
with high school, when two teachers persuaded
him to go to college, then switching from engineering to physiology after World War I, and
from industry to the research lab, from Chicago
to Harvard to Columbia.

I keep shifting all around; I go where the wind
blows strongest. I didn't plan any of these
things; they all just happened. I didn't dread
retirement but I didn't look forward to it. But at
sixty-three, I saw an opportunity to get out of
these administrative duties. The department
had gotten too big, it wasn't my department
any more. I came out here to go back into the
laboratory, which I enjoyed very much. I had
225 publications when I came out here; now
it's 300, a fourth of them after sixty-five. I had
the opportunity to do as much research as I
wanted on the subjects that interested me. I
quit lab work to take care of my wife after she

shattered her hip in 1973, until she died. I took over the shopping, cooking. I had to quit fishing when I got arthritis myself; my hands swelled. Now, I go to my office at the lab every morning, Monday to Friday, read the new scientific papers; young people come to review their research problems.

Dr. Hastings's recipe for age was simply "roll with the punches, don't resist it, use it for doing what you want to do."

Sam Jaffe, eighty-five, also made a shift. After taking early retirement as a Hollywood agent (one of the toughest in the business) twenty-five years ago, he was now being consulted as an "authority on retirement" in the land of the lotus eaters. When we met, he had an eager look—one is tempted to say "boyish"—though his bald head, snow white sideburns, and the wrinkles of age were there. But the brightness of his eyes, his step, his quick, eager speech were not what is usually meant by "old."

At sixty, I had enough money. I said to my bookkeeper one day, how much more money would I have in ten years, if I keep on breaking my ass, getting a nervous stomach on these deals? It wasn't enough money to keep going like that until seventy. I sold the business. So I took some classes at the college. I just sat in the class and the professors lectured, but I didn't talk. The kids had to write papers but I didn't. I wasn't stimulated. So I told my wife, my retirement is a disaster; let's get out of here. We sold our art collection and moved to London.

London was good for me because I was a nonentity. They didn't know I was a celebrity. If I kept on talking about those old movies, how I made *Born Free,* how I ran Paramount and Columbia, what would I get out of it? I'm not ashamed of the things I did, I'm proud, but I don't want to spend the rest of my life talking about my past.

Then they came back to California, because they wanted to get to know their grandchildren. And this time, still intent on getting the education he missed, Sam found the Plato Society at UCLA, where people over fifty-five meet in a modest building on campus and teach or study, in turn, the subjects they want to investigate in depth each semester.

I sit around a table with the other members of Plato. I could mesmerize them, talking about Betty and Bogart, but I don't want to think about the past. It's tomorrow I'm interested in. I give a paper—we're in East-West Literature this year—I go to the library, work for hours. These people are way ahead of me; they're in there for advanced learning; I'm a beginner. Suddenly, I find myself using new words I never used before in my eighty-five years. I expect I'll still be taking on new questions at Plato when I'm ninety. One man walks into Plato all bent over, can barely walk on two canes, but when he sits down, he doesn't talk like he walks; his brain is alive. Afterwards, I take that guy to lunch; he used to teach history in a college.

"People keep saying to me, 'You're eighty-five. How come you look so good?' " Sam went on. And then he told me that both he and his beautiful, witty wife of fifty-nine years, wearing a chic skullcap pulled down to her brows, have cancer. "Mine was a skin cancer; the doctor didn't treat it right the first time. It came back, then grew like a grapefruit, now it's cured. Hers isn't. She said she just had a nervous stomach over my operation, but I knew it wasn't just a nervous stomach." When his wife died later that same year, Sam shared his grief with his children and friends, and he kept on going to Plato. Then, he refurnished their bedroom "for a man alone" and put away her dressing table, their bed. He knew he needed to make another shift, again, at eighty-five.

• • •

It seems hard for men to think in terms other than another family, another profession. Even if they could go on in the same profession or career, even when they are not forced to retire, some know they need to "shift." A college professor told me: "I can't get it out of myself to teach one more class." Retiring from a life of public service as a United Nations bureaucrat, Roger Bayldon was intrigued by the gamble of Wall Street and teamed up with younger men to try his hand on the stock exchange. That didn't work. He started studying art history at Hunter. The course was geared to train museum curators, and he insisted on getting the requisite credentials, taking all the exams, meeting the requirements though, realistically, he knew no job would be open to him in a museum, approaching eighty. He got the degree before he died.

The either/or, win/lose dualisms of the power equation, so crucial to male identity as it has been defined, are, in fact, what make men afraid of becoming "non-persons" in age, if and when they lose their power in the corporate structure, as most know they must. ("I intend to die making a deal.") But if the equation is either to hold on to youthful power at all costs or to resign from society, disengage altogether from work and the social ties and pattern of days which it provides, no wonder the desperation. To move to a different mode, for men, may take a drastic jolt or happen by serendipity; it may involve trial and error, risks and mistakes, or some kind of outside help not easy to find from psychotherapists and counselors, themselves blinded by the mystique of age.

The trouble is that for counselors, psychologists, doctors, as for corporate managers and the media—as for all of us—the measuring stick based on youth is all we have so far. For men, who until now have been defined completely by that breadwinning, win/lose career role since youth, there has seemed no alternative but to continue on that same track, even when the power games can no longer be won or have long since lost their zest, and the work itself no longer challenges.

That women seem to have greater success in finding alternatives is not to deny the harsh economic problems they face as byproducts of the feminine mystique and of the sex discrimination that kept their generation from training for and advancing in good jobs and professional careers. Women now entering age were permanently handicapped in earning power, pensions, and Social Security by their housewife years—especially women who also faced divorce. The double edge of age and sex discrimination can seem especially painful to women still struggling with their youthful definition as sex object in a late life search for love or work. But if they become "sexually invisible" earlier than those powerful men, and lack the option of turning in aging spouses and reliving youthful roles with new young wives and babies, why then do so many women in their fifties and sixties feel better about themselves than they have ever felt before? Men grimly holding on to whatever power they have had in increasingly perilous jobs, or facing the no-man's-land of retirement, may even envy their aging wives, zestfully entering a new stage in their own personhood. A history professor complained:

I'm afraid I'm a bit envious of my wife. She went to work a few years ago, when our children no longer needed her attention, and a whole new world has opened to her. But myself? I just look forward to writing another volume, and then another volume.

Another couple began to feel like "non-persons" in a beach community near Los Angeles, geared—as such communities seem to be—to youth. They were heading toward sixty when his company was taken over and he, too, felt suddenly invisible, unemployable, being interviewed for jobs by young men who simply didn't "see" him. He got a reprieve when a former business competitor hired him for the very years of experience in the business which the young personnel managers had disdained. But his wife by now was taking other steps to find the more basic "change of life" she felt they needed. She wanted to move back east to Maine, which she had loved visiting as a child. She picked a spot on the map, sent for the local newspapers, and found a house that sounded right and that they could afford. She had already gone from her own housewife years to collecting and selling vintage clothes. She got her husband to go into business with her, in their new community in Maine. With so many of the young people leaving that village, the vital older people who remained or who came there like themselves to settle welcomed their energies. Ultimately she was elected mayor of the village. He, who "had to be dragged kicking and screaming out of California," helped her run the business; but his main concerns now were inventions and musical pursuits that he had never had time to try before when business was his whole life.

For far too many older men, the ending is not so happy. I was struck a few years ago by a headline in the *Los Angeles Times* (March 16, 1989): *"The Will to Die . . . Suicide Is a Tragic Search for the Elderly, Especially for Men and Even More So in California."* A former professor of engineering at UCLA, who continued to visit his professor emeritus office after twenty-one years in retirement, had taken off his slippers before sunrise and jumped from the balcony of his twelfth-story apartment. His case was "tragically typical," the newspaper reported:

The suicide rates among older males are strikingly high, increasing steadily after age 65. Nationally, there are 35.5 reported suicides for every 100,000 males from 65 to 74 years old, according to the National Center for Health Statistics. The rate soars to 54.8 from ages 75 to 84, and to 61.6 for those 85 and older.

In California, the rates are higher still. According to the California Department of Health Services, the rate of suicide per 100,000 males age 85 and over is 105.5.

For women, the rate of suicide per 100,000 females over sixty-five is less than 10, and even lower over eighty-five. The paper commented: "Authorities believe that suicide among the elderly, especially males, takes place much more than statistics show." But it is the men who commit suicide in age, not the women.

Graduate students, interviewing the aging San Francisco men and women in Marjorie Fiske's study,[7] applauded the women's struggle through anxiety and depression as they started to grope toward doing "something on their own." But they began to feel very sorry for the husbands, who came back from increasingly boring civil service jobs to watch television, and became more and more dependent on their wives because they didn't have many friends themselves. "The men got angrier and angrier as their wives over the years got more confident and began to do more things, instead of just taking care of them. The wives began to resent their husbands' demands on them. The men simply got more and more depressed," Fiske told me. The women had crossed over to new roles; the men had not.

Intrigued by the crossover he found in the aging men and women he studied in Kansas City, David Gutmann looked for clues in other cultures and found that some societies provide new roles for older men. Among the Druze— tribes scattered through the highlands of Lebanon, Syria, and Israel—the older male at the birth of his first grandchild gives up the active supervision of his flocks and vineyards to his wife and older sons, and is admitted himself into the ranks of the Aquil, the religious gerentocracy of Druze society, responsible for its commerce with the gods.

The older male Aquil experiences a kind of rebirth: he changes his garb, shaves his head, gives up liquor, tobacco and sensual concerns, and devotes himself to prayer and the contemplation of God. . . . His significant life is spent in the company of other prayerful men . . . his domestic life, with his wife, becomes quite secondary.

. . . The old man's emerging humility and submissiveness fits him to live in the dangerous interface between the gods and the mundane community, and, through his prayers, to bring life-sustaining forces into the community, so as to maintain and increase children, flocks and crops.[8]

The "disengagement" from modes of dominance so traumatic for men in late twentieth-century America could be seen as a transition toward some further stage of human development that is aborted in our society:

The [aging Druze male] relinquishes his own productivity, but not productivity per se. Instead of being the center of enterprise, he is now the bridge between the community and the productive, life-sustaining potencies of Allah. The old Aquil now carries forward the moral rather than the material work of the community. . . . The Druze case shows that the inexorable psychic developments of later life are not necessarily a prelude to social withdrawal and physical death; given a society which recognizes the emerging dispositions, values them, and gives them role articulation, the so-called passivity of later life can provide the ground for a later life revival, for a kind of social rebirth.[9]

But we are not the Druze, and the withdrawal of the possibility and even the desire for dominance, in work or love, may appear to American men in our time as a terrifying descent into a void—so beyond their power to control that even a death which they themselves could induce might seem a better out.

In searching for other clues about older men who were able to cross this void—from the Hindu tradition to sub-Sahara tribes, from Kenya and Australia to the Comanche of the American Southwest—Gutmann found anthropological records of institutionalized roles for older men. In "quite disparate cultures, young men are expected, through their own energies, to wrest resource and power from physical nature, from the enemy or from both; older men are expected, through rituals or through postures of accommodation, to coax power—whether for good or malign purposes—from the supernatural."[10]

Older Hopi men, unable to go to the fields, would knit, card wool, or make sandals at home. When a Pomo Indian (Mexico) became too infirm to serve any longer as warrior or hunter, he was compelled to assist the squaws, cleaning and taking care of children. In places as disparate as Israel, Colombia, Germany, the Yucatán, and the Fiji Islands, anthropologists have found older men moving toward values, interests, and activities which are "no longer stereotypically masculine"—taking on tasks, such as the garden, hitherto reserved for women; spending more time in church than women of the same age, a reversal of church patterns for younger men. But in all previous studies, the shift or crossover of American males toward more "feminine," "familial," "community" values in age had been reported as decline.[11]

Where cultures elevate young men's dominance to an overarching value, the repressed "passive" male potential is more likely to emerge as the basis of "midlife crisis," illness, and the disengagement that precedes death. And yet these same studies showed that the same shift which "appears to sponsor masculine passivity and early mortality," increased the "authority and freedom of older women." Brooding about this paradox, I suddenly realized that a "crossover" is not a sufficient explanation. For in our own society, women's greater strength in age—and their increasing edge in longevity—does not seem to be based on young men's power of dominance and possession, but rather on the ties of intimacy and social bonds which women are more able to sustain or recreate than men.

In studies of rural and urban blacks, of family ties in different ethnic groups in San Francisco and London, and other urban centers of the industrialized West, modified extended family networks are now found in all cities—based on ties sustained by the women—not the patriarchal extended family of the countryside and of the past. "The urban family is based on strong bonds between grandmothers, mothers and daughters. . . . We now find that urban matriarchy is founded in women's superior capacity for intimacy, rather than acquisition." [12]

Berkeley psychologist Norma Hahn, following up women and men, now in their sixties, who have been studied since childhood in the Berkeley-Oakland longitudinal studies, found women leveling off in their nurturance around thirty-seven to forty as they become more aggressive and assertive. Beginning in 1968, at around age thirty-seven, the women's self-confidence began to surge "up and up," as did their openness to their own feelings, she noted. Whereas before they were somehow constricted by dominant values of attracting and pleasing men, these women now began to express their feelings in all sorts of new and different ways.

But the men studied in those same years were struggling and often stuck with dramatically increased nurturant impulses they had repressed in the interests of upward mobility. One executive at forty-seven told Hahn: "I still have to pretend I want to be vice president or my company won't approve of me, but that's not what I want to be anymore." An engineer in his fifties said: "Ten years ago I wanted to get really high up in the company. Now I think I'd rather be a happy failure." This "letting go" of ambition is what permits men to bring out these other values, Hahn told me in her Berkeley office. "Both men said the women's movement had given them permission to let go. Before, the executive's main concern was to 'make a hell of a lot of money.' His wife's going back to school, her desire to do things on her own, relieved him of some of this pressure: her happiness no longer depended solely on his economic prowess."

Ten years later, in my own California interviews, I saw women in their fifties, who had gone back to school and started late but were moving with increasing confidence in their own professional careers, react with disquiet, dismay, even outright rejection at their husbands' decisions to retire at sixty or seventy, and their lack of interest in new business or professional ventures.

It's like at sixty, he said he was old enough to retire, he didn't have to keep on racing after new accounts at the agency. He said we had enough money, if we scaled down some. But I don't feel like scaling down. I'm not that old yet, I have my own plan for the next ten years, I'm still moving up.

Sam Osherson, working on a study at Harvard of men who quit their businesses and professions at midlife in order to pursue buried dreams of becoming artists or musicians, told me about his own midlife crisis when his wife finished medical school and became a doctor:

A career change like that is not the answer for me any more. That's the problem for men—the career is what we use to defend our sense of self. Our family, the way it used to be, I was clearly the most powerful and I thrived on that. I felt adored and the center of everything. This process is coming apart now. She's happy in her new career, I feel bored sometimes, and wish we could do more as a family. But the kids aren't so interested now in going ice skating with me after school.

I used to feel needed because I was needed, she was dependent on me economically. When she struck out on her own, changing our family arrangement, it was like she could make independent choices that I really never had as a man. The draft, the Vietnam War, economic considerations forced my early career decisions. That rush of enthusiasm over her new career is nothing I ever felt free enough to experience in mine. If I didn't have a family depending on me—and I was a good provider—I'd have to focus on all the garbage in my work.

I've come to the end of this career, and I've

got no enthusiasm to start another. All that performance suddenly seems oppressive to me. I've lost my motivation. I need to bring out the feminine side of myself, but how's a man to do that, in America, in the 1980s? I suppose that's why I'm spending more and more time on my garden, a lot of men my age are gardening now. But we don't have anything like the women's movement which gave our wives the tools they were denied before to feel comfortable with their masculine assertiveness. I think women have difficulty now in accepting or nurturing the nurturing side of men.

Does a man who shows that soft side of himself, after fifty, still have to be afraid of being a wimp? At seventy-two, Sam Beer was bemused about his own compulsion to accept a new professorship at a smaller college after his forced retirement from Harvard:

Do I see myself at eighty very seriously going to my office every day, driven, working all the time the way I always have? Couldn't I feel free now just to explore for myself? If I could get into that mood, everything would be different, thinking and feeling. Not just to vegetate, that's not what I mean, but to be human in a more fundamental way, really to contemplate your own humanity.

Once you get in the rat race, maybe you can never get out. But if you really could honestly de-rat-race your life, you would be in a different place. I have to be honest, though. I don't know what it would be like. Maybe you can't aim at it, like another career, because you'd just project what you've already had, the eager beaver. Maybe you don't know what the new place is until you get there.

Granted, there are simply no clearly defined and widely shared expectations as to what men should do during this period of life. But if they continue to view themselves and their possibilities according to youthful norms of power—career or sexual potency—then all they will see ahead is decline, closing down, the abyss of nothingness with an indefinite period of "uncertainty and aberration" en route. However, as Vern Bengtson pointed out: "Decrease in specific social requirements and expectations can also be interpreted as a gain in freedom." The very loss of norms and roles gives them an opportunity "to pick and choose among alternative behaviors—a degree of freedom from societal restraints that is perhaps greater than at any other period of the life cycle." [13]

Further, there is evidence that merely continuing the roles of the first half of life—the professional or political power goals or the sex games that drove a man's youth—will not necessarily lead to this "new place." Bengston found that men in their seventies showed low activity in such roles as club member, civic/political participant, and church member; a slightly higher pattern of activity in the roles of friend and neighbor; and the highest activity in family roles, such as parent and grandparent. But the predictions that decline in these activities would impair their aging were not borne out. "Only social activity with friends was in any way related to life satisfaction." [14] It seems clear from my own interviews, and from all this research, that only self-chosen purposes, projects, and ties with continued personal meaning are important beyond midlife (a deeper intimacy in marriage or friendship, a true confidant).

Disengagement from the roles and goals of youth and from activities and ties that no longer have any personal meaning may, in fact, be necessary to make the shift to a new kind of engagement in age. In my own life, and in the lives of many people I interviewed, what got in the way of the shift was the attempt to hold on to, or judge oneself by, youthful parameters of love, work, and power. For this is what blinds us to the new strengths and possibilities emerging in ourselves and in the changing life around us, and thus makes a self-fulfilling prophecy out of the expectation of decline.

Carolyn Heilbrun in *Writing a Woman's Life* (1988) discussed the kind of shifts it took—and still takes—for women to stop living as "female impersonators" or "heroines" of male romance, and discover instead "new stories for women." Until recently, the supposed sorrow at the "door closing behind us," the loss of youthful beauty, kept women from creating new stories about the door *opening ahead* into age. Heilbrun saw that passage to something new for women in age as *open-ended*—not the closure of "and they lived happily ever after." [15]

But can age free men finally from being male impersonators? Neither crossover into the man's world and role, nor the remnants of envy and rage at his previous power, will keep the fountain of age flowing for women very long. And it is even less possible for aging men in America today to find their own fountain of age by crossing over to women's previous role, when both men and women alike look askance at men who openly admit to yearnings and sensitivities, vulnerability and dependence. "If we are to avoid an intensified war between the sexes, we must be fully aware of mutual problems," Harvard psychiatrist Norman Zinberg warned. "Women have suffered from centuries of unwillingness on the part of a men's world to permit them to express their active side. . . . Men are beginning to suffer from unwillingness on the part of both men and women to permit men to find acceptable ways to express their passivity." [16]

That year at Harvard, I got to know Dr. Zinberg, one of the few psychiatrists to overcome the Freudian obsession with childhood and youth and deal realistically with aging patients' problems on their own terms, helping them break through the stereotypes of age and of youthful sex roles, which deny their possibilities for further growth. Zinberg was consulted by a sixty-four-year-old man because of his growing depression, his loss of interest in a highly successful business, his general sense of apathy, and the absence of any fulfilling or committing interests in his life. He was also suffering from occasional sexual impotence and increasing "sexual decline," but did not present these as problems to the psychiatrist. He so clearly accepted the cultural attitude that his sexual activity labeled him a "dirty old man"—and believed it proper that he should cease such activity—that he felt it unnecessary even to comment on it.

Only after that man had seen the psychiatrist several times did he mention his impotence which, at that time, was of almost three years' duration, coinciding with his depression. He no longer made any effort at sexual intimacy. He had been divorced ten years earlier after a long marriage to a dissatisfied woman with whom he had four children "but never had a mutually pleasant relationship." He had used prostitutes, and after his divorce had numerous brief affairs with much younger women, but mainly he "plunged into his business with ever increasing activity." His problems and depression seemed to have begun with a highly successful business venture that had made him, unexpectedly, a very wealthy man. "He felt there were no further goals to strive for after that. . . . He felt he had been happier before, and once he had accomplished what, from a financial point of view, was the pinnacle of his life, there was nothing left to live for."

During the therapy, this man began to see his aggressiveness in business as stemming from his fear of rejection of his wish to be cared for by women. A great deal of the energy he had spent "in acting against the outside world" was also "acting against his own dependent and passive wishes." The ease with which he had accepted his sexual decline began to seem "part of his rejection of his previously active and rigorous state."

He still felt depressed, but decided to leave treatment, and his business, to travel a while— an old dream he had never had time to realize. Six months later, he returned to the psychiatrist no longer depressed but tanned, confident, and obviously more cheerful. Visiting his son, he had gotten to know his twenty-year-old granddaughter, and in long discussions with her young friends was impressed by their ideas, which he contrasted with his own "traditionalism and rigidity." He had no direct sexual interest in any of them, but was particularly impressed by their attitudes toward sex. "It was his feeling that they saw beyond what his generation could envision, that is, sex could be a friendly, pleasant experience, characterized by neither the bitterness that had gone on between him and his wife nor the subterfuge and clandestine, shameful quality that had characterized his other sexual experiences."

For the first time in years, this man had a renewed interest in sexual activity. Instead of going to the traditional winter resort he had visited every winter for the last twenty years, he traveled to less conventional places, met a woman in her late forties, previously divorced and widowed, who seemed to share his granddaughter's "freedom." They became friends and began to date, but he felt great trepidation about trying sex again. Finally, he confided his fears to her—a considerable breakthrough for him. She laughed at his insistence that he was too old, and "indicated that if he had any real trouble she would be more than pleased to help him out." By the time he returned to the psychiatrist, he had been seeing this woman for several months, found himself quite successful now with her sexually, with none of his previous symptoms, including the depression and obsession about his business. He was planning to marry her, and to explore other long-buried interests.[17]

Another of Zinberg's patients, Mr. B., was brought in by his son two years after his retirement, at sixty-nine, suffering from a growing sense of depression, isolation, headaches, and a strong death wish. Married, with three children aged thirty-nine to forty-four, he said that "as far as he was concerned he was dead." He had chosen to retire from a business he had founded and run successfully, though his son did not want him to leave and insisted there was more than enough for both of them to do. Mr. B. had bought the stereotypes: that he had "earned a rest," that he "should get out," that it was "time to see the world." He believed that there was something wrong with him, now that he was miserable in his retirement, and felt guilty because he wished to stay in business, found travel without any goal boring, and simply could not keep himself occupied.

With Zinberg's help, Mr. B. realized that he had left the business only because he believed he should, because of his age. But it turned out that he had never liked being the head of the business and that "part of him longed for many years for his son to take over." Still, he had truly enjoyed "situations where he had brought certain people together and had generally made arrangements so that things could move along smoothly without his having to take over," and he had been "tenacious and competent" in organizing such aspects of his business.

He had felt it was not "appropriate" for him to stay on in his business after sixty-five. "The idea of returning to head the business—which his son quite freely offered him—was not possible for him. He felt he did not belong and was embarrassed, shy, self-conscious and otherwise ill at ease whenever he went into the front offices of the plant." But after a few weeks of exploring his real feelings about himself and the business, Mr. B. "began to devote himself to the question of what he could really do." From the moment he undertook the project of finding a new place in the business for himself, his mood changed perceptibly: "After only three weeks he learned that a portion of the plant was not functioning well. . . . He went back to the job of getting people together and trying to get things to work right, of being a 'facilitator,' as he himself described it." By the time he stopped therapy, he had found three other areas where he could work in the same capacity, and was no longer depressed.[18]

Both of these men, Zinberg said, "tended to cling to culturally stereotyped views of themselves," which kept them from responding to new clues in their environment, to the reality of their changing interests and the real feelings of others. It was as if they had to hold on to the sexual and business dominance of their youth —about which they had denied their own real feelings for years—or die. As a result, they became estranged from their own feelings about themselves, and from finding new and different areas to satisfy their needs for intimacy and work.

Men, in fact, are being told to hold on to modes of dominance in retirement as zealously as women are being sold those "female impersonator" face-lifts. A former CEO of a New York advertising agency recently complained in the column "About Men" in *The New York Times* about the question: "What will you *do?*"

It wasn't really a question . . . I couldn't be serious about retiring, they said. An obsessively dedicated executive, still in good health, still endowed with unflagging energy, still several years shy of 65—for such a man, was it possible to have a satisfying life after work?

When he said he was going to carry out a long-held dream to write a book about a neglected political hero of the last century, at first "that seemed to satisfy all those well-meaning people so concerned about my post-treadmill fate."

But with no mortgage to pay, and "no youthful illusions that the world was panting to read my work," he looked at this book as "simply a retirement project more purposeful than golf, more engrossing than whittling. Stimulation without stress." His friends and former associates weren't having any of *that.* He began to dread their questions—how was his book coming, when would it be done, did he have a publisher yet? "You are what you produce," a friend told him sternly.

Those looks I received—part pitying, part censorious—testify that admiration, these days, is reserved for elders who successfully challenge their biological roles with prodigious feats of energy and accomplishment: the grandfather in his eighties earning his first college degree; the sixtyish marathoner; the 70-year-old learning to pilot a plane.

But I am none of these, nor do I want to be. It wouldn't work for me any more than it does for so many others of my age— men who vainly attempt to stay young by borrowing visions that belong to a different generation, and investing in values not truly theirs. . . .

The numbers [of men who die several years after retirement] have convinced me that growing older can be far less painful than trying to stay young—and failing . . . I'm determined to avoid the expectations trap: accepting someone else's ideas about what I am, and what I should do, instead of shaping my own standards and setting my own pace.[19]

On the cutting edge of age, such men can glimpse—beyond that dread closing of the door of youth—*release* from the mandates of sexual and social, financial and professional competition, to express long-buried sides of themselves, to meet their human needs for love and work in new ways, to become finally and fully themselves. And while the women's movement to equality has released and enhanced strengths in women for age—and has helped liberate men from the machismo that keeps them from evolving to their own new place—it seems to me that past this crossover there is no need or room in age for man-as-enemy, for envy of or battle over that obsolete power which he no longer enjoys if it has not already killed him.

As the end of the Cold War removed the old enemy and left communism and capitalism in need of restructure and new purpose, so the old war between women and men dissolves in the sexual *glasnost* of age. But if our approach to age is no longer to deny it, holding onto outgrown youth as the end of life, how do we give it new structure and purpose? How do we move beyond a mere "crossover" to new ways of loving and working? How do we *live our age* as simply a new time of our life, a new period of our humanness, a new stage?

The clue lies in those individual differences that increase with age, for both women and men. The clue is the *personhood of age.* Defined less by biological programming, we now know from research, than at any other period of our lives, not necessarily programmed at all by the social roles and norms that defined our youth and middle age—in that normlessness that is at once the terror and the liberation of age—how do we live out our personhood? For if we see age as a *new* period of life, which each of us now must define for ourselves, we also know that we must find *new ways of living all the parts of our life* that are essential to our humanness.

We need to evolve new ways to sustain or re-create the ties of human intimacy and love we found earlier in youthful sexual encounters and raising children. We need to evolve new ways of working and learning—no longer defined by career—to give purpose to our days and keep us part of the human enterprise. But the first and crucial step for each of us is to break through our own paralyzing youth blinders and the dread of age that they engender. Only then will we become aware that we are in "a new place" and can move forward to find our own new ways to keep on loving, working, learning, choosing the care we want to get and give, and undertaking the risks and quests that age can free us finally to choose for ourselves.

Part III

*New Dimensions
of Work
and Love*

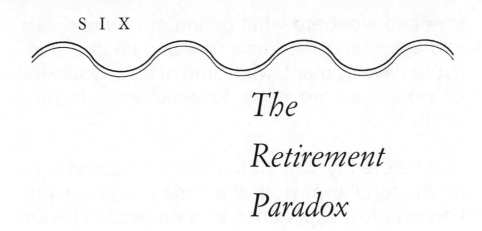

The Retirement Paradox

The two experiences basic to our human identity, Freud said, are work and love. But he was addressing explicitly the task of overcoming the sexual traumas and conflicts of childhood in order to be able to love and work in fully human ways in our maturity. Life expectancy then was barely fifty, and in the conventional wisdom and sophisticated scientific thought of Freud's time, we "retired" from work and sexual love in age. The parameters that defined our lives after we could no longer pass as young were "care" and the approach of death. How desperately we must hold on to youth, deny age, if that is the only way we are permitted to love or work. But if

327

love and work are what define our humanness, and age is accepted as a new and unique stage in our development, what kind of love, what kind of work, can we hope to experience beyond youth?

Just before my sixty-fifth birthday, I started a job on the regular payroll of a large university, putting my life's experience as a professional journalist and activist feminist leader to new academic use. Some forty years earlier I had turned down a fellowship that would have taken me to a Ph.D. in psychology at Berkeley, renouncing my serious interest and early promise in a professional career because of conflicts I didn't understand at the time but later conceptualized as the feminine mystique. I had felt guilt, and painful loss, for years over that path not taken. So there was something very satisfying about doing it at last, though now so differently.

As Visiting Distinguished Professor in Journalism and Women's Studies, I took a course already in the catalogue and turned it into "Women, Men and Media." Finding no books that I could use as texts, I assembled panels of living text from women colleagues on both coasts who, in their lives and their work, were changing the image of women. I was encouraged by male faculty at the University of Southern California to expand this into a national symposium, which led to a new nationwide watch, monitoring the representation of women in newspapers, magazines, television, and film. I also helped bring together leading feminist thinkers from all the disciplines—law, social work, literature, theology, and science—with policymakers, movie producers, and corporate leaders to confront new questions about equality, going beyond the male model. And then I joined the Andrus Gerontology Center to teach a seminar on the mystique of age. I was, of course, not on any tenure track, appointed only one year at a time, no "career."

But all of this somehow got me beyond the paralyzing conflicts and manipulations that, in fact, had forced me to "retire" from active leadership in the women's movement. I was now using whatever wisdom that movement had given me to conceptualize new questions, in my teaching, lecturing, writing. And yet I must admit I missed being out of the loop of active leadership. Then, in the face of new urgencies, with the Supreme Court retreat on abortion, I started holding mother-daughter dialogues in various cities for any of the organizations wanting to reach out to the new generation. And my own daughter and daughters-in-law worked with me, for the first time, trying to voice their need for real choices to have children and to work, beyond the question of abortion.

It was strange for me, at first, but also a liberation, finally, to work in a new way outside the competition for power in academic or political organizations. I had been paralyzed, and increasingly depressed, I now realize, bowing out or holding on, as long as I resisted and denied the changing parameters of my work. Serendipity—the accidental byproduct of a simple survival move, to leave New York in the winter because my asthma seemed to be getting worse as I hit my sixties—opened a new place in my work, after I moved to a new place physically. I'm not sure, now, whether my asthma got better because of the California climate or because I found new ways to work, beyond that rat race for power, which characterizes the women's movement as well as any other institution in this post-industrial world.

The assumption that we will all one day stop working, either by choice or because we are compelled to do so, has long been a fact of life in our society, which equates age with decline. Even further, as I discovered when I began to look into the whole question of retirement, our society exactly pinpoints the onset of that decline at age sixty-five. No one would presume to date so precisely the onset of childhood, adolescence, or adulthood, and reward—or punish—those who don't arrive or depart on time. Why age? And why us?

For many years in this country, retirement at sixty-five was mandatory, written into the law.

With the realization that it was arbitrary, that law was rewritten to counter what had come to be seen as "age discrimination." But did it? When the bill that extended the mandatory retirement age from sixty-five to seventy in private industry and removed it altogether for federal employees first passed the U.S. House of Representatives in October 1977, there were no opposing speeches, and the final floor vote was 359 to 4. There was the same remarkable lack of opposition in the Senate, and to the later bill that purported to abolish age discrimination and mandatory retirement altogether, except for tenured college professors, CEOs, deans, airline pilots, and other critical professions. At that time, some 23 million Americans, about 10 percent of the population, were sixty-five or over. And while the pressure on college admissions and professional training continued among the children of the baby boom, the ensuing "baby bust" was already manifest in a growing shortage of service workers. The lifting of the age of mandatory retirement might, in effect, have been the first step to force the lowest-paid workers in the dreariest jobs to keep working longer before collecting pensions. But at the middle managerial and executive levels, and in the professions, early retirement was now effectively being encouraged—or not-so-subtly forced—at ages far short of sixty-five.

In fact, the mystique of age still prevailed: the

man (or woman) who loses his job, for reasons of downsizing or takeover, at fifty or sixty cannot find another at the level of his expertise. And the "solution" which personnel managers or "human resources" vice-presidents now propose, for those sixty-five and seventy years old who do not voluntarily choose to retire or accept a pensioned buyoff at sixty, is to throw them into a temporary pool replacing service help on vacations or pregnancy leave, or in overload emergencies.

In August 1989, more than ten years after the mandatory retirement at sixty-five or seventy was supposedly abolished, I was asked to speak at a session in Washington on family policy and work at the Academy of Management, the organization of business school professors training young MBAs. In the face of the labor market shortage for service jobs and the "baby bust," they were ready to talk about the need for parental leave and child care to keep the younger women working. But even the most future-minded management experts have not considered new ways of using those men and women they can no longer force to quit at sixty-five or seventy.

Indeed, the focus is elsewhere: how to prepare for retirement, and how to survive it. Health experts have even developed manuals for prevention of "retirement shock." But so completely have we been "socialized" for retirement, so completely have we accepted the mystique of age that it comes as a surprise to be reminded that, not long ago, work and age were not severed. In colonial times, older people held the best jobs, and did not leave them until death or ill health forced them out. In seventeenth-century New England, 90 percent of the ministers and magistrates died in office. People showed their respect for age as power, then, by powdering their hair to look older than they were.

The idea that sixty-five is the appropriate age to retire began with the nineteenth-century German chancellor Otto von Bismarck, who invented the Social Security pension system in 1884. When he arbitrarily set the age for retiring at sixty-five, very few people lived that long. Life expectancy at birth was about thirty-seven years. In 1900, when life expectancy for men was 46.3 years, all but 16 percent of those years on average were spent working. In this single century, life expectancy has increased by thirty years for men (nearly forty for women), almost double its length in Bismarck's time. But our view of age and work is still dictated by that arbitrary, and obsolete, terminal number of sixty-five.

Paradoxically, the infirmities that used to plague age have virtually disappeared in the same years that people have been induced to "retire" at earlier and earlier ages. In this century, most of the diseases that used to shorten life have been virtually eliminated: smallpox has been reduced 100 percent, polio 99.9 percent, tuberculosis 99.5 percent, diphtheria 99 percent, and rheumatic fever 98 percent.[1] Chronic diseases have been compressed into later and later years. Even through their seventies, four out of five of the older participants in the massive Swedish longitudinal study were without serious handicaps. According to data presented in June 1983 to the Salzburg Seminar on Health, Productivity and Aging, at age seventy, 95 percent of that comprehensive cross section of the Swedish population was without physical handicap; at age seventy-five, 90 percent; and at age seventy-nine, 80 percent. Could it be that it is not physical or mental decline but the very fact that people are compelled to retire from work at or before sixty-five that forces their "disengagement" from society? Certainly the losses caused by retirement itself—the loss of identity, of power, of challenge to one's human abilities, of social ties and status, of simply being part of the active mainstream—are the bulwark of the perception of age as drastic decline from the peak of youth.

A woman named Pauline Ragan got her training as a gerontologist after her own "retirement" as mother, going back to college when her children were grown. After a while, she began to think of the "retirement counseling" she herself was now giving other women and men as a kind of confidence racket:

The reluctant or unprepared retiree must learn to give up the work role and self concept attached to it. . . . Even when formal age-mandated retirement does not exist, various pressures cause the older worker to retire. He (or she) may be subjected to subtle hints to leave or to blunt attacks upon his ability. . . . Sometimes financial incentives, "bonuses," are offered to induce retirement, and the underlying atmosphere is like the army joke—volunteer or else . . .

It is a tribute to the cooling out mechanisms at work that the process takes place so smoothly. . . . To the extent that in our system prestige and self worth are based largely on occupational status and income, occupational status is lost or relegated to the "former" category, and income is almost invariably reduced. . . . For many persons it is also a loss of a social network that is difficult to replace. And it is a loss for those individuals who derive intrinsic satisfaction from the performance of their work or profession. . . .

Persuading the American worker to retire gracefully and not rock the boat seems to be a relatively easy accomplishment, although some of those workers are now beginning to squawk. It is at least a lot easier than cooling the mark out must have been in those ancient or primitive societies in which the aged were set on an ice floe or on the top of the

mountain to die because the limited resources of the community could not support
them.[2]

The figures are startling. By 1950, according to
U.S. Department of Labor statistics, 46 percent
of men sixty-five or over held or were seeking
jobs. The exodus of older men from full-time employment increased over the next twenty-five
years until by 1970, only 27 percent of men sixty-
five or over and by 1976 a bare 20 percent—one
out of five—held or were seeking jobs. And only
8 percent of older women held or were seeking full-time jobs indexed by the Labor Department in 1976, just before mandatory retirement
ended.

An occasional poll revealed that as many as a
third might have wanted to stay on, or move to
some different work, if they could. But clearly
only the most desperate—or the boldest—succeeded. The mystique of age as "retirement" is
so thoroughly accepted that even today, most
people I talk to do not know that forced retirement at any age has been outlawed. When one
looks more closely at the research, it's fairly
clear that actual ill health (not decline) accounts
for a small minority taking early retirement, and
extreme financial need for another minority
working past sixty-five. But for the great majority
of men—and growing numbers of women—the
existence of Social Security and pensions, and

the pressured expectation of retirement (and decline), mask another self-fulfilling prophecy of "life after work" that can be terrifying in its lack of structure.

For blue-collar workers, assembly-line workers, and for women in menial service jobs, Social Security at least makes possible a "life after work" that is a release from hard physical routine or menial labor. But for executives, professionals, and increasing numbers of women, the picture is different. One psychology professor emeritus pondered "the challenge that retirement presents. Days have no beginning or end, there are no appointments, no meetings, little or no mail, no mutually-informing conversations or even mutually-assuring meetings. Without content it becomes impossible to 'keep up' with one's colleagues or institutional changes."[3]

And if compulsory retirement is traumatic, so is the situation in which the manager or producer is downgraded at the office for months or years, until he "chooses" to take his pension and quit. "Many companies already exert subtle and not so subtle pressure on older people to get them to retire," *Time* magazine reported (October 10, 1977) as the new retirement law went into effect, quoting a Detroit lawyer representing white-collar workers in age discrimination cases: "If they are going to do you in by age 53 and make you worthless, increasing the retirement age . . . means nothing." An ombudsman at the *Boston Globe* noted that the very expectation of retirement now seems to make people on his newspaper "lapse into premature senility. They walk around like zombies just waiting for the day they retire. Younger people behave differently toward the man soon to retire. They no longer respect him, and sadly, he does not respect himself" (*Time,* October 10, 1977).

It has been conventional wisdom that women "adjust" more easily to retirement than men, since their identity is less invested in work, and they have the role of homemaker to fall back on. Studies of women in clerical, sales, and service jobs—where, until recently, most women were segregated—seemed to bear this out; such women were much less likely than men to have enjoyed their jobs. But recent studies show women more reluctant than men to retire. Most pension plans, in fact, require women to retire at the same arbitrary age as men, although the women have entered their careers much more recently, can expect to live longer, and can less easily afford to retire. Older women are also less likely to be married and cannot therefore even pretend to retire to a full-time homemaker role. In fact, most of the generation now reaching sixty-five started their working careers only after they finished child-rearing, just getting going about the time their male counterparts began discussing retirement.[4] Such women have already had a lot of practice in "involuntary retirement"—from early jobs to marriage; from motherhood to the empty nest; from husband's retirement and widowhood to the new lives they must make for themselves. Even the new career women do not invest their total emotional energy in any one activity and are less likely than men to be *defined* by career. Still, the evidence suggests that retirement can be just as traumatic for many women as it is for men.

The eminent sociologist Erving Goffman pointed out that a pension enables a man (or woman) to maintain the illusion that he is leaving of his own accord. "A man can say to himself and others that he is happy to retire from his job and say this with more conviction if he is able to point to a comfortable pension."[5] Pension and Social Security are real factors, of course, in people's ability to *survive* "life after work"—or make new choices about work. And that is why there is so much political anger at any hint of tampering with the Social Security system, or taxing older people for Medicare. In fact, the suicide rate for older white males, which had been declining, is now on the rise again—perhaps because inflation is eroding the value of those pensions; perhaps because other realities of "life after work" are becoming clearer over time, beyond the grim bottom line of physical survival.

In her early fifties, Louvinia Smith was summoned to Personnel at the government agency in Mississippi where she worked and told that a reduction-in-force situation existed. "Since I was over 50 with more than 20 years service, I could take an immediate annuity, reduced, of course. Otherwise . . . a two-step demotion." By working hard and continuing courses, she had "clawed" her way out of the secretarial pool into the professional field, "only to have the door slammed in my face by the 'youth-quake.' When you work in this environment of unconcealed hostility and studied contempt, and you know that the invisible bar prevents chance of future advancement—in fact, holds a chance of demotion—you either look for another job or consider retirement."

She had applied for every vacancy that she could qualify for, but when they saw her age, "recruitment had closed the day before." Then she started interviewing fellow workers who had retired. "I knocked on Mrs. Moore's door at 2:00 one afternoon. She came to the door in her nightgown. 'Are you ill?' I inquired. She shook her head dully. 'No, I'm all right, I guess. There's no reason to get up, so I just stay in bed.' "

Louvinia Smith started to keep a daily log, and her supervisors realized she would have the basis for an age discrimination case. She does not intend to retire until she can enter "a new way of living, with new kinds of experiences and accomplishments which are beyond the possibilities of the young." [6]

When Robert Butler asked me to serve on the faculty for the Salzburg Seminar on Health, Productivity and Aging in the summer of 1983, I was drowning in the mystique of age. I had been part of the Harvard Medical School working group on ethical issues in aging, like when to pull the plug of life support systems on comatose stroke survivors or terminal cancer patients, or whether residents of nursing homes should have a voice in decisions about their own care. But I had begun to see that very focus on age solely as "problem" or illness requiring "care" as the crux of the mystique of inevitable decline. Removed from work, from active participation in the mainstream of society, people over sixty-five become statistically and socially important mainly as users of costly medical and nursing home care, and drains on the Social Security system.

To look at people over sixty-five in terms of work, health, and productivity would be to treat them like full people again, not just objects of compassionate or contemptuous care. It was in terms of work that the issue of the personhood of women was finally and fully joined—and the women's movement was born. I welcomed the opportunity to deal with age in such terms, for I was beginning to sense that the age mystique among gerontologists and advocates of "better care" for the elderly was more insidious even than outright ageism.

But the professionals and administrators of services from the dozen nations at that Salzburg seminar simply did not want to look at older people in terms of "work" or "productivity." No matter what Butler said about ageism, or I about the age mystique, no matter Alvan Svanborg and Jim Birren's strong statistical evidence that most older people do not now decline in mental or even physical abilities before their eighties if they remain active in their communities, no matter retired department store CEO Maurice Lazarus's business charts of bottom-line value to industry of older people's skills and experience (and specific ways they could be used), the professionals present kept wanting to talk about nursing homes and "care." They seemed positively outraged, threatened in some very basic way personally, and somehow affronted morally, at the very idea of subjecting older people to the same standards of "work" and "productivity" applied to the rest of society.

And, of course, most of those experts and professionals were themselves still "young," approaching middle age. Since their own careers were based on the "care" of the elderly, maybe they didn't want to see age in other terms. Or maybe, seeing older people only as pathetic objects of their "care," they had such a righteous dread of age they didn't dare look at them as people not all that different from themselves. And yet none of us wanted to deny the realities of age, or to pretend that we could stay forever young. In fact, as we proceeded—and did engage the issue of work, productivity, and active participation in society for people over sixty-five, we had to think in ways none of us had done before about the values of work. Beyond the bare necessities of subsistence—if pensions took care of that—why did people still need to work, or why might society need them to work; why, and under what circumstances, would they choose to work; and what might they be able to contribute to company, institution, or society? But it was very hard indeed to get beyond the model of incapacity and decline (after all, older people haven't grown up using computers, and how do we compensate for failing vision, or hearing, or slower reaction time, or muscular weakness?) and to think of using gifts that may evolve with age.

Still, dealing with the real world that we are all aging in, we saw that it would also be necessary to think in a new way about "productivity." If work is necessary beyond subsistence in order to have identity and status in society, to keep using and developing one's abilities, to stay healthy and alive, should it be measured and rewarded only in terms of the short-term bottom line?

Among the minority of men over sixty-five who continue to work, most are either at the bottom or the top of the occupational ladder, many studies show. Those at the bottom work from sheer financial necessity; they are not covered by pension plans, their Social Security will not enable them to meet expenses of family, children still in college, medical bills. But the increased availability of pensions has decreased the proportion of older men who work simply because they need additional income. The number of older men continuing to work for non-financial reasons has become greater. Why is it that some people at the top of the occupational ladder continue to work after sixty-five—and so many others say they would, if they could only find work?

A study was done in 1974 of retired male faculty at three universities where retirement was mandatory at age seventy and optional at an earlier age. At least three quarters found work for pay after retiring. Half of the others continued to work, writing and publishing papers, devising new scientific techniques, but receiving no pay. Most of the ones who worked did so part time. Those men who worked were more likely to claim "excellent health"; those who did not work tended to say that their health was "no better than good." The men continuing to work seemed to be mainly those finding new meaning in their work, or developing it in new directions. They were more likely to have given new courses or radically altered old ones. They were more active in a larger number of professional associations, and reflected "intense attempts to be aware of, transmit and advance new developments."[7]

Other studies showed that people who remain active at a later age are more "field independent" than those who do not; that is, they have a greater sense of their own identity, and are thus better equipped to act contrary to public opinion, where retirement is the expected behavior. Only people pretty sure of themselves, firm in their own authentic identity, can resist the overt pressures to retirement, and the denigration of their own abilities implicit in the stereotypes of age bombarding them from the media, not to mention the glances and tone of voice of co-workers and bosses.

There are legitimate reasons not to want to keep on doing the same thing year after year, which may be why, given the option, only professors who are developing new courses or material want to keep on teaching. And given the *pain* involved in meeting those stares and tones of contempt where there used to be respect, small wonder that so many seize on the dream of "retirement" if pension makes it possible. "You may not want to just keep on doing what you've been doing for forty years," said my frank old friend Liz Carpenter, "especially if you've once had real power, and now you'll just be doing what you are tired of doing anyhow, at a lower level. Better to get out completely and try something new."

A sixty-two-year-old assistant comptroller for a major corporation was repeatedly reminded by his department head of his approaching retirement. This employee checked with the personnel department, found out he could not be forced to retire at sixty-five, or even seventy, and got this pointed over to the department head, who stopped mentioning it. If this story was considered newsworthy (*The New York Times*, February 25, 1981), it was because relatively few men are that "field independent." But the dream of retirement is deceptive. If it does not lead to new purposes (which may look a lot like work), it can dissolve in suspiciously early death—or be experienced as living death. And, again, the mystique in place today enables only the most independent, or lucky, to find other purposes that will permit their continued development and use of the strengths of maturity.

In another 1974 study of sixty men and women (average age sixty) anticipating retirement within three years, "not all of the older men relished the thought of retirement," but only one out of five listed any further "occupational goals, generally limited to part-time employment." Though "freed from work and financial obligations, they often showed a resurgence of interest in earlier avocations and a desire to develop some latent talent or interest more fully," but most were unable to conceive of any further change in themselves beyond a focus on pleasure and "taking it easy" instead of work.[8]

Men who continued to have high career goals suffered anxiety and other "detrimental" symptoms in retirement. But "driving and successful career men, who find no meaningful challenges and feel compelled to pursue 'enjoyment' with equal vigor," also showed "low morale." The higher the men's capacities and the broader their horizons, the more likely they were to view "the undemanding goals of leisurely relaxation and freedom from pressures as unfulfilling and continue to experience the need for a sense of meaningful productivity and accomplishment." Thus the gerontologists now proclaimed that "adjustment" to retirement required a retreat from this need for meaningful accomplishment, which most men finally make.

According to this same study, the women were "considerably more open in revealing disappointments and admitting renunciations." They had hoped to make up for the goals of self-fulfillment seemingly in abeyance during the child-rearing years and, in the face of retirement, still mentioned goals relating to personal growth. But the findings suggested that most of the men had "successfully accomplished . . . [a] 'lowering of aspirations' and there were emotional repercussions for the few who did not." These men reacted negatively to questions about their goals for the future, "conveying clearly that the term 'goal' in their case was synonymous with tangible career achievements," and that no other activity merited "this appellation."

347

The women, on the other hand, did not seem to share the men's "adjustment" to this lowering of goals to "ease and contentment," showing "a keener desire for some further form of personal accomplishment." And yet, so imbued were the researchers with the mystique of age that they applauded the men's "adjustment" to a life of "ease and contentment"—despite their own re-iterated belief that "the ability to maintain viable values and meaningful goals" is essential to the adaptive process at all stages of human life.[9]

It may be worth remembering that mandatory retirement and Social Security were first intro-duced in the United States in 1935, during the Depression, not from humanitarian concerns for older Americans but because their forced re-moval from the work force would create more jobs for the young. The originators did not con-template the significance of being a non-worker in a society where status and identity, as well as subsistence, are closely tied to productive func-tion in the work force. Mandatory retirement grew in the years following the Depression and World War II because it was a simple and legal means for employers to rid themselves of their most expensive workers. From 45 percent to 61 percent of all retirees over sixty-five polled by Louis Harris in 1976 had not wished to retire. By 1990, they could not be legally forced to do so. But the "positive adjustment" to retirement is now kept in place by the mystique of decline which was created, in effect, by *the very removal of people over sixty-five from the productive labor force,* arbitrary as it was.

The suspicion that retirement does not necessarily lead to "ease and contentment" but to a kind of stress that hastens death keeps being raised—and denied—in gerontological research.[10] Stress scales developed by Holmes and Rahe on younger persons indicate that any major or drastic change in marriage, job, finances, or home can lead to increased susceptibility to illness or accident. Retirement involves major changes in work, social relationships, and daily personal behavior, all at once, as opposed to a mere change in job or marital role—stressful enough on the Holmes and Rahe scale. "Retirement marks the beginning of the roleless role, older persons being forced to create their own roles in the absence of socially defined ones."[11]

Researchers have noticed that cholesterol levels may remain normal during the period of anticipating job loss or retirement, and often for a "honeymoon" phase immediately thereafter, but they increase with the actual *experience* of unemployment or retirement. "Where a honeymoon phase does occur, it is often followed by a disenchantment phase, a period of letdown and despondency, as the retiree begins to cope with such problems as inadequate income, poor health and loss of friends. . . ."[12]

The *"disenchantment* phase," according to

this gerontological model, is followed by a *reorientation* phase, involving "an acceptance of, and adjustment to, the retirement role, including the establishment of a structured routine and a stable life in retirement." The last phase, *termination,* "may involve a return to work [but] more often involves . . . illness and disability, the retirement role being replaced by the sick and disabled role as the key organizing factor in an individual's life." [13]

An important study in Lancashire, England, revealed a steadily increasing incidence of illness requiring medical treatment in the two years before retirement, dropping from 50 percent to 30 percent immediately after the giving up of work, and then increasing again four to six years after retirement. This study was actually biased in the healthy direction since workers retiring because of ill health or disability were excluded. Another study, carried out in two U.S. rubber tire companies in 1977, found workers more likely to suffer serious illness, and to die, three to five years after retirement. Considering that "work satisfaction has been shown to be the best overall predictor of longevity" in research by Erdman Palmore cited earlier, it's hardly surprising that when retirement also involves a person's relinquishing his or her most meaningful social contacts, as it does for most men, and some women, it may shorten the life span. *Purposes* that organize one's days—and *social ties*—were, after all, discerned as the chief factors in vital aging in all the massive longitudinal research. On the other hand, some studies, mainly among better-educated volunteers at Cornell and in the Boston area, are often quoted in support of the view that retirement does not adversely affect health. (Since almost all of the people in this kind of study dropped out before it was finished, however, there is reason to believe that those who continued were healthier, better educated, and more likely to have remained active and purposeful.)

But there is no arguing with the grim statistics from numerous sources showing the highest incidence of depression in men from sixty-four to seventy. While persons sixty-five and over constitute over 11 percent of the population, they account for 25 percent of reported suicides. And though the suicide rate is higher among men in all age groups, the male-to-female suicide rate goes from three to one at younger ages to ten to one among those sixty-five and over. "The rise in male [suicide] rates around the time of their retirement [and] the much less conspicuous increase at this time in women . . . indicate that lack of occupation is a factor predisposing to suicide, and especially to suicide in the elderly male."[14]

The depression that leads to suicide, as gerontologists describe it, can be brought on by an irreversible progression of losses: "One, work is gone, and so are friends. . . . Self disdain has replaced self-esteem. Hope has disappeared. There is a sense of passivity and helplessness . . . loss and isolation." The individual least likely to cope successfully with the losses of age appears to be the white male. In the seventy to seventy-four age group, white men commit suicide at a rate nearly three times as high as that of non-white men and nearly five times as high as that of all women the same age. It is as if the very expectation and opportunity for success which drives that man while young makes him more vulnerable to its deprivation in age. "A man who has his sense of self confused with his work may come to think of himself as nothing when the work is gone," suggested Dr. Adrian Ostfeld, professor of public health at the Yale University School of Medicine.[15]

The aging of America's work force is viewed by employers only in "problem" terms permeated by the mystique of age. In 1988, some six hundred companies surveyed by the American Society for Personnel Administration and Commerce Clearing House were asked whether they were "experiencing problems related to senior employees" and to identify "policies they are implementing now to address current and future problems." Almost half (47 percent) of the companies reported experiencing "moderate to very serious problems associated with managing the careers of senior employees." But between the lines of that survey, most of those problems could be traced to the dead-end expectations that currently define work in age. Despite the fact that mandatory retirement is no longer legal, about one third of the companies reported having an "informal philosophy that retirement at or before age 65 is in the best interest of both the employee and the organization." Fewer than 10 percent had policies to accommodate "the special needs of older employees who want to stay on the job on either a full-time or part-time basis."[16]

The programs and policies recommended were all addressed to the self-fulfilling prophecies of dead end and decline. Though personnel managers acknowledged that most of the problems were caused by "senior employee loss of motivation," they continued to focus on "the difficulties senior workers may experience in learning new skills." The very comments of the managers conveyed both the stereotype and the corporate pressures that create those problems: "We must overcome the stigma associated with older workers and develop formal and informal policies to address plateaus and obsolescence" ... "Many senior employees lose interest and enthusiasm because the corporation has stifled them" ... "Dead-end professionals are generally those who have learned that doing what you are told ensures longevity and that taking risks is risky business. Bringing out innovative ideas from senior managers is a problem" ... "The company must convince them that they are slipping in performance. In some cases, we must persuade senior workers that they will not die as soon as they retire" and "We have no alternative but to demean a person's performance and force him or her to step down or out."

While the authors of the report, Professors Benson Rosen and Thomas Jerdee, and some of the managers could conceive of creating "new roles for senior employees," the "problems" caused by that stigma led them to a circular dead-end reasoning that kept in place an all-or-nothing policy of early retirement as best for the bottom line. The study revealed that most companies were not even attempting "innovative retirement policies," new roles, reassignment. And very few even use actual performance evaluation or medical evaluation to make that all-or-nothing decision. The exceptions were provocative. Instead of focusing on disabilities, a physician consultant to a major aircraft company developed a rating system that allowed the company to look at the actual capacity of people to perform various activities. He found that if you label a person's physical status in positive terms of what he can do instead of in negative terms of what he can't do, companies are more likely to keep that person on. But only 9 percent of companies reported even using performance appraisal as "input" into the retirement decision.

Why haven't more companies adopted a policy that allows people to cut back gradually in their work schedule, or move to new roles of job sharing, as mentors or consultants? Jerdee and Rosen answered their own question: "In the last decade there has been an emphasis on downsizing and companies have been looking at cutting costs by reducing the number of highly paid senior employees on the payroll and substituting cheaper younger employees."

Even though more companies are using part-time workers, the survey showed that most companies were not allowing senior employees to work part time, or to take part in job sharing, tandem staffing, and other flexible scheduling, which was what most older workers had said they wanted. One manager admitted that the senior employee was "somewhat penalized for continuing to work on a part-time basis, rather than opting for full retirement benefits. Because senior employees have often worked for the organization for many years, they have many ideas about what should be done. The organization should better utilize their experience. Even as consultants, the senior employees are often not brought into business meetings where they could offer valuable input."

This manager found an increasing "gap" or "disparity in values" between the senior group and large numbers of his employees under forty. He said: "It should be noted that the senior workers themselves are not creating the problem. The senior employees are a major stabilizing influence on our work force. They hold on to the basic values . . . are conscientious and accept a high degree of responsibility. Because of this, senior employees are very productive. [They] offer a wisdom that is not there among younger employees." [17]

Further, as the number of younger employees began to decrease, a few years down the road companies might need to bring back the very employees who were being offered early retirement. Accordingly, it seemed strange to these researchers that companies were not using tuition reimbursement for more training or different job assignments to prevent burnout or obsolescence, the so-called senior career problems. Most companies which offered tuition and career counseling for younger workers to master new technologies did not encourage or often even permit older employees to continue developing in such ways. "The costs of having people who are at a stage in their career where they feel like they are stagnating and they just start marking time" were not considered.

Almost half the managers reported that "plateaued" or "obsolescent" senior employees were moderate or serious "problems" in their organization. But "career plateaus" were, in fact, *defined* as the "cutoff of advancement opportunities." Career "obsolescence" was *defined* as "a situation where employees fall behind in their ability to use new techniques or master new skills." Clearly, the absence of encouragement or opportunity for the older worker to develop new skills, or move into new roles, would cause such problems—"Year after year you are passed over until it is obvious that you are not going anywhere." Research showed that many older employees would "love the opportunity to take on new roles, would welcome the chance to become involved in developing younger employees and to take on responsibility for special projects." But Rosen and Jerdee concluded that today's organizations "apparently do not have the flexibility to allow them to do these things."[18]

It becomes clear from all these surveys that a different approach to age and different policies of work would be necessary for most people to want to extend their careers. People approaching fifty now seem to *prefer* early retirement because they want a release from "rigid schedules and job related stress." Most said that they might extend their careers if their employers felt that they were making "a significant and valued contribution," but only under "more flexible work arrangements." Such arrangements would have to start with systematic annual performance reviews, and training and development opportunities for older as well as younger employees. "Late career options" envisaged by these researchers included job sharing, internal "temporary" help pools, retirement phase-in options, and training and mentoring roles for senior managers. And the few companies that have implemented such arrangements have found concrete corporate payoffs: increased productivity, improved morale, reduced start-up costs, lower pension costs, lower turnover rates, longer paybacks for training investments, and "full utilization of valued human resources."

Other "career-extending" and "career renewal" strategies that could replace "all-ornone" early retirement were pinpointed in further research by Rosen and Jerdee. In their later papers, they no longer accepted at face value the so-called problems of "late career management"; that is, the equation of age with decline in job performance, "obsolescence," or "burn-out plateau." Reviewing over sixty studies, they found that age is, in fact, positively related to most job attitudes. Some studies found older workers more committed than younger workers. Less turnover was found with age, and more overall job satisfaction.[19] Perceptions that job performance declines with age were also not substantiated by their research findings; while speed may decline with age, broad general abilities do not. When subjective criteria were used, a small decline was detected. However, "small declines in specific skills and abilities associated with aging appear to have little appreciable effect on job performance."[20]

And yet, Rosen and Jerdee found, "the fact remains that older workers do encounter career problems." Their research revealed that many of these problems were actually caused by "erroneous age stereotypes; that is, widely held beliefs about the limitations of older workers . . . 'deadwood,' 'out to pasture,' 'on the shelf,' and 'over the hill.' " When they presented managers with a series of hypothetical incidents, depicting younger and older employees under identical circumstances, the managers, viewing older workers as more rigid and resistant to change, gave them less feedback and less chance to improve on poor performance, and denied a request for training funds recommended for an identically situated younger employee. They were much more likely to send a younger worker whose skills had grown obsolete to a retraining course.

Hence the vicious circle: stereotypes regarding older employees' lower abilities, motivation, and learning capacity lead to restricted opportunities for training and development, and thus to "obsolescence" and career stagnation, to blocked promotion ladders and career plateaus. The perceptions that older workers were unable to meet job requirements, unwilling to adjust to change, and incapable of mastering new methods and procedures, "contribute to major mid- and late-career problems. Rather than watch their skills grow obsolete due to organizational neglect, many older workers opt for early retirement. . . . Others who for financial reasons cannot afford to retire early, remain on the sidelines . . . trapped in dead-end careers." And the critical juncture, leading to continued growth with age for some and "obsolescence, stagnation, and career decline" for others, is the period around age forty.

As they approached later life, those people who were still focused on status, recognition, and competitiveness were especially likely to report medical symptoms of strain and "career burnout." Once an employee was "marked as not promotable, a cycle of withheld career development opportunities, obsolescence and stagnation can be created." Rosen and Jerdee found that when "plateaued" managers were assigned challenging, satisfying, clearly defined jobs, they continued to maintain a high level of performance.[21] But "even the most ambitious and productive employee, once branded as plateaued, can fall into a corporate Catch-22 trap." It was still a stunning exception when a company like General Electric retrained older engineers whose skills were obsolete rather than replacing them with younger, more up-to-date engineers —even though retraining costs were estimated to be less than one third the cost of hiring new employees.[22] The *easy* way around the "problems" that the age mystique, in effect, creates is simply to encourage older workers to accept early retirement.

Currently, over half of American men and women are out of the labor force before age sixty-three and four fifths are out before their sixties are over. Between 1963 and 1983, the labor force participation rate of men aged sixty-two to sixty-four dropped almost 30 percent. A more recent survey by Rosen and Jerdee of managers and executives found that almost 40 percent planned to retire at or before sixty, with many opting for as early as fifty-five.[23] Even with the abolition of mandatory retirement, many organizations squeeze people out before they are ready to go, Rosen and Jerdee concluded. Despite the new law, managers can still exert pressures, subtle and not so subtle, on senior employees to retire voluntarily. They may still legally terminate senior employees in cases of documented need, such as organizational downsizing or failing individual performance. As Rosen and Jerdee put it: "How much choice does the individual senior employee really have? What procedures are available and used to protect individuals from unwanted pressures to retire? Are appeals procedures available to senior employees who have been denied opportunities to participate in various alternatives to complete retirement at a specified age?"[24]

It is significant that age bias complaints filed in federal and state agencies have more than doubled over the last decade . But the stereotype that restricts all our thinking about real possibilities of continuing to grow and develop after fifty, sixty, seventy, still keeps most older people from using the law, as women and minorities have, to challenge those practices of age discrimination which lead to career plateaus, obsolescence, and premature retirement. The law requires equal training and development opportunities for employees *of all ages.* Denying or limiting options for older workers to participate in "fast track" development programs or other training opportunities geared toward younger workers should be grounds for an age bias lawsuit. So should the denial of part-time and job-sharing alternatives to an all-or-nothing retirement—at levels commensurate with the older worker's actual abilities and training. But as it is now, even companies with such options still make the older worker retire from his own level, offering him part-time or consulting work at a much lower wage level, on a "temporary" basis. And, predictably, the personnel managers reported that the "stigma" attached to such jobs was such that most older workers did not find them an acceptable alternative to retirement for very long.

What surprised Rosen and Jerdee the most, however, was the fact that companies had not even attempted to evaluate the costs and benefits of providing new or further training for their "late career employees." They simply did not think of older workers in terms of the genuine changing bottom-line needs of the organization. And this blind spot is strange indeed, in the face of mounting shortages of technical, administrative, executive, and professional people as well as service workers in every field, the predictions of fewer and fewer young people able to fill those jobs in the next twenty-five years, and the increasing need for independent judgment and responsibility in service jobs, as compared to physical strength and routine following of orders. The mounting numbers of able, experienced men and women in their sixties who can look forward to ten, fifteen, or twenty years more of active life should be perceived as a solution rather than a problem. But the mystique of age is both cause and effect of that blind spot. If real work is seen only in terms of youth, or "young" middle age, men or women who no longer pass as young are not seen in terms of their actual abilities for work at all. Their new or different strengths in age are seen only as deficits.

It is an inexorable progression. Barred from continuing to participate in the mainstream work of society, at levels that would really use the abilities of their age and experience, older people inevitably are diminished of personhood. They are no longer perceived as active producers and shapers of the society, but as passive dependents on our compassion, and on the services that make and keep them dependent. It should not be surprising that, contemptuously denied the training that would let them master new technologies, and not consulted or used for their experience and wisdom, they might not want to continue in a rigid nine to five job if they had the option of retirement without desperate financial sacrifice, and might not be attracted to menial, low-paying jobs with even less autonomy and status. But those "human resource managers" in their forties simply do not see men and women over sixty as *people* like themselves in a new stage of development.

The all-or-nothing model of work or retirement —and some of the well-meaning attempts to "manage" the so-called incompetence or deficits of older workers—keeps us from taking seriously our own evolving strengths. Even well-intentioned advocates lock us into what in effect are "failure" models.[25] The incompetence model, focusing only on the deficits some older people have in comparison to youth, in its very attempt to relieve distress creates self-fulfilling prophecies of failure. If you refuse to buy into that compassionate model, "the only way to succeed at growing old is to stay middle-aged, or better yet, eternally young. Clearly, those who cannot continue to behave as though they were middle-aged or younger have 'failed.' "[26]

Any actual physical disability or mistake or temporary failure (no matter how irrelevant to the ability to carry on the work or career) is exaggerated by this process, in which finally we buy into that stereotype which holds that our potential for growth, development, and continuing engagement virtually disappears when we are "disabled" by age. People who counsel older men or women from such a focus, and those of us who accept it, become the victims of the low goals we then set for ourselves. Underestimating our potential for further participation in society, we narrow our own perception of choices, and gradually restrict our exercise of autonomy to routines of daily living, and the television set.

The pressures and pains of those seductive retirement offers, and the shame and rage that piteous mystique inevitably represses, finally make us collude in our own exile. They are hard to resist alone. A recent study of *Fortune* 100 companies by the General Accounting Office found that approximately 80 percent sponsored an "exit incentive" program between 1979 and 1988, with the percentage of those companies requiring waivers not to sue for age discrimination nearly tripling in that period.

Even so-called creative professionals can be induced by the age mystique into premature retirement. Increasingly, in my new bicoastal life, I encountered vital, able Hollywood screenwriters and directors in their fifties and sixties, with successful comedies, series, and dramas behind them, who decided to "get out of the industry" because twenty-seven-year-old editors or program vice-presidents "don't even see me," "can't hear what I'm saying," "don't get the meaning somehow."

There are rare exceptions. Though uninsurable because of emphysema, John Huston, at eighty, directed James Joyce's *The Dead* from a wheelchair—necessary to hold the oxygen tank without which he could not breathe for more than twenty minutes. He teamed with a younger co-producer, Weilland Schulz-Keil; his thirty-six-year-old son, Tony Huston, as co-writer; and his daughter Anjelica, starring. On a typical day when shooting ended early on *The Dead* because Huston got the crucial scene right in eighteen minutes, his sound mixer commented: "I just did a picture in Chicago where we had fourteen-hour days. Huston gets what he wants in eight hours. Also he knows what he wants. Do you know how rare that is?"

Older men in business often discover that they, too, have become invisible. When the company Albert Hunt was working for at fifty-five moved out of state, he found that his thirty-odd years of experience in sales and administrative jobs suddenly "didn't count." Employment agencies "just didn't cater to older people," he said. Through the "Ability Is Ageless" Job Fair, sponsored by the New York City Department for Aging's Senior Employment Services and the Chamber of Commerce, which gives employers the opportunity to see older people and break down some of the myths, he finally got a job as assistant sales manager for an import company.

Tired of the "revolving door of the younger worker," 130 companies came looking for "mature" workers at that fair in 1989, a 30 percent increase over the previous year. At first they seemed mainly concerned about the physical ability of older workers to keep up with job demands. But a marketing specialist at Interim Systems, a temporary agency, confirmed that close to 75 percent of New York's 1.3 million residents over sixty are in good health. "When you talk about seniors, you are not talking about people who are sick any more," she said, citing a woman messenger who was ninety years old. The "voluntarily" retired workers now flocking by the thousands to such fairs want to go back to work, not just for the money. "I'm alive again," said Arthur Fleming, a retired accountant now working for an insurance company. "I have purpose, I have security, I feel good about myself."

On the other hand, the mystique of age keeps us apologizing and denying that in age we might not want to work in the way we had to when we were young. In fact, we might have different abilities now that could better serve companies and institutions. Taking ourselves seriously in this new stage of life, we might make demands of the work we want to do different from the more onerous earlier demands of family survival, the immediate material improvement of our lifestyle, or the career ambitions that drove us in the past.

In arguing that investment in the training and development of older workers makes bottom-line sense, Rosen and Jerdee cited research showing that older workers have proven to be more stable, reliable, and careful; have lower absentee turnover rates (the average length of service for employees between fifty and sixty is fifteen years); and have very low accident rates. (Workers fifty-five and over make up 13.6 percent of the labor force but have only 9.7 percent of work place injuries.) Their research also indicated that older workers "enjoy higher morale and a greater sense of organizational commitment and job involvement than workers in any other age group." [27]

Thus companies like McDonald's and Travelers Insurance—faced with shortages of service workers, and finding that teenagers out of high school are unable to meet the demands for "independent judgment," "responsibility," and "capacity to analyze a situation" required for the new service jobs—are hiring back retired workers, as temporary replacements, in peak times, without benefits or security. These jobs are not likely to lead anywhere or to provide status. The autonomy they provide is simply the ability to control one's own hours or days of work, while continuing to earn and function in society.

● ● ●

Through all the paradoxes and contradictory complexities of the retirement research, one element pierces through again and again, the only constant. And that is the element of *choice.* Personal, individual control over the situation—regardless of when retirement takes place or how a job is left, replaced, or continued—makes the difference, in terms of health and life satisfaction.[28] The question is: How and why do men and women choose to work past retirement, when the whip of career no longer drives them? Can work fulfill personal needs and real needs of society when it is freed from that drive? The important consideration, then, may not be, is there life after work, but how might work, freed from the drives for power and success that have dominated men (and now women) through midlife, serve the evolving needs of human life in these new years of age?

A recent Louis Harris Poll of senior citizens indicated that even bombarded as they are by the mystique of age, most people over sixty-five see themselves not as dependent helpless victims but as "resilient survivors who want to keep making significant contributions to the mainstream of American life." [29] But they do not necessarily want to do so in the same way they did when they were twenty-five or fifty, whether or not it is a question of retirement—though the prospect of retirement sometimes forced the decision to "move to a new place," "try one last thing before I'm through."

For most of his adult life Wilbur Daniels had been a labor organizer, rising high in the ranks of ILGWU officialdom. He retired—and embarked on a completely new career:

When I heard myself telling the kids I worked with at the union office now for the third time that an idea was no good, we did that ten years ago, we don't have to invent the wheel all over again, I knew it was time to get out. But it all happened because of an umbrella. A guy I used to negotiate with across the table, we'd given each other a hard time but we became friends, took me out to lunch, and then to see his new office. He'd forgotten his umbrella, and walking back to get it he suddenly said, "What do you want to do when you grow up, Willy?" I laughed. It was like he'd read my mind.

Well, he asked me to try out for the job of running this foundation. Instead of trying to get more money out of people, I'd be in charge of spending it, for research and other projects that would advance the welfare of mankind. The funny thing is, I didn't have any foundation expertise, but they picked me for my people skills, and general shrewdness as a negotiator, I don't take any bullshit. It's been my Ponce de León. I mean, I'm learning again, all the time.

I'd really stopped learning in my job, I'd done it all so many times. It's given me such a taste for new adventure I began to change my whole life.

Given the present options open to them, and the general pressures and expectations of retirement, Americans through the 1980s were almost evenly divided on whether or not they would prefer to work past the age of sixty-five. According to the Harris survey, a "greater availability of regular full-time jobs" would interest less than half of workers facing their sixties (44 percent). But 80 percent would work if there were greater availability of part-time jobs—a job that allows a day or two a week to work at home, a job shared with someone else, or a flexible schedule that requires a total of seventy hours every two weeks. Only on jobs where people "learn new things," have "a lot of freedom to decide how to do my own work," and "have a say in important decisions" would substantially greater numbers prefer to keep on working full time rather than "retire completely."[30] Thus, with the age mystique still firmly in place, it appears that we must be truly exceptional, or exceptionally lucky, to keep on working in ways that are satisfying and productive.

I think about the many men and women I interviewed who have continued working past the usual age of retirement—and well beyond. They keep "moving on." They no longer do things the wasteful way they did when they were young. They, more and more, get the whole picture, with less and less patience for irrelevant detail. And, in the end, the ones who keep on growing seem to be moved to a deep embrace of what is "good" and "true," even if not conventionally moral, even at the risk of life and reputation. (Many of the young scientists who developed the atom bomb devoted their old age to warnings of nuclear holocaust and efforts for nuclear freeze and arms control.)

It is only by accident, now, that any U.S. industry, or government, fully uses these gifts of age, or that we ourselves find ways to keep on developing and using them. Yet it was men well over sixty who blew the whistle on Watergate, and acted, across party lines, to save the constitutional rights and the rule of law it threatened. It was Supreme Court Justices in their eighties—Brennan, Marshall, Blackmun—who defended freedom of religious conscience and speech, principles of equality, rights of dissent against the political pressures and dissimulations that sought to undermine them during the 1980s. It was Justice Harry Blackmun who warned of the danger to the "freedom and equality" of the new generation of women—and to the respect and authority of the Supreme Court itself—when, in the summer of 1989, a majority of the Court, mainly its younger members, voted to retreat from the constitutional protection of a woman's right to reproductive choice in the *Webster* decision, allowing states to restrict or deny abortion again.

The fact that Supreme Court Justices are among the longest-lived of all Americans is of interest here. They must continue to respond to new challenges in their work; they continue to be needed and to participate in the mainstream of society; they continue to be nourished by support and bonds of peers and younger men and women who respect them. And they are valued for the wisdom of their age, for their integrity and authenticity, for their sense of the true and the good. They are protected from rigidity and self-contempt by the ever-evolving demands of their work, and the respect it engenders. Rabbis are another such long-lived group, along with symphony conductors and artists.

Thinking about the groups that live the longest in our society, one senses the following: they are all involved in work that keeps them developing and using their abilities to the fullest. And their work demands and uses the qualities that emerge in age—the ability to see the picture whole, and its meaning deep, and to tell it true: wisdom. And it is *real* work that is needed and for which they are respected. They do not have to pretend to be young. They are not expected to decline in age in the qualities for which they are valued—and they do not. (In view of the stereotype of memory failure and age, how do symphony conductors in their seventies and eighties —Toscanini, Stokowski, Bernstein—accomplish the feat of learning whole new symphonies?)

Consider the depth and knowledge of historical precedents involved in a Supreme Court decision. Of course, clerks and aides do the detailed research and documentation of the cases. But, as we have seen from the research, the comprehension of the meaning as a whole is where age excels over youth. The justices' days are organized by complex purpose, and their work continually demands the exercise of individual choice and flexible response to change. They control the pace of their work, it is not the same work every day, and it demands their highest, most human capacities— reason and profound feeling. Many of the Supreme Court Justices continue functioning despite heart conditions and bouts of cancer. The continued exercise of those high human abilities is clearly conducive to their own continued vitality in age and longer survival—and, it would seem, to the vitality and survival of human society.

I do not think it is an accident that Supreme Court Justices are among the most visibly longest-living people in the United States. They are, of course, continually challenged by the new cases our constantly changing society brings to them for judgment, in ever-changing political and moral contexts. I got a concrete sense of this from personal conversations with Justice William Brennan, whom I had long admired, in his eighty-third year. His biographer, Stephen Vermiel, shared these observations with me from an intensive study of Brennan's life and development in his thirty-three years on the Supreme Court:

Justice Brennan is continually using his mind on something that is an absolute passion with him. He doesn't have a lot of other interests. He watches a little golf on TV, reads a little history, used to walk to the Court every morning with Judge [David] Bazelon, now he puts in a half hour on his exercise bicycle. His world is law and the Court. And the cases—which he picks personally, he doesn't delegate that to law clerks as some of the other justices do— continually challenge him to grow.

When he came on the Court, in the fifties, the term "sex discrimination" did not exist. He had a traditional marriage, his wife raised the kids, cooked the meals, the very concept of women as professionals, entitled to equal opportunity, wouldn't even have crossed his mind. But in the early seventies he was one of the first to interpret the Fourteenth Amendment, the equal protection clause, to prohibit sex discrimination as well as race discrimination. Until then no one had even tried to say it was unconstitutional to discriminate against women on the basis of sex. In 1971, Justice Brennan introduced the concept that not only was it unconstitutional for the U.S. government or the states to discriminate in employment against women but that the circumstances used to justify denial of opportunity to women should be subjected to the same "strict scrutiny" as racial matters.

When he came on the Court, it was interpreting the Constitution to desegregate schools, lunch counters, and public swimming pools. But nobody was talking about, even thinking about, creating positive employment opportunities for minorities, much less women. The Civil Rights Act of 1964 didn't specify or even talk about affirmative action. He was adapting constitutional thinking to new situations that hadn't existed before when he started writing the affirmative action decisions at the end of the seventies. The cases that had brought him to prominence, as a labor lawyer in Newark, representing employers' interests, reforming New Jersey court corruption, didn't deal with big social issues.

The man keeps growing. Otherwise, an eighty-three-year-old veteran of World War II wouldn't be defending your right to burn the flag. Otherwise, how explain his memo in 1963, urging the Court in the *Griswold* case to base the "right of privacy" in birth control, and later abortion, on the Ninth Amendment, which states that rights not specifically spelled out in the Constitution are "retained by the people."

Discussing cases, it's amazing how crisply he sees things. Maybe because he knows now what the cases are really about, maybe he isn't so concerned with irrelevant details. I'll study the case, ask him what about this angle, that angle, it's not that complicated to him. He certainly seems to see the cases more clearly than his law clerks do, young hotshots though they may be, 107 law clerks in 33 years have learned from him.

Justice Brennan conquered a bout of throat cancer at seventy-eight, with no recurrence, and then suffered a very mild stroke, which for a while affected his right hand. He couldn't give his usual firm handshake for a couple of years. On his evenings out, at eighty-three, he reveled in good food and drink, good lively talk and laughs—with old friends and new. "Is he lively enough for Bill?" asked my cousin Mickey Bazelon, about a man I wanted to bring to dinner with the Brennans. And after Brennan finally had to retire, the younger justices appointed for ideological conservatism claimed Brennan's influence when, in 1992, they upheld women's basic right to choose.

On the other hand, Justice Potter Stewart, who retired at seventy, "deteriorated like a bullet hit him when he left the Court," an acquaintance recounted. "After a year, he was visibly showing the symptoms of Hodgkin's disease. He would come back to the Supreme Court Building, all hunched over, his hair white, and it affected the other justices, so many of them like Brennan older than he, like seeing a ghost."

Employers have not yet asked how they might use the emergent qualities—the wisdom—of older men and women on the cutting edge of an evolving work force. But in places where, for whatever reason, this is happening—and from older people thinking in new ways about the work they want to do now—we get some hints.

Ben Kaplan was officially retired as Justice of the Supreme Court of Massachusetts at seventy, but two years later was called back to serve as full-time sitting judge of the next grade appellate court. The chief justice has the power to so call back retired judges in Massachusetts where, as in other states, there are never enough judges to catch up with the caseload. But such judges must be reappointed every three months. When word gets around that they are "getting gaga" or "hard of hearing," the letter doesn't come. At seventy-nine, Ben Kaplan's opinions had become increasingly more elegant and wise, his juniors told me.

I was curious as to how his judging had changed, in quality or pace, and how, perhaps, he used his young law clerks to make up for any deficits. "They're not that useful," he told me. "They don't have the experience, and they're so eager to impress, they load the opinion with so many citations that the meaning is obscured." Kaplan was not aware of any change in his own technical command of the law. But he had noticed, surprisingly, a change in pace—not a slowing down but a stronger, quicker path to the core of the decision. "I see the way clearer to the essential point than I did when I was younger," he said.

That ability to pierce through the bullshit to the real meaning—that nose for authenticity and insistence on being finally one's authentic self —may be why older people get reputations as crotchety troublemakers, "truthtellers." But such a nose for authenticity and meaning could possibly be of great value to an institution. For us, as individuals growing older, to try to keep on working the same way we did when we were young—to try to pretend that we are still young —may be to miss the signs of what we are growing into, the new work we might be capable of, and enjoy, to our own and our institutions' greater profit. "I've done that, I can't get that out of myself anymore," I kept hearing over and over again, from college professor, advertising executive, musician, nurse, feeling the need in their sixties, seventies, to move on to "something else," something new. The judge and the artist and the symphony conductor are able to keep moving on to "something new" in the same field. But for the rest of us, denial of the experience of our years and forced retirement may lead us to move into new fields.

The copious research cited earlier in this book shows that purposes and goals shaping one's days—and keeping one tied into society—are essential to vital age. But "use it or lose it" is only part of this. There is a continued development implied here that builds on and extends experience into wisdom. The increasingly authentic self somehow demands expression in work, goals that are *real for oneself.* "I can't pretend to go through those motions any more," says the lawyer. "I'm just not that interested in the agonies of adolescent rebellion any more," says the dean, retiring to concentrate on his own research again. "They have to get someone else to head the department, the title and the pay notwithstanding. Administration is a bore," says the chemist. "No, I don't play the same way I did when I was young," says the musician. Should he try his best to deny that, hide it, mourn the loss—or pay more attention to the new and different way he is able to do it now? It would be like the women lawyers, or rabbis or lieutenants, who at first tried to pitch their voices to male cadence, and then some got the nerve to pay attention to, and develop, their own style.

Ellen Langer has done many experiments at Harvard questioning the assumption that growing old is an irreversible, linear process of physiological decline. With age, the body diminishes in importance as a determining factor in a person's development, she has posited. If the mind continues to grow,

> the physical aging process need not operate like a force of gravity, inevitably dragging the person downward toward the end of life. . . . [But] to make changes in later life one must fight against all sorts of . . . preconceptions before they are "recognized" as growth.
> It is only when people are behaving "mindlessly" and thereby are relying on categories that were drawn in the past that . . . endpoints seem fixed. . . . A "mindful" mind can continually create expanded possibilities which influence the state of the body.
> Mindfulness is the type of cognitive activity that occurs when an individual deals with a new environment or deals with an old environment in new ways. . . . With age, the apparently routinized character of life dulls the person's sense of vital involvement. Mindful involvement has an enlivening effect upon

the person, while mindless involvement has a deadening one.[31]

Those earlier experiments in the nursing home, where very simple "mindful" acts such as watering plants and arranging the furniture made people age differently and live longer, convinced Langer and her colleagues that people should have "the opportunity to create their own development rather than being trapped in a pattern that is inescapably played out." In effect, she assumed it should be possible to completely reverse age and re-create youth. So she advertised for elderly men to take part in an experiment, and took those men, approximately seventy-five years old, on a week's retreat, with the hypothesis that if they would mindfully assume that they were fifty-five again, they would become "more bodily youthful."

The experimental group was told to be "psychologically where they were about 20 years ago"—to eat, talk, exercise, and think each minute as if they were fifty-five again, to talk about events that happened twenty years ago in the present tense. A control group going through the same days was told to focus on their past of twenty years ago, but from their present selves, not denying that they were now here, at seventy-five.

Half the eighty men were asked to fill out questionnaires, told to take part in discussions, complete tests of physical strength, perception, cognition, auditory and visual thresholds, and write about their likes, dislikes, attitudes, relationships, joys, homes, and so on, as if they were fifty-five again. They were not to include any of their history past that date. And they were told that they might well thereby improve their physical health as well as their psychological well-being—and "feel as well as you did in 1959." The other group did the same thing, but working up to the present at their actual age.

But the results were not what Langer expected. Both groups showed improvements in hearing, in memory, and in other tests of psychological functioning. Of course, all the men, in both groups, were not only actively involved in these tests and discussions during the five days but were actively involved in serving their own meals and cleaning up, etc. And the men in both groups were "treated with more respect and given more responsibility than is typical for the old." Thus, in line with her earlier experiments, she found that making demands that challenged these elderly men "apparently reverses many debilitations of old age."

But the group told to "become 55 again" did not show the dramatic improvement of the other group, and what differences did emerge were not necessarily positive. They became increasingly hostile and unfriendly. The second group that did the exercises as their present selves became more and more friendly and emotionally expressive.

In retrospect, Langer realized that her experiment itself was a manifestation of age bias in its determined search for the fountain of youth: those instructions to the seventy-five-year-old men to become fifty-five again. Would the seventy-year-old want to give up the experience and matured consciousness of his years, even though some of the health and strength of the earlier time is desirable? The real explanation of the improvement of both groups, she concluded, was the "mindful" activity required of them each day.

Thus, the view of aging as inevitable decline constrains psychologists' ideas about the limits of human capacity, constrains employers' ideas about the age limits of productive work, and constrains everyone's ideas about the limits of our own personal growth. "New theory and research suggest that there may be many more possibilities than we can now know," Langer concluded. It is only if we can conceive of such possibilities of vital change or growth in these new years of age that we, or any of our institutions, will take the steps necessary to let it happen.

The categorical imperative of work versus retirement begs the question. Much research has shown that the most important predictors of vital age are *satisfying work* and *complexity of purpose.* Those who continue working at jobs that have become mindless and routine forfeit the fountain of age. But the possibilities of further, vital growth can be seen wherever people continue after sixty in work that demands continual mindfulness. They also happen when people are challenged by retirement to find, or create, new projects whose very lack of imposed structure demands continual mindfulness. The mindlessness that results when people continue in the same routine jobs, or in jobs that no longer challenge them, may explain why many blue-collar workers, and teachers who do not develop new courses, opt for early retirement. The mindlessness of unstructured, purposeless days may also explain why retirement, for some people but not others, leads to depression, decline, suicide, or premature death.

A funny thing has been happening to the Peace Corps: more and more of the volunteers now have gray hair. The average age was twenty-three when John F. Kennedy started the Peace Corps in 1961. Today, over 500 of the 6,300 recruits are from fifty to seventy-eight years old, and someone recently retired at eighty-six. Odi Long joined the Peace Corps at sixty-five after he retired from his job as a lineman at Illinois Bell. Patricia "Sam" Udall went in at fifty-seven, and came out at sixty-one to start a new career as Senior Volunteer Facilitator. She told me:

The Peace Corps was designed for people fresh out of college; they'd get this vigorous Outward Bound physical training, and be sent off to Mozambique to dig wells. Many had never held jobs before, they wanted this adventure before going into their careers or professional training. Now we get the older persons at the end of their careers, with enormous experience professionally and in life. Their business skills are more and more what's needed in the Third World countries, where most people live in cities now and the problems are more complex than digging wells.

We've discontinued that vigorous physical training because it isn't appropriate any more. The major difference with the older volunteers is that they have the skills and experience the young don't have, and they insist on being constructive. At sixty-five, they've been pushed out of the American job market, and the Peace Corps offers an opportunity for them to be very productive and continue using their skills in society. It seems to revitalize older people, though physically it's still hard, and harder still to learn a new language, like Swahili.

One big thing we've got going for us is the respect for age in most of the countries we go to. We hear and learn a lot that younger people don't because people in other countries aren't that comfortable talking to younger people. The worst problem is that older people want to see results, because they recognize their time is finite, how they use their time is vital, they're not as willing to just be laid back, hang out. They take more risks too, if they've had to sell their homes, or quit their jobs, or have a health condition. But people over fifty don't seem to get "separated" from the Peace Corps at any higher rate than at thirty-five. The problems of placing an older person with a history of high blood pressure aren't any greater than a young one with a history of asthma.

At sixty-six, Bernie Lovitsky, an executive search consultant in Atlanta, recalled his depression, and deterioration of confidence, in his years of early retirement before he joined the Peace Corps. He had sold his discount store in Michigan after his wife died, and moved to a California beach community:

I wasn't working, and got very depressed, just sitting around in that beach lifestyle. Everyone seemed to be running away, living on the surface. I thought of starting a new business, but I was losing confidence I could do it again. Driving down the freeway, I heard a public service announcement about joining the Peace Corps, age didn't matter. Maybe the yuppies weren't volunteering enough.

They assigned me to Tonga and my daughter was vehemently opposed: "You may never see your grandchildren alive." The language training was hard, but I was determined to understand these people and have them understand me. I'd join their wedding processions, clap when they did, eat what they ate. I went to their feasts and fireworks, and danced with the women and men. I was supposed to help them set up a wholesale grocery distribution system. I found out they were being taken advantage of, high prices, bad merchandise. In two years their cooperative went from $20,000 a year to $2 million. Today they're doing $4 million and the business is being run by the Tongan people themselves.

Today, in my mid-sixties, I have more energy than I've ever had in my life. After my two and a half years as a Peace Corps volunteer, I got myself a job in an executive search firm, met my second wife who'll never stop either—we set up the only couples' shelter for the homeless, we've got fourteen hundred volunteers. I'll never retire again. But what's important to me now is not the work I do for money but what I do that isn't just materialistic, that really touches people's lives and makes a difference.

It would be wrong, I think, to see experiences like Lovitsky's as merely a chance to "start over again." There's an evolution involved here: the work of one's age does have to use one's human abilities, to challenge mindfulness, to have some personal meaning, to keep one part of society. But does it have to be paid, if one's needs are sufficiently met by other means? Does it have to have status to be real? Does it have to give one power?

This gets very complicated, in a society where money is the definition of worth, status, and power—and men's lives, and to some degree now women's, are judged by their scores in that race. Men are not necessarily being forced or seduced out of middle- or upper-level jobs by early retirement because they no longer have the ability but because younger men can be had for less money, and want their titles and power. From necessity—or some evolution of the self that seems more painful for men—those who continue to grow in age seem no longer driven by pursuit of the power that obsessed or exhilarated their youth. The continued pursuit of such power, or the failure to evolve beyond it, can equate retirement with suicide.

Ernest Hemingway evidently killed himself when, in his early sixties, he could no longer compete in the physical exploits, the machismo courting of danger in bullfighting and big-game hunting, and the carousing and sexual exploits that still defined his image of himself. He was also deeply depressed, suffering from cancer, and unable to write. A. E. Hotchner quotes Hemingway a few months before his suicide as saying, " . . . what the hell? What does a man care about? Staying healthy. Working good. Eating and drinking with his friends. Enjoying himself in bed. I haven't any of them. Do you understand, goddamn it? None of them."

Down through the ages, great plays and novels have been written about men's futile attempts to hold on to such power in age, or managing to transcend it, before their deaths, for some other, deeper meaning of what it is to be a man. King Lear, struggling to keep on playing king, and demanding flattery from his daughters after he has given them control of the lands, moneys, and troops that were his power, goes mad. But retirement can also *force* a restructuring of life to new purpose that does involve work, in and for society; that uses men's abilities in new ways. Such work may or may not be rewarded by money, status, or power. It often is found only after a man (or woman) has given up that pursuit. In fact, many of the people I interviewed who were continuing to work had already lost interest in the pursuit of power.

It was not easy for them to find meaningful work in their sixties or seventies when age was defined by the loss of youthful power—and that power was the gatekeeper. But one thing is clear. If our abilities are to continue to evolve, they must be used in some purposeful way. For vital age, a project that structures one's days and keeps alive those all-important human ties and sense of personhood is essential. Those forced by retirement to find such projects for themselves went in and out, into or around conventional lines of career and profession; but what they are doing may be on the cutting edge of the evolution of work. If the "pursuit of happiness" in our own or America's youth is reduced to the untrammeled pursuit of material wealth and power, age must surely require us to pursue other, deeper values in our work.

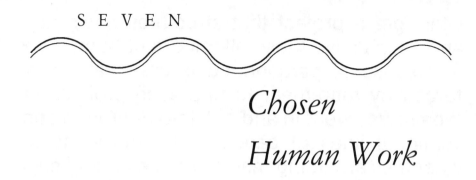

Chosen
Human Work

As I continued my search, I began to suspect that vital age involves some further crossover of the polarization of love and work, female and male. It was interesting to me that the most striking of my interviewees were somehow able to cross that divide, using feelings in their work, working now from choice (love), moving beyond old obsessions and restrictions. And in a few cases, where companies or institutions were wise enough to use this new wholeness, the organization also evolved in surprising ways, with specific bottom-line profits to show for it.

But the measures and values of such work may not be the previous ones. If survival is met by Social Security, the insistence on personal choice in pace and purpose marks the chosen work of age as a new liberation. It transcends both physical survival and conventional roles, evolving as the realization of a unique personhood in work that extends into the human future. Erikson called this "generativity versus stagnation."

Such work is not readily available although, as many observers have noted, it is easier for women to find or improvise purposeful projects in age (in addition to the routine daily housework that remains) than it is for men, who have never had to improvise that way, or been free to. The problem, and the possibility, of retirement for men is finding work that they can take seriously beyond the pursuit of power, which still controls most gates. But if age liberates them from that race personally, it may also enable them to slip through those gates, no longer a threat to others' power. Among the men I interviewed, this almost always seemed to involve a physical move from the place or field where they won or lost their own power. Otherwise, they got stuck in the pain and rage of its loss, continually reminded by their treatment of the contemptuous terms that game reserves for its losers, and kept thereby from moving on—from truly growing. For winners and losers of the power game, it seemed easier to find new terms in another field.

But that takes a mindful search, a willingness to risk the unknown again. It requires a new boldness, an ability to suffer the pain of rejection, and not lose confidence—to come back for more. Even in youth, one's armor against such pain is to avoid its risk—or rise above it with a pseudo-pompous arrogance that rejects before it can be rejected. Age must provide a comfort with the self that youth cannot imagine for men or women to take such risks. That many retreat into the isolation of retirement from the world of work altogether and wall themselves off from that larger rejecting society in "leisure world" ghettos is not surprising; it becomes harder and harder to find and sustain purposes and projects as "retirement" stretches out, year after year. But for those with the strengths to find their way beyond the gates of power, retirement can itself be a gateway to new life.

At the 120th birthday party of my friends Sally and Gene Kofke, celebrating their joint 60th birthdays with children, grandchildren, friends, neighbors, and colleagues from the various stages of his career, and hers, I got a clear sense of this shifting focus. Gene had been working for AT&T for thirty years, and was in the top 1 percent management group when he took early retirement at fifty-six, after the giant corporation split off from its component telephone companies. Now sixty, he recalled:

It was a scary decision, especially when you've worked for one big family-type corporation virtually your whole adult life. There's an inertia you build up after all those years—you're accepted, you're comfortable, you're recognized, you've got that corporate identity, and you don't realize how essential that is to your well-being until you strike out on your own and you get a few rejections. You have to learn not to let it get you down.

Sally was a lot more adaptable than I was. Not only was I around a lot more, she had to adapt to supporting me rather than the other way around. I had a vision that I would only work 60 percent of the time and play more, but I quickly realized that you either work full out or you have no control at all. In this new little company I work with now, I'm the most senior partner, by at least twenty-five years—everyone else is around thirty-five. I'm the only one without a Ph.D. They value the experience I bring to the company.

I've certainly had to change. I'm more self-sufficient now. I don't take a lot of things for granted that I used to. I take care of my own chores, the clerical work—actually I like it, the sense of self-sufficiency, that you don't need anyone to shore you up—and a lot of the housework. Now her career is expanding, I manage the house. If the question is, do I feel any loss of power—status power, informational power, the power that's imposed upon you by the way the public sees your organization—I guess I lost a lot of power. But in a way,

I have more power now. I have power over my own life. I don't buy that because you get older, you get less able; but the time you have left is shorter, what I do with the time I have left is important. You exchange one kind of power for another.

Forced out at sixty-three from the magazine job that had been her career for so long, my neighbor in Sag Harbor, Elaine Green, went into panic. She dyed her hair and spent $280 on a mini-skirt when a new young editor replaced her boss, but she couldn't really pass as young any longer. She would complain bitterly of her loneliness and depression, working alone at her typewriter at home, trying to freelance. "Even when I was a young mother at home with my children, there were other mothers to talk to." It had been some months since I had seen her when she dropped into my kitchen, talking so crisply and with such spirit that I didn't realize until she called it to my attention that she had a crisp new jawline. She had celebrated her sixty-fifth birthday with a face-lift. But, in fact, her new liberation had come from strengths called into being by that forced retirement which made the face-lift almost irrelevant.

I was so depressed by the hostility of the young women who took over the magazine, by those other young women not even looking at me when I went in for interviews, I felt like a non-person. As if they didn't want to wait on me at the pantyhose counter at Bloomingdale's because I had some disease repelling them that they didn't want to catch from me: my age.

Elaine was less interested in showing off her face-lift than the beautifully illustrated new book on decorating she edited as a freelancer, and the ghostwriting job she just turned down because she wanted to write her own book.

I was in a low blood pressure, plush-lined rut at the magazine. I'd be there still, with my white hair and my jaw dissolving into wattles, if I hadn't been fired. I had to reinvent myself, and I did. I'm glad now it happened, the challenge of it. It's as if something's been released in me. I know I was very good at what I did, but I feel as if I'm moving in a new way now, it's very exhilarating. It didn't happen because I got the face-lift. I actually got the face-lift because I felt optimistic about moving on to new ways in my life.

Several years later, her old magazine's main competitor brought her in to take advantage of her long experience to give it a new lift.

I met Jean Gollye at a reception of the Women's Forum, one of the new networks of successful women giving each other support and sharing problems as they move up in their careers. Facing fifty, Gollye was so devastated, forced out of her job as the only woman vice-president of the *Fortune* 500 company for whom she worked, that for a year she didn't have the confidence to look for another, or to freelance as a consultant. But back at work now in a different industry, doing public affairs for a major international music publisher, she was having new thoughts about work, and her life. Though she hardly looked like she was facing age (no lines or gray showing), she told me:

I realize now, maybe just in time, that I made a mistake. I made my career my whole life. It was my identity. I was so happy, working for that company, they thought I was good, and I was, and they kept promoting me, and all I thought about was their problems, the company's interests. I didn't pay enough attention to ever having a personal life. I didn't marry. I didn't have children. I had no trouble finding another job when I finally got hold of myself. I'm not that old quite yet, and it's a good job too, and the music industry is fascinating. But I'm not going to define myself by my work anymore. I'm making new friends, I'm going to a gym,

I'm going out to things where I meet different people. I'm working on a personal life for myself.

Like many other men, my old friend Mogey Lazarus had to reinvent himself in new ways, having been forced to retire in his sixties from his business career (chief finance officer of Federated Department Stores). In his seventies now, he was facing retirement again from his innovative volunteer career in health and hospital administration. I hadn't seen him in several years, and his color was so fresh and his face so unharassed-looking that I wondered if he, too, had had a face-lift. He had not. But throughout the many years of his so-called retirement, what had opened up for him personally was a less single-minded obsession with work:

I've changed a lot since I was sixty. When I realized I was going to be at loose ends, I had to find something I could zero in on, some concentrated productive activity, if I was going to keep mentally engaged, or I would fritter away my age with distractions. Until recently, if my calendar wasn't full, I'd be nervous. It was extremely difficult to go from a full, completely structured day to something unstructured—that really scared me—even though what structured it before was mostly not meaning-ful. I had to structure it now myself with things that had meaning for me.

You have to divorce yourself from your for-mer business. There can be second careers, but those careers come to an end, too. I had to retire from the hospital board at seventy-two. In the end, you're left with self-created careers, or projects that maybe shouldn't be called ca-reers and that do not depend on institutions. Maybe that's why writers, musicians, people in the arts who concentrate their efforts have a much easier time than people whose work de-pends on institutional support.

A lot of people when they get older close in, see the same people all the time. I see a lot of different people, make new friends. I have to, to keep my batteries charged. I think the more comfortable you become in older age, the faster you age. You've got to stay a little un-comfortable, keep the antenna out.

At seventy-four, John Kenneth Galbraith, after a long and distinguished career as economist and Harvard professor, with stints of political power as government administrator and ambas-sador, had just finished his second novel and was putting thought and energy into redefining national security and defense, with the end of the Cold War, into "common security" against poverty, crime, and violence. In his living room, he had been meeting with men and women half his age, advising them how the old peace movement, with its focus on nuclear freeze and arms control, might be replaced by a new political movement with a vision of community beyond war, transcending previous boundaries of right and left and single-issue organizational turf. He told me:

When I began to consider the fact that I wasn't going to live forever, I began to think about my grandchildren and whether they would live at all. Up to a certain age, I had an overwhelming preoccupation with my own career, my economic security, my own thoughts. I was preoccupied with myself. Until four or five years ago, it had not crossed my mind that I was not immortal. I always taught in order to write. I never had the courage to try to make it as a writer. By the time I discovered I could make a living as a writer, I was so deeply entrenched as a Harvard professor I just kept on doing it.

But the year before I was due to retire, the BBC asked me to do a series on "The Age of Uncertainty," and I happily gave up teaching and went on the road for two and a half years, with people half my age, taking on a new art form and a whole new world, from the edge of Scotland where my ancestors had been swept off by the sheep in the seventeenth century, to Singapore and the Silicon Valley. So far from feeling old, those years [of early retirement] made both me and my wife feel marvelously young. I could write books now free of the constraints of scholarly obligations.

Galbraith said he had long since gotten the "power bug" out of his system. But many men as well as women today can't seem to do that, even when retirement forces the issue. My young friend Cathy Wright, a brilliant lawyer herself, told me that her father, a powerful CEO, had nearly died of his forced retirement.

He had loved the power and the perks. He had said he looked forward to retirement—he would play golf, go fishing. He didn't do any of those things. My mother had left him, years before; his second wife had died. He sat there in his apartment, alone, and overnight he became old. They replaced him with a much younger man as president, but when the chairman of the board had a stroke, they asked Dad to come back. And he became himself again. Now he never intends to retire. He keeps saying the other guy is still young, he has a lot of learning to do—that guy is fifty, for heaven's sake! But my dad doesn't seem to have any idea of how to live without that power.

The gerontologist Robert Binstock, on the other hand, was forced by two heart attacks and open heart surgery at forty-two to move beyond the power track, and, surprisingly, to make a priority of a late baby:

The heart attack brought me to a new realization that it's my time, my life I'm wasting. It's a non-competitive thing. It's not me vis-à-vis other people, it's me vis-à-vis me. It's what I value for my life. That's a kind of maturity I doubt I'd ever come to without those illnesses. It's not that I go along thinking I'm going to die tomorrow. I don't get angry anymore over things I used to waste time, energy, effort, trying to beat out the competition that I might otherwise just enjoy.

Having a child at forty-six, I'm getting a lot more out of it. I'm not so concerned anymore about being a success or failure in my work. That's not my first priority now. I go out with my daughter on the weekend—I don't give a damn if I don't get the manuscript in by the deadline for the April issue. But if I don't play with her at thirteen months, she'll be fourteen months. I have a new sense of the importance of caring for people, valuing people, even though I can detect deficiencies in them. If I thought before so-and-so is dumb, that's irrelevant if I enjoy him.

I'm even thinking of moving to a university

no one has ever heard of, just for the spirit of adventure. I'm not going to take my identity from the institution anymore. To me, the thought of being in the same place, doing the same thing, fifteen or twenty years from now is stultifying, inherently depressing, even if it's good now. There's something inherently good in the idea that I can change, pick myself up and move to a new challenge. My body is certainly giving me an excuse to change.

When I saw Binstock several years later, at the gerontology meetings in Minneapolis in 1989, he had come into the hotel lobby where his colleagues in their suits and ties were making new connections over cocktails—and he was wearing running shorts. "Your health must be good now," I say, "if you're jogging in Minnesota in November." "My health is fine," he said, "but I'm not jogging. I just didn't feel like wearing a suit for a change."

Evelyn Shapiro, now seventy-eight, started college at forty-nine, after a long career as a professional violinist, in between bringing up her three kids. She told me:

I had taught and played, as concert mistress of the symphony at New Bedford, string quartets at churches, sometimes for money, sometimes for free. Then, I lost the flexibility of my left hand, the strength of my fingering hand. I couldn't play well anymore. So that's when I decided to go to college. I commuted an hour to the teacher training college in Bridgeport, graduated, got my master's, and began to teach. And I became independent. I never had a checking account of my own, my husband always paid the bills. Now I had my own checking account and I didn't have to ask his permission to buy something.

I got accepted at Brown for a doctoral program in teaching English, but I turned it down. I liked teaching the basics as I'd already started to do at the old-fashioned local high school, five classes, over a hundred kids, none of their parents had gone to college. You were supposed to retire at seventy; I was sixty-nine. My husband had died, so I sold the house and moved to the Cape, bought a condominium near my daughters. I went to the local high school where my granddaughters went and offered my services as a volunteer librarian. Then I went to the local community college and was hired as a part-time teacher. I was over seventy but now there's a law you can't discriminate. The first semester I taught three classes; now I only teach one because I like to do other things.

My whole life was my home and my children before I went to college. When I wanted to go somewhere, my husband always made excuses, "I'm not well enough," and then he had his heart attack. He didn't have the courage to do new things. Since he died, I've done a lot of traveling, took my granddaughter to Australia, New Zealand, fifteen days in a bus, a boat through the famous caves. It was the best trip of my life. . . .

Ted Mills, now in his late seventies, retired the first time at fifty-five from his job as television producer and vice-president of NBC in order "to pursue a crusade for meaningful work." In the early 1970s, he set up a Center for Quality of Work Life, helping corporations restructure their hierarchies to involve their workers in decision making. A few years later, with contracts in place with major American companies and unions, he gave the firm to his employees, retiring as president but staying on the board as director and consultant.

I retired as CEO at sixty-five, thinking that was what you should do. But after a couple of years, I found out what an idiot I was. My major surprise was to discover the whole syndrome of being young-old. You have all your juices, all your faculties, all your ability, but no obligations to go to work just for the money. With

Social Security coming in every month, and a pension, you can do work that really means something. It can be, it is the most productive time of my whole life because I'm not hassled by the distractions and compulsions of youth. I don't feel any older today than I did at thirty-five. No, I take that back. I feel a lot wiser and brighter than I was at thirty-five, and even my body is in great shape.

The problem is that power is hierarchical, and when you have for a period of years been elevated to a top status in the hierarchy, a lot of your value now is that power, not your abilities. And when you are removed from that authority or power, what you possess in the way of skills may not be that useful or valuable. When you are out of the power loop and you have shed the accoutrements of power, but you have the insights and the ability—what you should do is start something else. I'm extremely happy that I was able in the last two years to organize the Long Island Mobilization for Literacy, and make things happen with that urgent new problem. It's now got official government status. You can make things happen—not power, but influence—as much, more, at seventy or eighty as at thirty or forty, because you have more experience and a certain wise detachment. When you find your power to make things happen in age, because you have gotten rid of the idiotic trappings of the hierarchy, something tall comes out now, a serenity that is very useful.

Sitting on the dock at Sag Harbor on a September noon, over fish chowder, Ted Mills displayed that serenity himself, the lines in his tanned face, his ease in his open blue and white striped shirt, white chinos and safari jacket, brown loafers, bespeaking a singular lack of harassment and desperation, a sureness.

Power, that's all we're deprived of. All the richness may be there, the experience, but without the power, what do we do with it? In my case, I started a new initiative, but what happens to people who are not self-starters? Everyone climbing up that ladder is going to throw you out of their way if they can on age. But what almost killed me was my own death sentence of retirement.

To escape that death sentence, it sometimes seems as if men especially have to literally remove themselves from the scene of their power. Sometimes, with a couple, it's the woman who sees the next corner in larger terms than that defined by work; sometimes, for a man, that next corner is a frame of life in which work is not only, or even necessarily, different, but plays a less dominant part. More of his satisfaction now comes from that part of life he used to leave to his wife. There is truly a "crossover." Sometimes a woman, forced or freed by widowhood or divorce to embark on a career for the first time in age, discovers and uses professionally, for pay, abilities she had only used before in the family, or as a volunteer for the community, or for pleasure. She may experience new power in those years, but does not seem as driven or obsessed by it as some men half her age. In all my interviews, it seemed to me that the kind of work that fed the fountain of age did succeed in transcending that old polarization of work and love, career and family, play and seriousness.

At sixty-eight, Lee Mitchell reluctantly retired and followed his wife to Maine, where they bought a house and opened a gallery. Libby Mitchell said:

He wouldn't leave his job in Los Angeles, but I knew if we didn't buy a house while he was still working, we might not be able to move. Now we've sold that house for enough to give us something to live on besides Social Security, so we don't have to work anymore. It's nice not to have to answer to anybody for the first time in our lives. Both of us were cancer victims back then, but we don't have it now.

Lee sat behind a desk all his life, and in his later years he worked at the corporate level, with pressure and deadlines and quotas to fill. He would have just stayed in Los Angeles, as a merchandise manager in that home improvement chain, if the firm hadn't been taken over when he was sixty-four, and the old people all let go.

Lee said:

I looked for another job, but being in my sixties, I got a very cold reception. They seem to listen to you but it's as if they don't see you. You're a non-person. And then I became ill. I'd never had a sick day in my life before. I had cancer of the bladder [*caught in the early stages*]. *Then I said, That's it, I'll retire.*

"If you'd gotten that job in L.A., you'd still be there," Libby said. When Lee finally came to Maine, he started helping her in the gallery. He began building things, and had his own workshop in the basement. "I'm productive in a retired sense," he said. "I've always got some project to finish." They live on the edge of Acadia National Park. When they take visitors walking, "it turns out we oldsters get way ahead of them; they're huffing and puffing. It's gotten easier and better for us as we've grown older." Lee said, "There is a sense of community here. That decline you expect in age, it's gone the other way with us. Our mental attitude, our ability to think clearly—we're not nervous and anxious the way we used to be. Any problem that comes our way, it doesn't throw us now, we just handle it."

To have control over their own time, their own lives, at last, is what such people on the cutting edge of age are insisting upon. And not to be isolated, cut off from society. But if the work is merely designed to keep them "busy," it may not genuinely nourish their sense of themselves and their ties to community. Without institutional structures or support, those who have already had experience improvising and innovating are better able to start again. Women seem to have that edge now. Sociologists pondering men's lesser vitality and tendency to depression several years after retirement speak of the bureaucratic "routinization" of the jobs most men have held in recent years in corporate America, of the deadly narrowness of "specialization." Still, there are men who, in retirement, are able to innovate and improvise even within that institutionalized framework, and corporations that profit by it.

Asked by the Hallmark Company to come to the Midwest to give executive and creative personnel there a seminar on "The Evolution of the Family," I was surprised to discover that this future-oriented program had been the brainchild of an eighty-three-year-old man. The young design directors and corporate vice-presidents were clearly awed by him, as they ushered me into his presence. Later I went to Kansas City to interview him.

When Hans Archenhold retired at sixty-five, after thirty years at Hallmark, he was corporate vice-president for graphic arts. He told me:

I would have preferred not to retire, but at the time sixty-five was the retirement age for executives in our company. I took the first job that was offered me, to run a small printing company of no particular interest to me, though I ran it well enough. When Hallmark asked me to come back several years later, they did not really know why. There was a myth about using my experience and enthusiasm to influence young people. I was supposed to come back to my old job, but I felt an immediate wall there. I could not compete with my successors, imply that they weren't doing a good job. You can't go home again. Things change. The gap closes. Things are constantly in flux. You can't put yourself back in the same situation.

Then I hit upon a new idea. I knew that when Americans negotiate with foreigners, they feel culturally inferior, insecure. I came out of Germany, by way of Paris, Switzerland, London, in the nick of time, escaping Hitler. My American middle-class colleagues were well-educated executives, but it wasn't just languages they lacked. I decided to expand their brainpower to limits they never conceived of—not just records, but Beethoven at La Scala; not prints, the originals in the Louvre—to take those people selected for high office to Europe, and use all the humanities to break through their narrow-mindedness. They couldn't develop the new approaches needed by the company because they couldn't make the jump from yesterday to tomorrow. I gave them new dissatisfactions, new aspirations, new goals for our employees. You have to show them the greatest achievements, the miracles, and make them dissatisfied with mundane answers.

When you get older, you may forget names and dates, but you get better in your concept of the world and of problems, you strip down the unnecessary steps, and you don't exaggerate the importance of abstract knowledge or even statistics. You go more with your intuition. Most of the people who went through the program became more sensitive to other kinds of people, more sure of themselves, and more able to inspire the people who work for them to open their minds.

We set up a center for creating new ventures,

new products, spent $35 million to bring art-
ists, writers, engineers, craftsmen, architects
to live together with some of our best managers for half a year, a year, to create new
ventures, new kinds of Christmas-tree decora-
tions, new kinds of greeting cards. It increased
the profits of the company enormously. I
would not have dared it when I was younger—
I was too dependent on their approval, on my
paycheck, too concerned with my own future.
It changed the company. They don't hire people anymore who don't have the drive for innovation.

I ran the program for seventeen years after I
came back from retirement. I retired again at
eighty. I only go to the big meetings now. I'm
not as dissatisfied in my eighties as I was in my
sixties. You have to keep renewing your effort,
your vision. You have to see everything as new.
I have changed, from sixty to eighty. Before, I
was more concerned with myself, more critical, more rigidly disciplined. Now I commit myself more completely to people. All the
experiences I had over my lifetime prepared
me for that job after I retired.

In a sense, our society's linear look at work and
age and the insoluble dilemmas of work versus
retirement are *dictated* by the definition of work
solely in terms of the race for success and
power, those youthful games from which age

can finally free us. But, in much the same way as women's problems sometimes seemed insoluble as long as we could only see a male model of equality, so that rigid stereotype of work versus retirement may only seem insuperable according to the youthful model (which is still the male one). A horrifying concept emerged in the pages of the *Harvard Business Review* during the winter of 1989, proposing that women who couldn't follow the male, fast-track, single-minded career model because they wanted to have kids should be put into a different permanent "Mommy track"—forgoing advancement to real equality or decision-making power in their careers for the rest of their lives in return for some parental leave and flexible hours in those childrearing years. Women, young and old, who had managed (or hoped to manage) to raise children and advance in professions without such no-win choices were appalled.

But it was easier for those of us with the wisdom of age to see beyond that polarization to new possibilities. It seemed clear to us that more flexibility in work week schedules, parental leaves, and sabbaticals was indeed necessary, but not just for women. Permitted for women alone, as in the "Mommy track," it would surely lead to a perpetuation of inequality, segregating women in second-class ghettos outside the mainstream of career and profession. The need for greater flexibility in work schedules was made visible by the great movement of women into the work force. But that restructuring would also meet the needs of workers facing burnout or technological obsolescence and needing re-education and renewal, at midlife or in age. And men as well as women are now redefining "success" at work to demand more control over their own lives, including new priorities for family, personal growth, and pleasure, throughout their careers.

Until now, men's identity has been defined almost wholly by their work, as women's used to be defined by marriage and motherhood. And just as breaking through that narrow definition changed the aging process for women, signs of a similar breakthrough are multiplying for men. A 1988 nationwide study of over four thousand men—mainly executives and managers from *Fortune* 500 companies, plus some lawyers, accountants, doctors, twenty-seven to seventy-eight—looked at how men are questioning their roles, wanting to establish an identity separate from work.[1] The younger men, like women in the late 1980s, were now wanting to "have it all." Nearly half the senior-level executives admitted that they regretted spending so many hours at the job, and that if they were to do it over, they would spend more time with their families from the outset. Some 68 percent were happy in their professional lives, but felt their family life suffered as a result. "I know when I retire, my phone will stop ringing because no one will need anything from me then," said one CEO. "But as long as I come to work every day, I'm a happy man." But 58 percent in the middle management and professional groups felt that they had wasted years striving for and achieving success, only to find it "empty and meaningless." Where their fathers worked to "earn a living," the generation of middle managers today expected much of their "fulfillment" to come from their jobs. For the men over forty-five, success in their work was "all"; only 6 percent placed a high value on "personal growth." But 62 percent of men between twenty-seven and forty-five placed a high value on personal growth on or outside the job.

Like the suburban housewives I interviewed in the 1950s who wondered, "I'm my husband's wife, the kids' mother, but who am I?," the older executives asked, "Who am I, if not my job?" One sixty-one-year-old corporate vice-president said: "I wouldn't know how to survive on my own. I just wish there was more time for me to do my own thing. No, what I really mean is that I wish there were time for me to find out what my own thing is and then to be able to do it without fear of guilt, loneliness or loss of status."

Most of these older men felt: "Without my job, I'm nobody." The president of a major computer company, facing ouster by his board of directors, said: "I *am* the company. I can't bear the humiliation of dismissal. I'll be a non-person in this community." He suffered a serious depression and withdrew from life, even becoming suicidal. But the 23 percent who claimed to be "satisfied and happy" in the face of age had gone through a no-man's-land to a different basis for their identity. "Their self-confidence was a result of experiencing a period of self-doubt, a period of questioning their beliefs, values, and objectives. The satisfaction with their lives stemmed from a long search for inner meaning and from overcoming their dependence on external yardsticks for success. Their priorities included: having fun at work; valuing personal growth; cherishing family and friends." Status, fame, or money were no longer their main motivations.[2]

At the end of the 1970s, the Bell Telephone System began a new longitudinal study, comparing the current generation of college graduates being hired for management with those now facing age whom they had been studying since the 1950s. By midlife, the four-hundred–odd men in the original Management Progress Study were not exactly following the psychologists' predictions of midlife crisis and depression as their prospects of promotion and power narrowed. And the new generation of married women managers were much less likely to be defining themselves in narrow terms of career success and advancement even at the outset.

The 1950s generation of young managers began with very high expectations of what their lives would be like and how successful their careers would be.[3] Twenty years later, most of those middle-aged men had long ago given up their early dreams, and many couldn't remember how high they had aspired in the beginning. Describing that group, Drs. Ann Howard and Douglas Bray, who directed basic human resources research at AT&T, noted: "The photographs of that earlier group almost always show crew cuts, clean shaven faces, and skinny ties trimly adorning pressed white shirts. It seemed as if most of these men were political conservatives who wanted a homemaker wife, children, and to be 'Mr. Telephone' in their local communities. Off the job, they fished and went to church."[4]

At middle age, many were not interested in further promotions, even if they were available. About half resisted the idea of any future move for their family, even if a promotion went with it. There was also very little correlation between success (career promotions) and happiness. Perhaps because of "the aggravations of the additional responsibility" or "the politics they would have to endure at a higher level," promotion no longer seemed that much of a reward for the typical middle-aged manager. But there was no decrease in "motivation to respond to job challenge" with age, regardless of job level, and a great increase in "motivation for autonomy, or desire to be free and independent." Except for the minority still driven by ambition to move up, work diminished in "primacy": "The job is becoming less important in the individual's total life. . . . Other themes, such as the family or hobbies, were becoming more important. Satisfaction and interest in the job itself had also become more important than further advance." As long as even the lower-level men were putting in their hours, they would like them to be absorbing, useful hours. But even the minority, who were separated *out* as CEO material for their "high-flying ambitions"—they had been willing to make some sacrifices for career advancement, and to spend more time on the job or take extra courses—were no longer willing to relocate and wanted more autonomy.[5]

The new manager generation, from the beginning, was less involved with and less concerned about advancement. "Young managers entering the Bell System today simply don't have the lust to climb the corporate ladder that management recruits had twenty years ago," the researchers reported.[6] These new managers, including women and blacks now, were less conformist, less deferent to those above them, and much more "individualistic" than the 1950s managers. "Men are just as likely to be bearded as clean shaven. Wildly colorful informal dress is just as common as traditional business suits. Our new managers may be right-wingers, or Marxists, or disgusted with the whole idea of politics. The group includes women who want to be president and men whose hobby is home decorating."[7]

The *demise of the work ethic* was predicted by these researchers, unless there was a change toward more autonomy for the individual, more flexibility, and "participative management." Most of the new young managers simply did not identify themselves in terms of a lifelong career within that large corporation. "I want to lead a lifestyle that isn't all work," said one, who claimed he would secretly like to be "an actor or an artist." Some actually showed "negativism" toward advancement: "The higher you go up in management, the more time you have to put in your work. I plan to do my job the best I can, but my loyalty is to my family."

The findings of the AT&T researchers have been corroborated by comparisons in other companies between younger and older managers. A large survey done at the end of the 1970s by Daniel Yankelovich and his colleagues showed that in corporations and professions generally, "loyalty to the organization has been replaced by loyalty to the self . . . concern for work has been superseded by concern for leisure," and "identification with a work role" is no longer the paramount factor in younger men's identity. A survey of *Esquire* readers in 1979 found that men under thirty wanted more time for what they called "personal growth." Another study showed that new MBAs did not intend "to follow their fathers' footsteps in long years on a narrow corporate track." In the two Bell studies, the younger managers gave more importance to "inner harmony," "wisdom," and "true friendship." A more recent study suggested that high school seniors and newlyweds were nearly as active in exploring "leisure styles and commitments as they are in exploring potential work commitments."[8]

The "me decade" of the 1980s blurred some of these phenomena. But the younger generation's breakthrough from definitions of women solely in terms of family and men in terms of work advancement may blur the crossover in age. Men may share women's flexibility, as both balance career and family; women and men may need other new challenges to further development as they age. A professor at Yale Management School who left the practice of law altogether at forty-three said: "What we desperately need are new professionals who are consumed not with what they know but with what they must learn; who can work across various fields of knowledge; who make an avocation of looking for themselves . . . who are ready to challenge the pretension inherent in the offer and sale of 'expert' advice. Above all, we need new professionals who make their beliefs and ideals the bases

422

for their judgments and participation in public life."[9]

But these are precisely the values and ways of thinking which emerge most clearly in age—that "truthtelling" stubbornness, that impatience with irrelevant detail and data, and the zeroing in on questions of central meaning and basic value. Should a doctor alienated from the narrow technical focus of his younger colleagues retire, or be recruited in his wise late sixties for the larger questions of the hospital's ethics committee? Should there be a third house of Congress that is not corrupted by having to raise money to run every two or six years, whose sole function is to ask the larger questions? Could the growing need for such wisdom transcending narrow expertise in every field provide the pragmatic, social basis for the fountain of age? All we see now is the *accidental* use, by institutions, of that resource, and the *accidental* stumbling, by the most determined individuals, onto ways to keep on using their own abilities in society.

One institution which systematically uses the wisdom of age is professional baseball, our national sport, where players are, in fact, "old" before forty in terms of their physical ability to throw fastballs and run bases. But some of the best became the great managers of baseball history—Leo Durocher, Casey Stengel. Their wisdom and experience have been used to oversee and mastermind the deployment of young teams well into their own grizzled age. If companies could break through their own stereotyped vision, such "coach" or "mentor" use of older executives might be more cost-effective in terms of competition and productivity than "golden handshakes" to induce early retirement. And they would be given the same respect for their authority and wisdom as is accorded those baseball managers.

In politics and government, as well, there should be a way to tap into experience and wisdom freed from the narrow partisan concerns of keeping or returning the party to power in the next election. In their age, Nixon and Kissinger have advised the business and political leaders of many nations, for millions of dollars. Jimmy Carter, by contrast, emerged from agonizing political defeat and near financial disaster after his presidency, to sell his peanut warehouse and live in a four-bedroom brick house in Plains, Georgia, devoting his sixties to helping governments and warring tribes in the Philippines, Argentina, Ethiopia, Nicaragua, and Panama to resolve their conflicts and avert war. He travels ceaselessly, monitoring elections to strengthen democracy and human rights. He also teaches a Sunday School class at the local Baptist church. On a Sunday in 1989, at the age of sixty-five, silver-haired and relaxed, Carter took as his text the last chapter of the Book of Daniel, which he saw as "God's call to duty in the face of adversity." In what could as well have been a sermon for his own age, Carter said: "He is telling us, don't waste our time, don't waste our talents, don't waste our intelligence. We can have a faith that can transcend failure. . . . We can have an existence that has purpose . . ." (*The New York Times,* December 10, 1989).

If the study of age had begun with women, perhaps there never would have been that all-or-nothing concept of work versus retirement. In the short thirty years of the modern women's movement, new career patterns have already begun to emerge—or rather, a shifting mix of work and family commitments and other interests, involving continual improvisation and redefinition. Such patterns may culminate in even greater possibilities of fulfillment for older women, and for the men who join them.

Mary Catherine Bateson started out in rebellion against her famous mother, Margaret Mead, who subsumed three husbands and her daughter's upbringing to the demands of her anthropological field work, as one of the first women in what was then a man's career. Bateson married young and fitted her own degrees around her husband's shifting geographical career demands, as well as her own pregnancies. Starting from "a disgruntled reflection on my own life as a sort of desperate improvisation in which I was constantly trying to make something coherent from conflicting elements to fit rapidly changing settings," Bateson began to take seriously, and to conceptualize with respect, the actual pattern of her own and other women's lives, which simply didn't fit that single-minded linear career path. One woman, for instance, starting out as a dancer, turned during her pregnancies and her husband's academic travels to jewelry design, and then converted her dance and craft skill into a new technique of psychotherapy, collaborating finally with her psychoanalyst husband.

In her book *Composing a Life* (1989), Bateson points out:

Each of us has worked by improvisation, discerning the shape of our creation along the way, rather than pursuing a vision already defined. . . . It is no longer possible to follow the pattern of previous generations. This is true for both men and women, but is especially true for women, whose whole lives no longer need be dominated by the rhythms of procreation and the dependencies that these created, but who still must live with the discontinuities of female biology and still must balance conflicting demands.

Our lives not only take new directions, they are subject to repeated redirections, partly because of the extension of our years of health and productivity. . . . Sometimes a pattern chosen by default can become a path of preference. . . . Studying women's lives . . . we recognize common patterns of creativity that have not been acknowledged or fostered. . . . The model of an ordinary successful life that is held up for young people is one of early decision and commitment, a single rising [career] trajectory. . . .

These assumptions have not been valid for many of history's most creative people, and they are increasingly inappropriate today. The landscape through which we move is in constant flux. . . . Goals too clearly defined can become blinders. . . . It will become less and less possible to go on doing the same thing through a lifetime. . . .

Women have always lived discontinuous and contingent lives, but men today are newly vulnerable. . . . Thinking about myself and about other women I have known, some proud and contented and others embittered with envy . . . I . . . found myself questioning . . . whether indeed the model of improvisation might prove more creative and appropriate to the twentieth century than the model of single-track ambition.[10]

When I find men clearly partaking of the fountain of age, they also seem to be improvising new patterns for their lives. These may build on, or use differently, the skills and interests of their past careers. Even in the face of severe physical disability and actual decline of capacity, even at the very end of life, some find new strength and vitality, and a deeper sense of continuity. Such improvisation might lead men or women into a new career in their seventies or eighties, like my friend Earl Arthurs, retired insurance broker, wandering the world as a cruise ship host. But the projects of vital age may also lead further and further away from any resemblance to career, as for Norman Pease learning to play the organ, or I. F. Stone mastering Greek, in their eighties.

Joe Wilder, seventy-one, my friend and country neighbor, was in his youth an all-American, world-class athlete, Dartmouth's all-time highest lacrosse goal scorer against all opponents. As a boy in Baltimore, son of an immigrant grocer, he was expected to "succeed but never actually told how. Whatever happened had to be a matter of improvisation. But when I was nine, I learned I was a good athlete—a passport to all kinds of glories." Though he studied art and philosophy in college, he went to medical school and became chief of surgery at the Hospital for Joint Diseases in New York City at thirty-nine. He is currently chief of emergency services at Mount Sinai Hospital in New York. But he dates his "real life" as starting not with his career, but with an emergency phone call, when the comedian Zero Mostel, run over by a 20,000-pound bus and taken to the operating room for amputation of his severely crippled leg, refused surgery. Four major operations and six months later, Mostel thanked Wilder for saving his leg by upbraiding him for being a workaholic. "Come to my studio and draw on Saturday afternoons," Mostel commanded. Though famous as an actor, Mostel was also a serious painter. Wilder recalled:

I knew next to nothing about art. My life up to this moment was family and friends, sports, surgery, and being an "Indian Chief." He threw me a sketchpad and a piece of charcoal and shouted, "Draw!" A striking nude model was on the pedestal. . . . Three hours later I walked out in a daze, clutching my sketchpad like a newfound gold treasure. I was both exhilarated and frightened. I knew a door deep inside had been snapped open, and I could feel a dammed-up flood of emotions about to cascade. I was on the brink of a whole new world. The not knowing was as exciting as the knowing.

Three months later, Wilder had his own tiny studio on lower Broadway. He was amazed, after the years of "enormously controlled discipline and ritual as a surgeon and the stress and responsibility for the health and lives of others, dozens of eyes of my fellow physicians, residents, and nurses watching my every move as Chief of Surgery," to find out what it felt like to be "responsible only to oneself. What a joy to paint with abandon and total freedom any image that struck my fancy, without form, or discipline, or much knowledge."

After a year's painting orgy, Wilder became frustrated with his lack of technical knowledge. He registered for a class in basic fundamentals at the Art Students League and began to meet, observe, and question artists, the emerging "Pop" artists as well as abstract expressionists, and to become part of a network of artists, museum people, and critics.

As my confidence grew, I realized "Pop" imagery was not for me. I knew deep down that I wanted to paint athletes—the world I had grown up with in the Baltimore stadium—baseball, football, ice hockey, and lacrosse . . . the striking grace and artfulness of bodies in movement: bodies reaching out to overcome and break records. I left the mainstream of art and set out on my own. At just this turning point, I was invited to a Grand Prix race. Speed and solitude of the individual have long fascinated me, and I found both in painting the world of racing cars. I painted racing cars in all shapes and forms as well as drivers for ten years. Then it became too easy. My images were becoming too repetitive. At long last I decided to paint athletes in movement, in tension ... What excitement! I never tire of trying to create the wonderment and the miracle of the body in all its wondrous movements, tensions, grace, strength and muscular coordination, and the potential for overcoming adversity.

In these paintings, Wilder put together in a new way his background as a competitive athlete and his training as a surgeon, his practice as a teacher and instructor in anatomy and pathology. He was over sixty when the National Gallery in Washington, D.C., held the first major sports-image show ever held in an American museum, and his work appeared with that of Eakins and Bellows. A major art book publisher recently published his paintings of "Athletes," and medical journals used his paintings for their covers. At his seventieth birthday party, his friends from both worlds joined his wife and five children in toasting Wilder's new great painting of runners —all races and colors—which had been chosen as the official poster for that year's New York City Marathon. But when I went this summer to his latest opening, at a small Long Island gallery, he had shifted focus again: small, beautiful, intensely glowing still lifes, bowls of peaches and

431

cherries, flowers. To have achieved such success at the sports paintings, and then, at seventy, to change once again?

"When I sit down and paint," said Joe Wilder, retired athlete, soon-to-be-retired surgeon, "I am really a free man. All of nature, all objects, all creatures great and small are mine for the painting—free—to be painted when and how and what and where it suits me."

Hannah Arendt in *The Human Condition* cites the distinction that the ancient Greek philosophers made between "animal" work—the work of a slave or a woman (an *animal laborans,* or laboring animal), necessary to stay alive but leaving no mark behind, sweeping the floor that gets dirty again, cooking the meal that gets eaten—and "human" work. Human work, to those Greeks, the work of free men, involved courage: the risk of casting one's own being into the arena, in art, political contest, or any game of human skill in which you make your individual mark on your time. The concept of "hero" comes from that definition of "human work." Originally, it did not necessarily connote great physical bravery but simply the risk of freely chosen tasks or adventure in a community of equals, in which you dared to expose your true self.

The institutions of retirement, Social Security, and pensions have permitted many of the men and women I interviewed to transcend the necessities of physical survival, restrictive family roles, and to risk the adventures of "human work" in the last third of life. They, too, are "heroes" in the Greek sense. For them, the overwhelming value seemed to be *personal choice,* "doing what I want to do at last," "doing what I haven't had the chance to do before." And for many, this freedom finally to choose one's own human work meant saying no to paid work altogether, and choosing instead to work at play without consideration for what money (if any) it might make. Ted Apstein, at seventy-one, spends days rewriting one of his plays, to which he has happily devoted his retirement, or pursuing the hint of new interest that might get it produced. But he feels only "shivers of horror down my spine" when a younger colleague tells of having to rework a television drama of middle-aged love in Mexico into a "buddy" youth comedy on a spaceship. The last time that happened to Ted, he was in his mid-fifties, making a lot of money and in great demand as a film and television writer. He rewrote his "little gem of a love story, if I do say so myself" into a buddy comedy, but swore never again, and told his agent to get him enough soap opera work to retire at sixty and "write the plays I've always wanted to write." And so he has, for ten years now, without regret, though so far those plays have been produced only in regional or college theaters, Off-Broadway or its Hollywood equivalent, and made no money at all. He says he will not be satisfied until his plays get produced ("otherwise they don't become real"), but admits that it "wouldn't make that much real difference to me now" if they made money.

It's as if, once men and women break free from the old, rigid boundaries that once defined work, the fountain of age opens possibilities of change and life that need have no limits. And yet there is a pattern that becomes more and more clearly one's own, integrating previously unrealized parts of oneself, moving, even in the face of physical decline, toward a wholeness of spirit, realizing the mysterious self. Many philosophers of the mind have seen this—Jung, Maslow, Erikson. In the largest sense, in age, "work" is simply the vehicle of this development, expressing and even extending one's final life.

At the age of eighty-eight, Dr. Samuel Atkin, a psychoanalyst whose interest in aging began forty years ago, started a semi-autobiographical essay as "a participant observer, if you will, of the process of aging, and of the ongoing phenomenon of being old." His own aging process had been "complicated by several illnesses late in life, particularly Parkinson's disease and cardiovascular dysfunction, and the drugs needed to contain their symptoms. . . . Moreover, my debility has forced me into an almost life-and-death dependency upon others." But until his death, Dr. Atkin not only kept working, but he kept a journal "of my thoughts, ideas, fantasies, experiences and the vicissitudes of my physical and mental states," dictating his thoughts on a tape recorder all hours of the day and night. His son Adam helped organize this material, which he presented to the New York Psychoanalytic Society on June 10, 1986:

Though my life has outwardly become more drab, my perceptions have been enhanced by an astonishing freshness and vividness. . . . I am also subject to a new rhythm of energy levels and affective states, some now associated with creative drives used in this work enterprise, as well as in my continuing work as a psychoanalyst. . . .

Here I am, an old man approaching 90. The faculties I exercised, the physical powers I depended on, don't obey my will anymore. I am very weak. I must navigate with a walker. My equilibrium is uncertain, my control over my movements unreliable. . . . Working long and late on journal . . . when I feel desperate and low, as I did last night, I think: "What the hell is this all about? What the hell am I doing?" But I keep going. I can't walk. I can't see. I am half blind. But look! I hear, I see, I think, I remember. So I write down these notes. I am still Sam Atkin!

Adam Atkin recalled that several years before, when the Parkinson's became evident, his father was markedly depressed, and remained so for a long while. Several months after starting the journal, his depression lifted. Here are some extracts from that journal:

November 23rd—I discovered some time ago that there's been a change in me—I've come to enjoy living without any excuses! I am happy to be alive. . . .

Rigidity . . . Certainly, medical belief and psychoanalytic assumption have until recently characterized the old person as rigid . . . I believe that in the need for readaptation, a fundamental reorganization of my psychic apparatus has taken place, and that this is true for most, if not all, old people. Is this simply a matter of disease and illness? Or have I undergone some developmental transformation? . . . Forced to relinquish many preoccupations and functions and ambitions, one gains an opportunity to see things in a fresh way, things that were hidden or pushed aside by the pressure of "getting and spending."

September 9th—Just dying—this process I'm going through right now—is uncharted ground. Obviously, this can only be understood by going through it. . . . In seeking the meaning of Death I cling to life by forcing the I to live. I resist death. I relish this temporary immortality.

The old person is not merely a bundle of rigidities, increasingly unable to meet the demand for adaptation to his changing world. Rather, he is constantly adapting—more, perhaps, than when younger! . . . The old person gets great pleasure from learning new skills, from mastering the environment, however narrow. . . .

For example, because of my Parkinson's, I've had to learn to tie my shoes in a new way. I do it clumsily and it took me a long time to learn how to do it. But it is an achievement. Not to be dependent upon others to tie my shoelaces! That makes me very happy.

I have entered a new country—the country of the old. The unknown appears at every juncture. I used to live in a comfortable, civilized land. Now I am living on a frontier. Survival becomes a day-to-day, moment-by-moment focus of interest and satisfaction. Though I suffer great physical difficulties, often painful, though I am unable to do most of the things I spent a lifetime doing, I am pleasantly surprised by my changed world. Paradoxically, ordinary moments of life, the prosaic flow of experiences, have become newly interesting. I see things in a fresh way—the pictures on the wall, the pillows on the sofa, the tree outside my window. Existence has become adventurous.

I believe that one's developmental process continues beyond maturity . . . it continues until the end of life. I am obviously in a quite different place . . . from the Sam Atkin of twenty or even ten years ago: I move, see, think differently!

Dr. Atkin, despite his illness, continued to treat patients in his ninetieth year, though fewer than before. His psychoanalytic work had always been "central" to his life. But, he asked himself, did his old age affect his work, and if so, how? He was well aware that many of his colleagues looked askance, "disapproving, when they hear this old fogey is still practicing psychoanalysis."

Some days I come to the office in pain. I feel compelled to work a few hours a day whether I am physically ready or not. Knowing that I am still useful to my patients revivifies me. It also stimulates my intellectual activity. . . .

In the last few years I have discovered that despite my fatigue and slower response there have been some positive qualitative changes in my work, undoubtedly a reflection of the inner changes in myself. I am bolder, more forthright in my interpretations . . . I have been observing, thinking, working, creating. I do not intend to stop. In fact, Adam and I are already writing two further papers dealing with these themes and their theoretical implications, for presentation on the occasion of my 90th birthday.

Samuel Atkin died on March 5, 1989, nine months after the presentation of this final paper.

In my own mind's eye, I see the image of the double helix, those coils of DNA and RNA, entwining and unfolding around each other in ever-changing patterns, defining and redefining our humanness. I see love and work, the double helix of our humanity, finally, in age, coming together in the urge toward wholeness—stripped of mask, denial, irrelevant detail, to its essence. That urge to work, finally, not for power but for love, the pure pleasure of using one's abilities for chosen purpose, great or small, and the life force shining through at last pure and free in that work, strengthened by it. Fully human, choosing to work even in the face of death, and evolving into the freedom to use to the fullest one's unique human self, whole.

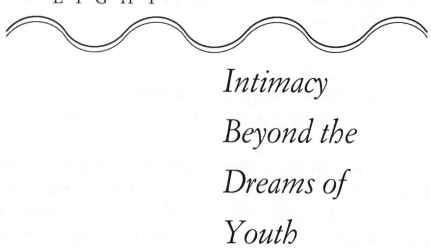

Intimacy Beyond the Dreams of Youth

I had a dream: In my house, propped up against a wall, pushed out of the way, was something quite large, all wrapped up in a rug. Like a mummy. And I said, "What is wrapped up in that rug?" No one was paying any attention to it, it didn't really get in the way. But I didn't want something wrapped up, hidden like that in my house. I insisted on slitting it open.

There was a woman wrapped up in the rug, and she was still alive! She was not young but she had longish light hair and a glint in her eye, and she was brandishing a knife in her hand. I woke up in horror and sat up in my bed. There was a live woman I had wrapped up in that rug, and she was going to kill me if I didn't let her out. So I went to see my old shrink, and I said, Given the realities, the numbers, my age, how could I live with the woman I had wrapped up in that rug? She was still alive, but how could I let her out without her exploding with rage—that knife in her hand? And I felt the pain of my own yearning.

Without love, the human self never develops at all, we learned from all those studies of Harlow's monkeys, and Bowlby's orphans in England, and children withering away in hospitals and institutions. Love sustains and defines the years of our growth to maturity. But is love not also essential to the continued affirmation of that human self—woman or man—in the new twenty-five to thirty years of life that have opened to us in this century? Is the problem really that men die too young, or seek younger women, and most women are therefore doomed to spend most of their late lives alone, without intimacy? Or could part of the problem be the sexual measures of ourselves as men and women held over from our youth, and the barriers to intimacy that they impose—which may indeed have something to do with men dying eight years younger than women? Could we see solution, not problem, in the mysterious endurance of women, the different ways they manage to sustain and renew intimacy, despite that seemingly insoluble sexual imbalance? If I am right, the problem is not the sexual imbalance but the fear and denial of age itself, which reaches its apex in sex: the inability of many women and men (single, widowed, divorced, married) to move beyond the youthful sexual measures—and the masks, fears, and shames—to an intimacy that may only be possible in age.

But it's not so easy to think, personally or politically, about putting it all together in a new way with love. For women like myself, for me personally, with our children absorbed in their own lives, our grandchildren in other cities a peripheral delight, old friends beginning to die, the former ties of profession and political cause loosening as one's own interests change, intimacy takes on new meaning. One stops enjoying the cocktail parties and big benefits and dinners, even if the invitations keep coming (and one suspects they might not). Can one really talk honestly to other women, to men, even to oneself, about that need still to touch, be touched. Intimacy with whom—if you're a woman alone, widowed, or divorced as more and more of us now are?

Do men have their own problems with intimacy, starting over again with new young wives and families, or seeking a new place in a forty- or fifty-year marriage? Are there false sexual either/or imperatives like that all-or-nothing paralysis of work versus retirement that blind us to the new possibilities of intimacy for which age frees us? Can we deepen our ties with men and women in ways that may not at all resemble our previous models of romance or intimacy? Must we forge different bonds with our children, and old friends, and keep making new friends to renew that vital intimacy? Not in the abstract, but in the concrete here and now of shared experience, are there answers for that yearning that we are now actually experiencing, without admitting it, because they no longer fit the old boundaries of love? Are there still other new adventures, of spirit and body, open to us from a new interface of work and love, that do not fit our previous expectations of either? Love and work, work and love, the two poles of our personhood in age as in youth? But must we, do we really want to love now the way we did when we were twenty, thirty, forty, any more than we want to work with the compulsions and obsessions of our youth?

"Be honest," my friend Martha said. "We all have the same problem, and there's no solution for it. All these women, widowed, divorced. The men our age are married, if they're still alive. And if they get widowed or divorced, they go after younger women, who still want them, if they have money, any power at all. No one even looks at us that way anymore. Of course, we have our women friends, the children, grandchildren if we're lucky. But it's not enough. It makes me mad just to think about it."

"I tell myself, forget it, there aren't any men out there, and if there are, they only want young chicks," said another friend. Widowed a dozen years, she was dropped by her one serious lover when she demanded "commitment," though in fact she was actually enjoying her new independence. "On the other hand, if I'm honest, is marriage really what I want now? I want something to make me feel more alive. Something is missing. But I sometimes think what I really need is to be deprogrammed of the fantasy man and the romantic happy-ever-after ending we all wanted when we were young. I need someone to share my life with now, more than my daughter and my friends; but does he have to be tall and powerful and rich? Does it even have to be a man?"

"If I'm honest," said a male friend, more chipper, full of piss and vinegar, at sixty-eight than he was in his fifties, despite (or because of?) his forced retirement from a bruising competitive advertising job and the replacement of the defective valve in his heart. "I've had it, living alone. But what can I do about it? I can hardly get married again. Ever since the heart attack, I can't get it up. I've no interest in a young girl, I doubt that would do it for me. But even with someone my own age, I'd be afraid to try. Not for fear of a heart attack—the humiliation of sex now." And we all say to each other, we women widowed, divorced, too long celibate: "But how could I even take off my clothes and get into bed with a man again, let him see my flabby body the way it is now?"

Woman or man, what we all need is some new way to touch, know, love each other the way we really are now, which is not for any of us the same as when we were twenty, thirty, or forty. Surely there is something else to be known and felt and said about love in age—yes, love, that gets beyond the insoluble dilemmas of the male/female imbalance, the youth obsession, the pressures and terrors of penetration, impotence, the measures of Kinsey and Masters and Johnson, the rages and jealousies that tortured our youthful and middle-aged sex. The fantasies and dreams of youth cannot sustain or satisfy us in age. Maybe new possibilities of intimacy have to evolve beyond the ways of our youth—inside or outside the old forms of marriage, friendship, family, community—if they are to nourish us in age.

But a clear-cut, no-win paradigm of sexuality in age is implied by even the most compassionate gerontologists. As Robert Butler and Myrna Lewis put it:

Many people—not only the young and middle-aged but older people themselves—simply assume that it is over. This is nonsense. Our own clinical and research work, the work of the gerontologists, the research of Kinsey, and the clinical discoveries of Masters and

Johnson all demonstrate that relatively healthy older people who enjoy sex are capable of experiencing it, often until very late in life. . . .

Should older people have sex lives? Are they able to make love? Do they really want to? Is it appropriate . . . "normal" or "decent" . . . or a sign of senility . . . poor judgment, or an embarrassing inability to adjust to aging with proper restraint and resignation? . . .

Older men judge themselves and are judged by comparing the frequency and potency of their sexual performance with that of younger men. . . . When measured by standards that are essentially athletic, older men are naturally considered inferior. . . . The predominant pressure on women comes from . . . that widespread assumption that only the young are beautiful. Many older people believe this themselves. When women's hair turns gray, and their skin develops wrinkles, and their bodies lose their earlier firmness and suppleness, they are very likely to see themselves as unattractive. . . .

There are others who have simply grown tired of sex. It may have been shared with the same partner routinely for many years, and they have compensated for its dullness by developing satisfying nonsexual activities. Other people may have stopped sex because of disabilities or serious illness. . . .

Whatever the reasons, it is possible to live a happy and satisfying life without sex if that is one's choice, and a good many older people do exactly that. American public . . . emphasis on sexuality has had the effect of making many of the young and middle-aged feel guilty, inadequate, or incomplete if sex fails to play a central role in their lives, and we do not want to place a similar burden on older people. . . . .

On the other hand . . . for many older people . . . [sexuality] carries with it the possibility of excitement and romance.[1]

This is the best of it, the rueful bittersweet resigned musings on the implications of the research that can be found on sexuality and age. The "problem" is clear enough, especially for older women. The "solutions" posited for the future—polygamy, younger men, celibacy, homosexuality, masturbation, longer life for men, a more sophisticated definition of beauty, androgyny, etc.—don't offer much immediate practical help for people struggling now with inadmissible yearnings that may or may not be what those researchers mean by sex. There came a time when I simply stopped having the old sexual fantasies. I no longer even dreamed of remarrying. I knew the odds, the numbers, only too well. I went on about my business—lectures, teaching, writing, conferences, children, grandchildren, friends, trips, dinners. And

I didn't let myself feel the panic: would I never know true intimacy again, would I ever take off all my clothes, be completely there with another being again? And sometimes I felt such a yearning, such a sense of loss, that I desperately tried playing the old game again. But it no longer worked. I couldn't do it. I couldn't risk the shame. Better to face the fact that this part of my life was over and take what pleasure I could in children and friends, women and men, without wanting or expecting it to end in bed, much less romance or marriage.

And I accepted, with some regret (I wouldn't let myself feel the pain), that I had simply stopped existing as a sexual being. But who was I kidding, then? Was this what I or anyone else could truly affirm as the fountain of age? Talking to those vital men and women who seemed to be fulfilling themselves in age, at first I had the hardest time even asking them questions about sex, intimacy. But when I did, I began to see a pattern in the insuperable dilemmas implicit in the research on sex and aging. I began to see a glimmer of hope, not only in predictable future patterns, but in the here and now of our daily lives, as women and men growing older at the end of the twentieth century in America. I glimpsed both the necessity and the possibility of intimacy and passionate sexual being/knowing beyond the dreams of our youth—the continuing necessity and possibility of making new existential choices in love, and of risking that existential pain, rage, and shame for as long as we choose to live.

The existing research on sexuality and aging (and its very lack) conveys an impossible paradox, the depressing divergence between capacity and desire, expectation and actual possibility, for both women and men. But what also emerges is the strong suspicion that false or skewed limitations are imposed on capacity, desire, and the actual possibility of intimacy, for both women and men in those new years after fifty, by measures of sexuality based on youthful male performance that may or may not be relevant in age. *Our denial of the personhood of age* —and its very definition as "problem"—ensures the virtual blackout of people over fifty as sexual beings, especially women.

There is, in fact, very little data on the sexual interests and experiences of older people, due, as Harvard psychiatrist Martin Berezin explained, to a "feeling among physicians, psychiatrists and research workers that it is . . . almost 'indecent' to probe into the sexual practices of persons old enough to be their parents. The myth of sexless older years held by young people becomes yet another self-fulfilling prophecy. A number of researchers report accordingly that many elderly people who find they have strong sex desires are overwhelmed with guilt and shame and feel that they are oversexed." [2]

In the two Kinsey reports (1948, 1953), out of

1,700 pages, only three are devoted to people over sixty, two on men and just half a page on women. In the seminal studies of Masters and Johnson in the 1960s and 1970s, only 4.5 percent of the total of men and women studied were over sixty-five. Significantly, when it comes to sex and age, that great pioneer of sexual study Alex Comfort pointed out:

> As in all fields of sexual study, it is the male, moreover, who is so far documented. His sexual "capacity" is marked by, and dependent on, an externally obvious erection, and research has been heavily motivated by male anxiety in this regard. . . . At least one standard textbook of geriatric medicine omits the discussion of female sexuality altogether, despite the large excess of women over men at high ages.[3]

Further, almost all of the existing scientific research on sex concerns measurable, quantifiable, physical sexual encounters and orgasms. As many critics have perceived, "the glaring omission in the studies of Kinsey and his colleagues was the denial of, and a lack of exploration into, the emotional aspects of the sexual relationship."[4] Kinsey measured sexual behavior in men along six variables: (1) ability to reach expected climax; (2) frequency of morning erections; (3) duration of erection; (4) angle of erection; (5) speed of reaching full erection; and (6) amount of precoital mucous secretion. Using these measurements, he reported that with advanced age there was increased impotence and decreased erotic responsiveness; that the sex drive in the human male decreases with age, primarily because of "altered physiological capacity," but "affected also by psychologic fatigue, a loss of interest in repetition of the same sort of experience, an exhaustion of the possibilities."

Kinsey was not as conclusive about the effects of age on female sexuality, explaining that since "a considerable portion of the female's sexual activity does not result in orgasm . . . there is little evidence of any aging in the sexual capacities of the female until late in her life." Reviewing all these studies, Martin Berezin reported his own difficulty in getting Harvard Medical School residents under his direction even to include questions about sex in taking older patients' histories. As for the research studies, "to assume that sexual intercourse is the only fact of a sex life is to oversimplify the problem. . . . Studies of sex in old age singularly have not referred to love, affection, tenderness and . . . relationships." [5]

According to their own "dispassionate and traditionally scientific" quantifiable measures, Masters and Johnson corroborated Kinsey's findings that "there is no time limit drawn by the advancing years of female sexuality," and that, in certain physical and emotional situations, the male maintains "a capacity for sexual performance to and beyond the 80-year-old age level." My Andrus colleague Ruth Weg found, in exhaustive reviews of longitudinal studies, "persistent sexual interest and capacity into the ninth decade of those elders in moderately good physical and psychological health," though the women had usually ceased sexual activity as a result of their male mates' "lack of libido," illness, or death—or the lack of a suitable partner. Studies from other countries showed a similar discrepancy between capacity and sexual activity, and a similar sharp divergence between women and men.[6]

The implications—pity the poor woman inevitably doomed to frustration of her sexuality and need for intimacy as she ages—are seldom spelled out. There are simply far more papers dealing with the sex life of aging males than those dealing with aging women. But there is concern, too, over "the dangers of preoccupation with sex by elderly men and women," the high numbers of sex offenders among old men, and the "touch hunger" and "starvation" of intimacy behind many older women's symptoms, from insomnia to overeating. "When careful physical and chemical examination yield very little in an older woman patient, the physician would do well to wonder if deliberate control, denial and repression of sexual feelings have not produced most of these symptoms," one doctor warned.[7]

A great many gerontologists have come to the conclusion that *helplessness*—being unable to control or affect one's own life—is the key to physical and psychological deterioration and decline. If intimacy is indeed crucial to that effective sense of self, then feelings of helplessness and lack of control should inevitably result from the sharp sexual paradoxes and forced denial detailed in the research. Yet women nevertheless continue increasingly to outlive men, and to maintain and renew ties of intimacy that keep them in control of their later lives much longer than men. The paradox is so sharp it may be more than paradox. What women who are married to men complain of— before and as they age—is not sexual problems of any sort, but lack of intimacy, lack of communication and shared feelings. And from remission of cancer to recovery from heart attacks, the *ability to share feelings,* the presence of a confidant (found in older women much more than men, with or without physical sexuality), seems to constitute the essential intimacy. Should we still see women only as victims of the sexual paradox?

If single, she is likely to outnumber the single men in her cohort (at times as high as 10 to 1) in the social situations in the community at large, at centers or nursing homes. Older widowers remarry quickly, and generally to younger women, whereas most older women who outlive men by eight years end up alone (5.3 times as many widows as widowers). Most older men are married—77%, as compared to 38% for older women. If she is still married but her mate has withdrawn from sexual activity, or has become involved with other, generally younger women, or he is ill, she may be . . . in starvation—for affection, touching and release.[8]

Still, if she is alive and he is ill or dead, could that masculine definition, which prohibits male sharing of feelings and intimacy except in the youthful sexual act, help explain his greater susceptibility to stress and his dying so much younger?

Consider the clues from other research:

• From childhood to retirement, males tend to have an extensive network of relations with others, but females tend to establish closer, more intense ties with a smaller number of friends.[9] Friendships between females have been found "emotionally richer" than friendships between males. Boys, as we know from Nancy Chodorow's work, have been forced from infancy to distance themselves from their own feelings and their dependence on their mothers—to "fight, win, compete, and not to cry"—in order to become men. Girls have been given permission to express feelings and have been socialized to be responsive to feelings. As numerous researchers and observers of women's and men's groups report, "the sharing of feelings, including hurt feelings, is more difficult for men." Ruth Weg concluded: "Women found care, concern and disclosure only among their women friends. What was lacking in man-woman relationships was a genuine connection—intimacy and support." She also asked: "Could the difficulty with self-disclosure and expression of feelings be factors in men's shorter life expectancy?"[10]

• With the years, incidence of chronic disease (coronary, cerebro-vascular, diabetes, arthritis) seems often sexually disabling for men. Frequently, treatment drugs "play havoc with libido and the capacity for erection." Anti-hypertensive medication may cause erectile failure and decrease in libido; beta blockers have also been involved in increased impotence. Investigators have found that 50 percent of diabetic males cannot stimulate erection by masturbation or any other method. Yet in a study of one hundred female diabetics, eighty-two maintained their normal sexual drive and orgastic capacity.[11]

• According to the Kinsey Report, the sharp decrease in sexual activity among women over sixty, including married women, is "controlled by the male's desires, and it is primarily his aging rather than the female's loss of interest or capacity which is reflected in the decline." A seeming *increase* in sexual interest after sixty-five was found among both men and women surviving to these years in the Duke studies.

Does this mean that both men and women who maintain sexual interest are more likely to survive after sixty-five? Perhaps the relationship of sexual intimacy to human health and survival has been obscured by that preoccupation with male erection and penetration. The male withdrawal from sexual intimacy and interest is certainly aggravated by the fear of impotence, and even terror of sudden death, intensified by the cardiovascular and diabetic conditions to which older males seem especially prone, although many studies have shown that there is less stress on the heart during intercourse than in a standard treadmill test (less than 1 death per 100,000 tests). The most common cause of male impotence is diabetes, though research indicates that this is not an endocrinological problem; since orgasmic response and an interest in sex have been found in some 80 percent of diabetic women, could the explanation simply be that male sexuality is equated with "erectile capacity," and not with total sexual responsiveness, which remains unimpaired in female diabetics? Might sexuality also remain in men, if so defined?[12] Recent studies indicate that organic factors are not likely to cause total loss of potency after prostatectomy in men, any more than mastectomy or hysterectomy desexualizes women, when such discussion is initiated by a doctor or counselor.

The real victims of the macho sexual obsession in age are only secondarily women. They may suffer from lack of "acceptable partners" because too many of the men their age are dead, and others seek younger women as stimulants of that waning youthful sexuality. But it is the excessive preoccupation with *youthful erection* which forces many men to give up that kind of intimacy too soon. And for many men, that is the only kind of intimacy they know. For men much more than women, the wife is the only "confidant," which is what the true intimacy of age demands, not erection or penetration. Alex Comfort reported that the main age changes in sexuality—the slowing of response, the increasing dependence of erection on direct penile stimulation, and the fact that orgasm ceases to occur at every act of intercourse—vary enormously among different men but show little further advance after sixty. The importance of such changes

is that while sexually active and unanxious men . . . experience them as a gain in control, men whose stereotype of virility depends on hurried erection followed by hurried intercourse may interpret them as loss of function and the consequent anxiety may induce failure of erection. It can be said with confidence that impotency is never a consequence of chronological age alone. Its increasing frequency with age is due to a variety of causes—the increasing prevalence of diabetes, of which impotency may be the presenting symptom; an increase in incidence of vascular-autonomic insufficiency; the increasing prevalence of conditions such as hypertension and prostatic enlargement, which may lead to problems through the use of medicines . . . of which impotency is a side effect; and above all the social expectation of impotence in age. . . . In spite of these factors, objective orgasmic loss of potency . . . is relatively rare at high ages. What may be seen . . . is a loss of interest in sexual activity reflecting loss of competitive self-esteem. . . .[13]

There is, of course, a "double standard" of aging, a remnant of the feminine mystique that defined women solely in terms of their biological role as mothers and as nubile sex objects. Simone de Beauvoir, Susan Sontag, Germaine Greer, and many others have expressed outrage at woman's victimization by this double standard. But it seems to me, now that we are emerging from rigidly defined sex roles, that men are as victimized in age by that lifetime of machismo as women by the feminine mystique. At least the women are still alive and open to new ways of intimacy, whereas the men their age, if not already dead, may still be barred by the remnants of that macho demand from any intimacy at all, except for, or even in, that narrowly defined genital role. In an Iowa study of 234 community residents over seventy, the older males had more frequent social contacts with their children, grandchildren, and spouses, but were less likely than older females to have intimate friends, and were less frequently able to replace their lost friends. The researcher suggested that the older men's higher suicide rate might be related to this finding.

Current research and investigations into sexuality and age—defensive, apologetic, and depressing indeed in their implications for women —have assumed continuation of traditional male and female sex roles constrained by "the need for heterosexual marital relationship, with the emphasis on sexual intercourse as sexual expression." But moving away from those gender roles and that "narrow focus on sexual intercourse," younger gerontological researchers have speculated that "other positive aspects of sexuality in the later years" could emerge, offering—theoretically at least—future solutions to the sexual dilemma of survivors:

The older woman, faced with a distinct shortage of available men her age, might expand the options that she defines as acceptable to include masturbation, a relationship with another woman, or a relationship with a younger man. . . . Some women choose a relationship with another woman as the preferred lifestyle and do not define it as an alternative to or substitute for a heterosexual relationship.[14]

But when they confront the actual situation of most older women today, the prospect is bleak:

There is no time limit for female sexuality. Women are physiologically capable of full sexual expression until they die. . . . Yet studies show a significant decline in sexual satisfaction and a lessening of sexual activity beginning in midlife. . . . Large numbers of older women live alone, their needs for intimacy unmet. . . . "How long has it been since someone touched me? Twenty years? Twenty years I've been a widow, respected, smiled at, but never touched. Never held so close that loneliness was blotted out. . . . Oh God, I'm so lonely."[15]

Unable honestly to visualize sexual solutions for aging women, most sex therapists and researchers today concentrate on measures to uphold phallic erectile potency in the male. A world-famous female sex therapist told me joyfully of a new hormone mix that might give three to four more years of phallic rigidity to the aging male, better than the prosthetic device that can be switched on and off like a light switch, the kind that sticks out all the time. Does he really get the same enjoyment, one wonders. Well, no —or if he does, and gives it, isn't the *mind* the real sex organ involved? "If only the problem were that simple for women," she joked.

Other researchers have sensed the limits of that youthful male sexual coupling:

Students of human sexuality [concur] that many couples may "have a lot of sex," but suffer from a lack of intimacy. . . . Much sexuality, to be sure, has the quality of intimacy. But genital orgasm can and often does occur without intimacy and even as an offense against it. While intimacy can emerge within the framework of sexuality, intimacy is never adequately defined by sexuality. To view intimacy only as an aspect of sexuality is a peculiar misjudgment of popular modern consciousness.[16]

In Marjorie Fiske's longitudinal research on men and women over four adult life stages in San Francisco, needs for more intimacy were expressed from youth on much more frequently among women than men. That did not surprise the researchers, considering our cultural emphasis from *Moby-Dick* and *Huckleberry Finn* to Hemingway and Fitzgerald—on men's "urge (or necessity) to escape from what is construed as yoking intimacy with women, to escape into parallel work, parallel play, fighting with men. Intimacy between men is warded off . . . in fear of homosexuality. . . ."

Their research confirmed that loss of a wife is more traumatic for men than widowhood for women. "We explain this on the basis that men are less likely to have other persons with whom they are intimate. In fact, men name their spouses as their confidantes—usually their only confidante—far more often than women do." Other psychologists have suggested that men's inability to disclose themselves intimately contributes to their shorter life expectancy. For the process of "disclosing oneself to another" is the essence of intimacy. It may be experienced or enhanced by physical touching, but the touching of the human heart is through words.

Such "reciprocal or mutual . . . trust, support, understanding, and the sharing of confidences" was especially significant for highly stressed middle-aged men facing retirement. In this high-risk population, five years after retirement, the men who showed the fewest psychological and physical symptoms were those with a high rating on "mutuality."

As current statistics show, they have a high rate of heart attacks and other cardiovascular problems, as well as mental health problems, dramatically reflected in the upward swing of the suicide percentages. It is precisely this group in which we found that the existence or absence of close interpersonal relationships was [critical]. . . . In addition to the fact that men in general do not have, but want, more emotional qualities within their close relationships, the middle-aged men who are "overwhelmed" rate themselves low on the capacity for intimacy and mutuality.[17]

New questions are suggested. Is coupling the only answer to intimacy in age? Though we are socialized from infancy to seek one "significant other" to share intimacy, those who study older women suggest this may be too risky in age. As older women, should our search instead be for a few intimate people in our lives—people to have fun with, to be responsive to our pain, and to give us the physical touching we need? Other researchers conclude that denial may simply be the wisest solution for older women; after all, denial of any sexual interest or need protects against depression which, in age as in youth, is the outcome of rage turned inward. But can one long deny that need for intimacy without paying a deep emotional, physical, and spiritual price? "I'm doing okay but I don't feel fully alive." The two great needs for vital aging are control over one's own life and those bonds of intimacy. Feelings of *helplessness,* of not being able to control one's own life, seem, in the research, often to depend upon the presence or absence of such intimacy. Does our very sense of *self,* the personhood that becomes clearer, more unified, *stronger* in age—if we continue to grow and develop after forty, fifty, sixty—still require the matrix of intimacy?

Yet, paradoxically, studies also show that older people, both women and men, often seem to be less lonely in the years after sixty than in their youth or any other period of life. Thus I realized that something more than denial may be involved here, and I circled back to my hunch that age's seemingly insoluble sexual dilemma—as the men die, or lose that phallic power, or select younger women in the hope of restimulating it, and the women live alone for lack of male sexual partners—is based only on that youthful male model of sexual intimacy, a genital sexuality that peaks in youth. If we ask how men and women who survive beyond that youthful peak actually experience intimacy, the paradigm shifts.

A student of mine, when I was trying to teach young would-be gerontologists at the University of Southern California to break through the age mystique, did her term paper on "Intimacy and the Later Years." Evelyn Sofko reported, in some puzzlement:

Interestingly enough, intimacy takes on different meaning as one moves through different stages in the life cycle, i.e., sexual intercourse to touch. Children are socialized to believe that becoming old means becoming sexless, unlovable and unloving, to dread the middle and late years [and] to fulfill this image when they too reach the later years. . . . The emotional and psychological pleasure of intimacy, the delights of caress and touch, physical closeness and the concept of intercourse and orgasm, has been reserved for the youth and early adult years.[18]

She observed that traditional attitudes, shared by doctors and other professionals, that older people do not need intimacy, especially intercourse, and that if intimacy does occur, it should be between a "heterosexual married couple," with the man older or the same age as the woman, are "old fashioned and not realistic options in the later years." But she found the "alternatives" which health professionals suggest for older women "uninviting," if not also unrealistic. Family, children, and grandchildren ("this kind of intimacy allows the older person to remember closeness and past expressions of love and physical holding"); neighbors ("intimacy in this type of relationship comes from dependency . . . getting a ride to the store"); service providers; spiritual intimacy with God and the church; and "friends who care for each other

. . . de-sexualized bonds." She asked six people over sixty how they themselves felt about the "alternative options" now being suggested by some professionals for sexual intimacy for older women: dating a younger man, other women, self-sex or masturbation, open marriages with older men, and "sexual satisfaction from means other than sexual intercourse." She decided:

Older people feel it is obscene to feel and express sensual and sexual feelings if they are bald, wrinkled, gray haired, fat, skinny and sagging. . . . Women feel undesirable as they see their bodies as no longer firm or supple, but sagging and not luscious. . . . Women feel they will be mocked by society. . . . [that] they cannot compete with the beauty of younger women. . . . Women have been raised not to be the initiator in courting men. . . . Furthermore, this present day cohort of older people grew up with a more close-minded attitude toward sex . . . that may prevent them from acting upon the suggestions for intimate relationships, especially sexual ones, such as with younger men, with other women, and/or a married man.

A seventy-two-year-old woman, married for thirty-five years, had had only one intimate relationship in the seventeen years of her widowhood—a "boyfriend" about six years older whom she "dated" for about three years. "Her intimacy went as far as cuddling and touching. ... Because her husband was her one and only love, she felt that having intercourse with anyone else would be disrespectful to their marriage." This widow was "aghast" at the "alternative options." She felt that younger men would never date older women; that older women would never be able to compete with younger women in terms of physical beauty and sex appeal; that men going through their midlife crises would go for a "much younger woman not an older one"; and that "anything younger than 40 would be seen as vile and abnormal" by peers of both the older woman and younger man. As for lesbianism, self-sex, open marriage, "most women of her age would never consider such an alternative ... and if they did, God would punish them."

My student interviewed one couple in their late sixties, who had been together for about thirty-five years, three kids, two grandchildren:

Their relationship was intimate but not in a sexual way. They have not had sex in about eight years, and they rarely touch each other as in cuddling, touching or fondling. But they talk a lot and share a lot of memories and secrets. They trust each other and are loyal to one another. And, to them, this is intimacy. Furthermore, this intimacy is a continuation of their past. They rarely had sex when younger, except when they wanted children, because they did not believe in using birth control.

A single man, sixty-seven, "married to his job," had dated numerous women, progressively younger, the most recent a woman of thirty-two. He would consider dating an older woman "only if she had the looks and body of a 30- or 40-year-old. Looks are very important to him. To him, sex is very important—not cuddling and touching—the sexual act. Currently, this man is dating a woman who is 35 years younger. He says that their relationship is very sexual, although she complains about the lack of other intimate aspects, such as talking and touching."

She also put these questions to a couple married for fifty-eight years, husband eighty-two, wife seventy-one, five children, eleven grandchildren, and two great-grandchildren.

This couple is as much in love now as they were 50 years ago. They enjoy sex very much, although they often do not finish having intercourse because they tend to get tired. But if they do not have intercourse, they love to cuddle and fondle each other. . . . They have always enjoyed intercourse and intimacy through touch, because it is how they express their love. While they do not have intercourse as much now, they have found more intimate, non-sexual gestures as a result. They did not think much of any of the alternatives, especially open marriage, but hoped that some day it would be acceptable that older people do need sex.

My student concluded sadly that to those actual older people she interviewed, "most of the alternatives for intimate sexual relationships were not acceptable . . . alternatives such as older women dating younger men and lesbians were not acceptable because these people were raised in a more strict period of time when sex was to be had only in a traditional marriage. . . . The acceptance of these ideas needs to be taught at younger ages." But all of her older people "enjoy intercourse in some aspect, whether sexual or not." She was now convinced herself that "older people are not sexless." And that "by changing the stereotypes of sexless older people, younger people will grow up with a more open-minded attitude about older people, and perhaps not fear growing old so much."

The younger students in my class seemed almost visibly to change their attitudes about those "poor old people" during this discussion of intimacy. Only the one older auditor, a woman in her seventies from the Andrus Volunteer Program, professed to be "shocked." The younger women shared the feeling that *their* generation in age would not have such inhibitions about meeting their needs for intimacy with younger lovers, or with other women. But even if she herself could not actually envisage "intimate, non-intercourse relationships," my student concluded:

Assuming that older people need or do not need to have sex is dangerous. Sex and intimacy needs to be a choice that each older person should be allowed to make, without pressure or guilt because of society. And this freedom to do as one pleases, whether it is having sex with a younger man and an older woman, two women or masturbation, should be an individual choice.

The question of sex and intimacy in age of course is not that simple. Even in youth, in the supposed peak years, we know that sexual intercourse can be experienced as transcending the boundaries of one's self, the ultimate closeness with the other. But it can also be profoundly alienating—the ultimate experience of loneliness, loathing and self-loathing, depersonalization, dehumanization. From interviews, research, and my own experience, it seems there comes a time when a woman cannot make herself "submit" to pro forma intercourse where there is no real closeness, no shared feelings—married or not married. And men, much as they may desperately want to, may not be able to go through the physical motions. If the basic change in people who continue to grow and develop in age is an authentic *wholeness* of self, transcending that masculine/feminine split in both women and men, then real intimacy must involve a sharing of that truthtelling, authentic self. The ultimate intimacy of such sharing eludes previous measurements of sexual orgasm—even multiple sexual orgasms—in women or men.

When Freud classified his three levels of sexual development—oral, anal, and genital—he was obsessed with reducing to scientific physiological definition a sexuality established by childhood and reaching its peak in early adulthood, forever determined by but finally freed from the Oedipal attachment to father/mother. The Kinsey measurements of genital sex—peaking before thirty in males, strangely immune to such counting in females—remained within that phallic paradigm. But when we start not with such measurements of phallic erection, penetration, and release but with the need of the whole person for intimacy, love, closeness (body and soul), is there a stage of touching beyond the purely genital as that person evolves in the later years to a simple, sure realization of self, a stage that can be seen in those who keep on developing instead of declining into rigidity or falling apart? Oral, anal, genital, *personal* stages of touching, sex, intimacy? Is it more than denial, and a lifetime of sexual inhibition, that makes some older people so sure about an intimacy

471

that is *not* centered on penetration and phallic intercourse?

The suggestion of a further stage in intimacy and a more complex relationship to sexuality comes from many of my own interviews of vital men and women who have grown beyond the needs that preoccupied their younger sexual games. From my interviews, I also sensed that the very fear or denial of age is both cause and effect of that desperate, doomed search for the sex objects, games, and hard-ons of our youth, which keeps us from risking new possibilities of intimacy and touch—the "knowing and being known" that is the essence of sexual love. And even that is unexplored territory beyond the male definition. "He knew her," the Bible said; never "She knew him."

Mike was seventy-four. When he was younger, I thought he looked like Humphrey Bogart. Now, his skin sagged under his chin, he was very brown and wrinkled and thin, but the sardonic glint in his eyes remained. We were lovers— could it be forty-five years ago?—and intimacy was still there. I could ask him, and he could tell me, things "I never somehow told my analyst." He said:

There is something new, different, about sexuality for me now. This medicine I take for my heart is debilitating in terms of erection. It's the actual organic effect of the beta blockers, they tell me. But in terms of the sexual experience itself, I'd say it is better than ever. Even though I'm technically impotent, I experience what happens sexually between Manon and me more intensely than ever. I lose myself more than ever before. There are other forms of sexual contact; I'm not exaggerating, the experience has become more intense—the sense of no boundaries, being truly together. It may have something to do with the technical impotence. I don't have to *perform* anymore, I can forget about it.

It's as though the penis as such becomes the whole body. My old image of the male as the thruster, the woman the receiver, that's gone now, but something better has taken its place. The whole body becomes sexual; there's a kind of losing yourself in the experience, not the old kind of orgasm, the ejaculation. It's as if two people become one person, whatever you're doing together, without any worry about performance, becoming one in the sexual experience.

Is it simply that sex now, for those continuing to become "more and more my real self" in age, differs from the sex of youth, not only because that may be no longer physically possible but because it means denying, not sharing, all that one has become? When the intimate private sexual experience—whatever the act of touch—involves that whole self, the intimacy that is reached surmounts all the sexual fantasies of youth, all those male/female power games and defenses. And surely it strengthens that sense of identity, aliveness, being in control of one's life, which is so essential to vital aging.

Within or outside of marriage, if sexuality is to be a fountain of age, it has to affirm and express that real self in intimacy. It has to transcend the old defenses and rages that come from playing those narrow male- or female-dominated power games, the masks that kept us from real intimacy in our marriages, the youthful "singles" pursuits. Sometimes a physical crisis, loss of erectile potency or nubile breast, even impending death, may finally force a breakthrough of masks previously preventing that intimacy, transforming a stale marriage or yielding the resolve finally to end one that does not meet that need for real intimacy.

One man facing sixty alone, Noel Perrin, a Dartmouth professor, candidly expressed some of the problems "when we take younger women out, and when we date our contemporaries":

> I, at least, often do take younger women out ... I do it because they have long shining hair and good figures. . . . Not only is some sleek divorcee of 38 likely to be better looking than women my own age, she's also likely to be more adaptable. She's got youthful

verve. . . . But take out such a woman, as I did all of last year, and you let yourself in for endless playacting and for a surprising amount of humiliation.

So why not take out women my own age? . . . Those first dates are hard. . . . There is not going to be that instant and spontaneous attraction that leads to second and third dates when you're young. For the young, sexual attraction serves as a kind of handy glue, keeping a couple together until other and more desirable bonds take hold. Shared memories, shared thoughts. . . . shared children. . . . But how do you get from first meeting to love, to what was once called being stuck on someone, with so little glue?

True intimacy is the whole purpose of middle-age dating. Only what took one date to accomplish at 25 may now take five or ten. By middle age, people have developed complex personalities, whole networks of obligations, settled habits. It would be naive to expect any quick meshing. . . . It's more work, of course. But then, we're deeper people now. With luck, we might wind up with the kind of rich and tolerant relationship we didn't even dream of when we were young.[19]

A friend of mine who had kept on playing the cute-and-pretty-young-thing into her forties, never talking very deeply even with her women friends, married—late—a handsome bon vivant equally concerned with appearance. When her breast cancer was diagnosed, some deeper need forced her to leave him. She became much more "real," more herself, and began to search for or renew deeper friendships with women and men she had known earlier, and to reveal more of herself in her work. Then she married a much less flamboyant man, with whom she clearly shared a more intimate, less defensive caring. When her second breast cancer was diagnosed, she called him, and he flew back from an important scientific conference in Germany. Ten years later, their intimacy seemed stronger than ever and her cancer had been in remission past the danger period.

In his late sixties, after forty years of marriage, another friend of mine experienced untouched depths of intimacy—"the most profound loving and touching and knowing of another person I would not have dreamed possible"—after his wife was diagnosed with inoperable cancer.

I told her, whatever happens, I promise to tell you the truth, to keep nothing from you, if you will tell me what you are really feeling, and what you want, whatever is happening. I thought it would be important for her to count on that. What I didn't count on was how it transformed me. Those were the most joyous, the most wonderful months of my life, with all the pain and the horror. They were shining, extraordinary, glorious moments, being completely open like that.

I thought we had a good marriage before, we both went our own ways, supported each other in our careers, were good parents, entertained. In all my years, so concerned with my business, with my boards, with knowing important people, doing the right thing, and never maybe feeling adequate to it all—was I ever that good a husband in her eyes? Suddenly we were there, that incredible strong thing between us, and I really knew what she was feeling, and that she really knew me.

He was a very desirable catch after she died, and dated a few younger, beautiful women. But he married a woman nearly his own age, a widow with serious purposes like his wife, and in his mid-seventies now was trying to achieve with her that intimacy of "truly sharing thoughts and feelings, not running away from them," he had experienced in those months facing death when he and his first wife dropped all the masks and really *knew* each other.

I have heard women my age expressing their rage over unfinished power battles in their marriages, the slights they may be experiencing in their careers or social life, and above all that unfair sexual imbalance and the lack of intimacy in their lives. But the rage almost built into those unequal, obsolete sex roles, the masks we use to hide that rage, and the subtle and not-so-subtle ways we express it, are all in themselves barriers to true intimacy. As can be rage over age itself. Men and women who still seek to fulfill youthful roles will be prevented by that rage from evolving to new levels of personhood and life-affirming intimacy. As the crisis of prostate or breast cancer can free a man or woman from no longer relevant roles that prevent intimacy, so age itself—if we will allow it—can free us from the defenses and rage such roles impose, to experience the pain of their loss and the liberation of moving on.

But marriage in American society, until very recently, has been shaped by rigidly polarized sex roles. And the rage they engender, exploding first in women in the 1960s and 1970s, with a backlash from men in the violent 1980s, has to be confronted if any marriage is to be a source of life-sustaining intimacy. The great increase in the divorce rate during this period (up to 50 percent before it stabilized a few years ago) stemmed partly from the explosion of that rage, as women broke through the narrow definition of their role, and men sought new, often younger partners to sustain their illusion of youth and dominance, or suffered midlife crises yearning for that intimacy.

From my own interviews, I sensed that confronting and transcending that rage is necessary if marriage itself is to be a source of the fountain of age. For many, rage is compounded by the dread and denial of age, and the futile attempt to hold on to the facade of youth. But the truth-telling compulsion to become one's real self (the hallmark of age-as-growth) and the yearning for real intimacy before it is too late can also precipitate the crisis that changes the marriage, or opens new possibilities of intimacy and identity beyond marriage (even for people who played those roles into their sixties and seventies). Where a marriage is held together by "false glue"—money, vicarious power or celebrity, fear of being alone, convention, children, specious economic considerations—the crisis of that exploding rage, and other existential urgencies in the face of age, may shatter the facade. Then both may seek intimacy in new ways, or rebuild the marriage on a more authentic basis.

Maureen's first husband was a powerful, charismatic man, a compulsive gambler, wealthy when she married him, making and losing several fortunes since. She was a striking, well-dressed suburban housewife, a volunteer for causes, an avid shopper. Though her husband was a "terrific sexual athlete," she never told him what she really felt about anything, and sought out adventure for herself in affairs with other men. When their younger son went on drugs, and nothing they did could stop him, the rage exploded "and the sham of our marriage fell apart." In her fifties, Maureen went back to school, got a degree in social work, moved, alone, to California, and gradually made new friends in a wholly different world from the comfortable suburban life she had enjoyed before. In her sixties, she married Kevin, a widowed former librarian and retired professor of children's literature, a calm, quiet man with lively interests in music, literature, art, who refused lucrative offers of consulting in order to pursue his own interests in his retirement. She said:

I can tell him anything, even when I think I've made a fool of myself, teaching a class, dealing with the dean, giving advice to a client. I would never have let my guard down with my first husband that way. Approval, the money, the social things that used to be important to me, somehow the sham of it all fell apart when our son went on drugs. I never would have looked at a man like Kevin in those days. I wasn't even that interested in him sexually in the beginning. I've had all that, the excitement, affairs. But he wanted it, and I wanted to be there for him. He is there for me in all ways. When I realize that I can really be myself with him, and I tell him these things that I never would have told anyone before, it's like wall after wall goes down. And the sex is getting deeper somehow, not the excitement of those affairs. But everything we do together is intimate.

Some of my feminist friends seethe with rage at aging husbands who turn in their old wives for younger clones. But such men, when they lose their own power, can also be hapless targets of the long-buried rage of newly empowered old wives. When Polly married Tom, he was a powerful aerospace executive. He was in his mid-fifties and she was in her forties, blond, beautiful, divorced with two children, and going back to school to get a professional degree in business administration. She loved their glamorous life. But when I met her ten years later, teaching in California, she was simmering with rage, for no apparent reason, at her husband. She continued to entertain his clients and colleagues, and to go with him to the beach club and benefits, but she was moving ahead ambitiously in her own career now. Over fifty herself, though she didn't admit it, she was exercising compulsively several hours a day in the gym, playing for the club tennis championship, so obsessed about her weight that her friends teased her about anorexia. But when he was forced out of his job, retiring at sixty-three, with a severance contract that kept him from working in the aerospace industry, her pent-up rage exploded. He wanted to cut down on their entertaining now, to be more frugal about clothes and other expenses, to "adjust to a lifestyle we can maintain in age."

"I'm not old, I don't intend to get old myself. I

481

weigh less now than I did when I was twenty-five," she said firmly. "My figure's better, I take care of my skin. I can't stand the change in him, the fear, the depression, this tightness with money." She started flirting with her colleagues, had an affair with a younger man, and decided to divorce her husband. In the face of age, even if she denied it, she still "dated" according to the rules we learned when we were young. For a while, she was "dating" a distinguished older doctor. His tennis game was great, he was good in bed, she said, and his friends were interesting. But on a weekend at his beach house, she picked up a book and discovered from the flyleaf that he was seventy-nine, and now she felt that rage at him. Again she exploded, told him she wouldn't go out with him anymore, it was "indecent" of him to chase someone as young as she when there were so many women out there his own age. "They don't interest me," he replied. "They are too old for me. I play tennis better than I ever did. I write as well as I ever did. I'm not really old. I don't even like to think about age." She said to me accusingly: "He *really* has a problem about age."

For some men, retirement and the mere release from preoccupation with success and power (and the erectile potency that often seems tied up with this in very complex ways) opens up new possibilities of intimacy, in new or old marriages. And for some women, rage subsides when they satisfy their own power needs in a later career and from choice, not passive martyrdom, achieve intimacy on a different basis with the husband and children they brought up. But for others, at this transition point in their life history, that crossover leads to a divergence in the face of age. She is preoccupied with that late self-realization in her career as he faces forced retirement and the need to move on from his own preoccupation with power, with perhaps a new yearning for an intimacy with wife, kids, or other men or women that he never felt before. And sometimes he seeks such intimacy with a younger woman and a new family because his own wife is too preoccupied with her own career needs now, or still too suffused with that rage for intimacy to be possible, or even sexual desire. Or perhaps he is still obsessed himself with youthful machismo, denying his own aging. Reminded of his age by his wife, and blaming his loss of potency on her, he tries to repeat the pattern of his youthful marriage with new young wife and children.

Research shows that in marriages where the success or power imbalance is very great, the sexual satisfaction and intimacy are low. (In one study of wives of successful men, 67 percent complained of unsatisfied needs for sexual intimacy. "He is like a machine, it's as if he isn't there.") As I discovered, unmasking the roots of the feminine mystique in the Kinsey figures, with each decade of improvement in women's rights, as more equality was achieved, women acquired more ability to experience sexual orgasm. Conversely, if men can indeed be liberated in age from their obsession with power and performance, their own human potential for sensitivity and nurturance can be released—and not only with a new young wife and children. In Hollywood, where aging all-powerful tycoons often sport young "trophy" wives, gossip confirms what other research reveals: they get it off from the power; the "trophy" wives are for show. Those excessively dominant males are reported to be less than dynamic in bed.

I met a former such tycoon who at midlife started growing in a different direction, in the interests of true intimacy. A graying, fast-moving, sharp-talking former go-getter in sweater and jeans, Frank McCarthy at fifty-seven was enrolled at the USC School of Social Work with his wife, cycling back to values he seemed to have given up during his thirty-year career in oil and show business. He had retired from producing television series, game shows, and monster movies.

My wife was a top model when I met her, a Miss Sweden. But she didn't like show business, the spotlight. She loves kids, cooking, our home, real people. The entertainment scene is alien to her, the bullshit. She wouldn't go to the parties; they love you when you're hot and don't know you when you're not. . . . She's an honest real person. Unfortunately, we didn't do a lot together when I was in the entertainment business. We have four children; two are teenagers now, growing up. She decided she wanted to do something serious with her life, become a social worker, but since English was her second language, she was nervous about going to graduate school. So I said, I'll do it with you. I was bored with show business, we could do homework together, drive to school together, eventually have a practice together.

So now I'm closer to my wife than I ever was. We've been together seventeen years, but I don't think we were ready before to be that close. Now I guess we're secure and comfortable enough in ourselves to accept the intensity of our intimacy. We have a deep, intimate, intense closeness now—the honesty of it, I never conceived of. We could be physically touching each other, close as in sex, but if you're not emotionally there, you don't really touch each other. Now everything has come together and both of us are really involved in our marriage.

I'm the oldest guy in the school here, the others are in their twenties. But emotionally, I'm different. I'm more patient, more tolerant, less strain, less stress. I have peace of mind. I can take the feelings I used to run away from. And because of that, my sex drive seems to have increased. During the movie business days, the pressures, I didn't seem to have that much sex drive. I put it into other things. Since I got out of those pressures, making money, I seem to get more stimulated sexually. In fact, I went to the doctor, am I crazy, I feel sexual all the time? Maybe I should just enjoy it, it's not a bad feeling.

When I first met Doris Cole, twenty-five years ago at a Presbyterian Church conference where I was speaking, she was a very tense, frustrated, angry minister's wife. A few years later, I met her again, her husband now a college president, and found her playing her role as president's wife with icy correctness and that seething rage underneath. As president's wife, how could she move as other women her age were moving now into their own careers? She should at least have a job title and a salary of her own as president's wife! When I next ran into her, on a plane from Washington, she had been divorced, and had become a college vice-president of development herself. And now, at sixty-eight, in a mellow old New Hampshire farmhouse surrounded by mountains, she was exultantly happy with her new husband—a widower who was also an old friend, both aggressively "retired" and exploring new paths together, surprised by their own new adventurousness in domestic intimacy:

This is the best relationship I've ever had. We enjoy each other, we both feel cherished. He knew I was going to an early meeting so he laid out breakfast before he went to bed. There just aren't any of those power struggles and resentments I used to seethe with when I was married before. There's just this lovely shining closeness.

A friend of mine in a long-term homosexual relationship, my neighbor Joe Pintauro, an ex-priest turned playwright, was facing sixty. Although he was gray, his face was very boyish, surprisingly unlined for fifty-nine years. He had some thoughts about sex and intimacy. From my own stereotype of the homosexual obsession with youth, I surmised that a purely physical, phallic definition of sexual intimacy would make age an even more terrifying prospect for some male homosexuals than for straight men or women. On the other hand, as Joe put it, and some of the research confirms, since nothing at all is *given* to assure homosexuals intimacy and support in age (without the conventional roles of marriage, parent, children, home), it's all existential. They are more likely to know that it has to be invented to happen at all (as, even for straight couples long married, intimacy has to be reinvented, consciously, to sustain that roleless age).

Over a dinner of leftovers at my table in Sag Harbor, Joe discussed this with me.

Intimacy? Intimacy can interfere with sex—not just among homosexuals—there's a fear of intimacy that allows sex and doesn't allow anything else. Sex can hurl you into the arms of a person and then when it's over, what am I doing here with this stranger? A lot of the promiscuity among homosexuals is the fear of intimacy. But sex can also lure you into those forbidden places of the heart.

With Greg, whom I've been living with over ten years now, I have intimacy, but no sex, not anymore. I seem to have a problem combining them. What I have with him is great love, commitment, dedication, but I can't see how to put that together with sex. I think I've come close to the heart of intimacy, but that heart is not sexual. There's some danger about intimacy, like going through a burning ring, something that one has to risk, give up. When intimacy occurs, it has that catastrophic effect of opening you up to a whole new life. If you achieve that bond with someone, do you walk away or make it the core of your existence? It's so funny that I'd be here talking about the heart and the fire and the danger of it, not the sex but the intimacy.

It's been a precondition of my adult life that I'm scared of intimacy. But in the last ten years, under the shadow of AIDS, there's been much more intimacy among homosexuals than there ever was before. AIDS has transformed the gay community. It has swept away the fear of age, obsession with youth. Gays are showing more courage, more idealism, more caring; they are more focused in their sense of reality now, faced by AIDS, than I would have believed possible. In the gay community, there is more complex intimacy; it's at a higher level now, a sharing of pain and fear and not just pleasure. A familial constellation forms among people when one of us dies. I can't tell you how many of my own friends have died—all of us who knew that person immediately bond as a result of sharing that loss. This bonding is happening over and over again among gay people now. You're linked to each other as a survivor, you're sharing the memories of him, the grief. It's all there is now—we are becoming more precious to one another, we are all afraid of losing one another; this incredible bonding that's taking place among gays now in the constant face of death could even be envied by heterosexuals.

In the play Joe was working on then, people are stranded on a boat that is slowly sinking in the middle of the ocean. The boat will ultimately sink, there is no way to save it. But they find some kind of mysterious balance, moving in continuous intense awareness of each other, that will keep them alive, afloat, indefinitely. It is a metaphor for AIDS, of course. But it also could be a metaphor for the dance of life in the face of age. That real glue of intimacy cannot save us from age or AIDS, but it can keep us *alive,* in intense touch with each other, finally *knowing and letting ourselves be known.*

That women, even in marriage, are more likely to have intimate, complex friendships ("confidantes") seems a significant clue to their greater vitality and survival strength. While women still buy the paperback romances that nourish their fantasies as heroines of love stories—the only stories, until recently, women ever could be heroines of—older women in real life now can see themselves as heroines of other stories and sometimes look beyond "coupling" for intimacy even when they have satisfying marriages.

In their fifties now, Blanche Wiesen Cook and Clare Coss recently celebrated their twentieth anniversary together by returning to the park bench in London where they decided to leave their husbands and move in with each other. They had met on the barricades of the peace movement in 1968 as young college instructors, unpublished writers. Now Clare was a playwright and psychotherapist, Blanche a college professor and distinguished biographer who had just finished her first volume of Eleanor Roosevelt's life. They told me they were both such "workaholics" and so involved in community activities that they made "dates" with each other, despite the fact that they have long shared a house, to nurture their own intimacy with enough time to talk.

When Blanche developed breast cancer, Clare organized a group of other women who had also faced life-threatening illness, to help see her friend and lover through it. Blanche's voice broke when she described how Clare's support "really saved my life." She had been so terrified and ashamed of her cancer, she couldn't even talk about it. So Clare, who as part of her group therapy practice ran groups on "Love and Lesbian Relationships—Bringing Out the Best in Each Other," quickly organized a "Living with Cancer" group. Clare said:

In the group, we were able to deal with it. That's what the lesbian community is about, a gang of intimate loving friendships, including single women, living alone because sometimes that's the best way, but always surrounded by intimate friends, not like a man walking away when the passion is ended.

Blanche reported, with humorous awe:

You're not going to believe this, but after Clare organized that group for me, my body actually created a gang of giant multi-nucleated cells that surrounded my cancer. A bunch of specialists from all over the city were coming around to look at my slides, my beautiful gang of cells. That's what I believe we need, a gang to support us in life.

When Clare leads her couple groups now, in addition to the sessions on "competition and equality," "romance and passion," "money and power," she includes "activism in the community." She said:

The more involved in a larger community, the more air in the relationship. Couples when they come together tend to merge. Once the initial bliss fades, these other issues emerge, and they begin to bore each other. Well, we still interest each other, we don't take each other for granted. I feel very strongly about commitment. We've gone through stages, we were not always monogamous, but for the last ten years, though we may flirt and have fantasies, we are committed to each other, we are sure about that.

When we have problems as a couple, we look to our group for help. We've learned to let each other know our feelings. When Blanche is upset about something, I don't take it personally anymore. I just listen, but I don't have to control what she is feeling. In our group, there is such respect now for our differences.

We have a new sense of the urgency of time; we want to spend our time with friends who are also interested in empowerment, in the things we believe in. We're blessed with friends who are in struggle but not gloomy. With the terrible frightening things going on in the world now, such friends are all.

Married or alone, straight or gay, such life-strengthening intimacy is not a given, it cannot be taken for granted in age. But if it is absent, or lost, or has deteriorated into boredom, apathy, alienation, or despair, or is blotted out by rage, fear, or physical illness, there is still time to make the choices that will transcend these losses and fears, and find other forms of intimacy to keep that ship afloat.

Dr. Helen Kaplan, facing her sixties herself now though she doesn't make a point of it, is a world-famous sex therapist, director of the Human Sexuality Program at New York Hospital—Cornell Medical College. She has seen in the last few years a great increase in the number of older couples—not newlyweds but men and women in their fifties, sixties, even older, in first or second marriages—wanting to "enhance" their sexual relationship. "In the early years of my practice, only younger people sought help from sex therapists," she said. "If fifty- or sixty-year-old women or men were dissatisfied, he had an affair, she played more golf and bridge. Now, they want to improve their sexual intimacy with their longtime partner."

And where that is their real desire, to have that intimacy with each other, we can help them. But if they don't really want to make love to each other, not even the most advanced penile implant will make much difference for very long. If you really want to have and give sexual pleasure, you transcend the limitations of the body by age or disease. If you are really conflict-free about giving and receiving sexual pleasure, and you're relatively secure and understand the physiological changes that make older men take longer, need more stimulating to reach an orgasm, then neither of them will panic, or feel unloved, or retreat, if he doesn't get the kinds of erections he used to. Despite our national obsession with that fully erect penetrating member or the firm, full, nubile breast, studies of women after mastectomy show that for most women there is no interruption of sex life, sexual pleasure, and their husband's desire is not affected, unless they have problems with sex, period. Then the mastectomy, the first sign of changed erection, "age" itself, excuses the retreat from sex, and a wall may go up against intimacy. Otherwise, in exploring new ways to touch and respond to each other, their intimacy may deepen.

More men come to me for help than women —in their fifties, and more and more over sixty —because they have become impotent. They read about the new technology and think it can be fixed. Women think they are no longer desirable or desired; they may be sad, like the men, but if they see no real alternatives, they resign themselves to it. Like giving up water skiing. The men may blame it on their aging wives and seek a younger partner, but often that doesn't work either.

The need for intimacy, or the desire for continued sexual aliveness, is usually not a hormonal matter, Kaplan said. Even for men, she suggested that testosterone injections, or the latest technological development (penile implants) can be as useful as a "contact lens, or hearing aid" in the service of continued sexual desire, but lead only to further depression if there is no real desire, no real intimacy, and if he has to deny his age.

If he thinks he is expected to perform like a man in his thirties, get an instant erection, hold it, do it twice, he becomes completely unable to perform, he's too afraid. Or she is afraid even to undress because her body isn't as firm as it was when she was thirty. Even with plastic surgery, no sixty-year-old can really look like a thirty-year-old; much better off to be a sexy sixty-year-old.

There are age-related changes in sexual functions, and once you understand them, they don't have to be disastrous. But if the older woman is insecure—am I undesirable, if he doesn't get an immediate erection he doesn't love me, I'm too old, I don't arouse him—it escalates into sexual avoidance. The longer that lasts, the more difficult it is to break the ice, overcome the avoidance. The older woman who is loving and sure enough accommodates herself to these age-related changes —they have oral sex, do it in the morning, whatever. But if she's preoccupied with her own insecurity, she thinks it's because I'm old, if I were only younger [and so may he].

I see many marriages now of older men and younger women with real problems. For a while, that younger woman sustained his fantasy of remaining forever young, all-powerful, a powerhouse. She had the image of this powerful man who can do anything. The paradox is, the older woman is likely to be much more accepting of his reality, and his vulnerability. A man can have millions of dollars but his penis is still sixty-eight years old. An older man can be a wonderful partner, a wonderful lover, if they both can get away from that obsession with the penis and the performance. In a sense, he has to become more like a woman, the total experience of the touch, the making love, not just that erection and penetration. He has to become accepting of his own and the older woman's need for more stimulation and responsiveness, and the reality of their less firm bodies.

We finally realize that phallic, performance-oriented definition of sexuality is both cause and effect of the sexual stereotypes that still limit all our thinking, personal and theoretical, about intimacy and age. And in fact, the prospect of real intimacy for women and men moving into their sixties today has been *enhanced* by the dramatic changes in our roles and expectations brought about by the women's movement, even though within marriage we seemed for a while to be embarking on sharply divergent, conflicting courses that might make intimacy almost impossible. The very intensity of the storm, and the deterioration of intimacy in conventional marriages of the recent past, testify to the buried rage beneath those masks of happy dependent housewife and all-powerful breadwinner we once were forced to wear. But I've observed, among women of my generation who have successfully moved into new paths of their own after raising their children, that the rage subsides, and the divergent paths converge again, if the marriages can survive. According to the research, the couples facing age with lowest morale and least sense of intimacy are those where the husband *still defines himself as family chief and provider,* and where the woman *still sees her identity only as housewife/mother.*

Many researchers report that hostility and marital dissatisfaction peak during the period preceding the "empty nest" and retirement—especially when the career directions of wife and husband are "out of phase"—and then, if the marriage survives, intimacy improves. The older women in the San Francisco study were "significantly more likely to perceive themselves as assertive and intelligent, and less likely to regard themselves as dependent, helpless, undecided or easily embarrassed. The older men were significantly less likely to perceive themselves as ambitious, hostile and resentful." While these married women were often "lonely" during the "empty nest" period, when the husbands were still preoccupied with success in their careers, now "it is the husband, rather than the wife, who is the more vulnerable partner needful of emotional support." In the face of retirement, "the men may rely on their wives for the affirmation of their self-worth and the continuity of their sense of identity." Middle-aged women give their spouses less importance as someone to "confide in" than do men. The fact is, women have "a greater choice of confidantes than men, who depend more highly—often solely—on the wife in this regard." Intimacy deepens with age as these men rely increasingly on the spouse as "someone to share interests and activities and to provide companionship." [20]

By their sixties, according to the anthropologist Paul Bohannon, they become a couple in a new sense—an autonomy in which neither man nor wife has any "dependency needs" but both choose to be "dependent and depended on for their mutual benefit." By that time, only a very small minority (14 percent) of the women in the San Francisco study felt that "my marriage doesn't give me enough opportunity to become the sort of person I'd like to be." Entering age, almost two thirds of these women were working, though almost none had "careers." Interestingly, neither husbands nor wives now gave much importance to their spouses' being "personally attractive" or providing sexual satisfaction. What was rated important now was "respect," "knows me well," "is comfortable to be with," "likes me," and "strong emotional attraction for each other."

The crossover of male and female sex roles in midlife may also enhance sexual activity in age. "Women, who have assumed submissive and passive roles generally, and in sexual behavior specifically, may become more assertive, instrumental, and initiating in their behavior."[21] One survey (1982) of 160 midlife women found them able to take the sexual initiative more often in a relationship (marriage or otherwise), and to appreciate their own sexual needs and desires rather than being primarily a participant in activity to please a partner. In another study, some women reported that they could no longer continue to submit to relationships with poor communication, lack of intimacy, and perfunctory sexual intercourse.[22]

The women of a more recent generation who focused on their own careers and did not marry or have children until nearly forty exhibited a comparable crossover, presaging new intimacy and perhaps an end to that "out of phase" career trajectory. When *New York* magazine (August 3, 1982) rounded up forty such women who used to put career first and were now marrying for the first time, in their forties and fifties, the one quality they seemed to have in common was "self-confidence." Such women appeared to have gone through a midlife crisis, like men, when their careers peaked in their mid-thirties or forties. Success in their work no longer was that fulfilling, and their goals were now "intimacy . . . bonding." They had enough confidence now—"often because of demonstrated competence on the job"—not to fear being "trapped" by marriage as their mothers had been. But they didn't look for the kind of man they might have when they were young. They no longer sought to marry the would-be-successful playwright or lawyer "instead of going to law school myself."

Esther was a top publishing executive when, at forty, she married Stan, a fifty-year-old psychologist with two grown children. She admitted: "He wasn't the kind of man I would have dated six years earlier. He wasn't as sophisticated and worldly as many men I knew. But he was strong and kind—he had a great sense of humanity. He didn't promise me the sun, the moon, and the stars. He promised me a healthy relationship, and that's what I value now."

Older men are more clearly seeking intimacy in their marriages now, the second or third time, if not the first. The *remarriage* rate for men in their fifties is higher than the first marriage rate for men twenty years younger. And the Census Bureau now reports that men over forty-five usually marry women who are only three to six years younger, and some even older. Stan Fisher met Esther shortly after his second divorce. He said: "I have no ability to be in a superficial connection with women, and with younger women, the connection was impossible. Esther and I were both mature and we knew how to deal with our problems. Younger women may be attractive physically, but they don't have the experience and exposure to life that makes older women more interesting to me."

Curves of mortality from many different diseases, taken from British census data, show higher mortality among men married to much younger or to much older women than among men married to women their own age or only a few years younger than themselves. They also show that women married to much younger or much older men generally experience higher mortality than those married to men of similar ages to themselves. The interpretation was that the younger spouse would shorten the older person's life by the simple pressure to keep up. But perhaps the lack of true intimacy or the extremes of dependence shorten the younger partner's life as well.[23]

The problems that older men and women are beginning to bring to sex therapists—including some very desperate older spouses after they have sought renewal with younger partners—often turn out to be byproducts of clinging to the youthful fantasy of sexual performance and attraction. Because they cannot restore sexual prowess, many therapists bypass that rigid youthful sexual definition to open the channels of intimacy and new pleasure it is blocking in older couples, or even the May-December ones. The real problem is usually the lack of or withdrawal from intimacy, which that youthful sexual fantasy obscures and obstructs.

Dr. Avodah Offit, former director of the Sexual Therapy Clinic at Lenox Hill Hospital in New York, told me:

The problem is, the ideals of our culture, even and especially in sex, make love in age very difficult. A seventy-two-year-old man comes to me because he doesn't get a complete erection. He was in love with a thirty-six-year-old woman who he thought was leaving him because of sex. So did she. It turned out that because he thought he couldn't perform, he had withdrawn from her, was no longer touching her or expressing his feeling for her. Because of his macho definition of sex, he wasn't giving himself the full freedom to be loving. I had to get them to be inventive, take chances in expressing their love.

Another woman, a California boutique owner, came into my office with what I thought was her son. She is sixty-two; for ten years she's been living with this adorable, delightful person. What is the problem? She can't let go sexually and love this fellow because she's afraid that at her age she's too unattractive, she's afraid that he'll leave her, find some younger sex object. It had been erotic at first, then she withdrew out of fear he would leave her for a young chick. But he has hung around for ten years, though they are not married, and it's not really a mother-son relationship. He is awfully mature at thirty, and he really does adore her. The problem was not sexual, it was that youth-age obsession that made her unwilling to risk really adoring this man.

It seemed to Cliff Sager, director of sex therapy for the Jewish Board of Family Services in New York, that older men are marrying or staying married to women closer to their own age than they did ten or fifteen years ago, when the divorce rate exploded. In his own practice and experience, he said he no longer sees so many men in their sixties seeking twenty- to thirty-year-olds.

I feel the men and the women approaching age now have begun to look for different values instead of trying to recapture their youth. Now they want a companion who understands and has lived in the world they've lived in. When I was in my late fifties, I dated women twenty to twenty-five years younger, and I found after a while I had very little in common with them. They didn't understand my history, I really wasn't where they were now, I'd had my kids. So I married Ann, who is not that much younger, who's a professional, has raised her kids, we could talk on the same level. I didn't think that was what I was looking for, but when it happened I realized how important it was. In second marriages, the matter of intimacy and respect is the important thing.

It seems to me, now, that not only in areas of sexual intimacy and marriage but with our children and parents, families and friends, we have to keep finding new ways, new rituals, to keep alive or renew those life-enriching bonds of intimacy in age. We need new social groups if the old ones lock us into stereotypes, or lock us out because of them. We must continually beware of our own tendency to try to repeat—or defend against—ways of loving that sustained or betrayed us in youth, retreating behind self-erected walls of isolation or frantic public activity to avoid rejection, humiliation, instead of risking, risking, risking the reality of intense, shared, intimate experience. Intimacy in age, maybe more than in youth, has to involve pain, mistakes, uncertainties. But we are free enough now and strong enough to embrace it all in ways we were afraid to before.

The crucial challenge in age (in and beyond marriage) is to continually make the occasions to deepen the touching and shared disclosure that is the true glue of intimacy—with friend, neighbor, or colleague; son or daughter; parent or grandchild; any lover. It can be done across generations and be kept alive despite thousands of miles of distance—and it can die, if left unnourished, among spouses occupying the same house, or next-door neighbors in Sun City or Sag Harbor. Those essential ties of intimacy may or may not resemble what we thought of as love in our youth; but whether we are married or widowed, living in the old city neighborhood or new retirement village, with children and grandchildren nearby or scattered over the continent, it now takes conscious choice to keep them vital and renewed.

Evelyn Duvall, whom I had known of as a pioneer in the marriage counseling field, heard that I was interviewing in Sarasota and invited me to the condominium from which, in her eighties, she informally presided over a loosely knit tribe of friends and neighbors in the Plymouth Harbor retirement complex, on the causeway overlooking the Gulf. "The most exciting thing in my life now," she said,

is interaction with other people—friends, sometimes even relatives—at levels of depth I've never conceived of before. For so many decades I was too busy with my career, my profession, getting married, having babies; the thrilling thing now is to get really close to people. I'm not afraid of exposing myself to other people anymore—men, women, young, old—you can get close to people now without all of the trappings that got in the way before. You're not born happy, it wasn't even given when your breasts were a perfect 36. Happiness here, now, is the end result of this dynamic I'm talking about, the intimacy you create and re-create by sharing life experience.

The ties of intimacy, the bonds of truly shared self ("confidants") are the crucial source of the fountain of age, the research showed. Deep, personal bonds with friends count more in vital aging than casual perfunctory family ties, or mere membership or attendance in social groups, new studies show. Shared history is a powerful starter with children and the friends of one's youth, as is the intimacy of bed and shared space in marriage. Projects and battles shared are a powerful promoter of those bonds in our midlife careers, political movements, community causes. But more and more now, in the later years of life, these ties can no longer be taken for granted. If we are no longer active in the battles ourselves, the memories alone are not enough. If we are no longer truly involved in office or profession or movement, the ties must be renewed in other ways, or replaced. If our grandchildren live a hundred miles away or a thousand, the phone call or occasional family visit is not enough. Some more organic or intensive way must be found to sustain real intimacy. Our "given" bonds—of family, school, profession, marriage, children, grandchildren—are no longer automatically renewed. And new bonds are no longer automatically given as we move into late life. It's all a matter of choice now. That's scary, but it's also liberating, if we are strong enough to admit our need for that intimacy, and keep on risking— pain, rejection, the unknown—to find new ways of creating these intimate bonds.

My friend Liz Carpenter started a "Baying at the Moon Club" when, after the death of her husband, and a long career in Washington, she moved back to Austin, Texas, and built herself a hospitable house with an ever-bubbling hot tub on a ridge overlooking the city. She rents a different cottage each year at holiday times, one year in Martha's Vineyard, another year in the California wine country or Mexico, and invites five or six of her friends to share it with her. One provides a piano, another the car, another takes care of the wine. Other holidays she spends with her children; she doesn't try to mix the two.

My cousin Mickey Bazelon takes one grandchild at a time on a trip to a country of her choice. She just took her youngest to Holland. The summer of her seventy-fifth birthday, she invited her son and his wife, the grandchildren, her brother and sister-in-law, her cousin (me), and six friends for a long weekend at an inn in Maine. We all had intimate ties with her to begin with, but most of us barely knew each other. Over breakfast, lunch, dinner, biking, shopping in Bar Harbor in the rain, arguing about politics, abortion, sharing thoughts about women, men, age, and new, common family and personal problems—non-stop talking, increasingly personal—we formed new bonds of intimacy with each other on that weekend. When I go to Washington now, I don't stay at a hotel, I sometimes stay with Mickey if she's there. I have dinner with her children and grandchildren when I go to visit my own in Philadelphia, and though they are cousins thrice removed, they now have bonds with each other.

On the white-pillared verandah of that inn in Maine, my cousin, looking incredibly radiant on her seventy-fifth birthday, confided she had only one face-lift, "years ago now." We compared notes on the ever-changing mysteries of our own feelings about ourselves as women, the men we have loved, and aging. She told me that day in Maine:

I'm coming into myself now. Finally, I feel accepting of myself, good about myself, I'm learning who I really am finally. Having you all here expresses it. All the years of my marriage,

I was concerned with my social position, my world-beating projects. I've been sloughing all that off like a caterpillar. But something essential, shining, is coming out now. I feel calmer somehow, certain of who I am. I'm not going to change the world anymore. I did what I could. I enjoy what I'm doing now, in the moment.

I started my own "family of choice" before I ever thought about age. I was forty-nine, had finally gotten divorced, and was afraid of being alone. I was not even thinking about getting married again—to end this marriage had been too terrifying—but I had no sense at all of how I was going to live my life. I still had one child at home, Emily, who was then thirteen. I didn't want to go back to our house on Fire Island, now for sale, where we had spent summers before. Life there was two-by-two, couples; it would be too painful, awkward, to go back there alone.

Two old friends of mine, both men, also happened to be in the process of divorce. I rang Arthur's doorbell in the city, unannounced, one morning when I was in his neighborhood and said:

You know what we really need—a commune, a kibbutz. We didn't do it right, this marriage thing. We are the type who don't like being alone. What's to keep us from making another mistake and getting married again from sheer loneliness? What will we really miss, not being married, that could open us to that? Not just sex, I think. It's living with someone, being able to sit around the kitchen table in your bathrobe without makeup on, letting it all hang out. Why don't we rent a big house together for the summer, and if it works out, keep it for weekends and holidays.

The first house, in Sagaponack, had five bedrooms. The two men, or the women they were then involved with, each had a kid. Two months of sharing that house, cooking and marketing for weekend meals, looking out over the potato fields at sunset over our gin and tonics, plotting a mythical scheme to loot the potatoes and distill our own vodka, and we knew our "commune" was working. Various friends, in various states of non-marriage, came for weekend visits and wanted in. We rented a larger house on a cove for two years. We began to develop our own "commune" family traditions, rituals, history. We had vicious family arguments over money. "Just add up what was spent on groceries and divide by six or eight"; not so simple: "My kid is only two, how can you say he eats as much as a thirteen-year-old?" . . . "I was on the Scarsdale diet this week, I didn't eat a thing" . . .

"How about that piece of Brie I brought from the city? Deduct that." We had turnover—when a couple broke up, or got married, when someone had too many scary fake heart attacks, or paranoid delusions, or was too sexually predatory.

Heidi, our Wall Street recruit, worked out a complicated wall chart to allocate the finances. Betty Rollin, when her magazine folded, took charge of housekeeping assignments with fancy titles like "Chancellor of Cleanup," "Duchess of Dessert," "Overseer of Hors d'Oeuvres." Martha Stuart and Dick Cornuelle with their various children moved in—my Emily and her Sally joined forces in defense against their overbearing mothers; his Peter, at thirteen, got a crush on me and we invented a non-alcoholic cocktail together. Men I dated were invited to join the commune, Dick for one, but I didn't like it when he invited other women for the weekend. Sexual jealousy, the age we were then, could have destroyed our commune; we developed unwritten rules to keep that from happening. Since most of us were in states of singlehood but sexually active, our "intimate others" had to be fairly strong characters to withstand this "family's" caustic scrutiny.

One weekend when we entertained a presidential candidate—we were all very involved politically in Democratic affairs—our proper Republican landlady came over to clip the hedge and do something about the torn couch slipcover. "What this house needs is a wife," she said caustically. To tell the truth, the men were more interested in the food, the planning of the dinners, at least, and even the cooking and the grinding of the special coffee beans, than the women. And just as interested in each other's children. To this day, when I call Betty Rollin and get her machine, I leave the message, "It's Other Betty," which is what Arthur's Matthew, who learned to talk in the commune, called me. When Bob started getting serious about Muriel, she tiptoed out after she'd stayed all night so as not to wake Emily, whom I had shipped out to the commune to recover from hepatitis her last summer in high school. And every Labor Day we engaged each other in deadly serious charades.

The commune lasted about ten years. One year, after a summer of unusually bitter battles, it split into two—but soon the two halves began entertaining each other, and the Labor Day charades became a bicommune duel. The most beautiful house, the one on Drew Lane, which we could have bought in the late seventies for $120,000, is now worth several million. We couldn't, then, figure out a way that four or more adults, unrelated by blood or marriage, could buy and own a house together, get the financing, and make some provision to buy each other out if one of us had to leave the state for a new job, or got married and we couldn't stand the spouse. But as, variously, we did get married, divorce, change jobs, move away, or buy, one by one, our own houses nearby, we became, most assuredly, a comfortable, trusted, all-too-well-known family for each other. We bring covered dishes, or cook together, for Thanksgiving, Passover, Christmas, and to celebrate each other's milestone birthdays or late weddings. We sometimes travel together; Dick and I made the others watch slides of our improvised African safari, and we talked of chartering a boat together in the Caribbean or Greece, but we never got around to it.

I dedicated *It Changed My Life,* which I wrote in the commune, to "my own family and my extended family of choice." We suffered each other's mastectomies, Arthur and Betty's divorce, Joe's cancer. We mourned our deaths—from cancer, AIDS. The commune gathered with great heart for Emily's wedding, and cheered when Wendy married Hilly and finally had her own baby at forty-five, and celebrated Steve's recovery from heart attack, and joined potluck fares to give Joe support for his cancer surgery.

A few years ago, we all met in my apartment to discuss, seriously, whether we shouldn't look for another house together for our age, "when what we'll really *need* is a commune." But we were at too disparate stages of our own lives again—some of us involved now in late parenting or new marriages; others too admittedly cantankerous, hunkered down in our separate houses. Still, since most of us have settled near each other, we can now at least envisage the day when we might rent those houses out and move in with each other for a time, or work out a plan to have more regular meals together, and take care of each other when we need it. I'm convinced that some kind of self-selected, chosen commune would be better, sooner or later, than keeping up these houses, each of us alone, when all our kids are gone. And better, surely, in the end than some impersonal "retirement village" or "nursing home." We have had that apprenticeship of shared space and housekeeping; we have our shared history and traditions; we know the worst of each other and the best—and we still *enjoy* each other. We have known and keep renewing that chosen intimacy together.

With my own children, and those of my friends, I have noticed an interesting development. In their twenties and thirties, they started coming back home again—Thanksgiving, Passover, summers—bringing wives, husband, their own children now, to my house in Sag Harbor. I relished the renewed sense of family which they clearly wanted again and enjoyed. I realized they were confident enough now, in their grown-up selves, in their busy careers and the rich texture of their marriages, fixing up their own homes which I loved to visit and taking delight in their own children, that they did not need to defend themselves any-more against their childish need for mother. And the richness of our family history is recorded in my albums of their weddings on my lawn in Sag Harbor, and the scary and joyous births, when I was still wanted, needed, flying back from Israel, Boston, California in the middle of the night.

When they came now, I took such delight in the richness of their being and their lives, and the loving way they bring up their own children, my sons as fathers, my daughter as mother, I *kvelled.* I delighted in my little grandsons, so like their father, my son, their mother, my daughter, so much themselves. But I sometimes felt a sadness I did not recognize. Did I want back my own years of that rich texture when I was changing diapers, cooking "gourmet" meals, picking out wallpaper, fixing up houses, improvising curtains, with their father and them? I missed the intimacy of someone to share that history with. On an impulse, I called their father, from whom I had been divorced for more than twenty years, and suggested we have dinner, to talk about those kids we share. The old bitter hostility was long gone; we had seen each other lately almost as strangers, at those weddings and births. But who else could I share that history with, our roots?

Still, as I realized when my own children met

some of their first cousins for the first time at the ceremony at my mother's grave in Peoria, a shared family history doesn't prove real unless we give it the glue of intimacy. My children hardly knew their grandparents, yet they are now passionately interested in their "roots." When my mother died, in a nursing home in Wisconsin, I thought we should take her home to Peoria to bury her. My brother, who still lives in Peoria, became closer to me when his first wife died, and his youngest daughter Laurie has now become my daughter too, in spirit. But we had never all gotten together with our kids. At the burial ceremony, we set up a picture of Mother during her young motherhood. And the children of her friends in Peoria, and my brother's friends and mine who knew her then, joined our children to share memories. Afterward, my sister and brother and I sat around on the gravestones, reminiscing about fights at our childhood family dinner table, and our kids took out their address books for each other's phone numbers—Philadelphia and Buffalo, Chicago and Minnesota, Los Alamos. We had used the ritual of Mother's death to create at least a little bit of the glue of intimacy for the children of her children. Like many of the first generation of descendants of immigrants, or even my generation, she herself had no interest in family roots. When my son Jonathan went to see her with his notebook to ask what town in Hungary her father and mother had come from, she said, "Oh, darling, I really don't know, I've never been interested in looking back like that."

Strangely enough, "family" and "roots" are a much more conscious, active concern of my children and the children of my friends than they were for my parents' or my own generation, when they were a taken-for-granted burden to bear conscientiously, or spend much of your life and fortune in psychoanalyst's fees to escape. Despite all the political hype over lack of "traditional family values," the concern of the new generation of young men and women for creating and sustaining family ties and values, and making occasions in their busy lives for family intimacy to take root, augurs more of that glue to sustain age than my mother ever had. My sons and daughter and their families come together to visit me, or visit each other in their different cities, almost every month.

And despite the media hue and cry about the disappearing family, the statistics show more older people today actually living with their families (spouses, sons, or daughters—mostly daughters) than all the people over sixty-five who were alive in 1920. Most prefer to live alone, but often move to live near their kids. I wouldn't want to live *with* mine, but closer would be nice. My friend Alex told me, in confidence, he wasn't too happy when, after his son-in-law got tenure, he and Alex's daughter found an apartment in his building. He was thankful when the negotiations fell through and they settled on another apartment several blocks away, then moved to the suburbs. He liked having them nearby, but not too close. He still wanted his own privacy, his independent identity. The point is, the ties of intimacy, even with family of blood, are now self-chosen ties, only as deep, real, intense, thin, or suffocating as we choose to make them. The existential burden of that choice is made easier, or more difficult, because the beginning is given with our family of origin. But the glue of intimacy comes from the activity, history, experience we choose and create occasions to share together.

In the gerontological literature, polygamy has been suggested as a future solution to that great excess of older women over single older men. "If a man could marry two, three, four or five women over age 60," such polygamous marriages would: (1) create the opportunity to reestablish a family group; (2) improve diets (married couples are found to eat better than widows and widowers); (3) pool funds (six can live much better and more cheaply than one); (4) prevent the need for nursing home care in illness since there would always be responsible people at home to nurse; (5) share and lighten the burdens of housework; and (6) solve sexual problems, "especially the legal availability of partners." [24]

My student, interviewing today's older people

for her paper on intimacy, found them not at all interested in such a possibility for themselves, neither the single nor married ones—"maybe for some future generation." But my own generation is only half-joking about it. Not sexually, seriously, but socially at least, it's happening. "Going out" is no longer necessarily two by two. You make a date, yourself, with a couple you like, to see a movie: three women and a man have dinner together, you make plans to travel together, two couples, two or three friends, woman or man, gay or straight, separate bedrooms, or if there's no room at the inn, twin beds. I often travel with my friend Dick, who shares my taste for offbeat countries, riverboats, trains across Africa. Long divorced, as I am, he's had a number of lady friends over the years, sexual involvements. Ours is not, though there is some chemistry ("There has to be chemistry," a widow friend my age insists). One Christmas Eve in Timbuktu, we slept on a ledge in a cave annex to the only hostelry; there was literally no room at the inn. Another night in Abu Dhabi we slept on ironing tables in the "guest house" laundry room.

The sharing of such travel, adventure, that *shared space,* creates ties of intimacy, enduring bonds, and history between friends who become more than social acquaintances, "intimate others." Without those bonds of intimacy—sharing one's naked self without the masks, sharing one's real feelings, joy and pain, fear and anger —even in marriage, women and men can feel "lonely." Sex can be a powerful enabler of that lovely, naked sharing. In a good long marriage, the glue of shared sex leads to shared space, building a home together, traveling together, having children together. And sharing all that pain and fear and joy, and the unlovely wrinkles and bulges of one's naked person, can strengthen our respect for and delight in that naked self "regardless." But the chemistry of friendship, love, and intimacy is just as essential to our sense of self in late life as it was in infancy. No longer automatically "given" by sex or our sex roles, by our professions or our social roles, as it used to be, even those ties now have to be *chosen* in new ways if they—and we—are to remain vital. It's all a matter of choice now.

Woman or man, we begin to know, before it is too late, that we can *choose* to tear down the walls we have built up against that joyous, painful intimacy, *choose* to take the risks of it, *choose* to create the experiences, reunions, that will keep it alive, over the distances of time and space. But space itself, and time too, must be created anew; we have to use it differently, move maybe to a different space, for the bonds of intimacy to continue to grow and nourish us in age. When our old communities no longer sustain that intimacy, when our children and friends have gone off or died, when the professional status essential to identity in that place is no longer our priority, when that big old house no longer suits us, we may have to find or create the *new space* that will enable us to keep or renew those purposes and intimate bonds which are the fountain of age.

NINE

Going Beyond

I knew the minute I heard about it that I wanted to go. Not necessarily for the reason that I gave myself or my friends, though I was too embarrassed to talk about it much. What was a sophisticated urban woman of my age doing, setting off on an Outward Bound wilderness-survival expedition in the North Carolina mountains with nine strangers? Of course, I had always had a secret yen for wilderness exploration, adventure; loved to read books about men sailing across the Pacific in a raft, or climbing Annapurna or Mount Everest, even though I personally was afraid of heights, and never could quite get the hang of sailing.

The traveling I had been doing too much, for too many years now, involved lectures, conferences, TV studios, fancy hotels, dreary motels, and banquets that were somehow all alike: Chicago, Los Angeles, Washington, London, Paris, Rome, Detroit. I had made a decade resolution, on my sixtieth birthday, that I was going to give myself some travel just for adventure, trekking in the Himalayas, or a boat ride down the Amazon, before it was too late. But that sort of thing didn't seem to appeal to my friends, and I hated traveling alone. Besides, I was always too busy: deadlines, social calendar, the women's movement, and this endless research on age.

Suffering, still, myself that denial and dread of age that made it so hard truly to celebrate my milestone sixtieth birthday, I had started seeking out individuals, environments, experiences that seemed to promise the different kind of breakthrough that I was calling the fountain of age. In a health spa in Mexico, I had come across a zesty woman whom I had thought to be around thirty-three until she came in to Christmas dinner with her children, grandchildren, and the "younger man" she was living with, a gray-haired architect. She mentioned that she had just signed up for an experiment in wilderness survival that Outward Bound was trying out in September, for the first time, for people over fifty-five. Would you send me their literature, I heard myself asking . . .

She had to be kidding! I read the list: "Standard Mountain Wilderness Age 16½+," "Managers-Executive Mountain Wilderness Age 22+," "Everglades Expedition Age 18+." And then, near the bottom, "Going Beyond—Intensive for Adults 55+." But was this for me? Besides an intimidating four-page medical exam form for my doctor to fill out, including an EKG, there were another four pages of instructions on "Physical Conditioning": ". . . work yourself up to 3 or 4 miles of continuous jogging for at least one month before your course begins. Do as many sit-ups, pushups as you can in one set on a daily basis, then add one every other day . . . pull-ups to build upper body strength. . . ."

I had never been able to do sit-ups, much less pull-ups. An athlete I'm not. I used to get all A's in school, except for D in gym. How I hated volleyball, tennis. Upper body strength? God knows I have enough to lug two or three too-heavy suitcases through crowded airports; my husband, every man I've ever traveled with, always complained about how much too much I packed; but, given feminist morality, I wouldn't let a man carry my bags for me anyhow. "You're more likely to get a hernia than I am," I would say.

On the other hand, how could I possibly carry all the stuff on the Outward Bound required clothing list on my own back? All this *wool* (pants, shirts, sweaters, "4 pairs of heavy *wool* socks," "*wool* gloves"), where was I going to find *wool* in August? "Several layers of light clothing will keep you warmer than one layer of heavy clothing." That's better, the layered look. I hated wool next to my skin anyhow, too scratchy. Several layers of sweatsuits and T-shirts should do. A whole page about boots— "above-the-ankle, leather or nylon upper, and a hard rubber lug sole which looks like a truck tire. . . . You will need to put about 30 miles on your boots to break them in. . . ."

I figured I would manage the whole thing by jogging three and a half miles every morning for a week, with my new mountaineering boots on. Twice around the Central Park bicycle track across from my apartment, which was three and a half miles, usually took me an hour; my friends called my seventeen-minute miles a "schlog." Even my doctor said I should try to make it more "aerobic." But when it came to filling out the Outward Bound medical exam, he said: "Are you out of your mind? This is for people who are physically tough. I can just see you halfway up some mountain cliff they'll order you to climb —it's an authoritative outfit—having an asthma attack."

Well, if he wouldn't sign it, I didn't have to go —honorably reprieved! "Come off it, Charlie," I protested. "It's a program designed for people my age. They're not going to have us climb rocks or anything dangerous like that." He called the doctor on the Outward Bound staff and they agreed I was not to do anything I didn't "feel up to." "You can go," my doctor said, "but I still think you're crazy."

In Central Park, people looked at me, jogging in those five-ton boots in the 80-degree heat, like I must be crazy. I would be a crippled mess of blisters before the boots were broken in. The last day, I saw an Army surplus store with a sign in the window: JUNGLE BOOTS. They felt much lighter, they didn't have to be broken in! I finally bought two pairs of red polypropylene long johns which the Outward Bound list said could be substituted for "warm though wet" wool. Packing, I added a gaudy striped Mexican cotton jacket to cover the dreariness, and my heavy-hooded white *wool* sweater from Ireland. Obviously, we couldn't be expected to carry all this on our backs; we would probably leave it at a base camp every night.

Suppressing second thoughts, I spent the plane ride to Asheville and the two-hour wait in the airport proofreading an overdue manuscript, which I dropped in the airport mailbox, with a scribbled note of instructions in case I didn't come back alive, and then dashed into the airport john to change into sweatsuit and boots —ready for the trail as instructed, with a last goodbye to modern plumbing. Among a crowd of blue-jeaned teenagers getting into vans, I saw a couple of sturdy Sunday School teacher types, a mustached man who looked like a spaghetti commercial, a hearty balding giant in suspender overalls (plumber, undertaker, small-town grocer?), and my friend Cecelia Hurwich! "You actually came!" she said incredulously. "Why not!" I growled.

SATURDAY: On the Outward Bound van, heading for our first campsite, we eye each other suspiciously. We were told to introduce ourselves first names only, and no "what do you do, where do you come from?" As we ride across the state line, into South Carolina, then Georgia, we are told that the Outward Bound experience requires leaving behind your professional role and past identity along with your city clothes, and dealing with each other on a "here-and-now" basis. As part of that immediacy, we will not be told where we are going and what we are going to do much before it happens. The three "leaders" giving out all this are lean, muscular, marathon-runner types: Dave, Judy, Keg. The seven of us victims introduce ourselves with hearty bluffness, nervous laughs, or (me) noncommittal blankness: Ruth, Letha, Jerry, Earl, Bob, Cecelia, an unglamorous-looking lot, long in the tooth middle-American, except for Cecelia, unbelievably chic in Army surplus jungle camouflage from head to toe.

At the first campsite, a grassy little hill off the road, our gear is handed out: backpack, poncho, sleeping bag, groundcloth, tin cup (which is to serve as eating plate, drinking glass, and washing bowl), spoon, water bottle, and iodine to purify it. We are to pack all this, plus our clothes, in the backpack, and our city stuff will be taken away in the truck and stored until we head back home. But, first, some warmup exercises.

We form what is later referred to as a "trust circle." Each person massages the neck and shoulders of the person in front, then pits her strength against his hand-to-hand, to try to force the other's arm down. Well, Bob with the mustache is clearly bigger than I am. I put my energy to it—and nearly knock him and myself over! "You're not supposed to go at it so intensely," he says, patronizingly. Then, one by one, in the middle of the circle, we stiffen our bodies, fall back, eyes closed, and let ourselves be bounced, from hand to hand, around and around. Next, each in turn, we fall backward off a four-foot stump, trusting that circle of waiting hands to catch us. The "trust fall," it's called.

And now a little sunset jog, three miles down the road and back. We are assured that Outward Bound is not competitive, each at his own pace. But everyone's pace is clearly a lot faster than mine. That mousy-looking Letha lags way behind the others but, to my horror, I can't even keep up with her!

Next, we have to divide and carry between us,

in addition to our own junk, the two kerosene stoves, tarpaulins for lean-tos, large water jugs for cooking, a week's worth of foodstuffs, mainly dried, in unlabeled plastic bags—dried potatoes, pasta, rice, dried bananas, apples, dried eggs, gray, brown, red, and yellow powders (soups, puddings?), large cans of tuna, tomato sauce, chicken, sardines, hunks of cheese, and loaves of heavy dark bread. We are supposed to organize our own menus, cooking, clean-up. They instruct us on the proper ecological use of the shovel for toilet, and the disposal of toilet paper, "though leaves would be better."

As instructions were given on how to put up the tarps and prime the stoves, I felt my customary mechanical ineptness set in. (To compensate for being too good in high school physics, I became so helpless, connecting electric wires, that the football team did my experiments for me, and I did their math problems. But what on earth could I do well at all, in this "going beyond" craziness I'd gotten myself into?) Nobody had touched the unappetizing mess of dried food bags. It occurred to me that I could organize a curry out of that canned chicken, dried bananas, apples, raisins, rice. There is, at least, curry powder, and plenty of dried garlic; also a couple of live onions and carrots. I'd never actually made chicken curry, but I've eaten a lot in Indian restaurants. Sex role stereotypes notwithstanding, I take over as chief cook—setting some of my new sisters and brothers to chopping up the onions and carrots and opening the cans. I even dream up an Indian-type yoghurt, cucumber, green pepper, and tomato salad. My "going beyond" mates are suitably impressed by the creative mix of fruit and fowl; they do not seem familiar with nouvelle cuisine. Craig Claiborne, Gael Greene, you should see me now! No wine, alas.

Judy, who affects me like those tight-lipped gym teachers of my rebellious youth, comes around to collect watches, money, and the clothes and cosmetics we won't need before our return to civilization; were we supposed to tell time by the sun? My stuff is all around me on the ground. I was so busy with that creative cooking I didn't test carrying it all on my back as I meant to. I turn in those heavy mountain boots, but I don't dare leave behind all that stuff on the list. After those years of overpacking on four continents, I get it all into the backpack okay, but will I be able to carry it? Policing my campsite, Judy glares at a piece of Kleenex. Ecological sin! In this pure mountain air, my asthma seems to have disappeared, but probably from lifetime habit, I still drip. Before the week is over, I am so haunted by Judy's ecological obsession that I pick up little pieces of white paper by reflex, even if they aren't my Kleenex, carrying a whole wad of such trash down a mountain in my pocket since there was no way to bury it in rock.

Around the campfire, we share why each of us is here, "going beyond." Ruth, a sturdy, sensible-looking woman, says with a perky gleam in her eye: "I've had the feeling lately my horizons are closing in. I've done my best for my kids. There aren't that many movies, plays, museums, restaurants, I want to go to. I want some new things to do with my life. I'd like to climb a few peaks before I settle for a rocking chair. I don't want the circle to close."

Earl, the huge southern hulk with the slightly pompous manner of a judge or minister or Rotary Club toastmaster, was attracted, quite simply, by "the risk of it. To come here for ten days, completely removed from anything we're used to, not knowing what will happen, who the others will be."

This is the first and only Outward Bound group where women outnumber men. In fact, women have only been admitted to such expeditions, which started as all-male, in the last few years. Even now, many more *young* men venture on these wilderness trips than young women. Do women become more adventurous with age? After they've lived through or grown beyond the feminine mystique, are women more likely to risk, or relish, new ways to test themselves than men? Could that be one reason women live longer? All the men admit they've had a yearning to do something like this for years—mountain trekking, river rafting—but wouldn't have dared come before for fear of being shown up by a lot of twenty-five-year-olds.

I smooth my sleeping bag over a flat, fragrant bed of pine needles. Since that little bottle of water we each carry is all we have to wash with, and drink (no stream near this camp), I congratulate myself on having brought along a big tube of Noxzema—I can "wash" my face, hands, underarms in the dark, without water, and wipe it off with Kleenex (or even leaves?). Lying there, looking at the stars from my sleeping bag, I feel surprisingly comfortable, free of the vague fears and guilts that keep me brooding, awake, at home. On this hard ground, alone, I don't feel dreary, gray, bitter, heavy, lonely as in those grim hotel-motel rooms. I give, and get, too much of my energy now in that impersonal public life, where strangely I sometimes have a hint of that old nameless feeling women used to complain of, "trapped" inside their role as housewives and mothers (or men in their breadwinner role). *I'm somebody's wife, somebody's mother; I'm a lawyer bucking for partner; I'm a spokesperson for women's liberation—but who am I myself?*

It feels good, to be stripped down to one's self, away from the role. It's a long time since I've had this feeling of trying something really new . . . not knowing what to expect.

SUNDAY: I wake up suddenly, in the black night. My psychological alarm clock works—it's 5:00 A.M. Jerry, who has volunteered to do breakfast,

533

is lighting the stove. I'm glad of the chance to go to the john, "wash," and get "dressed" before the others wake up. Does one get more or less inhibited, prize the dignity of privacy more as one gets older? Or does one lose the vanity, modesty, or sexual inhibition of youth? Each one of us here seems to map out her/his own space in this open place. At first, I go quite far away to change, behind a screen of trees or brush. After a day or so, I don't stray so far; I "change" inside my sleeping bag, and, like the others, merely avert my eyes, washing my teeth in the same water that will also clean my cup after breakfast.

The Chatooga River, where we head now for two days of shooting rapids, is where they made the movie *Deliverance.* We are handed out life jackets and hard-hat helmets. We pick up three guides, who show us how to paddle the rubber rafts, "drawing" right or left, and "ferrying" across the current by heading beyond where you really have to go, then letting the current swing you back. After lunch (sardines, bread, and cheese eaten sitting on a rock), all the guides and instructors get in one raft and our "crew" is on its own, in the other two. The rapids begin to get scary. We take turns in different positions. I do not volunteer to be captain. I'm glad no one here knows that I am supposed to be a leader of women. Sitting up in the bow, paired with that big guy, Earl, I begin to get the hang of it: the rhythmic swing of the paddle, the flick of the wrist, and when and how to set the blade against the current, or "draw" or "sweep" in longer circles. They have put Earl on the left and me on the right, because "draw left" is the crucial stroke to get into, then out of, most of these rapids. After we miss a few, it becomes clear that Earl, despite his brawn, does not have the extra upper body strength for a strong left draw. But if I sweep out to the right, and, Cece behind me backpaddles, Earl's left draw works okay. "Have you done this before?" asks Judy, surprised at my sudden competence. "In summer camp," I remember. "In college. And on my honeymoon. The Songo River." About fifty, forty years ago.

We head into Stage III of the river—not the most dangerous, but getting there. To prepare for tomorrow, when we'll be shooting rapids with drops of twelve feet and more—Corkscrew Rapid, Sock 'Em Dog, Screaming Left Turn, Five Falls, Jawbone—we are given a drill on what to do if you fall overboard. I lie on my back, stiff, with my feet up so they don't get stuck under a rock, and let myself be carried by the rushing current down the rapids like a log. At the bottom the entire waterfall roars over my head and up my nose. For a minute, I panic—I can't get my breath. But it's not asthma, just water. I finally catch the rope, get pulled into shore.

Now we go over Bull Sluice, a tortuous tunnel

rapid that seems to drop twenty feet at least. You have to lean into the raft, keeping yourself anchored under its rim so you don't get swept out as the raft slams from one rock wall to the other, is turned around, and then hurled forward and down by the roaring water. The guide gets in our raft for this one. "Drift forward. Draw left." Earl draws, I sweep right, we plunge over, there's nothing to hang on to, the raft is hurtling down, slamming into the wall, I lean in, lean in, dig my feet under the tube and lean in, we hit bottom, and paddle like crazy. Nobody falls in— but coming out of the turn we get stuck on a rock, have to get out in the water and push-pull the raft off.

Coming across a calm stretch to a small beach where we'll camp, I take in the cliffs and the trees and the tired soaking amazed exhilaration that I'm still alive—what a beautiful river! Deliverance indeed.

We hike up a hill above our campsite to a road where the truck has brought our backpacks. Carrying my backpack fully packed for the first time, I barely manage to get back down the hill to camp. How am I going to climb up a mountain with this pack on my back? I will have to get rid of more stuff. I also need to get back my second flashlight. In New York, I couldn't find one with extra batteries—only the disposable kind. It will never last another seven days. Last night in the dark, I walked off to go to the john downhill without a flashlight and got lost for ten minutes! But they say we can't get at our bags again until we go home; it's a rule. I have to get rid of that heavy white sweater, the extra sweatsuit, one of those long johns. I can do without the soap, towel. Others are also grumbling about the unnecessary stuff they're carrying, taking that "list" too seriously. At the "circle," where grievances, group decisions, and new instructions are reviewed each evening, I demand, with a mite excess of belligerence perhaps, a relaxation of that rule and ten minutes at our suitcases again before the truck leaves us tomorrow.

The troika says, In the wilderness, a rule's a rule, can't change your mind. But this isn't a life-and-death rule like not lighting a fire in dry underbrush. I've had a lot of years of rebelling against "rules" that don't make sense. Besides, their own wilderness-survival philosophy demands a flexible response to contingencies. The troika reluctantly puts it to the group, which, to my relief, rather nervously supports "more flexibility."

This night I do not sleep so well under the stars. Though I tell myself still that it was crazy to come on this expedition anyhow, and now I'll have a good excuse to back out, I know I really want to keep on "going beyond." But I'll never be able to climb a mountain with that weight on my back. Stage IV of the river will have really dangerous rapids; didn't men drown in the Chatooga in that movie? And tomorrow I'll have to take my turn at being captain and steering the raft. Considering the battles for power I've fought, win or lose, in nearly thirty years of the women's movement, I feel guilty, worrying only about my own survival. But the only thing I feel capable of taking responsibility for here is cooking. Tonight's dinner was chaotic and lousy. I volunteer to be in charge of dinners from now on. But then I have to carry the foodstuff involved. My menus will be geared to "light" stuff like pasta, garlic, the few remaining onions and cabbage; but I can't do without those heavy cans of oil and tomato sauce.

Cece has already asked Earl to carry her share of the heavy camp pots. As a feminist, I have to disapprove. "You're crazy," she says. "Those guys happen to be stronger than we are." Feeling rather foolish, I go up to Bob, the one with the mustache. He's volunteered to help me with the spaghetti tonight. I ask if he'd mind adding these cans of tomato sauce to his pack. He gives me a fishy look. He's probably thinking: "Women, they want equal rights and still expect us to be chivalrous and carry their tomato sauce."

At the "circle" before dinner, we take turns reading or reciting a "meditation" grace. Tonight, someone reads a passage from Thoreau from the back of the *Outward Bound Journal:*

I went to the woods because I wanted to live deliberately, to front only the essential facts of life, and see if I could not learn what it had to teach, and not, when I come to die, discover that I had not lived. I did not wish to live what was not life; living is so dear; nor did I wish to practice resignation, unless it was quite necessary. . . .

MONDAY: For Stage IV of this Chatooga River, a guide takes charge of each raft again. These next rapids are too tricky for novice amateurs to navigate—so maybe it wasn't just cowardice, my not wanting to play captain here. Starting out, I feel scared a bit still, but after that terrified moment, poised at the brink, I'm excited but calm underneath, paddling forward, then feverishly into, across the current, being twirled around, leaning in, bracing my feet, as we go over the falls, backwards—Jawbone, Shoulder Bone, Corkscrew, Rapid, Sock 'Em Dog, Screaming Left Turn—and then coming out of it, paddling frantically into that calm stretch at the bottom, soaking wet but not so cold today because of the socks Earl told me to wear under my sneakers. In the calm stretch below Five Falls, I take my turn as captain, and manage to steer the clumsy raft from the stern.

The young guides, who've spent years mastering each rock and rapid of this tricky beautiful river, tell us how they dreaded taking on people as "old" as we were purported to be. They figured we would hardly have the strength to paddle the rafts ourselves; they'd have to drag us through. They'd practiced CPR and emergency rescue drills and splints for our brittle, breakable bones. But, as it turns out, they didn't have to exert any extra effort and we are the first group in years where no one has fallen overboard!

At the "circle" before we take leave of the guides, they try to figure out what made the difference. "You weren't trying to show off and outdo each other, like the kids do." Maybe we've outgrown macho, even the men? "You have better balance and survival instincts." "We had to in order to have survived this long," Earl cracks. The guides had been sure we wouldn't have enough "power" for those tricky turns, and at first we didn't seem to. But in the end, we somehow acquired as much "power" as was needed. "You listened more intently," Dave ventured. "You cooperated more with each other, you weren't trying to show off, paddling in six different directions. I guess you made up for whatever actual differences in muscular strength by cooperation." Or, maybe, wisdom? "And will," Judy said; "you really wanted to do it."

Disembarking at the Outpost, we leave those young river guides in the warmth of mutual respect, rendezvous for the last time with the truck, get ten minutes to change out of our wet clothes and have that second chance at our bags (I change behind the truck, not even bothering with the ladies dressing room at the rafting outpost in my haste to get rid of that excess weight).

On the truck back into North Carolina, we practice complicated knots on ropes we are now handed, along with a compass and a whistle. The truck deposits us at a lookout point halfway up a mountain range. From now on, we're on our own in the wilderness; the vista is awesome, remote, but it no longer occurs to me to turn back. Earl helps me hoist my lightened(?) pack on my back, and adjust the shoulder strap. I'm embarrassed to discover that the belt, evidently supposed to go around my middle, won't buckle shut (that's where all my weight goes, my stomach). I manage to carry the pack down and across the road, though it still seems awfully heavy and keeps banging into my back. A good thing I unloaded the tomato cans on Bob, feminist ideology or not.

We leave the road, to climb straight up a short steep path to the ridge trail where we are supposed to camp tonight. And I literally double up under the pack. It keeps slipping down. I can't seem to get myself upright enough to climb at all. What's wrong with me? Age, after all? The others are doing okay. Maybe I've been whistling in the dark about having as much energy as I ever did. I literally cannot move, under that pack, even up the first few feet of mountain path. Dave comes back down to investigate. He says the pack doesn't fit me right. He says if I can just make it up this first steep part, the trail is level to the campsite, and then I can trade for a pack that fits me. I literally crawl, on my hands and knees, finally on my belly, under that ghastly bumping pack, up to the ridge. Even on the level trail, I can barely walk upright; that pack swings heavy, heavy against my back. I am delaying everybody. The rule of the trail is we are never to really get out of sight of each other, front to rear. It is getting dark already. How will they get me to an airport? I can't possibly climb eight miles a day like this. I feel a terrible disappointment. I don't want to quit "going beyond."

Cece and Bob have been sent ahead to scout a campsite. I dump that gruesome pack under a pine tree and head to the stove Bob is setting up, to mastermind spaghetti marinara with tomato sauce, spiked with soybean powder, green pepper bits and cheese, and a second choice of aglolio—sautéed with garlic, oil, and a smidge of red pepper—that I learned from my sculptor friends in Rome. And with Bob and Letha helping, I put together a smashing salad of the last of the fresh onion, cabbage, carrot, apples, and a few raisins, with the juice of the orange I didn't eat for lunch for dressing! But after that pack fiasco, I feel like such an abysmal failure, neither the food nor the flattery cheers me. Assuming I can go on at all, do I really want to if I'm always going to hold up the rear, slow the others down? This is what it must have felt like, being dumb in school. Dave brings over his own personal blue backpack to trade for mine. It's smaller and lighter, all right, and it buckles around my middle! Earl comes over to my sleeping bag and insists that I pack it all up and practice before I go to sleep. He helps me adjust the shoulder strap and the belt tight around my waist. I stand upright easily enough. The weight seems to be carried by my hipbones now. So it wasn't the feebleness of age, after all, but a matter of engineering!

This night, sleeping under the stars, breathing the piney air, I suddenly feel *solid*—and lighter about it all. I realize that even crawling on my belly, vertically up that ridge, I didn't get asthma. When we divide up the stuff again, I'll volunteer to carry the toilet paper. Joke . . .

TUESDAY: We squat on the ground, learning to take our bearings with map and compass. The troika leaves us to make our own way over the ridge, to our next destination, across Steele's Creek. It's clear from the map that we will have to leave the trail and bushwhack our way down the mountainside to the creek. Bob and Cece take the lead positions, trailblazers; Earl volunteers for the rear. He has been so effortlessly the leader, I figure he's holding back to give the others a chance. But I get very touchy when he keeps coming up behind me and offering me a hand, when there's a rock to climb or a steep slide to negotiate. I find a big stick to sort of lean on, climbing—it makes me feel more balanced. At least hand me that stick, he says, as I wriggle under a fallen branch, with that pack on my back. Oh well . . . Once we leave the trail, it's rough, scratchy, dense. Going down, you have to lean backward or it feels like the pack will overbalance you and fall on top. It's hard to climb under things with that pack. The stick doesn't really help. I go down from tree to tree, using branches as brakes. My pack begins to feel heavy again. I try sliding down on my behind —it works. The seat of my pants is now caked with mud, but who's looking!

It's getting dark already, surely it's not that late. It's been sunny and warm up until now; a storm is coming. The ridge we've been climbing down suddenly ends in a kind of precipice, no way down to the creek which we can now hear. We have to retrace our way back up that steep hill I just slid down and go over the next ridge. It starts to rain. The creek is wide, and not all that shallow. Those rocks look slippery. The three guys make a human bridge on the rocks, passing our backpacks across hand to hand. Earl falls in. I decide not even to try jumping from rock to rock. I'll go across in the creek itself; surely jungle boots, sweat pants won't take long to dry.

As we get out our boring bread, cheese, tuna for wet lunch, a "circle" is called. The troika, which has rejoined us, orders all food and common camp gear into the middle. What now? What's *now* is twenty-four hours of "solitary"— each one of us is to be deposited in our own little spot of wilderness along the creek, to survive alone for the next twenty-four hours. With four pieces of rope (to make a shelter out of our ponchos) and a ration of crackers, cheese, trail mix (raisins, sunflower seeds, granola), and an apple or orange. I've read about those solitary wilderness vigils but never thought they'd ask our age group to do it!

My spot is a dense jungle of black-green vines, wild giant rhododendrons choking tall trees (pine, spruce, whatever), rotting branches, stumps, rocks, and dank masses of vegetation rising rather steeply from the creek bed. Only one place, six or eight feet square, seems level enough between some trees to set up camp in. Some big fallen branches are clotting it up. I drag them out of the way, clear the rocks off my floor of decaying leaves. It's going to rain again, soon. I string up the poncho between four trees. Flat out like that, it doesn't seem like much of a shelter. Surely rainwater will just accumulate on top, or blow in underneath. I construct a diagonal roof ridge, knotting together the longest pieces of rope, and drape the poncho into a geometric tepee. Call me Francesca Lloyd Wright. I set up my groundcloth underneath, sticking out a bit on each side; put my sleeping bag under the central peak, and the pack with my clothes underneath for a pillow.

Then, I undress, go down to the creek, plop myself on a rock, and give myself a good cold clean splashing bath. Solitary survival rule: no swimming, no dunking in the creek beyond hip deep. But it's not warm enough to want to swim anyhow. In fact, it's gloomy dark already in this dank, rotting jungle—though it can't be much more than six o'clock. Nothing to read. They expect you to meditate, I suppose, but I never know what they mean by "meditate." I think by the seat of my pants, in action as it were. I read all the instructions in the *Outward Bound Journal* about edible thistles and tree ears. Oh, for a good mystery to read! I get into my sleeping bag; it starts to rain again. Hard. My shelter seems to work. Lying under my tepee, I move my hands all around and no drops are coming down at all. The rain is thundering on my roof, the creek is thundering below, but here I am, snug and warm.

Or so I tell myself. For some reason, I don't feel comfortable. I still haven't gotten the hang of turning on my side in the sleeping bag without the whole thing twisting on top of me—it feels like I am getting wet, from underneath! I seem to be lying in a river of water. Could I have slid down into the creek without realizing it? Lying in the wet, I am also beginning to feel a bit cold. What did they say about *wool—warm even though wet.* I fish my pack out from under the sleeping bag, strip, and put on, next to my bare skin, my entire supply of scratchy wool: turtleneck, sweater, the red long johns, and two pairs of socks. Then I put all the cotton sweat stuff back on top, pull the wool stocking cap over my ears, put the pack back under my head, knot the hood of the sleeping bag tight over it and me, and scrunch up in the smallest possible fetal position under my tepee ridge. I feel warmer now, except for my behind, lying in a pool of water. I remember those useless wool gloves which I forgot to put back in my suitcase. I stuff a wool glove under each buttock, inside my long johns. *Warm though wet!* In the interest of body heat, I eat all my provisions; they'll just get soggy otherwise. When it's light, I can look around for edible thistles and tree ears.

It's very noisy in these woods, crashing sounds. Did I hear Judy say something about bears? Should I sing to scare any animals away? At least, no rapists or other human beings will be prowling around on a night like this. The funny thing is, all my life I've been terrified of being alone. And now, I'm not even scared! Being alone is not my problem—it's how to keep my sleeping bag from getting wetter. I remember the warnings about hypothermia: if you get too cold and wet, your body temperature falls, and you could die even if you don't feel freezing cold.

After endless hours, too wet to sleep, I see a light approaching. It's Dave, checking, "solitary" or no. That's nice and flexible, in the face of such a storm. Am I cold? Oh no, I say cheerily, just a bit wet. From underneath, for some strange reason. He says it's because my groundcloth is sticking out beyond the edges of my shelter; it draws the water in. I should have tucked it under, all around. After he leaves, I kick myself for being so macho—and take an asthma pill, just in case.

But, strangely enough, even so wet and beginning to feel the cold, I don't get asthma. My natural adrenaline must mobilize in the face of real survival danger. Maybe all I have to fear is fear itself? If only this wet night would end.

WEDNESDAY: I don't think I slept at all. But suddenly the rain has stopped. I can see the creek again; it's getting light.

I climb out of my soggy sleeping bag. I drape that soaking bag, and my wet sweatsuit, T-shirts, socks, and sweaters over branches and bushes to dry. Now, with no sun? Stripped down to my bottom layer of warm-though-wet wool, I decide to try a little warmup jog. Can't—too rocky, stumpy. Try jogging in place. Uninspiring. Suddenly, I visualize a spin-dry washing machine. I take a wet piece of sweatsuit in each hand and, jogging in place, in my long johns, turn myself into a spin-dry machine, whirling those wet sweats around me. I even begin to sweat myself! As I'm spinning, Dave and the others appear on the trail—vigil over. I hastily pack my wet junk back in the pack, heavier than ever now.

Back at the campsite, the troika has made a huge fire and cooked a hot chowder. Judy has even baked gingerbread. I toast my wool-wet body by that fire until steam pours out around me. It starts to rain again; we make a circle under the tarp to share our solitary adventures. Letha had set up her shelter against a tree harboring a nest of yellow jackets. Stung, swelling, afraid of allergic-shock reaction, she blew her whistle. No one came. The troika was at the end of the trail, dropping the rest of us off. She found her way to the camp. They gave her some anti-histamine—and took her back to the same spot to resume her solitary vigil. Still swollen from the bee stings, she set up her shelter as far as possible from that nest of yellow jackets and "pretended it was a hospital."

Earl invented a plastic-container portable toilet ("at my age I have to pee a lot, I didn't want to get out of my sleeping bag in the middle of the night") and spent two hours "counting all my blessings," after which he slept through that roaring storm. Ruth and Jerry both thought they'd heard, or felt, the paws of bears on their backs. Far from giving us an easier solo than the younger groups, Dave says it was the worst storm in all his years of Outward Bound solos.

Bob and Earl both insist they didn't experience the "spiritual inner change" such solitary vigils are supposed to bring about. They "didn't have time to meditate." I who never have been able to meditate suggest that maybe what meditation really is is that intense total immersion in the actual experience which we all underwent, surviving that storm, without benefit of mantra. There is a new bond between us, that's for sure, an elation we all seem to share now, together again having survived the twenty-four hours alone.

I tell them about my lifelong terror of being alone, which I must have gotten over last night. I tell them about a dream I had before I came here—about a marvelous adventurous man I was secretly drawn to, but kept picking a fight with. Was that man my adventurous independent self, which keeps me "going beyond" even though I dread following it, in my fear of being alone?

Cece tells us how all her life she'd been "a terribly dependent person, leaning on my parents, my husband, even my children. I was a good hostess, dressed beautifully, did a little tennis, modern dance, interior decorating, but I never did anything really hard. Then, one day, I fell asleep driving; my car crashed and turned over; I nearly died. When I survived, I knew I had to start living my life." She went back to school, was divorced, started backpacking. "Now I'm so independent, I don't need anybody. All the things I used to need a man for I can do myself now—taxes, money, changing a tire. It scares me sometimes how independent I've gotten." Then she adds: "I like being back with you guys better than being alone, but being by myself isn't necessarily lonely."

Since this meal is clearly going to be both lunch and supper ("lupper," my kids used to call it, Sundays in that other life), we end our circle with "grace" before we set out again. Cece reads a passage, in the back of the *Outward Bound Journal,* called "The One-Inch Journey":

Always in big woods when you leave familiar ground and step off alone into a new place there will be, along with the feelings of curiosity and excitement, a little nagging of dread. It is the ancient fear of the unknown, and it is your first bout with the wilderness you are going into . . . the first experience, not of the place, but of yourself in that place. It is an experience of our essential loneliness; for nobody can discover the world for anyone else. It is only after we have discovered it for ourselves that it becomes a common ground and a common bond, and we cease to be alone.

Now the rain has stopped, and we set off for our next destination, an island in the creek's fork. But we cannot hike along the creek itself; we have to skirt some steep cliffs first. When the trail we thought we'd found peters out, we climb up through sticky thorny brush, until we get to another ridge. We climb and climb; it's getting dark, a wind is blowing through my still-damp sweats. My sleeping bag, nothing really got dry; the pack is heavier than ever. We are too high now even to hear the creek. If we climb back down and don't find that island, we will just have to climb up again. We are on a level spot on this ridge right now; why can't we camp here? Another one of those senseless rules? To my surprise, the troika agrees. We set up camp, in the windy dark, not very sheltered on this ridge, too windy for a fire, the troika says. They call another circle and warn of the real dangers of hypothermia for those of us with wet sleeping bags. They suggest we zip our sleeping bags together, alternating wet and dry, to pool our body heat. The women are willing, without re-gard to sex (or, rather, gender), but the men clearly don't want to. Earl says he is a "restless sleeper, snores, etc." Dave says Bob and Jerry will have to share, because Bob's sleeping bag is wet. "As long as you don't get too close to me," I hear Bob mutter. The women decide to pool our own heat, and let the men fare for themselves. But only Cece and I can mesh the zippers on our sleeping bags. The other two get on either side. With the damp bag on top, and the dry one underneath, and all that body heat, I feel much more comfortable than last night. Interesting that we women are more attuned to survival—transcending modesty, inhibitions about our bodies—than the men.

THURSDAY: By morning, between the shared body heat and the wind, my bag and clothes and even my jungle boots are dry. We set off again, with compass and map, taking bearings off various mountain peaks, heading for a poetic-sounding campsite called Starry Night. Trails keep petering out in precipices; we have to bushwhack again, slow, tough going, much signaling from front to rear, calling "circles" to consult. It no longer bothers me, bringing up the rear, though some remnant of pride makes me try to get a little ahead whenever we're on level ground. I discover I can save time by not taking off my pack at rest stops, just lean my back against a tree, standing up. Bushwhacking like this, it's going to take us two days. Then, Cece, who boasts she trekked over Kilimanjaro in Africa last year, finds a trail that isn't on our map at all, which leads us to a paved road. We get to a dirty campsite—which turns out unpoetically to be Starry Night—by the middle of the afternoon. There should be a brook, Dave says. All of us are out of water now. I volunteer for the water detail. Another expedition is sent off to the Outward Bound provisions depot to get food for our last three days. I tell them to return the sardines for peanut butter (ordinarily, I love sardines, but in our unwashed state we are all getting nauseated from the smell). Of course, by now, we all smell awful, to say nothing of the embarrassing continual farting from the starchy diet (or continual state of nervous fear); but after "solitary," we are so happy to be together, who notices smells?

As we sit around the campfire, groaning at Earl's increasingly bawdy jokes told with that parsonlike pomposity, two strange figures crash out of the darkness. Two blond girls (I do mean girls; they don't look fifteen) are introduced as Ann and Kitty, our "climbing instructors" for tomorrow. They don't look much like Hillary and Tenzing. "What are your-um-qualifications?" Bob asks, a bit gracelessly. It seems they are professional mountain climbers, who have been scaling rock and ice peaks all over America and the world for some years now.

FRIDAY: We are given hard-hat helmets again, and heavier ropes, to knot around our legs like diapers and secure with belaying pins. We simulate flat dry runs "on belay"—climbing a cliff with a rope around your waist, attached to the waist of a person at the top, secured in turn by a rope around a tree, as she belays your slack, or holds or hauls you up if you fall—and "on rappel," where you go down a sheer perpendicular cliff by bracing your feet against the rock, butt out, harnessed like an elevator to a rope which she plays out from above as you descend. Despite my fear of heights, I've always loved mountain climbing—on a trail. With my feet, and sometimes hands, on the ground. With trees nearby to grab onto, if necessary. But to climb perpendicular rocks with only a rope to keep you from falling?

Ann takes us on a follow-the-leader leapfrog practice climb over little rocks, eight, ten feet high, showing us how to traverse across a steep rockface, not clinging to the rock as you want to, but sticking your ass out to gain traction as you flatten your feet against the rock. But I don't seem to have enough strength in my upper arms to pull myself up to the top of even that eight-foot practice rock.

Now, one by one, we each have to belay up a sixty-foot practice cliff, and rappel down thirty feet or so on the other side. Cece is my belay partner. She looks like she's climbing up the walls of a four- or five-story building, as I belay the rope from on top, but she doesn't have any trouble. I can't even seem to get started myself. I finally find a quarter of an inch crevice for a toehold, and a teeny little rock nipple to get a hand around. It seems to take hours each time, to find another crevice, anything at all to hold on to. Tortuous. About ten feet from the top, four stories above the ground, with my toes on a ledge an inch wide and my hands spreadeagled on that too-smooth rock cliff, I get stuck. I can see a little knob farther up, but when I manage to get hold of it, I can't find a toehold, and slide back down again. My legs are beginning to tremble from the strain of holding on; I try to traverse sideways, with my butt out as per instruction, but there is nothing at all I can get my hands on.

I am terrified of looking down—everybody else seems to have finished, and they are all at the bottom now, yelling things like, "Come on, Betty, you're doing fine." I swear at them, with all the obscenity at my command, to shut up. It's enough of a nightmare to be spreadeagled on a cliff like this, without an audience! I manage to get my hands on something, but my feet don't hold, and I fall back down again until the belay rope catches. I manage to get my feet back on the ledge and just stand there, flattened out against the cliff, holding on now, in that mad embrace. An awful lot of time seems to have passed. I am tired, frustrated, angry—at myself, for being so inept, at those clods down there who did it so easily—and scared, not so much of falling as of not being able to do it.

Dave peers down at me from the clifftop. "Anybody else would have given up an hour ago." Is that a compliment, or a hint? Have I really been up here an hour? I am clearly holding up the whole operation—we are supposed to sleep on top of the mountain tonight. "Maybe I should give up," I croak. He figures I don't really mean it. He suggests traversing to the other side. My legs are getting so tired I'm afraid to move. But I can't just stay here. I am soaked in sweat, my heart is pounding, my mouth is dry. . . . How, I don't know, but I manage to creep sideways, finally get my fingers on something, and pull myself the rest of the way up.

It was so traumatic, being spreadeagled on that rockface for over an hour—the longest ever in Outward Bound history, I learn; everyone else has either done it by then or given up. And I am so angry at myself for holding the others up again that I rappel down the thirty feet like an automaton. You're supposed to walk your feet, braced against the rock, down the cliff, your right hand in a friction glove controlling the rope. It acts as a brake as long as you keep it behind your butt; you move it forward to descend. I keep losing my footing and swing on the ropes out of control, but thirty feet is nothing after that spreadeagle. I more or less kick-fall myself down that rock, *fast,* so I never really do get the hang of rappel or feel in control, as I finally did on the river raft; I just want to get it over with. It's not as if I ever intend to rappel down a cliff in my life again.

So now, late afternoon, we pick up our backpacks to climb Table Rock—a mountain with a flat rock on top like the one where the spaceship landed in *Close Encounters of the Third Kind.* Climbing that mountain, even with a pack on my back again, is practically a pleasure—it's a *human* trail, with ground to put your feet on. At least I can redeem my ignominy by concocting a gourmet dinner. Bob is lugging new cans of chicken and tomato sauce—curry again or chicken cacciatore? The trail climbs like a corkscrew to the base of Table Rock, up through a crevice, and around and around.

Finally, we come out on the top of Table Rock. The whole mountain range sweeps below us. The sun is setting. It's windy. No trees on top of this mountain, no soft pine needles, just hard rock. "Let's not bother with dinner," someone says. "Too late, too cold." Bob explodes: "I've carried these two heavy cans all the way up here, we're damn well getting dinner out of it!" I dump my pack by Cece and get to work on chicken cacciatore—I don't think Bob really likes curry. "Easy on the spices," he begs. While it cooks, we have our "circle" on a little rock porch jutting out over the very edge of Table Rock, with our sleeping bags around our shoulders against the wind. The moon is coming up, a plane flies by just beneath us. I read the meditation tonight, a passage from Tennyson's "Ulysses" in the back of the *Outward Bound Journal:*

> *Though much is taken, much abides; and*
>   *though*
> *We are not now that strength which in old*
>   *days*
> *Moved earth and heaven; that which we are,*
>   *we are. . . .*

Letha says: "It makes me wonder, all these things I've done this week I would never have thought I could do—it makes me wonder what other things I've never done that I could do now." I have a strange stunned feeling of really "going beyond" today—of risking something I was truly afraid of, and surviving. But it wasn't just the height, the falling, I was afraid of. I risked doing something I really was no good at—and survived. There's a headiness to doing something at this age you've never done before, when you don't have to prove anything anymore. But there is a pressure in Outward Bound—*no limits* to what anyone can do: can no one ever fall, or fail, or give up?

Cece and I anchor our sleeping bags under a stunted little bush growing out of a crevice, not to risk rolling off Table Rock in the middle of the night. But we keep rolling downhill into that crevice. Even with my entire grimy wardrobe on my back, two or more of everything, dirty or dirtier, I am cold. The stars and moon shine in my eyes. I do not honestly enjoy sleeping on this mountain peak. They say we won't be climbing any further tomorrow; why are we supposed to get up at dawn again?

SATURDAY: "We are going to take a shortcut down," Dave puts it. He wasn't literally lying before—not climbing higher, only rappelling down the sheer precipice side of Table Rock, a narrow cliff about as high as a twenty-story building and as steep, 300 feet down to the ledge below, falling off 2,000 feet on either side to nothingness. That rock we rappelled down yesterday was only 30 feet off the ground. Judy goes over first, stepping back off the cliff. "Yahoo!" The men are given the job of belaying our backpacks down to her. I cannot even bring myself to go near the edge and look down. I am truly afraid of heights like this, much more afraid of going down than climbing up. Dave says I have to go early this time because I'll only get more scared waiting. It does not really reassure me that Letha and I are strapped into special ribbon diaper harnesses instead of the ropes the others are belaying themselves in. The better to rescue us when we fall off that cliff? This is not like the nervous fear I felt before. I don't have the *feel* of this rappelling. I was too paralyzed yesterday, after my spreadeagled hour, to pay attention. By the time we went over the dangerous rapids in the Chatooga, my mind, my muscles had the feel of rafting.

Paralyzed still, I step back off the edge of the cliff onto a little ledge just below and dutifully brace my feet, stick my rear out, and cautiously move my hand in the friction glove up from the brake position to start the rope slide down the cliff face. But these ropes are heavy, not like yesterday. Of course, they have to be, to control a descent of 300 feet, not 30. *I can't control these ropes at all.* I am swinging out from the cliff face, I lose my footing, and I start swinging sideways, heading for the corner of the precipice, where it falls not that 300 feet down, but miles farther than one can even see from here. Dave says, rather urgently, that I had better traverse away from that corner. With my hand "brake" on, I manage to crawl back from the precipice edge. But it is clear that I don't have the upper arm strength or the knack to control these heavy ropes. If I am stuck again like yesterday, this high up, if I swing out sideways over that precipice again, I won't have asthma, I'll have a heart attack.

"I don't have to prove myself this way," I hear myself shouting. *"Get me out of here this minute!"* Dave stares down. "You really mean it?" "I mean it." I do not have the strength or the skills to rappel at this height. *And I don't have to prove myself on this precipice—I mean it this time.* "Then we'll take you off rappel," he says, leaning over the cliff edge. "You'll still be on belay. You'll have to climb back up." With no more danger of swinging out over the precipice, I manage to get back up those fifteen feet, and slide on my behind back, back from that edge. There is talk of my getting my breath and trying again. *No,* I say. The others rappel down one by one. I sit there, shaking in relief, and fear still, and, of course, self-castigation, humiliation. It felt nice yesterday, the way they respected me for hanging in there. Today I was right to "yield."

I had reached my limit. But I do not relish being cast out of the group.

I edge forward a bit to watch the others rappel down. I don't want to give in completely to my fear of heights. I watch Letha rehearsing, stamping the ground with her boots, getting the feel of those ropes, testing her harness. I can see that she is scared all right, but not terrified. She feels in control, she knows what she is doing. As she steps back over the edge, I catch her eye, and she smiles. "I get my courage from you," she says, releasing her brake. What on earth did she mean by that? Because I was such a coward, it made her feel brave? Well, she tells me later, she's been getting courage from me ever since she read *The Feminine Mystique* and heard me speak in Kansas City. And if I had the guts to say, "I don't have to prove myself . . ." and get off the rappel, she could surely get down that 300 feet. Unlike me, by now she did feel "in control" of the ropes.

I go down the trail and join the others again at the foot of the cliff. I envy their exhilaration. I wish I could have done it, but I'll survive. I eat a peanut butter sandwich but I'm not hungry, for here are Ann and Kitty again, and Henry, who is the chief climber. We're not finished yet? Well, it seems those ropes and cables strung nearly out of sight near the top of those trees we passed under during climbing practice are our last ordeal. You climb up a weird sort of tunnelish rope ladder, climb across a cargo net, shinny up a tall tree, fasten belay hooks on cables fore and aft, climb onto the Burma Bridge —two parallel ropes you hang on to while tightroping across a cable to a fallen tree from which you ascend to a higher tightrope bridge —this time only one cable for the hands, one for the feet. How does one get down? Like Tarzan, it seems. From a little platform near the top of the tallest tree, out of sight, you put your feet into one cable loop and your hands in another, and swing—oh, several hundred feet to the ground. No belay lines on this—you just hold on. You Tarzan, me not Jane!

Coward or not, I've gone through that sound barrier; my upper arm strength is clearly not up to such foolishness. I'll find out how far I can go and still turn around and get back down without playing Tarzan. So I climb the rope ladder and the cargo net okay, like getting back on the horse after you've been thrown. I don't exactly intend to "resign myself" to a life of timidity henceforth, after all. Then I climb back down the ropes and don't even envy the others, shrieking down that Tarzan swing. Someone once sat on that treetop platform for forty-five minutes before he got the nerve to jump. I'm glad that wasn't me! So now I know I really can do something very difficult that I've never had the nerve to try before if I try hard enough, though it will take me a lot longer than someone younger. But what a relief, at this age, finally, that I don't have to compete to prove myself—that I can live with the fact that I'll never rappel and that failure doesn't really matter one way or the other.

We're to end with a marathon run back to Outward Bound headquarters, where we're spending the last night. We change to shorts, running shoes, right there on the road, no one bothers with modesty now. "Go all out, this last time," Dave says. I schlog along as usual, but what the hell—I step up my speed on the home stretch and finally manage to pass someone (Ruthie, Letha?), and there on top of the little hill waits a crowd of young people. They've completed their own training, I guess, and are cheering us ancients. I sprint up that hill in real all-out style— and then stop at the top and put my hands on my knees to catch my breath. No real point to pass the finish line ahead of Ruth or Letha.

The seven of us go to the cabin where we'll spend the night, on bunk beds that look drearier than pine needles. The bonds between us jar against these room walls. The others go into dinner; I break ranks and take a shower, put on my one clean thing, the hiking shorts I never wore, my Mexican cotton jacket, and some lipstick.

Each group was to perform a skit after dinner. On the trail Bob and I had concocted a three-act drama called *Going Way Beyond,* trusting the others to improvise their parts. In our plot it turns out that offering Outward Bound to geriatric cases over fifty-five was a sinister scheme to collect the insurance they take out on all our lives, because the river rafting and rock climbing which only test the young are sure to kill us. So instead of toilet paper, the instructors say look for shiny three-petal leaves, etc. We survive, un-killable despite our years, until they direct us to take a "trust fall" off Table Rock. As one by one we back over the edge, the leaders weep: "What commitment!"

The kids howl. Enormous applause. A young girl says to me later in the washhouse, "That wasn't fair, you know how to do it better." She keeps staring at my white-streaked hair: "You people actually *climbed* Table Rock?" To my amazement, Cece seemed as nervous about im-provising her own lines as I was on the cliff. To each! Later, in a quiet back room, we old ones share finally our real-life identities—and the dif-ferences we will take away.

"After this, you feel you can do anything," says Jerry, who owns a computer business in Iowa. "But how do we keep on 'going beyond' back home?" He's fifty-six, and for the first time he and his wife are going to be alone together, with their last kid off to school.

"The people I know back home think I'm crazy for doing such things at my age," says Earl, who is seventy-two. He sold his prosperous insur-ance agency after nursing his wife for seven years before she died. Now, he goes all over the world, consulting on pension plans, taking jobs that will get him to new places where he wants to go. Getting a bit bored with travel, he's now thinking of volunteering at his local community college to teach illiterates to read. He also seems to have a number of lady friends he likes to take dancing. "I lead a double life," he says.

Bob, heading for sixty, let his partners buy him out of the Madison Avenue advertising agency he ran, and now runs his own one-man shop out of his home in New Jersey. He got tired of the commuting rat race. "I began asking myself what kind of life do I want to *live?*" he says. He's been trying his hand at a lot of things he'd never done before—sailing, gliding. "But this is a different kind of going beyond: to have been with a group of strangers—who became closer than family—for eight days, and to have seen nothing but noble manifestations of the human spirit. With all we went through, there was no jealousy, spite, meanness, cruelty, selfishness, artificiality; we were all completely open with each other, without boasting about or even knowing the jobs that define each of us at home."

"I learned here that I can be much more than I ever thought I could," says Cece, who amazes everybody by revealing she is sixty-four. She looks thirty-five—until you get close enough to take in the lines and wisdom of her face. "I was always a woman people looked at. Now suddenly I'm the oldest woman in the room. Now, instead of trying so hard to look younger, I want to explore my own aging process. I've been limiting myself. Now, I'm less interested in the outside, in being beautiful. I want to find new, harder things to do."

"Doing something like this opens a little window of the spirit you can go through when the walls seem to be closing in," says Ruth, who is a teacher in a Washington suburb, "getting itchy having to teach every kid how to perform the same way to please their ambitious parents."

Letha is a social worker in Kansas, a widow who got her master's degree after she nursed her own daughter through a serious illness, then started a Halfway House to help young psychiatric patients get back into the community. Now, she wants to go beyond that and run a hospice for the dying.

I am last in the circle. I say who I am. The women, it seems, have known all along, but had not broken my cover. "I never had much use for women's lib," Bob says in confusion. Earl is incredulous. "Then, you must be a celebrity," he says. "I just liked you for your gutsy spirit." I could have kissed him (and later did). I get paranoid about being liked for my "celebrity" instead of for who I really am—would they still like me if I lose it?

And then I had this glimmer about the fountain of age, which I shared with the others—that going beyond youth, we each might finally be able to celebrate being who we really are. "To be who you really are is to be celebrated," I suggest now to the others. The strength we found on this expedition into the wilderness to risk *being ourselves,* to go beyond those roles we've leaned on and hidden behind—and the wisdom, the compassion, the sensitivity and flexibility we've all seen, in ourselves and each other, on this expedition into the wilderness—are these perhaps unique strengths that can emerge in age, which we don't expect, or recognize, or value enough in ourselves or others if we only measure ourselves against the standards of youth?

"I forgot my age," Cece said. "I giggled again, which I stopped doing back home." Judy, our respected instructor, who is in her thirties (I had thought her older), says: "I'm confronting my own aging. People see me as old because I'm over thirty now." She's left teaching, where she could have "stayed thirty years and retired with a good pension, but I wouldn't have lived." This winter she'll work as a cashier at a ski resort and her husband as an instructor, to learn the ropes so they can branch out with a new life for themselves, in the mountains.

SUNDAY: We get up at first light again, though we talked until one. We have to scrub and return the pots and pans, unknot the ropes, turn in and account for all our gear, and change back into civilian clothes. To scrub pots with hot, running water instead of leaves and sand is practically a pleasure. I feel so light—clean hair, high heels instead of heavy boots, a skirt and pantyhose again—without whatever dead weight masks I've shed in "going beyond."

In our farewell circle now, tough Judy crying, Bob too, me too, Dave reads the Robert Frost poem:

> *Two roads diverged in a wood, and I—*
> *I took the one less traveled by,*
> *And that has made all the difference.*

During the next few years, after this first adventure in "going beyond," I began—more or less consciously, with a shifting mixture of exhilaration and fear, spurts of ease, bogs of dreary doubt—to move onto new trails in my own life. I certainly didn't "retire." I didn't actually even say to myself: *Face it, after sixty, after sixty-five, it's a no-win proposition, to keep on playing the old games, trying to beat the odds, to stay on top, in the old way, in work or women's movement politics—or in search of love partners, or dinner party invitations.*

I still got caught up in those games—maybe it was not possible to be completely free of them —and, I must admit, they got more and more depressing with age. Maybe because they didn't seem worth the effort anymore? But the sense that it was possible now to *go beyond* those games, in work and love, became more and more clear to me as I listened to men and women who were doing just that, and tried some new directions of my own. I had moments of panic when they didn't seem to be succeeding, or I couldn't see where they were leading. But I was surprisingly undismayed even when they failed, and I became more and more lighthearted at following serendipitous openings, at risking new ways.

It was a liberating revelation, "going beyond" on the Chatooga River, that we ancients, pooling our energies and the skills of our life experience, were able to surmount those dangerous rapids with fewer casualties and less need of outside care or rescue than any younger group. Evidently even in a task that demands the muscular strength easier to come by in youth, qualities that may emerge with age—wisdom born of experience, freedom from youthful competitive compulsion, cooperation, empathy—can more than compensate for whatever losses of muscle power or memory also come with age. I stopped worrying that I could no longer count on total recall of an interview if I didn't take notes; the significance was clearer, deeper, and not forgotten, months later—and I do take notes. To discover that even unathletic I, with some new training, could manipulate a boat around those rapids and bring back skills unused for forty years, convinced me more than any of my research that I might try new, completely different ways of working—in my writing, lecturing, teaching—or even, for a change, something I had never tried before, that I might not be very good at (the cello?). Of course, that is the real liberation of age: the amazing lightness and solidity of no longer feeling the need to prove oneself, to be the best, to outdo the others, to compete—and of being able to fail. What does it really matter?

It seemed easier, at first, to "go beyond" in a completely new place. When I moved to California to teach every winter, I was amazed to discover that I had lost my lifelong fear of being alone. Released from my old social routines, I felt nothing but exhilaration, alone in my new apartment by the Pacific, as I made new friends and tried new things, silly and serious, I never had time, or nerve, to try before. I even dreaded going back to my apartment in New York, my house in Sag Harbor, where I had always overscheduled every week to ward off those times alone. Now back home the panic and the dreariness came only when I slipped back into, or seemed stuck in, the old roles and fantasies. And I realized that it was when, and only when, I got stuck again in that youthful rat race, which no longer nourished my spirit, that I experienced still the terror of age instead of the simple exhilaration of "going beyond" in work and love.

I had a hunger now for further adventures "beyond"—spiritual, intellectual, as well as physical. After climbing back from that precipice, I realized we are able in age to take truly adventurous risks because we know our own real limits and are free enough of machismo/machisma to "just say no" as youth cannot.

My friend Marlene Sanders, who was the first woman vice-president of network television news, went on a similar river raft and mountain-climbing expedition with a group of women executives from state governments and corporations around the country. When their young "guides" scheduled them to climb another peak, after lunch, in the midday sun, and come back down again, she and some of the other veterans simply laughed and stretched out on the grass instead. Sunrise, sure, sunset; but not in the cancer-causing midday sun. "I've proved myself under Viet Cong fire, covering the Vietnam War, I've survived the brutalities of network television and corporate takeover, I don't have to prove myself in that kind of sun," Marlene said, comfortably. The next year, when her new thirtysomething boss called her in and said that as a result of the corporate takeover and downsizing she would have to switch to radio, on the overnight beat, she surprised even herself by saying no. She had been terrified of such a moment because she had felt her life depended on her handsome salary and corporate perquisites.

But the next year, becoming her own agent, she developed a whole new specialty of satellite broadcasting for business and professional organizations, wrote a book, developed a news program on city politics for public broadcasting —and finally found the time to use her own swimming pool.

On my expedition, it became clear on those mountain trails that Earl Arthurs, who turned out to be the oldest of us all, well into his seventies, was the strongest, and most effective, and sensitive in his leadership, of all our group. But his stroke alone was not really all that strong, we discovered in the rapids. And how gracefully he held back, climbing, to give the younger men and us women a chance to lead, and how unobtrusively and gently he helped me over those rough spots. I was becoming convinced now that such skills as emerged in Earl, and all of us, on that mountain trail "going beyond," could be discovered, named, nourished, and used in our day-to-day lives. I was almost certain they could be of value to the professions, corporations, government, or community service from which we are now expected to retire. I was sure there could be a liberation, with age, to use such abilities to meet real needs, and for real rewards, in our communities outside the bureaucracies of professional career. Somehow we have to "go beyond" that division between "love" and "work" that defined us in our youth.

As for love, in those ten days "going beyond," the bonds that developed among previous strangers, women and men, of disparate background and temperament—but with a common yearning and willingness to risk new adventure —were so solid and comfortable that no one felt lonely, unsupported; we became a kind of family. (Marlene's group meets every year now, for some new adventure. Ours is contemplating a canoe trip in the Everglades.) But these bonds were not based on the sexual coupling or the social competition or the rearing of children or even the shared memories that created and sustained the bonds of our youth.

After my expedition, I became more and more conscious of the need and possibility of nourishing such families of friends, for myself and other women my age, widowed, divorced, whose children were rightfully now absorbed in their own childrearing families and who were not likely to remarry. Surely, men had such needs too, that might or might not be met as couple, in the old way.

After, finally, coming to terms with the parameters of my own age, I became more and more convinced that it *was* possible—though it will not necessarily happen unless we make it happen—to "go beyond" one's previous limitations and pitfalls, the self-defeating, paralyzing traps and plateaus, in both work and love, responding to and using serendipity as it might emerge, or even painful tragedy, in the most surprising ways. But I didn't yet have a clear map. All I could do was try to make sense of my own and other people's experiences of "going beyond" the dreams, expectations, limitations, dilemmas, and problems that defined our youth to that new place that can expand, rather than restrict, the parameters of our age.

Part IV

New Choices

Coming into a New Place

$\mathbf{I}$t comes as a surprise, even at first almost a feeling of guilt: after a long time of being afraid, of not wanting to think about it, of pretending everything's the same, the delight, the sheer excitement of coming into a new place after sixty, after it's all supposed to be over. And it may not have come easily.

The pleasure was so intense in one woman, embarking on a riverboat exploration trip in the Everglades after three years of mourning the death of her truly beloved husband, that she had a heart attack carrying her camping gear through the airport. It took intensive hospital care, and some beneficent psychotherapy, before she could get into a new place in her work, love, and life. It took a lot of trial and error, and further traveling and more mistakes that didn't kill her.

For women, the strange ease of that new place comes especially as a surprise after the grief and loss of widowhood; and for men, after the panicky finalities of forced retirement or the unhappy realization that they can no longer deny age. One man watched his blood pressure escalate as he tried to hold on to his Hollywood career, competing in helpless rage with men half his age, producing for the "youth market." He focused all that rage on his wife, who made him feel like a failure because he had never fulfilled her dreams of fame and glory. Vowing finally to fulfill his own youthful fantasy of perfect love that his marriage had never satisfied, suddenly he moved out of their Beverly Hills house to a "temporary" basement apartment. Then, to everyone's surprise, he shifted gears. He stopped producing for the youth market—and pretending to himself about those youthful dreams of glory or love. He missed his wife. And in the reality of their big Beverly Hills house by herself, she missed him, and saw how much she depended on him, the way he was, not that fantasy Noël Coward. When he moved back in, both of them found a surprising delight in each other's company, without those dreams neither had been able to fulfill for the other.

It can come as quietly as waking up in the middle of the night in one's own house, alone, with a sense of new comfort after years of frantic fear of being alone. Or as simply as arranging one's furniture in a literal new place—a new apartment, a new city—with unexpected delight in the very strangeness. Or for women or men, it can start with setting out on some adventure never dared before—mountain trekking or wilderness river rafting, studying Italian or the cello, tap dancing or sacred scripture. Or simply stopping the practice of a profession or the pursuit of a power that has lost its meaning.

It comes, for some, from starting a new game they never dared try before for fear of losing. Or from suddenly speaking out against some accepted abhorrence or practice they had never dared object to before for fear of what others would think. The finding of oneself in a new place is marked for some by letting streaked blond or bright red hair grow out its natural gray. Or for others by being offered a chance to go on with, or back to, a job from which they had dreaded retiring—and to their surprise, not taking it, "I'm in a different place now. I've done that already." It's marked for others by sticking their necks out, suddenly, in an open invitation, or honest reaction, and being accepted or rejected—either way, it almost doesn't matter—without the usual shame or fear of humiliation.

However it comes, for others, for myself—and

it comes especially as a surprise after a long period of fear or worry, trial and error, seeming stagnation—*we know that we are suddenly in a new place.* But if we try to explain it by saying, "It's like being young again," that isn't really it. In fact, getting to that new place has something to do with the ease, the comfort, the new simplicity of not trying to pass as young or deny one's age at all. It's as if only by giving up those youthful illusions and demands, fears and dreams, by being your own age, by letting yourself know what you now know and who you now really are, that you have the strength to move on to that new place.

"I don't have that fear any more that they'll find out I'm a fraud," said Kevin McCarthy, playing in his seventies dramatic character roles, large and small, with much more range and diversity than the juvenile leads he was still playing into his fifties. "I know what I can do and what I can't do." When the movie roles seemed to be drying up, he put together and directed a play based on Harry Truman's life. He toured with a company, but "the logistics took all my time. It barely broke even. So I got rid of the scenery, and the stagehands, and the company, and turned it into a one-man reading. Just me and one chair on the stage. I didn't need all those trappings."

"Talk to my mother," said a Harvard colleague. "She started growing in all directions after she was sixty, and she doesn't stop." A sprightly, comfortable woman, neither thin nor plump, with light reddish-gray curls, Esther told me proudly that she was "going on eighty-two."

After my husband died, I sat down and said, I have to build a life for myself. I moved into a building where I had friends, and I made new friends at work. I didn't intend to sit back and be a burden to my children. I started going to the theater, to museums. I met another person at work, also a widow, we clicked, she likes to go places. We went to Europe, to Hawaii, to Israel, we drove along the coast of Italy. I don't kvetch, my health is good enough. Let's face it, I'm getting a little hard of hearing, but not enough to bother.

I got my first job in a department store, running the infant's department, at sixty-three. I had to officially retire at seventy-nine but I can give them 1,000 hours a year, so I work Tuesday, Friday, and Saturday until January and come back in April. Three of us go down to Florida and share a house. We joined organizations, do a lot of entertaining back and forth, other widows mostly, couples too. I think I'm very fortunate that I can live with myself. I'm proud of myself that I'm so independent. A lovely gentleman I knew sixty years ago came after me when his wife died. I had to fix him special foods. He'd fall asleep watching TV. If I married him, I'd be lonely. I wouldn't have the life with my friends. I'm in a different phase of my life now. I've lived a full life, with happiness, with sadness, with tragedies, with joys. I've had all the seasons. To tell you the truth, I don't think I ever stopped growing. If I didn't grow in one angle, I did in another.

At sixty-two, Hattie Price, having already lived through a major shift in her role as a woman, was consciously preparing herself for, and in fact almost looked forward to, another shift with age. She said:

I'm not at all tempted to relive my youth. That was a whole other era. But it's kind of stressful to be the first generation to age that isn't necessarily headed for dotage. I was a widow in my forties, I had to go back to school and get a B.A. So I got a job as Director of Housekeeping at the college. To put it all on finding a man, if you're older, is a dead end. The main thing, I always audit a course. I brushed up my French and began Italian. I audited American history, and now I'm starting on Chinese history. I'm not a bit systematic about it—do I really want another degree?

To be honest, I've become more centered in myself. Not my children, my house, my second husband—my own interests are now primary, for me. I didn't used to feel that good about myself. It took me a long time to get out of that sense of not being good enough, the way I was brought up in our Irish Catholic household, the hypocrisy of being such a sacrificial mouse. I get a kick out of how *good* women feel about themselves now. Thanks to the movement, which came in the middle for me, women can say, Well, now I'm rid of the kids. I'm free, this is what I feel, think, want for myself, without having that terrible guilt. You couldn't say that before. I certainly have a lot more self-confidence than I had when I was younger, and that's a blessed relief.

Bob L., an experimental physicist who has made more than one hundred important contributions to nuclear medicine, was sixty-seven when he told me:

I feel freer now. At my age, I don't have to pretend I'm still the same dashing irresistible lover. I never have been dashing. Age is freer, if you let yourself feel it. As long as you're denying it, you're not free. I was the oldest one in my section. I used to avoid conversations that would indicate my age: the Depression, the war. In the last few years I've gone in the opposite direction. I go out of my way to make it open, my age, I'm not embarrassed by it anymore. I recognize the feeling of freedom, being who you really are, the strengths of it. I don't want to be section chief anymore, spend the rest of my life on bureaucratic details. There are some new problems I want to work on now.

It's as if there has to be a relinquishing—which is sometimes more difficult than the forcible loss —of the previous focus for these new strengths to emerge. That mere relinquishing of youth— roles, games, standards—can actually liberate women or men to realize new or long-deferred dreams and get to "a new place" in age. Jim, at seventy-one, told me:

I no longer need anyone's approval but my own. You go through all kinds of evolution, and false fears and stops and starts, until you accept the process of change and transformation that I hope is going to keep happening to me until I die. Retiring, I do more than I ever did when I ran my business, but I don't *have* to do anything. I am dispensable, it will go on, but differently. Okay. Now, I can have more fun with my living instead of living my dying— which is what you do if you try to stay in the same place.

Sometimes, a physical, literal move to a new place registers, or enables, the change long building, long resisted. Germaine, a brilliant Washington hostess, had spent nearly fifty years shepherding, in infinite detail, her husband's career in law and government. She still remembered, and resented, his talking her out of going to law school herself—"Your kind of reasoning wouldn't hold up in a court, you're a woman, after all"—even though she had been head of student government at her Seven Sisters college. The women's movement came too late for her.

But in her sixties, she wanted a place for herself, something different from the hostessing she did for him and the committees she sat on. To her friends' surprise, she bought a condo in her own name in the town on the Gulf coast where they had sometimes gone for a winter holiday. She spent more and more time down there, in her new place, and began to take a leading role in an institute pioneering a new kind of education for people who wanted to study and learn in their age, but not in classes geared to children. She began to do a different kind of entertaining in that community where she was making her own place, and people hardly knew who her husband was. And then her husband became ill, and needed her in a different way.

Now, dividing her time between Florida and Washington, she found herself acting in quite a different way, on the committees which she once used to advance their social status. To her surprise, she found herself, at sixty-eight, confronting the chairman of the board of the Jewish philanthropic federation to which, under his sponsorship, she had been elected as the only woman member. She had raised a million dollars and she wanted it spent on "day care, which is a big need in Washington, with most children's mothers working—and not just for Jewish kids either. I wouldn't have had the nerve to stand up to the board before," she said. "I would have been afraid of making them mad at me, they might disapprove, they might stop inviting me."

She spoke, with surprise in her voice, and a note almost of fear of "feeling suddenly that I'm growing and growing after it was all supposed to be over." What was her fear—"of going so far ahead, where is it taking me?" Not exactly. "What if that hadn't happened to me?" she said, of any one of the moves she made that brought her to this place.

Because he was my dear friend, I watched Barney holding on, into his sixties, to the "security" of a corporate job where he once had high vice-presidential status and a measure of creative power. In these unusually turbulent last years of an always competitive television network, he had been stripped of the power and the perks he had truly enjoyed, and kicked into a programming ghetto from which he was expected to resign. He doggedly stayed on until he could collect his pension. During those years, treated with contempt by his colleagues and his rich second wife, whom he finally divorced, he drank more and more heavily, put on weight, and began to look like an ill old man. The day after his retirement he moved to Washington, went to work as a television consultant for a large non-profit institution, and married a healthy, sensible woman with a comfortable house and career of her own. When his kids were little, he had loved his garden. He turned her two acres into vegetables, flowers, filled its pond with fish, and acquired cows to graze its grass as well as chickens, so that they will always eat, even if his consulting stops.

When I saw him last, at seventy-two, he looked stronger, healthier, and happier than I had ever seen him. He had lost the alcoholic red nose, taken off the weight, and had one drink at night, without benefit of AA. "Since I left the network, I've stopped being afraid, even of death," he said, with that same note of wonder at "this new place I'm in."

There are so many things I want to do now, I don't have the time—I've started painting; I had that brainstorm about raising the cows, the fish; I'm working on a long-term project starting a cable system out here; I walk seven miles along the towpath every morning and do the gardens in the evening; I seem to have lost fifteen pounds without looking at the scales. I've got my daughters back again—we grew apart in those years—they all came with the grandchildren to my seventieth birthday. I wake up every morning and think how lucky I am. I finally have it all together, but the big change is I'm not afraid anymore.

Sometimes there are false starts. It takes trial and error, mistakes, to arrive at a new place. There can be an early failure of nerve, or emotions released—joy, fear, exhilaration, panic, guilt—at the breakout from the old place that can overwhelm and temporarily send one back. But having glimpsed that new place, one cannot really go back. So, Mary Ann, after the years of grief over the husband truly mourned—and resented for leaving her—after the river raft adventure was aborted by her heart attack at the airport, went for counseling. She took early retirement from her job teaching handicapped children and made a plan to study theology seriously and get her M.A. Not too late, at fifty-eight. She sublet her new apartment and went off to Jerusalem by herself, to study Hebrew, and explore. It was an adventurous summer—no heart attacks, she began to feel independent. A man she had flirted with for years wanted her to marry him. Though she had moaned to her daughter about the impossibility of going on alone, without a man, to her own surprise, she said no.

And then, drawn by some deep impulse, unfinished business from her painful past that she never talked about, she volunteered to do oral histories of other Holocaust survivors, to help make a permanent record of what happened before it was rewritten in history. On this project, she used her old skills in a new way, which truly excited her. She spent a day a week taking care of her own grandchildren, to help her scientist daughter get back to work. When another old friend's wife died and he sought her company, she didn't send him away so quickly. And when she set out on another adventure, renting a house in the Pyrenees sight unseen with three other widows, she didn't have a heart attack at the airport.

The "new place" evolves, takes and changes shape in response to what comes up in life. But it does not seem to be manipulated in opportunistic terms of career. Somehow, it expresses and integrates one's self in totality. It uses the accumulated skills and experience of the past to some new purpose that stretches into the future. In this new place, women or men report, in one way or another, that they are finally "putting it all together," "all the parts of myself," working

in a different way "with my whole self," somehow "becoming more truly myself than I have
ever been before."

The morning after the surprise party for her
eightieth birthday, Ida Davidoff showed me the
new wildflower garden she was planting—and
the plastic bubble she had just put over her pool
so she could continue swimming nude after the
weather turned cold. The birthday party had
been given by "all of her daughters"—women
twenty and thirty years younger than herself with
whom she had started a "woman's place" in
Connecticut at the peak of the women's movement, or worked with as colleagues or trainees
in her late-blooming career as a psychotherapist. I had first met her when, getting her Ph.D.
at Columbia at fifty-eight, she had done her
graduate thesis disproving the myth of the traumatic "empty nest."
　I came for breakfast that morning at 9:00 A.M.
She had already swum fifty-five laps and seen
two patients. She said:

The older you get, the more you get to be like
yourself. I have gained tremendously more
self-confidence even in the last four or five
years, become more integrated as a person
now, more together. My work has become
more daring, more spontaneous, more effec-

tive. I react as a whole person without thinking first whether I should or shouldn't try it.

It began for me with the women's movement. That was the first big change. Now, it's trusting oneself—accepting and using one's own best qualities without trying to suppress them. Everything kept women from trusting themselves before. In my work, I used to be always judging myself according to extraneous standards. Now, I don't need anyone to tell me what to do, I don't need their approval. What difference does it make?

I trust my own aggression now—following your curiosity, risking yourself in more ways is using this God-given drive for life. I finally trust this particular drive—you can call it aggression—which women have had to sublimate and men to exaggerate, to their own detriment. I react as a whole person now, as my self—reacting as a whole to the essence of the other person. Because you have this greater trust in yourself, your antenna picks up the messages you couldn't hear before. You can't hear it if you're full of your own self-doubt—worrying about whether you're saying the right thing.

All the memories you've stored up come into focus more when you need them if you're free of that old anxiety. My memory is better than it ever was before with my patients; I remember things they've forgotten, emotional memories. The freer I am, the more I act as a whole person

—which has come to me with age—the more effective I am in helping people get over their own anxieties.

Her own *authority,* sitting at her desk, poking among her wildflowers, presiding over "all of her daughters" at the birthday party, seemed organic, simple, unmistakable. She was living now with a rare, chronic immunological disease that used to be fatal. It was not curable, but cortisone controlled it.

Someone asked me the other day how I would describe my health. I said, superb, considering. If you need an excuse for not doing something, for staying put, for not risking, you use poor health, magnify it. That's why some women run to doctors all the time; it's a way of life that keeps them from really living. Most older people get depressed, not thinking in terms of the future anymore. I am constantly aware that I am living on borrowed time. Yet I live as if I'm going to live a long time. I'm planting bulbs, putting in shrubs that will take years to grow. Why deprive yourself of even an hour of beauty because you don't know how long you'll be around to enjoy it?

"She is my role model," her twenty-year-old grandson told me. "When I'm eighty-nine, I want to be giving lectures and swimming in the nude at midnight like she does."

Another woman, an elementary school principal widowed at forty-five, remarried after seventeen years of bringing up her sons alone. She had enjoyed traveling around the world with her new husband, being his hostess, decorating a big new house, "like a stage setting," and teaching at a nearby university. To keep that life, she thought she could handle "the humiliation of his continual affairs." Then, she broke her hip and developed severe back problems and a rare kind of arthritis that brought intense pain throughout her body and head. One night when her husband wasn't home, she felt an overpowering urge to get out an old Indian record she used to dance to—and she danced for an hour without any pain. She decided to leave that stagey big house. She told her doctor she was going to stop the cortisone, and when she went in for a test, her blood count was normal again.

I had to move. I was crippling myself to play that role, his lovely hostess, swallowing the humiliation from fear of being old and alone. I was denying my own spiritual core somehow. I had to let it go and be who I am. We divorced, and it was very frightening, the fear of a new life at this age. At sixty-five you're surely not going to get any job, you're too old to be hired. What do you do with your life? I'd kept this condo in Hawaii I'd bought to retire to before I remarried. My fear was, I'd sit on the beach with my old friends and do nothing. I was tired, I was spent.

Some weeks after she got back to Hawaii, she started REAL (Renewed Energy for Actual Living), a program "for older adults" at the School of Nursing at the university. Now, at seventy-two, she said:

I guess what I was really afraid of was that I wouldn't keep growing. I created an area of work that I could keep growing in, giving of myself. I don't need to cling to anyone, I don't even need a guru. I was always one of those people who has to control what happens. I don't need to do that anymore. I'm open somehow to receiving what's out there. I see it more clearly, more sides to it. I take it in, all in one piece. And I'm not kidding myself.

Her program is now being used in workshops throughout the islands and she was asked to keynote the Hawaiian Conference on Aging.

It did not seem to be coincidence that all of these people were consciously interested in age, and in the process of their own aging. There appeared to be something releasing, liberating about identification with one's own age, a conscious interest in age not in terms of resignation and decline but as a new stage of life with its own possibilities.

Frank Manning, eighty, had "focused" himself, and achieved a political effectiveness in the years since he was sixty-five that had eluded him in his previous up-and-down, uneven work life. I interviewed him in the cluttered headquarters of the senior citizens office which he founded in Boston.

At sixty-five, I was faced with a real challenge. I went down to a storefront, the Boston Center for Older Americans, in the Back Bay, where there were a lot of widows with no pensions, no health insurance. Some weren't even covered by Social Security. I got fourteen people together to start a Legislative Council. I did a survey, found seventy thousand people over sixty like that, called a meeting to get them covered by more Social Security. The only place I could think of that would hold enough of those people over sixty from all over the state to make their political clout visible was the racetrack. We got 160 buses to take them to the racetrack. We initiated hot lunch and home care programs so they could preserve their own lifestyles in the community instead of being warehoused in nursing homes. Now we've got 250 organizations in our council. We put out our own newspaper now. We started all kinds of VISTA programs run for and by older people themselves where before they had been exclusively for youth.

When I started all this, I didn't have too much confidence. The last time I tried something like that, I got by on my youth. But I must have some strength now I didn't have in my youth, because I've never had a hostile audience—even when the organization doesn't join our council, they follow our leadership, they work with us. We started a hot line on legislation affecting elders; now our state has the best record on elder legislation in the country.

Always before, I was really afraid to take on a big job. I turned down promotions; that's why I moved around so much. I think I was a bit of a coward, with no great confidence in myself. But after I was sixty-five, I realized my ability to get people to discover their own power.

His most recent project was "The Silver-Haired Legislature," an advocacy training program in which people sixty and over take out nomination papers, run for election, attend state legislative sessions, and then go into local community organizations to put the well-being of the elderly on the agenda. On this particular day, he had already had a meeting with people from different parts of the state on the problems of the homeless, and another on the loss of health care, and another on trying to get more affordable housing, and then he went to the State House to be sworn in—the council on aging which he started had become an official state commission. Tonight, "thank heaven I have nothing to do; I'm going to make my special spaghetti sauce for a few of my friends."

Only at the end of the interview did he mention that "I got Parkinson's late in life, just three years ago. No noticeable tremors—just a weakening of the legs." He also had a spur on his spine, which was causing him unendurable pain. He decided to have a spinal operation, despite a risk that he would lose the use of his legs. "I was back on my feet in a couple of weeks."

Norman Lear, sixty-five when I first interviewed him, was also moving to a new place.

I was going through a period where I was feeling so unsure. Everybody in the world was more certain than I about what he was doing next. When I sold off everything and the press called to ask why, I said, "The curtain is going down on the second act of my life, and it's rising on the third act." Suddenly, I began to feel terrific. The minute I saw that in print, something clicked in my mind. It's a Shake-spearean play, five or six acts; this is clearly Act III, but I'm sure it's not the last act.

"All in the Family," his great prize-winning television series, had in the previous year played its last tears-and-laughter episode. "Maude" and "Mary Hartman, Mary Hartman" were in his proud past. He had sold his studios, but was overseeing himself a slight sleeper of a movie about boyhood friendship. More and more of his energy and resources were now being devoted to People for the American Way, his organization of ecumenical clergy and lay people countering fundamentalist pressure on the media that they see as threatening constitutional rights of free speech and dissent. He had recently separated from his wife of twenty-odd years.

I have a lot of friends my age and they're much older. They may work out, play a lot of golf and tennis, but they begrudge age. They can't enjoy their age because they don't want to admit it. They can't accept being what and where they are. I'm beginning to deal with the totality of being older. I gave up all that power of the trappings of office, but I didn't give up the power of the person I have become.

Act III feels more like a time for growing vertically, from a deeper place, a more reflective place. Act III means less fear of being found out for who I really am. Maybe I could even get to the poetic side of my nature without being afraid of stuttering.

I used to be fearful that my competitors and colleagues would find out that I have a spiritual side. I'm far more tolerant in my third act of other people who express my own hidden questions, even on the opposite political side. I understand in my third act the intolerance of liberals like myself. I used to think that only the right was intolerant. Now in my third act I'm realizing the intolerant arrogance of arch-reflex liberals. I often think the fundamentalist evangelists have gotten their hold on the American public because too many liberals have written off the spiritual needs and values. We did not pay attention to a lot of cries in the night. We were ashamed of our own. Maybe that's the essence of the third act—to be able to look at what one really is, and know it, and say I like it.

He did not pretend to have become a serene, peaceful saint. "I rush a lot, I try to do too many things. I'd like to do less and savor it more." He did not, however, begrudge the time he had spent organizing People for the American Way, which now had 200,000 members, and was the only new, successful nationwide organization professing liberal values. "I really believe in the values of American democracy. It's all a lie, to use those values to rationalize abdication of government responsibility. Our government is bigger than it ever was, but we need a big government that will concern itself again with the common good, with the nerve to tell the truth about defense."

The "nerve to tell the truth," to "ask out loud" the question never asked before about some shibboleth or conventional wisdom accepted by those in power—in the committee, the corporation, the political party—is a strength once looked to from the young. It comes as a surprise that it could be a strength, instead (or also), of those in age who have moved to a new place. Some of the other men and women I interviewed whose "nerve to tell the truth regardless of the consequences" seemed to have quickened with age, were regarded as "troublemakers," too crotchety and uncomfortable to keep around. Some had resigned from the board of the civic group, the art museum, or the union in protest over what seemed a betrayal of principle or trust; they were seldom urged to reconsider. Several, on the other hand, had been brought back as consultants to their own companies or others in the industry to perform that very function—ask the question, give the opinion, based on a lifetime of experience in the industry, without regard to its effect on their own no longer relevant career.

Granted that my own interviews were hardly a scientific sample, the fact is I had no trouble finding people who were clearly continuing to evolve in their sixties, seventies, even into their eighties. I found them easily, in any city or suburb, community or institution where older people continued to reside and discover ways to remain active—even in some nursing homes or retirement villages, where people were really not expected to continue to grow and control their own lives, much less to "act out" that nerve to tell the truth in the larger community. And all of the people I talked to experienced age as a "shift," a "becoming my true self," "coming into a new place." But if this new place is not a rarity only an exceptional few can achieve, if it is a genuine possibility for a great many of us, how do we get there?

Some may never experience that "lightness" or the "nerve for truth," that "putting it all together finally," that concentration in age on "the things that really mean something to me." Some may never free themselves from the "concern with how the world sees me," never make the space in their lives to take care, finally, of long-postponed or unfinished business, or dreams. Some may never reach the authentic core of self that does not shrink from truth, never recognize or dare to try in late life the path not taken.

If we never transcend the boxes of our youth, never reconcile ourselves to the reality of where we are now, never let ourselves know that it's no longer important to attain goals that we set or accepted earlier in life, never explore the new possibilities, we will never get to that new place. But the very possibility of a "new place" in age, for any of us, has profound implications for our personal choices and public policy. The very possibility of a new place in age implies profound personal and social change.

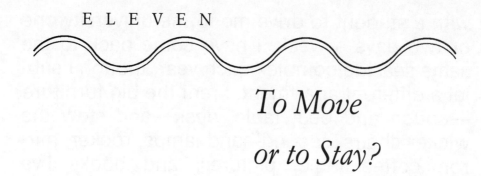

To Move or to Stay?

I was in my mid-sixties when I started coming to California to teach. It wasn't a career move in the old sense, nor a retirement one either. (I doubt if I ever will retire!) My asthma was getting bad, winters in New York. But I wasn't about to go to a winter resort or some "leisure world." I was welcomed at USC as a "visiting distinguished professor," though not on any tenure track. Because of the smog, I wanted to live near the ocean, which is miles from the university, but, terrified of the freeways, I did not want to drive in Los Angeles. So I chose to live in Santa Monica, where I could walk to stores, bank, beauty parlor, and the beach, and made a deal with a student to drive me to the university one or two days a week. I have come back to the same seaside complex each year, though I sublet a different apartment. I rent the big furniture —couch and bed, table, desk—and stow the wicker chairs, second-hand lamps, rocker, mirror, coffee table, pictures, and books I've amassed out here in friends' garages for the summer. Without my twenty to forty years of clutter, the lightness I feel here in this new home is *good.* Come to think of it, this move liberated me. It refreshed and energized me somehow, knowing I had to make new friends here, start new projects, plant my roots anew in journalist, political, feminist, and writers' groups (the interests of my past)—even try something truly new for me.

I had indeed moved to a new place now, both literally and figuratively, but I realized consciously I had to *keep moving,* even when I go back home; in any of the places which have been my home, I have to keep renewing and replanting the roots that sustain me. Older, we must move, and stay, and move again, to keep our life-giving ties alive, for this movement *is* our fountain of age. And there's a freedom in realizing this, a new freedom to move or stay, new necessities and possibilities of choice.

On what basis should we choose to move or stay, to cling to or renew old roots in place, or construct, redo the space from which to go and come back home? I knew already from my tracking of others through this space that there was no one answer to that question. We cannot simply stay where we are, the way we lived at thirty, forty, fifty, when we were young, even if we live in the same house, on the same street, in the same town as if nothing else has changed. Nor can we, in effect, deny age by removing ourselves physically from the streets of our youth, traveling rootlessly, or absenting ourselves from all reminders of the young life growing, changing all around us.

Whether to move to a new place, or simply to stay where we are, that is the deceptive, impossible metaphor of choice we put to ourselves facing age. Impossible because we *cannot* stay where we are. We have to move to a new place or forfeit our age—stagnate, denying change. But if we seek out this new place physically, we also face the necessity of creating new roots for the purposes and ties that are essential to our vital personhood in age. For the "place" we're in is not only metaphor—it is also enabler or restricter of our evolving self. If we do not move physically, we have to move in other ways to sustain our sense of purpose and renew, or replace, our vital bonds in that same old neighborhood, which has also changed as friends, mates, children move away or die.

For a while after I came to California, I felt torn, split, removed from my home, bereft of family, friends, and my political, professional networks, and yet exhilarated by the very need and possibility of creating new projects, ties, and pleasures—though not at home, yet, in this new place. And going back to Sag Harbor in the spring, I was no longer quite at home in the old place either, uprooted somehow, unsettled.

I recognize the risks now, the road signs, the dead ends and detours, from my own experience and from talking to so many who are, in fact, moving to a new place in the face of age: in Leisure World, Laguna Hills; in "mobile home parks" and luxury retirement towns in Sarasota, Florida; in small towns in Maine and Arkansas; in "life care" communities outside Philadelphia and "alternate" elder communes in Santa Monica, and back in Peoria, Illinois, where my old high school friends are aging in place. In different ways, they, we, faced the task of finding a place to *live* our age instead of forfeiting it in either a frantic clinging to the illusion of changeless youth or a passive embrace of the victim state, evading the risks of living for a guarantee of care until death. The choices themselves are bewildering, say the experts, trying to advise us whether to stay where we are and put bars in the bathtub, or move into a "retirement village" or "lifetime care facility," so our children never have to put us into a nursing home. But our real choices now are more complex than that.

• • •

Paradoxically, there is both a playing to the fear and denial of age and a literal acting out of the mystique of age that defines us solely as objects of care in the literature selling that "place to put Mom." The gerontologist Graham D. Rawles begins an essay on "A Place to Call Home" by describing eighty-two-year-old Nell's "adamancy" about staying on alone after her husband's death in the "spacious drafty residence" she had lived in for thirty-four years. "A recent attack from a 'doped' youthful intruder, a flooded basement, and increasing difficulty walking on the stony rutted pathway that led up the steep incline to her house on the hill had not weakened her resolve. This was the house where her children had been raised, where her husband had spent his last years, much of it sitting on the front porch as his soot-filled lungs progressively failed."[1]

Four years later, after a heart attack, Nell still refused to accept her son's offer of a basement apartment in his house in another state. When she left the hospital, she recuperated in her daughter's apartment until she was able to go home. Nell "remained firm in her resolve" to stay in her own home, "as long as I can get along by myself." After another attack, from which she never fully recovered, she died at eighty-seven. Was there something wrong in this scenario, staying on at home until the end? The gerontologist implied that there was.

Should Mom be supported in her wish to remain alone in the rambling old house? Should she be encouraged to move in with the family even at the risk of separation from her friends and at the cost of disrupting the family's lifestyle because such a move would necessitate doubling up the children and reducing the late night volume of the stereo? . . . Should Mom be encouraged to consider moving into an elderly housing project or to contemplate the life care facility chosen by some of her peers? At what point should institutionalization be considered? To what extent does the family have a moral obligation to provide assistance to enable her to stay in her home for as long as she chooses, regardless of the cost?[2]

People "aging in place" are pressured by failing health, deteriorating inner-city and suburban neighborhoods, loss of elderly neighbors, death of spouse, departure of children, and social isolation, the gerontologists warn. A "plethora of available options" are increasingly being offered for sale for "retirement living," for the "healthy elderly," for the "frail elderly," to move "Mom" into. The gerontologists now conceptualize a "care continuum" formula for people after sixty, in which a series of housing alternatives is "arranged along a continuum of increasing need for supportive social and medical services associated with increasing functional age and degree of frailty. . . ." In this scenario, the elderly person "is viewed as requiring residential facilities that progress from community-based individual and multi-family housing options through a variety of *congregate* alternatives providing a measure of practical and social support (including dining and service facilities) to nursing homes and hospital environments where primary emphasis is on medical care." [3]

For "them," the passive objects of a "care" sales pitch, it may indeed make sense to think of such alternatives as being arranged "along a continuum of increasing need" for support. But for *us,* who insist on *living* our age on our own terms, no less passionately though surely somewhat differently than our youth, that kind of formula misses the point. Home—the place where we choose to live—has to express and sustain our identity, the vital ties and purposes that make life worth living. Diagramming age along an abstract continuum of "medical needs," "social service needs," and "shelter needs"—with "costs per day" on one side and a baseline of "degree of frailty" from seventy to one hundred on the other—as gerontologists do, ignores their own studies spanning several decades which show that older people themselves express high levels of satisfaction with their own homes "even when the physical quality of the residence leaves much to be desired."

Perhaps in our later years, when we are no longer so completely defined by those roles of family and professional career that structured our youth, home—the place from which we come and go, the place with which we are intimately familiar, whose very furnishings express the roots and order of our being—is more important to our essential sense of selfhood and well-being than any gerontological "care." Whatever its gerontological shortcomings, mysteriously one's own home "maximizes a sense of personal competence," the gerontologists themselves admit. It can even sustain "the ability to maintain independence despite failing physiological and sensory capabilities. . . . An arena in which the individual is in control and over which he or she has mastery . . . residence in a place construed as home also plays a critical role in maintaining a sense of self-identity . . . as the individual engages in the ongoing creation and modification of home as a symbol of the self." [4] Because of all this, as many studies show, the great majority of older people expect and prefer *not to move:* 80 percent, for example, in a study of relatively healthy elders in Evanston, Illinois. Even for those who say they "probably will move" in the next two years, 44 percent would prefer not to.

In my hometown of Peoria, I was steered to Laura McCluggage as one of the most vital older people in the whole city. She had been a power on the County Board longer than anyone could remember, crucial to the reforms and innovations that have kept Peoria itself vital and changing though many of the farm machinery plants and distilleries that used to sustain its economy have closed down. She had been forced to resign from the board, not because of her age (eighty then) but because she had moved out of her big old house on the deteriorating West Bluff, where I grew up, to a small apartment in a new neighborhood, where her daughters insisted she would be safer and more comfortable. She told me:

I don't mind getting old. I just don't want to be bored. I'd be glad to be eighty if something comes along for me to do next. Since I've moved into this apartment, there's nothing for me to do. I can get out of bed in this apartment in my bare feet and the paper is in front of my door in the hall, and I put the coffee pot on and go back to bed again. When I had the big house, I got up and got dressed and went out to get the paper, maybe talk to the paper boy or one of my neighbors going to work, and I made breakfast. I always got dressed, ready to meet the day.

But the girls—I've got three daughters, eight grandchildren—thought living in that house alone with another winter coming on wasn't right, that I should sell it. It's a big square six-room house, and it got sold too soon. I wasn't finished with my County Board business. I had nuisance value on that board—they couldn't get around this old lady, popping off when something looked fishy. One of the men said, "You never know how Laura is going to vote, she votes with God."

They talked me into it, selling the house, so they wouldn't have to worry anymore. They're all busy people. The girls figured out where Mom ought to be living. They had an elegant condo apartment all lined up, Chateau Richford—swimming pool, elevator, all that stuff. To me it was like a mausoleum, carpeted floors, windows only on one wall. I like to live in a bright airy place where I can open the windows and let the fresh air in, with a nice little porch where the neighbors pass by and I can plant my tomatoes. I didn't want to pay the bill for all that fancy stuff. So I got myself an older little apartment with a porch where I can raise a tomato plant.

I very much resent people who think because you're eighty, you're getting kind of potty. It makes me cross, people trying to take care of me, acting as if I'm not all there, just assuming that you deteriorate when you get older. When old people do get handicapped, that's the time to start taking care of them. Actually, I've gotten better in some ways now that I'm older. I don't get gallstones over things the way I used to, I don't get uptight anymore, I take a crisis with a grain of salt.

It would have cost less than that fancy condo to hire a high school kid to shovel Laura's walk and drive her to meetings at night, instead of moving her from the house and community where she had a real reason to get dressed every morning. Was she more at risk of falling on those beloved hardwood floors than on the new carpeting she hates? Shouldn't that have been her risk to take? Would Nell have had a heart attack sooner or later if she had let herself be moved out of her own home to that basement apartment in her son's house far away? Was she not blessed that her kids respected her wish to stay on in her own home, until that last heart attack from which she didn't recover? Would she not have preferred to die that way?

The studies also show that most older people who choose to move are quite satisfied with the choices they've made—but *only* if they make that choice themselves. And there is no formula that works, once and for all. We may have to keep choosing to move, or stay, to sustain our sense of ties and purpose in the community— keep moving to a "new place," even if we stay where we are physically. Whatever choice is made, I've seen it work wonderfully, with people with a lot of money or very little; but they've all been willing to *risk* moving—or staying. There's no denying the risk. But when we stop moving to a new place and making it home, we seem to stop living.

That new place, as house/home, seems, strangely enough, to be as or more important for men in age than women. I have noticed it in my own friends, and in those I interviewed. The men, of course, have "retired" from the businesses or professions that once defined them. Even if they now seek to define themselves in terms of the feelings and relationships they used to have less time for, the children are no longer around for them to father most of the time; and their wives, busy with belated careers or with new interests of their own, joke that they married for "better or worse, but not for lunch."

When Erik Erikson began communicating with children through their play with blocks, he was struck by the way the little girls created enclosures, houses, and the boys built bold towers. In the early days of modern feminism, we were outraged at his assigning women to "inner space" and men to *doing,* as we fought to break through the exclusion of women from professions, careers, power in the public world. But now, watching the older men struggle to redefine themselves in terms other than external power in the face of age, I find some of these men focused on home, inner space, even obsessed with building a new house (as metaphor for self), while women sometimes simply want to pare down, get rid of a lot of possessions, simplify the clutter, and move on. So often, in my interviews and others' studies, it was the man who wanted to move to Arizona or Vermont, or a farm in Arkansas where he grew up, while she went along in protest, or refused to go at all. In such cases, the man who was kept from such a move simply withdrew inside himself, and "begins to die," as one therapist put it.

A *house,* a new place to just be, or find a new way to be, can be as powerful an enabler—of intimacy, purpose, ties—for an older man as a new job for a woman. After all these years of women struggling to define themselves anew in terms of what they "do," it was strange to see older men struggling to just "be." But what interested me was the way the women or men I've been tracking, whether they had moved or stayed, *used* "home," both to *stay themselves* and to *change,* as it seems they must, if they are to live a vital age. That home can turn on or off the fountain of age.

I have watched my own friends, in their sixties now, go back and forth on these polarities. Some built beautiful dream houses for their age, in the Hamptons, Arizona, or Palm Springs, and others scaled down, seemed even liberated by the need to scale down to a different kind of choice. But the "dream house" can turn out to be no guarantee of purpose or those all-important bonds of intimacy and community as we move into our third age, though for a time it may be a substitute. The move itself, to that new space, may be the enabler of new ties, identity, projects, but they do not come automatically with the territory. Some, after they had made such moves, saw more clearly what they really needed and wanted now, which may not be at all what they were sold or thought they wanted when they built or bought that new place.

My friend Richard, for instance, at seventy, has almost finished building a house which his friends agree is truly beautiful: long and low, along that pond he spent years searching for, ending in a flagstone- paved octagonal greenhouse-sunroom with corner cabinets made out of old barn doors and the garage a separate studio for his daughter. Every bit of hardware he picked out personally, subcontracting out the carpentry and plumbing. He went through thirteen architects before he put the final plan together himself, starting with two structures he had delivered COD. Though he had lived alone in a studio apartment in the East Seventies in New York for twenty-odd years since his divorce, spending summers and weekends in our commune or its aftermaths, it looked as if he built this house for his age not in terms of a single person or couple but big enough to house his own three grown kids and half a dozen communards.

Building that house had been his main project since he sold his business and retired several years ago. But now that it was nearly finished, and he was renting out his city apartment and more or less living out there, he was telling his friends he was already "bored." He would call or walk up my driveway at odd hours, complaining of "cabin fever"; he was just sitting in that house, reading, there was nothing to do. Don't sell it, we told him, it's so beautiful, it would be perfect for our commune Thanksgiving dinner. Maybe next winter we should rent out or shut down our own houses, he suggested, and all come and live in his. For, in fact, I began to suspect, he had built that dream house for a family still—for the children whose adolescence divorce had kept him from sharing, and who were too old now to spend that much time with their dad; or, unconsciously, for the "commune" extended family that gave him those ties he needed (we all need) now more than ever, as we approached age. He also needed another new project, now that the house itself was nearly finished. Thinking in old terms, I suggested that maybe he could make a new career of building such dream houses for others in his age.

In Peoria, my brother's friend Wally, whose wife, Louella, died several years ago, welcomed me to the beautiful small house he had built above a ravine with the Illinois River gleaming far below. He had brought up his family in the big house down the street. After they were grown and gone and he retired from his executive job in the declining farm machinery industry, which used to dominate the economy here, he and his wife moved to California near their children. He said:

We built a beautiful house, on a hilltop, with a swimming pool. It was half an hour from our kids. We joined the local country club. But after a year, we asked ourselves, what are we doing here? We weren't part of a community anymore. We missed our old friends. We came back and built this house, just for us, on this little piece of land in our old neighborhood. A great big bedroom for ourselves, and this one big living-dining room and open kitchen. A little office back there for me to work in. When our kids and grandkids come, we put them up in a motel.

Now Louella's gone, I'm doing more cooking myself. I invited another couple to come in last night, at the last minute, for potluck. I've got my old friends here to do that with. I've got the community organizations here that I helped build—the hospital, the mental health clinic, the symphony—they're glad to have me back to help out. I've got my old pals to play tennis with, I don't need to hire a pro, like in California, or keep up with the yuppies. I spent fifty years building these ties. They're what I need in my life now, more than the California sunshine. And I'll visit my kids, a week or a month, I don't need them living next door.

When Dick and Helen Dudman started going to Maine summers, fixing up a fisherman's shack on little Cranberry Island off Southwest Harbor, they thought they wanted some place "remote," removed from civilization and the omnipresent political density of their life in Washington. He had been Washington bureau chief of the *St. Louis Post-Dispatch* for many years, captured twice by the Viet Cong covering the Vietnam War, officer of Gridiron and National Press clubs. Before he was sixty-five, Dick knew he didn't want to stay on in Washington when he no longer had that journalistic power, as he had seen older friends do, hanging on. Dick said:

I had this romantic idea that we would move up to Maine and I would build boats from scratch, and help Helen run the radio station she had her heart set on buying ever since she was passed over for promotion at the station here. She couldn't do that from our shack on the island. That first year, until the station got in the black, she lived in an apartment we fixed up over the broadcast studio, and I stayed down in Washington, bringing in my paycheck, and commuting to Maine weekends. When the station began to make money, I took early retirement, ten years ago now. I was in my early sixties then, and she in her fifties, and it was her turn to go for it. Before, our life had been structured by my career.

As president and general manager of the radio station, Helen joined the Rotary, got involved with the Chamber of Commerce, discovered she "loved business, making a profit," and began to be asked to serve on boards of local industry and public utilities. Dick's project changed from his hobby of boatbuilding to new uses of his lifetime of journalistic experience, spending three months a year running a news service for Third World papers in Hanover, training journalists in Swaziland, doing visiting professor stints at black colleges in the South, bringing his former colleagues to Maine to star at benefits to build the local YMCA. When I visited them, nine years later (he in his early seventies, she facing sixty-five), they lived, with a mix of pleasure and irony, in a white-columned New England mansion with a great stretch of green lawn and evergreen woods. Inside, grandchildren's tricycles and rocking horses took away the stage-set look, their old furniture and relics from Washington mixed in with the early American antiques and quilts she has enjoyed collecting in their new hometown, population six thousand.

The new place, for Dick, as its outlines became clearer in Maine, was no longer his career but his changing, multi-purpose "being"—and sheer delight in Helen's mastery, running the radio station. For Helen, it was a chance to run the whole show, which she had never been given before. They worked together a lot, but she was the boss of the enterprise, and he clearly felt good about that, "in view of all the years she kept having to pull up stakes for my career moves, stay home with the kids, and then take starter jobs again. I see her flowering; she is so happy now. When the station made enough for me to retire and join her, she wanted me to be president, but I wouldn't dream of it." Then she started training her daughter, who had moved nearby, to take over the station management so she could travel with Dick again, on new adventures.

Sometimes, it was the woman alone who moved to the new place. The forty-five-year marriage of Peggy and Frank had seemed a romantic idyll to their college friends. They had four children, he had made a spectacular reputation very young with his early scientific work, then went into policy, administration, and she was an active church leader, a superb hostess, counted on for every civic cause. But in her late sixties Peggy quietly decided to leave their home in Ohio and move by herself into a new, experimental group living community. She told me:

We haven't really had a good marriage. It looked great, but that was a sham. On the public level, it was fine. On another level, he had continual sexual relationships with other women which he said had nothing to do with his feelings for me. I never let on how unhappy I was. I tried to commit suicide, but took tranquilizers not sleeping pills. I was afraid of living alone.

He won't accept the idea of growing old. I suppose that's what the women were all about, they get younger and younger, students, babysitters. I like the idea of living in a community. It will open in a year, it's for older people who want to make a real life together; you have to be healthy to get in, but you have that support in the changes that come for the rest of your life. I'm tired of taking care of this great big house for him. I resent the time it takes. I used to think I didn't have anything better to do. Now, I want to spend my time in things that are a real contribution. A lot of anger was in me all those years—mainly anger at myself, I would have these depressions. Now, I'm not depressed, I'm ready to move. Frank can do what he wants to, it doesn't hurt me. [He later remarried, a much younger woman, and, in his mid-seventies, was trying to adopt a baby.] This group living, I see it as a wonderful opportunity and liberation for me. In this new place I can replant my roots. I expect to start a political club there, get something done about affordable housing in the town. I'm going to use all the strengths I have now to help create that new community. I feel like a pioneer of age.

The most sensitive gerontologists increasingly respect, or at least pay lip service to, people's own preference, whether to move or stay. The ones who choose to, and can afford it, are moving to small towns, their old hometowns, university towns, retirement villages in the Sun Belt or on the outskirts of their own cities, mobile homes, or boats. Sometimes, such a move enables them to live more simply—with less money and effort. Some, forced to move for financial reasons, try to find a place they can afford, usually as near to the old neighborhood as possible. But more and more people are moving into "assisted living" or "lifetime congregate care" communities not because their health now requires it, but in anticipation or defense against the day their children might have to take care of them the way they had to take care of Mom or Dad in their final ailing years.

In my own interviews, as in the research, relocation does not seem to be a trauma when people choose to move. Even those who are forced to move seem to thrive if they have some choice, if they are *involved* in the moving process, or if they feel they are moving to a better way of life. In my own interviews, moreover, people's decisions to move often enabled them to create anew the ties or bonds or purposes that no longer worked for them in the old community. They remained or became vital in their age, even with physical ailments. But I got the feeling that people who moved while still healthy to ensure "care" for those expected months or years of physical infirmity were, in certain ways, forfeiting the fountain of age, along with the risks of continued choice. Even where physical problems exist, the decision to leave home and community where one has real ties may mean forfeiting the vital living of one's last years for a "care" that has to end in death.

When Jon Pynoos, my colleague at the Andrus Gerontology Center, was a graduate student at Harvard, he used to visit a neighbor, Mrs. B., who had lived on the third floor of his four-story walk-up in Cambridge for nearly forty years. He recalled:

She had created a very comfortable environment for herself—her mother's old wing chair and desk, old family plates on the wall. She would invite young persons to tea at four o'clock; she was driving her own car into her nineties. When she had several falls, and could no longer drive to see her friends, she agreed to move into a nursing home, though she would have preferred to stay in her own place until she died. After they moved her to the nursing home, she became very depressed. Few of her young friends visited her. She was never happy there, she didn't choose it, didn't want it, had to share a room with a dementia patient with whom she couldn't carry on a conversation, and so she became isolated though she herself was cognitively intact. She died at ninety-nine, but those last five years were not happy years. Most older people don't want to live with their children, or go into institutions. But what other choices do they have now? There's a lot of bewildering-seeming choices, but do we know what really works, and why, or what other choices we need?

I've followed enough people vitally aging in place—in that old home or a new place—and re-creating the roots and ties to life that keep them vital, to know that even now there are many ways to do it. Considerations of finance and physical health may seem crucial. But real choice may involve risking guarantees of lifetime financial security or health care.

Sally Page and her husband, both in their seventies, chose—like most of my old friends in Peoria—to "age in place," even though their health problems might have dictated a Sun Belt retirement. Sally said:

I don't like the climate here in the winter, but neither of us wants just to sit, play golf, unless we could find another community to really get involved in the way we are here. I don't see our friends doing that in Palm Springs. If you're ever going to know yourself, you do now. You know what you really enjoy, you don't have to do everything that comes along. Our biggest problem now is health—his high blood pressure is a big problem, my asthma. But my idea is just to keep on living as fully as we can, and if it's shortened a few years, so what. When our children were growing up, we had to be more cautious. Now we're free to live our lives the way we want to.

Plymouth Harbor, on the Sarasota causeway between two keys, where I interviewed Evelyn Duvall and her family of friends, almost went broke because they miscalculated the surprising longevity of people who moved to that "new place" in the community they created there—it was so much greater than the actuarial tables. As their Sarasota neighbor George Wolfe said to me: "They broke through the age barrier and just didn't die the way they were supposed to." I had a prejudice in advance about these tall, projectlike high rises, packaging the elderly away from the community, having lived in a high rise in New York for nearly twenty years without ever knowing my neighbors. In this one, the elevator stopped on every third floor—the individual studios and apartments opened off balconies above a common sitting area on that floor. Each such group of thirty apartments had its own community meeting, and sent its representatives to the larger board of residents that governed Plymouth Harbor. The day I sat in on that board meeting, in the sixth-floor community room, attendance was 100 percent. They were organizing their own seminars for the fall: architecture, astronomy, history of music. Rollin Posey, a former business administrator, said: "I have never served on a board in my life as active as this one, it drives you crazy sometimes, all these group decisions. We're not interested in doing good for old folks without regard to the larger interests of the community. Each one of us is living for the future, not the past."

Rose, another resident, said: "We have a pool here of our own resources to draw upon, retired people who supply voluntary leaders for every group—we don't have to go out of town to get a speaker—no one pays. It also gives each of us a chance to push our own interests. Two men whose only interest is boating pool their expertise and offer a course to younger people. A retired dancer finds a new way to use her skills."

Rollin said: "The thing about this group, we can afford to fail now. We are able to risk. Last year was the first time we took the risk of small group discussions about 'Great Decisions' as opposed to the larger lecture formula. The groups were oversubscribed."

They discussed how women in other condos talk constantly about illness and their ailments. "I've never heard a person here mention his or her physical symptoms," Margaret Ratz said. "We see each other coming and going, the Sarasota Players, the opera we got started here. If you have mental stimulation, you have life."

The administrator of Plymouth Harbor, Jack Smith, gave me statistics: 300 people in 250 apartments, a common dining room that served three meals a day (though most people also had their own kitchens), and a studio, card room, library, individual vegetable and flower gardens for anybody who wanted to plant one, a 42-bed nursing facility on the third floor. Average age was now eighty-two (from sixty-five to ninety-five), about 75 percent women, 25 percent men; only 18 percent were married, forty-nine couples out of three hundred people.

They have maid service, they don't have to mow the lawn. Our purpose is to simplify life, free people for the activities to maintain their own lifestyle as long as they can. Only three people moved out of here in the last ten years because they were unhappy. We have a bus to run people to shopping centers, the theater, concerts. We have home care service for people who need it. For that one-time entrance fee —$30,000 to $100,000—we undertake to take care of you the rest of your life. Costs run from $600 to $1,800 a month, depending on the size of the quarters, and the evening meal is included in the price for the small apartments. For the others, there are different plans. We sign a contract to give you these services the rest of your life.

Plymouth Harbor was the first "congregate living facility" I visited in the early eighties, when there were about fifteen hundred such facilities around the country. There was a system whereby they "check" people out every day. "If they don't check in, we call them, once a day." When it was set up as a not-for-profit enterprise, the bookkeeping was based on actuarial tables that surprisingly no longer seemed to apply. "Check in" or not, the residents didn't die as expected. They might have "sight loss, hearing loss, arthritis, a diet problem, diabetes," they might have a heart attack or stroke, and recover from it, but they just didn't die when the tables showed they should. Jack Smith said:

It seems that age isn't what we thought it was. We have to keep changing this place as we learn new things about aging. We changed our health care concept—providing services if possible in their own apartments keeps people out of the nursing home, the hospital. We changed the food service, put in a salad bar, a dessert bar. But what really makes the difference, I suspect, is the very powerful democratic structure they created themselves. That camaraderie among the aging, the ones who claim it, is something else. If you respond, I guess you stay alive. If you're secluded, pull the curtain down, turn inward, you stop living even though you're technically still alive. To survive past eighty the way people do here takes smarts.

In the garden, overlooking the waterway and the boats, I met Belle Bristol, over eighty-five, walking on the path, though I was told she has two artificial hips; another woman over ninety with a shattered leg (she had been told, "You'll never walk"—"Oh, yes, I will") was walking with a cane; and I chatted with a third woman of eighty-six who learned to speak again after a serious stroke, and was, in fact, now teaching French to a group setting out on a safari to France.

But Plymouth Harbor was not the fountain of

age for everyone. Peg, who was eighty-one, and trim in her slack suit, came with her husband because he was "tired of cutting grass and preferred to play golf." He died two years ago.

I don't have many friends here, I don't go down to the dining room. I'm a hausfrau, I love to cook, but now it seems I don't have any sense of taste or smell. I write back and forth to my kids and grandchildren but I haven't made any friends here. I figure they'll just keep dying, or they're healthy and I can't keep up with them, or they're not very bright or they can't hear, they can't see or they can't walk. I go to the exercise class, I walk twice a day, to keep fit physically. I go to some of the programs in the auditorium, but I don't take any of those Lifetime Learning courses because I don't want to be responsible for the work.

Dorothy was only seventy-four, but she was described to me as someone who was *not* in that stream of vital age. She said:

I've been here three years, and I've done less than any place I've ever lived. I used to teach teenagers Bible class, I used to do things, in the AAUW, in the League of Women Voters, in West Virginia. My husband died six months before I moved here. I'm ashamed I've just done so little. But I'd been involved in so many things before, the doctors said I'd worn myself out. I was like paralyzed all over before I was fifty, and I still held meetings right there in my bedroom. One of the last things my husband asked me to do was not get involved in anything. I tire very easily if I get involved in things because I'm a perfectionist. I go to church, to Bible class once a week, but I am utterly uninvolved in anything now. I've never had as few friends in my life.

Yet Edith Bowles, at eighty-two, remained involved, despite her inability to move quite the way she used to:

My values are the same, but I'm not able to carry them out the way I used to. The first year I was here, seventeen years yesterday, I was on five committees. I've had all the offices in the Community Association except president, and I'm going on the Executive Council again. The main thing I do now is tell people what happened in the past, our history. I'm one of the oldest residents and I've always been involved. I want to do things, I don't want to be a looker-on. I don't see so well anymore, so I had to stop driving. Now I go on the bus, or someone takes me to the meetings outside.

The Newmans were one of the youngest couples. They moved in several years ago after he retired from GE, and "livened things up" though she is nearly deaf. Ruth was seventy-four and Louis seventy-seven. She was a "colony" director of her three floors, he was president of the Residents' Association. Vivacious, with curly gray hair, Ruth said:

We retired here because we didn't want to be a burden to our children. We wanted to be in a place where we could take care of each other. If something incapacitates me, he can find people in the dining room to eat with. If a man has been married for many years, if something happens to his wife, he's lost.

Louis added:

All my life there were a lot of things I wanted to do and never had time to before. The first fifteen years of my retirement we traveled all over to places that are disappearing from the world—2,400 miles down the Amazon on a rubber boat; 1,000 miles above the Arctic Circle. But we're too busy here now for all that traveling. We'd been here only two weeks when they made me head of the Program Committee. It's an exciting life.

I found even greater camaraderie and vitality in a community of mobile homes where the residents, mainly from the Midwest, did not seem to have exceptional resources of either education or wealth. Something about the adventurous spirit made them buy a "mobile" home and took them to Sarasota every winter from the Midwest, even though some finally put that mobile home on a permanent concrete foundation—something about the space itself gave rise to a community that fairly sparkled with the fountain of age.

Trailer Estates had just celebrated its own silver anniversary as a community when I first visited it. According to the study it commissioned about itself for that anniversary, 65 percent of the current residents were married, 29 percent widowed (five times as many women as men). A few of the couples were widowed when they met each other at Trailer Estates. Their mean age was seventy; 32 percent were over seventy-five. Over three fourths of them had high school educations or less, a fourth had some college or graduate degrees. They had been teachers, salespersons, assembly-line workers, nurses, engineers, a doctor, an automobile dealer, policemen, firemen, postal workers, a golf pro, a watchmaker, owners of small businesses and assorted professionals and shop supervisors, and many housewives. They had come from either urban or small-town communities, mostly in the Midwest, where they had owned their own homes. Nearly half had lived in the trailer community ten years or more, and most had made significant improvements to their trailers and sites, which they owned. Sid Adler, the builder who steered me there, reminded me:

A community of mobile homes like this seems to create the greatest camaraderie of the aged. They are gregarious, they take care of each other, they get very involved in the community. They feel adventurous; even though most of their homes are set in concrete now, they keep the feeling that they could always pull up stakes and leave. A lot of them are union members. The UAW [United Auto Workers] research indicates that people like these, with strong commitments and interests, are more likely to stay healthy in their age and then just die, not linger on in long illnesses, debility or vegetative states.

I speculated about this. To commit oneself to a mobile home community—to a "mobile" way of life until one dies—is clearly not the same as committing oneself to "lifetime care." The residents of Trailer Estates opted for a *moving life,* not care. Apparently they didn't worry about a nursing home and evidently avoided it. Death seemed to happen in that community in the midst of life.

It wasn't luxurious-looking, that community of fourteen hundred families, but it was alive with activity. It had its own post office, volunteer ambulance, and fire department, boat marina; a shuffleboard tournament was in progress, a "self-defense" karate class was taking place in the community center, people were coming and going on bicycles and large "trikes" with grocery baskets on the handlebars, or sitting on the benches watching the shuffleboard players. A few were planting or weeding gardens around their trailers, or washing their cars. There was a lot more *visible* life than in the more luxurious Plymouth Harbor, probably because the mobile homes themselves were not that spacious; life was mainly outside, for all to see and easily join in. I was told by the recreation director, Helen Cross, that there was a long waiting list, that a lot of these trailers were actually quite old but had "appreciated in value because of the community." She said, "The true sense of community here gives it the value. They may not look like much, but the research shows people in these communities not only live longer, they are healthier in age."

These mobile homes had cost $25,000 to $45,000 with the land. Some had originally been pulled behind a car. They were lined up in uneven rows, with pine trees and patios, geraniums in pots, roses, hanging plants. At the community center, the shouts from the self-defense class on one side could be heard above the music of a ballroom dancing class on the other. They had regular dances every Saturday night, square and folk dancing on Tuesdays—white-haired women dancing with each other as well as traditional couples. It turned out that Helen Cross was a volunteer member of the mobile community, not a professional social worker. She was one of the pioneers here, came in 1965. When I asked her age, she laughed. "I don't usually tell. I'm eighty-one."

There were notices on the bulletin board for "Bayshore Funeral Home," "Horseshoe Pitching," "Square Dance Lessons 9:30–11:00," "Ladies Cards 1:00 PM," "Bible Study 7:00 PM," "Rehearsal Easter Pageant," "Blood Bank Meeting." There was a registry of volunteer nurses, and where to find one if anybody needed to. An art class, choir practice, "Park Improvement" and "Beautification" meetings. There were sign-up sheets for "Friday Crafts," "Thursday Crafts," and "Share-a-Craft" meetings where they taught each other ceramics, needlepoint, carpentry—no paid instructors here. Members of the Newcomer Club passed us on the way to see a new family who had just moved in.

Helen boasted: "Over 99 percent of the work here is voluntary. We don't have to hire much help." Helen herself came here with her husband, a retired GP, from Grosse Point. They heard about it, and it appealed to them.

People who really enjoy people come here. My husband who was a doctor said if you move to Florida, you add ten years to your life, if you move to this community, you add ten more years, because of all the activity, because of the community itself. You can't just stay home and feel sorry for yourself. There's something doing all the time.

One woman, who was riding a bike, stopped to talk to us.

To be shut in the house and not be able to get out, that's bad. I take my laundry down on my bike to the washer-dryer; you have a bike, you can go everyplace. Some weeks our car doesn't ever get used. I never rode a bike till I came down here. I now ride all the way to the Ringling Museum. I can walk to church, to the shopping center, to the bank. Somebody who's lost their husband or can't drive a car is not hemmed in, in this kind of place.

Roy Oxford, seventy-two, was an antique furniture finisher in Ontario before he moved down here in 1967. He taught square dancing and folk dancing, which he had been doing for his own pleasure for forty years. On the table in their trailer, his wife, Elsie, seventy-five in April, was working over a big ledger:

I'm the bookkeeper for this outfit, though it's usually the man looks after the finances. Five years ago they said I had osteoporosis and that my bones were softening with age and would break, but I keep dancing and playing the drums, I keep moving. We go birdwatching, camping. We drive down here from Canada in November and go back the end of April; up there we do a lot of gardening, here we go to concerts, lectures. I love playing my drums for the old people in nursing homes.

Her hair was fluffy white and she did nothing to hide the lines on her face. She got up from her ledger to go out to the vegetable stand, where farmers bring in fresh vegetables every day, stopping to talk to two old men sitting in the sun in front of the mobile home next door. It was a very small town; palpably there was more *community* here than in the more luxurious high-rise retirement condo tower on the beach where, despite the professional recreation director and well-equipped shops and studio in the basement, not much life was visible during the day and evening I visited. Here the mobile homes surrounded the recreation center: everything was visible as people went back and forth to the spaces reserved for bikes and trikes in the parking lot or their cars. The people here were clearly choosing "community" and life, as opposed to beachfront luxury and the discreet promise of "lifetime care" of the more expensive Plymouth Harbor.

My mother, Miriam Horwitz Goldstein Katz Oberndorf, spent almost the last third of her life —nearly thirty years—in Leisure World, one of the earlier and most famous retirement communities, in Laguna Hills, California. She was in her early sixties, younger than I am now, when she and her third husband sold their large apartment on Lake Shore Drive in Chicago and became enthusiastic pioneer residents of that walled city in the California desert. I boasted about her vital embrace of age; at seventy she buried her third husband, and, to supplement her income and Social Security, got herself licensed as a duplicate bridge manager and, for a time, a sales agent for biodegradable cosmetics. She had always been an avid card player; her grandchildren had gotten her interested in ecology and the environment. When I visited her in Leisure

World, she was busy, busy, busy! For a while, in her early seventies, she took up horseback riding. But mainly I remember the disciplined vigor of her daily hour-long walk, and the intricacies of those duplicate bridge games she managed three or four times a week, and played in when she wasn't managing. They were not social games, opportunities for chitchat and anecdotes about one's grandchildren. They were serious business, requiring the players to memorize dozens of different hands of bridge each day, as well as the incremental challenge to their competitive skill. Could a vital age be built around such games in a community walled off from the rest of the world?

"FUN and FREEDOM are a Philosophy for Best Time of Your Life," the resale brochure for Leisure World's "lovely manor homes" proclaimed, in the early eighties, when I first visited. The average age was rising, from sixty-three to seventy-three, in this "Planned Community for People 52 and Older," no children allowed (and *no really old* people visible), among the 22,000 persons enjoying "a completely carefree way of living, the world's finest climate . . . and peace of mind that comes with safety, privacy and security, plus more than $20 million in facilities for the pursuit of pleasure." "Total management services" provided all maintenance and repairs, all gardening, exterior plumbing, lighting, street and sewers, and "around the clock security guards." ("A capable security force of approximately 300 men at Leisure World maintains 24-hour protection of person and property. Entrances to the community are through gatehouses, where security attendants admit only residents, guests and commercial companies whom residents have called.") You also got to use "five magnificent clubhouses complete with hobby shops, game rooms, billiard rooms; three Olympic-size swimming pools; tennis courts; lawn bowling greens and shuffleboard courts; libraries and the most modern equipment for almost any social, educational or recreational activity, and no-fare mini-bus transportation anywhere in the community and to shopping centers. Small fees are charged for use of the riding stables and the 27-hole golf course." More than 185 clubs and organizations were already organized.

In the early days of Leisure World, suggestions of selling some of the homes to young families with children were soundly repudiated. More recently, suggestions of building a life care facility for older people no longer able to live a completely independent life were also defeated. Leisure World was only for "active" older people. The security getting past the gatehouse to my mother's "manor" was, as my grandson would say, "awesome." But on those winding "planned" streets, past the luxuriant blossoming shrubbery of the lawns and hedges, maintained as perfectly as promised, it was very quiet indeed; no one to ask directions of, no sign of all that heralded activity.

"The place was too quiet, even during the day," said one woman, who ultimately left. "What little bustling there is in Leisure World takes place in the clubhouses. The clubs give people a sense of identity. But I spent a lot of time alone there. I don't like to be around people just to be around people. That's what I didn't want to recognize when I was living there—a sense of alienation and separation."

Every day but Wednesday my mother managed or played duplicate bridge afternoons and/or evenings. On Wednesdays, she taught private bridge classes. She gathered some of her cronies in her yellow and green living room, decorated in the precise taste I remembered from our home in Peoria, and her apartments since. They all wanted me to understand that bridge was not just a "hobby" for them. "We're much too busy to go to the movies, or just watch TV." They boasted of their partners even coming to the bridge table hooked up to IV equipment, with oxygen tubes in their noses. My mother kept on managing a game while paramedics were working on one of the players on the floor over in the corner. "He had a nosebleed," Mother said. "He thought he was hemorrhaging. He was a bit hysterical. They took care of him. He was all right; nothing serious. We went on playing. In any other community, if someone started bleeding like that, a heart attack or stroke, everyone would be terrified. Here, we went on with our bridge game." Two people, in fact, had died during bridge games. "That's the way I'd like to die," my mother half-joked, "in the middle of a good bridge game."

But the stress on activity, the games, was deceptive, paradoxical. Some of the Leisure Worlders I met found in those games new purpose and a sense of identity, community; others found them isolating, alienating. Some felt "young at sixty-five" in a place where so many people were older, had more "things wrong with them." Others began to sense something frenetic, fake, and basically empty in all that activity. Some began to look for more serious purposes outside the walls of Leisure World, or in organizing the community itself. Some tried to combat what they began to see as a denial of the reality of age. Some gradually withdrew, behind closed doors. "When people first move into Leisure World, they sign up for everything," my mother said. "They join this committee, that committee, take the exercise classes, the dance classes, the ceramics, Spanish, the foreign policy discussion group. Then, they drop out. They don't find what they're looking for, I guess."

Helen Loring told me: "I came out here, joined this, joined that, went every which way, didn't know what I was doing. It wasn't me. I called it an adult playpen. I had to get out of that playpen and be a person again. I thought I'd had it with working. I'd been a social worker too long. I had to find a new way to do my own work. I guess you would say age freed me to do that."

They did a lot of denying of age in Leisure World, though in a sense they were obsessed with it. They had come here to escape the frustrations and dangers of age in their cities and hometowns. The ones I talked to were among those who had managed to make a new life for themselves here. But, sooner or later, they told me of the others, "the hidden Leisure World," behind closed doors in their manor houses, who have withdrawn from all that activity, or were never aggressive enough to enter it.

Jane Slavin, in her mid-seventies, had been living in Leisure World five years, the last two as a widow. She wore a gray sweatsuit, fresh from the strenuous exercise class she took twice a week, as well as the "Joy of Movement." She told me:

In Leisure World, there's a lot of resistance to any attempt to deal with the realities of age. The establishment here still insists on seeing this place as a center for vital, swinging adults; they refuse to face the realities that people getting older might need something beyond all that vigor. We tried to get a lunch program, a

647

drop-in lounge for all the people around here who are lonely and don't go bowling, an adult day care center for people with disabilities now that we're all getting older, a system of panic buttons or neighborhood teams just to watch out for each other—they refuse to deal with the fact that we are all growing older. I hate people who deny their age, but I don't want to be only with old people all the time. I don't want to be encapsulated here in Leisure World. I go down to Laguna Beach now to do things with younger people two to three days a week.

But these, the active ones, are in the minority in Leisure World, I learned. Maybe 4,000, 5,000 at most of the 21,000 residents went to the clubhouse, the lawn bowling and the bridge games, the clubs and committees. A lot more stayed in their manor houses, behind closed doors. They didn't have the nerve to keep going to the clubs, or they dropped out because they didn't find it "worth the trouble." I learned that the big chain-store supermarket sold more liquor in Leisure World than anywhere else in its chain. But it was thinking of shutting down its operation there, so many people coming in every day to buy a dollar or two of something, just to be with people.

Myra Nebin, the editor of *The Leisure World News,* insisted:

Even compared to a non-retirement community, this is a more vital community than most. But you do have a hidden population here. They may have been active at one time, gotten considerably older, maybe lost a spouse. Death is a big thing in this community, not talked about much. And depression. Behind closed doors, a lot of people in Leisure World, mainly women, are watching television with the shades drawn. And some, as they get older, can't quite cope, things are getting dirtier and dirtier, and they don't eat, they are getting undernourished.

Myra confirmed the obsessive denial of age:

When one of the clubhouse pictures was being taken the other day, a man keeled over. They propped him up to get the picture over and then they called the paramedics. There was a big controversy a few years ago about using some of the open land in Leisure World to build a facility for people who need more care and services so you wouldn't have to leave your manor home here when you get older. Our founder said, "We don't want all these old people here. You won't sell if people think this is a place for old people."

"He had a point," my mother said. "This place has a stigma as it is. It's a snobbish thing. People didn't want their friends to think they were moving into an old folks' institution." Even if they themselves were "moving in with all these old people" to escape that stigma—and found comfort in activities with people their own age or older—they clearly, many of them, bought the stigma. I wondered if the *denial of age,* so clear and so paradoxical in a place like Leisure World, got harder to maintain, and built a hidden rage that couldn't be dissipated in all that activity, the depression that no one wanted to talk about behind those closed doors. Did that walling off from the generations of the larger community relieve or exacerbate the rage that comes with denial of age?

Helen Loring, who had lived in Leisure World for over ten years, recalled her own ambivalence about age before she "got out of the adult playpen" and in her sixties trained to become a therapist herself.

The people who come to me depressed, because of loneliness, get medicated out of their gourd by these doctors here. Maybe 25 percent of the people here feel, I've paid my dues, I want to be taken care of. I get a little bit tired of their depressed unwillingness to move from one spot to another. I helped them work through their anger, but there was no desire to change, they hold on to the age rage. "It's too late, it's my rotten kids, it's a rotten world." I now have 80 percent of my practice outside of Leisure World, in the larger community. Those who say aging is a natural process and I'm going to get on with my life. To me, the most important thing is to be engrossed, not just busy, busy. I want to be engrossed in something that leads to something. I'm dying on the vine here, with all this hectic activity.

In a certain sense, the official Leisure World attitude was a Peter Pan denial of the very ability to keep changing that is the essence of the fountain of age. There was not much talk about people who leave Leisure World—for death or for life—but they stopped building new manor homes some time ago, and much of the denial of age here was explained in terms of the "resale" problem. "That's what I didn't want to recognize when I was living there—a sense of alienation and separation," said the woman who left Leisure World at sixty-five. Since leaving Leisure World, she had become involved again in the political life of the larger community, handling financial affairs for an anti-nuclear environmental group. My sense was that the ones who survived and continued to grow in Leisure World, finding a vital age there, turned some activity of the adult playpen into a serious project, became seriously involved in the governance or some movement for change in the community itself; or, in effect, they were lucky enough to die playing bridge.

I wish my mother had died running those bridge games, the way she wanted to. At eighty-seven, her doctor advised that she resign directing the games. It was too much stress, he said. They gave her a big retirement party. She also stopped driving, fell and broke her leg again, sold the manor house and moved to the Towers, which provided meals and services. Though it was virtually next door to Leisure World, the friends she had made there over bridge no longer included her in their games. She made no effort to keep on playing bridge, but got some small pleasure winning at Bingo. Suffering bouts of heart failure, she became terrified, living all by herself. My brother, who was closest to her, tried to work out a system of companions —nurses' aides—but Leisure World and its adjunct facilities wanted no part of the older people they supposedly were set up for when they no longer could take complete care of themselves. So, on Mother's ninetieth birthday, my brother, my niece Laurie, and I took her to lunch at the Ritz Hotel on the sea and discussed arrangements for her to move to a nursing home. There seemed then no alternative. They would not let her stay on in that "retirement hotel" outside Leisure World, just as she had not been welcome any longer in Leisure World itself. In nearby facilities for the frail elderly, everyone seemed so much more non-functional, impaired, than she was; more important, there would be no family, and no longer any friends to keep an eye on things, to visit her. Nancy, the grandchild to whom she was closest, was a social worker and her husband a hospital administrator outside Milwaukee. They found a "good" nursing home, church-run, only fifteen minutes from their house. Nancy and her little daughters could visit her there several times a week. The night of that birthday lunch, I had a severe asthma attack, for the first time in years. I knew Mother didn't want to go into a nursing home. And yet I certainly had no alternative to offer her in my own hectic life of travel, lecturing and teaching all over the country.

Laurie volunteered to pack up a few things that Mother could take with her to make her room in the nursing home less institutional, and to travel with her to Milwaukee. I arranged a midwestern lecture from which I could detour to visit her there the next week. She was very thin, though as beautiful as ever, impeccably groomed, and only too lucidly aware of her surroundings. There were not a great many activities to take part in, but she wasn't having any of them, and no one was doing anything about that. I mentioned to the nurses that my mother was a bridge master, and weren't there any people here she might play with? They looked blank. There was a cardroom but no one using it when I was there. I said, "Mother, why don't you start a bridge game?" "Oh, darling," she said, "it's no fun when people don't play seriously."

I had found out the woman across the hall was a retired biologist; my mother wasn't interested in meeting her. To get me off her back, as she walked me to the elevator after our lunch, she approached a woman in a wheelchair, not able to hold her head up, a stroke victim, or Alzheimer's—on this floor of the nursing home, very impaired people were put in with those who were unimpaired mentally, though most seemed to have some physical disabilities. Mother put her arms around the woman and said, "And how are you today, darling?" with that same tone of "compassionate" agism that was now being used on her, with an edge to it of the rage that must, I thought, have been eating her up. God knows, I had been fighting against my mother almost all my life; it seems that love-hate never dies. I didn't ever want to be like my mother, and I've often thought it was my awareness of her frustrations that drove me to do what I did. But I had come to admire her guts, her survivor's strength. Before she left Leisure World, and now again, this last time in Wisconsin, I was able to put my arms around her and say, "I love you, Mother," and mean it. And she said, "I know you do, darling, and I love you too."

I knew I would never see her again. She died a week later, just didn't wake up one morning. Died of what? I asked. Technically, I guess she died of heart failure. But my mother was always a strong-willed lady. She just didn't propose to keep on living in that nursing home. I only wish her doctor in Leisure World hadn't told her to stop managing those bridge games at eighty-seven to "save" her from stress. I only wish she had died while she was still tootling around in her busy life at Leisure World. I only wish she had been spared her final months in those increasingly impersonal, institutional surroundings, no matter the expensive professional care.

Strangely enough, though my mother spent the last twenty-five years of her life in a "retirement" community for "active" older people, devoted to play, walled off from the fears and dangers and problems of our changing larger society—walled off from change altogether, including the changed attitude toward themselves and other reminders of their own aging in the communities they left behind—that very denial of age and change left her helpless in its inexorable progression, torn from any semblance of home and personal, rooted bonds.

Newer retirement communities today are built around nursing homes, even if the facility is walled off from the rest of the community or hidden in a remote wing or top floor. I visited many of these new "congregate care," or "continuing care," or "lifetime care" communities, thinking they were surely the answer to denial, avoiding the trauma of the final months of my mother's forced move and decline before death. But, as I visited the best of them—near Philadelphia; in Charlotte, North Carolina, as well as in Florida and California—I began to wonder if there aren't worse things than denial. With increasing un-easiness, I began to wonder if the people I inter-viewed who had bought into these facilities to save their children from "having to put me in a nursing home" weren't defining themselves, too soon, as objects of such ultimate "care." Were they, in fact, somehow *colluding* in the process of denying their own personhood by withdraw-ing from the community into that "care" ghetto? They were defining their age, not in terms of purposes and choices and ties to life, but *in de-fense against* death, in terms of terminal care.

Morris and Frances Milgram moved into Attle-boro Village near Philadelphia when he was sev-enty-four and she sixty-three, his third wife of relatively recent vintage. The reason they signed up, no bones about it, was concern about ulti-mate "care." He put it this way: "Frances has high blood pressure and arthritis. I had a mini-stroke or two before we applied. I put down $195,000 for the largest two-bedroom apart-ment; that covers all the maintenance, one meal a day, and transportation to the train or local destinations. If one of us has to go into the nursing home and the other stays here, we still pay the same fee."

Morris, a prominent Philadelphia builder, was a national leader in moves for affordable and racially integrated urban housing. He had tried without success to develop some innovative intergenerational housing before his second wife died. Frances was an intensive-care technician herself, with no lack of professional opportunities and no wish to take on the role with her husband. On their first visit to Attleboro Village, she was charmed by the welcoming parlors with their white wicker chairs, plants, french doors opening onto green lawns—and by the assurance, "We'll drive your husband to the train, we'll feed him dinner, a release for me not to have to worry about taking care of him myself, a release for him not to feel he's a burden on me."

But Morris was struggling not to be defined solely in terms of "care." He was one of the very few residents of the life care community who still worked part-time—he went into his office three or four days a week. He, like many people in such communities, vehemently denied that they lived in a "nursing home"—even though the reason most of them moved there was to assure themselves of terminal nursing care. They insisted that the nursing facility be out of sight, in a remote wing or separate building, that people not be allowed into the dining room in wheelchairs or walkers. "This whole place is in denial," one of the Attleboro people told me. "They pretend the nursing home isn't there. When the question was raised, why couldn't people in wheelchairs come into the dining room and eat with everyone else, one woman said she would leave the community first."

Vivian Carlin was trying to break through the denial at Attleboro by training healthy seniors to work as volunteer aides in the nursing home. "The more people actually confront the reality of age," she said, "the more we get rid of the myth, the terrors. I never went into the nursing home facility when I first came here. I confronted my own fears, and went in. It's a part of life. Now I'm doing research for a Ph.D."

Vivian had become a virtual proselytizer for people to move into "life care communities" at younger and younger ages. "It's important to move in early enough—the younger you are, the easier it is to make new friendships, relationships. Of course, you have to be prepared for the 'poor dear complex,' people who think if you choose to go into a life care community, you're entering a nursing home. The main thing is, you admit you're getting old when you've chosen to come in here." I wondered. Intent as I was now on affirming my own authentic aging, my still and ever-changing self, there was a vitality to that which was not the same as the acceptance of age as deterioration and decline—or its terrified, desperate denial.

I went to visit my vital friend Earl Arthurs in another continuing-care community. Though he was still spending much of the year as a cruise ship host, he had moved in his early eighties into Southminster, a "continuing care retirement community" run by a corporation set up by the Christ Episcopal Church and Baptist Church on the outskirts of Charlotte, North Carolina, "to provide a residential environment in which older people may live as independently and as actively as their faculties and strength permit, secure in knowledge that support is available when and as it may be needed." The sales brochure was very persuasive, addressing head on that "voice in the back of your mind which still says, 'I'm not ready for *that* yet! And what will make you ready? . . . until significant illness or disability precludes [your] acceptance. Putting this decision off only increases the probability that decisions about where you live will be made by someone else. . . . It's much wiser to take action before a medical emergency narrows your choices, or impairs your ability to make decisions affecting your life."

Earl liked the country club atmosphere of Southminster. He had paid an entrance fee of $59,000 for a one-bedroom apartment ("It doesn't give me title to anything, it's not refundable to me or my estate, just gives me the privilege of living there"), with a monthly fee of $1,100 which included one meal a day (two or three would be only a little extra) in the restaurant-type dining room (two small private ones available for family celebrations), and the use of library, card rooms, parlors, chapel, art studio. That "immediate access to both emergency and long-term health care" was guaranteed by having a nursing home, and several floors of "intermediate nursing care," right there on the premises, but with separate entrances and doors locked off from access to the community proper.

Again, I was puzzled, as I was shown through this place, by the clear lack of any visible activity, or facilities for exercise, behind its expensive antique-decorated front parlors. I searched all over the grounds, but found only one small unused set of horseshoes behind the parking lot and one unconnected exercise bicycle in a little cubicle off the locked entrance to the "health care" unit. Southminster presented its beautiful upscale facade—Tara-like white porch pillars, Chippendale and Hepplewhite antique commodes in the front parlors—to the prospective seniors and their families, but did not even pretend to offer much in the way of activities or "organized joy." The staff insisted, as most of these places do, that people be "ambulatory and able to live independently" when they came in, but their whole "continuum of care" sales approach was geared to fears of helplessness, deterioration, and death.

I asked to look at the locked nursing home floors where people were immediately taken if they suffered an illness, attack, or worsening of a chronic condition, and placed on one floor or another depending on their respective classification as in need of "assisted living," "intermediate," or "skilled nursing care." One woman was up there because when she got down to feed her cat, her hip went out of joint. "They wouldn't need to be segregated to a room upstairs if we could give them one or two hours a day of help in their own apartments," the administrator said. But here, as elsewhere, there was a strong feeling against wheelchairs or walkers or crutches in the dining room because, "Let's face it," the administrator told me, "most people don't like to see themselves the way they'll be ten years from now."

Earl and the friends he had made at Southminster were among the youngest and the most active in the community—took meals, games, parties together. Some tried to "keep up with friends in town," spent Saturdays or Sundays visiting with son or daughter, grandchildren, living nearby, and went to their old churches. "You can still do what you want to do, come and go as you please, but knowing that continual care, what they call it, is there for the rest of your life is the main thing," as one woman put it.

There was not much pretense of the residents running the place themselves, though they had "used our influence" for the right to use some of their meal tickets for guests, get some friendly little arrangements of furniture in alcoves off the halls (those big, expensive, empty parlors notwithstanding), and obtain the use of guest rooms for friends and family to visit. They had organized a buddy system on each floor, to check up on each other; if the newspapers piled up outside the door, if you didn't come down to meals, someone would call every day. In the kitchen and bathrooms, little pullcords hung on the walls. The traffic was so heavy outside their gates that many were afraid to cross the street and walk out. They organized to get one traffic light at the corner and were lobbying the city for another at their entrance. But the local pharmacist who took over an area of the sundries shop so the residents wouldn't have to go out to buy medications and tranquilizers was doing a great business.

I did a lot of interviewing in such continuing life care facilities because of my own helplessness when my mother, in those last months, could not live by herself any longer. Many of my friends were now having similar problems of "what to do about Mom, Dad." But though I was approaching the age myself of some of the people I interviewed, I somehow could not see myself choosing to *resign* from active participation in the community at any age. The people in their sixties, seventies, eighties entering these facilities were trading off a large measure of autonomy and identity as a participant in that larger community, with all its problems, fears, and even painful reminders and rebuffs of their age, for a guarantee of nursing care if and when they need it. Given that only 15 percent will ever need "continuing life care," the voluntary embrace of an identity as a "care object" was indeed shortchanging their autonomy, their independent personhood, their active participation in the community.

What also struck me was how much even those dependent on some "care"—as, for example, pacemakers to be monitored—needed an identity beyond that to feel alive, needed actively to care for someone or something beyond themselves, needed some way to be part of the larger community of the living. When they controlled the facility themselves, that began to happen. Pennwood, a Quaker "life care" community, in Newtown, Pennsylvania, near Philadelphia, structured an Intergenerational Program with the George School next door. Dr. Juliette, a black retired math teacher, who helped organize it, played math games with a couple of kids who were having trouble in school. She told me:

I decided I could be more independent in my age by moving in here, rather than sitting every night alone in my little old apartment on that

663

dangerous street, or moving in with one of my brothers or sisters and their kids. Each one has invited me to move in with them—the black family takes care of its own; that's why you don't see us in places like this, that and the money, and, of course, some don't want us— but I don't want to live with their families, too many cooks ruin the soup. I want to be where I can be independent and they can come visit me.

Nearby, at Friends Village, a much more modest facility, there was no guarantee of "lifetime care." Singly and in couples, about sixty women and men shared a big old stone house, in single studio-type rooms or apartments or little cottages on the five-acre grounds. They took their meals in a common dining room, in tables of six to twelve, and they organized their own activities. Most of them still took part in the meetings of the larger community, giving each other rides when they were needed. They had their own medical insurance and doctors and knew the way to the nearest hospital. And, in informal ways, they took care of each other. But they did not define themselves as "care objects."

Anna Morse and Bent Andersen, both eighty-three when I talked to them, were not interested in any guarantee of "life care," though both had terminally ill spouses when they chose to move in here. His wife had Alzheimer's syndrome, her husband had leukemia. She told me:

We didn't want to go into a lifetime care community because dying is a natural thing. My husband died so easily, with all our children there, five years after his cancer was diagnosed. We were taking care of him at home; he passed away so comfortably, it was such a relief. We had planned what furniture to take here. Bent took care of his wife here five years. We had known each other thirty years. Two years ago, he moved into my studio. He took care of me after my hip replacement. The morning after, I stood up and walked four steps without pain, after two years of excruciating pain. Then, I became legally blind; he reads to me. He had some cancer in his bladder fifteen years ago, now it's spread to lumps in his neck. I took care of him through radiation therapy. He's taken care of me, and I take care of him.

We don't lock our door here, we don't lock our car, we live with faith in life. So many people live by fear. It's my belief that fear accelerates aging, in the worst sense, not just that aging accelerates fear. I must tell you that I've come alive in the last decade in a way I hadn't before. I have a new sense of freedom. For forty-five years, I lived under the shadow of a prominent husband from a prominent family. That's over, another part of my life. I'm Anna Morse now. For myself, I think too much effort is going into those elaborate facilities with all their security to keep affluent people alive a few months longer. We don't have that lifetime guarantee of care, just the chance to live our own independent life and to be a part of a larger community.

The people at Friends Village were as old or older than the ones I interviewed in the more luxurious "life care" facilities. But they seemed much less obsessed with terminal "care"—or with denying or shielding themselves from any reminder of death or other realities of aging. That was their *choice*.

To move or to stay—we keep having to make that choice as we age. There is no guarantee, ever, for any of these people, for any of us, that we will never have to move again, or that we can completely insure ourselves against illness, pain, death, or losing control of our lives. We keep having to move, and stay, and move again. From my own sense of it, and from many of the people I interviewed, *despite* the not-to-be-denied facts of life and death and physical aging, paradoxically, we can choose with more and more freedom and sureness of what we want — liberated now from irrelevant considerations that have stopped or driven us in the past—though we face obstacles surely as we move into this unknown territory of life. The access to good facilities of care, if and when we need it, is surely one consideration. But it should not be the main one in our choice to move or stay as we map that unknown territory. The awareness that there is no such final choice of "lifetime care" might free us, at least, to keep on choosing in terms of our own needs *now,* for the life we want to live, knowing that we can and must perhaps make a different choice, around the next corner, when we get to it. With no guarantees at all about when and how it will end, we can only choose to *live our age.*

TWELVE

At Home in a New Place

Somewhere in my search through this uncharted territory, I began to realize that, whether we move or stay, we can and must find or make a new place for ourselves in age. And there are traps and delusions to avoid, signposts to look for. Should we choose to live our whole age in terms of that dreaded mystique of deterioration and decline—which happens to most only in the months before death, if it happens at all—or in terms of *the life we want to lead,* in the community, in our late years, knowing that it and we will continue to change, and that it will end in death?

Beware the age mystique sell: We are its market, a boom market to take the place of our kids, who can't afford the houses they grew up in, and the receding numbers of "young" first-home-buying families. Hence the explosion of retirement communities, group residences, and "continuing-care complexes," all of which profit on the fear of being old and alone, the specter of age as inevitable deterioration and decline.

"As Alertness Outlives Vigor, New Kinds of Care for the Old," *The New York Times* headlined a front-page story December 2, 1990. The reporter noted:

When continuing care complexes first became popular 20 years ago, most were run by non-profit groups, and required that residents pay a large entrance fee, ranging from $30,000 to $100,000 or more, plus a flat monthly fee, in return for guaranteed lifetime nursing care. . . . But in the last five years, as developers have grown interested in the growing population of wealthy elderly people, most of the new complexes being built have been profit-making enterprises, charging no entrance fee but operating on a pay-as-you-go basis. Thus, people who require nursing care pay much higher monthly fees than those who need little assistance.

Rarely discussed, but often present, is a fear of outliving one's money, a fear that is likely to intensify as the industry switches increasingly to pay-as-you-go complexes. . . .

No one knows how many new profit-making continuing-care complexes are being built, but more and more real estate developers, hotel chains, and nursing home operators are getting into this market. Those who buy into it should be aware that their needs for companionship may not be met, and that the guarantee of terminal care may not turn out to be a guarantee at all.

Beware the final solution: There is none.

Item: "Increasing Numbers of Aged Return North from Florida. The number of elderly people returning from Florida to New York rose sharply during the last decade, a new analysis of Census Bureau data shows. Those returning were older, poorer and more likely to be widowed than those who moved to Florida from New York in the same decade" (*The New York Times,* March 15, 1984).

For some of those who have undergone the experience of "return migration," it was "the best among several unhappy choices," this report concluded. Mostly, the choice was made for "Mom" by her daughter or son, after "Dad" died. One such couple came back seventeen years later to Long Island from an apartment on the beach in Hollywood, Florida. "They had a wonderful life [down there]," their daughter said. "They were active and had a marvelous coterie of friends. Their investments enabled them to live comfortably."

When her mother was eighty-two, however, she developed angina and later broke a hip, was in and out of hospital for treatment and tests. Her husband's eyesight was deteriorating so he couldn't drive her. "It became more and more difficult for me since I'd have to go to Florida whenever there was a problem," said the daughter, who had three children and a career as a speech pathologist. "We all decided it would be better in the long run to bring them back here." She put them in an apartment five minutes from her home. A year later, the father died, and two years after that, the mother's health had "deteriorated to the point where she is in need of 24-hour care by nursing aides in her apartment." "It would have been horrendous if all of this had happened and they had been in Florida," the daughter said. "I think the average child would be better off to have parents close by." Should this be that "child's" choice, I wondered. And I began to understand why those who had had to make such a choice for "Mom" or "Dad" might make that same defensive move prematurely for themselves.

Questions do need to be asked about the geometrically multiplying hard-sell retirement communities, congregate living and life care complexes. Gerontologists once thought that such moves were the answer to "loneliness" and "isolation" for older people, that the "activities" of Leisure World and the like created a "culture of the aging" which enhanced health, long life, and well-being. The reality turned out to be more complex. Discussing "isolation" in the aged, psychiatrist Martin Berezin cited reports that many people who had moved to St. Petersburg, Florida—considered a Mecca for aged retirees—"suddenly feel lost without the support systems they left behind," especially those who move a long distance, between New England and Florida, say. "With many of these elderly people there appeared to be again and again a discovery of loneliness, a sense of missing things even when there were many people around them."[1]

When studies were done over the years of residents in places like Leisure World—many of whom had lived there far longer than they ever expected to, twenty-two of their seventy-seven or eighty-one years, for instance, "the longest I've ever lived anywhere"—the hypothesis that mere participation in all those clubhouse activities would provide the satisfaction and continued sense of self considered essential to vital age did not hold up. The activities of these retirement enclaves seemed to promote an "aged subculture but of a retreatist type." Those preferring to interact only with the aged turned out on the average to be less active, lonelier, less confident, and *less satisfied with life,* and also *less healthy* than those who preferred interacting with all ages in the larger community.[2]

In another study of people signed up to move into Leisure World, Vern Bengtson and his colleagues found not much relationship at all between frequency of activity and life satisfaction. Neither participation in formal organizations nor solitary leisure and household activities seemed to enhance such "satisfaction"—only "informal activity with close friends." Then researchers repeated the study, comparing people who had migrated in their sixties to the Ozark Lakes country, living in communities of all ages, to residents of "Carefree Village," as the researchers called the "lifetime care" walled enclaves, and to another group, also in their seventies, in a high-rise public housing project in a midwestern city.

Again, only "informal activity" with close friends, relatives, and neighbors was found to contribute significantly to life satisfaction. In fact, the greater one's *formal activity,* the less one's life satisfaction. This was especially true in Carefree Village, where the formally structured activity in age-segregated clubhouses seemed actually to *damage self-concept and lower morale.*[3]

Only activities that enabled or sustained personal ties, and a specific personal response, seemed to support the all-essential sense of self and satisfaction, Bengston argued.[4] Participation in a number of different formal organizations or activities was not a substitute for intimacy. In the Ozark small towns, where retirees now made a strong presence in community and church groups but did not live segregated by their age, 75 percent had three or more informal *personal* contacts with others in one day. In Carefree Village, only 60 percent, and in the urban housing projects only 21 percent had such contacts. Life satisfaction was higher in Carefree Village, however, than in the city high-rise housing projects, where 34 percent had no personal contacts at all in a single day.

When I was looking for research clues to vitality in age that year at Harvard, I sat in on a seminar on Loneliness given by the sociologist Robert Weiss. He identified two dimensions: emotional loneliness, the absence of an "intimate other," such as in love or marriage; and social loneliness, the absence of a community or network of friends to whom you feel attached. More and more psychologists have found that for older persons, loneliness is not necessarily linked to the death of a spouse or to how infrequently they see their children and grandchildren, but to the *absence of personal relationships with peers,* friends of their own age or any age who share their interests and with whom they sustain those roots of shared experience. Being married and living with one's spouse, without regard to the compatibility of the relationship, may still be the healthiest state of all, especially for men, many research studies have shown. But for the increasing numbers of men and women outliving or divorced from spouses, it is the fear of loneliness that often propels them toward institutionalized settings, with their promises of structure, activity, and care. Others scorn such ready-made connections, even as the social ties that used to sustain them unravel.

When Yale epidemiologists checked the survival of seven thousand Californians whose health and lifestyle has been studied since 1965, they found that, regardless of age, relatively isolated people had a mortality rate 2.5 times higher than people with strong social bonds, which researchers delineated in many combinations of marriage, friends, church, and informal affiliations. The most "intriguing" discovery, as the Yale University epidemiologist Lisa Berkman put it, was that "people could make substitutes or trade-offs. You don't have to have a family, but you do have to get friendship somewhere; you have to have something." Since one fifth of the American population now lives alone—and a far higher proportion over sixty-five—it is hardly surprising that "peer networks are emerging as very important and family networks are receding," said the Harvard demographer George Masnick. "The family does not dominate the entire rhythm of one's life anymore."[5] We are only just beginning to *name,* and therefore to *legitimize,* the new social and personal ties and structures we need for our continued vitality.

Wading through the research, and tracking

friends and strangers through this unmapped age, I came increasingly to see how places fostered or prevented or sustained those unnamed personal ties of intimacy and connectivity. This was easiest to see among my friends in Peoria, aging in place with friends they had shared life with since high school. Among women and men aging in cities today, the longer we survive, the less such ties are structured by family, marriage, or youthful roots. I found a zestful improvisation among the adventurous aging, who sought out or created new spaces and structures that sustained them, quite different from the institutional retreats like Leisure World. I admit again my own reaction of dread to those institutional settings, no matter that some vital members whom I interviewed there made them work for them. I take seriously the research which shows that people who choose to retreat to such enclaves, though they have more formal activities, and report more "friends" than those who move among all ages in the larger community, experience *more* "loneliness" and lower self-concept. I remind myself that informal, personal activities, which permit real sharing (disclosure of one's self and personal response), are what really count. And I discover that when communities and institutions are studied in terms of their effects on health and longevity, those that are least *total* in their control of people and permit more spontaneous, autonomous activity prove to be the best.

At the beginning of my own pursuit of the fountain of age, I spent some time with the gerontologist Morton Lieberman in San Francisco, where he had systematically analyzed the research on the effects of any kind of institutionalization on the psychological well-being and physical survival of older people. The numerous studies he surveyed were done in residential facilities, geriatric centers, and nursing homes —settings implying "permanent or indefinite residence involving a major change from a community living pattern"—and not the less centralized retirement villages. But the evidence of the "dehumanizing" and "depersonalizing" effects of institutional environments was overwhelming.[6]

"These studies clearly demonstrate that aged persons residing in a variety of institutional settings are psychologically worse off and likely to die sooner than aged persons living in the community," Lieberman concluded. Depression, unhappiness, rigidity and low energy, intellectual ineffectiveness, negative self-image, feelings of personal insignificance and impotency, low range of interests, withdrawal, unresponsiveness to others, and a tendency to live in the past rather than the future all seemed to go along with "a view of self as old" in such settings. On the other hand, elderly persons moving into apartment dwellings showed an increase in satisfaction and adjustment. One study showed that older persons "exhibit a generalized negative feeling toward all special settings for the aged," while another found that moving out of age-segregated environments "led to an increase in social interaction and emotional responsivity and toward improvement in mental functioning."

Despite the appearance of what seem to be "good" and "bad" institutions, Lieberman tentatively concluded that "those characteristics that are instrumental in influencing the behavior of the individuals residing in them are shared by all institutions." All told, these studies suggested that *the more total the institution* (scheduling of activities, rules and standards of conduct, decision making about the use of private and congregate property), *the greater its depersonalizing effects.*[7] Yet the developers continue to build, and profit-making corporations continue to promote and run, highly structured congregate lifetime care complexes, which inevitably share some of these institutional characteristics even though their marketing sell appeals to just that fear of "ever having to be put in a nursing home."

Yet, undeniably, people moved out of the community into such places because their genuine need for identity and intimacy, as well as their projected need for "care," was not being met where they were, or wouldn't be met in later age, they feared. Some may find those needs satisfied in such places; others may simply resign themselves to the choice they have made. Still others regret it and, if possible, seek further choices. Searching out alternative spaces and structures, I became convinced that it is possible in age to meet our continuing needs for intimacy and identity, love and purpose, *within the community* We do *not* have to buy into the dread of age and the fear of loneliness around which those segregated enclaves are structured, and which they perpetuate, even as they seem to defend against them.

It was people's personal and individual migrations and innovations within the community that registered sharpest on my Geiger counter in my search for the fountain of age. In Maine, a dean of nursing called my attention to the increasing number of elderly couples coming back from Florida, with all its sunshine, to settle in small New England towns that young people were deserting. Her own parents spent their winters in a Florida retirement village, where all the services and amenities were provided—the pool, the Bingo games, the "early bird" supper bargains. When they got off the plane in March, with the Maine snow still on the ground, beneath their tan they seemed so old, she told me. And then they got to work on their own little house— doing the repairs, planting their vegetable garden, taking on chores in the community, even braving that cold. They were needed, known in this community, respected for certain kinds of knowledge or skills not so easily found now among the few remaining young. And they interacted, from their roots there, with their daughter and the grandchildren, with new dynamics, sharp and personal and real, not just the pleasantries of ritualized visit. They seemed so much more alive and *themselves* again.

Improbably, despite my own stereotype about Florida, my Geiger counter clicked loudly in Miami's South Beach, no longer an age ghetto because gentrification and the influx of Latinos and other young people have forced out many older people. In the new cosmopolitan mix of swinging young, Latinos, and artists now drawn to the community, with its rehabilitation of Art Deco hotels and boardinghouses where grandparents used to rock on the porches, I found a new kind of age pioneer, who preferred this multi-cultural, multi-age mix to the quieter, secluded, depersonalized retirement villages and high-rise condos sprouting up in North Miami, Broward County, Fort Lauderdale, or on protected man-made "islands" on the way to Palm Beach. In the new-old, lively diversity, not yet completely jelled or altogether safe community rising from the old age ghetto of South Beach, I saw prophetic outlines for *revitalizing* American urban culture across generations.

Peggy Gordon, seventy-one, moved into Belle

Towers—a low, friendly-looking, oldish building overlooking the coastal waterway—twenty years ago, with her first husband. Now widowed and divorced, she wouldn't dream of moving out as some widows her age were doing for fear of crime and the other changes in South Beach. She even lived on the first floor, so she could walk out and drink her coffee on the common terrace. Her apartment was full of flowering plants, vivid paintings, an oversized wicker couch, soft pink and orange and purple pillows. She had become a serious painter in her later years. She told me:

About seven years ago I was sitting on South Beach with my brother and sister, all of us in our late sixties, and a very elderly woman passing by said: "It's so nice to see younger people here." Now South Beach is full of *really* young people. Here, the average age used to be sixty, sixty-five; now we have lots of yuppies, twenty-nine, thirty, though still not many children except when our grandchildren come to visit. A lot of older people my age down here are playing tennis now, though you'd think they can't even pick up the ball. The city is becoming alive again, things are happening that delight us elderly who are staying. We seem more alive now because we're part of a continuum.

In our building we now almost all know each

other. We don't intrude—we have no lobby so there are no people sitting around staring at you. I'm not afraid to live here by myself on the first floor; I go to Pritikin three nights a week for the aerobics and diet regime. There's also the exercise classes on South Beach; I take art lessons, play bridge, golf, do my volunteer work. I have my hot dates, it's nice to go out, you have more chance to meet people in Miami. I've been single ten years now. I'm dating two men at this moment; I could be two months without a date, I don't want the effort of meeting the needs of an elderly man. This summer I went on a mountain-hiking trip in Switzerland with three friends. I'm getting more adventurous now I'm in my seventies.

Paula Harper was one of the new younger people who moved into Morton Towers, another relic of the old South Miami Beach. They used to call it "Mortuary Towers." Looking thirty-something, Paula also was not afraid to live on the first floor. She took me to her apartment past two older women (dyed red hair, red and beige polyester slack suits), sitting in the airy lobby, saying hello to people passing by on the way to the pool or parking lot; several Hispanic children bouncing a basketball; a mother wheeling a shopping cart. Paula was forty-eight when she moved in there four years ago, though that made her virtually a teenager in Morton Towers then. She explained:

I wanted to live in South Beach. A friend had found an apartment here, big and safe and not too expensive; I liked it and moved in myself. People who came to visit me would say, How can you live here with all these old people, isn't it depressing? I don't find it depressing at all. I have some wonderful characters as neighbors. They don't play stereos loud, and they keep it safe. No creep or crackpot can get through our lobby past the old ladies. Unfortunately, my rent has just gone up 50 percent. New management here is jacking up the rents so the older people on fixed incomes will have to move out. Instead of $800, a real bargain for a three-bedroom apartment, now I'm paying $1,200.

The old people are still the most visible: they congregate in the lobby, play cards in the card room; but now I see more and more children, fashionable yuppies, Latino families. The new management wants to yuppify this place. I happen to like the mix myself.

Conventional wisdom had it that South Beach, deteriorating and dismal as an age ghetto, was being revived by gentrification. But Tamara Hendershot, the young woman who ran Variety Novelty Goods, loved the old people rocking on the porches next to the coffeehouses when she first came to the community.

There were maybe twenty hotels with older people on Ocean Drive two and a half years ago; now there are two left. They're remodeling everything so the older people will go; want to turn the Twelfth Street center, where the old people had their dances and classes and used to come and sing to each other, into a convention complex. Many of the hotels were rundown, but those older people were so independent, they had their own lifestyle, they didn't stay in their rooms, they came out to do all these things together, on the beach, along the streets.

Tamara thought the realtors were making a shortsighted mistake, trying to drive the old people out—they were such a vital part of the mix. "You don't see old people in New York this way. They come in here, they're interested, feisty, independent, and they're pushing them away."

Were realtors making a mistake, driving those feisty older people away? They and the urban culture they had created could be a vital, essential part of the new mix. Such a vital mix might be more attractive to a new market of adventurous older people than quiet, protected retirement villages and manicured age ghettos. In one renovated building, right on the boardwalk, I found an adventurous older person attracted by the vital urban mix of South Beach as much as by the sun and sea. Sam Kron, seventy-one, had been head of surgery in a major Philadelphia hospital. Sitting on the leather couch of his second-floor one-bedroom apartment, sliding glass doors open to the sounds and sights of the continual flux of young and old, retirees and vacationers and professionals on the busy boardwalk, he told me:

I'm really here because of my son. He's a fashion photographer, kept coming down here for location shots in the Art Deco area—fashion photography is a big industry here now. He kept saying, "Dad, you ought to move down here." I thought Miami Beach was the last place I'd go; my image was of a place you'd go to if you were old and sick and wanted to sit. But when I came down with my son, and stayed at one of the hotels here in the middle of the action, I thought the mixture of models, old people, Spanish, Germans, Italians, outdoor cafés, music, and the ocean was for me. I keep those sliding glass doors mostly open because I want to hear the ocean, and the action, the people on the boardwalk. But it's quiet and peaceful when I close them. I didn't come down here to sit; this place has the action I need for my body and my soul.

Sam Kron was attending courses at the University of Miami, and after having qualified for a state insurance license, had been hired by the largest insurance agency in Dade County.

They took me on as a consultant, not to sit around and write policies, but to go around and talk to people. It supplements my income, but that's not why I do it. I see a tremendous need for better financing of long-term care. So now I go to a lot of political meetings. My medical background plus being a licensed agent for a private insurance company gives me credibility.

I'm also teaching a course in fitness walking. I joined the Miami Runners and Walkers Club and I entered my first race at seventy. I win trophies now as a competitive race walker. Of course, there aren't that many men over seventy competing. I have a woman friend, a few years older than I am, with more energy than both of us, she's on the tennis court now. A good deal of my social life is spent escorting this lively wonderful woman to opera, ballet, concerts, parties. But I've been divorced twenty years and I don't know that I'll remarry. I just live an unconventional life, since I've moved to Miami. I love the freedom of it. I have friends in one of those deadly quiet condos in Boca Raton who think I'm nuts. I've met some adventurous older people like myself down here, but not that many yet.

Later, I learned that it was a woman in her sixties whom I had known forty years ago, when we were both young journalists home with babies, who had organized an army of senior citizens and students to save the old Art Deco buildings of South Beach from being torn down and the vibrant community of old people from being wiped out altogether. Some fifteen years ago, my old friend Barbara Capitman was wandering around South Miami Beach with her son John, whom I remembered as a baby when we were both pushing strollers, now the owner of one of those renovated old hotels. When I knew Barbara, she freelanced for an industrial design magazine. South Miami Beach, then, had deteriorated into a certified city slum; the median age was seventy-four; a lot of older people were living on Social Security in little "efficiencies"— hotplate, sink, bed, and toilet in those old buildings which hadn't been painted for fifteen years. But under the grime, Barbara noticed the gorgeous old Art Deco details. Two of the young students she got to help her save that community, Michael Kinerk and Dennis Wilhelm, were now carrying on the work of the Miami Design Preservation League (MDPL), which she started. They explained:

The way these Art Deco small hotels and boardinghouses had been constructed in the thirties was not only art history, but perfect for vital age—with their medium cozy height, large lobbies, and small rooms. The older people didn't spend much time in their rooms, gathering in the lobbies and on the porches and the rows of chairs on the sidewalks outside the hotels. Barbara and her son thought these old people seemed unusually sturdy. She found statistics indicating that they were living much longer than the average life expectancy. She thought it was because they were happy—not just the climate, the beach, but the camaraderie, not living in isolated little houses or high-rise condos where you don't know the neighbors, [but] exercising on the beach together, dancing and singing and walking on the boardwalk. She was very concerned about the gentrification, destroying the beautiful old historic Art Deco buildings for those concrete-and-glass high rises. Saving those historic buildings was her first priority, and she got a lot of us, who were art students then, to help her with that. But saving the community of older people was also her priority. And she recruited the senior citizens to do the necessary political work, along with the artists, architects, and design students like ourselves.

She started our organization, the MDPL, in 1976, went to the state and to Washington to get South Beach designated an historic district. The hotel owners and Chamber of Commerce tried to portray her as crazy. We thought she was crazy like a fox. There's a famous picture of her being dragged away by the police in front of the Senator Hotel, which the owners wanted to tear down, before she got the local ordinance passed enforcing protection of the historic district. It was the last year of her life, she could barely walk or breathe, but no one knew it. Everything she saw in her dreams is happening now. But the crazy thing is, now they want to turn the Twelfth Street center where the senior citizen dances and sing-ins and classes took place into a world-class convention center and name it after Barbara.

We want more older people to enjoy this place again. This is a unique place that needs to be cherished for its human-scale livability. We don't want T-shirt and souvenir shops and more rock and roll, skinheads cruising in hot rods looking for girls; we need our older people back.

• • •

Elsewhere in the country, adventurous older people are seeking out and helping to revive the small towns that were once the heart of American culture, more livable in scale than the big cities and car-culture suburbs, more hospitable to their individuality somehow than even the best of the institutionalized age ghettos. And in some of these towns the adventurous old are joining forces with the new kind of adventurous young, seeking a human-scale life.

I came to Eureka Springs, Arkansas, in the spring with my dear friend Maury Zolotow, in his late seventies then, thinking if his emphysema got worse he might escape the smog of Los Angeles by moving near his daughter Crescent, who had built a bed-and-breakfast into a gemlike little inn in that Ozark town. I knew from the research that many Ozark towns were attracting a brand of older people who did not want to live in age ghettos. Eureka Springs at the turn of the century had been a thriving resort town with thirty medicinal springs where fashionable Southerners came to take the waters. Most of those springs had become polluted, and during the Depression it was a deserted decaying ghost town. Then, in the 1960s, the hippies had discovered its beautiful old Victorian houses and hotels, never modernized and restored, and its deserted farms which they could rent for $25 a month, till their garden patches, and meditate.

Many of those former hippies were now restoring the town to a thriving art-and-craft tourist center, and they had been joined in recent years by a motley adventurous breed of oldsters.

Roger and Peggy Pettit, in their seventies, had come to Arkansas from Chicago to go fishing in the summer of 1975. He was a sales executive at Montgomery Ward, which had been bought out by Mobil. He hadn't yet thought of retiring, but was increasingly unhappy with the "depersonalization" of corporate culture. He talked to me on the deck of his house on Beaver Lake, surrounded by the low Ozark Mountains, fifteen minutes away from Eureka Springs.

Something about this area just spoke to us. We came down again, and the motel owner told us about this house on the lake for sale. We came over at midnight and sat out here in the moonlight, and I said to Peggy, "I'll make a bid on this house, and if they accept it, I'll quit now." If I'd stayed around and let them fire me, I'd have done better financially, but I don't regret it. I arranged not to close on the house for a year, and took early retirement. We wanted to live the natural life, live off the land, canoe the white-water rivers. Our kids and our friends all thought we were crazy. We joined the Ozark Society, became avid hikers, we ran the white waters, we climbed those crazy hills and hollows where the bootleggers used to hide. And then we joined the young people in trying to save this beautiful community from the power developers and polluters, and to help the rural poor in the terrible pockets of poverty in these hills.

After we moved down here, I got one of the artists to give me some lessons in watercolor painting. I've been accepted in some pretty good shows and won some awards. Peggy built up quite a business with her "organic sculptures," going out in the woods collecting what nature has cast off and recycling it— dried seedpods, bark, shells, nuts. We have a lot of friends here now, some older; a lot are younger; our concerns about the environment and art brought us together. This place has enabled us to be really ourselves. This is a place where people are free to be different.

But Peggy was worried, because now that her health was "rocky," their kids wanted them to sell the house in Eureka Springs and move near them into a Washington "lifetime care facility." But their life was here, and they held on to it. They hugged me vigorously at Clinton's Inauguration.

Louis Freund was eighty-four and Elsie seventy-eight when I talked to them in the historic fourteen-room mountain house they paid $2,800 for to keep it from being torn down fifty years ago. The house used to belong to the suffragette-prohibitionist Carry Nation. Elsie and Louis spent nearly fifty years, teaching at different colleges winters, sketching and preserving the history and the old houses of Eureka Springs and running an art school summers; and then, in the twenty-odd years since his retirement, building this new, vital community with the former hippies. Elsie recalled:

At first, the local people were menaced by those young folks with their beards. We were the intermediaries. Some were very talented painters, musicians, writers; they were really individuals to us, not hippies. We had been working with young people, teaching all those years. Some of those so-called hippies are still here, editing the newspaper, city council members, our present mayor; our town is flourishing now, and free of crime. It's romantic, as we look back from our age, knowing that some of these things we helped start here will endure.

Louis said:

We had no children of our own, so we got such satisfaction from other people's children when the hippies came. Watching them grow and develop was very satisfying for us. We're right in the center of things here. Crescent gave us our fiftieth anniversary party and the whole town danced in the street.

Susan Thomas was in her late forties when Eureka Springs came to her in a dream. She had passed through as a child. Her husband had cancer, her parents could no longer live alone. She told me:

This big old house was for sale, broken down into apartments as it still is. I was your original displaced homemaker, a minister's wife who went back to school too old to get a job, but here I could support myself sewing, something I always loved to do.

My husband's mother, in her eighties, was being driven crazy by her alcoholic son; she could have her own street-level apartment in this house, be near us but not really live with us. So she sold her house and gave us some money for our down payment. Two years later my mother and dad came down and moved into the apartment on the other side. My mother had made me promise I'd never put her in a nursing home. She was eighty-one when they decided they had to get out of their house in Baton Rouge; my father couldn't mow the lawn or fix the gutters on the roof anymore;

they were looking into a retirement village. My husband offered our street-level apartment to my parents and we moved down the hillside, with a kitchen and dining room we can all use on one level and studios for both of us up-stairs.

Caregiving for both our parents has been a challenge for us; we feel we have developed a unique living situation. We're meeting the challenge of our parents' age, but we're also creating a wonderful life for ourselves in this town. I stay open to unprecedented opportunities; you never know where they're going to come from. I love being my age now, though these circumstances aren't necessarily easy. I've got three eighty-five-year-olds and a disabled husband and I'm fifty-eight years old. But a lot of things that used to matter don't seem that important anymore. My fifties were better than my forties, and the sixties will be even better, I think.

In Eureka Springs, "What do you do?" was not the main question defining identity, which may be one reason why it was so nurturing to older people who felt finally free to be themselves. It was also, I noted, a place where space and structure sustained the personal and social ties necessary at any age. When Susan Thomas's first husband was dying, they kept, in effect, a community kitchen:

A couple with a baby, three gay men, a woman and her daughter, we cooked our own meals but the kitchen was a gathering place, and we'd cook a communal Sunday brunch. After Jack died, the people who cooked Sunday dinner with us helped build the coffin and dig the grave.

The more I looked into the movings and stayings that somehow structure our age, the more I sensed the serendipity—a seeming accident of space and time, seized on with a sense of recognition sometimes, less often consciously planned—out of which community may simply evolve. Arlie Hochschild, eminent Berkeley sociologist, did a classic study of the evolution of a subculture of vital age entitled *The Unexpected Community*—among widows, previously strangers, who moved into Merrill Court, a low-cost, low-rise California apartment building, in 1965.[8] As Freda, the first leader, told it, "There wasn't nothin' before we got the coffee machine. I mean we didn't share nothin' before Mrs. Bitford's daughter brought over the machine." As people came downstairs from their apartments to fetch their mail mid-morning, they looked into the recreation room, found six or seven people sitting down drinking coffee, and some joined in. A few weeks later the recreation director, who had formerly worked for a nearby bowling alley, "joined in" the morning coffee. Then, she

worked out a special season rate for older people at the bowling alley, always on Tuesdays,
and organized teams.

Half a year later Merrill Court was a beehive
of activity: meetings of a Service Club, which
was soon set up; bowling; morning workshops; Bible study classes twice a week;
monthly birthday parties; and visits to four
nearby nursing homes. Members donated
cakes, pies, and soft drinks to bring to the
nursing home, and a five-piece band, including a washtub bass, played for the "old folks"
there [as well as] a nearby recreation center
for Vietnam veterans. During afternoon band
practice, the women sewed and embroidered
pillowcases, aprons, and yarn dolls. They
made wastebaskets out of old Wonder Bread
wrappers, and Easter hats out of old Clorox
bottles, all to be sold at the annual bazaar.
They made placemats to be used at the nursing home . . . rag dolls to be sent to the or-
phanage . . . recipes to be written out for the
recipe book that was to go on sale next
month. . . .
   All the women were living on social welfare,
Social Security, or pensions, and in the eyes
of society they were not workers. They
earned no pay and had no employer, paid no
taxes, and punched no time clocks. . . . But if
you asked them, they would tell you they

were working. . . . If one of the regulars failed to come down, she was called and reminded. If people came only to talk, they were quietly handed work.

They used the money from the bazaar sale to "have fun," seeing a movie or musical, taking trips, eating in restaurants together, parties on birthdays, and holidays. Rituals, "our way" ceremonies—and "old hands" to pass them on—developed. And these customs gave the widows a lively sense of identity, "as opposed to the derogatory 'old people' normlessness."

If one was no longer a mother to a brood of small children, or a wife, or provider, one was at least the Birthday Chairman or the Treasurer or a member of the Flower Committee . . . with each new role came new customs. . . . For whatever reason, the widows built themselves an order out of ambiguity, a set of obligations to the outside and to one another where few had existed before.

The spatial arrangement of the apartments in Merrill Court fostered this enlivening sense of community. The living rooms and porches of all the apartments faced out on a common outside walkway, so everyone saw each other coming and going and knew immediately if something was wrong. Informally, the widows in good health took it upon themselves to care for the one or two in poor health. A "poor dear" hierarchy evolved within Merrill Court, based on health, closeness to children, loss of loved ones, along with a leadership elite, that embodied as well as countered the denigration of age they faced outside.

There was something special about the community bond in Merrill Court—"rivalries and differences . . . but not alienation and not isolation." Hochschild calls it a "peer bond" based on reciprocity, similarity, and equality (as opposed to the parent/child, "us"/"them" equations and the unequal equation between staff and residents in nursing homes). People the same age in nursing homes and other institutions did not develop this kind of bond, even if they were fairly healthy and socially similar.

The widows of Merrill Court took care of themselves, fixed their own meals, paid their own rent, shopped for their own food and made their own beds; and they did these things for others. They watched over each other's apartments when someone was away on a visit, and they took calls for one another. Their sisterhood rests on adult autonomy. This is what people in Merrill Court have and people in institutions do not.

Instead of playing the role of "old person," they felt free to "improvise new roles," as the sociologist put it, but they did not deny the less humorous social and physical realities of growing old, or the realities of their own aging. And, remarkably, *none of them* fulfilled the age mystique of deterioration and decline into senility before death.

It [death] was a fact of life in Merrill Court and there was no taboo against talk about it. Six residents died in the course of my three years of field work. . . . There was a collective concern with, as they put it, "being ready and facing up." . . . Strangely enough, five of the six deaths happened to people who had their social and psychic "boots on." . . . Rosie, an active club officer, died half an hour after returning from a Bible study class. Another two died while arranging with someone on the telephone for a meeting the following week. One died peacefully in bed and another in a chair, both after a day of activity. Only the sixth died in a hospital after a few days of not feeling well.

Actually, the only person who became senile in Merrill Court was one of the few who did not take part in the community. The remarkable absence of senility among these widows suggested to Hochschild what other research has shown—that "social isolation may well produce the senile behavior."
Hochschild was convinced that the widows,

and others inside an old age community "insulated by a community of peers, feel the sting of [the age] stigma less than most isolated older people." She predicted that future communities of the aged would be more middle class, and geared to leisure. But surely not, if the commercialized retirement and "congregate care" communities incorporate the implicit denigration of age, substituting depersonalization and total "care" for that self-respecting activity among equals and ties with the larger community that supports a solid core of authentic identity.

In Santa Monica, I found other "alternative" attempts to meet the need for independence and intimacy among older people, without denying the physical and economic realities of aging. These alternative patterns, arrived at by serendipity or necessity, seem to me much more appealing than the most luxurious retirement village or "congregate care" facility. They might even point to new possibilities for those of us intending to age in place, in our own homes or city apartments.

Alternative Living for the Aging (ALA) and Housing Alternatives for Seniors, as they are variously called, operated out of small storefront offices on the West Side of Los Angeles, a non-profit venture set up in 1978 to provide *shared housing options* for older people as an alternative to living alone or in an institutional setting.

"In most communities, two basic types of living arrangements are available to older people," said the founder and director Janet Witkin, now forty-four (she was barely thirty when she started it). "There are institutions—retirement villages and hotels, board-and-care homes, nursing homes, congregate care facilities—or independent living in apartments or houses. We also provide a third choice: a cooperative, extended family type of living."

Coop House I was remodeled out of two old duplexes, opening now onto a common dining room and small courtyard. The sixteen people who lived there, ages sixty-odd to ninety-one (twelve women, four men, one married couple), each had their own bedroom studios and baths and shared common living and dining rooms, kitchen and courtyard. For $450 a month, they got the joint services of a cook for the five dinners a week they ate together, and major maintenance services. Otherwise, they cleaned their own studios, shared the KP, kitchen clean-up and table setting, did their own lunches and breakfasts, each with a shelf in their common kitchen, refrigerator, and pantry (the second kitchen was used by the cook). Another structure, El Greco, was an old duplex apartment mews about to be torn down for a high-rise condo, which they moved onto two empty lots within walking distance of the Fairfax–West Hollywood shopping district, with its stores and cafés, theaters, gym, church and synagogues. In El Greco, people had their own kitchens in separate bed-sitting-room apartments, and no cook. They ate together at potluck dinners, which they organized, in each other's apartments or in the courtyard—which all their apartments opened onto, their common outdoor living room. There was no resident manager or "staff," or medical care. They used the hospital and clinic facilities of the community when they needed them, and the exercise classes and humanities courses offered by Emeritus College and other schools nearby. They organized their own "buddy system," monitoring each other for health emergencies, and, on their own initiative, often got concert and theater tickets for the whole group, arranging carpools among drivers and non-drivers.

I sat around a circle in the sunny courtyard of Coop House I, with two men and twelve women who, some years after they moved in, were still marveling: "Aren't we lucky?" "Aren't we smart to be living here?" "We're free birds here, independent!" They had been there six, seven, or more years, most of them. "I'll be eighty-two in March, I must be getting old," one woman said, laughing.

We all had our own apartments or houses before. We could only take what we could use in one bedroom—living room, which can get overcrowded. But when my husband passed away, I hated being alone. I heard about this on television. When we moved in, none of us knew each other. Everyone here is very independent, we go our own way; when we want to be together, we do things together. During the week, we all eat dinner together. Sometimes some of us like to go out for dinner, or invite people to eat with us here. On weekends we usually go out with our kids and grandchildren. We're independent but we're not alone. We have our difficulties, but we're doing just fine. We're congenial.

I could tell that by the way they teased each other. They did not make a big thing about the way they also took care of each other. But it was clear that without this "family," some indeed might be in nursing homes. It was also clear that though almost all seemed very close to children and grandchildren, they most emphatically preferred living with each other, in this new family-type arrangement, to living with their own children.

Rose had to take early retirement from the UCLA Engineering Department because of her health. She was seventy-seven, and had two sons and a daughter living in different parts of California. She told me:

I didn't want to be alone, but I didn't want to live with any of my children because I wanted all of us to be happy. I'm a very independent person. I visit them but I can't travel as much as I like now because of my emphysema.

None of us wants to live with our children, take away their privacy. They have their own interests, own friends. It wouldn't be so good for them or us. We'd be fifth wheels. It's wonderful to be independent and to live in such a good lively neighborhood. You can walk, take the bus, a little trolley, you don't even need a car. We know that in case of emergency, we're not alone, someone will be there for us. I have to be under oxygen sometimes fourteen hours a day. Someone asks right away, Can I help? I'm the only one in my own family who ever lived this old.

On the back of the common kitchen cupboard were names and phone numbers of doctors and people to call in emergencies for all the "family." The arrays of crackers, teas, soups, on their separate shelves were open to each other on an "honor system." But no one living here seemed to worry much about "care," or the danger of being put in a nursing home.

The apartments in El Greco, opening out onto the beautiful tiled courtyard with a fishpond running through it, were odd-shaped, beamed, with high ceilings and would seem charming to people able to shell out far more than the $450-odd a month the residents have to pay. The ALA structures were renovated with city and philanthropic money which Janet Witkin raised as a pilot project in low-cost housing for the elderly. A lot of people have been turned down because they had too much money. But when upper-income groups asked Janet to consult with them on building this new type of extended family structure "up-scale," it somehow didn't happen. "They have too many choices," she said. "El Greco and the Coops work because the people there know that is what they need and they need to make it work."

Max had lived in El Greco for three years. He moved to California at eighty-five to be near his daughter after his second wife died of cancer, but not to live with her. ("I married a younger woman so she'd take care of me in my old age and look what happened!") His daughter, Trude Armer, told me:

I was resistant about his moving, but he's very happy there. He shops for other people, shops for his buddy, but likes the fact that he has his own privacy. He's so proud that at his age, ninety, he's learned how to cook. He invites people over for dinner. He walks miles every day. This arrangement has allowed him to stay independent and even to take care of others which, though he complains about it, has been very important to him.

Edie, who was president of El Greco, was sixty-nine. She had lived there four years.

I was so lucky. I was being evicted after I retired. Where was I going to go, the rents are so high now in Santa Monica. I was a bit snobbish about moving in here. But I like this lively neighborhood, I like the feeling we have of living together here, doing for each other. I'm happier here than I can ever remember. We have an understanding of each other's problems and needs, we don't nudge each other. We're all very active, we want to live an independent lifestyle, but none of my children are in California, I'm totally alone here, so I need this community of my peers. The security of it; we're independent but safe.

In one way or another, they all considered communal living an "adventure." Jack Landis, who used to be president of Coop House I, said: "We've learned by taking risks. And by taking chances on this we've gained an advantage— companionship and support." But the fiercest

707

champions of this new shared independent living were those who had had the experience of institutional living in a nursing home or a retirement hotel. Garret Beattie, eighty-six, had lived in a retirement home on the upscale West Side. "It was terrible. I was there thirteen months and I had one roommate after another. There was no one to talk to and finally I became ill from the food. I told my son I couldn't take the loneliness any longer. I had to find someplace else to live."

Rose Becker, eighty-seven, said:

This is my home. I know that I'm happy here. When I was at the retirement hotel, it was like we were all sick people. It was so depressing. You'd hear the ambulance and get sick to your stomach. When I had to go into the hospital recently for special surgery, people from here called me every day or came to see me. When I came home, the others brought my meals to me and took over my share of the chores. I was back on my feet in no time.

There were five such shared houses in Santa Monica, which people seemed to leave only when they died. The local papers marveled at this experiment; that these women and men, aged between sixty-five and ninety-one, who two or three years before were strangers, now "consider themselves a family" and were "willing to be participants in a pioneering lifestyle for older people: group living." But the idea of a "commune" of any sort still seems so daring to Americans, even Californians, that the main demand so far has been the much more conventional couple-type sharing of their own apartments and houses by widows, or by older women and men with younger ones with meshing needs and strengths. They are, indeed, "odd couples," and sometimes it works and sometimes it doesn't; but never as long or as well as the really innovative larger "extended families."

Housing Alternatives for Seniors in Santa Monica arranged house or apartment sharing for older women or men who weren't able to continue living alone, for financial or physical reasons, but did not want to give up their independent lifestyle. Sarah Epstein's children had moved her into a "retirement hotel" and she was not thrilled about it, though her kids assured her, "You won't have to cook or clean; they'll do everything for you." "It was a lovely beautiful place but I just couldn't stand it," she said. "There was no place to go, nothing to do but just sit around. And I lost too much weight, maybe because I didn't like the food."

Concerned about her health, her children got her into a "lifetime care" facility. She spent three weeks there, getting out just before her month's grace period expired and she would have had to

709

give up her life savings for that assurance of "lifetime care." She said: "You had to be there three years to get a room by yourself, and *none* of the roommates got along. It was awful. Food was a big problem there, too. It was served off a turnstile, and the last person got almost nothing. I used to cry all the time, but my daughter kept saying I'd get used to it and it would feel better after a while."

Sarah didn't want to take that chance. When she went into the Housing Alternatives for Seniors' storefront, they matched her up with eighty-three-year-old Cele Rice Goldman, who had a different problem. Since her second husband died she couldn't afford to keep on living in her sunny, cheerful first-floor apartment, with its long, spacious living room, its two bedrooms and baths. And she had no desire to move in with any of her five children. She was in good health and fiercely protective of her independence. Soft-spoken but stern-looking, with a glint of humor, she had been introduced to two prospects whom she turned down. "I didn't think either of them would be able to take care of themselves," she said. She and Sarah decided to live together after only one talk, though Housing Alternatives encouraged several sessions of talk and a weekend or two of tryouts.

"We hit it off right away," Cele said. "I've lived through two husbands and they didn't divorce me. You have to live with someone to find out if it will work. I took a chance; she took a chance. You can't do this without risk. I figured, I'm alone and I need help, so I took a chance."

Once they decided to share Cele's apartment, the practical arrangements they made were simple and flexible. They split everything down the middle: rent, gas, electricity. Sometimes they ate together, sometimes they didn't. When they did, they took turns cooking. They each bought their own food, though sometimes they shopped together. "When family comes to take one of us out, the other is usually invited and usually doesn't go along." Sarah had the back bedroom, which was filled with her pictures and prized furniture, and a small television set. Cele got up very early and read the paper until the TV news came on at seven o'clock. Sarah got up then, and they usually had breakfast together before going about their separate activities. Sarah spent a lot of time as a "hooker"—she actually learned hooking rugs at the retirement home. So what was the difference? "Here, I'm my own boss—I hook rugs by choice; there, I did it because I didn't want to sit around the lobby waiting to die."

Most of the thousands of "matches" Housing Alternatives had made were between widows of roughly similar age, and a few widowers; but matches of older women with younger people, often students, had also been very successful. Although older men were open to being paired with a widow, the women weren't ("Old men just want someone to make their breakfast and wash their socks," they said). Widower Victor Arkins, an eighty-eight-year-old retired tool-and-die worker, became much more lively after he started sharing his apartment with Ben Himel, a widowed ex-schoolteacher ten years younger. About a month after meeting at the storefront and getting together several times for coffee and walks along the beach, Himel moved into Arkins's two-bedroom apartment in Venice. Four years later they were surprised themselves that they had drawn steadily closer. Said Himel:

We didn't have any common interests at all. He was a mechanic involved with tools, and I was interested in the arts all my life. And yet I find I am so pleased to be with this man. I used to dread getting out of bed in the morning because I was so lonely. Now getting up is a real pleasure. I was afraid of losing my independence, but I thought it was worth taking the risk. Now we blend so well, it's remarkable. Maybe it's because we're so different that we get along.

Janet Witkin told me that she began the crusade that led her to start Alternative Living for the Aging after her own grandfather entered a nursing home.

I was struck by the lack of spirit I saw in board-and-care homes. I was perplexed as to why people were in such institutions who did not need medical care. It became clear that they simply didn't have many options. I was appalled at what happened to my grandfather. Two people to a room, who don't want to be there, uprooted, giving up all control over their days, having to eat three meals a day whether they are hungry or not. He really went downhill fast. When I visited him, he said: "It's not good like this, I can't take care of myself." He died at eighty-eight. I figured there had to be some other way. I learned how to lobby, write grant proposals.

Witkin raised public and private money to start the non-profit Alternative Living for the Aging and organized the roommate matching pool of Housing Alternatives for Seniors by word of mouth and media, through senior citizen centers, churches, synagogues, clubs, schools, and gyms, covering all the bases people over sixty might touch. And she steadfastly resisted pressures to go the "lifetime care" route which all the for-profit retirement villages and congregate care facilities and nursing homes were now taking. She said: "We didn't want to provide everything. Then it would have become an institution. We're not taking care of these people. I believe strongly in the concept of maintaining independence through interdependence."

That's why ALA provides twice-a-month cleaning service for the communal areas of the houses, a gardener, and a cook for five nightly meals, but the residents are on their own for other meals (with full kitchen privileges), and are also responsible for the light housekeeping tasks, cleaning their own rooms, as well as monitoring each other's health through the buddy system, running the governance of each house themselves, and organizing for themselves whatever entertainment or cultural life they want to share. They run and live their own lives out in the city from this base they share.

Despite the enthusiasm of everyone who had been through Coop I or El Greco, Witkin had not been swamped with applications to move in, partly because of resistance to even considering the possibility that shared living with eight, ten, or fourteen other older people could work— which is why there was the alternative of "matching" seniors to share homes or apartments as roommates. That resistance which keeps older people isolated was often one of the reasons that they were already sick, Witkin believed.

If they would live with people instead of hibernating in their apartments, they'd have more of a reason to get well. By themselves, on their own, the possibility for endurance is less. Is this life about having everything in my kitchen just where I want it, or is it about sharing life with others and being there to help someone when they need help, and to receive help, and enjoy the company of others as you share the joys and burdens of life?

We resist that lifetime care age-as-sickness route. As long as they can manage to take care of themselves living here, with people helping each other, any way as long as it works out, it's okay. Some people finally die, but almost no one moves out from El Greco to go to a nursing home or because they're unhappy. Our low apartments around the courtyard don't give you the economy of scale of a high rise, but the quality of life is unbeatable. And it still costs a lot less than the for-profit nursing homes and board-and-care with two to a room. What we're about, of course, is building a community—not just a cheap apartment, or taking care of sick people. This place is for people to go on with life the way they want to, not isolated from the larger community.

We've matched up 3,500 people by now to share homes or apartments, with one and a half staff persons, a computer, and a lot of outreach to clubs and libraries and public service announcements. A lot don't work out, a lot do, but there's not the social structure to hold it together like the houses. And there's going to be a greater and greater need for all kinds of housing alternatives as the whole population ages.

In more and more cities, from Florida to Massachusetts, Philadelphia and Washington to San Francisco, older people were finding or creating different kinds of home-sharing arrangements. A model program in Plainfield, New Jersey, helped older owners convert part of their homes into accessory apartments, with an average conversion cost of about $10,000. Sometimes, the economic basis for the home-sharing arrangement involved only the sharing of rent and expenses; sometimes there was an exchange of service for rent.

In Florida, residents of Share-a-Home, developed by Jim Gillies in 1969 as an alternative to nursing homes, hired people to take care of housekeeping, cooking, and driving needs. The group houses, bought and organized by Share-a-Home Corporation, spread across the state. Residents paid $400 to $600 a month, compared to $1,500 to $2,000 for nursing homes in the same area. More and more of these "alternative living" experiments are also being organized by adventurous individuals, without landlord-tenant, social service agency, or other for-profit or non-profit arrangements.

In a comprehensive research survey of shared housing for the elderly, economist Charlotte Muller of the City University of New York found some evidence that people who made such moves survived longer, were less likely to enter nursing homes or be hospitalized, and experienced better health and well-being and fewer limitations on activity even if they were in poor health when they applied.[9] The worsening of health and deterioration assumed by the mystique of age *was not found* in these people who moved into shared housing in their seventies or eighties. In fact, they became less worried about their health, but they also seemed more realistic about their disabilities. Another study found that those who moved to shared housing participated more in activities, had more good friends and social involvement. They were more likely to "get out" and "dress up" than before. They participated and were more integrated within the outside community than residents of "care" facilities.

Many studies seemed to indicate that older people who actually moved—into group living, or alternative forms of independent community living—showed more life satisfaction, better emotional health, a significant increase in engagement, and a better view of the future than those who stayed on alone in apartment or house despite growing dissatisfaction. In a Philadelphia study, twenty-four people who moved into a shared living arrangement showed much better health, happiness, more friends, and fewer limitations of activity six months later than a control group of comparable status originally. Three years later, 67 percent of those who had not moved had died, whereas only 11 percent of those who had *moved anywhere* had died.[10]

This is the direct opposite, of course, to the dramatic lowering of life expectancy, satisfaction, and activity after moving into a nursing home or other such institution. There is a big difference, obviously, between those who move into institutional facilities and those who join with others in the shared housing they control themselves, with only informal and spontaneous social exchanges, informal health monitoring and mutual help, and cooperation in carrying out tasks that become onerous to do alone. The more "total" the institution, the more devastating to one's personhood. We know that politically now for whole populations; why should it not be true in individual aging?

There is a need, and a way, of moving that comes to new terms with life alone. "You won't catch me retiring to one of those places," Marlene Sanders told me emphatically. "I wouldn't ever want not to be part of things. I'll stay in my own apartment." But, in her sixties (though in her broadcast career she can't afford to look her age), she just made a very crucial move to a new apartment, geared consciously now to her life alone. It had been eight years since her beloved husband died of a brain tumor, and her son, long since moved out, had a family of his own now. But she had held on to that apartment, with its big living room and formal dining room, which she hardly ever used, its three bedrooms and maid's room, because, she now admitted, "I wasn't ready to say goodbye to all that, my married life. I kept thinking I might get married again, and if he had kids, we could use all those rooms. But I'm not thinking in those terms anymore. I doubt I'll marry again. My new apartment is geared to my life now, the way I'm planning to live it, for myself."

She spent all spring packing boxes of books and clothes and marking furniture to sell or give away. This apartment was only six blocks from her old one, so she didn't have to leave the West Side neighborhood which she loved, or even change her phone number. It seemed sunnier and somehow more spacious than her old one —though, in fact, it was smaller—and fresher, lighter. The old couch looked brighter; her paintings were stunning in the sunnier light, with so much of the old clutter gone. She took down a wall so the small formal dining room now opened into the living room in a large, light space. The lightest room in the house was her bedroom. The second bedroom was her study, with all the shelves she needed for her computer, reference books, and a couch that opened into a bed when friends sleep over. Like me, she was not charmed by the idea of cooking for herself, or eating out alone in a glitzy restaurant. But that can of sardines or tuna in the refrigerator can't really solve our hunger pangs. She had found four good, cheap ethnic restaurants within a two-block radius for her new entertaining plan—"We'll have a drink right here, and then go out nearby, no reservations needed, no sweat."

The move we must take now may not be final, permanent, because there is no final decision, no once-and-for-all move or stay that can ensure our age against risk, illness, and ultimately death. We may have to move again. But in order to be truly *at home* in that new place, it has to be shared in some way to enable us to experience our vital sense of self in human contact. It has to enable us to control our own lives, in privacy and in sharing, to feel rooted and safe leaving and returning, if we are to retain our personal identity. Though it can and maybe must take a different shape as our needs change in age, it must enable us to keep on moving and risking new adventures. Even if we have to live with some disabilities, they need not define us.

As for me, after exploring all the spaces and structures of age, I feel a sharper relish, but a new need for truthtelling, in my own moving back and forth between my apartment in the dirty, noisy city of New York, my little house in

Sag Harbor where I write and my children bring their children, and my sublet condos in California where I teach winters. I'll continue with all this moving; but I see now, more clearly than ever, that it is the deepening of my ties of purpose and intimacy that makes those places "home" for me, that nourishes my vitality in the face of age. Ever since I've started moving back and forth, my asthma has been getting better, my general health and energy—and my friends on both coasts now are more and more dear to me, even former enemies I've shared so many battles with. Until the end, it seems to me, I'll think in terms of the *life* I want to live, not foreshortening or shortchanging the *risks of living* to guarantee "care" in the months before death. I intend to find new adventures for my third age; and if I'm lucky, I'll die on the move, in the air, on the road.

I flew back from California to New York for my sixty-fifth birthday party, and it was wonderful. This time the party was not the surprise—my own happiness was. Remembering my reaction at my sixtieth birthday party, my friends had warned me, thinking I might be angry. They were going to hold it at the Palladium, a many-staircased Art Deco disco with flashing multi-colored strobe lights and ever-changing graphics, reborn from an old movie theater on East 14th Street. They had reserved a big room for the party, but we could stay on and dance with the regulars if we so chose. I enjoyed the idea of my friends' taking over that new and swinging place for my birthday.

And there they all were—my own children and the friends who were my great extended family of choice, come even from far cities. They did a sort of musical revue celebrating my "wonderful life," as they put it. They sang a song about the pains of being a bright girl growing up in Peoria when boys weren't supposed to like girls who were bright. And Jonathan, my second son, gave a humorous, barbed paean to my cooking, which wasn't long on apple pie or even chicken soup.

The men and women I had shared houses with in those years after my divorce did a song and dance celebrating the domestic details of our "commune." The women who have been marching with me through the battles of the movement sang in celebration of our liberating struggles. A friend from my college years came all the way from Rome—and men I have loved, and people who have given me grants and scholarly refuge, and my publisher and agent and editors and the hairdresser who finally got me to cut my hair. And when the disco opened, some of us went down, and danced and danced and danced. How I do love to dance now—I was much too self-conscious when I was young. A friend who flew in from San Francisco, looking younger than he did when we met twenty years ago, swung me around my gyrating kids and their spouses, under the Palladium strobe lights. Everybody seemed to be having a ball at my sixty-fifth birthday party. What a celebration of life! Was it possible age was to celebrate?

After they sang Happy Birthday (too many candles to blow out in one breath), I tried to tell them how it really felt, this surprising new place that I found myself in at sixty-five. I felt awash with love, closer to them than I had ever felt before. I felt the strength of the long years of old-and-new bonds in that room, the pain and pleasure of our shared lives, the mistakes forgiven, the wrinkles unhidden. I tried to tell them about the surprising joy I felt, and I saw they felt it too, celebrating the reality of *"l'chaim,"* at sixty-five.

Part V

Care for Our Vital Age

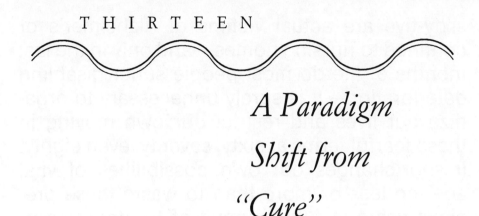

THIRTEEN

A Paradigm Shift from "Cure"

All along, I have resisted the intensifying campaign, in the media, by the burgeoning experts on age, and by what seem to be the vested interests they perhaps inadvertently serve, to define age as disease; I have refused to let myself, or other women or men after sixty-five, be defined as objects of "care," as at thirty-five I refused to let women be defined as sex objects. But I have come far enough in my own journey to know that we cannot, must not deny the reality, the actual possibility of the frailties, disabilities, chronic or sudden mishaps which age can entail. Nor indeed that it ends in death. Since, as we have seen, only 5 percent of Americans over sixty-five are actual victims of Alzheimer's or confined to nursing homes—and only in the last months of life do most people suffer disabling deterioration—it is surely unnecessary to organize our lives and restrict our own moving in these fearful terms at sixty, seventy, even eighty. It shortchanges our own possibilities of vital age, no less or more than to waste these precious years in futile pursuit of the fountain of youth.

We have to think in a new way about care. We have to break through the mystique of age that defines us only in terms of fearful, final deterioration and the disabilities we become victim to if we let ourselves be defined solely as objects of care. If I am right, there needs to be a different way of handling sickness, disability, and care in age.

Can our doctors treat our ills the same way they did when we were young? They'll surely overdose us if they do. Or not treat us at all for maladies they see simply as "the sickness of age." Is age a sickness, after all? Regardless of age, surely the point is to *cure* the disease . . . or is it? Does care itself, as well as love and work, have to be perceived in different terms in age? Can we also make new choices for care that neither deny the realities of age nor acquiesce in the often self-fulfilling prophecy of senile, isolated, infirm decline to death—a care that enables us to *keep choosing* the way we live our life, until the end? If we confront our own aging that ends in death as a part of life, how do we control our own care and sustain our power to choose? How do we live, how do we die, exercising our precious, mysterious, unique human being to the end as part of the ongoing stream of life?

The trouble is—as the demographics of age become more and more striking, and as more of us do live into our seventies, eighties, and nineties—the sheer size of the market we represent for the sellers of pharmaceuticals, and the practitioners of cardiac and cancer surgery and other costly high-technology medicine, is enormous—and enormously profitable. The expense of such care (most of it, we keep being reminded, for people over sixty-five) has become a huge drain on our personal and national resources. Further, it has engendered an intensifying war between the segments of our society that must, in one way or another, foot those bills. Health care plans, both public and private, proliferate. Costs of Medicaid and of Medicare, which is specifically designed for the elderly, seem staggering—as do the escalating doctor bills, hospital, nursing home, and pharmaceutical profits they mask. Yet that adamant assumption of age itself as sickness, debility, can keep us and our doctors from dealing concretely with symptoms of genuine illness that can be remedied in age as well as in youth, but may manifest themselves differently and require different treatment.

It is worth noting here that medical care prices are now rising at an annual rate of 8.2 percent, as cited in the House Committee on Aging report, *Emptying the Elderly's Pocketbooks* (1990). These huge increases "continue a seemingly never-ending upward spiral," the committee's chairman, California Congressman Edward R. Roybal, warned. "Since 1983, the medical care price index has grown over twice as fast as the overall consumer price index and over twice as fast as the average monthly Social Security payment. For America's elderly, the result is that out-of-pocket health care costs will reach one-fifth of elderly income in the early 1990s, much higher than the one-eighth level of the late 1970s."

Our own horror, fear, and denial of age is based on the spectacle of final months and years of costly, painful, vegetative decline when we can no longer control or take joy in life. There seems to be no way we can assure ourselves of care that we can control. But if we could sustain our own power to choose how we live and how we die, exercising our precious human autonomy, our personhood until the end, there has to be a way to bypass the indignities of the nursing home, the passive dehumanizing treatment by the medical experts and the institutions, whether they ignore our ills that could be cured or insist on curing us in ways that make life no

longer worth living even if they keep us technically alive. We have to confront our own fears
and confusion, and the traps awaiting us in our
obsession with—or denial of—the debilities of
age, in order to define for ourselves a care that
will free us from unnecessary preoccupation
with illness in age, in order to live its adventure.

I was told to bring in all the medicines I was
taking—pills, tablets, sprays, drops, prescription
and over-the-counter—in a brown paper bag. I
was surprised, slightly embarrassed, at how
many there were when I spilled them out on the
table. Before my blood pressure was taken, a
urine sample, my arm tourniqueted to draw
blood, I had to go over with a nurse not just
the usual medical history of my own and family
members' past diseases, but questions about
the structure of my every day—when I got up
and got dressed, who I saw, what I did, and who
I told my troubles to. Then I saw a doctor, and
before I left, even on that first visit, an appointment was made to come back to the same place
for a mammogram (without noticing it, I had let
two years go by since my last one), and also
an appointment to see a dermatologist about a
funny little non-pimple with a black spot on my
cheek which I had noticed for maybe a year now
and had even told my regular doctor about at
my last physical. "You get dark spots with age,"
he said.

I was putting myself, as a guinea pig, through

Robert Butler's Geriatric Management Clinic at Mount Sinai Hospital in New York. It was the only medical school in the country where geriatrics is a full-fledged medical department, on an equal level with internal medicine and surgery, so that all medical students, whatever specialty they are heading for, are required to do a regular rotation—not, as Butler explained, to "create another expensive specialty," but to give doctors of the future an educated awareness of the real dimensions of health and vitality in women and men over sixty. I knew that Butler's work on age implied a paradigm shift in care, a treatment of ills and ailments, chronic or acute, where the aim was not necessarily to cure the disease but to keep a person functioning at her/his own maximum potential, which defies not only the conventional stereotypes of age but also the patient's own acceptance of them.

I did not have a particularly high-tech experience at this major medical center, though the geriatric clinic had access to its facilities. It was all covered by Medicare. I was assured, in fact, that in this clinic, serving mainly low-income people from the surrounding community, which reached into Harlem, I would get a sense of a better model of care for older people than if I saw one of the doctors on their staff privately and was referred by him to separate specialists, rather than this "team" approach.

Dr. Jan Maby looked to me to be in her thirties,

in her last year as training fellow at the Mount Sinai outpatient geriatric clinic. She interviewed me at length before prescribing various tests and procedures, and again six weeks later after all the results were in. It interested me how methodically she went about getting the whole picture, head to toe, of how I functioned in all my different organ systems and in my daily life: all the medicines I'd been taking, how I was taking them, how they fit together, and the *changes* that may or may not have taken place in recent years.

Dr. Maby was less interested in the diseases of my childhood and youth than whether, in fact, I really needed to take all those pills for my asthma, and whether I used my inhalers efficiently (she demonstrated a way that more clearly got those whiffs inside the throat). And since my left eye was now functioning perfectly, after the lens implant seven years ago, why wasn't I considering getting that same use out of my non-functioning right eye? And was I aware of a heart murmur (which wasn't serious but required that I take antibiotics before any dental procedure)? She tested a hearing device that I should use when teaching or at theater and lectures—working well enough. And did I know that the angle of the bladder changes with age, did I experience "incontinence," involuntary leaks? Rather embarrassed, I admitted that "when I cough hard . . ." She said: "A gynecologist or a surgeon would recommend surgery because that's what they do. But stress incontinence can be handled with exercises," and she gave me an illustrated manual on Kegel exercises. She insisted that I have that mammogram, too long omitted, then and there, and also examined my breasts very carefully herself: "A mammogram does not take the place of really examining your own breasts and noticing any changes." She was interested in the fact that I went through menopause without taking estrogen, and also in my exercise regime of the last six years: forty-five minutes on the treadmill, four miles an hour, elevation of 10, 6:30–7:15 A.M., five or six days a week. She said technically I'm "at risk" of osteoporosis, being white, female, post-menopausal, and over fifty, but since I did exercise and didn't smoke, she prescribed calcium, not hormones. She ascertained that I had no signs at all of diabetes or arthritis though my cholesterol was borderline: 260, higher than it used to be, I should get it down to 200. But I'd already cut out red meat, cheese, and eggs, I told her. Discovering that I fly a lot, she warned about peanuts!

The little bump on my skin with the black spot turned out to be basal cell carcinoma (skin cancer, not serious if removed) and she sent me to get it excised. And, come to think of it, why hadn't the regular doctor pursued that little non-pimple? "You get dark spots with age" indeed!

"We got it all out," the dermatologist said, "but come back in six months, and wear sun screen number 30." Dr. Maby checked the pathologist's report on my second visit. This time she found my chest "clear as a bell," but didn't accept my fatalism about waking up in the middle of the night, those hours of not being able to get back to sleep. "Certain things people accept with age are not acceptable," she said, taking out a pad. But she was not writing any prescriptions for sleeping pills. She made a log for me to fill out: when I go to bed, when I fall asleep, when I wake up, for how long, the quantity and quality of my sleep every night for two weeks, and any unusual events. It was evidently not a good idea to just keep on lying there not sleeping, but I may not have been staying awake as long as I thought.

None of it was very dramatic. No arcane diseases were diagnosed or, in fact, on Dr. Maby's mind. But she was very interested in *changes,* if any—from bowel movements to headaches and muscle pains. I'd noticed no such changes; in fact, I suddenly realized, I'd been taking Bufferin less, actually "functioning" better than five, ten years ago. And I was particularly intrigued by the questions on the Psychosocial Screening Instrument (Multidimensional Functional Assessment Questionnaire) that had to do with my daily functioning and the texture and structure of my life:

"Do you have any friends/relatives whom you like very much? If so, who?"

"How many times this week have you been out of the house? Where did you go?"

"On the average, about how many hours do you watch TV?"

In addition to asking what I did on a typical day, from getting up to going to sleep, there were questions about "mood" that were pretty clearly aimed at identifying depression:

"Have you dropped many of your activities and interests?"

"Do you feel that your life is empty?"

"Do you prefer to stay at home, rather than going out and doing new things?"

"Do you feel pretty worthless the way you are now?"

The mini-mental state test was a very simple one, but not just a rote memory test; if I had lost the capacity for conceptual thought from brain tumor or Alzheimer's, I wouldn't have been able to do it. My "typical day," of course—writing, meetings, lectures, lunches and dinners with friends, treadmill and sauna, walks and talk— had plenty, still, of those complex structures and ties that the nurse and a social worker (both part of the mini-team that was unique in the "management" of the older person "as a whole" under Butler's tutelage) seemed to know were as important as vitamins for a vital age. They also ascertained that I had had no falls in the past six months, and that my medical problems did not limit my ability to care for myself.

I was given a once-in-a-lifetime pneumonia shot, which I didn't even know existed, as well as flu shots, and they very carefully explained to me how to make a living will, gave me the legal "health proxy form" which under a new law in New York "allows you to appoint someone you trust to decide about treatment if you lose the ability to decide for yourself." I appointed Emily, my daughter the doctor, as my "health care agent" "to make treatment decisions after doctors decide that you are not able to make health care decisions for yourself . . . in accord with your wishes and interests. If your health care agent is not aware of your wishes about artificial nutrition and hydration (feeding tubes), he or she will not be able to make decisions about these measures . . . often used to continue the life of patients who are in a permanent coma."

I wrote on this form about treatment I did not desire and/or those treatments I wanted to make sure I received. For example, "If I become terminally ill, I do/don't want to receive the following treatment. . . . If I am in a coma with no hope of recovery, then I do/don't want. . . . If I have brain damage that makes me unable to recognize people or speak, and there is no hope that my condition will improve, I do/don't want . . . artificial respiration . . . nourishment by feeding tube . . . cardio-pulmonary resuscitation . . . antipsychotic medication . . . electric shock therapy . . . antibiotics . . . psychosurgery . . . dialysis transplantation . . . blood transfusions, etc." But "pain prevention," that I did want.

I learned that I was in very good shape "for my age." Of course, I have that lens implant, and use those little things in my ears when I remember to, but I certainly seemed to be "functioning" at high energy. Still, I realized I would have been much better off if I had had such a whole-person scrutiny some years ago. I had been going piecemeal to different "specialists," and once I was almost put on treatment for high blood pressure and serious heart arrhythmia until I happened to ask the doctor if any of my asthma medicines could have that effect. It turned out the new medication the allergist had given me might indeed have had such an effect, which he promised he would evaluate on my next visit. On my own, I simply stopped taking that medicine. The next visit, my blood pressure was 120/80 and the arrhythmia had almost completely subsided.

Dr. Maby told me:

One of the worst problems when you're older is to have a lot of different doctors, a lot of different medications—the big problem is the medications themselves, their side effects. We try to cut down on the number of doctors and medications. Sometime we find older patients are getting medications because it's easier to prescribe them than to do a workup and find out what's really wrong. The doctors don't want to spend the time, so they treat dizziness with an anti-dizziness pill. A lot of problems in age are caused by all those medications because patients doctor-shop, and they don't like to pay doctors if they don't give them prescriptions to cure the disease. They and the doctors both look at being old as a disease.

Robert Butler, whose dismay with the way this country, including its physicians, treats older people led to his Pulitzer Prizewinning book *Why Survive?*, was most emphatically not in favor of creating an expensive new medical specialty of geriatrics, which might further ghettoize people over sixty. Rather, he insisted that every primary care and family doctor and specialty physician had an "absolute responsibility to understand the nature and the conditions associated with age." His Annenberg Institute and Department of Geriatrics at Mount Sinai teaches students from the beginning of medical school through their residencies to see older people as *people,* not only through their contact with patients suffering diseases of age (from osteoporosis, arthritis, and diabetes to Alzheimer's) but by regular contact with *healthy* older persons tak-

739

ing classes and seminars (theology, poetry, modern dance) at the nearby 92nd Street Y. Butler told me:

What they get out of it is to see older people as individuals, not crocks, and to see disease and disability in age as often *remediable* if not reversible. Just because they're old, you don't write them off as untreatable. Our overall principle is how to maintain the person's functioning, and restart it if it's been lost. When you take the functioning of older persons seriously, you can improve their quality of life from even modest changes as opposed to dramatic high-tech "cures."

There are a lot of low-tech powerful instruments of change like widow-to-widow groups —no money or space for it in the hospital, they insist, though it would cost much less than the high-tech new machines and fourth-generation drugs. But there's no insurance or Medicare category for group therapy, music therapy, any of these life-enhancing measures. We keep lists and refer our patients to those self-help groups I'm not allowed to run here. I even put myself at risk with my colleagues by insisting on a psychologist and social worker as well as doctors on the team. The most insuperable problem is financial, to get the older patient even seen; as it stands now, doctors don't want to see Medicare-Medicaid patients —people over sixty-five—because they get paid less for some procedures. There should be a single standard of medical practice, and it should be insured nationally.

Just as I had discovered a gerontological underground, I found an underground of doctors and health workers breaking through the mystique of age-as-disease. In effect, they are challenging not only the denial of the real dynamics of aging and its personhood but the total medical model governing hospitals and nursing homes, medical schools and government agencies in their dealings with older people. Nearly twenty years ago Mark Williams, as a young doctor rather improbably choosing to work with older patients in his advanced training at the University of Rochester, spelled out the radical challenge in a groundbreaking article in the *New England Journal of Medicine,* attacking "illness as the focus of geriatric medicine." He asked: "How critical is it to determine precisely the nature of the underlying disease when one is helping an elderly person cope with illness?" While the doctor's traditional quest "to define the disease responsible for a patient's distress is important when the disease is acute or potentially remediable," the fact is that most older patients aren't suffering from such "acute" diseases but chronic conditions such as heart failure or arthritis. The "remediable conditions" most often found by experienced internists and geriatricians in elderly patients are "drug toxicities and abuse of physical restraints" caused by the medical treatment itself.[1]

A "disease-specific focus," Williams insisted, deemphasizes what should be the dominant issue in older people's care, "the maximization of the patient's productivity, creativity, well-being, and happiness. This goal of improving patient function and satisfaction to the utmost is usually achieved without curing the underlying disease." He pointed out that accurate disease diagnosis and prognosis, which generally involves estimating the remaining life span, facilitates treatment decisions that are "especially toxic or risky . . . usually reserved for circumstances in which longevity is immediately threatened. Small reductions in life expectancy are a less important concern in the management of chronic disease and become nearly irrelevant in the elderly."

For instance, "approximately three-fourths of us will suffer low back pain . . . at least 25 percent of people who have serious impairment due to low back pain are over age 65. Particularly in the elderly, backache can compromise the ability to care for oneself (to dress and maintain personal hygiene), to move about and to retrieve objects; the result can be confinement, as well as the loss of independence in functioning." But despite the prevalence of low back pain, "physicians can only rarely identify a specific underlying disease." The management of low back pain involves exercise and environmental adjustments tailored to the individual patient. "Such advice is aimed at the reduction of pain and its impact on the patient's function. The definition of underlying disease is rarely accomplished, and if it is, it is a fact that many features of backache depend more on psychosocial influences than on disease."

On the other hand, Williams continued, "the ability to continue living independently is a critical issue for all elderly persons. Loss of this ability is a serious illness, which, in this country, often leads to institutionalization. Why should an elderly person with reasonably well-preserved visceral, mental, and musculo-skeletal function be afflicted with the illness of loss of independence?"

Bluntly, over and over again, Williams kept saying that the traditional medical model—the doctor's focus on *diagnosing and curing the disease*—was often beside the point in caring for older people. Older patients may be living with several chronic diseases, many of which are irreversible. In one study, three groups of women—white, well educated, relatively affluent—were living with chronic diseases such as hypertension, diabetes, and arthritis. What differentiated the women put in nursing homes from those living independently was not severity of disease but functioning dexterity. They were found to differ dramatically in their ability to perform simple manual tasks: opening a door, writing a sentence, stacking checkers. Defining their specific diseases might be less complicated than dealing with their concrete problems of hand function but, for such older people, it's that *enabling* of function that "constitutes healing."

When Dr. Williams and I met at the Salzburg Seminar, trying to look at age in terms of "health and productivity," he formulated two essential components of the paradigm shift from curing disease to *improving function* in older people:

1. Under optimal circumstances, serious disability or loss of function with age is not apparent until shortly before death.

Normal aging in the absence of disease is a remarkably benign process. . . . Erosion [of organ system reserves and homeostatic controls] is evident only during periods of maximal exertion or stress. [It] will eventually reach a critical point (usually in very advanced age) such that relatively minimal insults cannot be overcome, resulting in the person's death in a relatively short time. Consequently, any morbidity apparent to the person is compressed into the last period of life.[2]

2. Real aging changes in body tissues have to be taken into account if older persons are not to

be under- or overtreated. For instance, certain drug components remain in the bodies of older persons for a much longer time than they do in younger persons. But since "advancing age results in increasing differentiation and biologic uniqueness," prescriptions cannot be based on age criteria alone.

Doctors may also misinterpret symptoms of older persons if they examine them perfunctorily with measures based on youth. For instance, jaundice, a sign of hepatitis in young people, usually results from gallbladder disease or malignancy in an older person. Paradoxically, the equation of age with disease also results in the underreporting of illness and underutilization of health care services by older people. As Williams put it: "The belief that old age is inextricably linked with disability and morbidity . . . reduces the desire for health care since the manifestations of disease may be dismissed . . . 'What do you expect at my age?' " Since many older persons continue functioning with at least one chronic illness, symptoms of one condition may exacerbate or mask symptoms of another: angina may be absent or less dramatic in an older person with heart disease; an acutely ill older person may merely show confusion, unsteady gait, falls, or urinary incontinence, which are dismissed as signs of expected senility.

Williams spelled out the basic paradigm shift in ordering diagnostic procedures and prescribing drugs for older persons: "If the premise of the physician-patient relationship in the setting of chronic illness is to maximize productivity, creativity, well-being and happiness, the quest for the specific pathologic process becomes irrelevant. . . . The symptoms of many incurable chronic conditions can be successfully managed without modifying the disease process underlying those symptoms." He suggested prescribing drugs for older persons only with "an absolute indication and unequivocal necessity for treatment," "discontinuation of all unnecessary drugs," "simplifications to reduce the likelihood of drug interaction," and measures ensuring that "the older person know of the potential side effects of the medication."[3]

Nearly twenty years later, Williams today at Chapel Hill is still finding it necessary to warn doctors that functional assessment, not specific disease, has to be the focus of care for older persons:

An older person's ability to manage everyday routines cannot be determined confidently from the names of the diseases he or she may have or from the length of the problem list. For example, an octogenarian with systolic hypertension, congestive heart failure, maturity-onset diabetes, severe osteoarthritis and frequent urinary tract infections . . . might be an active political leader, a vigorous community volunteer or a severely disabled resident of a skilled nursing facility. [Yet] functional status measurement is not routinely included in clinical practice or in medical education. . . . Defining pathologic entities is often less complicated and more highly reimbursed than addressing function and reducing disability, but the latter constitutes healing, the ultimate goal of quality care.[4]

But it is not only the mystique of age-as-disease that deters doctors from the *personal attention* to the older patient's functioning that good care in age involves. When Williams did a survey of what practicing physicians in North Carolina rated as their most challenging geriatric concerns, the only frequently mentioned new topics were financial: "the failure of Medicare to pay the full amount of normal fee for office visits, creating a disincentive for seeing elderly patients at all"; and "the amount of time it takes to deal with elderly patients with multiple interacting problems and medicines faced with the paltry and regulation-intensive reimbursement."[5]

Unfortunately, the way doctors collect the most—from private health insurance, from Medicare—is by "curing" disease, or, rather, tests to diagnose a specific disease. A new version of the old-fashioned family doctor, trained to treat the whole person, is what is needed; but specialists prescribing new, esoteric, high-tech procedures and pharmaceutical cures for exotic diseases and terminal illnesses—or disabilities that can be lived with but can't be cured, or where the cure is more disabling than the condition—know where the money is. And that is what far too many older people get as depersonalized, passive objects of "care," instead of whatever it takes to keep them functioning actively in the community, in charge of their own lives, doing the things that give them pleasure, partaking of the fountain of age.

In 1990, the medical establishment began to come to grips with the paradigm shift involved in promoting *vital function* for people over fifty. There was, and is, continued outcry over the high proportion of medical resources, the excessive hospital dollars and technology used in treating elders' diseases (most of it in the last months of life)—that expensive, high-tech intensive care, chemotherapy and radiation which specialists prescribe to diagnose and "cure" incurable, terminal cancer and other diseases, extending life, and pain, just a few more days or months. But the Institute of Medicine of the National Academy of Science has at long last set up a committee on Health Promotion and Disability Prevention for the Second Fifty. Its report, issued in 1990 under the title *The Second Fifty*

Years, was written by a panel of "specialists" and thus did not fully meet the aim of its chairman, to go beyond the medical model to deal with the unprecedented possibilities of vital life for older people today. But it abjured doctors and health professionals to break through their own equation of age-as-disease. Dr. Robert Berg, Professor and Chairman of the Department of Preventive, Family, and Rehabilitation Medicine at Strong Memorial Hospital in Rochester, New York, had spent most of his own adult life trying to teach interns and residents that "what matters to the person is function, not the disease. . . . Disease is important only because it interferes with function—with people over 50, it is even more important for doctors to focus on function and not disease." As the groundbreaking report was introduced,

> For a layman to observe a halting step or nearsighted squint and say the person is "just getting old" reflects our culture's pessimistic attitude toward aging. When a health professional dismisses such impairments as "merely aging," he or she may be closing the door on counselling and treatment that could spare an elderly person years of discomfort, isolation, or disability.
>
> Our policies and practices—indeed, our most fundamental attitudes—relating to care of the elderly must undergo a significant shift

from the *pessimistic* to the *realistic.* When an older person begins to experience difficulty, there are a host of measures available to prevent problems from becoming disabilities— and to prevent disabilities from causing dependence and fear.[6]

Doctors and nurses must go beyond medicine's two traditional goals: "to cure disease and to prevent disease." Their goal now has to be to "preserve and improve the quality of life for the older person." Health professionals must shift their focus "from the way an organ or cell functions to the way a person functions—to view the [older] patient as a total human being, living in a home and participating in society." Out of thirteen risk factors and causes of disability which the panel of distinguished doctors decided to study, only the last was "infectious diseases." The others: misuse of medications, social isolation, physical inactivity, osteoporosis, falls, sensory loss, depression, oral health, screening for cancer, nutrition, smoking, high blood pressure. The report spelled out and disavowed the assumptions that growing old necessarily meant "frailty, sickness and a loss of vitality," that "older individuals were a burden to the state, their families, or even to themselves." It affirmed the concept of "quality-of-life years." ("Living is not the goal but living well," it quoted Seneca. "The wise man therefore lives as long as he should, not as long as he can.") Noting that 30 percent of Medicare costs are for care in the last year of life, it asked: "Should we continue to devote these resources to the provision of acute care, or should we allocate more of them to prolong independent functioning in a community?" (Unfortunately, the report did not stress that Medicare reimburses acute care and prohibits payment for preventive services.)

I interviewed Dr. Berg in his hospital office in Rochester and again over oysters at Grand Central Station, noting his "us" not "them" approach to vital age. He told me he was devising new forms of exercise for himself, well into that "second fifty." Prevented from the beloved squash of his youth by knee problems, he was looking for ways to make brisk walking less boring "with a variety of people to walk with" and "new games to play so my bones won't thin." He told me:

The real measure should be how many quality-of-life years or months you get from whatever treatment. In the second fifty, the drug or operation or chemotherapy cure of the disease may give you less quality of life than the original condition. There are doctors who keep operating on cancer of the bowel; there's a point at which you cause more misery than you help. Most people diagnosed with cancer have months, years to live, if they don't stop being active, just keep on doing whatever they do that gives them pleasure. Instead, most doctors want to operate, if there's something that can be done technically, do it. Listen to the patient—don't operate, operate, operate; keep her as fit and able to function as you can, but not so many operations, new medications that are worse than the disease. Doctors don't tell women how sick they will get from chemotherapy after breast cancer, so they can make realistic choices.

Doctors like to think of themselves as gods who cure. It was hard to get them to think about what can be done to prevent or ameliorate the burden of disability, instead of finding fancy ways to diagnose new diseases with exotic new high-tech instruments, or keeping patients alive a few months longer with terminal illness.

Data analyzed in *The Second Fifty Years* indicate that 42 percent of strokes in older men and 70 percent of strokes in older women are directly attributable to hypertension; increased blood pressure levels are the single greatest risk for heart attack and stroke in persons over fifty, accounting for most of the disability in age as well as deaths.[7] While "the benefit attributed to the [medication] treatment of high blood pressure increases with age," Dr. Berg's report pointed out, the adverse side effects of anti-hypertensive drugs in the elderly have not been sufficiently studied, much less their effect on quality of life: physical, intellectual, and sexual functioning, memory, social interaction. As for "non-pharmacologic therapy"—weight loss, salt restriction, aerobic exercise, relaxation therapy—"unfortunately, the only available studies of the efficacy of those measures have been conducted on young to middle-aged patients."[8] Dr. Berg said: "We need more research studies of what those drugs actually do to older people, compared to treatments like exercise and diet and meditation that aren't even prescribed for people in their seventies and eighties."

Though arthritis is the most common disability among older people, Dr. Berg bemoaned the fact that when an older person tells the doctor "it hurts" when she walks, the doctor says, "Then don't do it, don't walk," instead of giving exercises that would strengthen her muscles so it wouldn't hurt so much. "Doctors hardly ever prescribe exercise for older persons. They should ask at every visit, 'What are you doing for exercise?' If she says, 'Oh, doctor, I'm getting too old for that,' you tell her, 'But you don't necessarily have to do the same exercises as when you were younger.' "

Perhaps the most important finding was that all physical symptoms, including symptoms of

Alzheimer's, found in older persons "in the absence of detectable disease" may indicate "masked depression" or "somatic equivalents" of depression, even without "depressed mood." The report stated bluntly: "Recent advances have made depression an eminently treatable disorder; yet only a minority of elderly depressed persons are receiving adequate treatment. . . . Depression is seriously under-diagnosed and often mis-diagnosed. Vast resources are expended in fruitless diagnostic searches, in medical treatment of somatic symptoms without a detectable basis and in neglect of the underlying, treatable psychiatric disorder."[9]

The main "risk factors" for depression in older people are, in fact, not medical at all, or even "psychiatric" in the pathological sense. Losses of spouse, friends, and extended family, geographic isolation, unplanned retirement, lack of confiding relationships—all the conditions which "decrease social interaction" may cause "major depressive illness" unless "buffered" by new forms of social support, new roles, and activity.

Social disapproval constraining older people's sexuality—and medications widely used for high blood pressure and for the treatment of depression itself which diminish sexuality—are also significant risk factors for depression. Doctors were warned to watch out for sleep difficulties in older people, since early morning waking or frequent interruptions in sleep may be signs of depression. Above all, the report insisted that older people's depression can be treated, deploring the fact that doctors and families and the patients themselves "all too often may see the older person's deteriorating condition as an irreversible aspect of normal aging."

A survey in North Carolina cited in the report revealed that no more than 8 percent of such mentally impaired persons were receiving any professional mental health services, even though 20 percent of them were getting psychotropic medication from their doctors. A survey of an older Hispanic population showed that not a single person out of seventy-five suffering from major depression had ever received any professional mental health care. Also cited was a RAND Corporation study of eleven thousand patients suffering from eight conditions common in age: chronic angina, arthritis, back problems, coronary artery disease, diabetes, high blood pressure, gastrointestinal and lung problems, and depression. The disabling effects of depression on such routine activities as bathing, climbing stairs, dressing, socializing with friends, walking, and working were "comparable to those of a serious heart condition and greater than most of the seven other medical conditions. Only arthritis was judged to be more painful, and only serious heart conditions resulted in more days in bed." [10]

The widespread depression among older people, undiagnosed or diagnosed only in terms of those physical conditions it exacerbates, evidently has more to do than anyone realizes with the fact that older people, though only 12 percent of the population, utilize 30 percent of medical resources. The depression of older people, the end result of our own and our society's fear of age, leads to very large hidden costs arising from "expensive and often fruitless diagnostic searches for physical illness; the often risky medical treatment of somatic symptoms without a physical basis; and inadequate or delayed treatment of depression." [11]

But despite the growing media hype and manipulation of public indignation at "greedy geezers" using up too much of the burgeoning national health care costs, the health care establishment, for the most part, continues to treat the "diseases" of aging in terms of the old medical model of "cure," and aging itself as "disease," without regard for the costly burden of unnecessary depression and disability. The specialists on Dr. Berg's panel still considered treatment of depression mainly in terms of drugs: pharmacotherapy. While the panel reported that "psychosocial" therapies for depression in older people are just as effective—and safer, without the disabling side effects of the drugs—they simply concluded that psychotherapy is too expensive for most older people, not often offered by psychiatrists, and not reimbursable when delivered by non-physicians. Finally, the panel noted, almost as an afterthought, that an "innovative approach" to "change negative attitudes about aging and the aged" warranted "further research."[12]

The essence of the paradigm shift of care in age is, of course, not medical at all. It has to do with maximizing your own autonomy in your everyday life and in the control of your care. It is holistic, for real. And yet it is rigorously scientific in terms of medical cause and effect; all the research on the effect of purpose and intimacy, role loss and social support, activity, rage, and despair on the immune system is relevant. But the real-life exercise of this paradigm shift is deceptively simple; and, though it doesn't necessarily do away with the need for doctor and hospitals, it could do away with much of the need for costly and ultimately life-impairing medication and high-tech surgical procedures.

I first experienced the paradigm shift at the Pritikin Longevity Center in Miami Beach in December 1988. I had heard of their new rigorous approach to heart disease, diabetes, arthritis, and other killers of age, of their claim to halt and even reverse high blood pressure and cholesterol and blockage of arteries before or after bypass operations preventing heart attack and stroke. I had just been told that my cholesterol and blood pressure were "borderline—nothing to worry about," but instead of my decade-long stalemate of trying in vain to lose ten pounds, I seemed to have gained ten pounds. Research, sure, but, let's admit it, I went to Pritikin to dip into the physical fountain of age for myself. And oddly, I was a little sheepish about doing such a thing for basically preventive reasons, since I never have been a hypochondriac and used to ignore even an asthma attack until I needed the emergency room.

The first people I encountered in the unpretentious lobby of the small Hotel Flamingo were three men I knew personally, one of whom had already had a heart bypass and was there mainly to give moral support to his friend, on a life-and-death ultimatum from his doctor to lose 100 pounds. Most of the men I met at Pritikin came only *after* heart attacks or as a last resort before second bypasses or permanent invalidism from intractable worsening chronic disease. The women were there, in effect, to take new charge of their own aging, having stood by helplessly as their husbands' health deteriorated.

In 1957, when my father was first diagnosed as having coronary insufficiency, with a cholesterol level approaching 300, he was given medical advice common at the time: cut out all activity, take medications and stick to the "Good American Diet" of eggs every morning and steak every night.

He only got worse, so he began his pioneering research into the relationship of diet to heart disease. Within a short time, he lowered his cholesterol to 120, started running 25 miles a week, and led a vigorous, happy 12-hour-a-day work schedule until his death from complications in the course of drug treatment for leukemia in February 1985. . . . Though diagnosed with coronary heart disease 28 years earlier, his autopsy revealed that all his coronary arteries were wide open, showing a complete absence of cholesterol and fatty deposits, as reported by the *New England Journal of Medicine* in July 1985.

That account by Nathan Pritikin's son Robert was handed to all who entered the Pritikin program in Miami or Santa Monica. In my several visits to Pritikin in Miami in the eighties, I heard many more dramatic personal stories about reversal or amelioration of heart disease, crippling arthritis and late-onset diabetes, prevention of bypass surgery, and people taking new, active charge of their own lives after doctors had given them up in their fifties, sixties, seventies, even their eighties. Such evidence, of course, was only "anecdotal." Pritikin is austere and expensive, neither glitzy health spa nor New Age mystical shrine; the effectiveness of its simple regimes has been confirmed now by several independent research studies. But the important implication for me was that a paradigm shift from the passive medical model of "care" of older people to active control of their own aging actually, observably worked. Nathan Pritikin himself was not a doctor, though the programs he designed were now supervised by doctors. And the effects observed among the thirty thousand women and men who have attended the Pritikin centers since 1976 were recently confirmed in research reported by the American Medical Association.

During the first two weeks I spent at the center in Miami, the forty-odd men and women there ranged in age from twenty-seven to eighty-five, though most were over fifty. After a thorough medical examination by the director, Dr. David Lehr—including intensive blood workup and a stress test—I learned that my cholesterol and blood pressure were too high, that I had a heart murmur and arrhythmia probably exacerbated by asthma medication, but that I handled strenuous exercise on the stress test without any trouble. He figured out that that strange surge in my weight had begun three months after I stopped jogging the previous year, when I sprained my ankle. Even though I'd spent the same amount of time swimming (the breast stroke, sixty-six laps), he pointed out that this was not aerobic, and the resulting shift in my metabolism meant I would now gain weight on the same diet on which I had stabilized before. I was put on a diet of 800 calories a day, and started on four daily thirty-minute intervals of aerobic exercise. Over the first few days I built up to forty-five minutes. The basic exercise period on the treadmill was closely monitored, with frequent heart-rate checks. I could fill the four periods with any combination of treadmill, exercise bicycle, brisk heart-rate walks on the beach, pool and gym aerobic classes. The exercise periods were interspersed with lectures which spelled out in detail the causes and effects of high blood pressure and cholesterol, the disabling dynamic of diabetes and arthritis, and their specific relationship to diet and exercise.

Members of the Pritikin staff diagrammed what precisely happens when you have a heart attack. They explained precisely how exercise reduces the risk of a heart attack, decreases appetite, increases bone strength, slows or prevents development of osteoporosis and depression. They cautioned about setting "realistic goals." "If you walk twenty miles a week, you decrease the risk of a heart attack six times—an hour a day, four to six times a week." They warned us to "prepare for temporary slips," and showed us how to make up for them instead of giving up in guilt. Pragmatically, they advised, "*Plan* to exercise every single day so you can take a day off if you need to without guilt." And in a session on "Longevity: Playing the Odds," they questioned the simple goal of "living longer." "It could be a terrible ordeal for people to live this long, not being well, not living well. This comprises the bulk of the older people visiting doctors in America today. You can control a large part of this, you can change your lives, in your sixties, your seventies, even in your eighties, and can go on differently for twenty years."

The possible choices and "exchanges" to keep your diet within the limits prescribed were spelled out in detail, and cooking classes given on ways to eliminate the offending fats—butter, eggs, and cheese. Soup breaks in mid-morning and afternoon carried out their prescription of a number of small meals rather than one or two big ones. A "Shopping and Label Reading" workshop, with field work at the supermarket, illuminated the difference between "low-fat junk food" even at the health store and true 1 percent low-fat milk.

The drawing of our blood and taking of our vital signs each day was part of a demystification process. We learned what the measurements meant, what was dangerous (not just "well, at your age . . .") and what was not. Nobody was coddled. Pritikin was serious, stark, sometimes single-minded. But I lost those onerous ten pounds in the two weeks there. Back home, following Dr. David Lehr's recommendations "more or less" ("If you stick to 1,200 calories, you can have one drink; if you go over, make it up the next day. Do forty to forty-five minutes at your heart rate on the treadmill six days a week, you'll keep on losing"), I lost another seventeen pounds over the year. But the discipline was hard to keep up, traveling as much as I do. Gradually, I put half of it back on, but only half. And, perhaps not coincidentally, my asthma improved enormously, my blood pressure and cholesterol stayed down.

Like Weight Watchers, or any other mutual support group, we reinforced each other in our routines, those two weeks at Pritikin. It was harder, of course, once we went home. But the married ones had been encouraged to bring their spouses (without extra cost), who got the hang of the diet and the importance of the exercise. And the thrust to "take more control" seemed to lead to changes not only in diet and exercise but in lifestyle. In fact, they introduced the concept "lifestyle checkup." David Lehr had been a conventional internist and cardiologist with a big Miami practice when he was asked to go out to California to review the Pritikin program in 1977. He studied the program several months, then followed up twenty participants who had serious heart disease when he originally examined them. He told me:

I saw people getting better I wouldn't have been able to do anything about in my own practice. I didn't know why, but they were unquestionably getting better. A different premise was involved. The premise we all used to accept is, If you get to be sixty, seventy, everybody's got you programmed to disappear into the sunset, your mental powers will disappear, your physical powers, everybody writes you off. Yet now we know from research at Tufts on people fifty-eight to seventy-two that muscle mass can actually be increased 200 percent with exercise, even bone mass. You don't necessarily have to worry about dying until you're ninety; you can improve your muscle mass, your bone mass, your ability to do things; you can clean up your arteries; you can even improve your mental powers. You can improve your immune system's response, fighting cancer, with exercise and diet and purposeful activity.

And, of course, at Pritikin, if nothing else, exercise and diet became purposeful activities, under conscious control. Lehr went on:

In my traditional practice, people would slump in, they'd go through tests, I'd have them take a little pill, they'd slump out. That's what medicine has become; we treat symptoms with pills and more and more complex technology. When I came back and started talking to the doctors at the hospital here, that regression of cardiac disease and diabetes is possible, that arteries can be cleaned up, they thought I was crazy. So I continued my regular practice at the hospital but started the Pritikin program here. I hospitalize my patients now maybe 50 percent less than I did before.

I'm not sure it's just a question of longevity. It's as if they leave here physiologically younger, in spirit, in body, in risk factors. Not that we deny age. We say age is not a limiting factor of anything you really want to do. You can take control of it—no matter when you start, you can do more.

The first person I knew who underwent the Pritikin shift was my friend Joe Machlis, musicologist, composer, and writer. He started having angina and heart trouble in his early seventies, when bypasses were becoming hot. After his first stay at Pritikin, he began a daily regimen of an hour's swim and several miles' walk, and cooked his own Pritikin supper before going out on his nightly round of concert and opera, taking only fruit salad at dinner. After he was officially retired at Queens College, he started teaching at Juilliard, wrote the libretto of a new opera, and in addition to a new edition of his classic *Joy of Music,* started, in his eighties, writing novels. At eighty-one, angina finally began to impede his activity, but past the age when the operation is usually performed he had a successful triple bypass. The doctors agreed to do it because they said he was physically in his fifties! I went to see him in the hospital, and it was indeed a traumatic experience for him. But four years later, he celebrated his eighty-fifth birthday at a gala party, given by the publisher of his latest novel and yet another edition of *The Joy of Music.* Every August he went back down to Pritikin to gird himself for the next year's project.

I found that the diet and exercise were the easiest things to get under control at Pritikin, but the dramatic effects of that on your health might not last after you leave the program, unless you made more basic changes in your lifestyle. In the individual counseling, as well as the lectures between the monitored exercise sessions and medical exams, the point was made clear enough, based and backed up by medical research but not phrased in medical jargon. "Diet and exercise are *not* enough. If you don't change your lifestyle, change your life, it won't work." Dr. Robert Bauer, sixty-seven, had practiced internal medicine, cardiology, for over thirty years. He told me:

When we first started, we were dealing with people who were desperately ill. We saw people get better at various stages of these diseases after they started treating their body differently. Some doctors would still say, why even fool around with people over seventy, it's not worth it, you're not going to be able to change anything. Statistically I can't give you data to confirm the fact that they live longer, but they're getting more life out of their years. They seem to be more active, more alert, those with arthritis find the pain more tolerable, the disease process even if still there is ameliorated so they can enjoy life. In my previous thirty years, I was just keeping people alive to go downhill, keeping them alive to go to the nursing home and drain the whole family's resources, and yet we weren't supposed to let them die. Now we're not making people younger but we're getting them back on their feet to live a vital, different life.

It is important to realize that what I saw at Pritikin was not some magic guru New Age "cure" of heart disease, diabetes, arthritis, or medical "fountain of youth." It was merely an example of the paradigm shift in health care implied by the premises that age itself is not disease; that the older person, body and soul, becomes more and more her/himself *as a whole,* unique and integrated, and can't be treated either in terms of youth or of separate mechanical parts; that autonomy and control—of one's body, one's life, one's days—is biologically as well as metaphysically the key to the fountain of age.

In all of this, it seems to me now that the people of America are ahead of their doctors. Medical research has, of course, now shown that diet and exercise can indeed lower blood pressure and cholesterol, that the heart attacks and strokes which killed our fathers before sixty could be avoided. The great increase in conscious control of our bodies, our own aging, in the last ten to fifteen years is starkly visible in the numbers of people of all ages jogging, speedwalking, and taking up tennis or aerobics classes. Not only are there more people exercising, but the sight of a seventy-year-old woman jogging is no longer shocking. "Yo, Grandma!" some kid would yell at me when I went jogging in Central Park ten years ago. It bothered me. But not now. And the new diet consciousness has got even junk food processors advertising "no-fat," "low-fat," "cholesterol-free," the best restaurants as well as McDonald's competing with more and more gourmet fish, vegetable, and pasta dishes. The phenomenal decrease in heart disease in America in the last decade and a half, after that geometric increase of the previous half century, is attributed by every knowledgeable doctor to "lifestyle changes," not just changes in medical practice. But the paradigm shift implied is not necessarily happening in their own practices. The medical establishment evidently still prefers to "cure" heart disease with a bypass rather than prevent it.

Mark Williams trains his own medical students

at Chapel Hill differently now. He speculated why the medical profession as a whole has not yet shifted toward the new treatment of age implied by the research:

There has to be a clear reason why an older person goes to see a doctor, a particular problem. The doctor has been trained to deal with that in a very technical, mechanical manner, classification of the disease, abnormalities, symptoms, not how to size this unique person up so he can deal with his life. Even though lip service is now paid to holistic principles, the doctor feels more comfortable writing a prescription, ordering a diagnostic test, sticking to the technical aspects of medicine rather than intervening to help the person in his life. It's a knee-jerk reaction; it's easier to order an X-ray, a painkiller, rather than try to understand why the person is coming in at that moment and to change what's causing the problem. The irony is that it doesn't require more time to do that, it takes less time than these tests, because you're getting to the heart of the matter.

Williams found a "delicious irony" that cardiology research was finally "trickling into quality-of-life measures because they simply can't find statistical differences of outcome in morbidity and mortality" from their bypasses and other high-tech operations. It appalled him that in one year, at the end of the 1980s, 130,000 angioplasty procedures were done, increasing at a geometric rate the following year though it was "a totally unproven procedure." Huge amounts of money were being spent "fiddling at the margins," Williams pointed out, referring to many of the most expensive high-tech procedures.

A person having a first heart attack today has a 90 percent chance of living another five years. Everything we do, including bypass, angioplasty, and aggressive reduction of cholesterol, will only increase that chance to 92 percent. If you look at ten years, your chances are only a little less, but the most intensive surgical intervention will only increase those chances 2 percent. There is almost no data documenting the well-observed benefits of effective psychological treatment of depression, whereas thousands of patients have been randomized and followed after cardiac surgery though it has long been clear that the magnitude of the effect is very small, marginal.

When he took his own medical students on "geriaction" rounds, Williams said, he wanted no advance report as to what "disease" that older man or woman had. As he asked his patients questions, he thought out loud to the students everything he saw and heard, finding out who they were through his own observations—Sherlock Holmes at the bedside. Williams's "geriaction" is "a creative, active process—if I have been successful in seeing the truth of the older person and communicating back to him what he can do about it, he can take action to change the situation that has caused the problem. A lot of depressive symptoms can be very effectively treated by just having a sympathetic listener deal with what he hears in an effective way—not to jump to electric shock treatment or psychotropic drugs."

But Pritikin is expensive, and takes too much discipline to follow long without continual costly "refreshers." And Medicare will pay for bypass surgery but not, at this moment, for "geriaction" treatment of older persons in terms not of disease but of action needed to enable them to keep functioning and evolving in vital life, not even diet and exercise instructions, much less intangible lifestyle or "behavior therapy." The doctors collecting their fees in conventional private or group practice, HMO- or insurance-geared, increasingly refuse to take Medicare patients, or to allot personal quality time to give even paying older men or women enough "confidant" listening to spot the depression which apes and exacerbates every disease in age.

· · ·

In the many years of my search for the fountain of age, I have tracked the reverberations of a covert, accelerating war over the evidence accumulating in clinical research of a basic link between a person's own control of his or her life, the psychological supports of that control, and his or her immune system's resistance to disease or decline. This evidence seems to be a basic challenge to the medical model, which treats age itself as disease. At the very least, it implies a truly different mode of control over one's own aging and that paradigm shift in medical care which doctors now resist, and which the powerful medical establishment and the pharmaceutical companies may have good reason to resist. Studies have shown that factors such as isolation, lack of intimate companions, or malnutrition—found in surprising numbers of affluent as well as poor older people and often linked to depression—account for a much greater share of the decline in the immune systems of older people than is generally recognized.

Surveys in the decade 1975–85 found that anywhere from 15 percent to 50 percent of Americans over the age of sixty-five consume too few calories, proteins, or essential vitamins and minerals for good health, according to the Human Nutrition Center on Aging at Tufts University.[13] Many older people, the Tufts experts say, fall into "a spiral of undereating, illness, physical inactivity and depression," or a spreading "drug induced malnutrition," with four out of five people over sixty taking drugs for at least one chronic ailment, and some taking as many as five or ten drugs daily. They are admitted to hospitals and treated for dehydration, infections, or mental confusion, when the "prime problem" may simply be "inadequate calories or protein—which in turn may be caused by a life devoid of physical activity . . . meaningful tasks, and social interaction." For the depressed, dispirited aged, undereating can be "a way of committing slow suicide," they noted.

In that decade, the mass media, from newsmagazines to *Vogue,* disseminated the startling news from the U.S. Surgeon General's Report on Health Promotion and Disease Prevention that only 1 percent of Americans who die before seventy-five die from infectious disease.[14] If we are to live beyond seventy-five now, "it will be because of the way we have chosen to live . . . because we had the good sense and the discipline to make modest changes in our lifestyle, changes that actually make the difference between long life or early death." The 22 percent drop in cardiovascular disease in the previous decade and the 5 percent decrease in the rate of death from stroke every year for the previous five years was credited by the Surgeon General not to medical miracles but to measures people have taken to help themselves—changes in life-style that are the results of a growing awareness of the impact of certain habits on health.

Beyond fads of diet and exercise, a very recent study found that people who suffer a heart attack are more likely to die or suffer another attack within six months if they live alone and have no close friends.[15] Nearly 22.6 million people, or 12 percent of American adults, were living alone at the time of the 1990 census, the majority of them over sixty-five. New studies reported in the *Journal of the American Medical Association* found that living alone was "a major independent risk factor," comparable to physiological factors in heart disease: not divorce, separation, or death of a spouse, but the sheer fact of living alone. Unmarried patients without a close personal confidant were significantly less likely than others to survive for five years.

An annotated bibliography summarizing 1,400 scientific research reports on "Mind and Immunity" was published in 1985 by Dr. Steven Locke of Harvard Medical School and the Institute for the Advancement of Health, a clearinghouse for research on links between mental factors and disease. During the year I spent at Harvard, I sat in on the study group compiling this research. It was, indisputably, hard science. But simultaneously the resistance of the medical establishment to the implications of such findings was also building.

A furor was set off by a study indicating that cancer patients who received psychotherapy along with chemotherapy lived longer than did those who received chemotherapy alone. The evidence linking the brain, the immune system, and the course of disease had become so strong that advanced hospitals and social agencies had begun using support groups (of cancer or heart patients, of widows and widowers, similar to the support groups of people struggling to stop smoking or lose excess weight) and other forms of psychological intervention to "complement medical treatment." The resistance exploded in an editorial in June 1985, when the influential *New England Journal of Medicine* proclaimed that "our belief in disease as a direct reflection of mental state is largely folklore." The American Psychological Association and others attacked that *New England Journal* article as "bad science," "inaccurate and unfortunate," asserting that it ignored a substantial body of research findings that now corroborate the linking between psychological factors and health.[16]

At UCLA Medical School, at the University of California Medical School at San Francisco, at Harvard, and elsewhere, research projects continue to enhance patients' immune resistance to disease and even reverse it through psychological treatment, biofeedback, yoga, or meditation exercises that, in effect, move them from the state of passive victim (of disease, of aging) to some control over the quality of their own lives, even while under medical care. A number of studies, cited by Dr. Locke, indicate that *feelings of helplessness* may be associated with a poor survival rate, regardless of the specific disease. Overcoming his own cancer, Neal Fiore, a psychologist at the University of California, Berkeley, in a 1979 article in the *New England Journal* proposed methods for mobilizing the patient's own psychological resources by giving him or her more control over chemotherapy, helping decide the pace of treatment.

On the cutting edge of scientific research, it is becoming clearer just how these larger factors of purpose, meaning, intimate ties, and the expression of our real feelings affect the immune system that is the key to our health, vitality, and survival of all disease. At UCLA Medical School, Norman Cousins was invited onto the faculty after his successful experiment at curing his own supposedly fatal auto-immune disease through a purposeful regime of exercise and healing laughter. He raised $10 million for rigorous research in this direction, and when he died, approaching eighty, he left behind not only the accounts of his own self-directed care (*The Healing Heart* and *Anatomy of an Illness*) but careful studies now being completed by others.

Dr. George Solomon, one of the founders of the new study of psychoneuroimmunology— how the mind, stress, and the immune system interact—was brought to UCLA by Cousins to extend his research on long-term survivors of AIDS. He had found significant numbers of people who should have been dead of AIDS surviving and healthy, five years and more, despite fatally low T-cell counts. UCLA asked him to study healthy older people who, like long-term survivors of AIDS, were not sick despite extremely low counts of T-cells, which conventionally reflect an age-weakened immune system.

He chose fifty physically healthy older people —mainly through senior centers. Their ages ranged from sixty-seven to ninety-seven when he began; seventy-one to one hundred when I talked to him. All of them were "functioning very well . . . have no life-threatening illness"; if they had any cancer, they "have had no sign of it for five years, are not cardiovascular handicapped but could be on some medication. They are healthy but not superhealthy." All of them were "living independently" and cognitively intact ("they had their marbles"). He compared this group with a second group—twenty-nine healthy young volunteers, aged twenty-two to thirty-nine—and found the older people's immune systems functioning as well or better. The increased incidence of malignancy, cancer, diabetes, heart disease, arthritis, pneumonia, and auto-immune disorders with age has been linked to the decline of immune system function. Though the healthy older people's T-cell functions were down, their natural killer cells, which prevent metastases and kill viruses, were much higher than in the healthy young people.[17]

The measure echoed what Dr. Solomon found in the functioning long-term AIDS survivors. In both groups, he saw an extremely high correlation between immune system function and psychological factors—"hardiness," which involves "control, commitment and challenge." It had been established in other studies that depression and bereavement affect the immune system more severely in older people, "depressing" T-cells and natural killer cells. "Anxiety," "hopelessness," "despair" had strong negative immune correlations; positive immune effects seemed to correlate with "a sense of control and with the ability to express anger." He also found that exercise, releasing endorphins, increased both the number and activity of natural killer cells, and this effect was even more marked in the healthy older people than in the young ones.

In describing these older people to me, Dr. Solomon said: "They are future-oriented, focused on what they're going to do." He found in both survivor groups an "assertiveness, the ability to say no, the ability not to be masochistic and self-suffering, and to take care of oneself, one's own needs." This was the opposite of the "passivity, conformity, compliance and suppression of emotion, particularly anger," that has been found by other researchers to lead to an unfavorable prognosis of cancer.

Solomon gave as an example an AIDS patient who, after being diagnosed, developed a very severe, rapidly advancing lymphoma and was given a week or two to live. He was treated with chemotherapy; two years later, with no signs of lymphoma in his body, he returned to his work as a college professor. In the meantime, he had twice recovered from pneumonia, and had no evidence of the organic brain disease often associated with AIDS. What was happening? "He is feisty as hell," Solomon speculated. "He seeks out treatments. He takes charge of his own care. He doesn't put up with anything. He has the fiercest determination to live. . . . He has projects, he is involved. He has a marvelous support system . . . and his T-cell count is 28" (the normal count is between 500 and 1,500).

With geropsychologists Donna Benton, John Morley, and other colleagues at UCLA, Solomon continued to follow the group of healthy older people, only three of whom died in the four years of the study. One got cancer; the other two died suddenly, in the midst of life, with heart attacks. "The survivors are still future-oriented; they are involved in life; they find meaning in life; they are self-reliant; they are assertive," Solomon said.

But he also admitted "sadly" that studies like his, which have had a great effect on molecular biology, have had "very little impact on medical practice with older people." The implications for future medical care are clear: "The doctor must *know* his patient, what's going on in his life, with his family, his feelings." But, he added, "When a doctor gets $2,000 an hour doing a cardiac catheterization, how much time is he going to spend finding out what is really going on with the geezer or grandma?" Medicare doesn't even cover the minimal costs of peer counseling.

Thus it seems apparent that we, in age, must demand or somehow manage this paradigm shift in our own care. That move alone will have more impact on medical practice in general than the high-technology machines now keeping people alive a few extra weeks or months when they can no longer control or find purpose for their own lives—that prolonged, *terminal,* high-tech medical intervention which accounts for most of the billions in "catastrophic medical care" for which the "greedy geezers" are being blamed.

Again, we have to break through the medical establishment's definition of age as inevitable decline. If, for example, the decline of the immune system is not an inevitable, irreversible aspect of aging, but directly affected by the factors crucial to our total well-being—in age as in youth, love and work, our ties of social participation and meaningful tasks—then the increasing billions we now spend, publicly and privately, on high-tech medical care and prescription drugs might better be spent on social programs that increase control over our own lives.

At three o'clock in the afternoon the day before New Year 1992, maybe a hundred people were dancing, jitterbug and 1940s style, cheek-to-cheek and dips, rock and roll, and the good old fox trot. In the big open atrium of the Senior Friendship Center in Sarasota, Florida, where people usually waited to see their doctors, the comfortable wicker chairs and couches had been pushed back for this early New Year's Eve party. The doctors' offices and examining rooms were off behind the arches, and reasonably well equipped, though high-tech machinery was not much in evidence. But thousands of older men and women in Sarasota have been getting a kind of health care here—from retired doctors, nurses, and medical technicians—that they might not get from hotshot busy urban or suburban younger practicing physicians or HMOs, even if they could afford it.

Begun ten years earlier in Sarasota and now being expanded to sites around the state, the Senior Friendship Center offers health services embedded in a whole network of activities, involving eleven thousand volunteers, which give a lot of people who retire to Florida and might otherwise have withdrawn from life a new sense of purpose and community. Dr. Sam Warson, nearly eighty now, came down here to retire himself, but got involved again, organizing retired doctors and nurses to use their lifetime of medical experience and training in a new way: for their peers. The health care here is offered in the context of activities and services that keep older men and women stimulated, involved, and participating in the community as whole people. It seemed to me to embody the paradigm shift in medical care implied by the fountain of age.

The name was written large: SENIOR FRIENDSHIP CENTER ("The name says it all," said Sam Warson). The HEALTH SERVICES sign was over in one corner; a few wheelchairs were parked by the arched entrance to offices and examining rooms, but they hardly dominated the large atrium where people were dancing now, and where, on other days at various times Spanish classes, foreign affairs discussions, stretch and sketch exercises went on. Large screens radiated out from the entrance, that day displaying photography and artwork by the seniors themselves for sale for late Christmas presents. The room where the frail elderly came for "candlelight supper" was called the Living Room. A small trolley car stopped at the front entrance every hour, on the hour, to take people into the center of town. There were only two paid staff—the manager, who had just been made Florida Health Services Manager in order to develop similar centers for the whole state; and Bernice

Wilke, who took care of all the forms necessary to collect Medicare, Medicaid, and keep the government off their backs—an essential element that allowed retired doctors to volunteer their services and younger practicing doctors and specialists of Sarasota to take the center's referrals when procedures not covered by the retired doctors' special licensing were required. What was going on here was not "care" in the traditional sense; or rather, as Sam Warson puts it, "not just caretaking."

At first Sam and the founders rented space in a downtown building. Then they organized the older people themselves, as well as younger ones, to go down to City Hall, wearing yellow carpenter aprons someone donated, to lease unused land bordering a park for a dollar a year. They raised the money in the community to build the center. They had to get a special provision from the state legislature for the retired doctors and nurses to be able to volunteer their services, with a special licensing procedure, responsible to county health officers. The population of doctors retiring down here was increasing at a rate faster than the population as a whole. When I visited, six hundred active health profession volunteers were serving two thousand people a day at the Senior Friendship Center. These services "in kind" would amount to over $600,000 a year. But the doctors and nurses here worked "in a different setting than a medical one," as Doctor

Sam explained. It was not by accident that outside the examining room door stretch exercises or a photography workshop was going on—activities conducive to physical and mental growth, to better health. Sam said:

The thing these older physicians have that the young guys in practice now don't seem to have is time: they sit and listen, they take the time, they love what they're doing now, it's what attracted them to become doctors in the first place. They don't have to worry anymore about the overhead, the paperwork, the competition. They can give their full attention finally to the patient, really listen to him or her, here and now. There was a lot of resistance in the medical community at first, that we would be robbing local doctors of patients. But we're seeing people who couldn't afford local physicians' fees. And more and more doctors won't take patients on Medicaid and Medicare anymore. We keep in close touch with the medical community, we get many referrals.

[Patients] have to be over sixty and of limited income, and since we do not operate twenty-four hours a day, they have to be prepared to use the hospital emergency room or a local doctor nights or weekends. A lot of what we do is not the medical model, geared to cure acute illness or injury, it's preventive medicine.

Medicare and Medicaid, most insurance today, only covers them when they get sick.

The different kind of care offered at the Senior Friendship Center was exemplified by Bernice Wilke, the office manager, who scheduled appointments, filled out all the forms, and kept the insurance records and charts in order, and who, according to the conventional doctors in town, should be dead by now. She told me, with verve: "I'm the paperwork queen, trying to keep up with the government. Four years ago, I was told I'd be lucky to live a year with my cancer. I started as a volunteer here while I was waiting. Now I'm one of the few paid workers. But all the work here is done by loving, caring people. I think being part of a community like this makes you decide you're not leaving in a hurry."

Sister Luke Crawford, another one of the founders, stressed that their efforts were "thoroughly nondenominational," though as they have expanded their centers to other communities, they do use church fellowship halls. "Some people call me Sister, some call me Luke," she said. On the wall, a Japanese drawing from the seniors' art exhibit proclaimed in calligraphy, *"A bird can soar because he takes himself lightly."* One of the patients took Sister Luke off to the dance floor, and Brother Bill Geenen, who had "been around from day one" and who was credited by many with sparking the whole effort, took over. He told me:

From day one, we had a philosophy: anyone could come in the door, look around, participate or not participate as they will. There are no membership requirements, no fees to pay. Age is a lot of people feeling their way into a new situation; a lot of people have to make terrible adjustments, they've lost a spouse, lost their professional standing in the community, their financial status. All our volunteers are sixty-five and older; using their skills and abilities to help other people somehow keeps them younger. Whatever we do, it keeps people out of emergency rooms, hospitals, nursing homes. With our active volunteers, we can give people whatever help they need to keep them in the community. Maintaining independence is the number-one goal of everybody.

What I loved about the Friendship Center was the sense of lively life going on—no one wallowing in the victim state, no one parroting compassion for "those poor old people." Everybody was taking charge, taking care of themselves and each other. The band played on, and even those who hadn't danced in years were dancing.

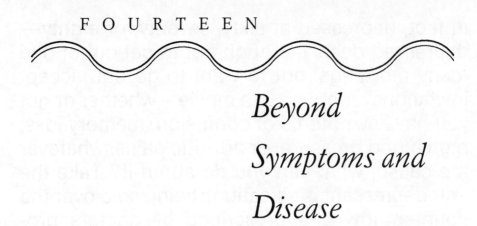

FOURTEEN

*Beyond
Symptoms and
Disease*

Again and again, in the literature, the research studies, the clinical data, and in interviews with doctors and gerontologists concerning care for older women and men, no matter what the symptom or disease—diabetes, arthritis, high blood pressure, heart—one finds behind it depression or despair. And, if diagnosed, depression is supposedly one condition to which the elderly are susceptible that can be effectively treated, with a much higher and longer lasting rate of success than the heart bypasses and organ transplants costing so many millions of patient and Medicare dollars.

But if you, or your older mother or father, are,

in fact, depressed at sixty, seventy, or eighty—depressed deeply enough not to get out of bed many mornings, not to want to go out, accept invitations, shop, go to a movie—whether or not you have symptoms of confusion, memory loss, high blood pressure, or arthritic pains, whatever the cause, what can you do about it? Take the anti-depressant medications being sold over the counter now and prescribed by doctors profusely? Go to a "shrink," who will tell you, "You're old. What can you expect?" if one will even agree to see you at all because of your age?

Given the reality of aging in America today—the loss of power in forced retirement, the subtle and not-so-subtle put-downs and denigrations of the youth culture, the growing sense of invisibility, the isolation and loneliness as spouse or friends die, the fear in the city streets, the real economic worries and physical symptoms—the wonder is all those studies in which older people report they are *not* lonely, unhappy, or angry most of the time. Knowing all the reasons we have to be angry, lonesome, or afraid, one can only suspect that an awful lot of older people are suppressing an awful lot of rage. And if, indeed, depression in old and young alike is defined as unbearable rage turned against oneself, small wonder that depression is endemic in older people, whether or not it is diagnosed or visible only in its physical symptoms: unexplained loss of appetite, weight loss, confusion, unkemptness, arthritic pain, high blood pressure, lower back pain, or panic breathlessness.

Ten years ago, starting out on this search, I had a hard time finding psychiatrists or psychologists around Harvard Medical School concerned with or even willing to treat older men or women except to confirm symptoms of senility, the dread Alzheimer's—for fear of which most older people resist the idea of even going to a "shrink" or mentioning emotional distress, depression, or despair in a regular doctor's visit. In Cambridge, as, more recently, in New York and Los Angeles, I was told that psychotherapists and psychoanalysts are loath to take on older patients. Of course, for all psychotherapists trained in any offshoot of the Freudian tradition, the causes of mental illness are rooted in childhood. And even if it were not a daunting project to trace back in memory for trauma sixty, seventy years ago, for any psychological descendant of Freud growth and change are considered barely possible after youth, impossible even to conceptualize, in Freudian terms, at or after midlife.

When it became known that I was interested in the psychological problems of older people, I was invited to the Boston Society for Geriatric Psychiatry. Naively, I spoke on breaking through the age mystique, on dealing with older patients not as objects of senile decline but simply as people in another stage of life. All the other papers tried to fit the symptoms of older people into Freudian categories, as if the whole point was to "cure" their emotional distress in age by tracing it back to the Oedipal conflicts and complexes of their youth. The nurses and social workers present, who actually dealt with older people's troubling physical symptoms of depression or despair, felt that these papers were somehow beside the point.

When David Gutmann stepped down as chief of psychology at Northwestern Medical School in 1973 and started an "Older Adult Program," he didn't get much support from the medical establishment. Because he insisted on treating people in age in "developmental" terms, studying and naming the crossover of men and women after midlife—the new assertiveness released in women and the new nurturing inner life and sensitivity of men—as growth to a new stage, he was not taken seriously by the gerontological establishment either. When he invited me to participate in a conference at his Medical School in Chicago on "The Unconscious in Later Life," I sensed a breakthrough: here at last were professionals dealing with the inner life of men and women in age on its own terms.

Reporting that he was able to find almost no articles in psychoanalytic journals on middle to old age, Bertram Cohler of the Tavistock Clinic in London reminded us that people are not supposed to benefit from psychoanalysis after forty; and according to Freud, women couldn't really change after thirty. At that time, Tavistock was the only facility in England offering therapy to "older" people, and that meant *over forty.* Cohler rather diffidently suggested that the significance of social relationships or their own inner life to older people themselves cannot be understood in psychoanalytic terms of the Oedipal complex and the "nuclear neuroses" of the childhood family, implying a linear model of continuity. Was it possible that there are, or can be, continuous transformations of personality in age as in adolescence, that even childhood memories can be reworked in age to serve new needs, he asked his audience of psychotherapists. (Are there new psychological needs and problems in age that cannot be dealt with in terms of memories of the past at all, I ask.) Could there be transformation in later life comparable to the identity struggles and conflicts of adolescence? If in the "transference" so essential to psychoanalysis, the analyst becomes father or mother target of unresolved conflicts, does the analyst now represent the child or grandchild? Or is that model, based on the childhood family, no longer relevant in age?

Gutmann described the Rorschach record of a fifty-three-year-old Polish-American woman sent to Northwestern for psychiatric treatment for depression. She saw two bulls, horns locked

in combat, blood spattering . . . a volcanic eruption . . . an eagle in flight, and finally "an explosion of something—a coming up of creation. It
looks like a butterfly, a beautiful butterfly, but
like it broke loose. It's coming out of its cocoon.
Out of eruption comes a work of nature. Looks
like it would be all rainbow colors, like Niagara
Falls. Out of eruption comes a spray of multi-
colors."

As Gutmann analyzed it:

Clearly, this is not the imagery of a truly depressed woman. These are images given by
a woman who is both fascinated and terrified
by the powerful "masculine" and alien energies—represented by antlered deer, fighting
bulls, eagles and volcanoes—that are eruptive within her. These energies could lead on
toward a rebirth (the butterfly emerging from
the cocoon) but rebirth necessarily entails
the token death of the established, familiar
self, as well as the possibility of combat and
destruction.

Psychiatrists typically blame this [older
woman] patient's kind of pain on outward
and imposed losses: of beauty, of procreative capacity, of the mothering role, or of
the husband. . . . In this instance, the patient
was literally poisoned, in the psychological
sense, by her own potential strengths. She
treated them as though they were foreign in-

vaders, and developed psychological anti-bodies which—just as physical antigens produce fever—in her case produced agitated, weepy depression. Because her early life . . . taught her to fear aggression, and because of her marriage to a husband who needs a submissive wife, her new energies could not move beyond the eruptive phase, and her shackled aggression turned inward, taking the form of self-punishing symptoms.[1]

Gutmann reminded us of anthropological studies of societies where that power of older women was feared as witch, or used as safe wise elder of the tribe. Cases like this, he told his colleagues, teach us that late-life, post-menopausal female psychopathology "can have a base in development rather than depletion, and that the causes are often reversible, rather than (as is commonly proposed) irreversible. The therapist's task here is simply to help the patient recognize and welcome her own assertiveness." He also warned of the "abnormal outcomes" that result when such energies do not achieve real expression and "are side-tracked into pathology. In addition, a view of the older woman that ignored her developmental potentials had its own pathogenic effect: when the more hopeful, growth-centered possibilities of the older woman are ignored . . . the 'depletion' view, the denigrating view of the older woman as perpetual victim, becomes paramount, stimulating further demoralization and regression."[2]

This woman had been coming to the emergency room with apparent heart attacks; then she began to have arthritis symptoms, grew more and more depressed, thought she was going to die. Her kids, in their twenties and thirties, unmarried, were upset when she got herself a job at Marshall Field and began to take trips with her woman friends. Her husband wanted her to quit work. When, at fifty, she thought she was pregnant and decided to have an abortion, she became obsessed with guilt, though in fact the pregnancy was psychological. As Gutmann recalled:

> In the beginning she would come and cry, she thought her symptoms were all physical, and I would give her pills and tell her what to do. She felt there was no absolution for her sins, nothing she could do with her life. She didn't want to keep on living as a mother to those kids the way she used to, she didn't want another baby to take care of, she was consumed with guilt. When they told her she'd have to learn to use a computer, she thought she could never learn it, and almost quit her job. When she did master it, she had a heart attack.
>
> I didn't give her pills. Instead of concentrating on the weeping, the depression, all those

supposed losses which weren't the real problem for her at all, I helped the butterfly emerge. I helped her see she could change. She could let the rage explode with me. She began to set limits with those overgrown babies, take risks with her husband. I gave her hope when she came in feeling stuck, helpless, hopeless. She could change, in her sixties. At her age, the doctor, the priest would give her the easy answer—your age, the menopause, the Rosary, absolution for her guilt—instead of really dealing with the problem: that she could learn the computer, even fail at the beginning, that she didn't have to be right all the time. She would move out, then not feel well, and get upset with me because I wouldn't go along with her idea of being hospitalized. She finally got to the point where she could empty her nest, as she needed to, and she moved to California.

A colleague interjected:

Sometimes it's hard when you have women, getting into their seventies, becoming comfortable finally with their aggression after a lifetime of masochism. Now all these fantasies of what they'd like to do with their lives. Well, okay, they surely seem energetic. But is it right to let those fantasies become a need when you know they're going to come up against the physical limitations of age?

That was not the point, Gutmann insisted. It was not physical limitations that stopped them, or needed to, most of them, in their sixties, seventies, even eighties.

But when they begin to try something new, and find they can do it, and realize "I could have done this earlier, I could have done it any time, why didn't I do this sooner?" They can still not do it, and blame it on the husband, or disease, and get really angry, and depressed. If we therapists find it suspect that they are really not that involved with their kids anymore, we keep them from making that shift. In therapy with older patients, you have to work through the pain of that insight, "I didn't have to do it that way, all my life, I was a fool." But later, they can see that even though they lived that way before, now they can do some different things.[3]

Sitting there that week, listening to Gutmann and his colleagues and residents talking in this new way about their cases, I saw indeed that the so-called physical limitations of age were not the point. Summing up what they did differently at the close of their staff meeting, Gutmann told me: "Mostly older patients get defined and treated as the sum of their weaknesses instead of being put back in touch with their own sense of themselves, their own strengths." He trained the young therapists who worked with these older adults to "serve as a catalyst for their own growth and their own strength." His center admitted "anybody that comes in not grossly brain-damaged, fifty to ninety, if we think they can benefit and, if they have chronic health problems, are able to get here and out by themselves. And we don't charge."

The men and women who came in were not "psychologically sophisticated." White-collar, blue-collar, lower-middle-class, housewives who had gone back to work but not "careers," they would hesitate to go to a psychiatrist: "I'm not crazy." They felt they should be talking to "my minister," "my rabbi," or "my daughter," but somehow couldn't do so, and they had been told to get help. They didn't have high expectations. But these brief sessions, where they were taken seriously as the people they had come to be and their problems were not dismissed as inevitable "losses" of age, could transform symptoms into new growth.

A woman came in whose husband was stricken with Alzheimer's. He had always taken care of her, financially and in every other way, making all the decisions, and now she had to take care of him and everything else. She had been an overly "good mother," always worrying about her children, and had been looking forward to the golden years when she could travel with her husband and think about herself. She came in, Gutmann said, depressed, feeling guilty about her own rage, that fate should have repaid her this way for being such a good mother.

Initially, she felt guilty about being so angry, and angry also at her children for not helping enough in the care of their father. And then she began to see she had a right to be angry, she had been put upon by fate, she had to put up with it, she didn't have to like it. She finally made the decision herself to put him in a home. Then she started thinking of herself as an individual, rather than a couple, and took on some of the strengths she'd looked to him for as her own.

The therapist, younger than that woman's daughter, did not play the authority, telling her what to do. She said:

I kept giving it back to her that she knew better than anyone else what she should do, to strengthen her sense of self, her own power. After he died, she told me: "You know, Leslie,

I can't believe how wonderful it is. I'm so free now, I'm so amazed, I really enjoy myself. When something comes up, I don't give it a moment's thought, I go." When he was still alive, he couldn't accept the fact that she was entitled to be a person in her own right, to have some time on her own. She is a real gutsy lady now.

Another of the young staff members was clearly aware that the way she now saw these older people was not the way she used to. She had shared all the stereotypes of age in the beginning. She said:

I'd worked almost totally with younger adults. My preconception was that older people are real brittle, that I wouldn't be able to deal with the painful part of their lives. It surprised me how concretely they could face up to situations that younger people spend their lives avoiding—even losses of spouse, a child, or if they're seriously ill, their own death. They are more resilient, more able to use what I can give them, more insightful than younger patients.

Another Freudian, H. Peter Hildebrand, chief of psychological services to older persons at the

Tavistock clinic in London, suggested that "as well as there being primal fantasies concerning birth and sexuality there is also a primal fantasy concerning the death of oneself and one's spouse." As he gradually extended the age range of his own patients from early fifties·to patients in their late seventies, he began searching for new clues to a kind of integrity or wisdom that could counter the "despair of the knowledge that a limited life is coming to a conclusion; and also the . . . disgust over feeling finished, passed by and increasingly helpless." By extending Freud's "notion of original fantasy so that it concerns not only the creation and birth of the individual but also his death," he felt it "possible to find for ourselves a role as analysts with older people which can be as creative and fruitful as working with younger patients."

In actually dealing with such older persons, Hildebrand, though previously a Freudian, saw the need for a developmental psychology of later life that was not based on infantile sexuality and "not based on deficit and loss but much more directed toward the major problems of the second half of life." In the later years, he said, a "false self" or a "sense of identity [that] has become parasitical on the role" is threatened by the actuality of the aging process. Dealing with "resistances to recognition of changes in sexual behavior amongst older people," he found that Freudian concepts of "castration anxiety" and other aspects of "infantile sexuality" were not useful. Hildebrand insisted:

In the second half of life therapists are faced with a population who differ markedly from the young people in the first half of life on whom so much of our current theorizing is based. However, the evidence does not support either Freud or received psychoanalytic wisdom when they say older people are not amenable to either analysis or analytical psychotherapy. . . . Freud stated that older people are too rigid for psychotherapy. Recent evidence suggests that, unless irreversible brain damage has occurred, older people have learned considerable flexibility in the use of their resources. . . . After all they have been there, in the way a 25- or 30-year-old has not. They have been hardened and tempered by life and where their defenses have not cracked they seem to have a good deal of capacity to delay gratification, allow problems to resolve. . . . Moreover, they often have much greater self-reliance than do younger people and can be left to get on with things by themselves. . . . Older people can use briefer experience of therapy than younger people. . . . Older patients do not have the time to hang about contemplating their navels, they want to get on with things —but different things.[4]

He then suggested that to deal with the real new issues of age, therapists themselves need to be free of the preoccupations with sex and aggression that dictate their work with patients in the first half of life. And so, though he had dutifully traced a seventy-seven-year-old widower's masochistic sexual preoccupation with his mean daughter-in-law to his childhood sexual fantasies about his mother, he realized that "what this man really wants now is to end his days in dignity and some comfort," to get free of his sexual preoccupation with his daughter-in-law and move to a place where he himself can control the care he needs. Reversing the Freudian sexual obsession of his own youthful training, Hildebrand suggested that sexual obsession in age may mask some other new, deep need.

Hildebrand had been seeing a woman patient in her eighties, and several men, all of whom were locked into obsessive sexual relationships with young lovers in their thirties. They were terrified of losing these lovers, who in fact were preying on them. He suggested that they could get free of such now terrifying sexual preoccupations if they could come to terms with the fact that they were going to die. Does death, then, take the place of sex on the psychoanalytic map of age? Or was he suggesting that, in fact, if in age he can help them get "free of lifelong sexual obsessions," they can not only come to terms with the losses but see "the whole value of their unique lifelong scenario as they've written it for themselves." And this, he insisted, was much "more important than the sexual problems which have been the preoccupation of psycho-analysis."

To be "vitally involved" in life in this new stage, as opposed to "stagnation," one has to be able to accept without despair this one and only life as one has lived it, and why one has lived it that way, accept the pain one has inflicted on others, and the strength and competency one has developed. Reconciling the opposing tensions that have split one before was newly possible in age, Hildebrand said, but can't be accomplished just by "dreaming and thinking, reviewing the life which [a person] has lived." It had to be worked out through one's active, present, vital involvement in the world, here and now, in one's seventies, eighties. "Whatever he has been in the past, what's important now is his ongoing involvement in the world."[5]

But these are most unusual forays into new territory, dealing with psychological conflicts and depressions of older persons with real respect for their integrative potential. David Gutmann has had a continual battle to get funding, office space, residents, and research help for his Older Adult Program, perhaps because he was attached to a medical school and yet insisted, for more than one reason, on departing from the medical model of age as sickness, age only as loss. He pointed out to his colleagues that a man or woman of seventy, seventy-five, might well be reluctant to go to a psychotherapist, even if a doctor suspected depression behind high blood pressure or worsening angina, diabetes, arthritis. For that person suspects, not without basis, that the psychiatrist will give her or him some kind of a test to prove that he or she is senile. In fact, patients themselves may secretly be afraid that the confusion, depression, or anxiety that can mark new growth in age, or mask real problems easier to deny than solve, may truly signify that decrepitude which the age mystique prescribes.

There is a vicious circle here that keeps older people from getting real help with reversible depression which might free them to confront real problems, now paralyzing them in rage and despair, before that feared decrepitude becomes a self-fulfilling prophecy. As Gutmann pointed out, psychiatrists and psychologists "continue to view the older patient in the most catastrophic and benighted terms," because older people, in their fear of psychiatry finding them senile, "tend to bring their emotional troubles, coded as physical symptoms," to their doctors, who prescribe pills to cure those symptoms and do not refer older people for psychological help until a patient becomes unmanageable.

"Accordingly the psychiatrist mainly sees

older patients who are drastically and even irreversibly damaged. In effect, he sees terminating, rather than aging, patients—and his clinical norms are based almost exclusively on this very special group," now truly pathological. Psychiatrists, therefore, "define the aging patient as a victim of irremediable loss," and the psychiatry of aging is "transformed, more or less unwittingly, into the psychiatry of termination." This predicament extends even to the middle-aged, who are seen as suffering from the irreversible loss of career for men, or procreative capacities for menopausal women. Thus "therapy with the aging—of whatever age—is . . . designed to reconcile them to inevitable loss, and to blunt (with medication) the pain and depression caused by loss . . . ignoring unique strengths of older individuals." Therapists then look at any older patient as possibly senile, unaware or forgetting that "research with normal populations makes the point that average expectable losses, while not pleasant, are certainly not devastating to most older individuals: the aging routinely tolerate chronic illness and even the looming threat of death, without becoming panicky, acutely depressed, or psychotic."[6]

In fact, if the older person does enter the office of such a doctor, he or she may well be given a "mental status questionnaire" used to screen for senility—a series of questions or a simple task, such as copying a geometric figure, with the numerical results compared to a standard-ized scale. My brilliant friend Mark Williams taught his students at Chapel Hill never to let such tests take the place of respectful attention to the person. "When determining mental func-tion, the clinician must accurately 'size up' the older patient as a person. Our premise is that everything about an individual . . . appearance, dress, behavior and language, represents a uni-fied presentation of self." As Williams pointed out:

> Most of the nouns and adjectives that perme-ate the literature on mental status assess-ment are based ultimately on pathological findings. . . . These are the only assessments we know of where a person has to prove their normalcy; usually normality is assumed until abnormalities are demonstrated. In other words, an attitude of "guilty until proven in-nocent" can be engendered, reenforcing dangerously misleading stereotypes of el-derly persons. Practitioners respond primar-ily to patients' errors on mental status scales and questionnaires; this tends to divert their attention away from careful evaluation of pa-tients' residual capabilities.[7]

It's as if, to break through that mystique of de-terioration-from-youth, these pioneers of what is truly *new age* (age-as-new?) have in effect to strip themselves of the very language of the medical model, the psychiatric model, the Freudian model, even the geriatric model, and create a new language, by carefully studying *the evolving thought and behavior of older people themselves.* After several years of working with the healthy men and women aged sixty to eighty in his Older Adult Program, Gutmann began discarding some basic psychoanalytic and gerontological formulations.

Older adults do not, need not, disengage themselves from involvement with others. But time is often needed for refueling—reengagement. I do not believe in reworking childhood conflicts—but working anew. I also do not believe in the notion of preworking death. This final stage scenario may not be totally valid—as life keeps extending, our notion of this may have to be reexamined. It does not leave enough room for innovations of development, what is new, unpredicted about age as longer life. A person with a relatively stable, integrated ego is capable of handling unpredicted unexpected events which is surely the task facing age today.[8]

But with rare exceptions, Gutmann said, it is not easy for psychologists to stop thinking about age in terms of deterioration and decline, about older persons as passive victims of imposed losses; even metaphors like "young-old" or "old-old" reinforce the dread of "old." He speculated that the "catastrophic view of the aging process" *causes* many of the very symptoms we associate with age, leading to treatment exclusively in terms of "symptom reduction," the overmedication which in turn can mock senility. Is the unconscious still an important part of personality, to be studied on its own terms in age? Gutmann thought so: "When we deprive an older person of an unconscious, we deny his personhood. We have to think of the unconscious not just as pathology but as a source of energy, strength, growth that may not have found expression before." In their work at Northwestern, Gutmann and his colleagues made "few assumptions as to what we may find" in this new phase of life. Studying men admitted for the first time after fifty to Northwestern psychiatric facilities, they found that most of them (77 percent) were suffering from emotional disorders, mainly depression, with only 10 percent suffering terminal organic brain syndrome (Alzheimer's). And most (59 percent) of the men with those emotional disorders were "not reacting to clear and irreversible losses of health, kin, work or career [but] suffering from depressions that may have dynamic, developmental and potentially reversible causes."[9]

Again and again, these therapists, taking seriously the unconscious of these older men and women in terms of their own personhood at this point in their own life span, used the word "shift"—a shift from playing out, yet again, the role of mother–father–dependent baby; a shift from an endless, narcissistic relationship with one idealized object to a more pluralistic, realistic framework; an identity of self less alienated and armored and hard even to conceptualize in the old terms. And they asked themselves whether the new freedom of women to express their assertive, aggressive selves in careers during their parenting years, or in sharing late parenting with husbands, would make the "crossover" of age a different, less traumatic experience for them.

It is hard to graft this new view of age, in which people become so much more authentically themselves, onto the old framework of depletion and loss, the old determinism of infantile sexuality. Gutmann and his colleagues were almost puzzled at how well their older women patients seemed to do now, with brief psychotherapy, fifteen sessions, compared to the men. "They seem to use it to free themselves of old guilts and go on, not so much from the development of insight, but something has been freed up, they are more at ease with themselves, comfortable with their new strength, they are freed up to explore this new and frightening source of energy and they carry it into life," Gutmann said. But they also warned each other that the possibilities for continued development they now could see and even help release in these older women and men might come into conflict with society's expectations of age: "Opportunities for generativity versus stagnation might not be present in old age. Strengths acquired in earlier stages might not be applicable to old age. Skills developed through the life cycle might have to be suppressed in view of the opportunities present in old age." Perhaps dealing with the late years, even more than the young, they hardly dared ask themselves, should psychotherapy go beyond *adjustment* to the age-denying realities of society now? But listening to them, I must ask: What happens to the rage if that new energy and strength of self we are finally free to use in age is denied any use at all by society?

There seems to be very little psychological theory based on the actual experience of older people. The "stages of life" rubrics reified by Freud and his followers, Erikson, Daniel Levinson, or Roger Gould, were based on lives, only (or mainly) of men, who came of age early in this century or in the 1940s and 1950s. For the most part, they were not followed into their sixties, seventies, and eighties. The few longitudinal studies, at Harvard and Berkeley-Oakland, of "normal" men and women followed from childhood into old age analyzed data according to conventional psychological rubrics based on youth. That people reaching seventy or eighty today had very different "shoulds" in childhood —different experiences with mother, father, marriage, jobs, women and men—from the baby boomers who will be sixty in the year 2000 is a truism.

The one great psychoanalytic pioneer who did concern himself with age was Carl Jung. But it is not easy to find even Jungian analysts or therapists who actually work with older people today, and who continue to evolve their theory and practice as the experience of men and women in age continues to evolve. Two Jungian analysts in San Francisco, Bruce Baker and Jane Wheelwright, recently made a thorough search of case histories and theoretical discussions by Jungian therapists based on actual work with older patients. To their surprise, they could hardly find any. They reported:

> Although old age is supposed to be the psychological culmination of life for Jungians, very few old patients are written about in the Jungian journals. . . . It seems that most analysts do not work with them. In a recent survey of Jungian analysts, 29% of the respondents stated that they try not to accept patients over seventy, and only 23% felt they worked well with this group. . . . Perhaps some unconscious resistance inhibits therapists from seeking or accepting old patients.

In effect, they suspected even Jungian therapists of dismissing work with older, "unproductive" people as "a waste of time," reflecting "our
society's present basic denial of the worth of
wisdom and experience." [10]

In their own work, Baker and Wheelwright
found the inability to adjust to the profound
changes—both internal and external—that are
inherent in aging at the heart of many psychological problems in the troubled elderly. *The insistence on seeing themselves as young, the
denial of age itself, was the crux of psychological troubles in older men and women.*

The changes that age brings are so basic and
so numerous that sometimes old defenses
and solutions no longer silence the new
kinds of anxieties that come with them. . . .
Long-cherished goals remain out of reach,
lifelong relationships break off, unsolved
problems grow urgent, unresolved past
transgressions become ever more painful
and former paths to satisfaction appear less
and less accessible. New adjustments are
called for, but unfortunately the awkward-
ness that any old person inevitably feels
when developing latent abilities and new attitudes usually makes [her] too uncomfortable
even to think about them. . . . Jung believed
that "the very frequent neurotic disturbances
of adult years all have one thing in common:

they want to carry the youthful phase over the threshold. . . . Whoever carries over into the afternoon the law of morning must pay for it with damage to his soul."[11]

But Jung also believed that "the greatest potential for growth and self-realization exists in the second half of life," that the disturbances of later life were due to the inability to be in touch with those unconscious images and feelings which, if fully experienced and examined, would bring one closer to one's real self. When such a growth change is blocked, symptoms emerge: depression, defensive dogmatism, cynicism, denial, quiet despair, "suffering designed to guarantee guilt-generated concern, obsession with the past, boredom, exhaustion, stagnation and all the physical and psychic woes arising from unacknowledged . . . tension."[12]

On the other hand, when older people who have been coping with life for many years *do* undertake analysis, they bring to it such strength and flexibility and rich remembrances that Jung himself preferred working with them. Baker and Wheelwright concurred:

Old patients, their childhood complexes now less affect-laden, do not worry so much about what others think about them. They feel they have "nothing to lose" by trying a new way of problem solving. Painful insight, once reached, can often be more easily integrated because of lessened resistance. In addition, many older people describe an increase of intensity in their feelings and in their connections to the world that make them more reflective. And, as death draws closer, patients often feel the pressure to solve their problems and realize themselves. As one patient put it, "I just hope I can grow up before I die." With their ego-involving problems of doing well and getting ahead relegated to the past, their relationships often less idealized, and their lessened energies forcing them to be more selective, old people can face the profound questions. . . . Their old age, especially with the help of analysis, can be a fertile ground for growth. . . . Results can be just as profound, if not more so, than with younger patients.[13]

But analysis with older persons differs from analysis with younger ones, they insisted. The reality of medical problems, and the effects of medication, have to be taken into account. So do different kinds of resistances: "At my age, what does it matter?"; the possibility of dependence on the analysis as a threat to patients' independence, which they see, rightly, as the keystone of their existence; the humiliation of having to turn to a younger person for help; the feeling they should have transcended their personal problems. Baker and Wheelwright added a word of warning here:

Many therapists want to protect older people from harsh realities, because they see them as "frail." . . . There is no such need to shelter older people: grief does not shatter them, because of the wisdom they have gained through the years. . . . Some therapists want to deny their own future selves as seen in older clients . . . or their own inevitable death. . . . When seen to be ill, weak, or helpless, old people make therapists feel similarly helpless and ineffectual. To regain their potency, therapists over-protect their patients, withhold painful insights, avoid conflictual interpretations, console too much, and are drawn into helping solve concrete problems in the outer world that are better left to the patients or others.[14]

According to the Jungians, there are seven tasks of age:

1. To face the reality of age and of death. "From the middle of life onward," Jung states, "only he remains vitally alive who is ready to *die with life*." Though "the startling reality of death" may cause panic in one's fifties, going into the sixties, "if the reality of death is accepted, further demands of life pull people around." The

healthy old seldom think about it, "focusing instead on living and accepting death as a part of life." [15]

2. The need to review, reflect upon, and sum up one's life. Baker and Wheelwright have found it remarkable how many old people feel an urgent need to tell their story before they die. Jung himself died shortly after writing *Memories, Dreams, Reflections.* ("I try to see the line which leads through my life into the world, and out of the world again.") [16]

3. Draw some conscious mental boundaries beyond which it is not reasonable to expend the remainder of one's time and energy. "Some careers, relationships, desired achievements, even cherished goals must be abandoned, with grace or pain." But this can also be an "unloading of self-imposed burdens and a deliverance from exhausting efforts toward unlikely goals . . . perhaps only half-wanted rewards. Consciously letting go of these burdens and aspirations lets one focus total attention and energy not only on what is attainable, but on what is one's truest concern."

4. Letting go of the dominance of one's ego. This process of "letting go" may be especially hard for those whose previous productivity was most rewarding.

A successful, unretired business magnate may persevere in ego-dominated actions for too long, and then be laid low by depression or physical symptoms that are messages to let go and contact the Self. [At first] the process of looking inward seems self-indulgent, weak and nonproductive. . . . Many others want to let go, but their friends and relatives insist they stay involved with the outer world.[17]

5. Jung's fifth task of aging, "a new rooting in the Self," involves bringing together the opposites in "the most complete expression of our wholeness, which is also our uniqueness"—"God within us."

6. Finding the meaning of one's life, or "the real meaning of human existence," according to Jung, involves coordinating, in old age, one's important memories, bit by bit, with important outer happenings, until "a sense of one's archetypal ground plan is revealed, and through it a reason for existence," which connects us to historical and universal meaning. Jung wrote: "A human being would certainly not grow to be seventy or eighty years old if this longevity had no meaning for the species."[18]

7. Jung's seventh, most far-reaching and most often uncompleted aspect of aging is a "rebirth," engaging unused potentials in a "dying with life." One emerges from this encounter with "a playful approach to life, using all the possibilities that life has to offer, not in an ego-domi-

nated way, but as a creative artist or as a child at play. . . . Living itself becomes the point, and the unexpected becomes the raw material of its exploration. . . . Old age becomes a time when one can be one's own authority and make a unique contribution."[19]

The final task of aging, therefore, is a creativity that can "allow one to say yes to the finality of death, and in so doing, ensure what transcends death." At this point, "aging, and life itself when entered upon fully, becomes a process of creativity." Jung himself became more creative as he aged. *Memories, Dreams, Reflections* has a much more human, personal feeling than his previous intellectual creations. "Acknowledging the imminence of his death," said Baker and Wheelwright, "and the limits of his existence, he recalled in great detail and with great intensity his entire past, immersing himself in it thoroughly . . . and by allowing . . . feeling to come to the fore, he created a moving human . . . testimony to his own essence and to the value of the human soul in general. . . . And, in doing so, he helped others to find the way to their own essences as well."[20]

In her eighties, Jane Hollister Wheelwright noted that her own fear of death, sharp to the point of panic in her fifties, was transformed into a deep curiosity and interest through working with people in age and terminal illness, as they themselves became more and more conscious of their aging as "a state of transformation." She decided Jung was right when he advised older people "to proceed as though they would live forever," that "in old age one tends no longer to have problems." As one becomes more and more one's deeper, true, unique self in age, "many ego-related problems tend to disappear. . . . Those who have struggled with their lives will find that the nagging self-concern of the past fades away, and it becomes possible to simply brush off many things that might once have been disturbing." She found people who are troubled and despairing in age "those who remain locked in the ego."

In fact, she came to believe that the *dominance* of youth, in American society, is responsible for the "exaggerated importance of the ego, which properly belongs wholly to youth, and less so to middle age, is extended throughout the whole of our lives." Instead of holding on to the pretense of youth, "what makes an old person seem young is rather the emergence after middle age of latent abilities and openness to new attitudes. . . . People who resist the demands of these new impulses pushing up from the inside and who cannot allow themselves to be temporarily awkward and unsure are likely to become unnaturally rigid and fossilized as they age."[21]

In a sense, the Jungians see age as paradigm shift. Whereas the meaning of the first part of life has to do with ego, career, and family development, new and different goals are required in the second half: the pursuit of meaning, wholeness, and the further creation of consciousness.[22] But to make this shift, one must not only overcome one's own resistance to change, but resist the dread of age and its stereotype as deterioration and decline. For those accustomed to steady advance in career, social status, prestige, and authority, it may be especially difficult. Symptoms and exacerbation of disease or emotional problems may occur "when transformation is necessary but not forthcoming, when the only security lies in change which cannot occur because of fear, or because no helpful initiation into the new mystery is available," as another Jungian analyst put it.[23]

New forms are being devised to aid this transformation that depart from the medical or even the orthodox psychotherapeutic model. They may indeed reduce or even prevent the physical and/or emotional symptoms of decline or disease now expected in age. In Santa Monica, since 1977, a Senior Health and Peer Counselling Center has trained hundreds of older people who are not doctors, nurses, or psychotherapists to help their peers through this transition to a new view of their own age. They have empowered each other in ways that had a direct effect on physical and mental health far beyond the center's original concept, which merely supplemented the annual physical exam (blood pressure monitoring, glaucoma and cataract screening, hearing tests, and medications evaluation) offered as a health service to people sixty and older at voluntary charges.

In her modest office in a non-clinical-looking, low and sprawling California cottage that houses these services, Evelyn Freeman, director and trainer of Peer Counselling, showed me their training manual:

> When we began our program in 1977, we saw peer counselling as a way to address the emotional issues of older people and to assist them in maintaining an independent lifestyle for as long as possible. We have come to see that, through peer counselling, when older people learn to view themselves as worthwhile, valuable citizens, they are likely to be healthier—both mentally and physically. Older people can learn that many of the images of aging are myths and stereotypes, that they have options, and that, as a group, they can have power. They can participate in the development of a new image of older citizens. They can be healthier, more productive, sexier and funnier than they ever thought they could be.

Men and women volunteers, fifty-five and over, selected not on the basis of medical or formal psychological training but for their "sensitivity, compassion and variety of experience," were trained by professionals "to help their peers face the challenges of growing old." Both trainers and trainees, far from the dispassionate, objective medical model, were enjoined to be, above all, authentically themselves; "to accept yourself as you are and to celebrate your individuality"; to accept the others as they are ("when we present ourselves authentically, we create the climate for meaningful connection with another"); and to establish "connectedness" with the older person they counsel by being "fully present," which meant being "totally attentive to the words, body language and intention" of that person. To be "passionately connected" with that older person, to really *see, hear,* and *know* her/him is, of course, what older people need, but do not get, from the doctors who see them through that blinding age mystique.

I sat in on one training session—seven women, two men, hair in varying shades of gray or gray-dyed-red, sweaters, slacks, sneakers, and sandals—discussing their "clients'" problems and giving each other lessons on getting more "real," more "connected." They discussed one client who was depressed and taking a lot of medication, "going downhill," though she'd been heavily involved in activities since her husband died. Did she ever really go through the grieving process? Who will talk to her? Another client had to be seen at home. She'd been so depressed that she had difficulty getting up in the morning; she wasn't sick, it was just that she had had little contact with anyone.

A volunteer in a white slack suit, blue shirt, told of a black elderly client, who cried "unbearably" during the counseling, was depressed for two days afterward, and didn't want to continue digging into all the troubles of her past. "I suggested that we don't dig too deep into those troubled waters, just enumerating those things she doesn't want to talk about got her upset again. I asked her if she'd like to join my growth group instead. She fit in beautifully, she really liked it, the idea of supporting each other for growth, at her age, instead of the painful digging in her past."

She asked their advice about another woman, seventy-six, who had been getting more and more depressed, always referring to her husband, who had been abusing her for years, as "the dear one":

The last few weeks she refers to him as "the son of a bitch," "the bastard." Something is happening. She realizes she can't change him, only herself. In her seventies, still beautiful, she had just been sitting there in that tiny apartment, taking abuse from the dear one. Now she's getting into the bus, going out herself. Last session she felt life might still have unexpected joys, and awful pains, but things can still happen. She left him twice but went back for fear of being alone. I gave her some literature on alternative housing she could share, on her Social Security. She said, "I'm seventy-six years old, I don't know if I can make that kind of change anymore."

Should she talk to the husband as well as the wife? Was it really just fear; or maybe she couldn't live without that hostility to sustain her?
Listening to these people empowering their peers to new possibilities of self-empowerment, even at eighty-one, I sensed a shift taking place beyond the medicine of pills and professional "care" among the peer counselors themselves (one was past ninety when she decided to go back to Indiana to live with her grandchildren). A young intern of thirty-seven who was learning from them said: "All I know is it changes me, just seeing that there can be changes in later life, that the possibility of change, of creating and re-creating your life is never ending. It has nothing to do with age."
The woman in the pink-flowered slack suit, almost seventy, had been doing peer counseling with older people since she was fifty-eight.

I came here because I wasn't content with the models of age I grew up with. I wanted to find another way to be old. All my life I've been afraid of what's going to happen next. All my life I have been afraid of being alone. My husband left, I came here for the counseling, I found out I was all right. I can make plans on my own now. I didn't want to leave my house and I didn't like being alone, so I started renting out my bedrooms; now I have three younger people living with me; economically I'm better off than I ever was before. It's like I have more choices now. I can choose to go on a trip at the drop of a hat—don't even have to stay to take care of the cat or watch the house, I have my three housemates to take care of that. I seem to be laughing a lot more but now I like crying, too. I don't feel cheated by life anymore—and I don't have to take out the trash. Periodically I get qualms when I hear that someone is going into a nursing home. I'm afraid of that. But I think now I'll manage somehow so that I won't even have to do that.

Some eight thousand people, aged sixty to ninety, come each year to the Santa Monica Senior Health and Peer Counselling Center. Originally they came for medical "care," but behind their medical symptoms was something else that had to do with age that could be changed. The crux of it, as they kept saying in the training group, was that "here we look at old age as another continuum of the life process. We give each other a role model for being *ourselves* in age as we may never have been before." As one of them put it: "We get more than we give. We are trained, not exactly as psychologists, but to share what we know from life. You make it okay for the client to feel what she really feels, you show that you've been through that same thing yourself, and already, she's stronger than she was before. There's an energy, a vitality, an optimism of fresh eyes in the peer counseling. They don't see 'younger,' they see *me.*"

Bernice Bratter, the director, came to run the peer counseling program several years after the center opened in the mid-seventies.

They started out giving physical exams to older people who weren't covered by Medicare or Medicaid because they fell between sixty and sixty-five, and because Medicare only covers disease, not prevention. It was originally called a "Health Screening Clinic for the Elderly," and it was a real grass-roots project, started right in the neighborhood by older people themselves who had been involved in health care before they retired. What they found out was that many people who came in with various physical symptoms were mainly depressed, not sleeping, anxious, frightened, lonely. There was no place to refer them. Most professionals in the area didn't want to deal with older people, felt they couldn't change.

We had no idea of how this was going to change the lives of the peer counselors themselves; there's research now that such volunteering releases endorphins that strengthen the immune system. We had no idea of how many people fifty-five and older would be excited about getting this kind of training. Evelyn Freeman, who is in charge of training, got her own Ph.D. at seventy and wrote this huge manual which is now used to train peer counselors anywhere. She is my role model. I find myself astonished when I come up against the conventional view that older people are rigid. There's a whole pool of retired people out there who are brilliant and creative, but they're not the twenty-nine to fifties everyone else wants. They are not doing this because it's a step in their careers, going to look good on their résumés, but because they love it. They want the stimulation and challenge of the new learning and to give something back, an opportunity to keep growing and changing themselves which they can pass on to others. The focus is not age as illness, the focus is on growth, and it's not just words.

The trouble is, for the sellers of pharmaceuticals and the practitioners of high-tech medicine, the focus remains firmly locked on age as illness, disease—and as a source of enormous profits. As a result, government policymakers and taxpayers see age only as an enormous drain on our economic and social resources. It does not seem to have occurred to anyone, except those actually living vital, useful lives in age, that it could be any other way.

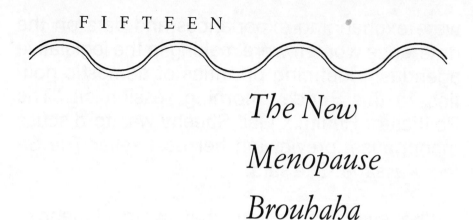

FIFTEEN

The New
Menopause
Brouhaha

In San Diego, California, in November 1991, I sat with about a thousand women at the Forum for Women State Legislators held every four years by the Center for the American Women and Politics of Rutgers University's Eagleton Institute. These were the vital, dynamic women, in their mid-thirties to sixty-plus, empowered by twenty-five years of the women's movement, who had been elected in vastly increased numbers in state legislatures in the last few years. We were meeting on the eve of the 1992 election campaign, tagged by Democrats and Republicans "the Year of the Woman." No longer merely concerned with sheer numbers, they were exchanging experiences and data on the difference women were making in the legislative agendas, redefining priorities of domestic politics. In this Sunday morning session on "The Politics of Health," Gail Sheehy was to discuss menopause, previewing her best seller *The Silent Passage.* She said:

Whenever I mention that word, "menopause," I feel a squirm, because it means middle age, I'm getting old, I'm losing my sex appeal, I'm depressed, a little crazy. There's a shame to it. It keeps us from ever realizing how much power we have. In the next few years, the boardrooms of America will light up with hot flashes. There are 43 million of us now between forty-five and fifty, the first of the baby boomers to reach menopause, and in the next decade this number will increase by half.

Because these women had broken through the feminine mystique and defined themselves in terms no longer limited by that biological sex role, I hardly expected them to be traumatized by menopause. I was slightly surprised when Gail, a personal friend, called menopause the "most profound change of our life" and made fun of "those women who tell me I haven't experienced much of anything, tra la, tra la. . . . She may be one of the lucky few, or obese, or she may be lying," Gail said, detailing symptoms of "unexplainable fatigue, feelings of sadness, free-floating depression, loss of sexual desire, mental confusion, hot flashes, changes in memory and brain clarity, unexplained nervousness, etc.," which sent her shopping from gynecologist to gynecologist, refusing to accept the "natural consequence of aging," until one prescribed estrogen replacement therapy. She warned that while some have defined menopause as "a natural biological process, not a disease," 75 percent of women experience the miseries of hot flashes, for two to five years, or "for the rest of your life" unless they go on artificial estrogen. She told them: "These symptoms can be controlled by hormone therapy indefinitely." She deplored both the lack of real, controlled studies of hormone therapy, and the fact that many women steer clear of estrogen because of fear of cancer (insisting that "women are ten times more likely to die of heart disease than any kind of cancer"). She explained that while the risk of breast cancer increases by 30 percent after fifteen years on estrogen, and endometrial cancer 400 percent, that kind of cancer "is very easily diagnosed and cured."

In the question period, one of the feisty legislators took the mike: "About these symptoms, I suppose I'm in the midst of menopause but I just don't pay attention to it. I couldn't tell you at the end of the day if I've had any hot flashes or how many. It's simply one part of your entire life, why not just live it?"

A state representative from Billingham, Washington, agreed:

We've been changing continuously up to this point. Why shouldn't we continue to change instead of trying to hold onto an old model? My grandmother died at eighty-seven. She never took estrogen. I'm struggling with hot flashes. I don't mind them that much. What I'm really getting wary of is women still being used as guinea pigs; they still don't know the long-term effects and yet it seems like all the doctors are now telling women, "you should take estrogen."

As I saw a new brouhaha about menopause intensifying, my own feelings of uneasiness and dismay increased. I didn't exactly suspect a new conspiracy against women, which was somehow coopting us. But there seemed to be a suspicious coincidence of the demographic emergence of this incredible market—50 million women hitting menopausal age—with the revived definition of menopause as disease. When I finally took the mike myself at San Diego, I asked if we didn't try to deny age but merely accepted it as simply another stage of life, if we didn't define menopause, which is undeniably the end of youth and reproductive function, as disease, why would we try to "cure" it; why would we risk those chances of cancer, however small or undetermined? Should we not indeed affirm this "change of life" and, at least, seek clearer information as to how and why to control its "symptoms"?

There's no question that doctors today almost universally insist that women should take estrogen, in combination with progesterone, from the time menopausal symptoms begin (until they die?), claiming the risks of cancer are "minimal" compared to the protection from heart disease and osteoporosis, and, of course, the relief from those "hot flashes" and the other "symptoms" of menopause itself. And yet . . .

In the first half of this century, menopause was considered a natural physiological event that seldom required medical intervention. It was only after scientists learned how to synthesize and manufacture the hormones estrogen and progesterone that twentieth-century medicine, deciding that menopause could be treated, defined it as a disease. Doctors thus extended the boundaries of their role beyond diagnosis and treatment to include the definition and management of a heretofore normal female condition. Defining menopause as a "deficiency" disease, like diabetes, gynecologists began prescribing estrogen for virtually all menopausal women for an indefinite period. By 1966, when Robert Wilson's book *Feminine Forever* was published, the link between estrogen and endometrial cancer was already known. His crusade for estrogen replacement therapy, from menopause to the grave, was funded by pharmaceutical companies (Ayers Laboratories, Searle, and Upjohn). Kathleen MacPherson, professor and dean at the School of Nursing of the University of Southern Maine, says that "Wilson was widely dismissed as a quack by his more sober colleagues but rarely in public and always off the record." Wilson's "prevention and cure" of menopause prescribed that a woman take estrogen and progesterone throughout her lifetime so that she would continue to have periodic bleeding; otherwise, "no woman can be sure of escaping the horror of this living decay." And medical books began defining menopause as a "deficiency disease only treatable by physicians with estrogen replacement therapy." [1]

By 1975, when a series of studies established that estrogen replacement therapy increased the risk of endometrial cancer, and that DES, the estrogen then prescribed in pregnancy, could cause cancer, Premarin had become one of the most popular drugs in the United States. Six million women were taking it to "prevent aging." There was a 40 percent decrease in estrogen prescriptions after the cancer risk became known. Several million women were probably still taking estrogen as prescribed by their physicians in 1978 when, despite opposition from the drug industry and the medical associations, regulations were passed requiring that all estrogen products contain a prolonged use warning.

In the early 1980s, seeking funds for a more definitive "prospective study of health promotion and disease in Leisure World," Dr. Brian Henderson, a biostatistician at USC, stated:

Few medical interventions have had as widespread application as . . . estrogen treatment in postmenopausal women. One survey indicates that more than half the postmenopausal women in one metropolitan area had used estrogen for at least three months. Such a high prevalence of use and the reported risks and benefits of such use have generated much controversy around the medical community of the appropriate place for estrogen replacement in the *therapeutic regimen* of the individual *patient.* [Italics mine, and a feminist question: If menopause is not a disease but a normal life development, why does it make a woman a "patient" requiring a "therapeutic regimen"?]

In the past five years at least ten studies have been published, all noting a positive association between endometrial cancer and estrogen use. In our own study conducted among the residents of Leisure World . . . women who had used estrogen replacement therapy were eight times more likely to develop endometrial cancer than those who had not (the risk ratio for conjugated estrogen was 5.6). . . . There now remains little doubt that the association between estrogen therapy and endometrial cancer is real. On average, endometrial cancer is found at an earlier stage in women who use estrogen therapy than in those who do not, and the case fatality rate is still about 10%.

The Leisure World study also found that women after approximately three years of daily consumption of 1.25 mg of conjugated estrogen were 2.5 times more likely to develop breast cancer than those not on estrogen. The study noted: "There is no reason to believe that the prevalence of specific menopausal symptoms in the community is unusually high, whereas the prevalence of treatment clearly is." [2] In those California women, none of the other breast cancer risk factors was extreme or significant, including family history, except for long-term use of estrogen. And the 2.5-fold increased risk for those estrogen-using women, an average age of seventy-two at the time, was doubled if they had any history of benign breast complaints. The team also noted that the indications for the estrogen prescriptions "were often ill defined . . . menopausal syndrome . . . lack of energy . . . hot flashes." Based on their study, they estimated the lifetime probability of getting breast cancer for a woman undergoing natural menopause at fifty who receives 1.25 mg of replacement estrogen therapy for approximately three years would increase by age seventy-five from 6 to 7 percent. They felt that "The benefits of estrogen therapy at this dosage level would need to be extremely great to warrant such risk."[3]

But by the end of the 1980s, with estrogen formulas now profit leaders in the pharmaceutical industry and the baby-boomer millions approaching menopause, the medical community seemed united in suppressing such doubts. Reporting on a conference of a newly established medical organization, the North American Menopause Society, Jane Brody wrote in *The New York Times:*

On the one hand, [women] hear, estrogen replacement can perpetuate their premenopausal immunity against heart attacks and it can stop the otherwise inexorable loss of bone with age, a loss that eventually leads to osteoporosis and debilitating fractures in millions of older women.

On the other hand, women are warned that postmenopausal estrogens can increase their risk of developing cancer of the uterus, gallbladder disease and possibly cancer of the breast as well.

They are told that the uterine cancer risk

can be negated by taking a second hormone, progesterone or progestin [which] continues menstrual-like bleeding each month . . . and may wipe out the benefits of estrogen to the heart . . . .

She noted that the conference was "clearly stacked in favor of hormone replacement, with no speakers adamantly against it."[4] A woman epidemiologist from Johns Hopkins deplored the fact that some women "choose not to take hormones [out of] fear of cancer," since "heart disease, not cancer, is far and away the leading killer of women after menopause. Heart disease takes an average 12 lives a year among every 2,000 women over 50 years old, as against two deaths a year from breast cancer. Even if hormone therapy doubled a woman's chance of getting breast cancer . . . it would not come near to canceling estrogen's lifesaving potential."

Dr. Wulf Utian, founder of the new society, and director of Obstetrics and Gynecology at the University Hospital of Cleveland, along with other experts at that conference, discounted a recent Swedish study suggesting that long-term treatment with estrogens can raise a woman's breast cancer risk, *especially* if she took both estrogen and progesterone. The *Times* report went on: "What the study really showed, they said, was that women on hormones who get breast cancer are more likely to survive than breast cancer patients who have not taken estrogens, possibly because estrogen users are more closely monitored and their cancers are detected earlier. As for cancer of the uterus, this is no problem for women who have had a hysterectomy." (Feminist health networks have long warned about the high proportion of unnecessary hysterectomies performed on American women, especially black women. But doctors in this new North American Menopause Society seemed complacent that "in many parts of the country as many as 40 to 50 percent of postmenopausal women have had the uterus surgically removed." As for the rest, they should see their doctors more often, so their cancers can be treated!)

"For those who still have a uterus and are taking estrogens without progesterone, Dr. Utian insists on annual sampling of the uterine lining to detect abnormal growth of endometrial tissue and head off a potential cancer. He pointed out that uterine cancer is a slow growing disease that is highly curable, especially when treated at an early stage."

There is no question that the medical establishment is hardening its stance in favor of hormone replacement therapy, and is annoyed at the "impasse" (as a Mount Sinai dean put it to me) created by women's fear of cancer and distrust of male medical "expertise." Doctors pay lip service to the National Women's Health Network's dictum that women must decide for themselves "which diseases they most want to avoid." But the National Women's Health Network continues to be "critical of the routine prescribing of hormones for healthy women because of the known risks . . . and the lack of complete data on risks and benefits," and the American Association of Retired Persons insists "since not every woman is destined to develop osteoporosis or heart disease or to be bothered by hot flashes, not every woman needs estrogen replacement therapy."[5] The trouble is, too many women, including myself, know other women who, many years later, did contract cancer because their mothers took DES, a hormone prescription for sleeplessness and other problems of pregnancy that once was similarly popular among obstetrician-gynecologists. And until recently progestogens were thought to protect against breast cancer, too. But by 1990, research in Sweden indicated that women on combination hormone therapy had the highest rate of breast cancer—more than twice the rate of women taking estrogen alone, and four times the rate of women who didn't take hormones. So, in 1990, the *AARP Bulletin*'s advice was: "You should take estrogen only for a specific reason, and when you're on it you should be closely monitored by your physician."[6]

Meanwhile, breast cancer's increase nationally seemed to approach epidemic proportions. In

1990, breast cancer killed more than 43,000 Americans. But the scientific establishment seemed only to strengthen its efforts to get every woman to take estrogen, for longer periods of time. In a story in *The New York Times* entitled "Estrogen's Benefits Exceed Cancer Risk, Scientists Say," the Leisure World study was again used to claim that "older women who take estrogen tend to live longer than other postmenopausal women, suggesting that the hormone's ability to prevent heart disease outweighs its risk of causing cancer, scientists say." On the basis of a new review of the Leisure World medical records, USC epidemiologist Dr. Ronald Ross was quoted, "The longer you're on estrogen the longer you live." The claim now was that women who used estrogen at some time after menopause had death rates (for any cause) 20 percent below those who never used the hormone, and women who took estrogen for at least the last fifteen years had death rates 40 percent below non-users. It was also noted that women in the United States were now receiving about 20 million prescriptions a year for estrogen.[7]

It was not noted in this new report that the women who chose to take estrogen in this study were better educated and of a higher socioeconomic group. But I learned later from other researchers that the women who took estrogen in these studies were less likely to die from heart disease because, being better educated and better off, they were more likely to be using the new knowledge about exercise and diet, and thus "probably a healthier group to start with" than those who don't take hormones. But the National Institutes of Health then insisted that it would be too costly, and take too long, to follow a group of comparably healthy women, half of whom take hormones, half who don't, over a ten-year period and also to look into diet and exercise in the same controlled fashion, in terms of risk and benefits, for cancer, heart disease, osteoporosis, hip and wrist fractures, and gallbladder disease. Instead, they sponsored another study on the effects of hormones alone on cholesterol levels in blood.

Still, doctors were joining in what began to seem a concerted campaign to counter the evidence linking estrogen to the increase in breast cancer, and specifically to dismiss the American Cancer Society's warning that women's odds of getting breast cancer had risen to 1 in 9. *The New York Times* reported on March 15, 1992: "The risks of getting breast cancer have been so greatly exaggerated that many women are needlessly taking potentially harmful drugs or even having their healthy breasts removed." Though "one in nine is the cumulative probability that any woman will develop breast cancer sometime between birth and age 110," many experts now insisted that "a woman's risk during most of her life is far lower . . . even women in their eighties do not face a one in nine risk of getting it in the next year . . . and a woman's risk of dying of it is even lower. . . . Even having two close relatives die of breast cancer is not a death warrant." (The American Cancer Society has said it will keep using that number, since 70 percent of American women do not get regular mammograms.) Even so, because of the risks, the National Women's Health Network maintained its opposition to "giving drugs (with known health risks) to healthy women."[8] Meanwhile, it was revealed that the estrogen in birth control pills and in post-menopausal hormone replacement therapy can set off or aggravate migraine headaches. "At least twice as many women as men are plagued with these life disrupting headaches which make them feel sick all over."[9]

I sensed a kind of schizophrenic split in all this, a cognitive dissonance in the messages to and from the baby-boom millions now entering menopause as market and those same women who for these past twenty-five years of women's movement have learned to take control of their own lives and health. But it is not simply the male medical establishment that is promoting these hormones. A measured account in *The New York Times Good Health Magazine* (April 26, 1992) noted a 1989 study from Massachusetts General Hospital which showed that "female doctors are 19 times more likely than male physicians to prescribe hormone replacement therapy." A woman gynecologist at the University of Utah School of Medicine was quoted: "I view menopause as an endocrinopathy. . . . It's just as if a patient came in with hyperthyroidism or any other gland failure. If a woman was at very high risk of osteoporosis but also had a family history of breast cancer, I wouldn't hesitate to put her on estrogen." A woman professor at Harvard Medical School, director of what is now called the Menopause Unit at Massachusetts General Hospital, complained that her efforts to convince her patients to take hormones were often unsuccessful: "When it comes to hormones, women are influenced by non-medical sources. . . . Yet when doctors tell people to take medicine to lower blood pressure, they take it, even though there are some side effects." One woman had a doctor tell her, "If you don't take estrogen you're going to end up with osteoporosis and no sex life."

The report concluded:

Many women in the baby boom population (which by the year 2010 will provide more than 50 million potential customers for hormone therapy) are not inclined to simply follow doctor's orders. . . . Many women feel uncomfortable with whatever decision they make about hormone replacement therapy. A Massachusetts survey found that one-third of women who are given prescriptions for hormones don't bother to fill them. Those who choose to take hormones are often apologetic and uneasy. . . . Women who decide against hormone therapy worry that they'll be sorry later on. The treatment can, however, be started at almost any point.

The upshot of this, and other reviews, is that some women "should obviously take hormones and another group should obviously not," but for the majority trying to decide whether to take hormones, the issues are less clear. "To sort them out, each woman entering menopause should have a physical examination and then talk with her doctor. . . . And because there is no one therapy that suits everyone, the wisest option for patients and their doctors is to resist irrational fear of estrogen as well as estrogen evangelism." [10]

The new three-year study finally begun at the National Institutes of Health as a result of a recent campaign led by the women in Congress will investigate the effects of drug treatment of women placed randomly in groups taking estrogen alone, estrogen and progesterone in three different combinations, or a placebo. Specifically, the study will measure the effects of the drugs on cholesterol, blood pressure, and bone density, as well as cancer of the breast and uterus. Another $100 million, fourteen-year study will track the incidence of heart disease, osteoporosis, and breast and uterine cancer in 25,000 post-menopausal women taking either estrogen or a combination hormone therapy. These studies are designed to yield clearer answers to questions doctors have about dosage levels for the dozens of medications they now prescribe for menopause. The fourteen-year study will also look into diet. But these studies, it seems to me, will merely refine the "medicalization of menopause." If menopause were not seen as disease, why would the studies start and end with hormone replacement therapy instead of the various aspects of *life after menopause* that contribute to vitality and health or seem to hasten debility and death?

On the other hand, for the growing numbers of experts on menopause-as-disease promoting lifelong hormone replacement therapy, the very strength and health of women undergoing "change of life" today is the problem, the very fact that "most women seem to pass through menopause with minimal discomforts or disruptions and seek no treatment," that only about 15 to 18 percent of post-menopausal women now take hormone replacements since many "who can readily afford hormone therapy are reluctant to try it."

The *disapproval* doctors express at women's "resistance" to hormone therapy jolted me, at first, for despite my own feminist suspicion of doctor-as-god, I respect many doctors, male and female, including some in my own family. And some of the doctors I truly respect accept the estrogen gospel and deplore the fact that people like me whose "word is listened to by women" question it. The feminist warnings, especially, are seen as "potentially dangerous." "It's a shame," the ubiquitous Dr. Wulf Utian, founder of that North American Menopause Society, told *Newsweek,* "because so many women are reaching menopause now and are getting information from non-experts." [11]

Perhaps because of such exchange of information, in women's health networks and other groups where women now talk about that once-shameful, never-discussed-out-loud "change of life"—and sometimes trust each other more than the medical establishment, or learn that each has been told a completely different set of "facts" by her doctor—most American women, so far, seem to be resisting the estrogen evangelists. As Jane Brody reported in *The New York Times:*

Despite renewed interest in estrogens to treat the sometimes depressing symptoms of menopause and its long-term effects on the health of the heart and bones, fewer than one woman in five who has reached that stage of life now uses hormone replacement therapy. . . . Even among those who start hormone therapy, only about one-third use it regularly, and many abandon the treatment after the most common immediate symptoms of menopause, hot flashes, subside. Also, many women are simply opposed to the idea of taking any kind of medication day after day, year after year, when they feel perfectly fine.

The overriding cause of this menopause mania is, of course, the sheer size of the market. Responsible health reporters have warned that the new breed of menopause mavens have personally profited from the expanding menopause market. Brody commented:

Pharmaceutical companies, meanwhile, are racing to develop more acceptable and safer hormone regimens in hope of capturing a market that already exceeds half a billion dollars and is still growing. If manufacturers and enthusiastic doctors prevail, upwards of 90 percent of women will take replacement hormones for three to five decades.[12]

There has also been a surge in over-the-counter menopause "remedies," particularly vaginal lubricants, and entrepreneurs are scratching their heads about what else women in this age group might be persuaded to buy. What's more, the *Times* reported that "with talk of menopause reaching a passionate pitch nationwide," medical debate has begun over treating men for the drop in their sex hormones after midlife.

A number of recent studies have suggested that testosterone levels do slump gradually with age, perhaps by as much as 30 to 40 percent between the ages of 48 and 70. . . . Scientists are fiercely divided over whether any of the effects of gradual testosterone loss are serious enough to merit treatment with hormone supplements, the male counterpart of estrogen replacement therapy in postmenopausal women. Some gerontologists suggest that many elderly men may benefit from testosterone supplements. . . . Others warn that the excessive use of male hormones could raise the risk of prostate cancer and cardiovascular disease, a large price to pay merely to hang onto youthful biceps and libido. They worry that normal aging among men will come to be viewed as a deficiency, and that men will be cajoled into taking expensive and potentially hazardous treatments they do not really need.[13]

A Boston University epidemiologist, Dr. John B. McKinley, warned that even though "there is no epidemiological, physiological or clinical evidence for such a syndrome, I think by the year

2000 the [male menopause] syndrome will exist. There's very strong interest in treating aging men for a profit, just as there is for menopausal women."

There is a growing body of information, however, which could dispel the obsessive fear of age that is at the root of the menopause mania. If in Gail Sheehy's *The Silent Passage* menopause is "a panicky, weepy episode, driving women to whimper, 'Won't I ever be me anymore?' "[14] the overwhelming evidence in research studies and in my own interviews strongly indicates that, in vital age, women as well as men *become more and more themselves.* The "natural" remedies for alleviating menopause symptoms—vitamins E and B6, herbs and biofeedback, continued sexual activity in all its diversity, endorphin-producing pursuits and projects, and above all, "regular physical exercise, which helps both the circulatory system and the bones"—also have their markets, but they are clearly less profit-generating than synthetic hormones. Buried after the hormone news are often the less sexy facts that "even for women well past menopause who have already lost significant amounts of bone, exercise can help to maintain and even increase bone mass."[15] "Exercise also increases blood levels of protective HDL-cholesterol, which helps to keep arteries clear of fatty deposits." Or at the very bottom of the page: "Studies of other cultures have found that the more women are revered in aging, the less trouble they seem to have with menopause—physically or psychologically." [16]

I am alarmed at this new epidemic of menopause mania. It seems to counter the effects of the women's movement of the last twenty-five years, erase our breakthrough of that obsolete feminine mystique which used to define the cessation of reproductive sexuality as the "end of life as a woman." The *personhood* of women, which is what the women's movement was all about, hardly ends with menstruation. And surely our self-esteem is based now on our total personhood, our participation in society, not just our sexuality and motherhood. We have asserted control over our own reproduction, no longer passive martyrs to our biological "destiny." But I am concerned that women's very wish to "control" our own lives, even some feminists' excessive embrace of (or reaction against) the victim state, may feed into the menopause mania. How can conscientious female obstetricians, gynecologists, and gerontologists not embrace the "overwhelming evidence" that estrogen not only relieves menopausal symptoms but lengthens life? It's hardly surprising that the women doctors as well as the men buy into the medical model, which up until now has, of course, been defined by men. Women have been moving in great numbers into these professions only recently, and even when they give new importance to women's experience, they still conduct their studies and treatment within the framework of that medical model: menopause, age, as disease.

Dr. Gail Greendale, a brilliant young internist and UCLA Medical School professor, has devoted her entire five-year research career to integrating all the studies on menopause and osteoporosis. Was it possible, I asked her, that women in these studies years ago may have been profoundly depressed in menopause because of factors that no longer exist? There's no question, she said, that women who don't take estrogen have higher rates of bone loss after fifty, and higher rates of wrist and hip fractures. But she warned: "The evidence that estrogen is helpful for this comes from observational reports, not randomized controlled studies of the same population."

Still, she herself was convinced by the "magnitude" of the effect, though she admitted that the possible role of exercise and diet in this was simply not known. As for the long-term effect, "you'd have to follow women for twenty years to find out if women who get estrogen at age fifty have fewer hip fractures at seventy, or any other effects." Similarly, the observational studies seemed to show those who take estrogen have one-third fewer heart attacks in their sixties than women who don't take it; but again, the women who took estrogen were healthier to begin with, and again, factors of behavior, exercise, diet, and mental health were not looked at. Hopefully, the Women's Health Initiative study will be free of this "prevention bias."

Dr. Greendale said:

Whether or not menopause actually causes declines in memory, attention, mood, there's evidence that argues in both directions. The studies that show an association of depression with menopause were done on women who went to doctors with the preconceived notion that menopause was going to cause depression. Of three major studies going on now in random populations undergoing menopause in New England and Baltimore, two out of three show no relationship of depression to years from menopause, the Baltimore study shows an association of "depressed mood" and not clinical depression. Many theories have been proposed to explain the mental and emotional changes in menopause, but whether or not these phenomena really occur is now in question.

The evidence of breast cancer risk from taking estrogen, on the other hand, suffered from something called "surveillance bias." As Dr. Greendale put it:

Any physician prescribing estrogen is going to make sure these women come in for mammograms and physical examinations every year. I don't want to explain away any benefit of estrogen itself. But women who don't take estrogen are not getting in to see physicians as much. Therefore, every single study that looks at the relationship of estrogen to breast cancer is biased to find cancer.

Actually, there are two studies that find a 30 percent increased risk of breast cancer after ten years of estrogen use, but the increased risk doesn't show up until after ten years so we conclude that there is no risk of increase in breast cancer for women who use estrogen up to ten years. We don't have data over fifteen years; very few women up until now have taken estrogen that long. But the prevention of heart attack only seems to happen among women *currently* taking estrogen.

You wouldn't want to give estrogen to a woman who had breast cancer, because it could make it grow. But even with a history of breast cancer in the family, we would now prescribe estrogen.

As for the increase in breast cancer (from one in eleven to one in nine), "probably detection" explains a lot of it "but not all." The doctors assure us that even if the benefits of estrogen on osteoporosis and heart involve greater risk of cancer, women who take estrogen are more likely to get "early detection" of cancer; but Dr. Greendale warned that "early detection doesn't necessarily mean increased survival."

She herself would prescribe estrogen to women coming to her with menopausal symptoms, in the belief that the "imperfect information" they must act on is of sufficient "magnitude," "consistency," and "biological plausibility" to warrant hormone replacement therapy. She said:

I believe 95 percent of the medical community would now agree with me that estrogen prevents osteoporosis. If they ask me if diet, exercise, calcium might not be just as good, without the risks of estrogen, I'd have to say we don't have that information. I tell them, if you want to live with the uncertainty—if after all the information I've given you, you'd rather stick with diet, calcium, and exercise—I'd say, if you can live with the uncertainty, okay, that's fine. At this time, 10 percent of my women patients are on unopposed estrogen; they need to have endometrial biopsies annually because we do know the risk of endometrial cancer is four times greater with estrogen. But earlier changes in the uterus precede that cancer. Then you have to either stop the estrogen, or combine it with progesterone, or do a D&C. Though there's some data that progesterone undermines the beneficial effect of estrogen on cardiovascular disease, about 40 percent of my patients are now on Premarin (estrogen) and Provera (progesterone). They have that bleeding once a month, just like the good old days. I tell them I'm comfortable for them to stay on that regimen up to ten years; after that, if I have more information, I'll pass it on.

Any woman who comes into my office approaching fifty, who hasn't had a period in a year, I ask about her mood, hot flashes, other symptoms, and has she thought about prevention issues associated with menopause. If she's never heard about estrogen and osteoporosis, cardiovascular risk, I tell her these are things women don't necessarily feel at fifty, but at sixty-five or seventy it may be too late. Most women who come into my office who've never given much thought to menopause don't leave with a prescription for estrogen right away. I tell them it's a major decision, to think and talk about it to friends and family, and then come back to see me, because the first time you hear all this, it's overwhelming.

I think there's been a major backlash against estrogen but it's time to swing back. I see an extremely biased sample of highly intelligent, highly educated women who've read it all. They are more informed about estrogen than most physicians. I lay down the benefits, the risks; I think being anti-estrogen is anti-feminist as much as being an estrogen evangelist.

You have to live with the uncertainty. The controlled studies that are being started now won't be finished by the time I reach menopause. As of now, I'll take estrogen, even though my mother had breast cancer and I also run an hour every day.

Dr. Greendale was not alone. Dr. Donna Shoupe, director for Gynecology, Infertility and Menopause at USC Medical School, also did a macro-study of all the diverse, confusing, sometimes contradictory research on estrogen replacement therapy and menopause. She became convinced that women on estrogen didn't seem as likely to be dying of heart attacks. She told me:

To be honest, I do believe in my heart there's a greater risk of breast cancer if women take estrogen replacement therapy. There does seem to be almost an epidemic of breast cancer. But the benefits of estrogen far outweigh the risks. If you put all the papers together, women feel better after menopause if they take estrogen. When the ovary stops making estrogen, changes are going to take place. If you stay on estrogen, you'll stay the same longer. There are many, many changes the body undergoes if you don't take estrogen.

I suppose there *is* advance, as well as the possibility of regression, in the new brouhaha over menopause. The fact is, women heading into age today are not passive, not easily manipulated—by doctors, pharmaceutical manufacturers, drug salesmen, or politicians. In the battle for control of their own reproductive choices, they learned a lot.

I sat in a conference room at the National Institutes of Health (NIH) in Bethesda with three of the women responsible for carrying out the new Women's Health Initiative study. Bernadine Healy, first woman head of NIH, had been implacable in her insistence that medical research make up for its previous male blind spot and focus on diseases, disorders, and conditions unique, more prevalent, or more serious in women, and on different risks and treatment of conditions which may or may not be experienced differently by women. The fourteen-year study by the Women's Health Initiative will finally investigate the long-term effects of diet, exercise, and other non-pharmaceutical measures on the health of older women. Dr. Florence Haseltine, who is in charge of the study and director of the new Office of Research on Women's Health, told me:

We had to separate out women's health from reproduction and sex, so we started with menopause, which nobody was doing any real research on anyway. Besides, our whole generation is heading into menopause now, which makes it a national emergency. We're the group that got our husbands into the delivery room—we're not putting up with this menopause!

You need a lot more information about women's health than just estrogen. You can't tell women now to do one thing or the other; if they don't have symptoms, they won't take estrogen. At the end of three years, our Postmenopausal Estrogen Progesterone Initiative will have studied four or five thousand women who are taking controlled doses of estrogen, estrogen and progesterone, or nothing at all, and we will know what effect it actually has on their bone density, their cholesterol level and lipids, and cancer. We'll have a better handle on preventing osteoporosis and breast cancer in older women. Rather than arguing without knowing the answers, we'll have the information, the data, so women can make real choices.

Given the confusing and contradictory information they are getting from doctors and menopause "experts" today, women have to make their personal choices on the basis of informed guess and gut feeling. My friend Martha, who

had been taking estrogen for eight years, decided to stop: "If I'm not taking it, at least it can't
feed a cancer—I exercise enough, my heart's
fine." Phyllis, a doctor herself, had real menopausal difficulties—painful, drying vaginal tissues, terrible mood swings—which estrogen
helped. She told Joan, a friend of hers whose
mother and aunts died young of heart disease,
not to worry about cancer. As long as she
flushed out all those cells with progesterone
every month, they couldn't grow into cancer,
could they?

My friend Ruth Spear, after breast cancer herself, started the National Alliance of Breast Cancer Organizations, which has led the battle
nationwide to give women more information,
and more control, from health insurance coverage for mammograms to more research on alternatives to estrogen. Her coalition, which ranges
from feminists and academics to female executives and Catholic nuns, takes action on information that they disseminate, such as early
warning on silicone breast implants and new
studies showing that breast cancer risk increases with the duration of hormone replacement therapy.[17] She reminded me:

By the time a breast cancer is detectable on a
mammogram, it has been growing for eight
years. Breast cancer affects 145,000 women

annually in this country. If you multiply this figure by eight, this means 1,160,000 women are walking around at any given time with undetected breast cancer. So who can identify who will not be harmed by estrogen? For some 70 percent of breast cancer, causal factors remain unknown. A number of researchers feel that the link for all the known risk factors for breast cancer involves the metabolism of estrogen. In 1971, about 70,000 women suffered breast cancer; in 1991, more than 175,000.

Armed with information like this, Spear's coalition helped pass laws in Indiana, Montana, Vermont, and thirty-three other states requiring insurance companies to cover screening mammograms and Medicare to cover screening mammography, and an annual exam for older women.

The studies that counter the medical model—of menopause-as-disease—are mainly disseminated through the growing women's health networks and burgeoning menopausal self-help or consciousness-raising groups, from *Our Bodies, Ourselves* to *Ourselves, Growing Older.* Inspired by feminist thinking, each such menopause self-help group is different, focusing on physical and social midlife concerns, health care problems and alternatives, as well as the effects of estrogen replacement therapy and the influence not only of hormones but menopausal stereotypes on sexuality and women's sexual identity. They share their own experiences and perceptions as older women, much as younger women did twenty-five years ago. Women are also emerging in the health care professions who are asking new questions. Self-help groups are giving extensive consideration to alternative health measures: herbs, vitamins, diet, and exercise. This sharing of experience itself seems a potent health measure. Members of the Menopausal Collective in Cambridge, Massachusetts, mentioned more than any treatment or drug their sense of being "part of a supportive community" as giving them "more self-esteem, less anxiety" about menopause, a "feeling of power" instead of "hopelessness," and, above all, "a more positive attitude about growing older."

In a newsletter called *Healthsharing* (Winter 1986), Ann Voda, a nurse with her doctorate in physiology, provided "Cool News for Hot Flashes": "My own work on the hot flash over the past eight years suggests that most women can and do deal with the hot flash as a normal part of life without resorting to automatic and regular estrogen use." The hot flash is, of course, "real," and her research indicated that 88 percent of menopausal women experience it, over varying periods of time, but its very commonness would indicate that it "cannot be abnormal or a symptom of disease." Research from her laboratory and others suggested that estrogen replacement therapy merely prolongs the transition, and prevents women's bodies from settling into a new biological rhythm as they otherwise will do after about a year. If estrogen is used and then withdrawn, menopausal sensations and changes associated with the transition reappear, and going through these at a later age can be worse.

An editorial in *Hot Flash* (Spring 1988), a newsletter for midlife and older women, warned:

> Osteoporosis is a "hot" issue for women today. It is the most severe, crippling disorder midlife and older women face. Although it now affects one out of four white women over age 50, the vast majority of us are not condemned to develop it as we age.
>
> A media blitz has convinced many of us that women are naturally . . . subject to this disorder because of decreased estrogen levels after menopause. All menopausal women are being advised to take hormone replacement therapy the rest of their lives, to prevent this devastating disorder. . . . All women (if they are lucky enough to live so long) go through menopause, but three-fourths of them don't get osteoporosis. . . . Why should women who are not at any known risk for osteoporosis take controversial hormones into their bodies for almost half their lives?

... Would aging men allow such experimentation with their normal hormone balance? ... Why don't many of us know that we have osteoporosis until we suffer a fractured wrist or hip? Why can't each of us go to our physician to require that our bone density and estrogen levels be accurately measured? ...

We do know that people who are physically active, even into old age, tend to have denser bones than sedentary people of the same age; that elderly women who start exercising even at age 80, can slow and even reverse some bone loss. What we need to know now is the kinds and amounts of exercise which are most effective.

At a conference for nurse practitioners sponsored by the State University of New York Health Science Center and Planned Parenthood, at the Hunter Health Science Center in New York, I joined some hundreds of health care professionals, mainly women, in a cutting edge symposium entitled "Women Growing Older: Breaking the Rules" in October 1988. Kathleen MacPherson, professor and dean at the School of Nursing, University of Southern Maine, discussed "the politics of estrogen replacement therapy," and others dealt with clues for early diagnosis of endometrial and ovarian cancer, cardiovascular risk screening, breast cancer update, management of menopausal symptoms, and urinary incontinence in women. At least as much time was spent on "Preventing Isolation and Loneliness in the Later Years: Lifestyle Options," "Staying Social," and other issues of "empowerment" to enable midlife and older women to take more control of their own lives and health. The nurse practitioners and other clinicians got professional credit for these three days, though many of the things they learned broke the rules of conventional medical wisdom.

Increasingly, recent reports indicate that "menopause plays no significant role" in the health of middle-aged women, except for the small, distinct group who have a surgical hysterectomy. In a Massachusetts health study of 8,000 randomly selected women in 1981–82, more than 70 percent expressed feelings of relief or neutral feelings about menopause; less than 3 percent expressed any regret, even among the surgical menopause group. Followed for nearly five years, 2,300 of the same women showed changes of attitude only from mixed or regretful feelings to more positive. Prior attitudes about or *expectations of menopause* were almost the only factor that affected their experience, and carried far more weight than hot flashes.

Despite health care professionals' belief that depression in middle-aged women is caused by endocrine deficiency after menopause and can be "cured" by treating them with estrogens, the only group of women in the Massachusetts study reporting an increase in depression were those who recently had a hysterectomy. The study indicated that "depression" in middle-aged women is associated mainly with "events and circumstances unrelated to the hormonal changes that occur at menopause."

MacPherson told the conference:

The myth of menopause as disease has been so successfully marketed to the American public that currently most women associate the word menopause with depression if not mental illness, osteoporosis if not cancer. Because menopause has been labeled a disease, women believe they must be "treated" by physicians with carcinogenic estrogens in order to be "cured." . . . Nurses must dismantle this metaphor and return menopause to their women clients as a natural and positive event. Nurses cannot naively expect physicians to admit to patients that they have been prescribing an iatrogenic [harmful, disease-producing] treatment. . . .

Once menopause was constructed as a disease by the American medical profession and . . . presented as scientific truth to the public . . . menopause as a normal and biological event disappeared. . . . Medical and psychiatric literature has presented the menopausal woman as frequently depressed, unstable, confused, tired, asexual, and overwhelmed by hot flashes. . . . The only scientifically documented menopausal experiences are hot flashes and night sweating. . . . There is no estrogen-deficiency syndrome, and menopause is not an illness.[18]

MacPherson further warned:

When hormones are used to treat known osteoporosis, the benefits can be weighed against the risks by a woman and her care provider. To recommend widespread use of hormone replacement therapy . . . to prevent osteoporosis . . . would be the same as recommending that everyone take antihypertensive drugs because so many people develop high blood pressure. For no other condition is anything as potentially dangerous as hormones being recommended as a preventive measure. Yet some physicians persist in supporting long-term hormone replacement beginning shortly after menopause and long before osteoporosis has progressed to fractures. . . .

If women stop taking prophylactic HRT there is a rebound effect causing them to lose bone as rapidly as if they had never taken the hormones. Once started on hormones women also become dependent on expensive medical services—regular pelvic and breast exams, pap smears, blood pressure monitoring, and endometrial biopsies.[19]

MacPherson did not claim that diet and exercise alone can prevent osteoporosis. She pointed out that the medical model overlooks social factors that put women at risk for osteoporosis, such as poverty, which induces a low-calcium diet, and violence, which causes lack of exercise for fear of walking alone. Finally, "continuing the myth that osteoporosis is caused by a flaw in women's physiology not only subjects women to hormone replacement therapy with its yet unknown long-term dangers for older women but leaves the situation of men with osteoporosis largely ignored." [20]

I do not think the dangers of the new menopause mania apply to women alone, or require us to mount or continue a war of women against men into age. Somehow the strengths in women that emerge with age enable us to live longer than men, and get better health care, even organizing self-help groups when we have reason to distrust the medical model. Women who survived cancer, not their doctors, organized the National Alliance of Breast Cancer Organizations to get mammograms covered by health insurance. And the women in Congress who fought for the Women's Health Initiative are finally getting the research needed to overcome the male blind spot in the medical model.

During the conference for nurse practitioners in New York, Lois Monteiro of Brown University pointed out that nearly three times as many women die of heart disease as cancer, yet heart disease is considered a men's disease, and women don't perceive themselves at risk. In fact, women may *not* be as much at risk for heart disease as men. The gender differences that are beginning to become clear are tricky in their implications. On the one hand, almost everything that is known by science about heart disease is based on research done solely among men, and treatment based on these parameters doesn't seem to be given as readily or work as well on women. But this may or may not turn out to be an advantage for women.

Men are four or five times more likely than women to undergo coronary artery bypass surgery, mainly because men are still much more likely to get heart disease than women. Findings that women hospitalized for coronary heart disease undergo fewer major diagnostic and therapeutic procedures than men may reflect "under use in women or overuse in men," the *New England Journal of Medicine* reported in 1991. Women with positive stress tests are referred for angiography less frequently than men, and women are referred for bypass surgery at a more advanced stage of the disease than men, resulting in higher mortality.

The *New England Journal* report speculated:

If women are more willing than men to adapt their lifestyle and use medications to avoid surgery, or if they are more averse to short term risks, they may decline most procedures more often than men. . . . [or] the differences may represent a sex bias in the delivery of medical care. Such a bias may compromise the clinical outcomes of women who undergo procedures at a later stage of disease, or in some men with less severe disease who undergo procedures that offer little or no marginal benefit over more conservative care.[21]

The relative differences between women's and men's access to new high-technology care was also reported for dialysis and kidney transplants, diagnosis of lung cancer, and catheterization for coronary bypass surgery.

Lois Monteiro questioned the prescription of estrogen as protection for women against heart disease, pointing out that that same hormone in the birth control pill sometimes causes blood clots and stroke. She wondered why doctors aren't asking:

Why does that female hormone which is supposed to protect women from heart disease, in fact, sometimes lead to blood clotting, myocardial infarction? The medical profession, which is still mainly male, hasn't asked or studied this. There has been virtually no research on this supposed hormonal protection from heart disease. I don't know of any study of those women on estrogen over a long period of time who definitively got more protection on heart disease along with the risk of uterine cancer.

What is more likely to protect women, she suggested, is that the stressful, hard-driving, pressure-packed Type A behavior pattern associated with men's heart attacks doesn't seem to work for women in the same way. Contrary to the predictions that women who entered male professions and careers would succumb to early heart attacks and strokes like men, a study released in the *American Journal of Public Health* (January 1992) by researchers at the University of California, San Diego, showed that working women, in an upper-middle-class suburb, Rancho Bernardo, had significantly lower risk of heart disease at ages, forty to fifty-nine, and fifteen years later, at fifty-five to seventy-four, than housewives or women who could not find steady work. Most of the women were managers, business owners, professionals or executives. After tracking 242 women from 1972 to 1987, researchers discovered that the working women had sharply lower cholesterol and blood sugar levels, and better blood pressure and in-sulin levels than women who stayed home. The working women also seemed to drink and smoke a little less, weigh less, and exercise more than women at home, but that didn't ex-plain the difference. The researchers speculated that working gave these women a psychological bonus that translates into physical well-being and ties with others "who can share the burden when things go wrong."

The only case in the Framingham Study in which Type A working women did have more heart attacks were women in dead-end jobs, with no ability to move or control the situation, upper-level clerical or secretarial jobs with no real autonomy, and a lot of responsibility on the job and in the family. Monteiro therefore had high hopes for healthy age for women who in recent years have been moving into careers. "They won't be in that kind of dead-end situa-tion. They may be in high-stress careers, but the flexibility, the adaptability they've acquired, jug-gling responsibilities, life priorities, shifting in and out of roles may be more important protec-tion than hormones."

The questions I have now about "care" in age go beyond the medical model, even if its sex bias is cleared up. I keep coming back to the first clue that set me off on this search over twenty-five years ago: my hunch, from those women who "didn't have menopause," that women who had broken through the feminine mystique, going beyond the biological role which used to define their lives to a fully human personhood, would experience a completely different aging process—that menopause would simply be another milestone of life and growth they would pass through. Now that I have confronted in full force in my own life and among the countless women and experts I have been interviewing the reality of this change, and the forces opposing it, I see that eternal vigilance is needed to ward off both a reversion to the feminine mystique, and a passive acquiescence to the medical model which reinforces the mystique of age as decline even as it seems to defend against it. The questions that still make me uneasy, after all my attempts to pierce through the research ambiguities of the menopause mania, come up again with renewed urgency when we face that unknown territory of age beyond the "change of life," which cannot be avoided, or even postponed forever, for women or men, no matter how much estrogen or progesterone is prescribed for us. To be blunt, do we want to organize our age around "care"—in an ultimately futile denial of death—or do we want to *live our life and our death* as part of the ever-changing mysterious larger life and world that will go on after us?

These new years of life beyond biological reproduction make us unique as human beings. Do we eschew the possible meaning of these years, *waste* our human age, if by estrogen or testosterone we try to keep ourselves from continuing to change, keep the semblance of estrogenic sexuality and testosterone-macho virility, though, in fact, both are shams at this point, no longer serving biological reproduction for survival of the species? Do we thereby prevent ourselves from maturing into some larger wisdom and generativity that anthropologists now surmise may be the evolutionary significance of age for our survival as human society?

Even in terms of our own lives, the Oakland Longitudinal Study and other research indicated that the stereotypical, polarized "masculinity" and "femininity" which seemed to best serve teenagers' adjustment, if maintained into age, were least conducive to well-being, development, and mental health. In the research on menopause, I was struck by the fact that women who had dieted obsessively to stay too youthfully thin were among the few with severe physiological symptoms at menopause. Drug companies and doctors are still trying to dismiss the horrifying spectacle of millions of women mutilated, and even endangering their lives, sold those silicone gel implants to mimic youthful breasts even though, of course, they would not yield sexual sensation or milk. Young, testosterone-rich males are at worst risk for death by car accident, as we know from the insurance tables, and that hard-driving, youthful "masculine" dominance, if rigidly maintained, characterizes the Type A male most prone to heart attacks in midlife. Could the decision to take the synthetic hormones that are related to these traits into age avoid, in effect, that masculine-feminine "cross-over," the knitting of those two halves of ourselves together that Gutmann and others found in those who do keep growing, changing, and becoming more fully themselves and whole as they age?

In mounting our battle for equality with men these past years, I, at least, never meant that women should exchange their frustrations as housewives, within the obsolete sexual parameters of their female role, for the heart attacks that twenty-five years ago were striking hard-driving American men down at ever younger years. And, in fact, that has not happened. We have seen that as men have changed their lifestyle and taken better care of themselves, as well as sharing more in the care of their children, their risk of heart attack has gone way down; and as women have moved to purposes beyond sexual attraction and the care of husbands, children, and homes, their mental health no longer declines but improves as they age. Women who work outside the home now are less at risk for heart attack than housewives. Those polarized sex roles were geared to reproduction, the social biologists say. If we try to prolong them, do we miss other liberating possibilities of the fountain of age?

What has all this to do with "care"? These aren't the questions we ask, or are asked by, our doctors. *In a certain sense the very premise of the "care" they offer us in age is that, insofar as possible, it will keep us from growing older, our bodies, ourselves,* or will keep on "curing" us, denying death forever. The "care" that tries to treat, cure, eradicate age itself as disease may inadvertently hasten our death. It also keeps us from facing our own *changed* needs for intimacy and purpose, diet, sleep, and exercise, instead urging us to buy those drugs.

I felt like cheering the first signs of paradigm shift at the nurse practitioners' conference in New York. Confronting the problems of drug abuse by older women, they considered ways to cope "with the loneliness and isolation many older women feel as they are forced to live out their later years alone," and "the creative lifestyle/housing options women around the country have chosen, or designed, so that they may continue to grow and thrive all of the years that they live." The nurse practitioners were asked to explore their own assumptions about sexuality in older women, and how these affect care decisions. A program for "Staying Social" designed to serve gay and lesbian elders in the five boroughs of New York City was studied for its larger implications: "All older women face the loss of loved ones, loss of friends, loss of mobility, and the loss even of control of their lives. Life becomes filled with outsiders—doctors, hospital health attendants, caseworkers. Survival is often dependent on not being alone—not being isolated in one's needs." Instead of tranquilizers and painkillers, the nurse practitioners discussed practical ways to bring about "networking, connecting, sharing."

As I was puzzling over all these questions about care, a woman of my own acquaintance, a successful film executive somewhere over fifty, suddenly committed suicide, throwing herself out of her high-rise apartment when an overdose of sleeping pills didn't kill her. It shocked the world of high-powered women in New York of which she and I were part, since no one even knew she was "that depressed." The Women's Forum, whose membership is solely based on career success, was moved to convene a special lunch to address the need "to be there for each other" and to "have someone to call" when, in the face of age that we have all been experiencing, any of us have "problems" or "concerns" that we need to share. For years, it seemed, nothing had been discussed at Women's Forum meetings, informally or formally, except advances in people's careers. It came out that many women simply stopped coming to the meetings when they had no career advances to report. They talked, now, of their need to share their own "pain," at or after divorce, putting parents in nursing homes, conflicts with grown kids, fears about cancer, and the sheer need of deeper, closer ties, to be with each other. These high-powered women, still dressing for success, most now in their fifties and sixties, some dying their gray hair, wanted to "come out" with their age, wanted to share with each other feelings beyond the ambitions that had fused their "new girl network" to combat "the old boy network" twenty years ago.

If we cannot solve the problems of age by a "care" that is based on denial, we must help give each other the care we do need to keep control of our lives, confronting the realities of our aging bodies, ourselves growing older. Can we really control all possibility of heart disease, osteoporosis, diabetes, cancer, all risk of any debility or decline? For how long? If we kept on those drugs which "prevent" or "postpone" menopause indefinitely, even if we didn't invite uterine or breast cancer, liver disease or stroke, would we forfeit the lucid glow, or what Margaret Mead called the post-menopausal zest, of finally being fully who we are ourselves? Whatever that hormone replacement therapy may or may not do, isn't our real need now to forge deep new purposes and bonds and nourish old ones, with man, woman, and child?

And must we not acknowledge the limits to our

own control—that life *is* change? That, beyond menopause, at sixty, seventy, eighty, vital as we may be, using our bodies, using our minds and hearts, in the activities that keep us human, there will still come a day when we are helpless, in the face of irreversible disease, in the face of death?

The Nursing Home Specter

We were sitting around my dining table in Sag Harbor, old friends, pooling leftovers in a homey communal midweek dinner, mussel soup cooked by Leni, the youngest of us (though she must be nearly fifty now), with mussels harvested off the ocean bottom by Si, an avid diver, who'll soon be seventy-five, just finishing his latest sociological tome on changes in the family. Cynthia brought bread and Linda wine, and I buttressed my leftover chicken and rice salad with fresh sliced tomatoes, sprinkled with balsamic vinegar, olive oil, and sprigs of basil from my garden. We were used to cooking together, since some of us had shared a communal house in our earlier, post-divorce years.

What we talked about that night was something I couldn't remember our ever having talked about before: how we want to end our lives. Well, of course, we had all been aging, and I, the oldest after Si, had been writing about it, though not talking about it, really, with my friends. Si said, *sotto voce:* "Some of us might talk about other people's aging, because we don't want to face our own." But Cynthia's father had just died, at ninety-one, from pneumonia, after two years of progressive disability and decline from a stroke. He had been fine, at eighty-eight, lively; he had even flirted with me when he visited two summers ago. The last two years, she told us, everything started to go—his eyesight, he'd get confused, fall in the bathroom. They needed, finally, to arrange for someone to be with him around the clock in his condo in Florida. He didn't actually have any major illness, no specific disease. It all started after her mother's death four years earlier. "Even though they didn't get along," Cynthia said, "she must have given some necessary structure to his life. But even then, at eighty-eight, he'd gone on a trip to Israel and made a really close new friend, a man of eighty-two, and spent fine times with him and his lady friends and then, the new friend died, and Dad seemed to lose it."

Her father had signed a very careful, detailed living will. The doctors, of course, had treated the pneumonia with antibiotics, which could perhaps have cured it. But it was evident that he could no longer function. Though he could not communicate with them at all, the living will made clear his wishes. The doctor, accordingly, was told to stop the antibiotics, and not to prolong unnecessary painful dying; the doctor himself suggested stopping the artificial feeding and hydration. It had been painful for Cynthia to give that permission, but she'd gone over it with her father before. And, I realized, my own living will was too general. "Could I spell it out, if and when I would not be able to talk, to walk, to eat, to drink, to move, to read?" "Well, maybe reading isn't that important." "Maybe you would want to go on living even if you couldn't walk."

Leni had put her mother, after a stroke, in a Long Island nursing home, where doctors said she would never be able to walk again, and would be dead in a few months. Leni's mother said she wanted to go back to her condo in Florida, to die at home, where she still had friends. Taking her mother back to her old doctor in Florida in a wheelchair to get a painkiller prescription, Leni told him that there was no point in trying to get her mother to walk again. However, the doctor insisted on asking her himself if she would like to try walking again. Her mother said yes, and put her whole mind to the exercises with the physiotherapist the doctor recommended, and did walk again, and saw her friends, and got around fairly happily for three months, when she fell and died.

Linda's father, eighty-nine, was back now in an apartment in his old neighborhood in Greenwich Village, liberated from a "continuing-care" facility, complete with nursing home, which Linda's brother had found for them near his own place in Chicago after their father had a stroke and could no longer take care of their mother who had Alzheimer's. Their father, forced to retire at seventy-six from the beauty business he had run, had found a whole new career for himself handling the accounting for a volunteer refugee agency he'd become active in. But he had refused to put his wife in a nursing home. Transplanted to the Chicago "lifetime care" facility, they both seemed to lose their identity. The mother started screaming, hours at a time, night and day, and had to be put in the nursing home. The father was miserable. He said the old Chicagoans in that facility weren't "sharp," he couldn't talk to them. They didn't even laugh at his jokes. The rules said he couldn't bring anything wool, how could he go out, do any business at all, with no nice suit—wash pants, already!

Linda flew out to Chicago to share Thanksgiving dinner with her father and brother, and knew she'd have to get him out of there. She found a small apartment in his old neighborhood, and someone to come in every day to clean and cook and take him out to do errands. And she herself was there, or on the phone with him, once or twice a day. His friends had dropped off. She felt in retrospect that if she'd talked him out of his "humiliation" at having to use a cane or walker, and kept him from resigning from the volunteer board, he wouldn't have declined so fast. Still, he was happy, back in his old neighborhood, his old newsstand, the barber shop, the corner grocery. It was only when he could no longer handle the cane, or even the walker, and had to use a wheelchair, that he said, "I can't walk, what's the use of living." But then, after another friend died and he realized he himself was *still living,* he decided to throw a birthday party for himself, on his ninetieth birthday, ordered the food from Zabar's and gave Linda a full list to shop for: candles, flowers, and pretty paper napkins.

Marlene Sanders's mother, Evelyn Fisher, at eighty-six had been doing fine in her condo at Coco Beach in Florida, where she'd been living by herself for fifteen years since her husband died. She played golf two or three times a week, drove around to friends and various community activities, had a regular volunteer job at the hospital. A stroke four years earlier had left her with a limp, but she still managed to get around in her car, which was also getting older. A year ago, after a lot of plane trips to see grandchildren and great-grandchildren in Pennsylvania, Arizona, and Connecticut, she contracted a virus, an attack of meningitis which put her in a coma. After a week she came out of the coma. But Marlene and her brother got rid of her car, which they felt was no longer safe for her to drive. Not knowing how she would be able to get around in Florida without a car, Evelyn decided it would be better to move back to New York to be near her daughter and the new great-grand-children. Marlene found a highly recommended senior facility "for independent living" near her own apartment. It wasn't a nursing home, resi-dents had to be able to carry their own meals on a tray in the dining room; but there was a nurse on duty twenty-four hours. They paid the de-posit, filled out the forms, and showed up for the required personal interview. Marlene told me:

We had to sit there waiting a half hour for the social worker. My mother looked at the other residents walking down the hall, and they all looked so gray, so dull, too old, feeble, lifeless. My mother is full of life still, stroke or no stroke. She wears red and yellow, bright col-ors, a striped pant suit, T-shirts, she colors her hair, she's a good-looking woman. She didn't think of herself as that old. It made her de-pressed just looking at those old people, who were probably younger than she.

Then, the social worker came and had my mother walk down that long corridor to her office. She didn't like my mother's limp. She said it might make her spill things, carrying a tray in the dining room. Therefore, they wouldn't take my mother. We were both relieved to get out of there!

We'd fixed up her condo in Florida, painted it, did the floor, new windows, to get it ready to sell. She decided to go back to Florida. And she feels so happy now to be back there. But she still misses her car. So I've found someone to come in and drive her whenever she wants. If she leaves now, it will be to a nursing home, but she's not ready for that yet. I hope she never will be. I hope she dies there quietly and suddenly whenever it's going to be. That's what she would like. But I also called my son Jeff that very day, and said: "I'm telling you right now, don't even consider ever putting me in a nursing home or any kind of senior facility for so-called independent living. I'll take my chances of dying outside on my own."

Talking with my friends in Sag Harbor, realizing we'd never discussed these questions with each other before, we all felt exhilarated, at a new place, more alive—and closer to each other. "I want to go on as long as I can, in control, and then to end it," Cynthia said. "But how?" "It's too tough and personal a decision, you have to make it for yourself at the time, or before" . . . "You have to make it while you still can, before you get too confused with Alzheimer's or whatever"... "At what point do you decide you don't want to go on living?" Si was the one who asked that, admitting, now, that he thought about it a lot, and maybe we *should* talk about it.

But how do we ensure such a choice, ensure that we "die with life," in the midst of life—given all the forces of our society that prey upon the elderly, stripping them of all but the most expensive, dehumanizing alternatives, high-tech invasive surgery and nursing home care?

ITEM: "Elderly and often confused Americans are being shockingly abandoned in small but growing numbers on hospital emergency room doorsteps across the country."

Sometimes they are abandoned by children who have come to regard aging parents as a nuisance, and sometimes they are dropped off by family or friends who are simply exhausted by the pressures of caregiving.

Whatever the reasons, people increasingly are leaving the elderly at emergency rooms and, at times, "bolting" as one doctor put it, telling hospitals they are relinquishing all responsibility for their aging relatives. . . .

Emergency room physicians say families are so stressed in part because Medicare does not pay for custodial nursing home care or at home long term care, because little respite care is available and because families in crisis rarely can discover what does exist. . . . When a hospital admits such patients, it can wind up holding an empty bag financially.[1]

ITEM: "A plan to protect the elderly against catastrophe has backfired on stunned lawmakers. . . . Some appear ready to wash their hands of the problems of the elderly."

Aged constituents have verbally pummeled their representatives in Congress in the summer recess over the Federal program to pay for insurance for catastrophic medical costs, a program they lobbied hard to get just last year. . . . They argue that the Medicare surtax imposed on retirees violates the promises of the Bush administration and members of Congress not to raise taxes. . . . Some members of Congress speak privately of the "greed" of the elderly, who have prospered in the last two decades but want others to finance their extended medical benefits. . . .[2]

ITEM: "I see by the papers, damn near every day, that I'm a Greedy Geezer. . . ."

The trouble with us geezers is that we live too long. If we don't bankrupt the country with our pensions, we'll do it with our medical bills. That is the theme of a campaign that has been going on for well more than a decade. It scored big with the Social Security "rescues" of 1977 and 1983, which cut benefits and raised payroll taxes . . . [and] with the Catastrophic Medicine Act of 1988. . . . The new ability of medicine to extend life by heroic measures has also served as an effective club to swat geezers. . . . We are . . . dying beyond our means.[3]

From the accumulation of such news items in recent years, I began to realize that the very possibility of real personal choice for any of us at the end of life has become mired in political and economic crosscurrents, in which people now entering age are becoming pawns and scapegoats. The exponential growth of nursing homes and the increasing domination of the politics and economics of aging by nursing home and "catastrophic" long-term care considerations is itself dangerous, threatening to preclude real possibilities of living out one's age in terms of personal choice and control within the community. Even the fundamental economic bases which seemed to offer all Americans (at least all who worked most of their lives) the possibility of a humane old age—Social Security and Medicare—are under attack now. In order to guarantee our ability to control our own aging, and to get the minimum health care we may need, we may have to fight the very proposals seemingly offered to "protect" us, and watch very carefully the campaigns that give us the "right to die." Consider:

The first warning was the hullaballoo, early in the eighties, over the Social Security "crisis." The unprecedented, increasing numbers of people living through their seventies, eighties was just beginning to be demographically visible. That these were not the "poor old people" of the stereotype, the mystique of decline, was also becoming visible. A lot was being made of the fact that most old people no longer were "poor" —and that, of course, was due to Social Security. But the relative prosperity of older people was simply, for most, the ability to "get by" on Social Security, but barely. At the same time, the economic decline of the middle class and the poor as a result of Reaganomics and the increasing flow of the nation's wealth to the upper 1 percent of the population was beginning to be felt but not yet articulated. The frustration was expressed as outrage over the budget deficit and rising taxes, both blamed on the oppressive costs of Social Security and Medicare for the elderly. Those soaring health care costs (and profits) were now burdening everyone but that upper 1 percent whose tax cuts were a main cause of the deficit.

Social Security, the one entitlement that covers everyone who works, was the finest accomplishment of the New Deal. When the Social Security Act was passed in 1935, promising to liberate old people from the poorhouse, old age security was declared a right, not a charity. At the time Social Security began, most old people were at the bottom poverty level. Under Social Security, the proportion of the elderly classified as "poor" declined to about one out of eight; without Social Security, not one eighth but *one half* of the elderly would qualify as poor.[4] According to a major study by the Social Security Administration, by the 1980s 38 percent of all income received by the elderly was the Social Security check. The Social Security check was the only income received by 14 percent and represented at least half the income for 62 percent. As for the media hype of greedy geezers riding about in golf carts at Palm Beach on their Social Security, the study found that 77 percent of the elderly in 1984 had total incomes below $20,000, and only 3 percent enjoyed incomes above $50,000.

In its first fifty years, Social Security took in $55 billion more than it paid out; but during the Reagan-Bush years, the government borrowed heavily from Social Security reserve funds, at low or no interest, to mask the growing deficit. The "panic" when the government threatened to slice Social Security was set off by a prediction by Alan Greenspan of a Social Security deficit of $150 to $200 billion by 1990. (This was, coincidentally, about the same as the estimate for the savings and loan bailout.)

The use of the greedy geezer as scapegoat for the nation's large economic problems reached a peak with the "catastrophic illness" fiasco, which, under the guise of "protecting" seniors, made them the villains of the exploding cost of health care. Medicare and Medicaid, as they were originally adopted twenty-five years ago, staved off demands for a national health system by providing welfare coverage and meager medical care for the very poor (Medicaid) and limited coverage for doctor and hospital bills for people over sixty-five on Social Security (Medicare), financed by yet another increase in payroll taxes, along with premiums paid by older people themselves, matching or exceeding those paid by the government. Further, Medicare permitted the agencies producing this care to determine the fees for which doctors and hospitals can be reimbursed.

Then, on the eve of the 1988 election, in an appeal for the vote of older people who had turned against Reagan-Bush for their attacks on Social Security, the White House suddenly asked Congress to extend Medicare to cover "catastrophic illness." Passage of the legislation helped elect George Bush. But it soon became clear that the bill would actually leave older people worse off than they had been before, with even less control of their health care. This so-called catastrophic Medicare would cover hospital or nursing home care only for certain acute disease or emergencies already covered by most people's insurance, *not* extended nursing home stays or home health care. This in the face of all the statistics which incontrovertibly show that the great majority of older people could live out their age and die in their own communities, without resort to nursing homes, with certain modest provisions for health care at home *which this bill did not provide.*

Further, the costs would be paid for entirely by older people themselves, with continual increases in Social Security deductions, plus an additional 15 percent income tax increase on all persons sixty-five or older who paid $150 or more in income tax. (One does not have to be very wealthy to pay $150 in income taxes. Census Bureau data at this time showed the median income of men age sixty-five and over at less than $12,000 a year and of women at $6,374, just above the poverty line. Those with incomes of more than $13,000 a year would have been worse off if the Medicare Catastrophic Coverage Act had remained.) The only real beneficiaries were the insurance companies, which would no longer have to pay the supplementary policies most older people bought, through their unions or the AARP, to cover the "gap" in long-term hospital stays and prescriptions beyond Medicare coverage. Since this would now make many older people pay higher tax rates than millionaires, there was an understandably angry rebellion of the "greedy geezers." Their outrage forced Congress to repeal the act in 1989, leaving geezers worse or no better off than before, but with a worse media image.

After that deceptive "catastrophic" long-term medical care act was repealed, with much congressional and media blame for the elderly (who saw through it), more and more services and programs that helped people age in their own communities were cut, without public notice, while Medicare itself was increasingly curtailed by provisions that directly or indirectly *deprived* older people of health care that might keep them out of hospitals or nursing homes. "Scattered reports from across America indicate that state budgetary slashes are impairing or threatening to impair hundreds of programs for the elderly involving community care, transportation, meals, and the affordability of prescription drugs," the *AARP Bulletin* reported in December 1991. In Detroit, older persons got 27,500 fewer meals, at home or in senior centers, because of budget cutbacks, hitting programs on aging the hardest. Pennsylvania's Jefferson County eliminated ten thousand meals for independent elderly after getting its state funds cut 15 percent; it then stopped subsidizing transportation that took older persons to grocery stores, doctors' appointments, and senior centers.

The Georgia State legislature trimmed its 1992 budget by cutting out Medicaid help in financing hearing aids, eyeglasses, and dentistry. The Florida legislature threatened to cut out the statewide transportation system, including the twenty-eight vans and buses that transport people every day to the Senior Friendship Center in Sarasota, to doctors' offices and grocery stores, and state aid for prescription drugs and other medical services at home. The Friendship Center's spokeswoman pointed out that these services "help people maintain their independence and live at home, where they want to live. If fragile older persons living in a community cannot get medicine to sustain their health, they'll wind up in hospitals where the cost is far greater."

As Medicare cuts proceeded, the media reflected an intensive campaign to deny the ill effects on older people's lives. "Hospital Cuts Aren't Hurting Care for Elderly, Study Says" was the headline in *The New York Times,* October 17, 1990, reporting an AMA study claiming that "measures imposed in 1983 to shorten hospital stays for people 65 years of age and older who are insured by Medicare have not disrupted a trend of improved chances for their survival." But giving the lie to its own headline, the *Times* then added:

But the cost-cutting measures did increase the likelihood that an elderly patient would be discharged in a medically unstable condition. The percentage of such patients rose to 14.7 from 10.3 before the measures began. . . . Those who were discharged in medically unstable conditions were 50 percent more likely to die within 90 days than were those who were medically stable.

Eight leading insurance companies filed a federal court suit in July 1992, charging National Medical Enterprises, one of the nation's largest operators of psychiatric hospitals, with a massive scheme to commit insurance fraud by admitting thousands of patients who did not need hospitalization and treating them at inflated prices. The insurers, including Prudential and Travelers, claimed that the hospital operators "systematically manipulated the diagnosis of patients to keep them in hospitals until their health insurance coverage was exhausted."[5]

Older people are especially vulnerable to such manipulation. In the absence of a national health care program that would give people real access to the care they need, older people, increasingly anxious over *control* of their own care, are now being sold costly private nursing home care insurance. At the same time, with the medical care price index growing over twice as fast as the national consumer price index—*and over twice as fast as the average monthly Social Security payment*—our own choices about health care are being taken over by outside "managed care" providers, increasingly used by companies and insurers to decide what treatments will be covered by what doctors, how long hospital stays will last, and other matters that used to be a question of private choice between the doctor and the patient.[6]

We have to take control of our own final choices from those who would profit from and exploit our fear of that final infirmity—and then make us scapegoats for the nation's economic crisis and unbearable health care burden. But it seems to me that we cannot preserve our own choices at the end of life by focusing on the single issue of "long-term" or "catastrophic" care, despite the fact that nursing homes have increasingly become the center of discussion on age policy in America. Furthermore, evidence has also increased that "family" is not necessarily a panacea for "long-term care." More than 1.5 million older Americans may be the victims of physical or mental abuse each year, most frequently by members of their own families, the House Select Committee on Aging reported in 1990.[7] A nationwide survey, based on data gathered by states in 1988, showed that incidents of abuse have been increasing and now touched one in twenty persons over sixty-five. The most likely victims were women over seventy-five, and the abuser was most frequently the son of the victim, followed by the daughter. The incidence of elder abuse has risen 50 percent in less than a decade, from 1 million victims in 1980 to 1.5 million in 1988. In Los Angeles County, reports of elder abuse have risen 300 percent in the four years since the state passed a law making it mandatory for doctors and others to report such cases.

Real "choice" in age must, of course, deal with present realities in terms of family or nursing home care. But it must also focus on alternatives and possibilities that do not now exist.

I admit my own overwhelming dread and prejudice against nursing homes. In ten years of research, no data has emerged to counteract my impression of nursing homes as death sentences, the final interment from which there is no exit but death. In some research I have seen, no matter their condition upon entering, men or women tended to die within six months of being put in a nursing home. Even if they were not dying, or in any state of terminal disease when they entered—merely no longer able to take care of themselves, living alone, like my mother —something happened, as a result of being put in the nursing home, that led to death. Of "no apparent cause," as they said of my mother. She died in her sleep "of old age"; she was ninety. I think she had no wish to live any longer, in that nursing home; no bonds, no people she cared about, no purpose to her days.

When I started out in this search, over ten

years ago now, I was appalled by the overwhelming preoccupation of gerontologists with nursing homes and their sick, passive, childlike, and ever more deteriorating senile patients, when only 5 percent of people over sixty-five were, in fact, in nursing homes. Since then, the preoccupation with nursing homes as the only answer to "long-term care" for older people has become a national obsession—preventing government, national, state, and local organizations, and older people themselves, from taking real, small steps that would ensure other possible choices.

The nursing home specter had become a self-fulfilling prophecy by 1990. The number of nursing home residents had almost tripled in twenty years. Total annual expenditures on nursing home care had risen from $4.2 billion to $34.7 billion. The probability of nursing home use had increased to 17 percent for ages 65 to 74, 36 percent for ages 75 to 84, and 60 percent for ages 85 to 94. The average age of nursing home residents was now 79.

It was estimated that 37 percent of those who died at 65 years or older in 1986 were in nursing homes. Some 25 percent died within a month of entering the nursing home, 50.8 percent within six months.[8]

An estimate in the *New England Journal of Medicine* based on National Center for Health Statistics data projected that one in seven men and one in three women who reached the age of 65 in 1990 would spend at least one year in a nursing home. "For persons who turned 65 in 1990, we project that 43% will enter a nursing home at some time before they die . . . 55% [for] at least one year . . . 21% [for] five years or more."[9]

Pointing out that nursing home patients tend to get worse after their admission to nursing homes—they develop urinary tract infections, eye and ear infections, and bed sores—Bruce Vladeck concluded in a 1980 study, "These are diseases not of age or frailty but of inadequate care."[10] He reported that doctors and even trained nurses were "largely absent from nursing homes" and that the ongoing care of chronically ill nursing home residents was "deficient." "They sit in these nursing homes, minds clouded by drugs, staring unfocussingly at daytime television and soon but not soon enough they are dead. . . ."[11]

Some 5 to 10 percent die simply from being moved from home or hospital to nursing home, he stated. "Many nursing home residents would be better off anywhere else."[12]

"The single greatest fear we have in this country is the fear of growing old, losing our mind, and being put away in a nursing home," my friend and mentor Robert Butler has been saying for years now. And women are more likely to enter nursing homes, unnecessarily, than men, according to the experts, because they are both less likely to have a spouse still alive to share their care and less willing to be a "burden" to their children; they do not want to give up their independence to be cared for by daughters or daughters-in-law.

Yet, despite the focus on "catastrophic illness," most people now die as the end result of chronic conditions they've lived with a long time. Medicare does not cover long-term care, except for acute illness, nor preventive medicine or almost any home care. Only people below the poverty level are eligible for Medicaid, which covers nursing home care as well as eyeglasses, hearing aids, dental and drug prescriptions. By 1983, there were some 50 percent more people in nursing homes than in community hospitals, many with waiting lists of a year or more. But despite repeated evidence that most older people would prefer to stay in their own homes, less than 3 percent of federal Medicare funds devoted to long-term care in 1990 was spent on home services.[13] And those nursing homes now cost over $30,000 a year. "Spending down" to poverty has become accepted as the way to get Medicaid to pay the nursing home bills. Reports in the media of what goes on in nursing homes increase our helpless obsession and denial: "When you enter a nursing home there's a feeling that this is the end. . . . You give up your home, your possessions, your autonomy. . . .

Most people leave nursing homes horizontally." [14]

Relatives often go to extraordinary lengths before they send a loved one to an institution. Social workers say they know of too many daughters working themselves to exhaustion trying to attend to an infirm parent while raising families of their own, and too many husbands and wives, frail themselves, struggling for years to provide gruelling 24 hour aid to a chronically ill spouse. [15]

The solution that the "care" experts now offer people is to "plan" and save to buy insurance to cover nursing home care, rather than question the entire specter.

One reason nursing home costs come as such a shock to so many people is simply that they have not planned for them. . . . Americans have not traditionally thought of saving or buying insurance to cover the expenses of long-term care. . . .
More and more, experts say, planning ahead for the possible expense of chronic care will have to be a customary rite of aging. [16]

Thus, we are advised to buy "long-term care" insurance we may not need, or that will profit a nursing home that could make us long for death. During my winter in California in 1992, the *Los Angeles Times* reported state "citations" of a "skilled nursing home" at Rancho Los Amigos for "violating new Federal regulations that restrict the drugging and physical restraint of patients and for providing so little supervision that some patients were found wandering along a highway."

Inspectors described the facility as reeking from a "musty, fetid" odor. Floors were debris-strewn and sticky from spills and messes. A drainage bag of body fluids was found on the floor of one room. Feeding pumps and suction canisters were encrusted with secretions. In another room, a restraining device used to tie down patients was covered with ants.

Stinking bedridden patients in dirty hospital gowns were routinely left unbathed. . . . Inspectors charged that nursing home staff failed to rotate patients every two hours to prevent development of painful bedsores and that they helped patients out of bed and into wheelchairs only every other day.

Inspectors observed one patient whose fingernails had grown so long he could not push a button to operate a mechanical device and another patient who was left in bed for four days, clothed only in a diaper.

According to state health inspectors the Rancho nursing home has flagrantly disregarded new Federal nursing home regulations [that] require nursing home staff to stimulate patients to attain the highest practicable physical, mental and psycho-social well-being.

Inspectors also faulted the nursing home staff for failing to adhere to new regulations that strictly govern the use of psychoactive drugs and physical restraints. . . . They witnessed one patient who was strapped so that the restraints tightened around his genitals. In another case, a patient given psychoactive drugs suffered permanent neurological damage as a result of the medication.[17]

The daily rate at that nursing home was $202 per patient. Its budget for 1992 was $6 million.

But with "family" seen as the only alternative to the nursing home, the *Los Angeles Times* also offered the following tips to avoid guilt in putting "Mom or Dad or whoever" into a nursing home:

The decision to move a relative to a long-term care institution can be one of the most difficult you'll ever make. . . . Health care professionals . . . who routinely counsel families on this subject offer these suggestions for easing the experience:

- Avoid making the promise, "I'll never put you in a nursing home . . ."
- Once your loved one is admitted, recognize his grief. Don't deny the enormity of what has happened. Let him talk about his loss the way you would let a grieving person talk about someone who has just died.
- Visit when you are comfortable with the idea and in an "up" mood . . .
- Don't over-visit . . .
- When visiting a patient with dementia, keep in mind that his reality is not the same as yours.
- Be advocates for the patient but don't overdose on a loved one's complaints . . . Don't try to make things perfect at the nursing home. An institution is not a home no matter how you cut it.
- Remember that this is probably not the first time you have felt guilty over the patient.[18]

The social workers complained that it was harder to "adjust" the family to "the institutionalization of a person whose perception, memory and judgment were intact" than one with Alzheimer's. ("Someone with a cognitive deficit does not recognize the difference in their surroundings.")

In the course of my search, I was plied with shocking statistics about the excessive use of physical restraints in nursing homes, denying patients any activity at all, any purpose. As to the prevalence of use of tranquilizers and anti-psychotics as restraints and their deleterious side effects, in the San Francisco Bay Area physicians' orders for such drugs in nursing homes rose by 10 percent in 1987, though the nursing home population rose by only 1 percent in that time—with documented evidence that the risk of falling increased among older people placed on such drugs.[19]

In a 1992 hearing on "the shocking problem of excessive and unjustified medication of elderly Americans living in board-and-care homes," Chairman Edward R. Roybal of the House Select Committee on Aging reported on a three-year investigation of nursing homes in Ohio, Texas, California, and Washington, D.C.: "Residents of these facilities were excessively medicated—over 85 percent of them were on three pre-scribed drugs a day, two of which were psycho-active, despite the fact that not one home maintained medical or mental health records to justify the residents' drug use. This form of legal-ized drug abuse often leaves the frail residents of these homes in a stuporous condition."

Lloyd Lewis, executive director of two continu-ing-care facilities, Kendal at Longwood and Crosslands in Pennsylvania, who boasted that "in 17 years of operating our nursing centers we have never owned or used physical restraints," wanted to mount a nationwide effort to "untie the elderly" as a major confrontation of ageism in America. He showed me data that restraints (belts, vests, jackets) supposedly intended to "protect" the elderly, but sometimes suffocating or strangling them, are used on more than a third of the nursing home population, at least a half million Americans every day. The *Minnesota Star Tribune* (December 2, 1990), in an eight-month investigation of deaths caused by use of restraints in Minnesota nursing homes, found "cases of people strangling in their chairs, dangling from their beds, hanging or falling or burning to death." This was sixteen years after a congressional committee heard "complaint after complaint about old people tied up like animals in nursing homes" and adopted rules to prohibit use of such restraints "for staff convenience," requiring doctors' orders that they were "needed to prevent injury."

A few nursing homes have been made to pay multi-million-dollar damages for deaths caused by "isolated acts of gross negligence." However, for the first time, a federal jury in Mississippi in 1990 awarded damages to families of two nursing home patients "whose last years were blighted by neglect at a home run by the nation's largest nursing home chain . . . the kind of routine neglect and abuse that do not kill but cause great suffering for thousands of nursing home patients every day."

The cases involved Beverly Enterprises, then operating more than eight hundred nursing homes around the country. The Jackson, Mississippi, jury awarded damages to the families of Margie Berryhill and Frederick Bolion for "what happens to residents in maybe 60 percent of the nation's nursing homes," as one expert put it. The jury assigned dollar amounts to the different kinds of neglect:

Fifty thousand dollars for leaving Mrs. Berryhill in her own excrement, $25,000 for verbal abuse of her by the staff, $15,000 for not bathing Mr. Bolion, $15,000 for keeping him in a smelly room, $60,000 for failing to give him the physical therapy he needed, and so on, coming to a total of $125,000 for each of them. The jury further found that Beverly Enterprises' failure to provide good care was so "willful, wanton, malicious or callous" as to merit another $125,000 in punitive damages to each claimant.[20]

Ironically, the verdict in one of these cases was reversed because the evidence in the other was so "inflammatory and shocking" that it had unduly influenced the verdict in the other. Ultimately, however, both cases were settled.

But nursing home "reform" may not be the answer. Even some of the best nursing homes, in fact, the very premises upon which nursing homes in America are run, *deny the personhood of age.* They merely represent an extreme case of ageism, reifying the image of age as inevitable decline and deterioration. We are right to dread the nursing home. If we are not seen as human beings, but merely "objects" to be disposed of, warehoused until death, then restraints, drugs, are not "abuse" but cost-efficient aids to our "long-term care."

Does denial and fear of our own aging explain our readiness to put Mom or Dad in a nursing home, despite these conditions, which are periodically brought to public attention by the media? The continued building of these nursing homes, and the demand that their exorbitant costs be covered by national health insurance, seems all the more suspect in 1993, when new data show that fewer and fewer of the elderly are suffering serious disabilities.

"The common assumption that old age in America brings with it unremitting deterioration is being challenged by a new study that shows disability rates among the elderly decreasing during the 1980s," *The New York Times* reported in a front-page story April 7, 1993.[21]

Findings by Duke University researcher Kenneth Manton and his colleagues challenged gerontologists' "idea of old age as a time of steady deterioration." The Manton study showed that while the population over 65 increased by 14.7 percent from 1982 to 1989—to 30.9 million from

26.9—the disabled increased by just 9.2 percent. The proportion of the elderly reporting no disabilities rose from 76.3 percent in 1982 to 77.4 percent in 1989. The number of older people requiring personal assistance (for basic needs like taking a bath, getting dressed, going to the toilet, shopping) declined by 10 percent even as the numbers of the elderly were increasing. And the improvement in health seemed to be greatest for those 75 and over, and just as great at 85 and over.

Family care as a viable alternative may also be an evasion of new realities. According to a 1987 survey by the AARP, 75 percent of the people who take care of elderly relatives are wives, daughters, and daughters-in-law. Most work full or part-time as well, often having to give up time at work to care for a parent. Nearly 40 percent also have children at home. My colleague Vern Bengtson, sociologist and director of research at Andrus Gerontology Center, estimated that half the thirty-five-year-olds today will have a dependent parent for at least twenty years before she (or he) dies.

The assumption that the "family" is the real answer to long-term care was used during the Reagan-Bush era to evade responsibility for innovating the social programs that are needed to prevent the nursing home specter just as it has been used to block a national child care program. But that assumption is wearing thin.

Working already at two jobs, women are still assuming responsibility for frail parents who need care. But more and more, it is becoming clear, mothers really don't want to move in with their daughters, to be dependent on daughters and daughters-in-law. The reports of "elder abuse" by sons, daughters, or daughters-in-law, along with the increase in child abuse, have mounted as economic and other pressures build up rage and frustration in American families, and that rage is too often vented on those who are the least strong and the most dependent.

The fear of "becoming a burden on my children" reinforces and is reinforced by the nursing home specter, focusing our attention on no-win alternatives that assume a medical model of dependence for our later years. It has become very clear that old people want to stay in their own homes, where they have bonds and projects, and can control their own lives, whatever disabilities they may have, which often don't involve serious declines in function until they are well into their eighties. Even in their eighties, when a sizable percentage of the elderly may have some disability, they continue to *function,* as long as they stay in their own community. Elizabeth Bartoch, eighty-three, of Cresskill, New Jersey, had amnesia after her husband died in her arms. She was "distressed" at her confusion. Her son closed up her tiny house, she said goodbye to her neighbors, and moved in with his family fifteen miles away. But after fourteen months, she decided she wanted to go home again. Her son said: "She felt she was intruding. She wanted to do things her way, but it wasn't her home." Back in her own home, she took in a boarder, and her son stopped by every day. "She's happy to be back in her familiar neighborhood where she can take walks without getting lost."

Over these years, I have visited some of the very best nursing homes, sparkling clean, where neither physical nor chemical restraints were used, and the halls and rooms certainly did not smell of urine and feces or that awful, all-pervading sweet smell of disinfectant. Run by Jewish and Catholic agencies, not-for-profit, some were doing their best to give the residents some "choice"—over the food they ate, which movie to see—and some control of their day, at least the illusion of some choice over when they wake or sleep or eat. But basically the institutional paradigm remained: They left the larger community of which they were part, and their identity in it, when they entered the nursing home. Within the institution, how much control could they have over their own lives, how much real choice?

The Jewish Homes for the Elderly or Hebrew Homes for the Aged, as they are variously called, are considered state of the art. But housed as they are in high-rise buildings, on the outskirts of a city, of sufficient scale to provide economies of service of food, linens, drugs, and medical care, they are inevitably too large and impersonal to seem like "home" and too cut off from the life of the city to be "community."

I have lectured at those Jewish homes, outside of Boston, and in the Bronx, and experienced the eager intelligence, the hunger and stubborn clinging to autonomy and identity in the questions of the residents—mostly women, a few men, most of them over eighty. In Massachusetts, they were housed in 934 units, in five buildings, and there was a gridlock of wheelchairs in front of the elevator—residents waiting for attendants to take them to their next scheduled routine. Ellen Feingold, educational director of Jewish Homes for the Elderly, the professional showing me around, insisted:

We could never build a smaller one, a hundred people or less, unless it was right in the middle of town, where people could really reach and use their neighborhood services. You need a certain amount of density for choice, autonomy. We have a communal cafeteria, but at least no more mandatory meals in a communal dining room. Nothing infantilizes people more than to be forced to sit down for dinner every night at 5:30, whether they're hungry or not. Now they have to get $40 a month worth of tickets, but they can choose how and when to use them.

This nursing home was a teaching facility of the Gerontology Program at the University of Massachusetts, but in recent years their focus has, indeed, been shifting from training professionals to take "care" of older people in such nursing homes to encouraging older people to go back to school themselves. More specifically, they trained healthy, active women and men in their late sixties and seventies, most of whom never went beyond high school, to serve as advocates for the frail elderly to get them the services they need from the comunity. Feingold said:

Instead of looking at older people through the microscope as objects, as gerontology has historically done, we've turned the microscope around and are training the older people themselves to deal with the political arena as critical players, not just objects. We're training them to name their own issues, set their own priorities, be their own advocates, but also to involve younger people in that work (though the young ones at first expected, and objected, to "baby-sitting" for the seniors).

Paul Houlihan, director of that gerontological institute, told me that this displacement of older people themselves, from "objects" of gerontological policy to definers of it, was "unsettling" to the young turks of academic gerontology. The "aging service" establishment was threatened by the idea of giving technical training to people themselves over sixty-five, not only for dealing with and serving as advocates for their peers in need of services, but with expertise for action on public issues affecting the community as a whole. The women taking these courses—widowed housewives, retired secretaries—instead of baby-sitting for their grandchildren, were getting the confidence to "take on the statehouse," acquiring skills that gave them a "sense of increasing control over their lives and their environment."

But inside the nursing home walls, autonomy can only exist within very narrow limits. At the Hebrew Home for the Aged in the Bronx, food items are voted on and off the menu every two years by the "powerful" nineteen-member Food Committee. In *The New York Times,* a delightful column about that nursing home, "Where Politics Is Thought For Food," quoted a resident:

Nothing is more important to people here than meals. It's just about all anyone talks about. Members of the Food Committee had been buttonholed by constituents for days before the meeting, people who wanted to lobby for the ouster of red cabbage or for the introduction of banana pudding.

There are many single-issue factions who want the ear of committee members, such as those seeking less sodium in the food, less sugar and more spices. There is the "no breakfast before 8:00 AM" group . . . the anti-cheese faction . . . and those pushing for larger portions.

"It is an awesome responsibility," said Naomi Schwartz, referring to making decisions concerning the daily meals served to 900 residents, 800 staff people in the home, and 400 meals delivered to the elderly outside the home. Mrs. Small said sometimes members think about leaving the Food Committee, but they cannot bring themselves to give up the power and prestige.[22]

The fear of the nursing home in reinforcing the dread of age was analyzed cogently by Elias Cohen, whom I met early in the gerontological underground. In fact, he tried to convince me that concentrating on keeping older people out of nursing homes, or reforming and financing better nursing homes, was a copout from affirming, for older people, the same goals of empowerment, self-realization, and participation in society that we had advanced in the women's movement for equality. He suggested that older people themselves "have bought into an elderly mystique which holds that the potentials for growth, development and continuing engagement virtually disappear when disabled." Seeing themselves already solely as passive objects of "care," "without high aspirations or even a sense that empowerment was a real possibility," once they enter or are "put" into nursing homes, they collude in that living death.[23]

Further, he said, the ageism of the long-term care industry and its advocates "stereotypes older people in terms of the characteristics of the least capable, least healthy, and least alert of the elderly," and sets standards and policy that make the stereotype a self-fulfilling prophecy:

It perceives the older person as, in effect, a relatively helpless and dependent individual who requires support service .... without adequate concern as to whether the outcome of this service contributes to reduction of freedom for the participants to make decisions controlling their own lives. . . .

The very language used in laws, rules, regulations, long-term care program guidelines, training manuals, etc., would have to be radically revised "to change what seems to be the commonly held view that disability in old age marks the point at which resignation, disengagement and acquiescence in the authority exercised by others is appropriate behavior."

The Live Oaks Regenerative Community, as it was originally called, was started in Oakland, California, by Barry Barkan, a former journalist and New Age activist, who described himself now as a "futurist and gerontologist." He did not come out of academic gerontology but from the civil rights movement of the sixties and from building therapeutic self-help communities for drug abuse victims in the seventies. He had become a consultant on health care organization, "building communities as support groups—putting the antibodies into the social system" to counter isolation, alienation from meaning, disconnection. The need for this in age came to him when his grandmother—who had gone from household to household as their family structure fell apart, moving from Brooklyn slum to separate suburbs—fell sick and was put in a nursing home in Long Beach, New York. He visited her there:

She had aged considerably since I had last seen her a month or so before. She was visibly smaller. . . . She didn't want to live anymore. She said it again and again. Not as a person letting go of the sweet gift of life and preparing for a mysterious connection to the God to

918

whom I remember she frequently prayed, but as a person betrayed.

Her life was culminating in a stiff, cold environment that had no knowledge or respect regarding who she had been, and, moreover, had no time to care. She was disconnected from her past. Her future had been presumed to be nonexistent and her present was relegated to a limbo . . . by a culture . . . . profiting usuriously from the infirmity of its elders.

When he visited her, morning or afternoon, she would be lying in her bed, alone, in a dark, smelly room. But the worst, as he described it to me, was that

Nobody knew her, nobody knew who she really was, or used to be. Nobody could, she was isolated, alone in her room. There was virtually no interaction of people with one another. The patients complained about the staff, and the staff's main purpose seemed to be to minimize the amount of work they had to do, to keep the patients restrained, tied down, drugged, so they wouldn't get in their way. It was a culture of dependence. In such an institution, it's easier to keep people completely dependent than independent or semi-independent. There was no community for her to be a part of. Everyone in my family felt helpless, guilty. She died in nine months, at eighty-seven.

After I went to work at the Home for Jewish Parents, I decided my life's work would be to create a regenerative community—not a nursing home. That implies pathology, but aging itself is not a pathological state. In a nursing home, patients are seen only in terms of their infirmities, not as the people they were and still are.

I sat in on the daily community council meeting at Live Oaks in the sunny atrium-courtyard around which the residents' rooms radiate. The residents and staff were dressed in diverse summer garb, no uniforms. They did some exercises together, discussed what was going on in the community, and also national politics and developments in the world. Told that I was going to visit, they had been discussing "women's issues."

Perhaps it was the sunshine, but despite the canes and walkers, Laura in her hot pink slacks, Harriet with bright red sandals, Helen in a blue-and-white checked slack suit did not look "old" and "sick" like the residents of other nursing homes I had interviewed. Helen's daughter, visiting, told me that her mother's "walking" over to meet me was new for her. "The doctor said after her stroke there was no hope she'd ever walk again; now she's recovered most of her balance." Anna in a striped pant suit strutting up to me was ninety-four. Four years ago when she came in with diabetes, she had to use a walker.

They were interested in hearing about the women's movement. "Women felt that they deserved to be known for who they really are," I told them. "As prejudiced as society was about women, its view of elders is even more distorted. They have to see elders not just as sick people." They nodded their heads with no less intensity than the students I had spoken to at Stanford the night before. One of the women told me she didn't agree with "women's lib," and one of the male minority said it should have happened a long time ago. They all acted as if their opinions still counted, and, in one way or another, with every issue raised, seemed to ask: "What can we do as elders here, now, to make a difference?"

Ken, a man in a green lumber jacket and plaid shirt, was teased about his crush on Dolly Parton. He was eighty-four and came to Live Oaks from a nursing home where he "got very disabled. I was ready to give up the ghost, I was hearing Gabriel's horn, not long for this world. Now, seems like I'm getting my strength back." He said men should take a more active part in the women's movement, "so it won't be a cat-dog fight, women versus men." I agreed. And they got into a big argument about whether there could be a woman president, and why women live so much longer now than men. The women, outnumbering the men there maybe five to one, were mostly widowed.

Anna said: "When the men get sick, they give up, they don't fight. When women get sick, they fight. But Ken here, Jim, I've seen them fight, even when they've heard Gabriel's horn." Ken said: "Women last longer because they do a better job taking care of themselves." Anna said: "Women had to take care of the children so they had to take care of themselves. Maybe women have spoiled men." They applauded vigorously. Someone said seriously: "Men use up their lives too soon. There's truth in it all."

The menu for the day was read out. It was not exactly nursing home food: chili, cornbread, fruit salad. A gardening group invited whoever wanted to plant some strawberries today. People were reminded that there was a four o'clock "Happy Hour" at the nearby Hawaiian Room. On the bulletin board, in the midst of their own drawings and paintings, which were also displayed in all the halls, were notices of pending events: "Strolls"; "Community Meeting"; "The Live Oaks Community Third Annual Memorial Day Yard Sale and Barbecue (Break out the good stuff! Household and personal items that don't quite do it for you anymore, but somebody else would love to own)"; "Mother's Day Morning Concert."

Unlike the nursing homes and "lifetime care"

facilities I had visited, the halls and inner courtyard at Live Oaks were full of people and colorful things (no fancy don't-touch furniture or institutional spick-and-span enamel), plants flourishing or scraggling, and people walking purposefully or ambling, socializing, in chinos and jeans, cotton shirts and T-shirts, fringed flowered scarves trailing over walkers or wheelchairs, people in running shoes and using canes. The residents of the "skilled nursing" wing mingled with the others; wheelchairs and walkers were not hidden away or barred from the dining room. The people there probably had the same range of disabilities as in any nursing home, and most were in or on the verge of their eighties. But the ambiance was of a lively, living community. (Somewhere along the way they had changed their name from Live Oaks Regenerative Community to Live Oaks Living Center.) It was a little messy, a little sloppy, but the people, even those using walkers and in wheelchairs, seemed *alive* and somehow *part of each other.* Barry Barkan told me:

We encourage people to wander the halls, whatever their disability. Even if they aren't up to independent living when they come in, and start in the skilled nursing facility, as soon as they get better, we move them into the living center. Besides, we don't segregate them, as in a nursing home. Most of the meetings, classes, workshops are held right in the skilled nursing facility to give a sense of reality, of still being part of the community. When people do need nursing care here, they keep their identity —they're not just known by their disability.

We have a real memorial service for everyone who dies here. We don't just strip the name off the door and wheel the body out in the middle of the night, as they do at most nursing homes, no ritual, no acknowledgment of the person who was with us, as if her life didn't mean anything. To know that your life means something, to say how we will remember that person, gives support to the spirit. The family members come and bring early photographs to share with people here at our service.

One man in an intermediate stage of Alzheimer's hadn't been out of a wheelchair for three years. Our staff got him up and walking. The light came back to his eyes. People can continue to participate in our community meetings in different stages of confusion, they can just sit there, and if something comes up they can relate to, they become part of the world again.

The sense of "community" rather than packaged-for-death nursing home was manifest not only in the groups strolling and talking to each other in the halls and the promenade outside, but also in the interplay with their neighbors on both sides—little black kids in red sweatshirts and running shoes, old and new California families trying to stave off industrial "development," and the wildflowers and deer overflowing the canyon below. The Live Oaks folks have joined their neighbors in the battle to save their environment from pollution. The low, sprawling spaces of Live Oaks, the manageable size, might not present the same "economies of density" as the profit-making nursing homes—the piano and TV in the living room looked secondhand—but the three hundred–odd members of the Live Oaks Community acted as if they lived here, as if it really was their "community."

It seemed more than rhetoric, the commitment at Live Oaks to autonomy. I saw a woman whose right side was paralyzed after a stroke, teaching herself to do needlework again with her left hand. A woman, ninety-eight, who had been confined to a wheelchair, was getting physiotherapy to stand on her own legs again. I heard her tell the therapist, "You forgot the other leg." I talked to nurses who had worked in nursing homes and gotten "burnt out." They seemed to stay at Live Oaks. Barry told me:

You're dealing with elders who give you hope. They still want to be in charge of their own lives; you have to just give them what they need to take care of themselves, not run every day for them according to a chart. Here every day is different. There's more interaction with family members—some come here every day, eat with us, become friends, members of the community.

We don't cut up the fruit for people here, we put fresh fruit on the plate, they like cutting it up for themselves. A lot of the medical disabilities they came in with had to have been depression. They didn't want to live, they didn't have anything to live for, they didn't want to come out of their rooms, when they first came here. We don't ignore the disability, but we relate to what's well in the person.

I commented on all the people "wandering the halls" at Live Oaks, compared to the empty gray corridors of a nursing home. Barry explained: "In an ordinary nursing home, someone with Alzheimer's starts wandering, maybe pushes into someone else, they would tie her down; she'd deteriorate fast after that, never leave her wheelchair. Here, maybe we get them walking with one of the others, hand in hand."

I was struck by the *joie de vivre* of the staff members, as compared to the oppressive, professional "cheeriness" of a nursing home staff. I was struck too by how comfortable the alert residents, with "all their marbles," seemed to be, pushing the wheelchairs of the more disabled ones on the promenade. "It disempowers their fear," Barry said of this matter-of-fact acceptance of age, in all its diverse reality. The sense that they still counted as *people,* even at eighty, eighty-five, ninety, whatever their physical condition, must have been the difference.

Dr. Carol Winograd, clinical director of geriatrics at the Stanford University Medical School, explained to me why a community like Live Oaks was *physiologically* more conducive to vital age than a medical model nursing home:

People able to take control of their lives can get better; people who buy into the medical model—I'm old, I'm sick, aging means being a sedentary vegetable, being taken care of, no responsibilities, no place to move—they stop moving, they don't do well. What we're trying to do now in our clinical work is really work on a person's ability to take control, make decisions. We see people very late in life able to make very important changes; that's not an ability that is lost with age.

The medical model has to change to foster "aging-in-place"—wherever you live, whatever level of services you need, to be available to you where you live. You don't have to move out of your home, your own community. You could have shared cardiac monitoring, shared dining—eight or ten people who live nearby, not a huge institutional meal—shared exercise classes, even memory retraining. There are very few places now which make it easy for older people to develop new skills. With communities developing models that enable people to keep participating, using their skills and even acquiring new ones in age; sharing services but keeping control of their own activities, with facilities for temporary care at different levels where and when they need it, a real support system in their own home or in the community, we could do away with nursing homes.

In Oregon, state policy and programs are geared to a much broader range of "choice" for people in age who need some support or care. By whatever combination of the individualist spirit, pioneering western tradition, and anti-bureaucracy concerns of economy, at the beginning of the 1980s, after studying the needs of its elderly, Oregon adopted a program of assisted living apartments in which older men and women could lock their own doors and control their own lives, with help at home as needed, and a kind of "foster care" program in which two to five old people live together in private homes whose owners help care for them. "We knew that the rising numbers of people going into nursing homes was going to break the Oregon bank real fast, and we found that many wouldn't go into homes if other support was available," a senior service administrator said.[24]

In the assisted living program in towns throughout Oregon, people bring their own furniture into private apartments, with showers and kitchenettes and keys to their doors. Meals can be taken in communal dining rooms, and nursing, housekeeping, and personal assistance is provided when needed. The emphasis is on enabling people to maintain dignified, comfortable lives as part of the larger community. Clara Pratt, director of Oregon State University's Gerontology Program, and a younger college student shepherded me around the rather ordinary-looking houses and apartments where older people, some disabled, were living much like everybody else, most definitely not in nursing homes. She explained:

Maybe it's the Oregon mystique—we're a state of very independent people, and we're also very community-minded. Way back in the sixties, we got the idea of spending federal money earmarked for nursing homes for community-based services. For people who can mostly take care of themselves, it's cheaper. When people are seriously impaired, it's not necessarily cheaper, but it doesn't cost more than nursing homes and it gives people more

choices and control; even people with Alzheimer's need an opportunity to function, need
choices, to be the person they still are and
want to be.

Our main effort at first was to keep people in
their own homes. At a certain point when they
need twenty-four-hour care, they need alternatives—not just alternatives to the nursing
home, but a whole system of possible choices
where even the nursing homes become more
rehabilitative. People in Oregon nursing
homes now come in because they're discharged from the hospital; 50 percent now
leave the nursing home after two weeks or a
month because they do have other choices of
assisted living.

Joanne Rader, a nurse with impressive graduate training, was very conscious of the fact that
"care" for older people in Oregon was a departure from the medical model.

In Oregon, we allow registered nurses to teach
unlikely people to give injections for diabetes,
for instance. It allows a diabetic person to
choose where she wants to live, and if there's
no one in her family to give injections, she can
move into an apartment, and the nurse can
teach her next-door neighbor or someone in

the foster home to give the injection. Other states allow families to do this, but supposing you don't have a blood relative to live with, you have to expand your concept of family to give older people more options, more choices where to live.

In Oregon, I was told, more people are receiving long-term care Medicaid support *outside* of nursing homes than anywhere else in the United States. There are fewer regulations and bureaucratic jobs. As might have been predicted, the for-profit nursing home chains organized a campaign to shut those alternatives down. In 1981, an independent study was commissioned, which found that most older people in Oregon preferred not to be in nursing homes; for themselves they valued independence, flexibility, and freedom. Others wanted nursing homes. Oregon decreed that the state had the responsibility to give older people options of the "least restrictive environment." Rosalie Kane, who worked under Dick Ladd in developing this departure from professional long-term care standards, told me:

It's not really a question of better care. People who want to stay in the community, with assisted living, foster housing, don't get worse care. In acute illness they are more likely to go to the hospital, which probably levels out to healthier days most of the time. Basically, it's the issue of choice—at a certain age, who makes the decision about your life, doctors, nurses, family members, everyone but the person herself? The struggle going on now is to let the older person herself make the decisions, how much choice should she have? When it becomes an institution, the institution has all the power.

"The dignity of risk," Clara Pratt suggested as a necessary value in age: "There is a dignity in allowing people to make choices, and take risks." Joanne Rader had the job of giving nurses statewide new training to stop using restraints, to stop treating older people "by the rules" but as individuals, according to "principles of shared responsibility, choice and dignity."

The mixture of privacy and community was evident in the "pioneer" assisted living quarters I visited. Each of the twenty-five residents had their own mailboxes, the warm, comfortable armchairs in their living rooms weren't covered with plastic, the fireplaces looked used. There weren't a lot of "activities" scheduled on the bulletin board, but there seemed to be a lot of traffic of the older people in and out of the one-story building. Two neighbor boys from down the block came in, looking for a friend. Sam, who was a hundred and one, caused a little stir when he stood on a chair to fix some curtains. They brought him a step stool. I counted three cats and a dog underfoot. People were allowed to bring and take care of their own pets.

Most of these people, living independently in their own apartments, were over eighty, and many would have been seen as "frail" and "disabled" nursing home candidates. About 40 percent got some assistance with dressing, 80 or 90 percent with bathing; some were even getting catheter care, in their own apartments, and daily injections. They seemed to be feeding themselves and getting where they wanted to go. Ribbons or pictures on some of the doors evidently helped those "confused" by stroke or Alzheimer's to find their own apartments. No one was expected to share an apartment with a stranger-roommate, but they could entertain family members or friends any time of the day or night. They got housekeeping help, but "controlled their own space, day and night." "They negotiate with us how much care they want and pay less the more they take care of themselves," Joanne told me.

With an average age of eighty-seven, there were only eight deaths last year. "They knew they were dying, and wanted to die here," Joanne said. "A ninety-three-year-old woman, cancer of the liver, it was messy, a lot of bleeding at the end. Her whole family was in the room with her when she died." Until that point, "basically she was free to live the life she wanted to live here, and let us know if she wanted some help." A resident, Connie, told me: "I've had lots of trouble, but I'm still here. I try to mind my own business, but if somebody needs help, I try to help. You never know when it's your turn. Everybody knows everybody; you won't find nicer, more interesting people. No talking behind your back, we come right out with it."

There hasn't been a new nursing home bed in Oregon in over ten years. When people need help with specific problems—injections for diabetes, can't dress or bathe themselves, confused, malnourished, afraid of heart attack in the middle of the night, or just needing some structure in their lives—they can get that help without being walled off in a nursing home. They are given the "least possibly restrictive choice."

Karen Wilson, a private consultant for Concepts in Community Living in Portland, differentiated "home" from nursing home, a virtual contradiction of terms: "Home is a sense of space, space in which you can control what happens to you personally. You can get more money in nursing homes by making people more dependent, powerless, which is crazy, and affects the outcome of any illness."

People in Oregon who give "foster care" to

frail older people in their own homes are paid by Medicare—$250 a month for room and board, and $300 to $500 for care, more for private patients. They are given eighteen hours of training in dietary and care planning, the insurance paperwork, and principles of choice. Karen said, "We're looking for people who respect independence and will create an environment where people can come and go and do what they want to do." Juanita Shepard, who runs two such adjacent houses with her sister and brother-in-law, got into this when her own mother, back in Montana, could no longer live alone but didn't want to go into a nursing home. "I took her to live with me and discovered I liked it. I quit my job as a receptionist because I couldn't leave her alone, so I took in three other women to keep her company, and help pay the expenses, and then I got my license. The people who supervise this program, like these ladies here, keep a close watch on us. I feel I can rely on them if I have a problem."

Juanita was caring for five elderly women when I visited her. Four out of the five seemed to get around quite capably by themselves; one, the youngest, used a walker. She was recovering from brain surgery. "Emotionally she's getting better, not physically," Juanita said. "But we're drawing her out, she's talking and laughing more." When the women become conscious of each other's problems, they are very helpful, she said. Incontinence, which in other states puts people in nursing homes, Juanita has helped them handle in different ways. "I like it that I can help keep them out of a nursing home."

Family-style, the women ate a "leisurely breakfast" in their bathrobes, read the papers; Juanita did the housework and helped them at different stages of getting dressed and making beds. At 10:30 or 11:00 A.M., family members dropped by to take them shopping, or back to their old neighborhoods. Juanita tried to get them to go over to crafts and classes at the nearby senior center but they didn't want to. They seemed to prefer to read, or go out for walks, by themselves. Things there were "kind of homey," though not the same as their own homes. Elsie, ninety-two, who had spent her last two birthdays in hospitals, said, "I feel better here. Sometimes I go back to bed after breakfast, sometimes I take a walk. I read when I feel like it, go to sleep when I want to." Juanita felt she herself got "emotional support" from those ladies—"they help me, too, like families do. We help each other."

Joanne Rader proudly took me to the Benedictine Nursing Center in Mount Angel, Oregon, where restraints of any kind were no longer used, and from which new principles were spreading that could banish the nursing home specter. She told me:

It's been the most exciting thing in my profession career, the stopping of restraints. It makes you realize other things that could be changed if you really looked at them as people, even in the nursing home. We'd like to close down all the nursing homes left for two weeks and reeducate all the staffs to experience themselves the "care" they've been giving to the "crocks"—make them see what it's like, being tied down in bed for eight hours. They have to be able to identify with these older women and men *as persons like themselves* to give truly personal care. They have to figure out what the unmet need is behind the problem, instead of categorizing it under fixed rules. What is she really looking for, wandering every night? Instead of restraints and medications to keep her quiet, isn't what she needs real connections, real activity?

Taken on a tour of the Benedictine Center, I saw the transformation in process. Next to a room where a person in a high hospital bed was kept from falling by iron bars was an older person on a regular mattress on a low frame near the floor, with an orange quilt and no bars. In another room a chair with a restraint belt had been replaced by a rocker and a recliner, which "eases agitation," placed with a good view of the TV set. The "security area" was not locked;

even patients "coded" for terminal care and Alzheimer's could come and go. The corridors opened onto small closed courtyards, so people in wheelchairs could go in and out and wander around, without being assisted or getting lost. Twice a week, specific activities for people with short attention spans were programmed to keep people, with Alzheimer's, after stroke, using their human capacities. Instead of waxing the corridors shiny clean, they were working on reducing the glare of that inhospitable shine, which also invited falls. A woman truly wobbly from two years of being restrained in her chair after a fractured hip was no longer tied down; if she wanted to get up from her chair, she had a beeper to summon someone to help her.

Many on the staff were single parents, and a child care center sat right in the middle of everything, enticing a degree of commitment and expertise among the staff which nursing home salaries don't usually command. The children mingled with the elders in a few intergenerational activities—gardening, storytelling, some movies. High school students were recruited as after-school and summer volunteers. There was a five-year plan to "deinstitutionalize" the look of the Benedictine Center, and its meals—no more eating on trays, napkins instead of bibs, pads not diapers. "We're looking at everything with a whole new set of eyes, personal eyes—getting rid of the 'us' and 'them,'" Joanne said.

The difference it's made, seeing the patients as persons, treating their so-called cognitive impairment by having someone they like talking to really listen to them—it's a powerful experience for us to begin to see them as our teachers in how to age. We've got a grant now to adopt our model for use in all Oregon nursing homes. We weren't able to transfer all nursing home patients into assisted living or home care, some were just too frail. Nursing home bashing—to make the nursing home unthinkable—is not the answer.

At the Benedictine Center, where I saw the frailest of the elderly thrive, released from restraints, living with the "risk" of falling, health professionals from all over the world were recently invited to think through the paradigm shift involved in long-term care in the future. After finding that 60 percent of all New York State nursing home residents were restrained physically at least part of each day—more than double the 25 percent reported in 1977—a social worker from Rochester, New York, recast his mission from helping his clients "adjust" to the "transition from home to institution" to "truly radical change reflecting a conversion of the whole attitude to chronically impaired older people—from that of being viewed as more or less passive recipients of a set package of care to that of being viewed *and* dealt with as responsible adults in charge of their own lives.''

As Carter Williams reviewed this shift for his colleagues at the Benedictine Center, it involved not only a multitude of services and policies that would keep people in charge of their own care at home with disability, for which today they would ordinarily be put into a nursing home, but a radically different approach to patients living in alternative homes, as he had observed them in Sweden and Denmark.[25]

In the Scandinavian nursing homes he visited, he found ''growing emphasis on the nursing home resident who has the usual rights of an adult.'' At Graberget in Sweden, with 210 residents, and at Skoevinge Health Center, Denmark, with 55 residents, he was introduced to a ''truly radical change'' in nursing home practices. Importance was placed on the nurse's firsthand knowledge of the resident and his/her needs—to get to know *each individual,* his customary daily patterns of living, and to incorporate them into the nursing care plans. Each group of nurses continued caring for the same residents. Variety, and individuality, dictated the physical environment, as well as safety. Residents brought furniture from home not only to their own rooms but the common rooms. Beds were low enough for short legs to reach the floor but could be raised electrically for treatments. New opportunities for choice were created: time of awakening, what residents wished to wear, and what and with whom they wished to eat. And daily small activities were worked out with each individual resident rather than a schedule of large group activities.

After a while, the Skoevinge staff had come to the conclusion that the very structure of the nursing home based on "taking care of" older people was inimical to the idea of the individual man and woman, in age, being able "to continue taking responsibility for his/her own life." In effect, they "did away with the nursing home and turned the former nursing home rooms into sheltered flats."

Now, wherever one is living is considered fully his/her own home with all that that signifies, and there is only one care giving service in the community, bringing services to chronically sick people of whatever age, in their own homes, including the flats in the institutional nursing home. Since the nursing home as such was terminated, the nursing home staff and visiting nurse staff became one organization capable of offering up to 24-hour service to people at home.

Such rights as one naturally has in one's own home, such as keeping one's own medications, are maintained. If and when disability and loss of function increase, these practices are appropriately adjusted, but adjustments have to occur on an individual basis.

Furthermore, "Swedish geriatricians view the restraint of a person as an invasion of a right which is basic to all human beings, sick or well, old or young—the right of freedom of movement. . . . Nurses particularly work with families to help them understand . . . why it is better to do some risk taking than to deprive a person of freedom of movement." The people in these Scandinavian communities were as sick as residents of U.S. nursing homes, around 30 percent having severe Alzheimer's; but Williams found no use of drugs as restraints, and only one or two among 210 in "life threatening" situations in a belt restraint in any year.

Could such principles, based on "the radical affirmation of the full adulthood and personhood of all old people regardless of health status," be adopted in the United States? Would the model of the Benedictine Center and Skoevinge permit nursing homes to become life-enhancing and not life-destructive? A number of efforts in this direction have been made in different regions in the last few years, some motivated by sheer repugnance of the nursing home specter, some by simple revulsion at its costs, and some by a genuine shift in attitude toward older people. At Morningside House in the Bronx, New York, nursing home administrator Thomas R. Clarke originated advisory committees composed of elderly residents and their relatives and friends to give them a voice in matters affecting their daily lives. Before he died, at forty-three, he gave two thousand practicing health professionals concepts in the care of the elderly that encouraged self-reliance and reduced dependence on institutional treatment with community living support services. Monroe County Community Hospital opened the doors of its geriatric clinic two afternoons a week to the elderly of Rochester, New York, who were on the verge of entering nursing homes. Here, these people and their family or friends could get advice and even solutions for care that would enable them to stay home. Dr. T. Franklin Williams, who initiated this program, later became head of the National Institute on Aging.

At St. Vincent's Hospital in New York, doctors and nurses made regular visits to over two hundred older patients in their own homes, and social workers helped arrange such things as hot meals and housekeeping assistance. The head of community medicine at the hospital, Dr. Philip Brickner, estimated that the cost of caring for these patients at home totaled about $18,700 a year, which is about 60 percent of what nursing home care costs.[26] Instead of the usual prognosis after hip fracture or stroke or other major illness in age—"long hospitalization, nursing home, further decline and death"—the Jewish Institute for Geriatric Care in New Hyde Park, New York, changed its focus to rehabilitation and return to autonomy, even at eighty or ninety.

In one year, it admitted about five hundred aging patients who had suffered strokes or hip fractures or who had had legs amputated after diabetic complications. About three hundred were able to return home within a year. "That percentage reflects our willingness to believe that people, even into their eighties and nineties, can overcome severe physical problems," said the institute's administrator, David Glaser.[27]

During the past few years, the Robert Wood Johnson Foundation has developed a number of alternative housing and health care service models that enabled older people to stay in their homes. "Service credit banking" and "volunteer caregiving" were organized, some through churches. Many suburban communities in Westchester County, New York, have been moving away from the medical model in caring for older people, matching them with local volunteer or paid caregivers if necessary so they could stay in their own homes. In Essex County, New Jersey, some 100 non-profit agencies provide services ranging from transportation and meals to housekeeping, shopping, banking, and home repairs to 35,000 residents over sixty. Connecticut, through its Promotion of Independent Living Program, has provided such services to 5,000 people over sixty in a year, free or on a sliding scale according to income. An Expanded In-Home Services for the Elderly program enacted in New York State to reduce Medicaid costs has sent licensed workers into the homes of about 17,000 people to assist them with bathing, cleaning, cooking, paying bills, and transportation.[28] Whether or not these programs saved the state money on medical or nursing home care, they made it possible for older people to retain autonomy and individual control over their lives in their own homes and communities.

There is also new evidence that health is best served by a reciprocal exchange of satisfaction and benefits in family care relationships— daughters or daughters-in-law, less often sons, taking care of frail parents, older wife or husband caring for chronically ill spouse. At Oregon State University, Alexis Walker and Clara Pratt found a continuum of reciprocal aid in which older women who received care from their daughters are seen as "making important contributions in return . . . the psychological aid of love, information, and advice, and the tangible aid of money. Furthermore, most daughters found the aid they received to be valuable." Noting other studies documenting the contributions that elderly people make to their adult children, the Oregon group urged practitioners "to view elderly care recipients as active participants in social relationships" with possible life-and-death effects. The mothers who were perceived as actually giving aid to their daughters and not just passively receiving their care were, it seemed, in better health. Other research confirmed that "beliefs about helplessness, passivity and dependency . . . may be particularly destructive to the elderly. In contrast, conscious recognition of one's continuing positive contribution to relationships," which led to positive feelings about oneself and positive interactions with others, seemed to enhance health.

Of 133 pairs of widowed mothers, average age eighty-four, and caregiving daughters, average age fifty-two, half of both mothers and daughters perceived that the caregiving situation had a positive impact on their relationship, and only 5 percent reported a negative impact. Daughters valued the greater closeness of the bond with their mothers, regardless of the type or amount of care given. The daughters who were negatively affected by caregiving were the ones who reported less intimacy, lower quality and less closeness in their relationships with their mothers. "Caregiving daughters who were encouraged to facilitate autonomy in their mothers and to promote their own emotional fulfillment reduced their feelings of caregiver burden and reported better quality relationships with their mothers."[29]

In these and other studies, the element of *conscious control* over one's own body, diet, exercise—and of active and mutual *caring,* as opposed to passive isolation and mere receiving of care—seemed to reverse many pathologies of the aging process. But whatever reforms of nursing home care or innovative services meet our physical needs, however long they keep us physically alive, we can still be trapped by our own resignation from continued risks in love and work, whether we voluntarily isolate ourselves in a "life care facility" with the nursing home on the premises or spend our sixties, seventies, eighties technically in the community but withdrawn in obsessive preoccupation with our physical decline.

I recently had a drink with Flora Lewis, a distinguished former foreign correspondent and columnist for *The New York Times,* who had come from Paris to visit her mother, in her nineties, in a nursing home in Santa Monica. Flora, well over seventy herself, horrified me at first by smoking a cigarette despite a continual rasping cough. After her retirement from the *Times,* she stayed on in Paris, writing a column for the *International Herald Tribune* and lecturing on foreign affairs, which enabled her to pay regular visits to her mother. The condition of her mother in that nursing home clearly depressed her, though she felt she could not have disrupted her mother's life in California and the lives of the relatives who visit her there by moving her to Paris.

Lighting another cigarette, she told me, "I do not intend to organize my own life to live as long as possible. I have no wish to live as long as my mother. I'll live the way I want to now and let the end come when it may."

To live a vital age as a part of life requires consciousness and choice until the very end. And we cannot free ourselves from the nursing home specter or those death-denying obsessions with terminal care unless we are able to live with death, accepting death as part of life.

SEVENTEEN

Dying with Life

In the dawn of the modern women's movement back in the 1960s, I had been one of the first to insist that we confront the issue of abortion, then outlawed as murder, in terms of a woman's right to choose when, whether, and how many times to bear a child; I felt that right was as basic—as the Supreme Court later ruled in *Roe* v. *Wade*—as any right spelled out in the Bill of Rights when our Constitution was first written, of, by, and for the people, who were men. They were young men, too. Life expectancy, then, was barely forty years. Today the technology that gives us a life expectancy verging on eighty can also keep us breathing on machines and alive even when we can no longer think, speak, move, respond, or make our wishes known—no longer conscious human persons. Should the choice of when to die also be a basic human right?

There is a movement, now, to that end. And I believe the "right to die" may be as essential to the personhood of age as the "right to choose" was, and is, essential to the personhood of women. But at this point in our history, "choice," which I believe essential to the personhood of age, seems to me personally and politically more complex than the question of when to turn off the machine in the intensive-care ward, just as I now see "choice," essential to the personhood of women, as transcending the question of abortion.

A few years ago, I took part in a seminar at the Harvard Medical School and Hastings Center, directed by Daniel Callahan, on "Ethical Issues in the Treatment of Age." It struck me as odd, somehow, that the main "ethical" question troubling these doctors, medical experts, and professional ethicists about treatment of age was when to turn off the machine: who, at what point, and by what principles, decides? I'm still leery when the new gurus of the "right to die" movement—or rationed "health care management"—crusade for the old *only in those terms:* the "right to die." It could be as misleading as the euphemism "right to life" for those who put

the life of the unborn fetus above the personhood and life of the woman, concerned with
protecting life *only before birth,* with no interest
in whatever happens afterward. On the other
hand, the question of choice is crucial to the
personhood of age, though it does not begin, or
maybe end, with who decides when to turn off
the machine. To confront personally the reality
of *death as a part of life,* as I believe we must in
order to truly *live our age,* we must break free of
the political manipulation and exploitation of
this issue, which plays to society's fear and denial of age.

In the sagging economy of recent years, there
has been more and more talk from Washington
about the disproportionate sums going to health
care, Medicare, Medicaid, and Social Security
for the elderly—the "prosperous," "no longer
poor," elderly—at the expense of the young.
When former governor Richard Lamm of Colorado first suggested that older people, ill or disabled, have "a duty to die and get out of the way,"
people were shocked. But when Daniel Callahan
published *Setting Limits* in 1988, a detailed blue-
print for limiting health care for the old in order
to free up economic resources for the young, it
got respectful attention. Callahan's proposal to
ration health care for older people would stop
all development of life-extending technologies
and prohibit the use of high-tech devices now at
hand for people who outlive their "natural" life

span, say the age of seventy-five (life expectancy now averages seventy-two for men, nearly eighty for women). At the same time, older people would be granted more painkillers and more nursing home and home health care services to make their dying more comfortable. As opposed to pushing expensive high-technology operations and procedures on older people, without real hope of giving them more years of quality life, this would seem a step in the right direction.

But, as my old friend Amitai Etzioni has warned, the idea of limiting the care the elderly receive is already a slide down a "slippery slope." "Once the precept that one should do 'all one can' to avert death is given up, and attempts are made to fix a specific age for a full life, why stop there? If, for instance, the American economy experiences hard times in the 1990s, should the maximum age be reduced to 72, 65—or lower?"[1] Callahan and the Hastings Center had already redefined death from the time when the heart stops beating and the lungs breathing to brain death, the point at which care should stop even if it means turning off life-extending machines, because people who are brain dead do not regain consciousness. They are dead as persons. But Callahan now suggested turning off life-extending technologies for all those above a certain age, even if they could recover their full human capacity if treated. He would withhold mechanical ventilation, artificial resuscitation, antibiotics, and artificial nutrition and hydration. But if health care has to be rationed because of limited national resources to pay its mounting costs, why should age be the criterion? Why not likelihood of recovery to full function at any age? Why not stop all interventions for which there is no hard evidence that they are beneficial, such as coronary bypass operations? Why not limit funds for plastic surgery that has no life-saving function—face lifts—for instance? Or limit the exorbitant profits made by the owners of nursing homes and leasers of dialysis units?

In the course of my search, medical eminences such as Nathan Keyfitz of the Center for Population Studies at Harvard, Ed Schneider at Andrus, Jack Guralnik at the National Institutes of Health, and many journalists have barraged me with data that have dangerous potential for intergenerational conflict, and a turning of the growing economic frustration of the middle class against the elderly, especially when it is discovered that most of those dependent on Social Security, Medicare, and Medicaid are now women. I've been warned that with all the millions now being spent on cancer research, a "cure" would, at best, add a few more years or months to people already over seventy, who are the great majority of those now suffering from cancer. Or, didn't I realize that the great majority of people with "disabilities" in the United States

are people over sixty-five, and that those growing numbers of people now living into their seventies, eighties, nineties have the most
disabilities? And most of the people with those
disabilities are women!

I, of course, countered with the data that most
of those older people living longer are *healthy,*
that they suffer fewer episodes of acute illness
than the young, that most of them *function* with
those disabilities, as long as they stay active in
their communities, and that relatively inexpen-
sive non-medical services not currently covered
by any health insurance would enable them to
stay in their communities without the need for
costly nursing homes, or hospitals with their
costly high-technology procedures, which do indeed account for too much of this nation's excessive doctor bills. And if my gerontological
and journalistic colleagues take this accusatory
tone of voice about the growing number of older
people with "disabilities" (*living* with these disabilities into their eighties and nineties where before they might have been dead) or the
disproportionate number of older women *living
with disabilities* (whereas the men their age are
dead), what might happen if the "duty to die"
becomes an adjunct to the "right to die"?

The medical model, with its focus on "cure"
of "disease," whether or not it embarks on that
slippery slope, will not help us here. In a paper
pointing out that while women now live eight

years longer than men, the number of disabled women counterbalances the number of dead men, Jack Guralnik and his colleagues made the point:

> As mortality rates decline and the average age of death is postponed, there will be a marked expansion in overall population morbidity levels if the onset of disease and disability is not postponed an equal or greater number of years. . . . Active intervention in areas which promote healthy aging might lead to an aging population which retains high levels of function for a longer proportion of their lives and is therefore less dependent on families and the health care system.[2]

But the problems implicit here are, for the moment, being addressed mainly by the mounting campaign to give older people the "right to die," and *not* for the non-medical measures that would give them real choices to age in relatively good health, independently, in their own communities, with purposeful days and loving bonds. The changing consciousness that is enabling us to break through the dread of age and its denial must, of course, confront the reality that it ends in death. And the "right to die" legislation recently proposed in California and appearing in many other states may give us certain choices we need, beyond the "living will," to resist being kept alive by aggressive, costly, painful, dehumanizing measures if there is no hope of our being able to continue or resume functioning at what we ourselves consider a human life. But this is such a grave, complex, and ultimately personal decision that who else but ourselves can decide it for us? If there is any way we can make our wishes known, ahead of time, to our families or those who may be treating us, we must take, and increasingly are taking, steps to do it. But I am leery of any laws that give that choice over to the state, hospital administrators, doctors, spouses, children, or anyone else except the person, or whoever that person delegates in advance should they not be conscious when the need comes. I'm afraid of that slippery slope; I'm worried that we will use our yet not fully tested political power in age too narrowly in terms of final choice, as if that one decision—when to turn off the machine, or even the right to get a doctor's help to take our own lives—will give us control, choice, and autonomy to the very end, and somehow defy death itself.

Politically, I'm afraid of that focus on the "right to die" as too narrow an approach to the basic question of retaining our autonomy, independence, and real opportunity to continue to participate fully in life. This must involve not only defense of Social Security and a genuine national health system for everyone, but new policies of access to housing, education, political participation and transportation for older people, and innovations of community service geared not to terminal, dehumanized medical "care" but to maintaining vital health, our own autonomy and participation in life until the end. The work of Elisabeth Kübler-Ross and others is a giant step beyond our national denial of death. But surely here we enter an area where the right of privacy—involving our most deeply held individual beliefs and values, religious, spiritual, existential—must be established and prevail. Because our "right of privacy" in death may be as important as it is in bringing life into the world, I believe there's a real danger in defining it only in narrow terms of turning off a machine.

"Conscious dying" was a headline that hit me, from the pages of the *Utne Reader* ("the best of the alternative press"). Was it possible, I wondered, to consciously *choose to die with life*— or rather, to *live a conscious aging,* not waste a minute of it in futile defense and denial?

Along with Dr. Elisabeth Kübler-Ross, Stephen Levine and his wife, Ondrea, have spent the last fifteen years in "deathwork," guiding hundreds of individuals toward "conscious dying." They point out that 75 percent of the population take their last breath in hospitals or other institutions where "death is considered the enemy." Stephen Levine said:

I have seen many people approach death in physical and spiritual isolation, seldom encouraged to embrace this experience in any way other than fear, cut off in heart and mind from the loved ones who might share this precious moment. . . . I have watched many people cling desperately to a rapidly degenerating body, hoping for some incredible miracle, anguished by a deep longing for fulfillment never found in life. [3]

He spelled it out:

To let go of the last moment and open to the next is to die consciously. . . . One of the remarkable things about confronting death is the depth at which it gets our attention. Focusing on death is a way of becoming fully alive. Because wherever the attention is, wherever awareness is, that is where our experience of life arises. . . . When we take death within us we stop reinforcing our denial, our judging, our anger, or continuing our bargaining.

Perhaps the first recognition in the process of acknowledging, opening, and letting go that I call "conscious dying" is when we begin to see that we are not the body. We see that we have a body but it is not who we are. One fellow remarked that he could see that he was "creation constantly in the act of becoming" . . . and that there was nothing he had to do about it. . . .

The death of the body is accompanied by less agony than the death of the ego, the separate self. The death of the self is a tearing away of everything we imagine to be solid, a crumbling of the walls we have built to hide behind. . . . It means the death of everything we have learned to be, all the thoughts and projections that so enamoured us in the past and created someone for us to be in the future. All is allowed to die back into the flow of life. . . . We experience the deep satisfaction of no one to protect and no one to be . . . and clear acceptance of what is. . . .[4]

I remember my own terror, as a teenager, when the realization first came over me that one day I would no longer be. The thought of death was unbearable to me. I remember my terror of flying, as a young reporter and then a mother, in those years when my work first demanded that I fly on assignments between cities. And I remember, when I started having to fly even more frequently, after I finished writing *The Feminine Mystique,* in those years I was organizing the women's movement—and I suddenly realized I was flying with no fear at all. I began to have a special sense that the fear of death had something to do with not really living, with evading life. Because in writing *The Feminine Mystique* I had had the mysterious experience of using every part of myself, my present and my past,

959

putting all of it together in a personal truth and then using that truth to help change the possibilities of life for those coming after me. And, while I would not have phrased it so grandly at the time, I was not afraid, after that, of big new challenges of living. Only obsolete fears, left from childhood, still got in my way, in work or love—using a word processor, driving a car—though less, much less, now as I consciously aged.

I remember the first time I felt the comfort of accepting death. Mark, my very beloved brother-in-law, died of heart disease, barely sixty, and even though I was divorced from his brother, I had truly loved him and went by myself to his funeral. As I watched them carrying out the coffin, my own younger son one of the pallbearers, what came over me was a strange combination of sorrow, and yet comfort, at his death. His wife, Pepi, could not really forgive him for dying and leaving her—if he had only stopped smoking, which he had refused to do, and paid more attention to diet and exercise, he might still be alive, he might not have left her alone with the rest of her life to live by herself. I could understand her anger. But what I felt was the strangest sense of how wonderfully and fully he had lived his life. I had shared some of its critical moments, after he lost his arm in the early years of Israel's nationhood, his loving support of me in the early storms of my marriage and motherhood, the amazing adventure of his romance and courtship of Pepi, his joys and pains as a father, and the gusto of his animal research and his clock collecting. For some strange reason, that warm compelling sense of the *aliveness* of Mark's person in my mind made me feel a new ease about death. So, Mark is dead, and one day I will be dead, too.

It's said that our fascination with airplane crashes, deaths by fire or flood, assassination or war, the sudden inexplicable violence that fills the pages of the newspapers, is a heightened sense of our own survivorship. It enhances our illusion of immortality—that death will never happen to us. But, in recent years, as my personal friends have begun to die—as the obituaries I now scan in the *Times* every morning often include a man or woman whom I have known or admired—I have felt, with increasing ease, that now familiar feeling of loss and sorrow, and yet that comfort, acceptance, at home with death. I have lost my terror and denial of death. I can live with its reality.

A number of my friends have had good deaths, struck suddenly in the midst of life. I think of Maury, dying of failed heart and lungs, with a page half written in his typewriter, preparing to go to Las Vegas the next weekend to initiate a younger writer into the mysteries of the gambling world he had so loved writing about. He was dying with life to the very end. I expect, also, he had been consciously dying for some time.

The emphysema from his lifetime of smoking, though he never called it that—"my breathing problem"—had been getting so much worse that the previous May, when I'd said goodbye to him at the end of my California teaching semester, I wasn't sure he would still be there the next winter when I got back. But just as, when his eyes became so bad he couldn't drive anymore, he had recruited a host of willing ladies and old male buddies to hitch a ride with, so, suddenly, he simply stopped taking all those medicines that were doing him no good, and making him feel so bad, and he began to breathe much better, most of the time, with an oxygen tank at hand when he couldn't get his breath.

That previous spring vacation we had spent together at his daughter's inn in Eureka Springs, Arkansas. He had shown me the particular tree he planned to be buried under. "That's Maury's tree," his daughter Crescent would tell her guests. An Alcoholics Anonymous buddy, seeking his help, was the last person to see him alive. But he had been on the phone only an hour before to Charlotte, from whom he had been divorced twenty years, his closest friend with whom he spoke every day, though they lived continents apart. At his three memorial services, in Los Angeles and in New York and in Arkansas, Crescent played a videotape of Maury teaching one of his writing classes—conveying the sheer zest with which he approached each new assignment, the surprises that he knew lay in wait in the new, as yet unknown material. He *lived* so fully that every time I get back to California and go to the movies with our friends without him, we feel his presence, his loss.

My friend Joe Haggerty found the lump in his neck only months after he and Susan got married, after twenty years of living together. Retired as a cement contractor, putting his energy now into a foundation supporting treatment of autistic children, guiding his own five children through youthful storms, gardening with Susan and vigorously sailing and playing tennis with a disparate bunch of old and new cronies, he sought the best medical help to fight the cancer. When he was warned that surgery might mean removal of his voice box, he urged that it not be done if other means were possible—and underwent devastating chemotherapy. After a lifetime of heavy smoking and drinking, he stopped both, cold turkey, and, with Susan's help, found a priest who had been a childhood friend to help him mobilize his spiritual resources. (The Catholic chaplain at Memorial Hospital had refused to give him communion, when Joe informed him of his divorce and remarriage, unless he had his marriage to Susan annulled and they lived together "as brother and sister.")

We marveled at them both, the next three years, remodeling their home, with an unusually beautiful master bedroom and bath, a massive old wicker bed in the very center of the room, Susan virtually putting her career as photographer on hold to plant a new garden and sustain Joe. We marveled at his continuing to sail, even in stormy weather, even after his voice box had to be removed two years later. We marveled at how he mastered that "damn voice box," and laughed at his inimitable jokes even though he did sound like HAL in *2001*. We had the twentieth reunion of our commune at a long table in their garden. When a new lump appeared on the other side of his neck, he resumed the chemotherapy, and rented a big house in Ireland for the coming summer, to take all his children and grandchildren.

In June, he had to have surgery again; the cancer was no longer responding to the chemotherapy. He ordered the doctors to do whatever they could so he could get to Ireland. If a more drastic treatment might give him a month or year more but leave him too weak to take that trip, forget it. They brought back wonderful pictures of their Irish summer—the kids so elegant, all dressed up for a ball, Joe and Susan presiding in their evening clothes, and bagpipes brought in. He died very suddenly—or at long last—before Christmas, only hours after he started hemorrhaging, in the middle of the night, in his own bed. And he died consciously, with Susan and his children in the room.

In recent years, some of my women friends

have confronted death in different conscious ways. After her second mastectomy, Ruth Spear put the energy she used to spend writing gourmet cookbooks and giving elegant dinner parties to organizing NABCO (National Alliance of Breast Cancer Organizations), which has forced health insurance to cover mammograms in most states, and provides a network of information and support for women to monitor their own cancer care. A distinguished woman diplomat, diagnosed with terminal cancer in the midst of an international crisis, chose not to have the drastic operation that might have given her another year to live, though in and out of hospitals. She continued to work on the political crisis, not even telling her friends of her cancer, until the end. Another woman, a painter, also chose not to have the drastic operation. When the pain of her terminal cancer became intense, she invited her friends and family to join her in a final party, and received them sitting in a coffin filled with flowers, with much toasting of them to her and her to them before she swallowed the lethal dose. (She even had her husband and a friend videotape her death party as our daughters now videotape their births.)

I had to admit my own mixed emotions at some of this—admiration, shock, distaste, and wonder. Maybe I was still in denial, maybe I was not close enough yet to embark on "conscious dying" personally, or liked to think I was not. At least I made a will and a living will, and sent copies to my kids. I had mixed feelings when they told me they had already discussed how they would jointly run the house in Sag Harbor, which I was leaving to the three of them as a continuing family retreat. I found it easier to fantasize about my funeral than specifically, concretely how I wanted to end my own life. All I knew was that I didn't want to end it in a nursing home, or in one of my kids' homes either. All I knew was that the *conscious aging* I had embarked on, in talking about these things to others, in writing this book, had liberated me from the denial and fear of age, to a kind of curious wonder, facing each new development as it came—the surprise of it, the unexpected good, and the admitted pain, which so far, in their actuality, had balanced out.

My friends and I had only just begun to talk about these things to each other, and I noticed that such talks seemed to make us feel more intensely alive. We seemed to be a little kinder to each other, a little more attentive to subtle clues of distress or well-being. Could we manage our age, each of us in our own houses in the country, where we now spend our vacations, weekends, and holidays, and live close enough to each other to easily pool leftovers and cook together on a summer evening? Should we begin planning ways to pool our resources more seriously, in the future, when we may not be able to handle all the details alone? Or should we trust ourselves to face all that when the need arises? Certainly, I would not consider leaving this community of friends and doings, walks and waterways that I know so well, to segregate myself in some "lifetime care" facility, no matter how it is gussied up to look like a country club, merely to ensure whatever medical, nursing, or other "care" I might need at the end. Maybe I would be lucky enough to die with life, as Maury did, a page half written on my open pad, with a sudden heart attack or in an airplane crash.

Still there is the reality of one day not being able to live alone any longer. Could Joe have had that good death without Susan making his care her career those last years? Admitting there is no way to insure ourselves against terminal age and death, I sensed that instead of spending too much time and energy worrying now about that dreaded terminal care, what we must do—the only thing we can do—is *to make the changes we need to make in our own lives to give them meaning to the very end.* That is the best insurance for our vital aging, and for dying with life.

I served for five years on a commission set up by the Harvard Community Health Plan to wrestle with principles that might be applied by HMOs (health maintenance organizations), increasingly being used by employers to "manage" the health care for which their employees and pensioners are insured and the new rationing dilemmas they face. Composed of an illustrious group of medical school professors, judges, economists and philosophers, educators and theologians, the LORAN Commission (named after the submarine underwater guiding device of World War II) was asked to devise a guiding set of principles by which decisions could be made as to use of limited insurance funds for the new, extremely costly technology now being developed that can extend life in ways undreamed of before —not only kidney dialysis and coronary bypass, but heart and liver transplants. If a single liver transplant costs $500,000, on what basis should an HMO cover it, compared to, for instance, a smoke-ending program that, for the same amount of money, would help one hundred people stop smoking, with measurable benefits in length and quality of life, preventing the need for future costly medical and hospital services? I was the only woman and the only lay person on the commission, and inevitably became an advocate for the interests of women as well as people in age.

We were, respectively: David Banta, World Health Organization; Robert Cushman, retired CEO; Douglas Fraser, President Emeritus, United Auto Workers; Robert Freeman, Director, Eastman School of Music; Judge Ben Kaplan; Frederick Mosteller, Harvard School of Public

Health; David Nathan, Physician-in-Chief, Children's Hospital; Albert Rees, economist; Hays Rockwell, Episcopal priest; Robert Sproull, scientist; Dr. Marshall Wolf, Brigham & Women's Hospital; and the Reverend John Paris, Jesuit priest and professor of medical ethics.

We heard witnesses from the nation's leading medical schools on the dilemmas HMOs and doctors now faced, keeping premature babies alive, for instance, with misplaced hearts or missing or damaged vital organs, with virtually no chance of living normal lives; their own questions about the hundreds of thousands of dollars spent on high-tech breathing and feeding and other devices to keep older patients alive an extra month, with no hope of walking again, or even talking. Economists and public health experts shared their expertise in developing "quality-of-life" measures, ranking new devices and technological innovations in terms of cost per number of people helped per quantity and quality of life years or months extended. All of it made sense, and all of it was a slippery slope. How do you justify insurer or doctor saying no to the plea to "do anything that needs to be done to keep Mom alive" or to "save my baby"?

On the LORAN Commission, I had to face the larger ethical, moral, and social implications of my own personal wish to live as long as I can really *live* and then, somehow, get what help I need to end my life, in dignified conscious dying, not as a comatose vegetable. The personhood of women implies, requires the "right to choose," according to our private conscience and values, whether and when to give birth, as we learned confronting the issue of abortion. In the historic decision *Roe* v. *Wade,* the Supreme Court decreed reproductive choice a basic right to be decided only by the woman herself, up to the time when the fetus could live viably outside the womb. The new technology that can sustain premature fetal life outside the womb but with no guarantee of full human development complicated that issue. So the new technology that can keep us breathing, by machine—when we can no longer speak or write or move or share our pain or joy—forces us to confront the personhood of age, and to think, at least, of the possibilities of "choice" at death, of defining a point for ourselves beyond which we cannot conceive of wanting to live.

And just as, in the beginning, the question of abortion was discussed only in terms of the doctor's right and duty, not the woman's, so terminal care of age tends to be discussed in terms of doctors' duties, needs, and costs. Father John Paris put the case to us bluntly:

With Blue Cross (or Medicare) blunting the jolt of out-of-pocket expenses, nothing is considered too good for Granny. Granny herself, as part of the fastest growing segment of our society, is proving an exacerbation of the problem. Older people constitute an ever larger proportion of chronic care cases. . . . Is it ever ethically appropriate to put constraints and limits on the amount of money expended on the aged? . . . It is not discrimination . . . but prudent choice to say, "Yes, you have had 90 good years of life, and so we are not going to continue to put the same amount of resources into your care as that of a newborn or a 20- or 40-year-old.". . .[5]

Noting the huge increase in health care costs (from 4.5 percent of gross national product in 1980 to over 10.8 percent in 1984 and nearly 15 percent today), with vast amounts spent on high-tech intensive-care items where "the potential benefit is very low," and with a relatively small percentage of patients (15 percent) consuming 50 percent of the costs, most of them "chronically or terminally ill," he asked:

Does it really make sense to spend 25 percent of our health care dollar on the last three months of life? Is it true quality care when . . . an elderly patient [is] admitted to a prestigious Manhattan hospital and placed in the ICU [and] on the fifth day . . . slipping closer and closer to death, her lungs begin to fail; she is put on a respirator; two days later she needs a tracheotomy. Finally, on the twenty-fifth day, she suffers cardiac arrest. CPR is instituted; it doesn't work. She dies. The bottom line is that after 25 days of . . . technology which can prevent dying, but not restore life, the patient dies. Her hospital bill alone is $47,000. . . .

Physicians in this country have already begun to realize that aggressive treatment of many terminally ill patients is often pointless. . . . The illusion that we could achieve . . . immortality through medicine . . . and the yet more devastating illusion that cost was never to be a consideration . . . produced a system that allowed us to resuscitate a terminally ill cancer patient 52 times despite his plaintive pleas "to be let go." It led us to transfer end-stage liver patients to the ICU, and it permitted us to keep brain-dead patients "alive" on respirators for months in the hope of a miracle. . . . It was an abuse . . . of technology . . . of the patient and above all an abuse of society and its resources, resources given to us by God, not for useless struggles against the inevitable, but for the upbuilding of the entire community.

These patients, on whom we spend the greatest amounts in the last few months of life, account for one out of every seven dollars currently expended on health care. If, once the diagnosis and prognosis were clear, we changed from aggressive interventions to a program of keeping the patient comfortable through the dying process, there would be a multi-billion dollar reduction in the present cost of health care.[6]

The exercises we went through trying to devise standards by which an HMO should decide whether or not to cover high-tech heart and liver and kidney transplants were instructive, given the growing emphasis on "managed" health care to save the employer's and insurer's dollar. But these exercises were not particularly concerned with age, since most of those insured in the Harvard Plan were merely aging baby boomers, in their thirties and forties. I could not even get them to consider not just "nay saying" to liver transplants and other means of aggressive terminal care, but saying yes to the kinds of services that enable older people to stay independent and age vitally in their communities. The home services covered by the Harvard Community Health Plan had to be "essential to treatment" of "conditions which are medically unstable or progressively deteriorating," but not as "an alternative to health center—based medical management," hospital, or nursing home— nor as a substitute for "long-term custodial nonmedical placement" (nursing home), and specifically not "supportive services for patients with chronic stable conditions who have reached a rehabilitative plateau and/or require only assistance with activities of daily living," "companionship," and "safety." Their memo on Home Care specified: "Coverage of home care is based on medical necessity not social need."

The trouble is, as health care costs continue to increase, and employers and insurers as well as families become increasingly desperate to cut or control them, "managed care" becomes a mechanism not for improving but for limiting the care people thought they were insured for. The extremely profitable, "aggressively entrepreneurial" managed-care companies—Blue Cross, Blue Shield; Humana; and other HMOs—contract with employers to review doctors' decisions and discourage hospitalizations and other services, eroding the coverage people think they have. And the "greedy geezers" are especially vulnerable to this.[7] "Managed care" is rationed care, and once such rationing is contemplated, the rationale is inevitably age. In his testimony before the LORAN Commission, Father Paris cited many authorities to this effect.

In trying to establish just and humane standards for deciding whether or not HMOs should cover expensive new health care interventions and technologies, our commission was introduced by Robert Berg to an index of "quality life years" saved. If Program A treated 100 people at a cost of $10,000 per patient, and 10 people survived who would otherwise have died, then the cost of saving a life ($100,000) would make it superior to Program B, costing $200,000 to save a single life. But Berg pointed out that this kind of thinking, in terms of national resources, "leads to funding the treatment of aged persons who will die soon in any event. It leads to the same priority for programs aimed at saving the life of an aged person compared to programs aimed at saving the life of a young person."

Alternatively, he proposed an index of "life years saved." If Program A treated 1,000 aged patients at a cost of $10,000 per patient (total $10 million) and saved 500 life years (i.e., giving 500 people an average extra year of life, or 250 an average of two more years), it would cost $20,000 per life year saved. If Program B treated *1,000 young people* at a cost of $25,000 per patient, the total cost would be $25 million. But if 2,000 life years were saved for three young people, it would cost only $12,500 per life year saved, and give that program priority even though its actual cost was two and one half times as great per patient, Dr. Berg told us. (In terms of national priorities, the Centers for Disease Control recently changed its method of ordering the importance of killer diseases from "lives saved" to "life years saved," and therefore replaced cancer, heart disease, and stroke with "accidents in young people" as the most significant American health problem.

Berg spelled it out bluntly:

One patient's life may not have the same social significance of another, an evaluation mostly related to the age of the respective patients. If there must be a choice, the 40-year-old will usually be preferred to the 90-year-old. This has led to the use of life years saved rather than lives saved. . . .

On the basis only of life years saved, would you give the next spot on an artificial kidney to a 90-year-old or a 40-year-old? Most of you would select the 40-year-old. But what would be the choice if there were only time or resources to save either one 40-year-old man from a burning building or two 65-year-olds? . . . The maximal number of life years saved would result from saving the 40-year-old (34.3 life years versus 2 x 14.8 years = 29.6 life years for the 65-year-olds). This leads to an action favoring one life saved over two lives saved—troubling. . . .[8]

We on the LORAN Commission, civilians and doctors, were thrown into turmoil when such dilemmas were made explicit. It clearly wasn't fair to endanger the limited resources of this or any "health maintenance organization" by spending millions or even hundreds of thousands of dollars on new, big-ticket, high-technology procedures that might or might not give one or a few otherwise dead individuals a few more months or years of life, of what quality? But how, indeed, to make such life-and-death distinctions? And these questions were particularly critical at the two ends of life, after birth and near death. Already, far too high a portion of America's exploding health care bill was being spent on neonatal and terminal care, keeping alive premature babies and dying elders with no real hope of developing or sustaining full human capacity.

After sessions of futile debate, the commission gave Hays Rockwell, now Bishop Coadjutor of Missouri, and me, as advocate of particularly vulnerable women and older people, the job of drafting our consensus on "Limits of Health Care at the Extreme Ends of Life." We didn't get very far, as distinguished a group as we may have been. We could agree on the "brain death" criteria to determine death (not heartbeat or breath or vegetative life). We could recommend as a current guideline that "no delivered conceptus shall be sustained if it weighs 600 grams or less *and* is 24 weeks or younger, since, at this time, even when extensive costly measures are taken, fewer than one percent of such deliveries survive" and only a fraction of them in anything like a whole state. But as to "issues surrounding the end of life," all we could agree on was an educational program around the concept of the living will (still not legal in Massachusetts and other states at that time) to provide people with "the means of defining the limits of their lives *as they wish them to be.*" All hospitals and health plans ought to have an ethics or review committee, we suggested, made up of people from medicine, law, and philosophy as a body to which patients' family members can turn as a last resort in making decisions about sustaining human existence when terminal and irreversible illness or injury make recovery unlikely. We also thought such a committee should be guided by "some version of a calculus which seeks to take into account all the factors by which life can be measured and defined"—such as the method proposed by Dr. Berg. But we were not clear enough ourselves, after three years of study, even to peg "the issue of defining life that is worth continuing," unequivocally, to *individual choice.*

The living will that Hays Rockwell proposed, addressed to "my family, clergyman, lawyer, physician and medical facility," specified the new morality:

If the time comes when I can no longer take part in decisions for my own future, let this statement stand as the testament of my wishes:

If there is no reasonable expectation of my recovery from physical or mental disability, I,   , request that I be allowed to die and not be kept alive by artificial means or heroic measures. Death is as much a reality as birth, growth, maturity and old age—it is the one certainty. I do not fear death as much as I fear the indignity of deterioration, dependence and hopeless pain. I ask that medication be mercifully administered to me for terminal suffering even if it hastens the moment of death. . . . Although this document may not be legally binding, you who care for me will, I hope, feel morally bound to follow its mandate.

Signed, dated, with two witnesses, such a Living Will Declaration can also include a Proxy Designation clause, specifying someone to "make treatment decisions if you are unable to do so."

In less than a decade since we started thrashing these issues out on that commission, law, medicine, and public opinion have moved further and further toward a "right to die" consensus, respecting individual choices as expressed in such living wills. But in 1986, a Massachusetts judge ruled "no" when the family of fireman Paul Brophy, in a "persistent vegetative state" with prognosis for recovering virtually "non-existent," wanted his life support discontinued. Brophy, a fireman and emergency medical technician, had helped to resuscitate many dying people, and had seen some return to their families barely human, "their bodies kept alive by tubes and machines." Before his own burst cerebral aneurism, he made sure his whole family knew he did not want his life prolonged in such circumstances. His wife, five adult children, ninety-one-year-old mother, and seven brothers and sisters all agreed that if he could express himself, he would want any efforts for continued life support to be stopped. But doctor, nursing home, and probate court refused to remove the gastrostomy tube because Brophy was not "terminally ill." On "brain death," the AMA now agrees, "one was disconnecting a corpse from a ventilator, not withdrawing life support from a living human being." But there is still disagreement about turning off the machine for patients who do not meet the criteria for brain death, yet show no signs or hope of recovering from coma —much less patients diagnosed with irreversible Alzheimer's or in great pain from terminal cancer who seek medical help in consciously terminating their own lives.

Ruling that dying people had a right to refuse food and that guardians or designated surrogates could make the decision for people who were not able to act on their own, the Florida Supreme Court, on September 13, 1990, decided that dying people and their surrogates need not have a court's approval before they stop forced feeding. The decision was based on "the right of privacy." The woman in the case, Estelle Browning, spent the last one and a half years of her life hooked up to a feeding tube in a nursing home despite a living will in which she specified that she did not want to be kept alive under such conditions. She was not comatose, but she could neither swallow nor communicate and was considered "incompetent." With five of the seven justices concurring, the Florida court stated: "The decision to terminate artificial life-sustaining measures is being made over and over in nursing homes, hospitals and private homes in this nation. It is being made painfully by loving family members, concerned guardians or surrogates, with the advice of ethical and caring physicians, or other health care providers. It is being made when the only alternative to a natural death is to artificially maintain a bare existence."[9]

Thus, our consciousness of aging and of death and dying as a part of life is evolving, with a new morality. In early October 1991, a poll showed that 61 percent of probable voters in Washington State supported Initiative 119, which would have permitted doctors to help terminally ill patients commit suicide or even kill them at their request. Only 27 percent opposed the "right to die" measure, and 12 percent were undecided. A month later, voters defeated the initiative by a 54 to 46 margin. An emotional and bitterly fought campaign, in which the backers of the proposal spent three times as much as its opponents, evidently made Washington voters think more seriously of "the gravity of the step they were considering," an analyst reported.

From the first, the force of calls for "death with dignity" was evident, as was the widespread revulsion against the use of medical technology to prolong dying pointlessly. Yet these powerful sentiments evidently paled before moral qualms and practical fears.

Authorizing physicians to give lethal injections was simply a line that many Washingtonians would not cross. And once they read the fine print, a good many voters apparently began doubting whether Initiative 119 contained enough safeguards against abuse. . . .

But another message was that people want to assert control over dying because they profoundly distrust contemporary medicine's capacity to respond to terminal illness or protracted, painful debilitation.[10]

A nationwide poll by the *Boston Globe* and the Harvard School of Public Health showed that 48 percent of the public thought giving lethal injections upon request should be "allowed but not required" of doctors. Some 30 percent thought such injections should be "prohibited." A similar ambivalent uneasiness was elicited by the women who sought out Dr. Jack Kevorkian's suicide machine in Michigan after being diagnosed with Alzheimer's disease—"not the mentally competent and demonstrably dying patients [but] those who have already lost the mental capacity to choose for themselves [and] those still able to choose but on the agonizing brink of what they or their families know will be an inexorable decline into physical or mental helplessness."

In our final report, submitted in 1988, the LORAN Commission expressed its belief that

the concept of quality care does not always demand that death be regarded as an enemy to be fought with every weapon at a physician's disposal. An obsession with quantity of life can adversely affect its quality. The case studies made clear to the commission that there are instances when the vast array of medical technological interventions available to treat certain individuals with certain conditions ought to be limited; that there are times when graceful death with dignity is preferable to lengthening torment."[11]

During the three years that we agonized over such decisions, our own thinking changed. We commissioned the Louis Harris Organization to take a poll of a national cross section of the United States on these questions, as well as polls of employers, union leaders, state political leaders, and members of Congress, and also doctors and nurses currently involved in making such decisions. All of these groups changed their minds about people's right to get medical treatment, no matter how expensive, and their "right to die." In the Harris Poll, if forced to choose between a treatment that would cure fifty dying children or one that would save the lives of a thousand seventy-five-year-old people and give them each three or more years of life, the overwhelming majority (81 percent) of adult Americans would opt to save the fifty children. While half the general public thought that doctors should "do everything in their power" to preserve the life of a newborn baby, "even if it is very seriously deformed and will never be able to live a normal life," a majority felt that a terminally ill patient's family should not have the right to demand that the patient be kept alive by very expensive life support systems.

In the summer of 1992 a number of different doctors told me, unsolicited, that they or some of their "colleagues" were no longer going to accept patients over sixty-five. In light of new Medicare payment standards, some of them said, "I simply can't afford it." But, they would quickly assure me, "Of course, *you* could always get treatment . . ."

My own obvious ambivalence about the "right to die" movement is partly the result of long experience with the issue of reproductive choice, at the other end of life. While the "right to choose" whether or not to give birth did and does seem essential to the personhood of women, the narrowing of that issue to the single question of legal abortion in the last dozen years has paralyzed the women's movement in mortal combat with fundamentalist religious and political groups, and diverted our own energy and attention from larger questions involving the rights and welfare of women, and the health and future of their children and themselves. The personhood of age surely does imply that we make our own choices about a life worth continuing, and decide in the privacy of our own conscience which we make public in a living will, recognized by our family, doctors, and the law, under what circumstances we do not choose to be kept alive by machines. But when to turn off the machine is only one small issue in the whole new range of public policy and moral choices implied by the personhood of age. The "right to die" a human death must mean the right to live a human age, participating in the larger life of our communities. It must mean the right to get the health care, housing, and other services we need to keep our autonomy and our own control of these unprecedented new years of life, through our seventies, eighties. And to that end, eradication of the age stereotypes and barriers that would exclude us from the ongoing work and play of society's mainstream is far more important than turning off the machines.

I am concerned that our own energies will be diverted from those larger issues by a "right to die" movement advocating only that final choice. I am concerned that such a movement may pave the way or serve the interests of powerful forces who need scapegoats to divert people's attention from desperately needed reforms in our economy and our educational and health care systems. I am concerned that the "right to die" will be seen not as an individual choice but as a socially acceptable form of euthanasia. Helen Kaplan, the eminent sex therapist, pointed out to me that the Holocaust began in Nazi Germany and her native Austria with "euthanasia" to purify the race of unproductive older people, the elderly and the retarded or urgenically unfit, before the 6 million Jews.

With over 500,000 copies sold, *Final Exit,* Derek Humphry's explicit how-to manual for taking one's own life with minimal pain and trouble, was at the top of *The New York Times* best-seller list for months in 1990. The head of the Hemlock Society, then in his early sixties, advised against guns and hanging—too imprecise and messy; instead, barbiturates should be taken with Dramamine so they will stay down, with a "plastic bag over your head" as a backup measure. And this specific advice was carried to many more millions by *People* magazine and the full-scale national media and television campaign that launched the book. But when Humphry's ex-wife Ann, forty-nine, committed suicide, after helping her own aging parents to die—and undergoing a bitter divorce from Humphry in 1990, when she was diagnosed with cancer—she claimed that he had driven her to kill herself.

Questions began to be raised about pressures that might be used on people, men or women not terminally ill, but suffering from depression, as so many must who face society's denial of their very personhood in age.

The suicide rate of people sixty-five and older, which had steadily declined in the half century after Social Security was passed, has been rapidly increasing since 1980. A 25 percent increase in the suicide rate among those sixty-five and older from 1981 to 1986 revealed 21.6 per 100,000 people taking their own lives, or twice the national average. It was the only group showing that kind of increase. Health care experts were puzzled, since older people today are so much healthier, more financially secure, and know they will live so much longer than their forebears. Was this unprecedented increase in elders' suicide evidence of "more of an attitude that suicide is an acceptable solution to life's problems, especially those of the elderly," [12] or of clinical, curable depression among older people, and implicit or explicit collusion by family and society in hastening their termination?

A new study of elderly suicide by the American Association of Retired Persons noted that white males sixty-five and over have the highest suicide rate (43.1 per 100,000), nearly four times the national average, with the ratio of male to female suicides increasing from 4 to 1 at ages sixty-five to sixty-nine to 12 to 1 by age eighty-five. And the report indicated that the cause may not be clinical "depression"—the treatable mental illness that precedes suicide in most younger people—but "an accumulation of losses that just keeps getting worse," according to Dr. Susan O. Mercer, professor of social work at the University of Arkansas, who prepared the AARP report. "It's loss of spouse, friends, health, status, and a meaningful role in society," she said. "More older people are committing suicide not out of depression, but because they just don't want to go on living. They are projecting what's ahead, and just don't want to go through with it. They're living longer, but the quality of life is not that good."

And here, the fine line becomes visible between the "right to die," "death with dignity," "final choice," "rational suicide," and subtle or not-so-subtle coercion. "The concept of rational suicide is gaining credence," stated Dr. Seymour Perlin, psychiatrist founder of the American Association of Suicidology. " 'Rational suicide' often masks the complicity of grown children, who tacitly agree with an ailing elderly parent, aware that his medical treatment is draining the family resources, that 'you would be better off without me.' By not protesting, children encourage the parent to commit suicide." [13]

"An awful lot of suicide in old age doesn't get reported as suicide," my friend Dr. Robert Butler, who keeps tabs on changing trends, told me. The AARP study also said that, unlike people in other age groups, when older persons decide to commit suicide, they are likely to succeed. "The elderly can more easily commit 'covert' suicide by starving themselves, terminating life-sustaining medications or overdosing on prescribed medications. Such suicides may also be disguised as fatal accidents."

Further throwing into question the widespread advocacy of "final exit" or euthanasia as appropriate responses to age and its problems were studies revealing that a great majority of people over sixty-five who actually do take their own lives are, in fact, clinically depressed, whether with or, more often, without a painful illness or infirmity. In a study of all the cases of suicide in the first ten months of 1990 in Chicago by people sixty-five or older, only 14 percent had a terminal illness, and 23 percent a chronic medical condition. In all but two of the seventy-three cases, the person taking her/his life was, in fact, clinically depressed. Dr. David C. Clark, psychiatrist at Rush-Presbyterian-St. Luke's Medical Center in Chicago, who did that study, stated:

A person who is severely depressed can't think rationally about suicide. The book *Final Exit* paints a picture, which we know is false, that most people who are in chronic pain, incapacitated or infirm want to kill themselves. Distinguishing between depressive illness and the pain and sadness of a serious illness is very tough, but with rare exceptions you only find suicidal thinking in the five to 20 percent of such patients who have an acute depression.[14]

While the "right to die" or "death with dignity" legislation was supported in the state of Washington by the American Civil Liberties Union as an issue of "privacy," many doctors opposed giving their colleagues the "right to kill" ("active euthanasia") older patients, even with the safeguard opinions of two doctors that they have less than six months to live, and must be mentally competent and have requested such help in writing. They pointed out that all doctors could make such decisions—even outside their own specialties—that the cause of such deaths did not have to be reported, and that there was no mandatory waiting period to determine if the patient was indeed mentally competent rather than clinically depressed. They worried that such laws could open the door for "the coercion of elderly or poor patients to accept [lethal injections] as a way of relieving family pressures."[15]

We can and must resist being kept alive, hooked to machines, past the point where it could ever be a conscious human life worth continuing. But we also can, and must, resist letting our final exit be controlled, unconscionably hastened or delayed, by political, bureaucratic, or economic dicta of church or state or doctors or even our own families, for motives of their own profit or convenience or making us scapegoats of frustrations caused by economic problems. Even those who support "death with dignity" initiatives must be conscious not only of their possibilities for dangerous misuses but of their practical limitations, when it comes to real choice in age. For they are no substitute for, and may divert energy from the real initiatives needed—in health care, housing, education, and employment—to guarantee that we can live out our lives, independent and active in our communities, with the bonds of love and projects of purpose, the respect and self-respect and human nourishment that make life worth continuing.

As for death, new research shows that for almost everybody, its actuality is not as painful and terrible as our denial, and the terror it masks and sustains, has made us fear. A new body of articles and books about "near-death" experiences—people who have "died," heartbeat and breathing stopped and then revived—report euphoria. A nationwide Gallup Poll conducted in 1982 found that a third of the 8 million Americans who reported near-death experience "recall being in an ecstatic or visionary state." They typically say that they felt themselves rushing through dark space, saw their lives pass before their eyes, and then entered "a realm of light," with "intense feelings of joy, love and peace." [16]

Without regard to theories of an afterlife, doctors, in fact, have been reporting for years that death itself is non-traumatic. The great physician Lewis Thomas, former head of Sloan-Kettering, noted that in all his years of practicing medicine, he had observed only a single agonizing death, from rabies. A *cause* of death can be painful—cancer, heart disease, multiple sclerosis—but "physicians who regularly tend to the dying agree that death itself is not all that unpleasant." In his book *The Medusa and the Snail,* Thomas suggested that the entire biosphere is a single, unified organism, like a living cell, in which dying is an indispensable part of living. In such an ecosystem, where everything depends on everything else, "You would need some mechanism that made death and dying acceptable. Pain is useful for avoidance, for getting away when there's time to get away, but when it is end game, and no way back, pain is likely to be turned off, and the mechanisms for this are wonderfully precise and quick." [17]

Once we suspect that our obsession with "care" in age comes from *denial* of death, once we accept our own and our parents' deaths as a mysterious part of life, we can, I think, protect ourselves from the futile, hopeless, often excruciatingly painful and humiliating procedures that play on our false illusions and denial to give us a few more days of life no longer human or worth continuing, and to deny us the peace and possible radiance of that *conscious* kind of death, that we can choose, in the company of people we love.

The "hospice" movement is growing today in many cities, often under church or hospital auspices—a place that is neither hospital nor nursing home, sometimes merely offering services and help to people who want to die as painlessly as possible at home. Housed in an intimate brownstone with a garden when it opened in 1980, Cabrini Hospice moved into a self-contained unit within Cabrini Medical Center in New York in 1982, but eleven members of the original hospice team still worked there ten years later, caring for terminally ill patients basically in their own homes, with brief stays at the Center when intensive therapy was needed. Over six hundred patients and their families were made comfortable as they approached death there in 1990. The home care nurses, social workers, nuns, and devoted volunteers of all races whom I met there were drawn to hospice work because they felt the needs of dying patients were not being met in the traditional hospital or nursing home setting where they had worked before, or where family members had been placed. As one nurse put it: "Hospice tends to the patient as a whole rather than focusing on technical care alone."

Originally a Catholic institution, Cabrini Hospice serves people of all faiths, and those who work and volunteer there share the exhilaration of "working on a new and exciting idea," a sophistication about hands-on care, "physical and spiritual comfort," and a sense of "the personal growth and development which has resulted from their work with the dying"—"the feeling that I touched someone." [18]

Mary Cooke, the nurse who has directed the hospice from the beginning, explained:

Our purpose is to offer comfort both to the patient and the family when they are beyond being cured—comfort not only of physical symptoms and pain but emotional and spiritual. The understanding from the beginning is that we don't offer cure. The patient signs a statement that he understands no heroic measures will be taken to resuscitate him; we use technology and surgery only if the doctor thinks it will significantly improve the quality of his life until the end.

When a cancer becomes so extensive that a patient's bowels are completely obstructed, nothing can get through, he is vomiting, not eating, in pain—and surgery could relieve that, or a tube, or intravenous feeding—the choice is up to the patient. One patient wanted absolutely nothing done, a couple of times a day she vomited and she died in a few weeks. We gave her pain medication, counseling, spiritual support; she preferred to vomit a couple of times a day rather than spend her last days hooked up to all those tubes.

Overall, our philosophy is to help people finish their lives with grace, dignity, love—to enable people to say they love each other, some who have never been able to do that in their whole lives. It's as if the patient needs to say something, hear something, say they're sorry, to let go. We don't know what that "something" is, but the nurse or doctor knows something is wrong, the patient isn't getting the relief she should from the physical medication.

Doctors sometimes refer patients to us when there's nothing more to be done. But we may think a lot more can be done to help them die. We find often so many things are unspoken —between patient and spouse, daughter, son, lovers, friends—something needs to be spoken, acknowledged. Even if the patient is in a coma and can't physically respond at all, we tell the family, friend, to say what they need to say; even if she can't answer, she may hear. Sometimes it's about things that happened twenty-five, fifty years in the past, but still gnawing at them; they put it out of mind years ago, but they still feel guilty about what happened. Sister Loretta helps them see that whatever they did, they did the best they could, that the life they lived was meaningful.

Most of the hospice patients die at home. The nurse comes once a week, reviews everything with the family, usually an aide comes in a few hours a day to help with the bathing, feeding, dressing, changing the bed linen— sometimes five days a week, or three, or seven. That woman with kidney cancer told us: "The good thing about my illness, it gave me a chance to teach my husband how to take care of himself." She taught him how to use a washing machine, he cooked for her, he helped her use the bedpan whenever she needed it, they didn't want an aide. Finally, she told us: "When I die, he'll be okay. I've taught him how to take care of himself." We were amazed how long she lived on, the kind who'd done everything, now she seemed content just to let him take care of her, like two loving beings in space, comfortable together. She didn't go into a coma. It was her decision finally to stop the transfusions; she knew she would die then. Her husband was sad at her death, but he felt good that he'd taken care of her so well. It was his chance to give back all she'd given to him in life.

The hospice seemed to me a true final affirmation of our personhood, of death as a part of life, as opposed to its futile denial and that dehumanized, technological, and futile obsession with "cure." There was no attempt to gloss death over with sweetness and light. In fact, there was a specific warning against any attempt to deny the reality of death—or to isolate the person dying from ongoing *life:*

Be aware that a "conspiracy of silence" can surround someone who is dying. Family and friends, with good intentions, often feel the need to "protect" the dying person from the truth. This protective silence and avoidance, rather than making the experience easier, usually causes the dying person to feel alone, isolated and cut off from those whose genuine love and support is so desperately needed.

It is important for someone who is ill to continue to participate in life: making decisions, enjoying hobbies, pastimes, holidays and social occasions; exercising as much independence and self-mastery as possible and maintaining relationships of intimacy and understanding.

And it is important for you as the person who may have the closest relationship to the dying person to remember: the feelings you are experiencing are quite normal, you needn't feel you are going insane. . . . Do not be afraid to express your own needs to friends and family members. . . . Be genuine with your loved one. He/she needs to know there is someone unafraid to be real. *You are not alone; others who share and understand your experience can be a great source of support.*

On the cover of the Cabrini Hospice handout on facing a terminal illness in your family was a quotation: "In a crisis of life and death, we may meet each other. This is the hope and this is the ultimate reward." In such a hospice, Medicare benefits covered both home care and inpatient services for patients who were either experiencing a medical crisis or whose caregiver required a respite. The admission criteria were an advanced illness, as certified by a physician, "a preference for palliative rather than curative treatment," a desire to remain at home, and "the availability of family member or friend to be a primary care person." To ensure "the opportunity to maintain control over the remainder of their lives and to live that time to the fullest . . . a plan to meet each person's needs for medical and support services is worked out with that person, his family or intimate other, and the hospice team and coordinated by a nurse, with nurse and doctor available by phone 24 hours a day, seven days a week. Specially trained volunteers are available to provide companionship to the patient, deliver medical supplies, and provide respite for family members."

Sister Loretta Palamara told me:

When it's possible, we don't let anyone die alone. When I go to someone who is dying, I try to give my full attention to that person leaving. You don't have time to practice what to say, to look it up in a book, and besides, it might not be in a book. You do it with the spirit present, for that person.

One thing the hospice does is recognize that a person's life is precious and affirms that life, living with dying. It's the people who are *present with you,* the ability just to be there for the person. The new buzz word in the medical literature is *presence*—how to be present with someone, help the patients to stay focused. [*Living their dying?*]

The hospice movement has grown from a single program in 1974 to over a thousand programs in 1985 to seventeen hundred in 1992. But, as Father John Paris warned us on the LORAN Commission, hospice programs are available to only a small fraction of Americans who are terminally ill: "Most critical and terminally ill patients continue to be cared for in institutions in which aggressive intervention and treatment of acute episodes is the norm." [19]

It is still not easy, in the United States, living-with-death, dying-with-life, to exercise our personhood, our choice, until the end. Establishment law and establishment medicine get in the way, financial considerations motivate the prescription of costly high-tech procedures and tests when there is no real hope for cure, or even moderately comfortable life. In the state of New York, as late as the summer of 1992, a woman in a coma, after she choked on a sandwich and fell unconscious on her kitchen floor, was being kept alive by a feeding tube that snaked from her nose to her stomach, and a breathing tube taped into a hole in her throat, though her husband and son had spent a wrenching year trying to persuade doctors that she would not want to be kept alive this way. Nearly every state now recognizes living wills, but the vast majority of people never sign such documents. Most states also recognize a family's right to decide to remove life support for someone they love who is no longer conscious, and doctors quietly work this out with families. But New York and some other states require "clear and convincing evidence" of what a patient would have wanted and leave it to each hospital to determine exactly what that is. The husband of Rosemarie Doherty, the woman in the coma who was moved after a year from hospital to a Brooklyn nursing home, told a reporter: "They said I'd need five people to swear Rosie had specifically said she would never want this tube, that tube, this antibiotic, that transfusion. We never talked like that. Who talks like that? But I know she wouldn't want to live like this. No one would. Would you?"[20]

The friends and family members who are needed to support people who want to control their own dying, with or without hospice help, may also be stopped by their own fear and denial of death. "I see that all the time," said Dr. Fawzy I. Fawzy, professor of psychiatry at UCLA School of Medicine. "People are uncomfortable being close to a person they think is dying. For some, it's too painful. They want to be miles away. For others, they have misconceptions about getting infected with a disease. What if they touch something and catch it?"

At least, it is being talked about now, it is becoming conscious: that many of us are terrified of getting close to people who are terminally or seriously ill—we "recoil from touching those who need it most."[21] The support groups for AIDS patients and their families are making that attitude conscious, which is the first step toward transcending it. Ginny Fleming and Carolyn Russell, who directed support groups for AIDS and cancer patients and their families in Los Angeles, argued that the best way to deal with that fear was to not shy away from people who are dying.

Fear exists, and it's very strong. We can't see someone else dying without seeing ourselves there, and we know it's going to happen to us. And the best way not to think about it is to physically avoid that person. If people can just get past their fear enough to look it in the eye, it can help them come to terms with mortality. They will realize, "Yes, death will happen to me, so how do I want to live my life. Death will always be a mystery, but the closer I've looked at it, the less afraid I am."[22]

Perhaps that is why hospice volunteers and staff members seemed so committed and "transformed" by their work with the dying, why sensitive doctors and nurses spoke of "learning" from their dying patients, even of "teaching" sessions. Two eminent doctors, who had been students of the late Dr. Maurice B. Strauss throughout their medical careers, recorded what they learned when summoned to his "last teaching session" less than a week before he died of inoperable cancer of the esophagus.

He remained at home, as was his strong desire, and spent what time he could arranging his affairs and writing friends about various matters, including frank discussions of his illness without pretense or sentimentality about its inevitable outcome. . . . The single most important item concerned a patient's right to participate as actively as possible—and with all pertinent information at his disposal—in decisions relating to the management of his terminal illness.

Another was his very firm wish to avoid hospitalization so that he could live out his remaining days in the familiar and satisfying setting of his own apartment. He pointed out to us how many times he would mentally have been disturbed . . . by uncomfortable and debilitating diagnostic procedures every time his fever spiked . . . had he been in any modern medical center during the previous six weeks. . . .

Maurie wished, as do most people, to face death with dignity and self-respect, and he did do so courageously. However, the extreme pain he had experienced during much of the preceding month or more, together with an awareness of his intermittently confused mental state, had apparently stripped him bare of these vital attributes that are so essential for any human being to face himself, much less others. Accordingly, it was of major importance to him that pain be adequately controlled. . . . When we saw him he had eliminated the problem . . . receiving morphine routinely every four hours, which was preventing the pain without noticeably depressive side effects. . . . Here was another lesson . . . that successful control of severe pain is of paramount importance [for] patients with painful terminal illness and that in frequently failing to provide it, we physicians deny our patients the opportunity to face death or even to face their families and close friends with self-respect and dignity.[23]

The critic Anatole Broyard started living his own dying and writing about it "in a Boston hospital, propped up in bed with an intravenous feeding tube in my arm and a catheter in my urethral canal after undergoing surgery for prostate cancer."

I've been feeling exalted since I heard the diagnosis. A critical illness is like a great permission, an authorization in absolving. It's all right for a threatened man to be romantic, even crazy, if he feels like it. All your life you think you have to hold back your craziness, but when you're sick you can let it out in all its garish colors.

Broyard wanted, above all, "to make sure I'll be alive when I die."[24]

For me, for more and more of us I hope, facing and overcoming our fear and denial of age and death, refusing to waste our last years on futile efforts to ensure ourselves some kind of mythical terminal care away from home and friends, outside of society, we can set about risking, as we have never been able to before, new adventures, living our own age. We need not wait until we face that fatal diagnosis to so free ourselves. If we face now the reality, at sixty-five or seventy, seventy-five, eighty, ninety, that we will indeed, sooner or later, die, then the only big question is how are we going to *live* the years we have left, however many or few they may be? What adventures can we now set out on to make sure we'll be alive when we die? Can age itself be such an adventure?

Part VI

Transcendence:
The Freedom
to Risk

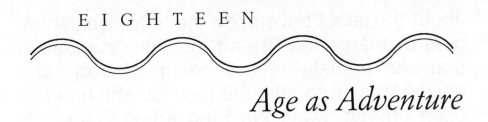

Age as Adventure

"I'll sum it all up for you," said my friend Ed, sixty-seven, taking off for a four-week solo wandermonth: London–Vienna–Budapest–Paris, train, plane, and rented car, after spending all summer getting his garden ready for his youngest daughter's wedding—despite trouble kneeling since his leg operation—and then, still mourning his wife's death, letting his daughter arrange her own wedding in a hotel. "As the guy said, I'd rather die on my feet than live on my knees, and I do not intend to go gentle into that good night." "If we're not careful, we could actually live until we die," said my friend Jerome, seventy-eight, consoling his wife, Rita, sixty-five, about the latest bulletin on the unforeseen dangers of margarine (!) and her own trepidation that she actually enjoys being "retired" and does not want to take the new job she had just been offered. "Can We Stop Aging?" the *Life* cover demanded in October 1992. "There are scientists who believe we can and will—but would we really want to?"

I went down to Washington to have high tea with my friend Milton, celebrating his eightieth birthday, as tall, gray-dark, and handsome, with those bushy sexy eyebrows, as full of new personal projects and political criticism as when I first admired him thirty-five years ago—but so much less heavy and pompous, so warm and witty and wise in the amazing fullness of his age. He reflected:

I'm more and more myself. But I'm more comfortable with differences, not uptight about them. I suppose along the way I got a larger vision, somehow. I've more desire to browse in the library stacks and learn now than ever in my life. I'm not envious of anybody else and I'm not anguished about my own failures. I also know if I were there again I'd fail again, so what. People kept asking me on my birthday what would you change about your life. That's the silliest of all questions, you can't change what you did, you can understand why, maybe.

After a lifetime of practicing law in New York, Milton had come to Washington in his sixties to run a National Center for Administrative Justice, to reform the handling of Social Security claims and public school discipline. With two marriages behind him, five children, and multiplying grandchildren, he made a home for himself alone out of a little townhouse in Foggy Bottom, getting great satisfaction out of choosing every decorative detail, from the Art Deco chairs to the teak elephant on his stair landing. ("I like my home, I like coming home. All these career women I take out now, they don't seem to want *homes!*") When the Reagan administration discontinued his administrative justice project, Milton, then in his seventies, used his base at George Washington University to develop an ongoing forum of "citizen discussion" of public policy in terms of "social values," involving Supreme Court justices and lay leaders like myself to lead dialogues about the Constitution: "What Would the Founding Fathers Do About Cases They Never Dreamed Of?," "Rationing Health Care," "Educational Choice," and "Women, Men and the Good Society," crossing old lines of liberal and conservative, left and right.

Last summer, he summoned all his kids and grandkids, his sister's brood, and his own former wives for an extended family conclave in the old farmhouse on a cliff on Block Island he had fixed up fifty years ago. If they would all agree to sell some of the land off now, they could keep the house for the next generation. He told me: "If I sell off those plots on Block Island, I have my eye on land on the Eastern Shore, in a little town called Milton, if you believe, which I could subdivide, and put in streets, and build a little getaway house for myself. I know just the piece for it, on a river that goes out to Delaware Bay."

When I first met him thirty-five years ago, he was using his legal skills, off hours, to develop a community for fellow ex-GI's and families on land they had bought communally, Hickory Hill in Rockland County. Most of the other families have deeded their houses to their children now, and moved to Hickory Hill II next door, an enclave of suburban granny condos they developed for their age. Milton took me through there, but that wasn't adventurous enough for his age. He wanted to develop something new, in the larger world he was comfortably part of, changing still.

Nell, in her mid-seventies, wearing one of those white foam rubber collars because she broke her neck slipping on the bathroom floor, was setting off on a red-wine-tasting tour of France with her new husband, my old friend Mogey, who believed red wine was better for his shingles than the medications doctors had been sedating him with. Her doctors had told Nell that if she fell again, she would be paralyzed from the neck down. So, she would wear that collar when they drove. Her only bow to the danger seemed to be an extra edge to her advocacy of legislation empowering doctors to assist people seeking painlessly to end their lives when they can no longer function. She was being very careful indeed to *live* until she dies.

We approach age in our own way, sensing it first as a loss of former roles and responsibilities, personal and social ties. The gerontologists approach the question of loss gingerly. Vern Bengtson, my distinguished colleague at Andrus, said:

> The lives of older people can be characterized sociologically by a theme of loss—of social positions (roles), of expectations (norms), and of reference groups. . . . However . . . one consequence of the decrease in social expectation may be the increase in personal freedom. Enhancing the competence of older individuals [no longer involves] adequate role performance [but] adequate coping plus doing what the individual himself wishes to do. . . .
>
> How often do we as professionals allow patients to decide for themselves what they want to be doing . . . ? Imagine a home for older persons run entirely by a board of residents. In this home the middle-aged professionals have only the caretaker responsi-

bilities specified by the residents themselves. . . . In the year 2000 there will be many more healthy and virile persons in the senior citizen category. They should not be forced into an unnecessarily dependent position. Older persons should be free to choose their own interests. Such freedom will have two consequences: (1) elderly persons will define what is right for them; and (2) having the freedom to choose, they will feel more competent.[1]

Well, yes, of course. But that still defines the old as "patients," objects of care, which would make them feel better if they had more voice in it themselves. But is bare coping, mere competence, the most that we can expect of ourselves in age, or that will be expected of us? In 1982, Robert Butler challenged the first United Nations World Assembly on Aging to confront the evolutionary implications of the thirty years by which human life has been extended in this century. This unprecedented extension of life is not the product of biological evolution, but social evolution, he pointed out. To unleash the unimagined resources of people growing older all over the world, to make productive use of those new years, is the next step in society's evolution. But ten years later, Butler had to admit, to a pitifully small UN gathering, another World Assembly on Aging having been postponed indefinitely, that there had been "no significant response." It is only in the individual experiences of people and groups finding new use for their own unexpected added years that we get hints of what might be possible for us all, the unheralded pioneers of age. Some we know about and dismiss as "geniuses" whose example can't possibly apply to us (in fact, may even *depress* us); some are stumbling on new paths, doing their own thing, without sensing its implications themselves. Now that I know to look, I see it everywhere: age as adventure.

But first, there has to be an *openness,* a sense that something new *can* happen. Maude Ann Taylor, a Jungian analyst facing seventy herself, predicted to me in California that the generation that grew up in the 1960s will be more open to age as adventure, to continuing to grow in their own sixties and seventies and eighties than people that age now.

People over sixty whom I see in my practice now are too bound by the old image of age, even in their dreams, to act on the impulse to develop further, to know parts of themselves that have never appeared before. That's what's so exciting to me about growing older now. But people now in their fifties are finishing with one stage of life—career, families—and thrashing around, longing for something new. Often one can see in their dreams little impulses to a new direction.

If people have a sense that nothing more can

happen, they won't move on to find that new thing. I've learned much more myself in these later years than I ever did earlier. But I don't have many patients now over sixty; they don't have a view of the world that permits them to pay attention to these new impulses, or even their own dreams anymore.

The transformations they experience are often triggered by some shocking event: your husband dies, you get cancer, you face death, you're forced to retire, it throws you into total distress. If you can stay with that discomfort, something emerges from that distress that may lead you to a new way of being. A new part of your personality may emerge, separate from the ego that governed your previous role. The old system needs to begin to crumble before the new can emerge.

Taylor was nearly sixty when she started practicing as a Jungian analyst, interpreting her own and others' dreams not in the Freudian terms of repressed material from childhood, but as new inner voices driving them to move in new ways, new avenues of possibility. It led her to a very different life in what was technically now her age, a new life work, a new search. It did not strike her as paradoxical that, at seventy, she felt both "comfortable" and "excited" by "the pull of the psyche to develop further, the power of realizing there's a spiritual dimension beyond the material one that seemed all there was to my generation."

Suzanne Wagner, another Jungian analyst, had worked with people in their seventies, eighties, even nineties, "letting go" of their previous roles—in profession or family—and "letting go of the body in a very deep way, discovering a whole new thing about yourself." She, too, saw age as an adventure:

A growing, deepening, knitting together of your life, a consciousness of what you have lived needing to come together in a whole picture, as if you have to integrate your whole life to prepare for the sloughing off of the body, as if in age the soul is getting ready to take off—the big adventure. Maybe you start traveling in a different way, or you stop traveling and do something you never did before, sit still. Your dream life now can reveal a very positive process going on, not quite identical with the body. In fact, your body may be slowing down, a different energy goes into self-reflection now, a deeper understanding of what you have lived; there's a gathering of all the parts, to knit them together consciously. You embrace all that you have lived, let go of old grudges against yourself and others. If you're open to it, there's a need now to open doors that have been slammed shut.

Our fear of dying has thrown us into a spasm

of wanting to control everything, but death is one thing we can't control. Why not accept your own age as a part of nature and find out what it really is instead of tampering with it? The problem is, we don't often listen to older people, we don't recognize that wisdom, flowing like a fountain.

I can recognize it in other people now, I can listen and see different ways they enter on that adventure. The driver sent by the car service to take me down the mountain from the retreat at Lake Arrowhead turned out to be a woman, maybe older than I was. I tend to get a bit dizzy at hairpin turns at such heights, but she handled them competently, comfortable in her slacks and lumber jacket. Was this her regular job? Well, she was on call for night trips like this which the guys who run the service don't want to take themselves, she did it for the extra money. Her regular job, for the Rangers, the Forest Service, was more adventurous. We drove past her cabin on the way down to Los Angeles, and she told me how she got to this mountaintop at "sixtysomething":

I got laid off at Rockwell, after fourteen years, just months before I'd get a pension. I was a glorified secretary—they called me an administrative assistant—to six quality-control engineers. Six years ago, after my husband passed away, I came up here on a ski vacation and fell in love with this mountain. I went to a real estate agent and said I couldn't afford more than $500 a month and I want a home up here; it's only a mile from town, and room for my son to visit. I couldn't live anymore down the mountain on that.

Most of the people up here are retired and don't go out much, or very young hippies. It was hard to find someone to be friendly with. One day I was walking along the lake and saw a little building sitting back in the woods with a sign that said: "Senior Citizens." I never thought of myself as a senior citizen, but I went in and I said to the lady. "I'm very happy to be here, but I need friends." She said there's a dozen ladies just like you come here, their husbands go fishing or work in Los Angeles all day, and a few gentlemen too. I met a wonderful gentleman whom I go fishing with, his wife died last year. I'm not lonely anymore, two lovely women friends, we go down the hill, do our shopping together, save on groceries that way.

I make about $30 a week working for the Rangers and maybe $8 to $10 doing these bad-weather trips those three young men don't want. I'm the front desk receptionist for the Rangers, except they know I get bored at the front desk so now they send me out on the trail too. I took my Social Security at sixty-two, because I was considered over the hill down there, couldn't get a job at all. I get the minimum, $600 a month, but between the Rangers and my driving, I made $6,800 this year. I'll take odd jobs, shoveling snow, clean someone's house, take care of people's dogs when they go away, drive people to the airport.

On the mountain now, every time I find a new road, I go up it. You'd be amazed how many people like me who can't afford to live down the hill anymore are living year-round in these cabins on the mountain now.

What started the new adventure for Bob Monroe in his sixties, after a hectic lifetime in show business, as actor on both coasts, agent, radio producer, scriptwriter, television producer—no children, no encumbrances, a failed marriage— was literally a fall down a flight of stairs, crushing his heelbone. I met him in an unchic Hollywood "snack and chat" joint, after my friend Gloria got him to direct a reading of her play. White hair, his bony face looking somehow stern and serene, he told me:

When I was an actor, which I always wanted to be, I was so monomaniacal I never could see the whole picture. Then I fell down that whole flight of stairs and things just fell apart for me. A friend said he didn't want to insult me, but they needed a dialogue coach. I was so broke I took it. I was a very lusty guy, and my dick went dead on me at the same time. And the people I coached kept asking me would I refer them to some good teacher like myself. So half my life later, I'm a teacher and now even a director for my students, and all this knowledge, all I've learned in all these years, is coming out of me for them.

I think I had to fall like that to get real myself. I don't think I'm a failure as a human being now, even if I haven't attained as much recognition in my profession as I wanted. When I broke my heel, had to sit with my leg up in the air for eight months, something in my spirit took over. When I started working again, an acting teacher, no more big deals, it's been the most fulfilling thing I've ever done. I love directing these kids, and the ones who sure aren't kids anymore but don't give up, I truly love getting something real out of them.

For some, the adventure involves an affirming, finally, of a piece of themselves they were afraid of or uncomfortable with before. Abe Rosenthal, five years after his retirement as editor of *The New York Times,* decided to have on his seventieth birthday the bar mitzvah he had never had at thirteen. Over breakfast at the Regency, where for years he did those power breakfasts, he looked amazingly healthy—thinner, calmer, and more collected than I used to find him. A lot of people expected him to *just die* or fade away in fury after he lost all that power. I asked him why he had a bar mitzvah at seventy.

I'd been feeling for some time that something was missing in me, something I needed. My father, whom I loved, died when I was twelve. He hated religion. So I had no religious training, though there's never been a question that I'm a Jew. My name is Abraham. But forty years on *The New York Times* I was A. M. Rosenthal, not Abraham. A few years ago, I realized something was missing. I missed knowing things Jewish. I felt uncomfortable attending seders, that kind of thing, everybody reading Hebrew, felt irritated at my father for me not knowing these things. And then I was over sixty myself, and I didn't want to be irritated at my father anymore. And it began to seem to me that being bar-mitzvahed was an elemental thing, a gesture of respect and appreciation and connection as a Jew that I had never made. But at sixty-five, sixty-seven, sixty-nine it would be ridiculous; you do that at thirteen.

I didn't consciously do it because I was seventy. But the idea you can't learn new things in age is wrong; the desire to learn more, be more, intensifies. I do more reading now, not because I have more time, I'm still running around, working on my column, but there's a sharpness and intensity to the learning now. It may come from dropping all the clichés, the shibboleths about age—you're lightening yourself to the extent that you get rid of certain things about aging you had in your head like fears that when you get older you're not going to be as good, as smart, learn much, be sexual anymore, your brain cells are going. Well, you realize, if they're gone, they're not the ones I needed. I feel sharper now, lighter in the head, like when you stop smoking, you enjoy food more. I was able to drop some ballast—like that irritation at my father, that uncomfortableness about the missing Jewish piece.

That bar mitzvah was something I wanted like a kiss, a kiss for my father and for myself, for being Jewish. It's an adventure for me now to speak my own mind and my own thoughts, after twenty years as a reporter and foreign correspondent, and twenty years as an editor, conforming to that journalistic tradition of objectivity, not even always aware of the power that masked. When I began writing in my own voice, my own openness, the column they gave me after retiring as editor, I felt awkward at first. I thought I'd do a different topic every time. But as the background noises and stresses of being the editor of the whole paper began to subside, what I was really interested in began to be clear, and it surprised me.

What happens if you're lucky when you get older—I still don't like that word "old," it's like a static definitive thing—you get rid of all the things that aren't important, and do the work and spend your time with the friends that you're really interested in.

I've seen my feminist women friends also grope for ceremonies, rituals, at sixty, sixty-five, or seventy, to affirm finally all those essential pieces of themselves and make a new commitment to the community, from the new place they were in. In my feminist think tank in California last year we tried it, but somehow couldn't get beyond the discomfort and the rage: "When Sleeping Beauty woke up, she was sixty years old!" We knew we had to think in new ways, beyond marriage and career, but found it hard. I've sat with Jewish, Catholic, and Protestant religious leaders, trying to translate that need into rituals that would liberate the spirit in age. But the rituals of the bar mitzvah, the confirmation, the graduation, the wedding, celebrate the entrance to prescribed, traditional roles of work and love. The place we enter now is unknown.

I somehow knew, on my own sixty-fifth birthday, that I was making a signal to myself, my family, and my friends that I was in a new place, ready to move on to my next adventure. But then I could not really conceive, concretely, of new ways to work, or love, or live differently—only a yearning, an expectancy, a sense of new possibility, of not being necessarily tied down anymore to what I'd been and done before, even old problems and fears that I might never resolve. It was like deciding to take a kind of trip you had never had the nerve for before, to a country no one really knew anything about, no guidebooks, maps you could trust—an adventure that was scary even to think about.

If there are countless industries and professions that profit on age as decline and deterioration, there is one burgeoning industry in America that plays to and profits on age as adventure: the travel industry. And, in fact, for many of us groping our way to the new adventure we need in age, travel to new places—continents and cities never visited before, voyages at sea, exotic islands and deserts and mountain treks—is the direction we may take at first. More and more of the passengers on ships and airplanes, package tours and cruises now are older, over fifty, sixty, not the Pepsi generation, not necessarily or only because in age people have more time to kill, or money to spend, and nothing better to do. Their travel may also symbolize a kind of necessary exploration for paths of possible new adventure in life. The trip removes us from the familiar routines and landmarks that we may still follow in our work, in our relationships, our professions or communities, even if they are no longer required of us, no longer nourish or challenge us. The trip takes us away from the familiar parties, meetings, social events with which we fill up our spare time, even if they no longer sustain us, or which have been taken away from us by retirement or death, or the changes in the neighborhood, or by the stigma of the age mystique we may still be trying to avoid or deny.

It jolts us out of mindless, futile yearning to repeat routines that have already gone stale on us in love or work. The trip expresses and opens us to our need for new adventure, in purpose and project and intimate ties, new exercise for our bodies and our spirit in age, even if it does not often begin to meet that need itself. The taste for such new adventure may be more intense, and even addictive, as we grow older, since it's not really a *place* we ever arrive at. But we may learn how to travel more adventurously, and we may also learn from such travel the possibility of other adventure beyond the trip itself that we never dreamed of in ourselves before.

Jean and Harold Berlfein picked me up to go bicycling on the long path that runs by the ocean from Santa Monica to Venice and all the way to Palos Verdes and beyond. Sometimes they went as far as they felt like and spent the night at some unplanned spot, they told me, whetting my appetite along the way with tales of longer bicycle jaunts they had made, in most of the fifty states and a dozen other countries by now. Harold, recently retired from a partnership in a big accounting firm, gave me his new business card —instead of CPA, the letters after his name were DNO. "Discovering New Options," he said with a smile. He and Jean were wearing T-shirts from their "Over-70 Ski Club," where last winter they had bicycled up the mountain and skied down. He had recently put a message on his answering machine: "When you're over the hill, you pick up speed."

They took their first bicycle trip in France nearly twenty years ago, already in their fifties. They had to go all over Paris to find someone who would rent them bikes, which they then carried onto a train to Provence. They got stared at: "What are those old people doing on a bicycle trip?" Jean, who had been a traditional house-wife and volunteer in the community when their kids were young, had since begun to take her photography more seriously and was making educational videos and filmstrips. On their trips, she told me,

I'm the instigator, he's the implementer. I have these weird ideas; he's at first reluctant, then he makes it happen. We like to leave it open, don't plan more than thirty-five miles a day, leave ourselves room for adventures along the way. We keep trying to convince compulsive types it's not how far you go but what you see on the way.

On a group trip, we're always the last in of an evening, not because we're the oldest, but we stop so many times to talk to people on the way. At Todi, the shortest road went almost straight up, a two-kilometer climb. The young people took that road, but we found a longer one that wasn't so steep. The young ones had to walk most of the way. We biked all the way and got to the inn first. When you're older, you do it smarter.

We've learned to say, "Pleased to meet you," in thirty-three languages by now. On our fortieth anniversary, there's a stretch up to La Canada that took us four hours when we first did it, all those years ago, and we made it in two hours now, in much better shape—this idea about your physical ability declining with age is open to question for us!

The freewheeling, adventuresome mode honed on these trips was carried into their everyday year-round life after Harold retired. Wary of getting in Jean's way, now that he would be working out of home, he converted one of the kid's bedrooms into a large office for himself, with a separate phone and answering machine. Since his ostensible retirement, he has started a grass-roots organization to promote energy conservation in Los Angeles and a Clearing House for Voluntary Accounting Services, getting retired accountants to volunteer their services to activist and community organizations. And he holds "retirement" seminars, which offer no laundry list of rules and procedures, but try to pass on that DNO mode to evoke everyone's own directions. As Jean, in their particular crossover, spent more and more time on her photography, he, without realizing it was happening, seemed to be spending more and more time on relationships with his new men's group and with his family, all three generations of it. He had also taken over most of the preparation of meals.

When I was working, I never really had time for my family except in the evening. Yesterday I spent part of the morning with my grandson. I'm having lunch today with my daughter. Jean and I often do errands together now on our bicycles, go out for breakfast together. I'm also becoming a mentor to some younger people. Life has lots of new possibilities now, it seems. We picked up a little book about sex in China, about how when you're older it can be much better because the orgasm isn't the most significant part of it, so it can be a much longer, more enjoyable experience. That's what we're working on now.

The concept of "adventurous aging" was something Eva and Boaz Kohana, gerontologists at Case Western Reserve, came up with when they found strong resemblances between their hardy fellow survivors of the Holocaust and older people who *chose* to leave their homes and roots to strike out for new lives in far places. In both instances, the previous roles that defined one's humanness were stripped away and life itself could no longer be taken for granted. What the adventurous aging had in common with the Holocaust survivors was what they called a "pro-active" mode. They didn't just passively react, go along with the terms they were given—inescapable as they may have seemed—nor did they blind themselves to the realities of their new situation, trying still to follow the old routines, as if life could go on as it had before. They were or became "pro-active" about tasks and ties that gave meaning to their lives, finding new sources of purpose, more consciously conserving family ties, or building new bonds of intimacy.

In such extremes (is age itself such an extreme?) does survival demand a kind of *evolution,* an active creation or re-creation of those ties and purposes that are evidently as essential to our humanness as food and water to our physical existence? That something as unessential as a trip can be a rehearsal or a preparation for that kind of evolution seems far-fetched. But consider the growing relish and demand for trips that involve physical challenge, if not actual danger, travel that involves an inner journey, intellectual challenge, as well as exploration of new places and cultures.

Wealth is not necessarily the key to such adventure in age. It was striking in my interviews how often, especially for women, the opening to new adventure in age came with the loss of a certain kind of economic security or social status, through widowhood or divorce. I met Jeannie Roth in Aspen, where she was helping out at a conference registration desk. My suitcase zipper had sprung, and there was hardly time to get it fixed before my plane. She said she had a big blue bag taking up too much room in her little apartment that she would let me have, and drive me to the airport too. She was sixty-five. She had been a housewife and a volunteer until her husband left her for his young secretary. At sixty-one, she went to work for the first time, as a receptionist and telephone operator for a ski company. She had come to Colorado to an Elderhostel in Durango and just stayed on, renting a little apartment over a garage on a year-to-year basis, turning down her landlord's offer to let her baby-sit for part of the rent. She preferred the variety of people she met at the ski company to babies now. But the Elderhostels had become a way of life for her. She had just come back from three weeks in Turkey, learned to speak French in Montreal, studied whooping cranes in their natural habitat on the Gulf of Mexico, and went on an archeological dig in Kenya. She told me:

I went by myself to that first Elderhostel, asked for a single room. But in the Elderhostel, you live in a dormitory, no frills; you meet so many lively, interesting new people. By now, I've joined with three different people I met in Elderhostels to try other things together. I've taken eight different people to their first Elderhostel. One in her seventies didn't think it was for her and she loved it. A lot of people hear about Elderhostel but are afraid to make the leap by themselves.

You sure don't go there to meet men, though you might find a man, now and then. I love my single life, I call it "single-blessedness." I love to travel, visit my children and friends as a single person. I've gotten to Europe every other year lately, but now that I'm sixty-five, I'm going to do it more often, make it count, stay a while. How much time do I have left?

She was thinking of leaving Aspen. "It's getting too ritzy." Should I send her back the suitcase, then? No, she said, she was traveling light now. I admired her outfit: an African silk scarf, a quilted paisley jacket she got at a thrift shop, knitted pants and sweater she picked up in Maine, a gold bracelet from Greece, a wonderful soft black leather bag she found in Turkey. Except for an occasional broken ankle from skiing, her health had been "great." She was not sure where she would head for when she left Aspen. A seventy-four-year-old widower who had just buried his wife of forty years was after her. Her friends thought she was crazy not to marry him. "The month after they get divorced, or leave the husband, they're looking for another, but not for me!"

I got much more than that suitcase, which I still use, from Jeannie. I sent for the Elderhostel catalogue myself and read descriptions of the courses and trips available to "elders," geared not just to exotic tourism or "adult education," I discovered, but to learning something really new. I had never been particularly interested in cruises, nor, in recent years, in taking courses. But there was something that intrigued me about one program: an intensive five to six days at the Peabody Institute in Baltimore, studying all the symphonies and the chamber music of Beethoven, and relating them to his life and the society of his time. I considered a program "Arguing with God—A Jewish Tradition" at the University of Judaism in Los Angeles. As "expert" in my own field, did I really want to face my vague ignorance, and real desire to learn more, before it was too late, about the mysteries of my religious roots, or music, which I now enjoyed "mindlessly"? What would it be like to go to concerts mindfully?

Other programs in the catalogue caught my attention: "Winter in Yosemite . . . for *hardy* hostellers. . . . Participants will be able to hike five miles a day on easy to moderate terrain . . . with naturalist guide. . . . Learn about the geology, flora, fauna and human history of the Sierra Nevada . . ." or "cross-country skiing, sleeping four or five to a room, with home-cooked meals served family style." Or Spanish for Travelers, or Introduction to Watercolor and Perspective Drawing at Ghost Ranch, where Georgia O'Keeffe painted.

I was intrigued by the very idea of an elder hostel, as opposed to a youth hostel. But did I really want to brand myself *elder* hosteler? Still, Elderhostel seemed to have study groups in out-of-the-way places, in France and Italy, India and the Amazon, that I hadn't gone to professionally (which had dictated most of my travels before), or hadn't particularly wanted to go to all by myself (as I've traveled mostly since my divorce), and seemed somehow to promise more active, curious, adventurous companions than a cruise. Or should I try a cruise, which I had always scorned as a passive, static drift when, in fact, in our age, what was needed was a new quest?

ITEM: *Washington Post,* January 8, 1990:

> Some travel agents already are calling it the Gray '90s. . . . Familiarity will breed contempt for familiar destinations, both in the United States and abroad . . . with adventure trips and travel to remote destinations filling the itineraries of the '90s. . . .
>
> Older Americans will seek a more active, participatory kind of travel. Ten years ago, senior citizens' travel was thought of as just one thing: little old ladies with blue hair on buses. . . . Now, as lifestyles have changed, people have come to realize that being older doesn't mean being passive.

I joined Earl Arthurs on the Caribbean lap of one of those cruises on which he now spent most of his time as host. For him and the other sixty- or seventysomething hosts, there was a sense of purpose on that cruise. Not exactly a "career," but they prided themselves on their sensitivity, for instance, to the needs of the widows who, it seemed, returned again and again to the same boat, going to the same ports—Bermuda, San Juan, St. Thomas, Guadeloupe. The boat had become a kind of home for them. Talking to women and some couples for whom this was their tenth or fifteenth such cruise, I saw that at least for the weeks on board, they got structure for their days and the comfort of social bonds, without the risks and difficulties of real intimacy or really adventurous travel.

It was not for me. Pacing twenty times the circumference of the boat in order simply not to get too fat on all those boring, rich meals, I felt claustrophobic and increasingly bad-tempered even with Earl.

The travel agencies and special services proliferating to meet the yearning for adventure, teased but somehow never satisfied by such cruises, even promise to "find seniors a travel companion or partner—traveling alone can be lonely." "There are now about 85 million adult singles in North America, but ever since Noah's Ark, the travel industry has been 'double occupancy oriented,' and it's a real problem for solo travelers, especially seniors," said Jens Jurgen, who operated Travel Companion Exchange, Inc., a ten-year-old agency which will help you get around that $500 to $1,000 penalty for single occupancy, plus the dreariness of sightseeing and dining alone, by finding "a pre-selected compatible companion for all types of travel, ranging from sharing local day trips to travelling by car or motorhome or even around the world." "It's more difficult for a single woman to travel alone," Jurgen allowed, "they feel more secure with a male companion." He claimed several hundred of his female subscribers later married their travel companions. He thought up the idea of a match-up service for single travelers when he traveled alone after his own divorce, and was lonely.

If companionship, protection (or romance) are not your top priorities, another service—"Going Solo," the "Newsletter for People Travelling Alone" (to which I now subscribe)—provides tips on traveling "Tuscany on Your Own," pensioni to stay in and better restaurants with communal seating, for hardy adventurers, female or male, who actually want to explore the possibilities of single-blessedness. From Japan to Sweden, Israel, Switzerland, Grenada, the guides steer you to "friendship programs" that match you with local families, "friends overseas," or mature native citizens who have volunteered to serve as companion-guides to visitors, matched on the basis of common interests or occupations. Other services enable you to swap your house or apartment for a comparable one in another country. My friends Doug and Ida Palmer satisfied their urge to explore their Scottish roots by swapping their house in Seattle, and were provided with car, list of friends and pubs, and guest membership in a local lawyers' club the month they spent in their doppelgänger's house in Edinburgh.

Among the most inveterate travelers I know are Bob and Ruthie Easton, my old, dear friends from childhood and high school in Peoria. He was the first boy I ever kissed, we left Peoria for Smith and Harvard together, but he went back to Peoria, after medical school, married Ruthie, his high school sweetheart, and has been an eminent pediatrician in our hometown ever since. The Christmas letter from Ruthie about "our recent, exciting trip on the Amazon" was equivocal. After recounting an erratic combination of luxury hotels, "yet another Hilton," dirty, buggy-jeep rides, walks on muddy jungle paths, or a lodge where there was no electricity, cold-water showers, and outside toilets, she wrote they had sworn off such trips, but added a post-script: "Shortly after we got home, Bob signed us up for a two-week bird-watching trip in Thailand this February." But when I saw him at our fiftieth high school reunion that same year, I sensed another deeper reason for his urge to travel, again and still, and his frustration when the destination was just another Hilton, or even a buggy jungle camp. He told me he was tired of practicing, had stopped studying the new developments. Even the big new hospital which he had helped build was not where he wanted to go anymore. Too many doctors "hustling" now, with all their subspecialties. But he was losing his zest for the kind of travel that hadn't really brought him to a new place when he returned home.

I've talked to other older men and women, who after some years of intensive travel have come home again with some new purpose in life. Frances Ann and Frazier Dougherty spent their fifties sailing around the Greek islands and came home in their sixties to a new life of gritty small-town community involvement. Forced to move their house in East Hampton farther from the ocean because of beach erosion, they began to take an active interest in town planning and environmental issues. Meeting resistance at first, Frazier filmed the Town Board meeting; he was going to call it "democracy in action." He took it to the local cable station, which refused to show it. Cable television was just getting under way and nobody else seemed to know that according to the law a certain amount of time has to be completely open to community access. Complicated battles ensued, which ended in Frazier's being asked to run for the Town Board himself, on behalf of the environmentally concerned, and the cable station putting him in charge of "community access." Frances took over the local theater and cultural center, and Frazier joined with some younger people in guiding LTV (Local Television, Inc.) into a pioneering entity that has trained five hundred local citizens to use television as a tool, filming every Town Board, trustees, and planning meeting in the surrounding towns, plus developing their own plays and operas.

Frazier said, whimsically:

So here I am working seventy hours a week again. Whereas people before thought community-access television meant blue porn shows, now I think it's changed their whole sense of community, and community participation. A recent survey showed 80 percent of the people now watch the Town Board meetings. It's "democracy in action" all right, though I'll probably be seventy-eight before I have time to finish that movie.

It was that long voyage around the Greek islands that got them to this very different place in their lives, both believed. "We couldn't go back to the same old life. We don't do things now that are socially or politically correct that we don't really want to do. You become less superficial. Every day is a challenge now. I call it freedom."

Does the travel, trip, adventure have to lead to a new place at home to be a fountain of age? It seemed to me that for some people it did. But there is also, for many, a sense of new enjoyment in the trip itself, physical, intellectual, or spiritual. Elderhostel and auditing or taking courses at one's old college or the local community college, the art center, or the Institute for Retired Professionals do not necessarily have to lead to a new "career" to be satisfying. The satisfaction comes from a new sense of meaning in one's life, a new path of meaningful activity. To the surprise of psychologists reviewing longitudinal studies of men and women now in their seventies who had been followed since they were teenagers fifty years ago—studies done at Wesleyan, Berkeley, and elsewhere—satisfaction with life, in age, seemed to depend less on the achievement of a long-held goal than on "how much time people are able to spend doing things they find most meaningful, are most competent at and take the most pleasure in." Reviewing such research, Rutgers psychologist Daniel Ogilvie found that, for middle-income people, finances, and even marriage and health, "account for a trivial degree of people's satisfaction with their lives after retirement," compared to how much time they can spend doing things which "give them the greatest sense of meaning and allow them to express most fully who they consider themselves to be."[2] He found that, on average, people's opportunity to spend time in meaningful activities was three to four times as powerful a predictor of satisfaction with life than health was!

The "action" that is involved here, and the ties of friendship outside the family that often result, may start with a single Elderhostel adventure, taking this course or that trip. But there is more and more consciousness, with the new experience of longer age, of the importance of *continued* growth, and *active,* meaningful participation over the long term on such adventures, if they are to keep replenishing the fountain of age, even though no longer driven by career.

Curious to find out more about Elderhostel, I went to see Marty Knowlton, in his seventies, white-bearded and longish white hair in the counterculture style, who had started the Elderhostel movement in 1975. Elderhostel does no advertising, but has grown, by word of mouth, from a handful of older men and women on a New Hampshire college campus into an international network of 1,800 participating universities and cultural and environmental centers, marine biology field stations, and archeological digs in every American state and Canadian province and over forty-eight foreign countries. Each year, 335,000 people over sixty participate in intensive study experiences "from Cicero to computers . . . politics to poetry . . . from Maine to Manitoba . . . Wollongong to Wales." Its catalogue states:

Elderhostel is an educational adventure for older adults looking for something different. The later years should be a time of new beginnings, opportunities and challenges. Elderhostel offers you a way to keep on expanding your horizons with people who are interested in the same things you are. . . .

Elderhostel may not be for everyone. But all you need is an adventuresome spirit and a yearning to be challenged by new ideas and experiences. . . .

Marty Knowlton had "run away" from his conventional life in Boston, teaching high school, then college, alienated and frustrated as a social activist after the Vietnam War and the breakup of his family. He went backpacking in Europe for four years, earning whatever money he needed as a "pick and shovel laborer," outside the system in which he'd been advancing and protesting. He recalled:

I needed that, to escape the system. When I came back, I was unemployable—too old, and too far out. An old friend directing residential life at the University of New Hampshire said I could run their youth hostel that summer. Thinking of myself, and all the older Americans I'd met aimlessly traveling in Europe, I said what's needed is not more youth hostels; why not an elder hostel?

I came up with the idea of a six-day experience, living on the campus, for people of "retirement" age, taking three intensive college-level courses with no formal requirements or credits. Such things had been tried before, and failed, in Europe and in the United

States, because older people wouldn't go. They had been filled with the myth, generally accepted at the time, that age means you don't learn anymore. Their own educational experiences hadn't been great, and were completely associated with youth. I kept saying, you're going to learn as well or better than you've ever learned, but they didn't believe me. But the first brave souls who experienced it went home and told their friends, and it grew from 20 to 220 that first year, evolving as we went along.

The colleges liked it because it was a way of using empty dorms in the summers. Then the demand grew for Elderhostels during the school year, so we branched out, to environmental study centers, and cultural conference centers, or intergenerational experiences, using guest houses or motels on the edge of college campuses.

I'm not a good administrator myself. I finally retired, totally and completely, in 1982. Now I'm trying to develop the Elderhostel idea into something more than an educational adventure vacation, an ongoing way for older people to pool their experience in new thinking, looking at things in a different way. "Gatekeepers to the Future," I call it, acting as an ombudsman for people not yet born. The problems our whole society will face in the new millennium can't be solved in the way we think about problems now. A lot of older people get scared by the organizations that are supposed to deal with age, the government, the gerontologists, telling them how fragile they are, all they harp on is the problems of older people, all their power turned inward. Actually, the people who come to Elderhostels are more liberal than the young yuppies, people willing to go new places with their minds. People leave Elderhostels like junkies—they need another fix. Maybe a way to actually work on problems that will face coming generations, becoming advocates for the future.

Bill Berkeley, who took over as president of Elderhostels when Marty Knowlton retired again, to start "Gatekeepers to the Future," saw new implications of the Elderhostel experience. When I talked to him at Elderhostel headquarters in Boston, he told me:

It's also an opportunity to make new friends, sharing this kind of adventure, at a time when you are losing friends and opportunities to make new relationships. But now our people feel the need to go beyond these individual educational vacation adventures, to harness their energy to new adventures for society. We're working out ways to do that now with

Habitat [for Humanity], building housing for the homeless, with the Oceanic Society, where volunteers will do formal research needed on environmental problems, and with Global Volunteers, to use older people's experience in developing countries, like the Peace Corps. We're also establishing an Institute Network, to help older people organize ongoing educational adventures in their own communities, with some help from us and from the local college or university, but which they themselves will run, taking turns studying and teaching, deciding which subjects they will pursue each year, and meeting in unused classrooms, or their own living rooms.

Many of the most vital people I have known in my life, or come across in this search, seemed to be getting involved in such new, more-or-less formal, ongoing structures or networks, pooling and focusing their wisdom in age on new and old problems of our society. I visited some of those pioneering institutes: the University for the Third Age, which Peter Laslett started in Cambridge, England; the Institute for Retired Professionals, started under the auspices of the New School for Social Research in New York; the Institute for Learning in Retirement in Cambridge, Massachusetts; the Plato Society in Los Angeles. Elderhostel had helped to start about sixty of these institutes, doubling the number by the end of the 1980s. The "learning junkies" are now put in touch with the nearest local institute after they've done the Elderhostel trip. Berkeley said:

People have a hunger for more than a learning vacation; some older people seem to have a hunger now to learn all the time they have left, and they like the idea of controlling it all themselves. They make a real commitment, that's how they want to spend their later years, as students. And they don't want or need outside experts. Most of the time, they find in their own group the knowledge and the experiences they need to teach each other now.

Like the University for the Third Age in Cambridge, these institutes require that every member rotate learning and teaching, undertake an original or ongoing research investigation, and be actively involved in at least one project of service to the community. The implications of such new adventures in education for a longer, vital age can already be seen. Sarah Petri's data showed unpredicted extension of both *lifespan* and *healthy, vital* age when she used the members of the Plato Society as control group for her study of Alzheimer's victims. Mary Osborne, eighty-five, had spent two years bedridden when she signed up for a "Senior Net" class in Dallas. Taught basic computer skills by a sixty-nine-year-old former beauty parlor operator, she discovered that she "wasn't sick, just bored to death." She bought a word processor and started writing the history of her life. Others were using the computer senior network to locate missing relatives, organize congressional lobbying campaigns on catastrophic health insurance, or merely logging on for companionship in the middle of the night.[3]

During a trip to England, I visited the University for the Third Age in Cambridge, organized over ten years ago by the eminent sociologist Peter Laslett as he was approaching his seventies and Britain was officially becoming an "aging society"—where at least 15 percent of the people are over sixty. By 2020, one out of five people will be over sixty in all advanced societies, Laslett said. He told me the University for the Third Age was the first new university in Cambridge in nearly five hundred years. Though it does not mainly meet in university classrooms, 400 people came to lectures, 250 to sessions every week. As Laslett outlined it, the First Age is learning as preparation for work and family roles; the Second Age is the active reproduction of family and production to support it; and the Third Age is learning for oneself, to develop, grow, and use one's abilities in work from which one will never retire. The University of the Third Age was not run by Cambridge University for older people, as most such programs have been in France and the United States, but by elders for themselves. They met in each others' homes, paying £10 a year for expenses of mailings and such; all the work was done by volunteers, and each one committed her/himself to teach, learn, do original research and some social service for the community.

That same three-pronged principle, I've noticed, was practiced, perhaps not coincidentally, by many who seemed to me to be in the fountain of age flow. I talked to Dr. Karl Menninger one afternoon at the Chautauqua Institute in upstate New York, after he had spent the morning in a three-hour painting class. That afternoon he was going to give a lecture on psychological issues. He was still involved in research. Menninger told me:

Life is growth. When you stop growing, you die. I've been coming to Chautauqua fifty to sixty years now, teaching and learning. My talks lately have been built around poetry. I think poetry is more important for people now than some of the psychological stuff I used to lecture about. They want the word from on high. Instead, they should keep asking new questions.

Some educators have seen that demographic revolution, that Third Age, as their own salvation and cutting edge. Others are still blinded themselves by the youth obsessions, the age mystique. One of the top officials at the Chautauqua Institute told me that that summer, despite the overflowing audiences for Dr. Menninger's lectures, they were disturbed by a survey showing half of their participants were well over fifty-five; the next-largest group was under twenty-one. Like magazine publishers and broadcasters, they were only interested in twenty-one to forty-nine. And yet their mix of modest cottages, apartments, rooming houses, and dormitories, lakes and country trails and fields and rivers to canoe in, classes, seminars, lectures, all kinds of educational adventures, and communal meals, was a perfect, non-segregated, intergenerational setting, clearly attractive to those seeking such adventure in age.

The Chautauqua Institute, one of the oldest adult education traditions in America, started in 1874, but was about to go under in 1970 when descendants of the founders came back to rescue it, and tapped into the new age boom almost reluctantly, as the official told me.

Yes, the over fifty-fives are attracted to come here. They have the time and the money and they don't want to just sit on the beach. We have 375 different programs in the 65 days of summer and others all year round. Painting, acting, ceramics, lectures, or some program every night. It's a hotbed of continued learning, self-improvement. Everything is offered but nothing is required. We don't program them. It's up to them. Older people love that freedom. They even walk out of a lecture when it bores them. But we want a better balance, to attract the younger people. I don't want this to be a haven for old people. They complain about the bicycles, the noise; the kids complain the older people won't get out of their way. Still, that mix of generations is what makes it healthy, vibrant, vital.

The older people who made up half the inhabitants of Chautauqua seemed to thrive on that intergenerational learning. There wasn't much focus on medical "care" there; the fifty-two-bed nursing home was actually closing down the summer I visited. Was it because the older people who came there were unusually healthy, or because that continual diet of intergenerational learning kept them healthy? The resident doctor said:

The older people I see here seem sharper and more healthy than the average. Well, we all know that if the body and the mind aren't active, they deteriorate. So it stands to reason if you keep using your mind and are active, participating as they do here, you don't deteriorate. As a matter of fact, they seem to be a little less sickly and more active than ten years ago. Maybe because there are not so many older people here now—except, from the figures, that's not so, is it? Maybe they just don't look old.

A new development in the United States is whole communities of older people settling around universities with such programs, moving to college towns—sometimes back to the college they went to in their youth, sometimes merely to one noted for its programs, in a good climate. The president of Dartmouth, where the trickle of alumni retirees to Hanover has become a flood, said: "Of course, we welcome them all, but they have made it all but impossible for junior faculty to find affordable housing near campus. . . . Most college-educated retirees can live in these towns on $20,000 a year almost as well as they lived in the major cities where they had worked."

Universities are also opening their doors now to growing numbers of people over sixty who are taking regular college courses, alongside the eighteen-year-olds, for degrees—B.A., M.A., and Ph.D. " 'College Age' Means Almost Any Age Now," *The New York Times* reported (October 25, 1989), noting that about 6 million students, from their mid-twenties to their nineties, are pursuing degrees, making up about 45 percent of current college enrollments, a stream that has doubled since 1970. "While many of their retired contemporaries were fishing or puttering around the house," the *Times* also reported, "Angelo Kochules, a 66-year-old retired sporting goods salesman, completed a degree in history, *magna cum laude,* from Queens College. And Carol Nieland Sinclair, 65, graduated from Columbia with a degree in theater arts."

Once resistant to such unconventional students, administrators are now seeking to fill seats left empty by the decline in undergraduates at the end of the baby-boom cycle. Almost 1,000 colleges now permit elderly people to take classes for credit or to audit them. Last year the City University of New York had 2,082 students over 65 years old, double the number in 1980. For a flat fee of $125 a semester, elderly people can attend as many courses as they want, as long as there are vacancies.[4]

At the Institute for Learning in Retirement at Harvard, meeting in the basement of one of the ancient catch-all administration buildings when

I visited, real estate businessman Fred Rosenbaum, seventy-five, was leading two groups: European History, Nineteenth and Twentieth Century, and International Problems. His wife, Barbara, who stayed home for eighteen years raising their three children (eight grandchildren now), then went back to work in advertising, had led six study groups but took the last semester off from "leading" because she had to go to the hospital. She had a "heart problem" and Parkinson's, though it didn't keep her from participating in "Foundations of Western Civilization." Thelma Tyndall, seventy-four, slipped on the ice and broke her hip, but it hadn't kept her from coordinating an Opera Group and attending French Literature. Dorothea Chickering, seventy-two, spent the first year of her retirement as a social worker fixing up a new apartment; the next year she volunteered to do remedial reading with eight- to thirteen-year-olds in the public school, but she didn't "come alive" again until she joined the institute.

Carl Kane, sixty, who retired from the construction business "at a very young age," said that this kind of participation study "reverses the shrinking world of the elderly to an expanding one. You're surprised at how many new things open up, and you make them your own. Socially, too. People who come here have lost their spouses, lost their friends, some friends have become senile, can't play cards anymore, and suddenly you're with people *alive*, people with imagination. All of a sudden your world is growing again instead of shrinking."

Carl was surprised at the way he keeps on changing since he turned sixty:

I've become more interested in each person, talk to them, learn about them, become involved. I didn't before, I just ran the business. Now I cook and shop, take care of things around the house while my wife still works, and I find that my mind is ranging wider, over many new fields, I have more time to think. My creative thinking is better than it was, I'm speaking more directly to the subject, more succinctly, no matter what you hear about older people.

I interviewed alumni of Penn State who had moved back to State College, the small town in rural Pennsylvania where forty or fifty years earlier a whole new world had opened for them. They had come from farms, the first persons in their families to go to college. But the "roots" they were renewing in their condos in that college town—or the old houses they were buying that were big enough for all the grandchildren to visit—meant more to them now than the farms they had grown up on. They weren't reliving their youth here. But a community in which they could continue to grow along with growing young people seemed more "real" to them, less artificial, than the Leisure World type of retirement community.

This new sense of adventure which age may force or free us to can *lighten* us of unnecessary weight and burdens we've dragged too long from our childhood, the frustrations of our youth that we swore never to face again. How strange not even to worry about them anymore, to find old pain strangely dulled, or even if sharp, bearable after all. How freeing, not to have to worry about, or maybe even feel, those old conflicts, about success and failure, in work or love. And if that lightens us, lights our path, surprisingly, in what had seemed so dark, dreary, gray, and murky, this third age we're entering now, that lovely, liberating *lightness* may be a serious sign —a signpost for survival, a signpost of evolution. For if so many of us are experiencing it now, even if we have no name for it, it can't be just *personal*.

The adventure we are free now to choose in age—though we can forfeit it or refuse its possibility—may begin with travel or study, but it ultimately involves new ways of work, and new ways of love, that are important not only for our personal survival but also for society—as if, in our third age, which is new for the human race, we are previewing new possibilities for society as a whole. It may be a nagging vestigial guilt, or truly significant, that the people I've interviewed, as lightened as they may be of previous expectations and rigidly prescribed roles, feel the pull to use whatever they have found or newly made of themselves *in society,* in old or new *community,* productive still, even if no longer fitting the old boundaries of career. Perhaps it is a serious blind spot, part of the social and political paralysis that has permitted our society to fragment and our economy to stagnate and decline—the cutting off of a vision of change, evolution, beyond youth, new ways to strengthen the raveling bonds of community that are more necessary than ever to our personal survival, and the survival of the human race.

When I spent my year at Harvard in 1982, starting with a seriousness I did not yet admit my own search for the fountain of age, I audited as many courses as I could find on evolution. From Stephen Jay Gould I glimpsed the fascinating mystery of how evolution happens, not in steady progression, but in leaps and long plateaus, sometimes in response to sudden outside crisis or catastrophe, or intensified by isolation from the larger population. From E. O. Wilson, whose course I also audited, I learned that age itself—unique to our species, and advancing still, these years after reproduction—must have evolutionary significance. How does it, could it contribute to the survival of the species?

In the winter of 1992, we saw the lifetime work

of Henri Matisse spread out in retrospective, and the pictures of him working through his late, late years, painting with a long pole even from his bed. And we felt something strong and powerful in that late work. Not as wild perhaps, not the same riotous feeling as his early work, no longer as brilliantly flamboyant. But something else—a simple wholeness, mind and feelings no longer separate. Winston Churchill became prime minister for the last time at seventy-seven. Grandma Moses started painting at seventy-nine. Michelangelo was creating his great sculpture until the week before he died at eighty-nine. Albert Schweitzer was working with the lepers in his hospital at Lambarene at ninety. Oliver Wendell Holmes was making landmark law on the Supreme Court at ninety. Barbara McClintock kept doing her brilliant, groundbreaking work in cellular biology throughout her sixties, seventies, though it so went against the grain of accepted scientific thought that she stopped submitting it to scientific journals. She was in her eighties before its enormous significance was recognized and she was awarded the Nobel Prize.

But they were geniuses, we tell ourselves. What can we learn from their late work to help us find our own? Still, if people do continue to create and elucidate principles unifying and guiding society onward with new wisdom—as these artists and scientists and statesmen have done—if there is a common pattern to their evolution in late life, it could guide us to certain principles of discarding or enlarging in our own lives.

It has been taken for granted, in modern times at least, and accepted as a scientific fact, that creativity inexorably declines with age. Setting out to reexamine records and research, Dean Keith Simonton, professor of psychology at the University of California, Davis, recalled:

In ancient times, and in most traditional cultures, aging was often synonymous with the acquisition of wisdom. . . . Within the last few centuries, the notion has become ever more prevalent that there is an optimum age for exceptional achievement, after which an inexorable decline sets in. . . . In the 20th century, when the onrush of socio-cultural change attained such a pace that knowledge became obsolete at an almost dizzying rate, the prime of life for achievement was sometimes made yet more youthful. . . . Accordingly, Einstein, who won his Nobel Prize for a major advance on quantum theory that he published when merely 26 years old, said that "a person who has not made his great contribution to science before the age of 30 will never do so." . . . What is the truth of the matter? Is it really the case that the odds of creative achievement decline after an early peak?[5]

When the actual empirical research that has been done on age and creative achievement was reviewed, there was indeed an "age curve." If one plots output as a function of age, across the fields of endeavor, "productivity tends to grow quickly to a conspicuous peak, and thereafter to gradually decline." But on closer examination, this average conclusion masks the fact that, in any field, the young and middle-aged always outnumber the aged. Furthermore, most fields have been expanding, with population growth, so that the number of competitors increases with age. If one plots creativity against age in terms of *individual* life curves, among the growing numbers of men and women who live and continue to work into their eighties, the outcome is much more various, and the apparent decline spurious or insubstantial. Replicating and extending the basic studies begun by H. C. Lehman in 1953[6] not just for creativity but for leadership, Simonton and others found a more complex picture: sometimes a double peak, or two separate peaks—"after a long decline a secondary upswing in creative output may emerge roughly around retirement age if not later. This second wind in the sixties and even eighties is rare."

But the age curve held true only as an aggregate across large numbers of separate careers. "At the individual level the age trends express nothing inexorable . . . from which an individual career may depart for all kinds of reasons." Further, that age curve of creativity seemed related less to chronological age than to years in that career—and it varied enormously in different fields. The peak around the late twenties or early thirties with steep descents thereafter was found in pure mathematics and theoretical physics. In other fields—novel writing, history, philosophy, medicine, general scholarship (and statesmanship)—a more gradual rise to the fifties was found, with a minimal if not entirely absent drop-off thereafter.

Even when individuals displayed no peak resurgence of activity after midlife, the decline was "not all that much"; they were usually more productive in the years after sixty than in their twenties. The productivity of scientists sixty and over was still almost 60 percent of their peak years. In a study of sixteen different fields, historians, philosophers, and scholars in their seventies produced at 84 to 90 percent of full capacity. Only in fields with very early peaks did the output during the last years seem substantially less. Yet even that decline can be spurious. After receiving the Nobel Prize, many laureates produce work of equal or superior quality. Thus Einstein earned a Nobel Prize for his research on photoelectric effect at twenty-six; his general relativity theory did not come until a decade later. But in the years before his death, he was working on his theory integrating all that was known on relativity, gravitational, magnetic, and small and large physical reactions into a unified field theory. It was dismissed as a fantasy vagary of his dotage by the physicists of his own time. My own son, who is a theoretical physicist, is working on "superstring theory" now, forty years later, in the terms that were dismissed as Einstein's follies of age.

After reviewing all these studies, Simonton concluded:

> Contribution for contribution . . . age becomes utterly irrelevant in the anticipation of creative impact. . . . The amount of decrement is seldom so substantial as to convert a person from a creative individual to one noncreative by the cover's close. Usually creators in their sixties and seventies are at least as productive as they were in their twenties. . . . Even in those favored proving grounds of youth, an octogenarian can still hope to make important contributions, albeit at a slower rate. Furthermore, those engaged in creative activities that favor early peaks and quick declines always have the opportunity to switch fields, entering domains of achievement where more maturity (even wisdom!) is a desideratum.[7]

When psychologists study the "late style" of those who do continue working, even more intriguing paradoxes emerge. The departure from convention, from the accepted wisdom or technical styles of the time, sometimes seen in older artists or thinkers, the simplification or unification of previous contradictions, the welding of emotion and thought in undefinable wholes is often cited, even by the older people themselves, as evidence of decline and vagary. In fact, it seems to be a characteristic of further evolution, an aspect of wisdom of which younger people are incapable, integrating disparate elements from a lifetime of experience into a truly new holistic vision which is only really understood a generation later.

Rudolf Arnheim, Harvard Professor Emeritus of the Psychology of Art, spent the most productive years of his own life studying late style. He pointed out:

> The unorthodox and uncompromising qualities of late styles in the arts have been attributed often and conveniently to the failing powers of their makers. The Renaissance biographer observed that Titian ... would have done better if in his last years he had painted only as a pastime, in order not to diminish, by weaker works, the reputation of his better years. Most of us, nowadays, however, admire Titian's late works as his most original, most beautiful and most profound.[8]

Arnheim related the late style "found often, but neither necessarily nor exclusively, in the end products of long careers" (all older people are *not* necessarily wise; some young people, including artists who have died young, exhibit the same characteristics) to the evolution of civilization itself. From the primitive stage, in which "there is little differentiation between the self and the other, the individual and the world," to the "conquest of reality"—exploration of the environment in order to master and control it—to "a world view that transcends outer appearances to search out the underlying essentials."

Another symptom of what may be called the late phase of the human attitude is the shift from hierarchy to coordination . . . the conviction that similarities are more important than differences, and that organization should derive from consensus among equals rather than from obedience to superordinate principles or powers. . . . Democracy, the most mature and sophisticated form of human community . . . presupposes the greatest wisdom even though in practice, more often than not, it makes do with much less. . . .

In later musical works, e.g., in Beethoven's last string quartets, timbres of the various instruments blend into the rich sounds of a kind of superorgan, and the antagonism of phrase and counterphrase gives way to an articulate flow. . . . The assimilation and fusion of elements, indicating a world view in which the resemblances outweigh the differences, are accompanied in late works of art by a looseness of the work's fabric, a diffuse-looking kind of order. . . . The late style fuses the contributions of the objectively given in a unitary world view, the outcome of long and deep contemplation.[9]

Arnheim based these insights on the late works of Goethe (his *Faust*), Rembrandt, Rodin, Titian, Cézanne, and Monet.

Perhaps because the problems of our own "declining" society, and the crises of its corporations and institutions require wisdom not necessarily gained by statistical MBAs, there is new professional interest in studying "wisdom." Paul Baltes and his colleagues at the Max Planck Institute in Berlin, in language as devoid as possible of subjective feeling, stated: "There is some evidence that older adults may be superior in some tasks of cognitive reasoning associated with questions of social and practical intelligence and the integration of affect (feeling) into cognitive reasoning." Still, "there is no empirical evidence that older adults *on the average* are better than younger adults on any task that has been brought under tight control in the laboratory." The problem is "extant measures and criteria of performance quality are youth-oriented."[10]

In order to study "wisdom," they had to get beyond those simple linear laboratory right-wrong tests to problems of life: life-dilemmas, life-planning, life-review. And the responses to their questions were necessarily evaluated not in terms of "right" or "wrong" but "rich" factual knowledge, rich procedural knowledge, "contextualism, relativism, and uncertainty." On problems of such complexity, dealing with *life,* older adults were among the top performers. Older adults showed "a greater understanding of life's uncertainty compared to younger adults." On the basis of such findings, they argued that "wisdom" is, in fact, rare today but that, while "not all older persons will be wise," there will be a much larger proportion of wise older persons than among the young. Because of "limitations in cultural evolution, the opportunities for older persons to display characteristics of wisdom are limited. However, because we define wisdom as an expert knowledge about the nature of human development and the human condition, we expect that the acquisition and maintenance of wisdom are facilitated by living longer." [11]

The questions and *contradictions* that emerge from the studies of creative genius and wisdom in late life are of real significance to all of us, growing older. Does professional training, which is geared to youth, use and impart wisdom, in dealing with the human condition, to doctors or lawyers or even teachers and businessmen? Though ordinary people are supposed to get more set in their ways as they grow older, some men and women from many walks of life thrive in age by doing "unsettling and unpredictable things," like the woman who celebrated her seventy-fifth birthday by a parachute jump "because that's something I hadn't done before." What enables some people in their seventies and beyond to continue "to burn brightly at their projects, despite age, despite infirmity, despite adversity"? They are not only painters and composers and scientists but ordinary people, their careers seemingly over, who resist "the temptation to become increasingly routinized and seek the comfort of the familiar," who find "serious play and infinite limits" in some work or project, and for whom a long-term relationship can take a new and exciting turn, or a lifestyle can be transformed into "both a deeper and more spontaneous communion with inner and outer reality"—ordinary people who become "fired with the passion to convert personal experience and skill into a new painting, a new poem, a new career or a new type of interpersonal relationship."[12]

Despite gerontologists' seeming preoccupation with older people only as problems and objects of "care," *Generations,* the journal of the American Society on Aging, devoted a whole issue (Spring 1991) to "Creativity in Later Life."

It was edited by Robert Kastenbaum, the Arizona gerontologist who opened my eyes to "habituation," which, in both love and work, "obscures our ability to recognize what is new or original in ourselves or in the world around us." He proposed a new seriousness, and a new playfulness, in age about "the creative impulse: why it won't just quit." It was a mistake, he insisted, not only to assume that creativity necessarily declines in old age, which the studies cited here question, but that creativity in age "is either a trivial pursuit or a pursuit undertaken by trivial people." This attitude tells us "less about the true nature of creativity in later life than it does about our society's discomfort with the prospect of dealing with an active, imaginative, unpredictable and therefore dangerous senior generation." Even in age, the creative person is "open to new experience. . . . Creativity can be the aging individual's most profound response to the limits and uncertainties of existence. . . ."

"Personal journals" written by people in their seventies and eighties and longitudinal studies cited in *Generations* indicated such creativity in late life as a culminating process of *individuation*, the development of self. Florida Scott-Maxwell: "I know my faults. . . . They are me. I am myself with ardor." May Sarton wrote at seventy that she was more herself than she had ever been, and better able to use her powers, no longer having "to prove anything to ourselves or

anyone else. We are what we are." These peo
ple's journals also revealed that such creativity
transcends and even challenges physical decline. Their writers do not fear death, but only a
prolonged dying, "the long weariness of being
cared for while deteriorating mentally and physically." They also revealed the need in later life to
focus and redirect one's energies and to structure time. "Decisions about ways in which energy can be directed and time structured cannot
be made once and for all. Successive physical
losses require people to redirect energies." Sarton wrote: "The challenge through a thicket of
physical problems is to believe in ascension still
and manage to throw the crutches away, so to
speak, and the more helpless in some ways the
more of a triumph to keep carting away non-
essential things and climbing toward death in
naked joy." Elizabeth Vining shifted from bird
watching to tree watching, as her vision
worsened; Florida Scott-Maxwell gave up drawing roots and seed pods and flowers, when it
strained her eyes, for rugmaking. When her
hands became too arthritic, she began to listen
to music.

These people affirmed and monitored their experience of age but were not "preoccupied by
the thought of being old." The "feeling old"
which so many people experience at midlife, imbued by that dread of age, may in fact be a signal
of the need to "switch" from habituated modes
of love or work. Sarton, in her early sixties, wrote

in her journal: "It is not only the coming on of winter, but the coming on of old age that I shore up against these days." After creating a new life for herself, in her house by the sea in Maine, she recorded a new "excitement" about being alive. "It is quite incredible that I am seventy and that I feel so young." After recovering from a stroke, four years later, she wrote: "I am no longer the very old woman with a very old dog I was all spring and summer." There seemed to be an ebb and flow in the lives of these writers, in all our lives. We feel ourselves succumbing to that mystique of *being old,* and then those strengths that have no name bubble up again: the fountain of age.

The return of "wonder" in old age is illustrated in "elder tales" down through the ages, in all cultures, showing older people doing something apparently outrageous or foolish after years of being practical and predictable. This increase in "mythic awareness" and "magical" thinking in age was initially interpreted as regression—a senile reversion to childishness, the intellectual deterioration that was thought to be inevitable with old age. A growing body of new research has revealed the reverse: wonder as an essential element of wisdom.

Complex, subtle forms of reasoning, which are missed by traditional psychological tests, develop in maturity. . . . Wisdom appears to invoke the return of wonder and mythic delight in the world. . . . Central to the attitude of wonder is an affirmation of life just as it is in the present. The individual neither hankers after a lost past nor a future yet to be . . . an affirmation of one's life just as one lived it, for better or worse . . . an affirmation of one's past, the return of wonder invokes a similar affirmation of the present, down to its small, ordinary events.[13]

I found, in my interviews, and even casual reading of the daily newspaper, that ordinary people are quite capable of making this kind of affirmation of themselves, discovering new sources and directions for their own creativity and wisdom. And I found myself lightened of my own denial and dread of age, by the sense of wonder, listening to them.

Bea Wattenberg would never have dreamed of becoming a dancer—in her sixties! She wrote me, from her home in Silver Spring, Maryland, when she read about my search for "the fountain of age":

When my husband died in 1983, I had no idea what to do with my life. The grief was overwhelming, but somewhere, lying dormant, was this reservoir of strength that I had no idea I possessed, and I was able to literally start a new life.

Just a year and a half ago I joined a group of dancers known as Dancers of the Third Age, formed about ten years ago by a young woman named Liz Lerman. She has gained national recognition by her seemingly single-handed battle against ageism in dance. I have become a member of her touring company, which consists of five young dancers and five seniors. Much of our work has a social message, through political satire; some has the poignancy of true life experiences. I have found myself performing with this revolutionary group on stages in Yugoslavia, London, Dartmouth College, Dallas, Chicago, and even the Kennedy Center, much to my amazement.

After forty-one years at Magic Chef selling appliances, Eli Finn was forced to retire; at the time he was eighty-three. He got himself a job at Unity Stove, taking the 7:04 train from Norwalk to New York every morning, even in a blizzard. His customers were appalled when he retired again—to go to college. At one hundred, he drove his '78 Cadillac down the congested I-95, weaving in and out of traffic, to study history at Fairfield University. When they got past the Civil War, the professor planned to have Eli, who remembered Teddy Roosevelt and first voted for Woodrow Wilson, teach the class.[14]

An acquaintance of mine who won beauty contests in her youth, and whose midlife was driven by enormous ambition, professional and political, and obsessive sexual passion for younger men, survived a personal catastrophe in her sixties and began working out of the limelight on larger issues involving the future of her people. When a cable network asked her to host a new celebrity talk show, she stewed a while and, to her friends' surprise, turned it down. "I thought about the hairdresser every day, booking the guests, the ratings pressures—and for what? So I designed myself a charm bracelet with the letters IDTA—I've Done That Already."

My sister Amy Adams retired at sixty-five as a teacher of gifted students in a Long Island public school, a job she had held for the thirty-odd years since she divorced. A painter, she had started out as a primitive, sketching at the Art Students League, and developed mastery and her own style, but she had never become part of the art world in New York, and almost never got a chance to show or sell her paintings. She had decided to stop painting several years before her retirement from that teaching job, consigned all her paintings to an auction gallery, and started taking writing classes. With her sons and grandkids now living in the West, she gave up her apartment in Fresh Meadows, tried but didn't like Florida, and settled in Chapel Hill, North Carolina, where she could take serious creative writing courses at Duke University, and become part of the Peer Learning Community, where she is now a member of the board and coordinates a popular contemporary writers' program. She wrote me:

I am serious about wanting to learn to write good fiction but I don't want to spoil it for myself by making it into a "should." I am serious but if I take it too seriously I'll kill it for myself, paradoxical but true. It's going to take a huge amount of work and time to go from being a very amateur writer to what will satisfy me. I've no desire to be a writing equivalent of a "Sunday painter." I want to reach the same level of competence I reached in painting but that happened over many years. However, I've got the rest of my life, and the process itself is what I want to focus on. The outcome—well, whatever evolves will evolve—nothing depends on it, no one to please but me. But I'm *choosing to do it, so it's OK. It's out of the same part of myself as the painting—my deepest self.*

"We have no role models for the new kind of age," one woman complained. I think it's more that the *denial of age,* the age mystique, has kept the images of people embarking on adventurous new pursuits—at sixty-five, seventy, eighty—out of the public eye, as the images of earlier women artists, pioneers, and doctors, even the women who fought one hundred years to get the vote, have, until recently, been kept out of the history books. A younger feminist writer, trying to overcome that symbolic annihilation, wrote to me about Elizabeth Peabody who, at sixty-three, after four decades of writing history texts and publishing the *Dial* with Emerson, had saved enough money to spend a year traveling in Europe studying experimental schools. In her journal she described that sixty-fourth year as her "wandering year, closing my apprenticeship to life." She came back to Boston and began an entirely new career as founder of the kindergarten movement in the United States, which occupied her until her death at ninety.[15]

The first conference on "Aging and Creativity" in America, bringing together gerontologists and scholars on art history, at Wingspread in Wisconsin in 1985, expressed some concern about promoting the very notion of "creativity" in later life. The conference asked: "Why don't artists, writers, composers consider retiring as many people do?" It also asked: "Could the idea of a creative old age be the beginning of a new myth about aging that places another burden on old people?"

The report on the Wingspread conference pointed out:

In our society there are strong social expectations that old age involves a decline in creativity. Most conference participants rejected those negative expectations yet it is not clear how to combat them. In trying to overcome stereotyped limits, it is all too easy to exaggerate in the opposite direction: as if creativity of old age were a kind of compensation for other losses of old age. . . . If we are unclear about the meaning of creative development in old age, nevertheless it is possible to recognize "depletion of the self" as the opposite of creativity . . . the danger of stasis and stagnation . . . people stay where they are because there is no place else today, no role expectations or possibilities envisaged for later life. In a period of rapid change, there is a need for models.[16]

Models do exist. Artists in all fields still producing in old age sometimes seem to be, in effect, kept alive and *vital* in their age by their work, despite physical infirmities that would otherwise cripple or kill. At eighty, Agnes de Mille, ten years after a severe stroke, told a reporter: "I can't do dancing anymore. I'm held together with spit and Scotch tape." Since that stroke, she had written three books passing on her wisdom about dance, and was working on a fourth. But Gian Carlo Menotti, who did not produce "late style" music, continued to exploit the accoutrements of his earlier success yet did not really "enjoy." He told the same reporter: "I loathe my body. The liver spots, the sagging flesh." [17]

Louise Nevelson, who didn't begin her career as a sculptor until nearly fifty, was still creating those mysterious constructions in her late eighties, wearing daring black satin pants, gold blouse, black lace stockings, dark eyebrow pencil calling attention to her lined face and brilliant eyes, in her studio and to openings—and still working, working. "I've never been lifted," she said, "but I do like a bit of glamour." Above all, "I still want to do my work. I still want to do my livingness. And I have lived. I have been fulfilled. I recognized what I had, and I never sold it short. And I ain't through yet." She died in the midst of that livingness.

M. F. K. Fisher kept writing until her death at eighty-one—not only her marvelous books about food but mythic tales of age, though she was slowed by Parkinson's disease in her seventies, could no longer type or use her right hand but lay awake "writing all night in my mind" on the sleeping porch in her California ranch, taping her stories the next day. Martha Graham, ninety-one, said: "I believe one thing, that today is yesterday and tomorrow is today and you can't stop. The body is your instrument in dance, but your art is outside that creature, the body. I don't leap or jump anymore. I look at young dancers, and I am envious, more aware of what glories the body contains. But sensitivity is not made dull by age." Only months before her death, *The New York Times* (October 1, 1990) announced: "Martha Graham, at 96, Does Something Different." She premiered a new dance, the lighthearted "Maple Leaf Gala." A seemingly "playful, almost giddy romp," close to jazz, which she'd always avoided before, "a dance of prancing young lovers drawing close and pulling apart in nonstop, acrobatic movement."

Robert Motherwell, in his seventies, claimed it was that "endless quest" which kept artists and writers going. "One wonderful thing about creativity is that you're never satisfied with what you're trying to do. There's always the anguish, the pleasurable challenge. For me, to retire from painting would be to retire from life." Aware that time was running out, they seem more afraid of losing their "wonder" and openness to the "new idea" than of death—afraid of repeating themselves. Hardly able to speak after throat surgery, Robert Penn Warren told a reporter: "You're not moving on if you imitate yourself." William Schuman, after a heart attack and triple bypass surgery, delivered a work of music fourteen months before it was due "so hot I couldn't stop." [18]

Retirement from a structured job or profession that they had long enjoyed (and to which, perhaps inevitably, they had become "habituated") permitted some of the people I interviewed to experience that same mysterious impulse—the "endless quest" that drives the artists. Woody English, whom I knew years ago in Rockland County where he ran the mental health center, retired at seventy-seven after forty-five years as a practicing psychiatrist. I hadn't seen him in twenty-five years at least, but he seemed if anything more sprightly and full of energy than I remembered. In late life, he had become a collagist, he told me.

Five years ago I took a class in collage on the Cape, at Truro Center for the Arts, and I knew that's what I had to do. In my youth, I had done watercolors, acrylic, won a competition in high school for an art school scholarship, but I was never satisfied with anything I did. I thought about being an artist but my father said no, you'll never earn a living as an artist, you should be a doctor like me. I never liked medicine, but when I found psychiatry, that was it, and I was good at it. Like when I found collage, that was it. And I am good at it.

Is it a career? Yes, unquestionably, and no. The nice thing about collage, you can do it anywhere, all you need is scissors and some glue. My previous career dealt entirely with people, this one deals with materials, but in both careers you're really solving problems all the time. It's exciting, doing something new. It made me feel enthusiastic, alive in a new way.

It struck me that what both Woody and my sister Amy were talking about, and many of the other people I interviewed, was perhaps akin to the artist's "late style." The word "adventure," which kept coming up until I adopted it myself, did not imply something as passive as watching television, but it didn't imply anything as grim and judgmental as "career." It implied work, not just pleasure, and meaning and complexity and challenge, and it surely implied participating in society, but it didn't necessarily imply status. I came across the concept of "flow," which for twenty years Mihaly Csikszentmihalyi, a professor of psychology at the University of Chicago, had been looking into, a state of "involvement" that lies between boredom and anxiety. A person in flow is mentally involved in the challenge and intrinsic pleasure of an activity yet lacks self-consciousness and anxiety about performance. Flow takes energy and effort; it's not the passive "go with the flow." People usually experience it when pursuing a goal. Csikszentmihalyi claimed that most people spend their lives alternating between work they don't necessarily like but are obliged to do, and passive leisure activities that require no work but offer no challenge. "As a result, life passes in a sequence of boring and anxious experiences over which a person has little control. With flow, in contrast, alienation gives way to involvement, enjoyment replaces boredom, helplessness turns into a feeling of control, and psychic energy works to reinforce the sense of self, instead of just being in the service of external goals." [19]

My friend Joe Machlis, who began writing novels in his seventies after nearly fifty years as a musicologist, exulted in experiencing that flow:

You've finished with the great disquietude, the discontent, the big ambition. You accept yourself. The question of wanting to be this or that, keeping up with whomever, it's finished. You stand back from the yearning and the ambitious striving and the discontent, and you look around and realize—these are the golden years, quietude of the spirit—you accept what you are and where you fit into the scheme of things. That's why I like my eighties, all that running and seeking and yearning is behind you. When I was in my twenties, I wanted to be a writer. I acquired the biggest collection of rejection slips. So, I became a music teacher. Now, I have no fear writing, no insecurity. I do it comfortably. It flows.

Youthful dreams finally realized, without the accoutrements and anxieties of career, can be the surprise adventure of age. Facing sixty, Charles Ballard took early retirement as branch manager of the Bank of America at Altadena and began passing the requisite courses to get into the two-year nursing program at Pasadena City College. The oldest graduate by far, he was offered several jobs, and chose the graveyard shift in pediatrics at the Huntington Memorial Hospital because "I like sick babies, and night was when the openings were." When he was a young student at Pomona College, Ballard said a tough course in zoology drove him out of pre-med studies and into business school and banking. "But I never totally gave up wanting to be in medicine, and with an opportunity for early retirement, I was reading about the nursing shortage. I thought: 'Oh, yeah! Here's a way I can get back into it.' There's a heavy demand for nurses, and I figured that once I graduated, I would have five to ten years to put into a career." His friends found it incongruous that a banker would want to become a nurse, but his wife, who is chairman of Pasadena's English Department, his two grown kids, and grandchild all thought it was great. Ballard himself "had some doubts. I wondered how I would be accepted. But I found it very easy to let go of being a banker and get absorbed in this. I've had a ball."

What's missing, in all the thinking about the problem of age today, is the need for the people indubitably living with new vitality through their sixties, seventies, eighties to use those evolving abilities in society—and society's need to use their wisdom and larger vision and truth-telling to confront its own problems of polarization and decline. That missing piece affirmed can transform individual decline into new adventure, life-long inner conflict, disquietude, and raging yearning into new wholeness. But as Erikson and others have groped to express it, the individual's task in age seems not only to involve integrity and authentic selfhood, abandonment of mask and denial and paralyzing defense, but *generativity.* To be part of the community, to be part of something larger than oneself, to contribute somehow to the ongoing human enterprise, to pass on some legacy to the next generation, is, it seems, a burning need of vital age, different from the parenting of one's children yet just as essential to survival of the human species.

That our society, at this crucial stage, has a compelling need to use those unnamed strengths of age is less clear. The jagged pieces of the jigsaw puzzle haven't come together yet, but I sense they fit. It is difficult to see the real possibilities of the third age in terms of particular solutions, the way society is structured now. But from the personal departures from expectation, one can see the necessity of new kinds of participation in the community in the third age, transcending present insoluble rigidities and paradoxical dilemmas.

In the youth of our society, architects used to say, "God is in the details." The young and middle aged are groaning under the pressure of these details. Holding on to win-lose games and the masks of their own youth, too many of our recent U.S. presidents, who seemed to be living their age in denial, were perhaps kept by their own lack of integrity and generativity from the necessary new vision. In their current dilemmas, business leaders sometimes covertly summon back the larger vision of those they have forced —one way or another—into retirement, as Exxon did after the Alaskan oil spill. The possibilities for society of this new third age can hardly be seen now, obscured as they are by misconceptions and prejudices—age-as-"problem." They have to be seen as *solution* and not just problem for change to be possible. And we have to name our own need to move in society in new ways in age to make it happen.

NINETEEN

Generativity

Just as in their "late style" artists and scientists, creators and great thinkers seem to move beyond tumult and discord, distracting details and seemingly irreconcilable differences, to unifying principles that give new meaning to what has gone before and presage the agenda for the next generation, so it seems to me age can free us all, personally—and our aging society politically—to a new wholeness, previewing in the serious or the seemingly irrelevant efforts of our late years new dimensions of life for the next generation. It's as if we need to break out of the very rubrics of our previous thinking about both love and work, which have always been defined *separately* by Freud and our psychological and spiritual counselors, and by Marx and Keynes and the political economists. It's as if, both personally and politically, we have to move beyond concepts of love hinged to the childhood fantasies, traumas, and sexual obsessions of which we have seemed to be helpless victims, beyond the endless wrestling with that passive sexual victimhood for women, beyond that brutal machismo so bruising to men, beyond concepts of work based on the industrial technology of society's youth, to a new wholeness of approach.

Erik Erikson, finding a dearth of meaning in age in our own time, conceptualized "integrity" as the polar opposite of "despair," and "generativity" as the promise beyond "stagnation." But he was limited in his own thinking by the psychoanalytic construct that ends in "genitality": the metaphor of biological sexuality, beginning with the baby at the breast and ending with the genital sexuality that peaks, with men, as we now know, by thirty. The surmounting of the obsession with one's own childhood trauma, and the love-denying defenses against its pain, is only now beginning to be contemplated in new ways by psychological and spiritual counselors. A new kind of counseling of elders— "life review," "spiritual eldering"—enables one to *affirm it all,* one's life as a branching tree, as gerontologist Jim Birren put it, which releases finally the generativity that can truly flow from the wholeness of age.

The very lack of rigidly proscribed roles, or forced "retirement" from those rigidly separate sex roles of our youth and the parenting years, can make possible a new kind of wholeness in the third age. But that is achieved now often only painfully, or can find no expression, because the age mystique, and the circling of the economic and social wagons around it deny us new possibilities. At this point, it takes real strength, and a compelling drive to generativity that *surprises* us, and those who study us in age, to break through that mystique and find ways, outside the mainstream, to express such wholeness in society. Some retreat in bitterness, or find what meaning they can in the routines of daily survival and the trivial pursuits prescribed for "senior citizens." But others, in their work of love, express a generativity that, as much as any truly revolutionary artistic creation or scientific discovery, may preview for a future generation new values and directions.

Since its inception in 1967, the Senior Concert Orchestra of New York has played almost 90 free concerts to over 100,000 citizens in high schools and colleges, as well as a free concert in Carnegie Hall, attended by many who may never have been to a concert before. Begun by the Senior Musicians Association under the auspices of

Local 802, American Federation of Musicians, it now includes retirees of the Philharmonic, the Metropolitan Opera, the NBC Symphony under Toscanini, and seeks the funding it needs to do its work as "a viable symbol for benign aging and productivity." The Seasoned Citizens Theater Company plays at senior centers, nursing homes, and hospitals. Their motto is: "We do not stop playing because we grow old . . . We grow old because we stop playing."

At the St. Mark's Episcopal Church on Capitol Hill, my old college friend Mary Jackson Craighill, in her early seventies, leads the Professional Senior Company, a group of dancers who have been working together for many years now, in "religious dance alongside secular dance." They perform in Washington and Virginia public schools, hold workshops for teachers and students, and in recent years held dance series, followed by conversations with the audience, at veterans' hospitals, soldier's and airmen's homes, and nursing and retirement homes, as well as church performances as part of the Sunday liturgy.

Forrest Behm, now 74, had a secret hobby while he was setting up plants in 45 countries as head of Corning Glass International Operations: "seeding change." He studied other companies which had broken out of the old linear dominance-and-control model, and tried small experiments of his own—far from corporate central where he sensed rigid hierarchical structures were threatening the company's future.

Forrest Behm, full of vibrant, adventurous authority, mesmerized CEOs at a retreat of the Leadership Institute of the USC School of Business in April 1993, with his tale of how he was brought out of retirement to "make change happen" at Corning. The new president, Jamie Houghton, summoned him out of retirement as his "coach" to transform the entire corporate culture at Corning Glass—from the top down —into an organization of autonomous, flexible, independent thinkers and doers capable of responding to change. By getting rid of obsolete bureaucratic procedures, passive, order-taking workers, and "business as usual" executives, they achieved their end. Now Behm responds to such SOS's from harassed CEOs in diverse industries who've heard that this guy in his seventies can help them "make change happen," though he refuses to set himself up in the "consultant business."

"I won't write reports and I won't stick around to teach them after I've got the process going. I'll come back in six months or every year, to take their temperature. Yeah, they pay me, but I do it for fun."

At 87, Arthur Fleming, the first U.S. Social Security chief, electrified gerontologists at the Anaheim conference of the National Conference on Aging in April 1993 with a passionate warning of the danger to the future of Social Security. Listening to him in awe, I found myself wishing that Clinton would bring him back, to save and evolve Social Security in his and the nation's nineties.

At a conference called "Farewell to the Chief (The Role of Former Presidents in American Public Life)," sponsored by the Herbert Hoover Library in West Branch, Iowa, in 1989, Daniel Boorstin, Librarian of Congress Emeritus, proposed a new national institution: a Council of Elders, consisting of past presidents of the United States and our most experienced retired leaders in labor, business, science, literature, education, and the arts. Using satellite television for an ongoing forum on pressing national issues, those wise elders could participate from their own living rooms, and even use the new technology to interact with other citizens in theirs. Boorstin proposed that such a council would pool their wisdom and experience "to address the nation's unfinished business, freed of the usual political considerations of getting re-elected or pleasing 'special interest groups.'" They would deal with long-term problems such as education and the environment, rather than current questions of policy.

Boorstin conceived of such an institution in historical terms of "saving a national resource." He told the assembled national dignitaries:

Our American strength, we have often been told, has been our youth. Ours is, or until recently was, a young nation. . . . It was the young in spirit, we say, who had the strength and the will and the flexibility to leave an Old World, to risk an Atlantic or Pacific passage for the uncertain promises of a still uncharted America. The framers of the Constitution provided that a person 35 years of age was old enough to be President, a Senator needed to be only 30 . . . the twenty-sixth amendment to the Constitution lowered the voting age to 18. We have been ingenious, too, in devising institutions—like our Land Grant colleges and the GI Bill—to make the best use of our youth resources.

But as our nation has matured—some would say only aged—as the need for immigrant courage is less general and life expectancy has increased . . . our ingenuity in meeting the needs and opportunities and demands of youth has not been matched by any similar ingenuity in devising initiatives to employ our older population. . . . The most conspicuous American institution directed to senior citizens is the so-called Leisure City, a place not of creation but of recreation and vegetation. Our concern for the special needs of our ailing, idle and disoriented aging has been admirable. But we need to refocus our attention on how to employ the special talents and resources of our most experienced citizens.

It seems significant that, even in the absence of such institutions, older leaders in many fields, as if driven by some larger generative impulse, may move beyond the battles of the special interests, the politically correct agenda or ideological imperatives that have consumed them for decades, risking isolation from their previous community as a result. They seem almost driven to use their wisdom to reconcile implacable differences that are consuming and wasting our human resources.

Heading for seventy, my friend Stanley Sheinbaum, economist, unrepentant liberal, and card-carrying ACLU member whom I first met twenty-five years ago campaigning for Eugene McCarthy against the Vietnam War, handed over his board chairmanship of the ACLU in California to a younger man. He began instead to direct his energies toward healing the growing chasm between the police and the diverse and increasingly polarized community of Los Angeles, on the one hand, and the insoluble conflict between Israeli and Arab interests in the Middle East, on the other. When he brought Israeli and PLO leaders together for the first time in the early nineties in Sweden, some of his outraged Jewish neighbors in California dumped the corpse of a pig on his driveway. As chairman of the civilian police commission, he took responsibility for seeing justice done after the Los Angeles riots of 1992, and for mobilizing the community to tackle root economic causes as well as real fears of increasing crime and violence, and real concerns for a law and order that would not make a mockery of justice, instead of venting their rage and frustration in hatemongering, group against group. To do that, he had to reconcile the liberal focus on the rights of criminals and minorities, his own responsibility for law and order, and his awareness of complex and economic realities not likely to be solved in the current political climate.

Looking drawn and pale, a few weeks after the riots in the summer of 1992, Stanley told me:

I came in with an ACLU cop-hating reputation, so I had to work very hard to win over the rank and file. I worked hard to get the police better working conditions, better equipment, and to show them I was concerned with their side of the problem. I'm no longer a liberal intellectual, talking from above the fray. On the line, it is that lifetime experience of knowing how things work that is critical now. All my liberal West Side friends expect me to treat the police union as the enemy. But that liberal talk is no good when they give lip service to "root causes," but won't do anything that means giving up some of their own wealth. The police department can't do anything about the root causes. But it can function with a concern for the community, which has been neglected, and the community has to take more responsibility itself to stop the drug dealing.

You can't deal with these crises in terms of labels; you have to apply some wisdom to the problem, look beyond the facts with some sense of the direction you want to go in. You can't solve the problem in Los Angeles without talking about the economy as a whole and real change in Washington.

When Norman Lear, approaching the age of seventy, gave a speech to religious leaders at Anaheim, California, in 1990 about the need to "nurture the sense of the sacred that underlies all religions" in American young people, it made a lot of his former community of liberal followers "uneasy." While the headline read, "Longtime Foe of Religious Right Urges Schools to Teach the Sacred," Lear did not reverse his belief in the separation of church and state, or his opposition to prayers in public schools, or teaching "creationist theology." "While we civil libertarians have been triumphant in most of our legal and constitutional battles," he said, "I am troubled that so many of us remain blocked or blind to the spiritual emptiness in our culture which the televangelists exploited so success-fully."[1]

On a Sunday night in February 1992, Lear meditated out loud to me:

The thing I find most on my mind, I believe that we have gone so far in a cold, quantifiable direction, where we're ruled by numbers, that we've lost our connection to our inner selves —our sense of the sacred, why people listen to the fundamentalist preachers on radio and television. There is no civic authority to respect, the American corporate ethic is the dominant influence of the culture. We've raised a generation of kids with no sense of values, of doing your best, of wonder—if you're not a winner you're a loser.

My liberal friends and my Hollywood buddies raise their eyebrows at my new concern for matters of the spirit. I'm not a mystic. I didn't suddenly have a vision. There's no stained glass in my system at all. But you reach a point where you realize life isn't about success as we think about success generally. The success I had with "All in the Family," it took me fifty years to get to that. It's taken me another twenty years to get to where I am now: the one irretrievable sin is not living in the moment. The moments of connecting are what count. And not needing to win anymore, not needing the immediate results of everything you do. The joy in the doing, the faith in the possibility, even if you can't see it yet, that's what keeps you alive.

When Jonas Salk stepped down from the presidency of the institute he established at La Jolla after discovering the live polio vaccine, his efforts to examine larger mysteries of the evolution of the human mind, and to make a scientific study of spiritual vision, were derided. His subsequent books, *Man Unfolding* and *Survival of the Wisest,* were virtually ignored by the popular press as well as the scientific community. But he continued his work, in his own laboratory at La Jolla, even though he no longer involved himself in institute or scientific politics, carrying out his own sense of professional commitment to the larger, evolving community. In the face of the AIDS crisis, he defied scientific opinion by undertaking research, again using live virus, despite the scientific dismissal of his work when his live polio vaccine was replaced by Sabin's laboratory vaccine.

Generativity is expressed in more mundane terms whenever "senior citizens'" talents are truly used as a community resource, or where they are allowed or encouraged to use their wisdom in work with younger people. In Fort Ord, California, "foster grandparents" go into Army homes where there are problems of child abuse as the mainstay of the Army Community Services Child Abuse Program. They follow formal procedures, including written and verbal reports, and are valued by the Army agency because they go in as "respected, non-threatening presences and help the mothers learn to care for their children without violence."[2]

At age seventy-one, George Kreidler, a former linebacker for the Green Bay Packers who retired at sixty-five after thirty-one years supervising the construction of oil refineries and chemical and nuclear power plants for Bechtel Corporation, was supervising house construction for the homeless for Habitat for Humanity. Retiring to Asheville, North Carolina, he was described as part of "a new breed of active, independent retirees, for whom a need to help society at large is as important as personal enrichment." Through the North Carolina Center for Creative Retirement, he also served as the mentor to a young college athlete, not to win more games, but for his "academic performance and future direction." Others tutored grade and high school students. Asked his qualifications for tutoring grade school students, a retired locomotive engineer wrote: "I have my act together."[3]

In the early years of the women's movement, after we broke through the feminine mystique and began to take ourselves seriously, in the "consciousness-raising" groups where we talked about our own experience as women the way it really is, we recognized possibilities in ourselves that we hadn't dared to put a name to until we heard about them from each other. The personal is political, we said, as we began moving to break through the barriers that had kept us isolated from society. We had no real role models then, because our mothers and the women who went before us hadn't faced the new road now open to us. We had to be role models for each other. The same holds true now, I believe, for women and men facing this new, unprecedented, and uncharted territory of age. We have to tell each other *the way it really is, growing older,* and help each other name the possibilities we hardly recognize or dare to put a name to when we sense them in ourselves. I think we need new kinds of consciousness-raising, to make that evolutionary leap into new age, to help each other move on new, uncharted paths.

How do we help one another finally to affirm, woman and man, the integrity of full personhood at last—that radiant inner self that seems to carry the mystery and meaning of our life—and to break through the barriers that keep us from really using what we dimly recognize as our own unique late style? How do we find ways, as we feel we must, to use the wisdom we have derived from the painful, joyful experience of our lives as we have lived them, *in society,* so that we may live out our generativity?

Part of the answer to these questions, for each of us, has to be personal; and yet it may be very hard to find, in isolation, against the total blankness of that uncharted age, that expectation only of decline, and the age ostracism—the graylash. There are some groping attempts now on the part of a few psychoanalysts and psychotherapists, spiritual counselors of mainstream church and synagogue and New Age gurus, to deal with age, but mostly, since they try to fit it into schema based on youth, coming to a dead end, a resignation: abdication from society, the whiling away of leftover months and years of life in trivial pursuits. Gerontologists have also come up with ways of affirming the totality of the life each one of us has lived as a necessary "life review" before death, or as a legacy for one's children and grandchildren. But no one has seen the generativity of age for what I believe it is, or could be: *a stage of evolution,* in our own lives, that could also be key to the evolution and survival of our aging society. And since the personal is political, I think part of the answer has to be a political movement that will effect the changes necessary for society to use productively the wisdom and generativity of age.

Acceptance, however, must first come from ourselves. And the need to affirm the missing pieces of ourselves and transcend the paralyzing conflicts of our youth and middle age can be met, finally, in age, without wallowing in the childhood traumas that may have caused them, or repeating them in a compulsive endless search for restitution, as the analysts say we do. Life has put us in a different place; but we might need help from each other, or new kinds of professional help, to recognize it.

In the spring of 1992, I heard June Singer, a Jungian therapist who seemed to me to evoke a new feminist wisdom, speak of transcending, in age, our condition as "the walking wounded—warriors and victims." Looking back on thirty years of psychoanalytic practice, she now suggested that wallowing in those wounds from early childhood in a certain sense encouraged disengagement rather than connection. And Maslow's definition of self-actualization as the highest form of human development—which, I might add, first-stage feminism echoed—made connection seem almost pathological. Those 1960s and 1970s encounter groups—"I do my thing, you do your own thing, I'm not in the world to meet your expectations"—may have been necessary as we struggled to break out of obsolete roles, but were they sufficient?

Lecturing in a Los Angeles hospital to health professionals and others, young and old, interested in the spiritual dimensions of healing, Singer said:

Nobody talked about taking care of someone else's needs. A whole generation grew up thinking the most important thing was self-actualization, getting rid of relationships that didn't meet our needs. So many books now on the "dysfunctional family," "co-dependency." We have pathologized the *need to take care of other people's needs,* the relationship between women and men. We dwell on the deep wounds we brought into those relationships, selecting someone who reminds us of father or mother, replaying how we lived it early in life, re-creating it over and over this time to make it different.

I no longer work with the baby part of people. We may have looked to our marriages to take care of those baby needs still crying in us. As long as he or she was around to meet those needs, or be blamed for not meeting them, we had the illusion of security. When that ends, and those childhood wounds are uncovered, we live in fear the lie of our lives will come out.[4]

Was that part of the isolation of age, I asked myself, or could age let one stop living that lie and *accept* childhood wounds, no longer needing to defend against them? Singer went on: "To heal the wounds requires a connection with a variety of people, a *community.*" Listening to her, I asked myself: Could age, at last, release us from the narrowness of that arid room mother-father-child? Does not "the isolation, if we do not have a partner to meet all our needs," which is part of our dread of age, come from that childhood-bound demand of our mate "what one person cannot give"? In age, at least, we can finally recognize that "we need a community, not just the perfect relationship."

The "adventurous elders" whom the Case Western Reserve gerontologists Eva and Boaz Kohana studied making a new life for themselves in Florida after retirement had developed more and new sources of social support and intimacy beyond the family, which seemed to enhance their vitality and well-being. Compared to their peers back in Cleveland, who sought security by staying in their old neighborhoods, or moving nearer their children, those adventurous elders who took the risks of moving had created new non-family sources of security for themselves. In other research, the bonds of friendship beyond the family seemed as or more important for longevity and vital age than those with spouse or children. In Florida, and in Sun City, friends and neighbors who had developed a give-and-take mutuality would be chosen over family if help were needed. The Kohanas called this "self-evolving behavior"—"All my life I've done for my children, now I do for the *community.*" Such "pro-active behavior" in age, as opposed to the expected passive decline and disengagement, seemed to "enhance their self-esteem and their psychosocial well-being which has an actual effect on their health," the Kohanas reported. And through their new work in the community, they develop more new sources of social support.[5]

The missing pieces of the wholeness of self and the new adventure of generativity seem often to involve the crossover to new forms of intimacy and engagement for men, and new active enterprise for women. But I think this crossover is misunderstood if it is seen only as a reversal of the old conventional masculine and feminine roles of our youth. Is the man who in late life, at or after the peak of his career, marries a younger woman and has babies merely trying to deny his age, play young still, as women biologically have no choice to do? Or can he now risk a new intimacy, affirm a nurturing side of himself, as he could not do before, bound by the dictates of youthful masculinity, the machismo that masked the missing pieces of himself?

When Christie Hefner heard of my search, she urged me to talk to her father Hugh Hefner, then sixty-five, and see how *Playboy*'s founder had evolved. With fantasies of nude bunnies cavorting in hot tubs and artificial grottos, reawakening lust in paunchy males, I went to see him at the Playboy Mansion in Los Angeles. Life-sized stuffed toys, teddy bears and tigers, a stroller and a playpen and a kiddy-swing were strewn around the erotic statues, on the lawn and in the great hall, which once I supposed was the entranceway to orgies. Hefner, in pajamas at midday, came into his study to talk to me—not, I gathered, from an orgy, but from a romp with his year-old son, who was born on his sixty-fourth birthday. His wife, Karen, was twenty-six. Hefner told me:

One can reinvent oneself in many ways. I'd spent most of my life running away from a Puritan home, trying to relive the boyhood I never really had. Now I'm in a different place. I lived out those adolescent fantasies through my fifties. I had a mild stroke in 1985; I was almost sixty. Call it a stroke of luck. I used that stroke as permission to put down the baggage of my life, quit trying to prove something to myself or anyone else, either by all that calculated defiance of sexual repression or proving myself in work. Continuing to live up to someone else's expectations, even by defying them, is a limited way of living. What was I trying to prove? What's important is living, the connections that are your real life.

My lifestyle changed totally. I started looking for a more traditional one-to-one commitment instead of the Playboy lifestyle. It took me a long time to get there, but what gives me the most satisfaction now, strangely enough, is my relationship with my own wife, and my kids. I don't have to prove anything anymore. Nothing was sweeter for me than passing the Playboy baton to that brilliant feminist daughter of mine. She *enjoys* being Chairman of the Board more than I ever did.

To my own and everyone else's surprise, I'm savoring this autumn season of my life most of all. The stroke taught me "the only thing you really have is life itself." Once you recognize that, you can savor it, all of it, you don't have to complicate it, you can be open to what comes.

But Hefner had also moved to a generativity beyond that which he was belatedly experiencing with his own kids. The Hugh Hefner Awards given every year to people and organizations defending freedom of speech and the First Amendment were his act of conscious "preservation for the future" of the basic principles of democracy now under attack.

In the gerontological underground, I was tuned in to "elder tales," a body of little-known folk literature in which psychological growth in late life is portrayed in stories that go beyond "they get married and live happily ever after." The wicked old witch, the fairy godmother, the wise elderly wizard are familiar enough in children's stories. But newer "elder tales" seem to concern personal self-confrontation and transformation. An older woman steals the magic towel which had made her young daughter-in-law more and more beautiful. That towel made the old lady more ugly. Wiping off the outer mask, confronting the shadowy, hidden, dark side of oneself, or the monstrous growth, and reconciling the dark and the light, in elder tales, lets the old woman (or the old man) find the way that seemed lost, and even dance, the way a child might, on that previously murky path. Such elder tales do not end with finding the bag of gold like the fairy tales of youth, but often start with it, and end with the transformation of that dead gold to living fish. The psychologists and gerontologists see in elder tales metaphors of self-confrontation and transformation, growth in age from material gain to spiritual concern with the meaning of life, to "wonder" and generativity.

My friends in the gerontological underground, Bob Butler, Jim Birren, B. J. Hately, Leah Buturain, and others, have hit on the technique of creative autobiography or "journal" sessions, to help elders today break through the denials and compartmentalism of their youth and middle age to see the *totality* of their lives. This search is not the same as psychoanalysis or psychotherapy; it does not necessarily concern itself with "problem" or "pathology," but seeks to find "the meaning of one's life as one has lived it." Butler calls it "life review," which he sees as a task of age in itself, not just as a legacy for one's grandchildren.

Studies of grief and mourning show the way meaning *changes* in late life. The ways people make meaning out of their lives and the changed understanding of their lives become clear in longitudinal studies of different generations and cohorts. I've been struck by that myself—how one's religious, psychoanalytic, or feminist paradigm changes the very sense of the meaning of one's life. But the categories of meaning into which we organize our experience can no longer come from stories, theories, or beliefs based only on youth.

The Judeo-Christian religions are belatedly coming to this task. Ten years ago, all I could find at the Harvard Divinity School of a spiritual model for age were funeral services, doctrines of the afterlife, heaven or hell, and a concept of "the Christian gentleman" that ended before fifty. Feminist theologians were just beginning to struggle for concepts of divinity that did not imply God as he, but the "goddess" was an earth mother, young. A Catholic theologian pointed out to me that Jesus crucified was a *young man.* Of course, Judaism has been blamed for creating God in the image of a white-bearded patriarch, but its monotheism, "the Lord our God, the Lord is One," actually implies no such image at all. The Hindu and Buddhist traditions more clearly proscribe the laying down of administrative details, power games, and domestic concerns in age in order to embark on a spiritual journey into the meaning of life.

But it is worth noting here that whether the metaphor is psychological or theological, rooted in old tradition or New Age search, there is a sense that the mystery and the meaning of life is one's ultimate quest—to be achieved somehow by a wholeness, an integration of the self, a naming and atonement of sin, an accounting of the use of one's talents, and some achievement of "amazing grace" that does not imply religiosity or stained glass.

Rabbi Zalmon Schacter-Shalomi, founder of B'nai Or Religious Fellowship in Philadelphia, has been developing programs for "Healthy Spiritual Eldering" based on Jewish tradition. He claims his map is "derived from the tradition of Jewish mysticism." At a retreat where some of us helped him work out these techniques, he told us:

The God I'm talking about is neither the Old Man with the flowing white beard nor the Great Mother giving birth to the universe. . . . In this instance, I mean God as the Verb energizing the universe, God as the Source of all movement. . . . We place ourselves before God and open ourselves to the Godding—fully disclose our tears and laughter; weaknesses and strengths, certainties and doubts, the parts of ourselves we love and the parts we despise, our prides and shames.

In doing this, we open ourselves to the world, to our fellow humans. We take down the barriers, drop our masks, and join with the rest of creation in the unending effort to live the good life. . . . The value you get from talking to God is in the conscious, intentional act of presenting yourself—thoughts, feelings and all. It is standing naked before that Presence, and saying, "HERE I AM! THIS IS ME! THIS IS HOW I AM." [6]

This stress on "spiritual empowerment" distinguishes such programs from orthodox church or synagogue "ministries" to the aging, with their "care" visits to nursing homes and their acceptance of the age mystique of passivity and stagnation. Though they adapt rituals from the Jewish or Christian traditions, they also use "experiential process and meditations facilitating individual inner work in the spiritual realm" to arrive at the integration and affirmation of the total self, which they consider the path of God.

On the "path," another New Age direction I explored, techniques of group therapy and encounter and "guided meditation" were used to elucidate your own naming: taking off the "mask" to confront the denied dark side, your "lower self," enabled you to recognize and strengthen your "higher self," and to put them both together in a wholeness and simplicity and new energy not possible when the lower self was denied. It occurred to me such exercises could be a useful part of elder counseling, without any implications of pathology.

At a desert retreat center, a house of prayer near Tucson, Arizona, a Dominican nun had "facilitated" that "inner journey to myself." She recounted her own lifelong struggle to name herself: "I am a lesbian nun. If I had a choice, I would be exactly who I am." She told of the long years when she had no close friends at all.

Friendship was connected to an evil inclination in me. That evil must be kept locked up. If it escaped, if I let it surface, I'd be sent away.

After final profession, I did graduate work in pastoral theology. The rug was pulled from beneath me when I realized that one cannot love God if one cannot love another person. . . . My strict guard fell, and I let my feelings for another sister surface. . . .

But guilt paralyzed me, and within three months I was unable to get out of bed to teach . . . I requested help and was sent to a psychiatrist, who medicated me with eight Valium a day. After four years of his prescription, I began to dislike the zombie effect and dropped both the Valium and the psychiatrist. . . .

I became a workaholic in order to suppress my feelings. My superiors appreciated all the work I produced; but I was a robot, an efficient machine with no warmth, no sensitivity to the needs of others, and no will to live. Then two years ago, I requested from my superiors an extended retreat time . . . I went to a desert house of prayer. There, with the help of a skilled facilitator, intense prayer, a woman I came to love, and a series of transformative dreams, I finally named and then claimed who I am. . . .[7]

She told how four "dream journeys" when she was approaching sixty had pushed her to "confront the fear of some unknown, to face the parts of myself that were terrifying me." She had dreamed of a thief trying to break in her door, of a pond filled with debris, an immense whale emerging from the water, opening its cavernous mouth, and sucking up the debris. In a terrifying final dream sequence, she climbed down the sides of a great black spiral hole, declined offers of a ride out, and when she could climb no farther, leaped into the hole and fell, banging the sides, being bounced back and forth.

I have let go of everything. I realized that what I was so terrified of was claiming my lesbian identity. . . . I began coming out to selected members of my community. In both my dream life and my waking life, I am taking risks I never could have dreamed of before. I am daring to be myself! . . .

I am overflowing with joy. I have faced my worst fears, descended into the depths of my nightmares, and emerged with my Self, alive and whole. My waking life and my dream life have let me know that I can no longer separate my spirituality from my sexuality. I cannot trust God while being terrified of my self. God has called me to be who I am . . . To deny the lesbian in me is to live in the fear of the mouth, the thief, my own face and own voice, the spiraling hole of my unconscious, and the ocean of my being.[8]

Gerontologists, like poets, grope for metaphors to guide men and women now in their sixties, seventies, eighties to find meaning in their own lives and sense where it is leading. B. J. Hately and Jim Birren, in the course on Guided Autobiography they taught at the Andrus Institute of Gerontology, used various metaphors of self. "Describe your life as a branching tree," they encouraged. "What kind of tree is it? How does it grow and branch?" Participants sometimes substituted their own metaphors. "My life is a river fed by many tributaries, meandering in different directions, at various points deep and quiet, sometimes crashing over rapids," commented one man, at a workshop Hately gave in Boston, which I attended.[9]

The guided autobiography approach was not a personal narrative in which one began at the beginning, "I was born in Nebraska," and proceeded through all one's life details to the present. Like the Jungian journal, it sought to reorganize this life material with questions from the participants that unlocked important events and feelings, allowing people to reintegrate their past at a higher level. Older people who came to these sessions were often letting go of previous relationships, roles, friends, values, and homes, Hately said. "Through guided autobiography, life review, many are able to accomplish their letting go, and then turn to embrace the future."

Robert Butler has claimed "the universal occurrence in older people of an inner experience or mental process of reviewing one's life." Yet this mysterious internal drive, perhaps propelled by one's no longer to be denied awareness of the imminence of death, almost insists on a new or more intense meaning to one's life in age, some new direction leading into the future, but to be acted upon in one's community now. As Victor Frankl, the great existential psychologist, put it:

Only under the threat and pressure of death does it make sense to do what we can and should, right now. That is, to make proper use of the moment's offer of a meaning to fulfill—be it a deed to do, or work to create, anything to enjoy, or a period of inescapable suffering to go through with courage and dignity. . . . Live as if you were living for the second time—and as if you had acted the first time as wrongly as you are about to act now. Once an individual really puts himself into this imagined situation, he will instantaneously become conscious of the full gravity of the responsibility that every person bears throughout every moment of his life—the responsibility for what he will make of the next hour, for how he will shape the next day. . . .

The one big question, Frankl said, "facing the transitoriness of human existence—how is it possible to say yes to life in spite of death?"[10]

Life review, whether it is accomplished alone or with the help of others, is a way to say yes to our lives, and can lead us to "integrity" of self, but not, I think, to "generativity," new roles for older people in society. That will take a lot of us saying no to the age mystique and demanding a continuation of our human birthright—to move in the new years of life as full persons in society, using our unique human capabilities as they have evolved through years of work and love, and our new capacities for wisdom, helping society transcend decline and move in new life-affirming directions. That, in turn, given the way our society is now, will require creating new social structures and political policies. One thing is certain. We cannot even begin to help create the new patterns that are needed if we are barred in age from participating in the institutions that carry society forward. It is only now that women are reaching critical mass in every field and institution that we can even glimpse the possibilities of style and structure, policy and practice, previously unnamed problems and new solutions for society itself that were hidden when the very rubrics were defined solely in terms of male experience. The "different voice" of women is only now beginning to be heard in new political and economic, psychological and theological terms, transforming the male model, in theory and in practice, in medicine and law, university and business, and every church and academic discipline. And it is only now that the *empowerment of women* can be seen in its evolutionary significance—as solution, not just problem, in the crises of family and church, economy and government, threatening the very fabric of our society.

For these same reasons, we must seek the *empowerment of age,* new roles for people over sixty, seventy, eighty in work and business, public and private sectors, church, synagogue, and the volunteer cutting edge of the community, which use their wisdom to help solve the problems of our whole aging society. But I do not think we can seek the empowerment of age on the same terms as the women's movement, or the black civil rights movement, or the labor movement, or the revolutions against oppressions of the past. There is a danger in seeing age as a "special interest group," even though it has already become clear how much power it might mobilize.

The American Association of Retired Persons, with its 33 million members, 1,000-plus employees in its Washington, D.C., headquarters, and 10 regional offices across the country is a powerful political force, though Horace Deets, its executive director, assured me its power is "vastly exaggerated." It can get "information out in a hurry," provide all kinds of services—from insurance supplements to Medicare to organizing volunteers to give free personal income tax preparation to older low- and middle-income taxpayers. It organizes cruises, monitors use of hearing aids, gives out nursing home information, and is even now asking its members to get involved in local coalitions, "to be catalysts for helping those older Americans who want to stay in their own homes or within their communities" by expanding eldercare options in their own communities.

AARP disseminates information and research on age widely. But its focus is mainly on improving "care" for the elderly, not on mobilizing the political power of people over sixty to demand new roles in society, or to change the political priorities of the nation. Of course, its *assumed* power is continually evoked, to defend Social Security and demand cost-of-living increases, to protect Medicare and Medicaid and protest cuts, and in support of the Older Americans Act, even though, in the recent years of economic recession, the exploding claims of age discrimination have hardly been enforced. But the leaders of AARP do not seem to see it as their mission to confront the larger social and economic questions in terms of *radical* change. And the debacle of the catastrophic health care insurance bill they supported seemed to increase public resentment of the "greedy geezers" as another potential scapegoat for the growing economic frustration of middle-class Americans and the working poor, white and black.

Deets told me that in the Reagan years, he could hardly get in to see anyone in the White House. Trickle-down Reaganomics and "deregulation" *repudiating* government responsibility for the problems of any and all people—women, children, the poor, students, the homeless, the elderly—discontinuing public programs of child care, housing and health care and aids to education, making social welfare and civil rights, liberalism and feminism dirty words, was the polar opposite of "generativity" and ushered in an era of clear "stagnation" for this aging nation. President Bush, preoccupied with foreign policy, failed to notice, let alone address, the problems of a nation falling into even deeper decline. He twice postponed the White House Conference on Aging, which had been called for 1991.

In the 1992 presidential campaign, Deets told me AARP asked both Bush and Bill Clinton what they were going to do about health care, the budget deficit, Social Security, age discrimination, and educational and employment opportunities for people at all ages. But it made no political endorsements. Deets said:

We don't have a Political Action Committee. We don't either endorse or target candidates for support or defeat. About 40 percent of our members are Republicans and 40 percent Democrats and the rest are independent. Health care is our number-one priority. But health care has become a political football. And if you bring out the statistics—the fact that even if only 12.5 percent of people over sixty-five are living in poverty compared to 35 percent thirty years ago, 25 percent of single women over sixty-five are living alone in poverty, and 45 percent of minority older people, or the fact that older people are still paying as much for health care as before Medicare because it doesn't pay for long-term care, nursing home care, home health care, or prescription drugs—you only reinforce that image of "poor" older people as sick and infirm, instead of a resource of talent and ability. And we fence ourselves off and isolate ourselves.

Deets told me he believes that older people need to "empower themselves in their own communities"—to get "out of the fence business, into the bridge-building business," and find ways to work together with other groups "to change a lot of society's problems." He was proud of the fact that AARP joined forces with the Children's Defense Fund, protesting the cuts in prenatal and child health services as well as Medicare. But the 1992 AARP vision statement "Toward a Just and Caring Society" dealt primarily with "service" and "care" of older people behind that fence, with a commitment to protection of the environment "for future generations."

I have been enormously impressed by the *possibilities* of AARP, on the issues it does, safely, address, and its power to market to and inform that huge and growing population of older Americans, to help bring about the paradigm shift necessary to break through the age mystique. It stated in 1992 that "more appropriate housing for disabled older persons can enable them to live at home rather than move to an institutional setting." But I am not sure that any model for age as a special interest group comprises the needed political paradigm shift: a new movement that will use the wisdom and resources of older women and men, who by the year 2000 will be the dominant population group of our aging society, not so much for protection of their own Social Security and health care, but to set new priorities of evolving life, and new measures of bottom-line success, in business and the national budget, new integrations of work and love, new policies and structures to meet the needs of all members of all families to grow and to care for each other—and new visions of generativity for our stagnant society.

The Gray Panthers pointed the way. At the first White House Conference on Aging in 1971, they drew attention to the fact that there were no African-Americans represented by organizing a "Black House Conference" just ahead of the official one. Then they got together with Ralph Nader to expose the hearing aid scam. The next year, they organized a national coalition on "Health Care as a Human Right" and paid a "house call" on the AMA Convention in Chicago, demanding action. They set up a National Media Watch task force to monitor constantly for age stereotyping, getting the Television Code of Ethics amended to include "age" along with race and sex. By the end of the 1970s, they were mobilizing people to expose and document nursing home abuse in their own communities. They were surely responsible for enactment of the Age Discrimination Employment Act, raising mandatory retirement from age sixty-five to seventy. They filed and won a federal lawsuit to get "gobbledygook" out of complicated Medicare forms, speed up the appeals process, and get the Food and Drug Administration to monitor the hearing aid industry for fraud. By 1990, they had achieved an intergenerational amendment to the Older Americans Act that expanded opportunities for older people to nurture and assist children in their community through volunteer programs in senior centers.

Among many items of unfinished business, in addition to achieving a national health care plan, accessible to all, that is equitably and publicly financed, the Gray Panthers are continuing to work for affordable and adequate housing for all, elimination of homelessness, and innovative work concepts that include flexible work/retirement schedules: job sharing, flex-time work, mid-career retraining, and a shorter work week, emphasizing "full involvement of people of all ages." The Gray Panthers now put increasing emphasis on the importance of an intergenerational network and coalition, the awareness that what happens globally and locally—in peace, the environment, housing, health care, and aging itself—has to involve people of all ages, has to be done by and for the *whole community.*

I visited Maggie Kuhn, founder of the Gray

Panthers, in the big, rambling old house on a busy street in Germantown, on the outskirts of Philadelphia, which she had shared for thirty years with a shifting "family" of students and other young people. With the house next door, it also served as away-from-the-Beltway headquarters for the Gray Panthers. Wearing a black bolero vest, soft white silk poet's shirt, and green paisley pants, her hair swept to the side and up in a simple, elegant chignon, she had just celebrated her eighty-seventh birthday in a two-day gathering of housemates, old and new. They gave her a soft, fuzzy stuffed giraffe for her birthday, a token of "the International Giraffe Appreciation Society honoring those who stick their necks out."

Kuhn had organized the Gray Panthers with six other women who were forced to retire at sixty-five. But they did not organize it to fight for older people alone. When they recently cornered the presidential candidates, it was to press for a national health care system to protect everybody, old and young, families and children. Some years ago they stopped fighting to save Medicare, which insures older people separately and inadequately as everybody's health care costs spiral. They had no patience with pseudo-solutions like the "catastrophic" bill or "pay or play," which divide the old from everybody else and divide the middle class and small business owners and workers from the poor. She told me:

The adventure in my case is breaking ground, the opportunity to move in new directions, to envision what could be. I had no idea when six of us organized the Gray Panthers in 1970 to oppose the war in Vietnam that we would become a worldwide network. The issue we took on, at first, was not age but the war in Vietnam. From the beginning we worked with the younger people, we were intergenerative. We called it the Consultation of Older and Younger Adults for Social Change, but after we had a joint meeting with the Black Panthers, the name Gray Panthers stuck.

I was doing a demographic study, and realized the life span in America had almost doubled in this century, and that could be an enormous force for social change. AARP wanted to organize older people just to keep them together, as a lobby on old folks' issues. Our philosophy was using gray power with the young for issues on the cutting edge of social change. I think we've established the fact that old age is a triumph. There's a freedom today —at my age I can speak out, be really radical. I've set myself a goal to say something really outrageous every day, and I've outlived my opposition.

What we've done is establish the intergenerational bond necessary for real social change, the continuity of life. The old and the young need each other. We're opposed to the segregation of older people out of society. Older people have so much to give to society, it's wrong to sell them places just to play, to keep them out of the way. There ought to be a moratorium on building more retirement facilities, Leisure Worlds, nursing homes. Shared housing avoids the need of such institutionalization.

"You also have to have a little fun." She took hold of her cane, and sort of swung herself, in a back-and-forth jig, up from her chair. "I call it the rock of ages." She smiled at me. And I felt those involuntary tears, as when I watched Casals conduct a rehearsal—the wonder that the presence of a fully realized human being evokes in us: the self, generative. I told her that, and hugged her goodbye.

A few days later I went to hear her at the United Nations. It was a twentieth-anniversary celebration of the UN's first consultation on age, held in a basement conference room. I recognized the white heads of many of the women and men I had met in the gerontological underground. Butler, Deets, and the other speakers admitted nothing had really been done in these decades by the governments of the world to face the enormous changes implied by the aging of the whole human society, the millions and millions of people now living those unprecedented new years of life. Governments had been too preoccupied with old nationalist rivalries, racial and religious wars, the brutal competition of the culture of greed, it seemed, even to think about their aging societies. But Maggie Kuhn was more concerned, that afternoon, about the future of the world itself, the decline of vision in and about the United Nations. "We need to bring the young and old together to get the word out about one world," she said. And then, with her "rock of age," she led her audience in the Gray Panther exercise: "Open your eyes wide" to keep watch over what is really happening in the world; "open your mouth" to growl and shout at continued injustice and oppression and wrong direction and blind stagnation; "open your arms" to embrace it all; and "shake your fists" to get results.

The movement that flows from the fountain of age cannot be a special interest group. It would be a violation of our own wisdom and generativity to empower ourselves in age only for our own security and care. It would be a denial of the true power of age. As we find and use that power (and we are beginning to do that), all the energy that has been put into denying age, personally and politically—the face-lifts, the false focus on age as "problem," the warehousing of "them" in Leisure Worlds and retirement homes that profit their promoters and keep us out of sight and participation in society, the "care" that profits its providers and prolongs pain but cannot prevent death—all that energy and generativity can and must be put to work, alongside the young and middle generations, to solve the new problems facing our whole society.

Our empowerment has begun. Even now, in Asheville, North Carolina, Los Angeles, and the Bronx, many supposed retirement enclaves are evolving into subversive pools of new activism, combining play and learning with work, volunteer or paid, by new measures guaranteeing service for themselves when necessary, to meet each other's and the whole community's needs for care. And companies on the cutting edge are meeting their own new problems by calling us back to work out of retirement, or giving us new options that will use our abilities beyond retirement in new tandem with the young. The flexibility, autonomy, and meaning that we now demand of work, the responsibility that we insist on sharing, is what, in the face of unprecedented technological change, industry and professions, public and private sector, now urgently need for their own survival. Such flexibility and shared responsibility and shorter working hours are also urgently needed now by families, two-paycheck or single-parent or three-generational, to put together the work they must do for pay and professional advance along with the work of caring for their own children. The new President of the United States has at last signed into law the family and parental leave act, and promises to innovate new kinds of health care, child care, and job programs, using the abilities of both age and youth in national service to repair the holes in our social fabric, pioneering new models of flexibility and shared responsibility in work and community. The new momentum for social change—bringing together the movements of polarized, often warring, ethnic and religious groups, the blacks and gays and the women's movement, who have concentrated until now on their separate special interests, rights, and oppressions—must transcend the victim state, as the Gray Panthers have done in age and, with unity and integrity, pool their own empowerment to bring about the "change" the entire community now yearns for.

Before he died suddenly at seventy-four, my dear new friend Maury Leibovitz, having retired and moved on from three careers (in finance, psychology, and art), used his wealth to run a national contest, asking older people everywhere to submit, as the "legacies" they would leave their children and grandchildren, the most significant moment or discovery of their own lives. He was going to have me join him in reading the winning "legacies" on television. Over a salad lunch in his office, the last time I saw him, he told me:

The adventure continues and will continue as long as the energy flows, and as one continues being involved in the changing interests of the community, the energy flows from new sources. All this talk about people losing neurons of their brains in age, all that's really about is people closing doors on all the sources of energy that open up with new ideas and hopes and feelings.

I believe the essence of life is change. With every new adventure you change. Without change, the whole organism dies. That's why I'm interested in new things all the time. You have to be open to the new possibilities of living. Our life has to have some meaning. Instead of looking back at the way your childhood messed you up, your mother, your father, or all the things that oppressed you, look back at the significant events and experiences that make you feel you have something yet to give to life, what made and still makes you grow. Accept the pain of the bundle you've been given, and see where you've taken it. Instead of letting it weigh you down, your back all bent over, take it in your hands, look at it, admire and wonder at its meaning, and hand that as a legacy to your grandchildren.

I thought once again about evolution. This new explosion of human age has to have some function in the survival of the whole community, stretching into the future. In evolutionary terms, the function of age has to go beyond reproduction to contribute in some other way to the survival of our species. It has to go beyond our personal future; if we spend our energy in age, or waste it, only in trivialities and play, *killing time,* denying age and death, we forfeit that wisdom and generativity stretching into the future. Our "legacy" has to be more than those memories of meaning we write down for our grandchildren. We cannot prophesy that future. It is only by continuing to work on the problems confronting our society right now with whatever wisdom and generativity we have attained over our own lifetimes that we leave a legacy to our grandchildren, helping to shape that future, expressing and conserving the generativity of the human *community.* We have to live our own age, generatively, as part of the community. In the wisdom of age, my ancestor Hillel said: "If I am not for myself, who will be for me? If I am only for myself, what am I?"

And through our actions, we will create a new image of age—free and joyous, living with pain, saying what we really think and feel at last—knowing who we are, realizing that we know more than we ever knew that we knew, not afraid of what anyone thinks of us anymore, moving with wonder into that unknown future we have helped to shape for the generations coming after us. There will not have to be such dread and denial for them in living their age if we use our own age in new adventures, breaking the old rules and inhibitions, changing the patterns and possibilities of love and work, learning and play, worship and creation, discovery and political responsibility, and resolving the seeming irreconcilable conflicts between them.

I began this quest with my own denial and fear of age. It ends with acceptance, affirmation, and celebration. Somewhere along the way, I recognized, with relief and excitement, my liberation from the power politics of the women's movement. I recognized my own compelling need now to transcend the war between the sexes, the no-win battles of women as a whole sex, oppressed victims, against men as a whole sex, the oppressors. I recognized that my need to reconcile feminism and families comes from my own generativity, my personal truth as mother to my children, and my commitment to the future through the women's movement. The unexpectedness of this new quest has been my adventure into age. I realized that *all* the experiences I have had—as daughter, student, youthful radical, reporter, battler for women's rights, wife, mother, grandmother, teacher, leader, friend, and lover, confronting real and phantom enemies and dangers, the terrors of divorce and my own denial of age—all of it, mistakes, triumphs, battles lost and won, and moments of despair and exaltation, is part of me now: *I am myself at this age.* It took me all these years to put the missing pieces together, to confront my own age in terms of integrity and generativity, moving into the un-known future with a comfort now, instead of being stuck in the past. I have never felt so free.

Notes

CHAPTER ONE

1. Jack Levin and William C. Levin, *Ageism* (Belmont, Calif.: Wadsworth, 1980), p. 111.
2. Ibid.
3. Ibid., p. 115.
4. Ibid.
5. Ibid.
6. See Rena Bartos, "Over 49: The Invisible Consumer Market," *Harvard Business Review,* vol. 58, no. 1 (January–February 1980).
7. Ibid.
8. *Media Decisions,* vol. 12, no. 10 (October 1977).
9. Elissa Melamed, *Mirror, Mirror: The Terror of Not Being Young* (New York: Linden Press, Simon & Schuster, 1983), p. 147.
10. Patricia Morrisoe, "Forever Young," *New York* magazine (June 9, 1986).
11. "How a Man Ages: Good News and Bad About Getting Older," *Esquire* (May 1982).

12. Jane O'Reilly, "A Candle at 50, for Accomplishment," *New York Times,* July 10, 1986.
13. Levin and Levin, op. cit., p. 75.
14. Joy Spaulding, "Old Age in America, Altruistic Suicide?" Paper presented to the Gerontological Society, San Francisco, November 1983.
15. John L. Hess, "Confessions of a Greedy Geezer," *The Nation* (April 2, 1990).
16. "Our Elderly's Fate?" *New York Times,* September 20, 1983.
17. Judy Foreman, "Making Age Obsolete," *Boston Globe,* September 27, 1992.
18. John J. O'Connor, "He's Not Getting Better, He's Only Getting Younger," *New York Times,* July 16, 1991.
19. Elizabeth Mehren, "Women in Films: Age of Anxiety," *New York Times,* June 18, 1991.
20. Bernard Weinraub, "Angela Lansbury Has a Hit, She Wants Respect," *New York Times,* December 1, 1991.
21. Bill Carter, "Networks Turning to Old Reliables," *New York Times,* November 16, 1992.
22. N. R. Kleinfield, "Grace Mirabella, at 59, Starts Over Again," *New York Times,* April 30, 1989.
23. Angela Johnson, "Magazine for Older Readers Looking Robust," *Los Angeles Times,* November 3, 1991.
24. Ken Dychtwald and Joe Flower, *Age Wave: The Challenges and Opportunities of an Aging America* (Los Angeles: Jeremy Tarcher, 1989).
25. "Advertising: Stuart Elliott's Quaker Oats Spotlights Vigorous Elderly," *New York Times,* November 13, 1992.
26. Suzanne Cassidy, "New British Magazine Doesn't Serve Youth," *New York Times,* February 27, 1992.
27. See Arnold Arluke and Jack Levin, "Second Childhood," *Communications Review,* vol. 1, no. 2 (Winter 1982).
28. See Mary Gresham, "The Infantilization of the Elderly," *Nursing Forum,* vol. 15 (1976), pp. 196–209.
29. Ibid.
30. Martha Tyler John, *Teaching and Loving the Elderly* (Springfield, Ill.: Charles C. Thomas, 1983), p. 164.
31. Levin and Levin, op. cit., p. 102.
32. Jerry Jacobs, cited in Levin and Levin, p. 101.

33. Payne, Gibson, and Pittard, 1969, cited in Levin and Levin, p. 108.
34. Ibid.
35. "Getting There Ahead of Time," *Psychology Today* (December 1971).
36. Spaulding, op. cit.
37. Judith Rodin and Ellen Langer, "Aging Labels: The Decline of Control and the Fall of Self-Esteem," *Journal of Social Issues,* vol. 16, no. 2 (1980).
38. "Exposing the Myth of Senility," *New York Times,* December 3, 1978.
39. Muriel Oberleder, *Avoiding the Aging Trap* (Washington, D.C.: Acropolis Books, Ltd., 1982).
40. Vern Bengtson, "Loss and the Social Psychology of Aging," in *Aging Two Thousand: Our Health Care Destiny,* C. M. Gaitz et al., eds. vol. 2 (New York: Springer-Verlag, 1985), pp. 62, 1 f.
41. Levin and Levin, op. cit., p. 100.
42. *Prime Time, By and For Older Women,* vol. 5, no. 5 (1976), p. 13.
43. Rodin and Langer, op. cit.
44. Muriel Oberleder, "Study Shows Mindset About Aging Influences Longevity," *Washington Post,* September 15, 1982.
45. Levin and Levin, op. cit., p. 103.
46. *Prime Time,* op. cit.
47. Levin and Levin, op. cit., p. 104.
48. Jerry Jacobs, *Fun City: An Ethnographic Study of a Retirement Community* (New York: Holt, Rinehart & Winston, 1974), p. 26.
49. Ruth H. Jacobs and Barbara H. Vinick, *Re-engagement in Later Life* (Stamford, Conn.: Greylock, 1977), p. 128.

CHAPTER TWO
1. David Gutmann, *Reclaimed Powers* (New York: Basic Books, 1987), pp. 2, 7.
2. Robert N. Butler and Herbert P. Gleason, eds., *Productive Aging* (New York: Springer-Verlag, 1985), p. 7.
3. John Rowe and Robert Kahn, "Human Aging: Usual and Successful," *Science* (July 1987).

4. *Introduction to the Study of Human Aging* (Rockville, Md.: National Institute of Mental Health, U.S. Department of Health, Education and Welfare, 1971), p. 17.
5. Rowe and Kahn, op. cit.
6. Ibid.
7. Ibid.
8. S. Groneck and R. D. Patterson, *Human Aging II: An Eleven-Year Biomedical and Behavioral Study.* U.S. Public Health Service Monograph (Washington, D.C.: Government Printing Office, 1971; cited hereafter as *Human Aging II*), pp. 59 f.
9. Ibid., p. 122.
10. Ibid., p. 115.
11. Ibid., pp. 61 f.
12. Gisela Labouvie-Vief, "Intelligence and Cognition," in *Handbook of the Psychology of Aging,* J. E. Birren and K. Werner Schaie, eds. (New York: Van Nostrand Reinhold, 1985), pp. 500–30; see also K. Werner Schaie and Gisela Labouvie-Vief, "Generational Versus Ontogenic Components of Change in Adult Cognitive Behavior: A 14-Year Cross-Sectional Study," *Developmental Psychology,* vol. 10 (1974), p. 305.
13. Alvar Svanborg, "Biomedical and Environmental Influences in Aging," Butler and Gleason, eds., op. cit., pp. 16–20.
14. James Birren, "Age, Competence, Creativity and Wisdom," in ibid., p. 33.
15. E. Cumming and W. Henry, *Growing Old* (New York: Basic Books, 1961).
16. Erdman Palmore, *Social Patterns in Normal Aging: Findings from the Duke Longitudinal Study* (Durham, N.C.: Duke University Press, 1981), pp. 47 f.
17. *Human Aging II,* pp. 61 f.
18. Ibid., p. 60.
19. Palmore, op. cit., p. 65.
20. Ibid., pp. 65 ff.
21. *Human Aging II,* p. 95.
22. Ibid., p. 96.
23. Ibid., pp. 101 f.
24. Ibid., p. 114.
25. Ibid., p. 68.

26. Ibid., pp. 73 ff.
27. Ibid., pp. 87 ff.
28. Ibid., pp. 73 f.
29. Ibid., p. 89.
30. Gutmann, op. cit., p. 92.
31. Ibid. See Chapter 4, "From Warriors to Peace Chiefs: Age and the Social Regulation of Male Aggression," and Chapter 9, "Elders as Emeritus Parents."
32. Ellen Langer and Judith Rodin, "The Effects of Choice and Enhanced Personal Responsibility for the Aged: A Field Experiment in an Institutional Setting," *Journal of Personality and Social Psychology,* vol. 34, no. 2 (1976).
33. Ellen Langer and Judith Rodin, "Long Term Effects of a Control-Related Deterioration with the Institutional Aged," *Journal of Personality and Social Psychology,* vol. 35, no. 12 (1977), pp. 897–902.
34. Ellen Langer and Judith Rodin, "Aging Labels: The Decline of Control and the Fall of Self-Esteem," *Journal of Social Issues,* vol. 36, no. 2 (1980), pp. 12–29.
35. Labouvie-Vief, "Intelligence and Cognition," p. 506.
36. See Rowe and Kahn, op. cit.
37. Ibid.
38. Marian Diamond, et al., "Plasticity in the 904 Day Old Male Rat Cerebral Cortex," *Experimental Neurology,* vol. 87 (1985), pp. 309–17.
39. Marian Diamond, "The Changing Brain: Age, Sex and Environment." Address to the Commonwealth Club, San Francisco, August 1986.
40. Ibid.
41. Ibid.
42. J. L. Horn and G. Donaldson, "On the Myth of Intellectual Decline in Adulthood," *American Psychologist,* vol. 31 (1976), pp. 701–9; see also, "Cognitive Development in Adulthood," in *Constancy and Change in Human Development,* O. G. Brim and J. Kagan, eds. (Cambridge, Mass.: Harvard University Press, 1980), pp. 445–529.
43. Labouvie-Vief, "Intelligence and Cognition," p. 503.
44. Schaie and Labouvie-Vief, "Generational Versus Ontogenic Components of Change in Adult Cognitive Behavior," pp. 305–20.
45. Labouvie-Vief, "Intelligence and Cognition," p. 506.

46. J. F. Fries, "Aging, Natural Death, and the Compression of Morbidity," *New England Journal of Medicine,* vol. 303 (1980), pp. 13–135; see also, J. F. Fries and L. M. Crapo, *Vitality and Aging* (San Francisco: Freeman, 1981).
47. Labouvie-Vief, "Intelligence and Cognition," p. 507.
48. Ibid., p. 508
49. J. E. Birren, "Toward an Experimental Psychology of Aging," *American Psychologist,* vol. 25 (1970), pp. 124–35.
50. Labouvie-Vief, "Intelligence and Cognition," p. 512.
51. Ibid., p. 515.
52. Ibid.
53. P. B. Baltes and R. Kliege, "On the Dynamics Between Growth and Decline in the Aging of Intelligence and Memory," in *Neurology,* K. Poech, et al., eds. (Berlin and Heidelberg: Springer-Verlag 1986).
54. Labouvie-Vief, "Intelligence and Cognition," p. 518.
55. Baltes and Kliege, op. cit., p. 8.
56. Ibid., p. 8.
57. Ibid.
58. Ibid.

CHAPTER THREE
1. Paul B. Baltes and Sherry L. Willis, "The Critical Importance of Appropriate Methodology in the Study of Aging." Paper presented at Boyer-Symposium VII, "The Evolution of Old Age Related Changes and Disorders of Brain Functions," Gross Ledder, West Germany, 1978.
2. Gisela Labouvie-Vief and Fredda Blanchard-Fields, "Cognitive Aging and Psychological Growth," *Aging and Society* (Cambridge University Press), vol. 2, part 2 (July 1982), p. 191.
3. Labouvie-Vief, "Intelligence and Cognition," in *Handbook of the Psychology of Aging,* Birren and Schaie, eds., p. 522.
4. Gisela Labouvrie-Vief, David Schell, and Shelly Weaverdyck, *Recall Deficit in the Aged: A Fable Recalled* (Madison: Wisconsin Research and Development Center for Cognitive Learning, University of Wisconsin, 1974).
5. "After Selfishness: Developmental Progressions in Adult

Thought." Paper presented at the annual meeting of the Gerontological Society of America, San Francisco, 1983.

6. Gisela Labouvie-Vief, "Dynamic Development and Mature Autonomy," *Human Development,* vol. 25 (1982), p. 186.
7. Daniel Levinson, *The Seasons of a Man's Life* (New York: Knopf, 1978), p. ix.
8. Ibid., p. x.
9. Ibid., p. 28.
10. Ibid., p. 34.
11. Ibid., p. 213.
12. Roger Gould, *Transformation: Growth and Change in Adult Life* (New York: Simon & Schuster, 1978), p. 310.
13. Ibid., p. 311.
14. George Vaillant, *Adaptation to Life* (Boston: Little, Brown, 1977), p. 226.
15. Ibid., p. 329.
16. See Jane Loevinger, *Ego Development* (San Francisco: Jossey-Bass, 1976), and B. C. Neugarten, *Middle Age and Aging* (Chicago: University of Chicago Press, 1968).
17. See Gisela Labouvie-Vief, "Growth and Aging in Life Span Perspective," *Human Development,* vol. 25 (1982), pp. 38–88.
18. Lissy Jarvik, "Aging of the Brain—How Can We Prevent It?" Paper presented to the Gerontological Society of America, Washington, D.C., November 1987.
19. Margaret Clark, "The Anthropology of Aging." Paper presented to the American Anthropological Association, Denver, 1966.
20. Ibid.
21. Ibid.
22. Bernice Neugarten, "Dynamics of Transition of Middle Age to Old Age," *Journal of Geriatric Psychiatry,* vol. 4, no. 1 (Fall 1970), pp. 71–87.
23. Robert Kastenbaum, "When Aging Begins," *Research on Aging,* vol. 6, no. 1 (March 1984), pp. 105–17.
24. James E. Birren and V. Jayne Renner, "Concepts and Criteria of Mental Health and Aging," *American Journal of Orthopsychiatry,* vol. 51, no. 2 (April 1981).
25. "Erickson, in His Own Old Age, Expands His View of Life,"

New York Times, June 14, 1988; see also Erik and Joan Erikson, *Vital Involvement in Old Age* (New York: W. W. Norton, 1986).

CHAPTER FOUR

1. Alvan Svanborg, "Biomedical and Environmental Influences on Aging," in *Productive Aging,* Butler and Gleason, eds., p. 23.
2. Ibid., p. 22.
3. Lois M. Verbrugge, "Sex Differences in Health Behavior, Morbidity and Mortality." Address at the National Institute of Health Conference on Gender and Longevity, Washington, D.C., September 18, 1987.
4. Lois M. Verbrugge, "Sex Differences in Morbidity and Mortality in the United States." Address to the Population Association of America, Seattle, 1975.
5. Ruth Benedict, "Recognition of Cultural Diversities in the Postwar World," in *An Anthropologist at Work: Writings of Ruth Benedict,* ed. Margaret Mead (Boston: Houghton Mifflin, 1959), p. 446.
6. *Human Aging II,* p. 120.
7. G. Baruch, R. Barnett, and C. Rivers, *Lifeprints: New Patterns of Love and Work for Today's Woman* (New York: New American Library, 1984).
8. Bernice Neugarten, "A New Look at Menopause," *Psychology Today* (December 1967).
9. Bernice Neugarten. "Dynamics of Transition of Middle Age to Old Age," *Journal of Geriatric Psychiatry,* vol. 4, no. 1, (Fall 1970), pp. 82 ff.
10. N. Datan, A. Ontonovsky, and B. Maoz, *A Time to Keep: The Middle Age of Women in Five Israeli Sub-cultures* (Baltimore: Johns Hopkins University Press, 1981). See also Bernice Neugarten and Nancy Datan, "The Middle Years," in *American Handbook of Psychiatry,* vol. 1 (New York: Basic Books, 1974)., chapter 29.
11. Margaret Lock, "Ambiguities of Aging: Japanese Menopause in Culture," *Medicine and Psychiatry,* vol. 10 (1986).
12. See M. F. Lowenthal, N. Thurnbar, and D. Chiriboga, *Four Stages of Life* (San Francisco: Jossey-Bass, 1975).

13. Marjorie Fiske Lowenthal, "Psychological Crises: Now and Then," in Lissy Jarvik, ed., *The 1990's and Beyond* (New York: John Wiley & Sons, 1978), pp. 33–35.
14. Marjorie Fiske Lowenthal, "Psychological Variations Across the Adult Life Course," *The Second Stage,* vol. 15, no. 1 (February 1975).
15. Ibid.
16. Marjorie Fiske and David Chiriboga, *Change and Continuity in Adult Life* (San Francisco: Jossey-Bass, 1990), p. 73.
17. Teresa Brenner and Pauline Ragan, "The Effects of the Empty Nest on the Morale of Mexican-American and White Women." Paper presented to the Gerontological Society, San Francisco, November 1977.
18. Linda Burton and Vern Bengtson, "Black Grandmothers: Issues of Timing and Continuity of Roles," in V. Bengston and J. Robertson, eds., *Grandparenthood* (Beverly Hills: Sage Publications, 1985), pp. 61–77.
19. Stephen Sternheimer, "The Vanishing Babushka: A Roleless Role for Older Soviet Women." Paper presented to the Gerontological Society of America, Boston, November 1982. See also *The Plight of Older Women Caregivers: Report of Brookdale Institute on Aging,* New York: Columbia University, vol. 17, no. 2, (1987).
20. Helena Lopata, "Self-Identity in Marriage and Widowhood," *Sociological Quarterly,* vol. 14, no. 3 (1973), pp. 407–18.
21. Ibid.
22. Ibid.
23. U.S. Department of Commerce, Bureau of the Census, *Marital Status and Living Arrangements.* Current Population Reports, Series P-20, No. 349 (Washington, D.C.: U.S. Government Printing Office, 1979).
24. Margaret Gatz, "Older Women and Mental Health." Address to the Western Psychological Association, Sacramento, California, 1982. See also J. F. Ball. "Widow's Grief," *Omega,* vol. 7 (1977), pp. 307–33, and F. M. Berardo, "Survivorship and Social Isolation: The Case of the Aged Widower," *The Family,* vol. 19 (1970), pp. 11–25.
25. Neugarten, op. cit. (1970).
26. Chrysee Kline, "The Socialization Process of Women: Im-

plications for a Theory of Successful Aging," *The Geron-tologist* (December 1975), pp. 486–92.

27. Ibid.
28. Gatz, op. cit.
29. Lillian Rubin, *Women of a Certain Age* (New York: Harper & Row, 1979), p. 14.
30. Ibid., pp. 39–40.
31. Sandra Levy, "The Adjustment of the Older Woman: Effects of Chronic Ill Health and Attitudes Toward Retirement," *International Journal of Aging and Human Development,* vol. 12, no. 2 (1980–81), pp. 93–110.
32. See Pauline Bart, "Depression in Middle-Aged Women," in V. Gornick and B. K. Moran, eds., *Women in Sexual Society* (New York: Basic Books, 1971).
33. Nancy Datan, "Women of a Certain Age and Beyond." Address to a conference on "Le Vieillissement de la Femme," Paris, June 1977.
34. Myrna Lewis, "Older Women and Health." Testimony at hearings of New York State Assembly Standing Committee on Aging, New York, March 23, 1983.
35. See Gatz, op. cit.
36. See L. Srole and A. K. Fisher, "The Midtown Manhattan Longitudinal Study versus the Mental Paradise Lost Doctrine," *Archives of General Psychiatry,* vol. 37 (1980), pp. 209–21. See also H. J. Dupuy, "Self-Representations of General Psychological Well-Being of American Adults." Paper presented at the annual meeting of the American Public Health Association, Los Angeles, 1978.
37. See Gutmann, *Reclaimed Powers,* op. cit.
38. Cecelia Hurwich, "Vital Women in Their Seventies and Eighties." Thesis presented to Antioch University West, San Francisco, June 1982.
39. Ibid.

CHAPTER FIVE
1. See Nancy Chodorow, *The Reproduction of Mothering* (Berkeley: University of California Press, 1978).
2. Jeanne Block, "Reconceptualizing Some Psychological Constructs in View of Recent Research on Sex Roles." The Bernard Moses Memorial Lecture, presented at the University of California, Berkeley, January 1972.

3. Ibid.
4. See J. Loevinger, *The Meaning and Measure of Ego Development* (San Francisco: Jossey-Bass, 1976).
5. Cited in Jeanne Block, "Conceptions of Sex Role," *American Psychologist,* vol. 28, no. 6 (June 1973), pp. 512–26.
6. Florine Livson, "Changing Sex Roles in the Social Environment of Later Life," in Graham Rowles and Russel Ohta, eds., *Aging and Milieu: Environmental Perspectives on Growing Old* (New York: Academic Press, 1983), p. 140.
7. Marjorie Fiske, "Tasks and Crises of the Second Half of Life: The Interrelationship of Commitment, Coping, and Adaptation," in *Handbook of Mental Health and Aging,* James Birren, ed. (Englewood Cliffs, N.J.: Prentice-Hall, 1980), pp. 337–373.
8. J. Cole and D. Gutmann, "The Late Life of Druze Women: ATAT Investigation," *Totus Homo* (Milan), vol. 7 (1976).
9. David L. Gutmann, "Alternative to Disengagement: The Old Man of the Highland Druze," in *Late Life: The Social Psychology of Aging,* F. Gubrium, ed. (Springfield, Ill.: Charles Scribner, 1974), p. 285.
10. David Gutmann, "The Cross-Cultural Perspective: Notes Toward a Comparative Psychology of Aging," in *Handbook of the Psychology of Aging,* Birren and Schaie, eds. (New York: Van Nostrand Reinhold, 1985), p. 305.
11. Research by Lipman (1962), Giambra (1973), De Grazia (1961), Lorold (1962), Wolff (1959), Meerloo (1955), Zinberg and Kaufmen (1963), and Berzin (1963) reviewed in Gutmann, ibid.
12. Ibid., p. 311.
13. Vern L. Bengtson, *The Social Psychology of Aging* (Indianapolis and New York: Bobbs-Merrill, 1973), p. 18.
14. Ibid., p. 28.
15. Carolyn G. Heilbrun, *Writing a Woman's Life* (New York: W. W. Norton, 1988), p. 101.
16. Norman Zinberg, "Changing Sex Stereotypes: Some Problems of Women and Men," in *The Woman Patient,* M. Notman and C. Nadelson, eds. (New York: Plenum Books, 1982), p. 73.
17. Norman Zinberg, "Social Learning and Self-Image in Aging," *Journal of Geriatric Psychiatry,* vol. 9 (1976).

18. Ibid.
19. Austen Ettinger, "The Retiring Kind," *New York Times,* May 28, 1989.

CHAPTER SIX

1. See J. F. Fries, "Aging, Natural Death and the Compression of Morbidity," *New England Journal of Medicine,* vol. 303 (July 1980), pp. 130–35.
2. Pauline Ragan, "Socialization for the Retirement Role: Cooling the Mark Out." Paper presented to the American Psychological Association, San Francisco, August 26, 1977.
3. Mortimer Herbert Appley, "The Professional Retiree." Paper presented at a conference on the Changing Patterns and Prospects of Aging and Retirement, Georgetown University, Washington, D.C., September 20, 1985.
4. Ragan, op. cit.
5. Erving Goffman, "On Cooling the Mark Out: Some Aspects of Adaptation to Failure," in *Human Behavior and Social Processes,* A. M. Rose, ed. (Boston: Houghton Mifflin, 1962), p. 496.
6. "No Early Retirement for Louvinia Smith," *Prime Time,* vol. 3, no. 4 (September 1975).
7. Gerda Fillenbaum and George L. Maddox, "Work After Retirement," *The Gerontologist,* vol. 14, no. 5 (October 1974), pp. 418–24.
8. Majda Thurnher, "Goals, Values and Life Evaluations at the Preretirement Stage," *Journal of Gerontology,* vol. 29, no. 1 (1974), pp. 89 f.
9. Ibid.
10. See Meredith Menkler, "Research on the Health Effects of Retirement: An Uncertain Legacy," *Journal of Health and Social Behavior,* vol. 22 (1981), pp. 117–30.
11. Ibid.
12. Ibid.
13. Ibid.
14. Menkler, op. cit., p. 125.
15. "Research Begins to Focus on Suicide Among the Aged," *New York Times,* January 2, 1979.
16. "Managing the Aging Work Force," in *Newsletter: Human*

Resources Management, ASPA/CCH Survey (Chicago: Commerce Clearing House, June 28, 1988).

17. Benson Rosen and Thomas Jerdee, "Managing Older Workers' Careers," *Research in Personnel and Human Resources Management* (JAI Press), vol. 6 (1988), pp. 37–74.
18. Ibid., p. 44.
19. Ibid., p. 47.
20. Ibid., p. 50.
21. Benson Rosen and Thomas Jerdee, "Investing in the Older Worker," *Personnel Administrator* (April 1989).
22. Ibid., p. 47.
23. Ibid., p. 50.
24. Ibid.
25. R. Kalish, "The New Agism and the Failure Models: A Polemic," *The Gerontologist,* vol. 19 (1979), pp. 398–402.
26. Elias S. Cohen, "The Elderly Mystique: Constraints on the Autonomy of the Elderly with Disabilities," *The Gerontologist,* vol. 28 (1988).
27. Rosen and Jerdee, op. cit. (1989), pp. 70–74.
28. Thomas Blank, Diane Hyland, et al., "Retirement: Timing, Initiation and Satisfaction," *Proceedings of the Gerontological Society of America,* Washington, D.C. (November 19, 1987).
29. "Poll Shows Most People Over 65 See Themselves as Resilient Survivors," *Wall Street Journal,* February 17, 1983.
30. Ibid.
31. Ellen Langer, et al., "Nonsequential Development and Agency," in *Higher Stages of Human Development,* Charles Alexander and Ellen Langer, eds. (New York: Oxford University Press, 1987), p. 117.

CHAPTER SEVEN

1. Ron Halpern, *Quiet Desperation: The Truth About Successful Men* (New York: Warner Books, 1988).
2. Ibid., p. 114.
3. Ann Howard and Douglas Bray, "Career Motivation in Mid-Life Managers." Paper presented to the American Psychological Association Convention, Montreal, September 1980.

4. Ann Howard and Douglas Bray. "Today's Young Managers: They Can Do It, But Will They?," *The Wheaton Magazine* (University of Pennsylvania, 1981).

5. Howard and Bray, op. cit. (1980).

6. Howard and Bray, op. cit. (1981).

7. Ibid.

8. See also Lowenthal, "Toward a Sociopsychological Theory of Change in Adulthood and Old Age," in *Handbook of the Psychology of Aging,* Birren and Schaie, eds., op. cit.

9. David W. Brown, "Professional Virtue, a Dangerous Kind of Humbug," *Change, the Magazine of Higher Learning* (Washington, D.C., November 1985).

10. Mary Catherine Bateson, *Composing a Life* (New York: Printing Press, 1989), p. 616.

CHAPTER EIGHT

1. Robert N. Butler and Myrna L. Lewis, *Love and Sex After 60,* rev. ed. (New York: Harper & Row, 1988), pp. 1–7.

2. Martin A. Berezin, "Sex and Old Age: A Review of the Literature," *Journal of Geriatric Psychiatry,* vol. 2, no. 2 (1969), p. 132.

3. Alex Comfort, *A Good Age* (New York: Simon & Schuster, 1978), p. 197.

4. Ibid.

5. Berezin, op. cit., p. 147.

6. Ruth B. Weg, "Sexuality in Aging," in *Principles and Practice of Geriatric Medicine,* M. S. J. Pathy, ed. (New York: John Wiley and Sons, 1985), p. 134.

7. D. Renshaw, "Sex and Older Women," *Medical Aspects of Human Sexuality,* vol. 16, no. 1 (1984), pp. 132–39.

8. Weg, op. cit, p. 137.

9. E. Maccoby and C. Jacklin, *The Psychology of Sex Differences* (Stanford, Calif: Stanford University Press, 1974).

10. Ruth B. Weg. "Intimacy and the Later Years," in *Handbook of Applied Gerontology,* Gari Lesnoff-Caravaglia, ed. (New York: Human Sciences Press, 1987), p. 135.

11. Weg, op. cit. (1985).

12. Nan Corby and Robert E. Solnick, "Psychosocial and Psychologic Influence on Sexuality in the Older Adult," in

Sexuality in the Later Years, Ruth Weg, ed. (New York: Academic Press, 1983), pp. 896 ff.

13. Comfort, op. cit., p. 201.
14. Pauline Robinson, "The Sociological Perspective," in *Sexuality in the Later Years,* Ruth Weg, ed. (Academic Press, 1983).
15. Jane Porceno, "Growing Older Female: With Love, Sex and Intimacy," *Generations* (Fall 1981).
16. T. C. Oden, "Intimacy: A Definition," in *Sexuality: A Contemporary Perspective,* E. S. Morman and V. Borosage, eds. (2nd ed. Palo Alto, Calif.: Mayfield, 1977), p. 468.
17. Marjorie Fiske Lowenthal and Laurence Weiss, "Intimacy and Crises in Adulthood," *The Counseling Psychologist,* vol. 6, no. 1 (1976).
18. This and the quotations that follow are taken from Evelyn K. Sofka, "Intimacy and the Later Years." Unpublished paper, May 1, 1990.
19. Noel Perrin, "Middle-Age Dating," *New York Times Magazine,* July 6, 1986.
20. Majda Thurber, "Becoming Old: Perspectives on Women and Marriage." Address to the American Psychological Association, San Francisco, August 1977.
21. Robinson, op. cit., p. 96.
22. Ruth Weg, *Sensuality/Sexuality in the Middle Years* (Academic Press, 1983), pp. 35 ff.
23. A. John Fox, Lak Bulusu, and Leo Kinlen, "Mortality and Age Differences in Marriage," *Journal of Biosocial Science,* vol. 2, no. 2 (April 1979).
24. Berezin, op. cit., and V. Kassell, "Polygamy After 60," *Generations,* vol. 14 (1990).

CHAPTER ELEVEN
1. Graham D. Rawles, "A Place to Call Home," in *Handbook of Clinical Gerontology,* Laura L. Carsteusen and Barry A. Edelstein, eds. (New York: Pergamon Press, 1987), p. 335.
2. Ibid., p. 336.
3. Ibid., pp. 337 f.
4. Ibid., pp. 339–40.

CHAPTER TWELVE

1. Martin Berezin, "Isolation in the Aged," *Journal of Geriatric Psychology,* vol. 12, no. 1 (1980).

2. Kent A. McClelland, "Self-Conception and Life Satisfaction: Integrating Aged Subculture and Activity Theory," *Journal of Gerontology,* vol. 37, no. 6 (1982), pp. 723–32.

3. Charles F. Longbro and Cary S. Karl, "Explicating Activity Theory: A Formal Replication," *Journal of Gerontology,* vol. 37, no. 6 (1982), pp. 713–22.

4. B. W. Lemon, V. L. Bengtson, and J. A. Peterson, "An Exploration of the Activity Theory of Aging: Activity Types and Life Satisfaction Among In-Movers to a Retirement Community," *Journal of Gerontology,* vol. 27, no. 4 (1972), pp. 511–23.

5. Quoted in Judy Foreman, "Friends: As Vital as Family," *Boston Globe,* February 3, 1982.

6. Morton A. Lieberman, "Institutionalization of the Aged: Effects on Behavior," *Journal of Gerontology,* vol. 24, no. 3 (1969).

7. Ibid., p. 335.

8. The extracts that follow are taken from Arlie Hochschild, *The Unexpected Community* (Englewood Cliffs, N.J.: Prentice-Hall, 1973), pp. 38 ff.

9. Charlotte Muller, "Shared Housing for the Elderly," in *Health Care of the Elderly,* Marilyn Petersen and Diana L. White, eds. (Newberry Park: Sage Publications, 1989), pp. 329–81.

10. Elaine M. Brody, et al., "Intermediate Housing for the Elderly: Satisfaction of Those Who Moved and Those Who Did Not," *The Gerontologist* (August 1975), pp. 350–56.

CHAPTER THIRTEEN

1. These quotations, and the ones that follow, are taken from Mark E. Williams and Martin M. Hadler, "The Illness as the Focus of Geriatric Medicine," *New England Journal of Medicine,* vol. 308 (June 2, 1983), pp. 1357–60.

2. Mark E. Williams, "Clinical Implications of Aging Physiology," *The American Journal of Medicine,* vol. 76 (June 1984), pp. 1049–51.

3. Ibid.

4. Mark Williams, "Why Screen for Functional Disability in Elderly Persons?," *Annals of Internal Medicine,* vol. 112, no. 9 (May 1990).

5. Mark Williams and Nancy Connolly, "What Practicing Physicians in North Carolina Rate as Their Most Challenging Geriatric Medicine Concerns," *Journal of American Geriatric Society,* vol. 38, no. 11 (1990), pp. 1230–34.

6. *The Second Fifty Years: Promoting Health and Preventing Disability,* Robert L. Berg and Joseph S. Coosells, eds. (Washington, D.C.: National Academy Press, 1990), p. 3.

7. Ibid., p. 35.

8. Ibid., p. 44.

9. Ibid., p. 202.

10. Ibid., p. 212.

11. Ibid., p. 211.

12. Ibid.

13. *New York Times,* August 13, 1985.

14. Ibid.

15. See "Solitude Can Be Hazardous to Health, Research Finds," *Los Angeles Times,* January 22, 1992.

16. See "Debate Intensifies on Attitude and Health," *New York Times,* October 29, 1985.

17. Henry Dreher, "The Healthy Elderly and Long-Term Survivors of AIDS: Psychoimmune Connections, a Conversation with George Solomon, M.D.," *Advances,* Institute for Advancement of Health, vol. 5, no. 1.

CHAPTER FOURTEEN

1. David Gutmann, "Beyond Nurture: Developmental Perspectives on the Vital Older Woman." Paper presented at the Conference on the Unconscious in Later Life, Northwestern Medical School, Chicago, October 8, 1983.

2. Ibid.

3. Ibid.

4. H. Peter Hildebrand, "Psychotherapy with Older Patients." Paper presented at the Conference on the Unconscious in Later Life, Northwestern Medical School, Chicago, October 8, 1983.

5. Ibid.

6. David Gutmann, et al., "Developmental Contributions to

the Late-Onset Affective Disorders." Paper presented at the Conference on the Unconscious in Later Life, Northwestern Medical School, Chicago, October 8, 1983.

7. Thomas Jones and Mark Williams, M.D., "Rethinking the Approach to Evaluating Mental Functioning of Older Persons," *Journal of the American Geriatric Society,* vol. 36, no. 12 (1988).

8. Ibid., p. 249.

9. Gutmann, et al., op. cit.

10. Bruce Baker and Jane Wheelwright, "Analysis with the Aged," in *Jungian Analysis,* Murray Stein, ed. (La Salle, Ill.: Open Court, 1983), pp. 257–58.

11. Ibid., p. 258.

12. Ibid., pp. 258–59

13. Ibid., pp. 259–60.

14. Ibid., pp. 261–62.

15. Ibid., pp. 265–66.

16. Ibid., p. 266

17. Ibid., p. 268.

18. Quoted in ibid., p. 270.

19. Ibid.

20. Ibid., pp. 272 f.

21. Ibid., p. 273.

22. See C. G. Jung, *The Stages of Life. Collected Works,* vol. 8 (Princeton, N.J.: Princeton University Press, 1969).

23. Baker and Wheelwright, op. cit., p. 274.

CHAPTER FIFTEEN

1. Kathleen I. MacPherson, *Menopause as Disease: The Social Construction of a Metaphor* (Rockville, Md.: Aspen Systems Corporation, 1991).

2. Thomas M. Mock, et al., "Estrogens and Endometrial Cancer in a Retirement Community," *New England Journal of Medicine,* vol. 294 (June 1976), pp. 1262–67.

3. Ronald K. Ross, et al., "A Case-Control Study of Menopausal Estrogen Therapy and Breast Cancer," *Journal of the American Medical Association,* vol. 243 (April 25, 1980).

4. "Personal Health," *New York Times,* October 12, 1989.

5. Robin Mrorority Henig, "Estrogen Roller Coaster," *AARP Bulletin* (February 1990).

6. Ibid.
7. "Estrogen's Benefits Exceed Cancer Risk, Scientists Say," *New York Times*, January 5, 1991.
8. *Los Angeles Times*, April 30, 1992.
9. Jane E. Brody, "Migraine Headaches and the Estrogen Connection," *New York Times*, January 8, 1992.
10. "Pros and Cons of Hormone Therapy for Menopause," *New York Times Good Health Magazine*, April 26, 1992.
11. "Menopause," *Newsweek* (May 25, 1992).
12. "Can Drugs 'Treat' Menopause? Amid Doubt, Women Must Decide," *New York Times*, May 19, 1992.
13. Ibid.
14. Quoted in Barbara Ehrenreich, "All About the Raging Hormone Express," *New York Times Book Review*, June 7, 1992, p. 7.
15. *New York Times*, May 20, 1992.
16. *Newsweek*, May 25, 1992.
17. *NABCO News*, vol. 5, no. 3 (July 1991).
18. MacPherson, op. cit.
19. Kathleen I. MacPherson, "Flaw in Women or in Science?," *Health Values*, vol. 2, no. 4 (July–August 1987).
20. Ibid.
21. John Z. Ayanian and Arnold M. Epstein, "Differences in the Use of Procedures Between Women and Men Hospitalized for Coronary Heart Disease," *New England Journal of Medicine*, vol. 325, no. 4 (July 25, 1991).

CHAPTER SIXTEEN
1. "Granny Dumping: New Pain for U.S. Elders," *AARP Bulletin* (September 1991).
2. Martin Tolchin, "Older Americans Faced with Higher Premiums and Surtax for Expanded Medicare Coverage," *New York Times*, August 30, 1989.
3. John L. Hess, "Confessions of a Greedy Geezer," *The Nation* (April 2, 1990).
4. See John L. Hess. "Social Security Woes: Confessions of a Greedy Geezer," *The Nation* (May 21, 1990).
5. "National Medical Enterprises Stock Plunges on Word of Racketeering Lawsuit," *New York Times*, July 31, 1992.
6. "Money and Medicare, the New Math. As Costs Expand, Patients Find Their Freedom of Choice Shrinking," *Wash-

ington Post, national weekly edition, September 30, 1991.

7. "Abuse of the Elderly Rises Dramatically," *Los Angeles Times*, May 1, 1990.

8. *Discharges from Nursing Homes: 1985 National Nursing Home Survey*, National Center for Health Statistics, Hyattsville, Md., March 1990.

9. Peter Kemper and Christopher Murtough, "Lifetime Use of Nursing Home Care," *The New England Journal of Medicine*, February 26, 1991.

10. Bruce Vladeck, *Unloving Care: The Nursing Home Tragedy* (New York: Basic Books, 1980), pp. 14 ff.

11. Ibid., p. 266.

12. Ibid., p. 209.

13. "America's Neglected Elderly," *New York Times*, January 30, 1983.

14. Ibid.

15. "Care of the Elderly: Hard Choices . . .," *New York Times*, March 27, 1990.

16. Ibid.

17. "State Flunks Care Facility in Downey," *Los Angeles Times*, March 14, 1992.

18. "Tips to Avoid Guilt in Putting Mom or Dad or Whoever into a Nursing Home," *Los Angeles Times*, January 26, 1992.

19. Carter Catlett Williams, at symposium on "The Future of Long Term Care," sponsored by the Benedictine Nursing Center, Mount Angel, Oregon, November 6, 1987.

20. Tamara Lewin, "Neglect at Nursing Home: In a First, Suits Are Won," *New York Times*, July 12, 1990.

21. Felicity Barringer, "Disability Rates of Elderly Drop; Study Finds Challenging Theory," *New York Times*, April 7, 1993.

22. *New York Times*, August 15, 1987.

23. The quotations that follow are taken from Elias S. Cohen, "The Elderly Mystique: Constraints on the Autonomy of the Elderly with Disabilities," *The Gerontologist*, vol. 28, Supplement, (1988).

24. "Array of Programs Helping Homebound Elderly to Avoid Nursing Homes," *New York Times*, November 24, 1989.

25. The quotations that follow are taken from Carter Catlett Williams, "The Experience of Long Term Care in the Future." Paper presented at the international symposium on "The Future of Long Term Care," sponsored by the Benedictine Nursing Center, Mount Angel, Oregon, November 6, 1987. *Journal of Gerontologic Social Work* (Winter 1989).
26. "Older Americans: New Programs Seek to Care for the Aging in Their Own Homes," *Wall Street Journal*, March 8, 1983.
27. Ibid.
28. "Array of Programs Helping Homebound Elderly . . .," *New York Times*, November 24, 1989.
29. Alexis J. Walker and Clara C. Pratt, "Daughters' Help to Mothers: Intergenerational Aid Versus Caregiving," *Journal of Marriage and Family,* vol. 53 (Feburary 1991), pp. 3–12. See also "Perceptions of Relationship Change and Caregiver Satisfaction," *Family Relations,* vol. 39 (1990), pp. 147–52, and "Perceived Reciprocity in Family Caregiving," *Family Relations,* vol. 41 (1992).

CHAPTER SEVENTEEN

1. Amitai Etzioni, "Spare the Old, Save the Young," *The Nation* (June 11, 1988).
2. Jack M. Guralnik, et al., "Predictors of Healthy Aging," *American Journal of Public Health,* vol. 79, no. 6 (June 1989).
3. Stephen Levine, *Who Dies?,* quoted in *Utne Reader* (September–October 1991).
4. Ibid.
5. John J. Paris, SJ, "Responsibility for Quality Health Care in an Age of Last Containment," *Connecticut Medicine,* vol. 49, no. 2 (February 1985).
6. Ibid.
7. Robert Kuttner, "Sick Joke," *New Republic* (December 2, 1991).
8. Robert Berg, M.D., Testimony Before the LORAN Commission.
9. "Dying May Refuse Food, Court Rules," *New York Times,* September 14, 1990.

10. Peter Steinfels, "Belief," *New York Times,* November 9, 1991.
11. Report of the LORAN Commission to the Harvard Community Health Plan, Boston, June 1988.
12. Martin Tolchin, "When Long Life Is Too Much: Suicide Rises Among Elderly," *New York Times,* July 19, 1989.
13. Ibid.
14. Daniel Goleman, "Missing in Talk of Right to Die: Depression's Grip on a Patient," *New York Times,* December 4, 1991.
15. Nat Hentoff, "Deciding Who Dies," *Washington Post,* October 26, 1991.
16. Timothy Ferris, "Death as Cosmological Event," *New York Times Magazine,* December 15, 1991.
17. Lewis Thomas, *The Medusa and the Snail: More Notes of a Biology Watcher* (New York: Viking, 1979), p. 105.
18. *Cabrini Hospice Newsletter* (Fall 1991).
19. John J. Paris and Frank E. Reardon, "Dilemmas in Intensive Care Medicine: An Ethical and Legal Analysis," *Journal of Intensive Care Medicine,* vol. 1, no. 2 (March–April 1986).
20. "New York Rule Compounds Dilemma Over Life Support," *New York Times,* May 12, 1992.
21. "Scared to Death," *Los Angeles Times,* January 14, 1992.
22. Ibid.
23. Walter Hollander and T. Franklin Williams, "Dr. Strauss' Last Teaching Session," *Archives of Internal Medicine,* vol. 135 (October 1975).
24. Anatole Broyard, "Good Books About Being Sick," *New York Times Book Review* (April 1990).

CHAPTER EIGHTEEN
1. Vern L. Bengtson, "Self-Determination: A Social-Psychological Perspective on Helping the Aged," *Geriatrics,* vol. 28 (December 1973).
2. Daniel Goleman, "Meaningful Activities and Temperament Key in Satisfaction with Life," *New York Times,* December 23, 1986.
3. "Whiz Kids with White Hair," *Time* (February 12, 1990).
4. "New Look on College Campuses: Gray Hair," *New York Times,* November 12, 1987.

5. Dean Keith Simonton, "Does Creativity Decline in the Later Years?," in *Late Life Potential,* Marion Perlmutter, ed. (Gerontological Society of America, 1990), p. 83.
6. See *Age and Achievement* (Princeton, N.J.: Princeton University Press, 1953).
7. Simonton, op. cit.
8. Rudolf Arnheim, "On the Late Style," in *Late Life Potential,* Perlmutter, ed., p. 113.
9. Ibid., p. 116.
10. Paul B. Baltes, et al., "Wisdom: One Facet of Successful Aging," in *Late Life Potential,* Perlmutter, ed., p. 74.
11. Ibid., p. 75.
12. Arnheim, op. cit., p. 115.
13. Allan B. Chiver, "The Return of Wonder in Old Age," in "Creativity in Later Life," *Generations* (Spring 1991).
14. "A Man of His Age, and Still Driving in the Fast Lane," *New York Times,* June 9, 1990.
15. Letter from Megan Marshall, May 2, 1985.
16. "Conference Report, Aging and Creativity," *Human Values and Aging Newsletter,* vol. 1 (September–October 1985), Brookdale Center on Aging of Hunter College, New York.
17. Nan Robertson, "Artists in Old Age," *New York Times,* January 22, 1986.
18. Ibid.
19. Mihaly Csikszentmihalyi, *Flow: The Psychology of Optimal Experience* (New York: Harper & Row, 1990), p. 228.

CHAPTER NINETEEN
1. *New York Times,* November 20, 1990.
2. *Elder Press,* Elnora Lewis Foundation, Soquel, Calif. (Summer 1987).
3. "For some, 'Retired' Is an Inaccurate Label," *New York Times,* November 29, 1990.
4. June Singer. Comments taken from interview, Spring 1992.
5. E. Kohana and B. Kohana, "Environmental Continuity, Discontinuity, Futurity, and Adaptation of the Aged," in G. Rowles and R. Ohta, eds., *Aging and Milieu: Environmental Perspectives on Growing Old* (New York: Academic Press, 1983).

6. Rabbi Zalman Schachter-Shalomi. Adapted from *The First Step: A Guide for the New Jewish Spirit* by Zalman Schachter-Shalomi with Donald Gropman (New York: Bantam, 1983).
7. Sister Pat O'Donnell, "Dream Journey to Myself," in *Lesbian Nuns: Breaking Silence,* Rosemary Curb and Nancy Monahan, eds. (New York: Warner Books, 1985), pp. 301–3.
8. Ibid., pp. 303–5.
9. Shepherd Bliss, "Your Life as Branching Tree," *Whole Life Times* (March 1983).
10. Victor Frankl, "Facing the Transitoriness of Human Existence," in "Aging and the Human Spirit," *Generations* (Fall 1990).

Index

1163

National Institutes of
Health (NIH), 842, 845,
858
National Medical
Enterprises, 896
National Women's Health
Network, 839–40, 843
NBC, 86
near-death experiences,
991–92
Nebin, Myra, 648–49
nerve cells, of brain, 154–
162
Neugarten, Bernice, 193,
205, 238–45, 255,
263–64
Nevelson, Louise, 1077
New England, menopause
study in, 853
*New England Journal of
Medicine,* 242, 741,
759, 775, 776, 869–70,
899–900
Newman, Louis, 635–36
Newman, Paul, 85
Newman, Ruth, 635–36
new place, coming into,
579–604
false starts and, 626–
627
interviews on, 580–604
Newsweek, 59–60, 83–84,
847
New York, 53, 70, 500–501

New York, N.Y.,
Department for Aging
of, 366
New York, State University
of, Health Science
Center, 864
New York Psychoanalytic
Society, 435
New York Times, 72, 80–
81, 258–59, 320, 346,
425, 669, 670, 837–39,
841–43, 847–49, 895–
898, 909, 915–16,
1053, 1078
*New York Times Good
Health Magazine,*
843–44
Nicholson, Jack, 54
Nixon, Richard M., 424
normal aging, 98, 744
brain and, 154–62, 198
decline and, 171–72,
198–99
"disengagement"
theory of, 131–34,
199
longitudinal studies of,
125–34
pathological aging vs.,
121–22, 141, 199–200
studies of, 119–41
North American
Menopause Society,
837–38

Roybal, Edward R., 730, 906

Rubin, Lillian, 259

Russell, Carolyn, 1001

Sager, Cliff, 504–5

St. Vincent's Hospital, 943

Salinger, J. D., 55

Salk, Jonas, 1096

Salzburg Seminar on Health, Productivity, and Aging (1983), 38–39, 117–18, 334, 340–343, 744

Sanders, Marlene, 60, 572–73, 718–20, 884–886

Sanford, Leda, 88

San Francisco, Calif., aging studies in, 250, 303–4, 307–8, 461–462, 498–500

Santa Monica, Calif., alternative housing in, 701–16

Santa Monica Senior Health and Peer Counselling Center, 820–27

Sarton, May, 1068–69

satisfaction, 677, 717, 718, 1040–41
retirement communities and, 672–74

work, 134, 350, 358, 384, 392–439

Schacter-Shalomi, Zalmon, 1108–9

Schaie, K. Werner, 128–129, 164–71, 177

Scheibel, Arnold, 160, 162

Schneider, Ed, 953

Schulz-Keil, Weilland, 366

Schuman, William, 1078

Schweitzer, Albert, 1058

scientific creativity, 211, 213, 1059, 1061–62

Scott-Maxwell, Florida, 1068, 1069

Seasoned Citizens Theater Company, 1088

Seasons of a Man's Life, The (Levinson), 187–190

Second Fifty Years, The (report), 748–49, 752

segregation, compassionate ageism and, 92, 105, 110–11; see also nursing homes; retirement communities

self-actualization, 291, 1100